No other monument so embodies the nation's ideals of political freedom and economic potential as the Statue of Liberty. See chapter 8. © Jon Ortner/Tony Stone Images.

A relatively undiscovered New York treasure, the Morgan Library houses one of the world's most important collections of original manuscripts, rare books, master drawings, and personal writings, from Gutenberg Bibles to handwritten scores by Mozart and Beethoven. See chapter 8. © Kelly/Mooney Photography.

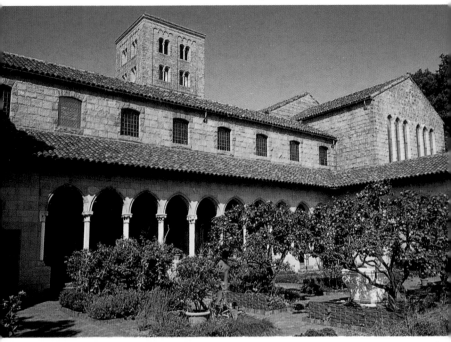

Visitors can discover the art and architecture of medieval Europe, from the famed Unicorn tapestries to an authentic 12th-century chapter house, at the Cloisters, a branch of the Metropolitan Museum of Art overlooking the Hudson at the northern end of Manhattan. See chapter 8. © Rudi von Briel Photography.

Shoppers will find a world's worth of merchandise in New York. Whether you're a foodie in search of the finest cheeses or a fashion maven on a quest for this season's latest look, the Big Apple's got it all. See chapter 10. Photos above and below © Catherine Karnow Photography.

Central Park is New York's most famous place to play. Its 843 acres provide city residents with an escape from the urban frenzy. On a sunny afternoon, there's no better place for biking, in-line skating, sunbathing, and people-watching. During the holidays, Tavern on the Green, located in the park, is a festive place to celebrate. See chapter 8. Photo above © Catherine Karnow Photography; photo below © Kelly/Mooney Photography.

New York has become downright family-friendly. Your kids will love newly revitalized Times Square and the fabulous dinosaurs at the Museum of Natural History. See chapter 8. *Photos left and below © Rudi von Briel Photography.*

New York is the world's premier performing arts city, and Lincoln Center is its premier cultural institution, with offerings that include opera, symphony, dance, jazz, theater, film, and more. See chapter 11. © Kelly/Mooney Photography.

Little Italy is shrinking as neighboring Chinatown outgrows its old boundaries. New York's traditional Italian neighborhood is now limited mainly to festive Mulberry Street, which is lined with traditional Italian restaurants and cafes, and a few offshoots. See chapter 7. © Rudi von Briel Photography.

The Guggenheim Museum, the only Frank Lloyd Wright building in the city, is more noted for its controversial design than for the collection of modern art it houses. See chapter 8. © Rudi von Briel Photography.

After a masterful $175-million renovation that was completed in 1998, Grand Central Terminal has been reborn as one of the most magnificent public spaces in the country. See chapter 8. © Bob Krist Photography.

The Flatiron Building, a triangular masterpiece that was one of the city's first skyscrapers, measures only 6 feet across at its narrow end. See chapter 8. © Rudi von Briel Photography.

A New Star-Rating System & Other Exciting News from Frommer's!

In our continuing effort to publish the savviest, most up-to-date, and most appealing travel guides available, we've added some great new features.

Frommer's guides now include a new **star-rating system.** Every hotel, restaurant, and attraction is rated from 0 to 3 stars to help you set priorities and organize your time.

We've also added **seven brand-new features** that point you to the great deals, in-the-know advice, and unique experiences that separate travelers from tourists. Throughout the guide, look for:

Finds	Special finds—those places only insiders know about
Fun Fact	Fun facts—details that make travelers more informed and their trips more fun
Kids	Best bets for kids—advice for the whole family
Moments	Special moments—those experiences that memories are made of
Overrated	Places or experiences not worth your time or money
Tips	Insider tips—some great ways to save time and money
Value	Great values—where to get the best deals

We've also added a **"What's New"** section in every guide—a timely crash course in what's hot and what's not in every destination we cover.

Here's what the critics say about Frommer's:

"Amazingly easy to use. Very portable, very complete."

—*Booklist*

"Detailed, accurate, and easy-to-read information for all price ranges."

—*Glamour Magazine*

"Hotel information is close to encyclopedic."

—*Des Moines Sunday Register*

"Frommer's Guides have a way of giving you a real feel for a place."

—*Knight Ridder Newspapers*

Frommer's®

New York City 2003

by Cheryl Farr Leas

with research assistance by Nathaniel R. Leas

Wiley Publishing, Inc.

About the Author

Cheryl Farr Leas was senior editor at Frommer's before embarking on a freelance writing career. She also authors the *Frommer's New York City from $90 a Day* and *Hawaii For Dummies®* travel guides, and has contributed to *Best Places Los Angeles* (Sasquatch Books) and numerous other travel guides. Cheryl also writes about travel, real estate, interior design, and other lifestyle subjects for *Continental,* Continental Airlines' in-flight magazine; *Daily Variety; Bride's;* and other publications. When she's not traveling, she's at home in Park Slope, Brooklyn. Feel free to write her directly at rncleas@yahoo.com.

Published by:

Wiley Publishing, Inc.

909 Third Ave.
New York, NY 10022

ISBN 0-7645-6622-9
ISSN 1090-7335

Editor: Lorraine Festa
Special thanks to Elizabeth Albertson & Stephen Bassman
Production Editor: Suzanna R. Thompson
Photo Editor: Richard Fox
Cartographer: Elizabeth Puhl
Production by Wiley Indianapolis Composition Services
Chapter 2 illustrations by Rashell Smith & Kelly Hardesty

Front cover photo: Detail from Grand Central Terminal (left) and the Chrysler Building

For information on our other products and services or to obtain technical support, please contact our Customer Care Department within the U.S. at 800-762-2974, outside the U.S. at 317-572-3993 or fax 317-572-4002.

Wiley also publishes its books in a variety of electronic formats. Some content that appears in print may not be available in electronic formats.

Manufactured in the United States of America

5 4 3 2

Contents

List of Maps

An Invitation to the Reader

In researching this book, we discovered many wonderful places—hotels, restaurants, shops, and more. We're sure you'll find others. Please tell us about them, so we can share the information with your fellow travelers in upcoming editions. If you were disappointed with a recommendation, we'd love to know that, too. Please write to:

Frommer's New York City 2003
Wiley Publishing, Inc. • 909 Third Ave. • New York, NY 10022

An Additional Note

Please be advised that travel information is subject to change at any time—and this is especially true of prices. We therefore suggest that you write or call ahead for confirmation when making your travel plans. The authors, editors, and publisher cannot be held responsible for the experiences of readers while traveling. Your safety is important to us, however, so we encourage you to stay alert and be aware of your surroundings. Keep a close eye on cameras, purses, and wallets, all favorite targets of thieves and pickpockets.

New! Frommer's Star Ratings & Icons

Every hotel, restaurant, and attraction listing in this guide has been ranked for quality, value, service, amenities, and special features using a star-rating scale. In country, state, and regional guides, we also rate towns and regions to help you narrow down your choices and budget your time accordingly. Hotels and restaurants in the Very Expensive and Expensive categories are rated on a scale of one (highly recommended) to three stars (exceptional). Those in the Moderate and Inexpensive categories rate from zero (recommended) to two stars (very highly recommended). Attractions, towns, and regions are rated according to the following scale: zero stars (recommended), one star (highly recommended), two stars (very highly recommended), and three stars (must-see).

In addition to the rating system, we also use seven icons to highlight insider information, useful tips, special bargains, hidden gems, memorable experiences, kid-friendly venues, places to avoid, and other useful information:

Finds *Fun Fact* *Kids* *Moments* *Overrated* *Tips* *Value*

The following abbreviations are used for credit cards:

AE American Express	DISC Discover	V Visa
DC Diners Club	MC MasterCard	

FROMMERS.COM

Now that you have the guidebook to a great trip, visit our website at **www.frommers.com** for travel information on nearly 2,500 destinations. With features updated regularly, we give you instant access to the most current trip-planning information available. At Frommers.com, you'll also find the best prices on airfares, accommodations, and car rentals—and you can even book travel online through our travel booking partners. At Frommers.com, you'll also find the following:

- Online updates to our most popular guidebooks
- Vacation sweepstakes and contest giveaways
- Newsletter highlighting the hottest travel trends
- Online travel message boards with featured travel discussions

What's New in New York City

New York will never be the same, of course. The city suffered a devastating blow on September 11, 2001—a blow strong enough to buckle lesser cities. Now, the Twin Towers no longer dominate the skyline, dazzling visitors and locals alike with their soaring presence, and thousands of our fellow New Yorkers are gone forever. But, despite the violation that New York City has endured, the city that awaits you stands strong and sure.

ACCOMMODATIONS New hotel development has slowed following the late 1990s bubble, but 2002 still has a notable yield of brand-new hotels.

Global giant Starwood's boutique brand, W Hotels, has infused hipness into a whole new territory: Times Square. The **W Times Square,** 1567 Broadway (✆ **877/W-HOTELS;** www.whotels.com), has all the W hallmarks—luxurious designer style, a sexy restaurant, a hipper-than-thou cocktail lounge—plus one extra-special perk: an A-1 location. Starwood's **Westin New York at Times Square,** 255 W. 42nd St. (✆ **800/228-3000;** www.westinny.com), is scheduled to debut in November 2002. The Westin may not be quite as over-the-top sexy as sister hotel the W, but you can still expect stylish rooms—and there's no arguing with Westin's signature Heavenly Bed, which really *is* 10 layers of heaven.

Even lower Manhattan has its own brand-new hotel: the **Ritz-Carlton New York, Battery Park,** 2 West St. (✆ **800/241-3333;** www.ritzcarlton.com), a soaring contemporary tower boasting ultraluxurious comforts and stellar views of New York Harbor and Lady Liberty. These things seem to be happening in twos this year: Look for a midtown sister, the **Ritz-Carlton New York, Central Park,** 50 Central Park S. (✆ **800/241-3333;** www.ritzcarlton.com), to be presiding over Midtown like a grande dame by the time you arrive.

Ian Schrager's perennially stylish **Royalton,** 44 W. 44th St. (✆ **800/635-9013;** www.ianschragerhotels.com), is slated for a major makeover that will last throughout the life of this book. While the hotel will remain open, I suggest sparing yourself the drama. Style hounds who don't mind putting up with the nuisance for a bargain, however, may want to check for deeply discounted renovation rates.

RESTAURANTS The restaurant scene is still going strong, with an emphasis, happily, on midprice meals among newcomers. Another positive development: It seems to be easier to get reservations these days than it used to be; still, special-occasion meals and coveted tables at restaurants such as **Jean Georges** should still be booked a month in advance.

Standouts among the yearlings include TriBeCa's **The Harrison,** 355 Greenwich St. (✆ **212/274-9130**), the best of the new breed of midprice comfort fooders; **Craft,** 41 E. 19th St. (✆ **212/280-0880**), the standout of the season thanks to chef Tom Colicchio's simple yet sublime true-blue American cooking; sexy, Southeast Asian **TanDa,** 331 Park Ave. S.

(© **212/253-8400**), this year's see-and-be-scenester; and elegant, exotic **Ilo,** chef Rick Laakonen's new tour de force in the Bryant Park Hotel, 40 W. 40th St. (© **212/642-2255**).

Ultraglamorous **Alain Ducasse at the Essex House,** 158 W. 58th St. (© **212/265-7300**), is worth noting because, even though it debuted in 2000, the restaurant really came into its own this year. The Michelin three-star chef has massaged this temple to conspicuous consumption into the city's finest special-occasion restaurant, earning three precious stars from the *New York Times.* Wildly expensive, but worth it.

SIGHTSEEING The museum scene has been equally lively, with a spate of renovations, temporary relocations, and debuts.

The biggest news is the temporary move of the **Museum of Modern Art,** which is closed for renovations until 2005, to an interim facility across the East River called **MoMA QNS,** 45-20 33rd St., Long Island City, Queens (© **212/708-9400;** www.moma.org). This is no shoddy venture: MoMA QNS is an architectural transformation of an old Swingline stapler factory into a gracious 45,000-square-foot (4,181-sq.-m) exhibition space showcasing the best of the museum's permanent collection, from Picasso to Warhol.

The grandest of openings has been that of the glorious new **American Folk Art Museum** (© **212/595-9533;** www.folkartmuseum.org), which unveiled its new home at 45 W. 53rd St. in late 2001. This ultramodern boutique museum has been called no less than the city's greatest new museum and best work of architecture since Frank Lloyd Wright built the Guggenheim in 1959, so I highly recommend adding it to your itinerary.

The **Asia Society,** 725 Park Ave. (© **212/288-6400;** www.asiasociety.org), has also reopened after a $30-million renovation. Also back in business is the restaurant at George Washington's old watering hole, the historic **Fraunces Tavern Museum,** 54 Pearl St. (© **212/425-1778;** www.frauncestavernmuseum.org).

Finally open after a lengthy gestation is the **Neue Galerie New York,** 1048 Fifth Ave. (© **212/628-6200**), whose mighty impressive collection of 20th-century German and Austrian art and design works is housed in a Carrèrre & Hastings–designed Vanderbilt mansion that's worth a look unto itself.

You may yet encounter some ongoing museum construction while you're in town. The **Museum of Jewish Heritage,** 18 First Place (© **212/509-6130;** www.mjhnyc.org), is working on a new wing that will triple the exhibition and events space and add a Family History Center; it's not slated for completion until 2003, but the work should not affect your visit.

Under exile until spring 2003 is the **Isamu Noguchi Garden Museum,** which also relocated to a temporary, albeit strictly indoor, space at 36-01 43rd Ave. in Sunnyside, Queens (© **718/204-7088**). Still, don't pass it up if you're in the neighborhood visiting MoMA QNS; the free weekend **Queens Artlink** shuttle will connect the dots for you.

Continuing repercussions from the September 11, 2001, terrorist attacks include, at this writing, the continued closure of the New York Stock Exchange to the public and limited access to the Statue of Liberty; you can take the ferry out to Liberty Island, but the statue itself is closed to visitors pending increased security procedures.

In fact, be prepared for tighter security everywhere you go. For the latest, most up-to-date information on what's open and what's not, as well as **Ground Zero** viewing access, check with **NYC & Company,** New York City's official tourism office, at © **212/484-1222** or www.nycvisit.com.

1

The Best of the Big Apple

Any attempt to define New York recalls the Zen wisdom that you can't step in the same stream twice. The city is so mutable, so constantly changing, that it's almost impossible to get a fix on. Restaurants and nightclubs become trendy overnight, and then die under the weight of their own popularity. (Yogi Berra had the perfect comment for that very phenomenon: "Nobody goes there anymore; it's too crowded.") Broadway shows, exercise fads, city politics, even neighborhoods are all subject to the same Big Apple fickleness.

But within this ebb and flow lies the answer to why we New Yorkers persist in loving our city so much, despite the high rents, the noise, the crowds, the cab drivers who don't know Lincoln Center from the Lower East Side: No other place keeps any of us on our toes quite like this difficult, magnificent city does. Nowhere else is the challenge so tough, the pace so relentless, the stimuli so ever-changing and insistent—and the payoff so rewarding.

The Big Apple has its own special magnetism, unrivaled by any other city. New York remains the nerve center of world finance and trade; the international hub of advertising, publishing, entertainment, and fashion; and the creative core for the arts. Just about every language and any dialect is spoken here, from Mandarin to Brooklynese, and no other dot on the map is quite so ethnically, culturally, socially, and economically diverse.

Despite its almost overwhelming diversity, the city's sense of community is strong. In fact, it's stronger than ever before. Yes—despite the devastating terrorist attack of September 11, 2001, New York is still a marvelous place to visit.

After the planes hit, we were devastated. The destruction of the World Trade Center left an empty hole in the Lower Manhattan landscape, and an irrevocable gash in the hearts of New Yorkers. But the city managed to start moving again within a week of the event—believing that we must, as a community, forge ahead, even with tears in our eyes.

Now, at this writing—just six months after the attack—the city is back in full swing, and its spirit is robust. We have not forgotten; we will never forget, but we know we must move onward. So subway lines reopen, new restaurants debut, museums move forward with scheduled exhibits and expansion projects. As talk of memorial parks and redevelopment heats up, and its streets begin to bustle with tourism and commerce once again, even Lower Manhattan looks forward to a bright future.

Come witness New York's astonishing resilience for yourself—it's reason enough to visit.

1 Frommer's Favorite New York City Experiences

- **Sailing to the Statue of Liberty.** If you have time to do only one thing on your visit to New York, make it this. No other monument so embodies the nation's, and the world's, notion of political freedom and economic potential more than Lady Liberty. As silly as

Paying Your Respects

As you rush about the city, pause to reflect and remember those who were lost on September 11, 2001. You can head down to lower Manhattan, study the remembrances on the gates at historic **Trinity Church,** and see **Ground Zero**—but you don't have to. You'll find tributes to the city's lost throughout New York, at sightseeing attractions as diverse as the ***Intrepid* Sea-Air-Space Museum** and the **Cathedral of St. John the Divine.** The bronze sphere that once stood on the plaza between the two Twin Towers as a symbol of global peace now stands—severely damaged but still whole—in **Battery Park** as a temporary memorial to the victims of 9/11. The **New York City Fire Museum** is an ideal place to pay tribute to 343 of New York's bravest who were lost in one tragic day. You can also check the calendars at museums such as the **New-York Historical Society** and the **Museum of the City of New York** for profound and insightful 9/11-related exhibits. Or just stop to shake hands and say a heartfelt thanks to the NYPD officers you see keeping the city's streets safe—they'll appreciate it.

For more on sightseeing attractions, see chapter 8, "Exploring New York City."

this may sound, the view never loses its power. The ferry that takes you out to **Liberty Island** also stops at the historic federal immigration station on **Ellis Island,** gateway to America for nearly half of the nation's forefathers. The museum's exhibits illustrate with moving simplicity what coming to the promised land was all about. If you want the view but prefer to skip the tourist crowds, consider catching the free Staten Island ferry, a city icon unto itself, instead. *Note:* At press time, visitors can tour the grounds only at Liberty Island; the statue itself had not yet reopened to visitors. Whether this status will change is unknown at press time. Even if it doesn't, standing at the feet of Lady Liberty makes a more-than-worthwhile journey, especially in these reflective, patriotic days. See chapter 8.

- **Spending Your Days at the Museums.** Museum hopping just doesn't get any better than this; the number of masterworks housed in this city is mind-boggling. If you've never been before, the place to start is the **Metropolitan Museum of Art,** the best art museum in North America, and one of the best in the world; even if you spend every day of your vacation here, you couldn't exhaust the possibilities. The new **Rose Center for Earth and Space** at the **American Museum of Natural History** is an A-1 standout for its new breathtaking Harrison Ford–narrated space show. Even though the Museum of Modern Art will be closed for renovation throughout the life of this book, 20th-century art and design can take heart at the **Whitney Museum of American Art** and the **Guggenheim.** And don't just stick to the biggies; New York boasts a wealth of smaller, lower-profile museums that speak to specific interests—from folk art to photography to financial history—and house some phenomenal treasures. For a complete rundown, see chapter 8.
- **Walking the Brooklyn Bridge.** A marvel of civic engineering when

New York Metropolitan Area

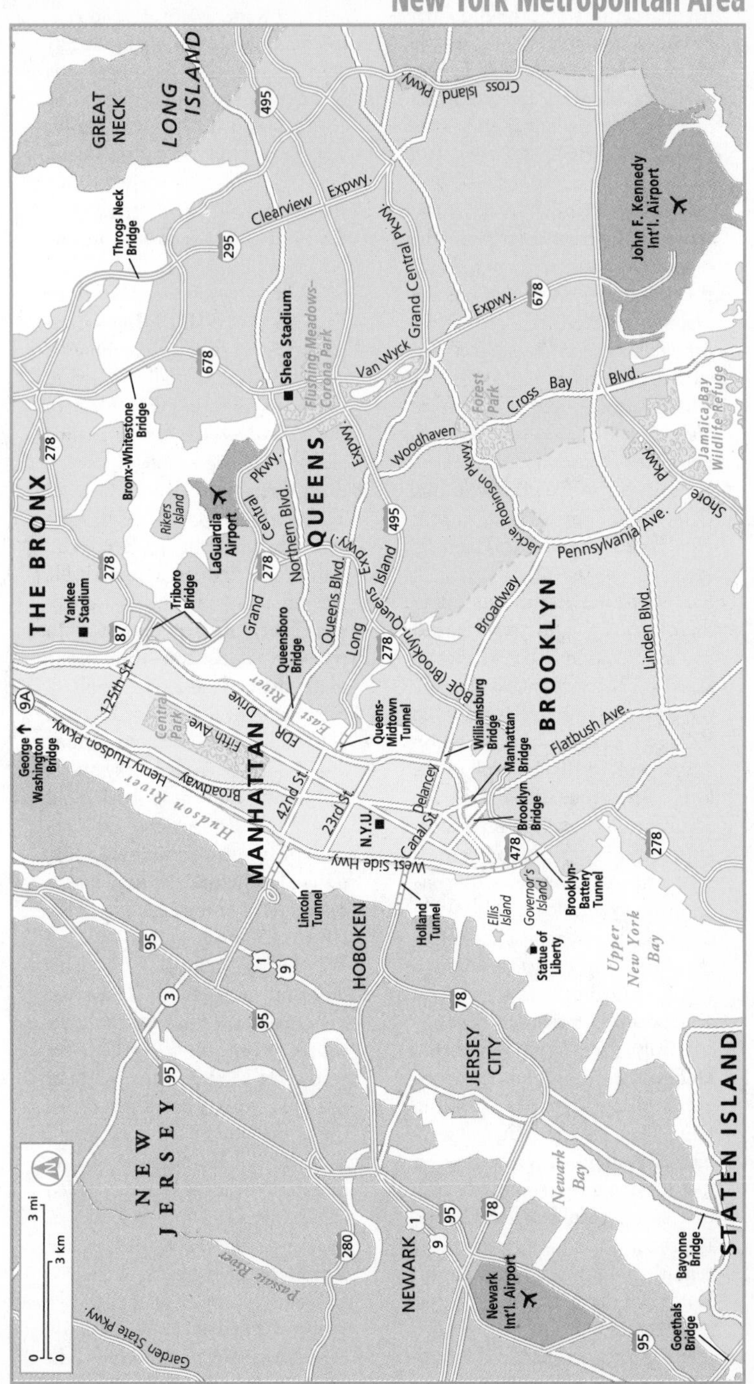

it first connected Brooklyn to Manhattan in 1883, the Brooklyn Bridge is still able to inspire awe even in jaded New Yorkers. I never tire of admiring its Gothic-inspired stone pylons and intricate steel-cable webs. Get an up-close look, and some marvelous—and now devastatingly poignant—views of Manhattan, by taking the easy stroll from end to end. Readers often tell me that this was the highlight of their trip. Start at the Brooklyn end for best effect and consider preceding your walk with a stroll through historic Brooklyn Heights for a leafy, lovely afternoon. See chapter 8.

- **Strolling the Neighborhoods.** One of the greatest things about New York is the distinct character of each of its neighborhoods. Rather than trying to quick-scan them all, I highly recommend picking one and really getting to know it. Wend your way through the historic streets of **Greenwich Village,** saunter the cast-iron canyons of **SoHo,** or explore the lovely, trendy **Flatiron District.** All you really need is a map and a sense of adventure. If you prefer a little structure, consider taking one of the many excellent guided walking tours that are available—there's no better way to get to know a neighborhood than with an expert at the helm. See chapters 5 and 8.
- **Visiting the City's Art Deco Delights.** Nothing embodies New York's historic sense of optimism more than its streamline masterpieces. And nowhere is the Art Deco style more passionately realized than at **Rockefeller Center,** the business-and-entertainment center at the heart of Midtown. You don't have to be highbrow architecture buff to appreciate this place; you can ogle the skyscraping Christmas tree or skate on the legendary ice rink in winter, or wave to Katie, Matt, Al, and Ann in the *Today* show studio at any time of year. The most romantic of the city's high-rises, the chrome-topped **Chrysler Building,** is another Art Deco gem; look for the gargoyles, looking suspiciously like streamline-Gothic hood ornaments, jutting out from the upper floors. And when you visit the marvelous **Empire State Building**—once again the city's tallest building—don't miss the streamline mural in the lobby in your rush to get to the top, where spectacular skyline views await. See chapter 8.
- **Star Gazing at Grand Central Terminal.** Always a beaux arts gem, this majestic 1913 railroad station underwent a remarkable face-lift that has made it a must-see. Every surface glitters with renewed optimism—but none more than the masterful ceiling, once again brilliant with 24-karat gold zodiac constellations against a gorgeous blue-green sky. Walk in, throw your head back, and watch the stars gleam. Or consider dining at **Michael Jordan's–The Steak House,** which opens onto the stellar view. See chapters 7 and 8.
- **Wandering Central Park.** This beautiful accident of civic planning makes the otherwise uninterrupted urban jungle tolerable for workaday New Yorkers. Without this great park, I couldn't imagine life in the city. Be sure to seek out Strawberry Fields, the living memorial to John Lennon, which exhorts us all to IMAGINE. Shakespeare in the Park, the annual theater-under-the-stars festival, is another greenbelt delight. See chapters 8 and 11.
- **Watching Your Favorite Talk Show Being Taped.** If you have

the forethought (to send away months in advance) or the patience (to wait in the standby line), you can watch Dave, Conan, Jon Stewart, the ladies of *The View,* or even Regis and Kelly work their TV magic. If sketch comedy is more your speed, try your luck at acquiring tickets for the holy grail of live TV tapings, *Saturday Night Live.* To start planning, see chapter 8.

- **Heading Uptown to Harlem.** If it's good enough for Bill Clinton, it's good enough for you, right? This once-again-hip neighborhood is actually one of its richest in history and culture. Harlem is full of wonderful possibilities: Latch onto one of the many architecture and history tours of the neighborhood for a bit of background; visit the Studio Museum for an insightful survey of African American and Caribbean art; head to the Abyssinian Baptist Church for a rousing Sunday service, followed by a soulful brunch at Sylvia's; or come uptown for a Creole dinner at Bayou, followed by a night of jazz at the Lenox Lounge. See chapters 7, 8, and 11.
- **Dining Out.** New York is the world capital of great eating, with the finest fine dining in the entire world. Consider splurging on a meal at Chanterelle, Le Cirque, Nobu, La Grenouille, or one of the city's other top-flight restaurants, a surprising number of which are capable of creating lifelong culinary memories. But the true beauty of New York's restaurant scene is that you don't have to spend a fortune to eat well. You'll find cheap but dazzling Chinese in Chinatown, pastrami to die for at any number of Jewish delis, pasta that even your Italian grandmother could love . . . the list goes on and on. See chapter 7.
- **Shopping 'Til You Drop.** There's no more glorious shoppers' paradise in the country—maybe even the world—than New York City. You want it? New York's got it. Check out chapter 10 to find it.
- **Watching the Curtain Rise on a Play.** There's nothing like the immediacy and excitement of a stage production in action. Movie and TV stars know it, which is why more and more are strutting their stuff on the New York stages. Make it a priority to catch a live theater production while you're in town. If musicals are your thing, stick to the Great White Way; if you prefer cutting-edge drama, try Off Broadway. See chapter 11 for tips on getting tickets.
- **Barhopping & Nightclubbing.** It doesn't matter whether you're the Ketel One martini or the draft beer type, whether cabaret or stand-up comedy or electronica is your thing, New York has the after-dark hangout for you. They don't call this "The City That Never Sleeps" for nothing. See chapter 11 for all the options.
- **Celebrating the Holidays in the City.** As millions of my neighbors head out of town to the shores and the mountains, I love to stay behind. On July 4th, a peaceful hush comes over the city—until the fireworks explode overhead, lighting up the night sky with patriotic flair. On Halloween, more than the usual ghouls walk among us in Greenwich Village. The huge hot-air balloons of the Macy's Thanksgiving Day Parade bring out the kid in all of us. No place is more festive than Rockefeller Center at Christmastime. And on Chinese New Year, a bright dragon promises great fortune ahead. For details on these events and others, see the "New York City Calendar of Events" in chapter 3.

2 Best Hotel Bets

This city boasts some of the best hotels in the world—and, believe it or not, some great affordable choices, too. For the details on these and other New York City hotels, see chapter 6.

- **Best All-Around Hotel:** In my book, nobody can hold a torch to **Le Parker Meridien,** 118 W. 57th St. (✆ **800/543-4300;** www.parkermeridien.com), which blends style, service, amenities, food, and plain old-fashioned fun better than anybody else. No other hotelier has been so successful in giving a fresh, new look and feel while maintaining consistency of reputation and service. The Scandinavian-sleek rooms are smartly designed and gorgeous, and both the health club and in-house dining are the best of the Big Apple's hotel scene.

  First runner-up is **Swissôtel New York, The Drake,** 440 Park Ave. (✆ **888/737-9477;** www.swissotel.com). This Depression-era dowager has also benefited from a savvy reinvention; it's now the most stylish roost on Park Avenue. Thanks to Rhys Rosenblum's terrific Q56, the Drake also shines in the dining department, plus its spa and fitness center is top-notch, and the staff is superb.
- **Best Landmark Hotel:** The Plaza may be more famous and the Waldorf more fabulous, but the exquisitely restored **Algonquin,** 59 W. 44th St. (✆ **800/555-3000;** www.algonquinhotel.com), is the winner. The birthplace of The *New Yorker* and home to Dorothy Parker's legendary Round Table in the '20s, this venerable beauty has managed to re-create the glamour of the past without pricing itself out of the reach of regular folks. Even if you don't stay here, stop into the wonderful oak-paneled and velvet-seated lobby—one of the most comfortable and welcoming in the city—for afternoon tea or a post-theater cocktail.
- **Best for Classic New York Elegance:** There's lots of competition in this category, but the low-key **Sherry-Netherland,** 781 Fifth Ave. (✆ **800/247-4377;** www.sherrynetherland.com), steals the show. This gargoyled neo-Romanesque residence hotel is the epitome of understated service and elegance. The rooms and suites provide a chance to experience the glamour of uptown apartment living, and the location—at the southeast of Central Park, presiding grandly over Fifth Avenue at its most fabulous—couldn't be more spectacular. Quintessentially New York in every way.

  First runner-up is the landmark **Waldorf=Astoria,** 301 Park Ave. (✆ **800/WALDORF;** www.waldorfastoria.com), a glorious throwback to old New York glamour—and often surprisingly affordable, considering the pedigree and the top quality of the accommodations.
- **Best Trendy Hotel:** Nobody does it better than **The Mercer,** 147 Mercer St. (✆ **888/918-6060;** www.mercerhotel.com), which continues to reign supreme among visitors who have an eye for style and pockets deep enough that they can afford to stay anywhere. Coolly chic Christian Liaigre interiors, a heart-of-Soho address, a celeb-heavy clientele, and a restaurant overseen by New York's top toque, Jean-Georges Vongerichten, make the Mercer the unrivaled epicenter of downtown chic.

For wallet-watching style hounds, superstar hotelier Ian Schrager and enfant terrible designer Philippe Starck have created the scene to end all scenes at **Hudson,** 356 W. 58th St. (© **800/444-4786;** www.ianschragerhotels.com). Who cares if the rooms are minuscule and the service is less than exemplary? Not the fashionable multitudes, who have turned this newcomer into scene central.

- **Best New Hotel:** The **W Times Square** (© **877/W-HOTELS;** www.whotels.com) gets kudos for bringing high style to a whole new territory. Never mind the touristy location—the style is chic, sleek, and 100% sexy. What's more, rooms are both ultra-beautiful and supremely restful; *New York Times* two-star winner Blue Fin is one of 2002's hottest new restaurants; and nightlife impresario Rande Gerber (Mr. Cindy Crawford) has reinvented his legendary Whiskey Bar as a seductive subterranean space.
- **Best Service If Money Is No Object:** For the ultimate pampering, you'd be hard-pressed to do better than the **Carlyle,** 35 E. 76th St. (© **800/227-5737**), where the staff-to-guest ratio is a phenomenal two-to-one; you won't want for anything here. The Upper East Side's Carlyle gets a run for its money from the West Side's **Trump International Hotel & Tower,** 1 Central Park West (© **888/44-TRUMP;** www.trumpintl.com). Your very own Trump Attaché will fulfill your every whim, keeping meticulous notes all the while for your next stay, when you won't even have to *ask.* Of course, such personal attention in Manhattan doesn't come cheap—but you'll be in supreme comfort as you max out that platinum card!
- **Best Service for the Budget-Minded:** The professional staff at the **Broadway Inn,** 264 W. 46th St. (© **800/826-6300;** www.broadwayinn.com), just may be the most helpful in the city. They're so committed to making their guests feel welcome and at home in New York that they give you a hot line number upon check-in so you can call when you're out and about if you need directions, advice on where to eat, or any other assistance. When you come home from your long day of sightseeing, they'll be happy to order in delivery from any of the nearby restaurants for you. And you thought New York wasn't friendly!
- **Best-Kept Secret of the Theater District:** With artistic interiors and anticipatory service that makes every guest feel like a VIP, **The Muse,** 130 W. 46th St. (© **877/THE-MUSE** or 212/485-2400; www.themusehotel.com), is the hidden jewel of the Theater District. An adult ambience and a stunning restaurant that's a star in its own right, Sam DeMarco's District, only adds to the Muse's luster.
- **Best for Business Travelers:** The **Regent Wall Street,** 55 Wall St. (© **800/545-4000;** www.regenthotels.com), is the best hotel in the Financial District, with an ideal location, gorgeous rooms, and first-rate amenities, including a full-service spa. If your expense account isn't quite that big, consider the **Holiday Inn Wall Street,** 15 Gold St. (© **800/HOLIDAY;** www.holidayinnwsd.com), whose 8-foot (2.5m) L-shaped workstation with desk-level inputs, an ergonomic chair, fax/copier/color printer, dual-line

portable phones with direct-dial numbers, and the kind of office supplies you never bring but always need, like paper clips and tape; SMART rooms even feature a Toshiba Satellite laptop computer so you don't have to cart your own.

In Midtown, the **Peninsula–New York,** 700 Fifth Ave. (© **800/262-9467;** www.peninsula.com), is the ultimate address for power brokers; each room has a terrific L-shaped executive workstation with desk-level inputs, direct-line fax, and dual-line speakerphones, plus other high-tech amenities for ladder-climbing execs. There's also the **Benjamin,** 125 E. 50th St. (© **888/4-BENJAMIN;** www.thebenjamin.com), which offers similar 21st-century technology and luxury-level comforts for a lot less. Or stay at the **Doubletree Guest Suites,** 1568 Broadway (© **800/222-TREE;** www.nyc.doubletreehotels.com), where you can get a two-room suite with all the comforts of home *and* office for the same money you'd pay for a standard hotel room; there are even some conference suites available if you want to hold an en suite meeting.

- **Best Inn:** If you're looking for something ultra-romantic, book into the **Inn at Irving Place,** 56 Irving Place (© **800/685-1447;** www.innatirving.com), an Edith Wharton–era jewel with some of the most beautifully outfitted B&B rooms you'll ever see. Another excellent choice is **Country Inn the City,** on West 77th Street (© **212/580-4183;** www.countryinnthecity.com), one of the most impeccably done guest houses I've ever seen—and superbly located in prime Upper West Side territory.
- **Best for Families:** The **Doubletree Guest Suites,** 1568 Broadway (© **800/222-TREE;** www.nyc.doubletreehotels.com), isn't just for business travelers—it's great for families, too. There's an entire floor of childproof suites, complete with living rooms for spreading out and kitchenettes for preparing light meals. And your young ones will love the Kids Club (for ages 3–12), which boasts a playroom, an arts-and-crafts center, and computer and video games.

  If you have baby in tow, there's hardly a better choice—especially at the moderate price level—than the **Gorham,** 136 W. 55th St. (© **800/735-0710;** www.gorhamhotel.com). Parlor suites have alcoves that are perfectly suited to cribs, and the hotel's Baby Concierge will make sure Mom and Dad have everything they need—including a stroller, so you don't have to cart your own.

  For more kid-friendly suggestions, see "Family-Friendly Hotels" on p. 136.
- **Best Moderately Priced Hotel:** The **Hotel Metro,** 45 W. 35th St. (© **800/356-3870;** www.hotelmetronyc.com), is a Midtown gem that gives you a surprisingly good deal, including a marble bath. On the Upper West Side is the **Lucerne,** 201 W. 79th St. (© **800/492-8122;** www.newyorkhotel.com), a sophisticated hotel that's big on comforts and service but not on price.
- **Best Budget Hotel:** If you don't mind sharing a bathroom, the charming **Chelsea Lodge,** 318 W. 20th St. (© **800/373-1116;** www.chelsealodge.com), offers impeccable comforts—including your sink and shower!—at a bargain-basement price. The **Larchmont Hotel,** in the heart of

Greenwich Village at 27 W. 11th St. (✆ **212/989-9333;** www.larchmonthotel.com), is another excellent choice.

If you want your very own facilities, your best bet for the money is the brand-new **New York City Howard Johnson Express Inn,** 135 E. Houston St. (✆ **800/406-1411** or 212/358-8844; www.hojo.com), a spanking-new hotel with rooms and staff that are much nicer than they have to be for the money. If you won't care for the HoJo's Lower East Side location, or you need space to spread out, head uptown to the **Hotel Newton,** 2528 Broadway (✆ **888/HOTEL58;** www.newyorkhotel.com), which doesn't expect you to put up with a minuscule room or a just-graduated-from–Burger King staff just because you don't have a king's ransom to spend.

- **Best New Year's Eve Lookouts:** Hotels boasting great views of the Times Square action include the **Hilton Times Square,** 234 W. 42nd St. (✆ **800/HILTONS;** www.timessquare.hilton.com). But none of Times Square's monoliths can beat the intimate **Casablanca Hotel,** 147 W. 43rd St. (✆ **888/922-7225;** www.casablancahotel.com), for vantage. This charming Moroccan-themed hotel has a wonderful rooftop deck (for guests only, natch) that couldn't be better situated for watching the ball drop—it's practically a private show.
- **Best for Gay & Lesbian Travelers:** New York is such an important center of gay life that virtually all of the city's hotels welcome gay and lesbian visitors. But if you're looking for like-minded folks, try the **Colonial House Inn,** 318 W. 22nd St. (✆ **800/262-9467;** www.colonialhouseinn.com). In the heart of gay-friendly Chelsea, this friendly B&B caters predominantly to gays and lesbians, but it extends hospitality to straight travelers, too.
- **Best Health Club:** It's hard to beat the **Peninsula–New York,** 700 Fifth Ave. (✆ **800/759-3000;** www.peninsula.com), which boasts a trilevel 35,000-square-foot (3,252 sq. m) fitness center with a gorgeous pool and complete spa services. But **Le Parker Meridien,** 118 W. 57th St. (✆ **800/543-4300;** www.parkermeridien.com), comes close: The mammoth 15,000-square-foot-plus (more than 1,400 sq. m) Gravity is a comprehensive fitness center, with state-of-the-art equipment on two levels (including a dedicated free-weight room), squash and racquetball courts, spa-treatment rooms, and more—including personal trainers, aerobics classes, and nutritional counseling. If that's not enough to occupy you, head up to the 42nd floor, where the pool has marvelous skyline views, or to the rooftop sundeck or jogging track.
- **Best Suite Deals:** The **Kimberly,** 145 E. 50th St. (✆ **800/683-0400;** www.kimberlyhotel.com), offers full-fledged one- and two-bedroom apartments—complete with full kitchens—for the same price as most standard Midtown hotels. Free access to a fabulous full-service health club and complimentary sunset cruises in summer add to the fabulous value; visit in the off-season, and the suites are so cheap that you'll feel like you're stealing. On the Upper West Side, one of the city's most desirable residential neighborhoods, the **Hotel Beacon,** 2130 Broadway (✆ **800/572-4969;** www.beaconhotel.com), also has spacious suites that boast all the comforts, including microwaves

in the kitchenettes and well-furnished living rooms with pull-out sofas. Most New York families don't live in two-bedroom apartments as big as these.

- **Best for Travelers with Disabilities:** Tops for travelers with disabilities is the **Waldorf=Astoria,** 301 Park Ave. (© **800/WALDORF;** www.waldorfastoria.com), which has a ramp entrance and nearly 20 oversized rooms designed to accommodate wheelchair-bound guests. Rooms feature low beds and peepholes, and spacious bathrooms with raised toilet seats and grab bars; some have roll-in showers as well. What's more, the solicitous staff is always ready to lend a hand.

  There's also the **Fitzpatrick Grand Central Hotel,** 141 E. 44th St. (© **800/367-7701;** www.fitzpatrickhotels.com), which has 10 rooms specifically designed for the physically challenged; or the newly constructed **Benjamin,** 125 E. 50th St. (© **888/4-BENJAMIN;** www.thebenjamin.com), whose 10 ADA-compliant corner suites have lots of space for wheelchair negotiating, including huge bathrooms.

  On the affordable front, the comfortable, budget-minded **Skyline Hotel,** 725 Tenth Ave. (© **800/433-1982;** www.skylinehotelny.com), has seven wheelchair-accessible rooms, ramps, and fire-safety alarms for deaf and blind visitors, plus free parking.

  If you are disabled, or your travel partner is, also refer to "Tips for Travelers with Special Needs" in chapter 3 before you plan your trip. And always call the management directly at any hotel you are considering for your stay to ask questions pertinent to your needs.

3 Best Dining Bets

One of the great joys of being in New York is that there's fabulous food at nearly every turn. You can flex your gold card on some of the most memorable fine dining in the world, or go ethnic to indulge in the best cheap eats you'll find anywhere. For the details on these and other terrific New York City restaurants, see chapter 7.

- **Best Overall Restaurant:** Setting the standard in the finest restaurant city in the world is **Jean Georges,** in the Trump International Hotel & Tower, 1 Central Park West (© **212/299-3900**), Jean-Georges Vongerichten's glorious modern temple to 21st-century French cuisine. Jean Georges isn't just about the food, or the setting, or the service—it's about all three, orchestrated for perfect harmony. In a star-studded scene, this *New York Times* four-star winner shines above all others. Book well before you leave home.
- **Best Spot for a Celebration:** For understated elegance, perfect service, and sublime New French cuisine, there's **Chanterelle,** 2 Harrison St. (© **212/966-6960**), which can cause even the most jaded gourmands to swoon. For the ultimate break-the-bank celebration, you can't do better than the divine **Alain Ducasse at the Essex House,** 158 W. 58th St. (© **212/265-7300**), whose Michelin 3-star chef offers the city's most fabulous—and most expensive—night on the town. For a somewhat lower profile special-occasion experience in the classic French tradition, book a table at **La Grenouille,** 3 E. 52nd St. (© **212/752-1495**), which has been hosting elegant celebratory parties since 1962.
- **Best for Romance:** Reserve at **One If By Land, Two If By Sea,** 14 Barrow St. (© **212/228-0822**),

where candlelight, lush piano music, and tuxedoed service in a pre-Revolutionary Greenwich Village town house take you back in time and put you in the mood for love.

- **Best Newcomer:** This year's winner is **Craft,** 41 E. 19th St. (✆ **212/780-0880**). Chef Tom Colicchio (also of Gramercy Park Tavern) has set the perfect tone for the post-glam era with a gorgeous craftsman-meets-modern interior and simple yet superb New American cooking.

  Almost equally splendid is chef Rick Laakonen's **Ilo,** in the Bryant Park Hotel, 40 W. 40th St. (✆ **212/642-2255**), who gives New American cooking a dramatically sexy setting and a joyfully exotic flair.
- **Best Spot for a Business Lunch:** Always terrific **Cité,** 120 W. 51st St. (✆ **212/956-7100**), built its reputation on business lunches, and continues to be the preferred choice of those who want to seal the deal. If you prefer more casual and want to impress with your New York acumen, head to the legendary **Oyster Bar & Restaurant,** in Grand Central Terminal (✆ **212/490-6650**), a bastion of old school cool.
- **Best Spot for a Ladies-Who-Lunch Lunch:** What's more decadent than lingering over three courses—with wine—in the middle of the day, when regular folks are hard at work? Daniel Boulud's elegant **Café Boulud,** 20 E. 76th St. (✆ **212/772-2600**), is the ideal place to rub elbows with the Upper East Side society dames who've made this meal a way of life.
- **Best for Celebrity Spotting:** It's the luck of the draw, really. But for the best odds, head to **Le Cirque 2000,** 455 Madison Ave. (✆ **212/303-7788**), where the crowd is full of big-name movie stars, politicos, and socialites; I spotted Whoopi just moments after walking through the front door. Your other best bet is **Tribeca Grill,** 375 Greenwich St. (✆ **212/941-3900**), where DeNiro, Keitel, Miramax's Harvey Weinstein, and other gold-plated celebs hold court on a daily basis.
- **Best Service:** With an almost-unheard-of 27 (out of a possible 30) rating for service from Zagat's, **Chanterelle,** 2 Harrison St. (✆ **212/966-6960**), simply can't be beat. The service somehow manages to be impeccable without being too formal or stuffy. Other restaurants try, but this is how it's supposed to be. A magical experience, and worth every penny.
- **Best Wine List: Veritas,** 43 E. 20th St. (✆ **212/353-3700**), boasts what must be the most enthralling wine cellar in town. Serious oenophiles can download the full list—market *and* reserve—for advance study, and then call up to have their choice opened and decanted for dinnertime.
- **Best Wine Deal: Cité,** 120 W. 51st St. (✆ **212/956-7100**), offers a nightly deal after 8pm that's almost too good to be true: For $60, you get a three-course meal—your choice of appetizer, main course, and dessert—and you can enjoy unlimited quantities of the four wines on offer *at no extra charge.* And you're not getting the cheap stuff: Recent choices included a '90 Mondavi Cabernet, a '97 Acacia chardonnay, a '94 Chalone Vineyard Pinot Noir reserve, and Taittinger brut for celebrating. These deals should still be on while you're in town, but call ahead to be sure.
- **Best Spot for Breakfast and Brunch:** Nobody does breakfast

Site Seeing: The Big Apple on the Web

The New York Convention & Visitors Bureau's official site, **www.nycvisit.com**, is an excellent online resource offering tons of information on the city, from trip-planning basics to tips on where to take the kids. But there's much more to be learned about New York in cyberspace than the official line.

Citysearch (www.newyork.citysearch.com) is the city's hippest and most comprehensive general-information site, with reviews and listings for restaurants, shopping, hotels, attractions, and nightlife. It's not quite as up-to-the-minute as it used to be, but it's still an excellent source for current happenings. Also, beware the frustrating search engine; if you're looking for a specific restaurant or shop, say, you're best off heading to the "Restaurants" or "Shopping" page and searching from there—and it still may take a few tries to find what you're looking for.

New York Today (www.nytoday.com) is the online arts, leisure, and entertainment arm of the venerable *New York Times.* The *Times* created this site as a gift to those of us who wanted access to access to their excellent cultural coverage and restaurant reviews without having to wade through the main site (www.nytimes.com), which requires you to register and pay archiving fees on past articles.

Tops these days just may be **New York Metro** ★ **(www.nymetro.com)**, the online arm of glossy weekly magazine *New York.* Able to draw on the magazine coverage as its primary resource, New York Metro is currently the most up-to-date site covering happenings in the city. (Although keep in mind that these things can change by the moment in the fickle, poorly funded Web world.) The site is particularly strong in restaurant and shopping coverage; in fact, the magazines shopping columnists update the site daily with news of sales and bargains.

Each of the city's high-profile weeklies also maintain sites that are very useful for current happenings, including:

- *Time Out New York:* www.timeoutny.com
- The *Village Voice:* www.villagevoice.com
- The *New Yorker:* www.newyorker.com
- *Paper:* www.papermag.com
- The *New York Press:* www.newyorkpress.com

For more on these city-focused magazines, see "Publications" under "Orientation" in chapter 5, "Getting to Know New York City."

Digital City New York (www.digitalcity.com/newyork) is much like Citysearch, and good for an alternative view. **About.com** also maintains a somewhat useful New York page at **www.gonyc.about.com**.

For the most up-to-date information on Lower Manhattan and Ground Zero, visit the website of the **Alliance for Downtown New York,** the stellar Business Improvement District so productive in Lower Manhattan both before and after 9/11, at **www.downtownny.com**.

You'll find subject-websites listed in the appropriate chapters of this book.

better than **Norma's,** at Le Parker Meridien hotel, 118 W. 57th St. (✆ **212/708-7460**), a soaring, ultramodern ode to the morning meal. Both classic dishes and creative interpretations are first rate. And, best of all, breakfast lasts until 3pm every day!

- **Best for Pre- (or Post-) Theater: Aquavit,** 13 W. 54th St. (✆ **212/307-7311**), offers a three-course pretheater menu for just $39—and their light Scandinavian cuisine won't weigh you down in your theater seat. Caviar lovers shouldn't miss the terrific prix-fixe value at legendary sturgeon importer **Petrossian,** 182 W. 58th St. (✆ **212/245-2214**). Lincoln Center–goers have sublime **Jean Georges,** in the Trump International Hotel & Tower, 1 Central Park West (✆ **212/299-3900**), where the faultless wait staff will make sure you're wowed well before curtain time. After the show, **Joe Allen,** 326 W. 46th St. (✆ **212/581-6464**), is the ultimate Broadway pub—and the meat loaf is marvelous.
- **Best Dessert:** There are many impressive pastry chefs in town, but few of them can top the remarkable confections at **Payard Pâtisserie & Bistro,** 1032 Lexington Ave. (✆ **212/717-5252**), which is well located for a pick-me-up during a day of Upper East Side museum-hopping or shopping. For down-home indulgence, head to **Bubby's,** 120 Hudson St. (✆ **212/219-0666**), where the classic home-style pies are to die for.
- **Best Chinese Cuisine:** With all the culinary wonders that Chinatown has to offer, this is a tough choice. But I can't stop thinking about those steamy soup dumplings at **Joe's Shanghai,** 9 Pell St. (✆ **212/233-8888**). **New York Noodletown,** 28½ Bowery (✆ **212/349-0923**), runs neck and neck with Joe's, where anything that's salt-baked is guaranteed to be sublime.
- **Best French Cuisine:** Downtown, magical **Chanterelle,** 2 Harrison St. (✆ **212/966-6960**), is the obvious choice, serving ethereal French with welcome contemporary twists. Uptown, longtime favorite **La Grenouille,** 3 E. 52nd St. (✆ **212/752-1495**), serves the classics with elegant perfection.

  For more affordable French, your best bet is also from the Chanterelle folks, whose **Le Zinc,** 120 Duane St. (✆ **212/513-0001**), shines among the stiff bistro competition with globally inspired bistro cuisine. If you want *très* traditional bistro fare, try **Balthazar,** 80 Spring St. (✆ **212/965-1414**), where the beautiful-people scene glitters almost as brightly as the gorgeous raw bar.
- **Best Italian Cuisine:** With **Babbo,** 110 Waverly Place (✆ **212/777-0303**), Food Network chef Mario Batali has created the ideal setting for his exciting northern Italian cooking. The room is beautiful, the service warm and gracious, and the food excellent. Nobody does pasta better. If you're watching your wallet, head instead to **Frank,** 88 Second Ave. (✆ **212/420-0202**), both authentically Italian and one of the city's best dining values.
- **Best Japanese Cuisine:** In a category all its own is inventive **Nobu,** 105 Hudson St. (✆ **212/219-0500**), where unusual textures, daring combinations, and surprising flavors add up to a first-rate dining adventure that you won't soon forget. For something completely different, try **Sugiyama,**

251 W. 55th St. (✆ **212/956-0670**), where master chef Nao Sugiyama recreates the delicate, palate-pleasing magic of Kyoto's kaiseki tradition.

- **Best Home-Style Cooking:** No other restaurant warms my heart more than the aptly named **Home,** 20 Cornelia St. (✆ **212/243-9579**), where the cumin-crusted pork chop sits in a bed of homemade barbecue sauce that's better than Dad used to make, and even Mom would tip her hat to the silky smooth chocolate pudding.
- **Best Jewish Deli: Katz's Delicatessen,** 205 E. Houston St. (✆ **212/254-2246**), is the choice among those who know their kreplach, knishes, pastrami. No cutesy sandwiches named for celebrities here—just top-notch Jewish classics. The all-beef wieners are the best in a town for known for its top-quality dogs.
- **Best Burger and Beer:** Ask a hundred New Yorkers, and you'll get a hundred opinions. But for my money, there's no better choice than **Old Town Bar & Restaurant,** 45 E. 18th St. (✆ **212/529-6732**). Whether you go low-fat turkey or bacon-chili-cheddar, the burgers at this venerable 19th-century pub are perfect every time. The fries are addictively crisp, the Buffalo wings are slathered in spicy sauce, and there's a whole selection of great beers on tap.
- **Best Old World Atmosphere: Baldoria,** 249 W. 49th St. (✆ **212/582-0460**), may be relatively new to the Theater District dining scene, but it feels like it's been here since Sinatra made the bobby-soxers swoon down the street at the Paramount. It oozes old world atmosphere—and don't be surprised if you spot a Tony Soprano look-alike at the next table.
- **Best Pizza:** Pizza doesn't get any better than at **Lombardi's,** 32 Spring St. (✆ **212/941-7994**), which has been baking up its own coal-oven pies since 1905. If you're feeling adventuresome, head across the river to **Grimaldi's Pizzeria,** 19 Old Fulton St., Brooklyn Heights (✆ **718/858-4300**), where you'll be rewarded with stellar views in addition to real Noo Yawk pizza.
- **Best Seafood:** The black bass ceviche alone—not to mention everything else that comes out of its blue-ribbon kitchen—keeps **Le Bernardin,** 155 W. 51st St. (✆ **212/489-1515**), at the top of the world's great fish restaurants. If your budget isn't quite big enough to handle such a splurge, head instead to SoHo's **Aquagrill,** 210 Spring St. (✆ **212/274-0505**).
- **Best for Families:** If you're traveling with a kid you want to impress, don't pass up an opportunity to eat at **Serendipity 3,** 225 E. 60th St. (✆ **212/838-3531**), a classic ice-cream parlor, but better. Sure, they have real food so you can *pretend* to be there for a real meal, but Serendipity is all about getting to the sweet treats. For more kid-friendly suggestions, see "Family-Friendly Restaurants" on p. 217.
- **Best for Vegetarians:** A perennial favorite among vegetarians is the Asian-inspired fare at **Zen Palate,** 34 Union Square East (✆ **212/614-9345**). But I prefer **Pongal,** 110 Lexington Ave. (✆ **212/696-9458**), which re-creates the flavorful and pleasing vegetarian fare of Southern India—and thanks to a daily visit from a rabbi, it's kosher, to boot. Everybody has to splurge

once in awhile, of course; vegetarians should visit **Café Boulud,** 20 E. 76th St. (✆ **212/772-2600**), where celebrity chef Daniel Boulud dedicates an entire daily menu just to you.

- **Best Late-Night Dining:** Chef Sam DeMarco pioneered the concept of quality late-night dining back in the early 1990s, and his **First,** 87 First Ave. (✆ **212/674-3823**), is still going strong. The atmosphere is energetic, the "Tiny Tinis" make perfect late-night cocktails, and the menu offers a large selection of sharable finger foods is both yummy and fun. Dinner is served Sunday until 1am, Monday through Thursday until 2am, and weekends until 3am.

  Another top-flight choice for late-night dining is TriBeCa's **Le Zinc,** 120 Duane St. (✆ **212/513-0001**), which offers beautifully prepared bistro fare until 1am weeknights, 3am Fridays and Saturdays.

  In a neighborhood notoriously underserved in the late-night department, newcomer **Pigalle,** 790 Eighth Ave. (✆ **212/489-2233**), deserves special mention for offering affordable French fare to after-hours Theater District crowds.
- **Best Stop for a Quick Bite:** It's hard to beat **Emerald Planet,** at 2 Great Jones St. (✆ **212/353-9727**), whose wraps and smoothies are made with all-fresh ingredients and a world of ethnic influences. A second location in Rockefeller Center makes a delicious, healthful, and easy lunch stop during a day of Midtown sightseeing.

2

A Traveler's Guide to New York's Architecture

by Lisa Torrance

New York City contains a wealth of architectural styles, from modest row houses to ornate churches to soaring skyscrapers. Constructed over 300 years, these buildings represent the changing tastes of the city's residents from colonial times to the present. A brief look at the city's most popular styles provides a unique perspective on the city's past, present, and future.

For the locations of the buildings mentioned in this chapter, see p. 19.

1 Georgian (1700–76)

This style reflects Renaissance ideas made popular in England, and later in the United States, through the publication of books on 16th-century Italian architects. The most-studied Italian of this period was **Andrea Palladio** (1508–80), who had freely adapted classical Roman forms. Georgian houses are characterized by a formal arrangement of parts employing a symmetrical composition enriched with classical details, such as columns and pediments. In the United States, the style was seen as an appropriate expression of the relative prosperity and security of the colonies. It was a sharp contrast to the unadorned Colonial style that preceded it.

Georgian buildings share the following characteristics:

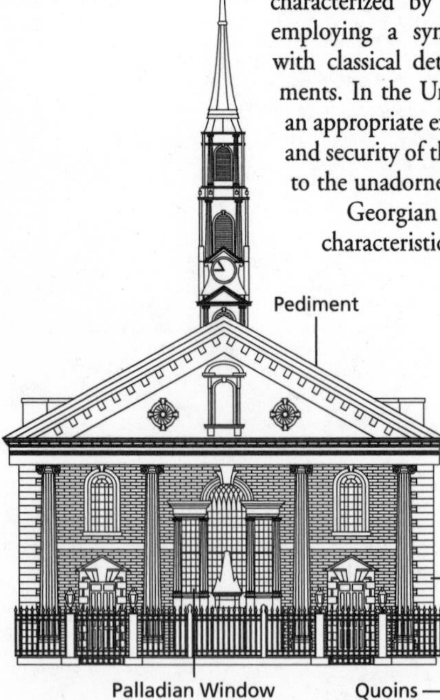

St. Paul's Chapel

- A formal, symmetrical arrangement
- A roof with four uniformly pitched sides
- A *balustrade* (a railing with balusters, or posts)
- A central projecting pavilion topped by a *pediment* (a low-pitched triangular feature) and supported by colossal columns or *pilasters* (rectangular columns projecting only slightly from a wall)
- A transom light above the front door

New York Architecture

American Surety Company **22**
Chrysler Building **9**
Empire State Building **12**
Federal Hall National Memorial **23**
Flatiron Building **13**
Fraunces Tavern **27**
Grand Central Terminal **8**
Gunther Building **18**
Haughwout Store **19**
Jefferson Market Library **14**
Lever House **4**
Majestic Apartments **1**
Metropolitan Club **2**
Morgan Bank Headquarters **24**
New York Public Library **11**
Racquet and Tennis Club **5**
Radio City Music Hall **7**
Rockefeller Center **7**
The Row **15**
St. Paul's Chapel **21**
Seagram Building **6**
SoHo-Cast Iron Historic District **17**
Sony Building **3**
Trinity Church **25**
United Nations Headquarters **10**
U.S. Custom House **26**
West Village **16**
Woolworth Building **20**

- Palladian windows (see illustration)
- *Quoins* (cornerstones in a distinctive material)
- Double-hung sash windows

St. Paul's Chapel, on Broadway between Vesey and Fulton streets (1764–66, Thomas McBean), the only pre-Revolutionary building remaining in Manhattan, is an almost perfect example of the Georgian style, with a pediment, colossal columns, Palladian window, quoins, and balustrade above the roof line (see illustration). Although it's a 20th-century reconstruction of a formal English house built here in 1719, **Fraunces Tavern,** 54 Pearl St., is another fine example of the style.

2 Federal (1780–1820)

Federal was the first truly American architectural style. It was an adaptation of a contemporaneous English style called Adam-esque, created by Scotsman **Robert Adam** (1728–92), which included ornate, colorful interior decoration. Federal combined Georgian architecture with the delicacy of the French rococo and the classical architecture of Greece and Rome. The overall effect is one of restraint and dignity, and may appear delicate when compared to the more robust Georgian style. Federal was popular with successful merchants throughout the cities and towns of the eastern seaboard. Its connection to the prosperous empires of Rome and Greece was seen as an appropriate reference for the young United States.

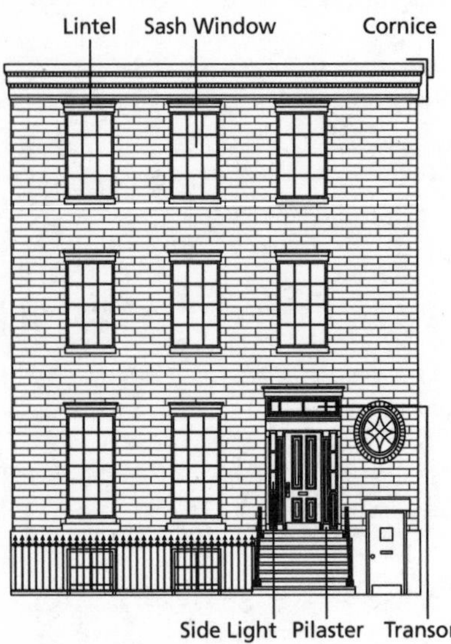

Typical Federal Exterior

In New York, the Federal style was popular for row houses (see illustration) built after the 1811 creation of the city's grid pattern of avenues and streets. These houses often share the following features:

- A height of two or three stories
- Prominent end chimneys
- A red brick exterior
- A steeply pitched roof
- *Dormers* (upright windows projecting from a sloping roof) with pediments
- Double-hung sash windows, often with a flat *lintel* (horizontal member over a window which carries the weight of the wall above it; commonly of stone)
- An elaborate doorway with sidelights and a fan or transom light (see illustration)
- Pilasters or columns flanking the doorway

- Delicate, exterior ornament of Roman origin, such as swags, urns, sheaths of wheat, and garlands
- A high basement

Federal Doorway

In the **West Village,** near and along Bedford Street between Christopher and Morton streets, are more original Federal-style houses than anywhere else in Manhattan. House numbers 4 through 10 (1825–34) on Grove Street, just off Bedford, presents one of the most authentic groups of late Federal–style houses in America. Notice the pedimented dormers and doors surrounded by pilasters and transom lights. Local carpenters created these buildings from plan books, probably published in England. In adapting the styles, they pared down the detail from the more delicate Adamesque in order to adapt to the needs—and pocketbooks—of their American merchant and craftsman clients.

3 Greek Revival (1820–60)

The Greek Revolution in the 1820s, in which Greece won its independence from the Turks, recalled to American intellectuals the democracy of ancient Greece and its elegant architecture, created around 400 B.C. At the same time, the War of 1812 diminished American affection for the British influence, including the still-dominant Federal style. With many believing America to be the spiritual successor of Greece, the use of classical Greek forms, particularly the Greek temple front, came to dominate residential, commercial, and government architecture. The style was so popular it came to be known as the National Style, and was used for numerous state capitols, as well as the U.S. Capitol in Washington, D.C.

Because ancient Greek structures did not use arches, the arched entrances and elliptical fanlights so popular in the Federal style were abandoned. The Greek Revival is most distinguished by a Greek temple front with the following:

- Classical orders specifying the use of three different column types: Corinthian, Ionic, or Doric (see illustration)

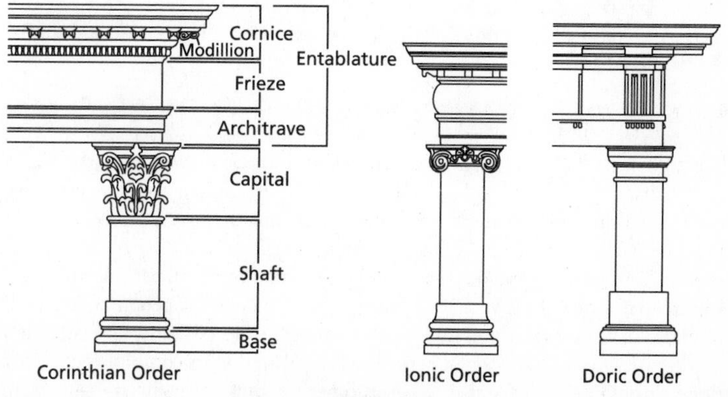

Classical Orders

- A full *entablature* (a set of roof parts, usually supported by a column, consisting of an architrave, frieze, and cornice)
- A low-pitch pediment
- White exteriors (it was not known at this time that ancient Greek buildings had been polychrome)

In New York, Grecian columns and orders were used mostly to decorate entrances on row houses, but whole buildings were also created. Perhaps the city's finest Greek Revival building is **Federal Hall National Memorial** (1834–42), at 26 Wall St., at Nassau Street, the site where George Washington took his presidential oath in 1789 (see illustration). The structure has a Greek temple front, with Doric columns and a simple pediment, resting on a high base, called a *plinth,* with a steep flight of steps.

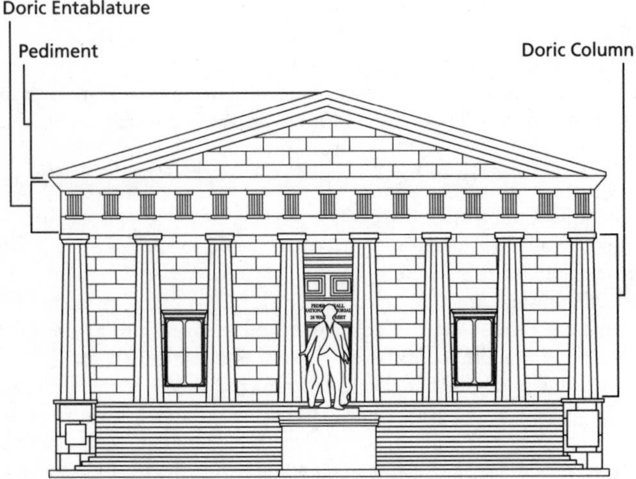

Federal Hall National Memorial

The Row (1832–33, with later alterations), numbers 1 through 11 on Washington Square North, is an imposing block front of early 19th-century town houses. Note the stately entranceways with carved wooden and marble columns; the brickwork, called Flemish Bond, which alternates long and short brick in each row; and the Greek motifs, such as obelisks, lyres, and honeysuckle adornments, called anthemia.

4 Gothic Revival (1830–60)

The term *Gothic Revival* refers to a literary and aesthetic movement of the 1830s and 1840s that occurred in England and later in the United States. A pervasive current within this movement was known as Romanticism. Adherents believed that the wickedness of modern times could benefit with a dose of "goodness" presumed to have been associated with the Christian medieval past. Architecture was chosen as one of the vehicles to bring this message to the people. The revival style was used for everything from timber cottages to stone castles and churches. Some structures had only one or two Gothic features, most commonly a steeply pitched roof or pointed arches, whereas other buildings, usually churches, were accurate copies of English Gothic structures.

A derivative style called **Victorian Gothic** (1860–90) became popular after the Civil War. Influenced by the writings of English theorist **John Ruskin** (1819–1900), this style is distinguished by contrasting colors of brick and stone in bold polychromatic patterns and decorative bands. This more freewheeling interpretation of the Gothic was well suited to the florid decorative approach of the late 19th century.

Gothic Revival is characterized by:

- Asymmetry
- Pointed arches
- Large pointed windows with tracery and colored glass (see illustration)
- Steeply pitched roofs
- A curvilinear gingerbread trim along the eaves (on houses)
- Towers
- *Battlements* (a fortified wall with alternate solid parts and openings; used for defense or a decorative motif)
- An overall picturesque quality

Gothic Window

Trinity Church, at Broadway and Wall Street (Richard Upjohn, 1846), is one of the most celebrated, authentic Gothic Revival structures in the United States. Here you see all the features of a Gothic church: a steeple, battlements, pointed arches, Gothic tracery, stained glass windows, *flying buttresses* (an external bracing system for supporting a roof or vault), and medieval sculptures. This was the tallest building in the area until the late 1860s.

The **Jefferson Market Library,** at 425 Sixth Ave. (Frederich Clarke Withers and Calvert Vaux, 1874–77), is a magnificent structure in the Victorian Gothic mode. Built as a courthouse, the asymmetrical structure sports striking bands of red brick and white stone, stained-glass windows, pointed arches, and a dramatic clock tower.

5 Italianate (1840–80)

The architecture of Italy served as the inspiration for this building style, which could be as picturesque as the Gothic or as restrained as the classical. This

Rival Revivals: Architectural Styles in the Late 19th Century

On the eve of the Civil War, the United States was a country of diverse tastes, interests, and cultures, and its differences were reflected in the country's architectural styles. During the latter half of the 19th century, several modes—including Victorian Gothic, Italianate, Renaissance Revivals, Second Empire, and even the exotic Moorish and Egyptian Revivals—coexisted. What these styles share is a certain eclecticism and picturesqueness. Mid-century architects reasoned that no age had produced the perfect architectural expression, so why not borrow freely from the best of the past and even mix different styles on the same building?

Although some of these styles were popular, none became dominant. In the 1870s in Chicago, technological advancements and imaginative design were coming together to create the world's first skyscrapers—*the* style that would one day dominate New York and the country's other urban areas.

adaptability made it immensely popular in the 1850s. In New York, the style was used for urban row houses and commercial buildings. The development of cast iron at this time permitted the inexpensive mass production of decorative features that few could have afforded in carved stone. This led to the creation of cast-iron districts in nearly every American city, including New York.

Italianate buildings often have a formal symmetry accentuated by pronounced moldings and decorative details. The commercial buildings resemble Italian palaces and tend to be rectangular buildings of several, spacious stories well suited to their original purposes as work spaces. The facades usually have the following features:

- A flat or low-pitched roof
- A bracketed cornice and an elaborate entablature
- Windows rounded at the top (flattened arches above windows are common, too)
- Large moldings over windows, called *hood moldings*
- Columns or pilasters flanking, or separating, windows
- Decorative keystones
- Quoins
- Balustrades
- Belt courses or entablatures at each story
- Vertical rows of windows and horizontal belt courses giving the building a very regular, compartmentalized look

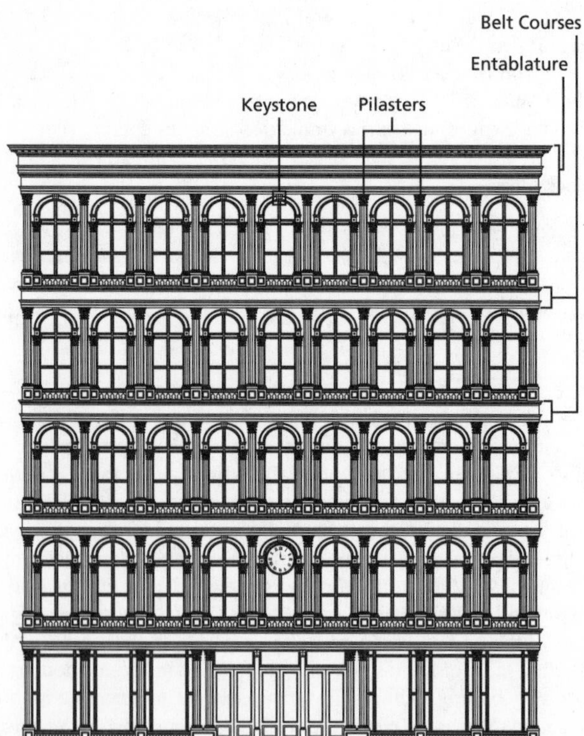

Haughwout Store

Impressions

New York is the perfect model of a city, not the model of a perfect city.

—Lewis Mumford

New York's **SoHo–Cast Iron Historic District** has 26 blocks jammed with cast-iron facades, many in the Italianate manner. The single richest section is **Greene Street** between Houston and Canal streets. Stroll along here and take in building after building of sculptural facades. At Greene and Broome streets is the **Gunther Building** (Griffith Thomas, 1871), a fine example of the Italianate. The most celebrated building in SoHo is the **Haughwout Store** (John P. Gaynor, 1857), at the corner of Broadway and Broome streets, a New York version of a Venetian palace (now housing a Staples store, of all things). The handsome facade with cast iron on two sides has a window arrangement—two small, Corinthian columns supporting an arch over each window—based directly on a 15th-century, Italian design (see illustration).

6 Second Renaissance Revival (1890–1920)

Buildings in this style show a definite studied formalism. A relative faithfulness to Italian Renaissance precedents of window and doorway treatments distinguishes it from the much looser adaptations of the Italianate. Scale and size, in turn, set the Second Renaissance Revival apart from the first, which occurred from 1840 to 1890. The grand buildings of the Second Renaissance Revival, with their textural richness, well suited the tastes of New York's wealthy Gilded Age. The style was used for banks, swank town houses, government buildings, and private clubs.

Typical features include:

- A cubelike structure with a massive, imposing quality
- Symmetrical arrangement of the facade, including distinct horizontal divisions
- A different stylistic treatment for each floor; with different classical orders, finishes, and window treatments on each level
- Use of *rustication* (masonry cut in massive blocks and separated from each other by deep joints) on the lowest floor
- Quoins
- The indication of additional floors with small windows
- The mixing of Greek and Roman styles on the same facade (Roman arches and arcades may appear with Greek-style pedimented or straight-headed windows)
- A projecting cornice supported by large brackets
- A balustrade above the cornice

New York's Upper East Side has two fine examples of this building type, each exhibiting most of the style's key features: the **Racquet and Tennis Club,** 370 Park Ave. (McKim, Mead & White, 1918), based on the style of an elegant Florentine palazzo; and the **Metropolitan Club,** 1 East 60th St. (McKim, Mead & White, 1891–94).

7 Beaux Arts (1890–1920)

The style takes its names from the Ecole des Beaux-Arts in Paris, where a number of prominent American architects (including **Richard Morris Hunt** [1827–95],

John Mervin Carrère [1858–1911], and **Thomas Hastings** [1860–1929], to name only a few) received their training, beginning around the mid–19th century. These architects adopted the academic design principles of the Ecole, which emphasized the study of Greek and Roman structures, composition, and symmetry, and the creation of elaborate presentation drawings. Because of the idealized origins and grandiose use of classical forms, the beaux arts in America was seen as the ideal style for expressing civic pride.

Grandiose compositions, an exuberance of detail, and a variety of stone finishes typify most beaux arts structures. Particular features include:

- A pronounced cornice and ornate entablature topped by a tall parapet, balustrade, or attic story
- Projecting pavilions, often with colossal columns grouped in pairs
- Windows framed by freestanding columns, a sill with a balustrade, and/or entablatures with pediments or decorative keystones
- Grand staircases
- Grand arched openings
- Classical decoration: free-standing statuary, ornamental panels, swags, medallions
- A heavy *ashlar* (squared stone) base

New York has several exuberant beaux arts buildings, exhibiting the style's key features. The **New York Public Library,** at Fifth Avenue and 42nd Street (Carrère & Hastings, 1911), is perhaps the best example. Others of note are **Grand Central Terminal,** at 42nd Street and Park Avenue (Reed & Stem and Warren & Whetmore, 1903–13), and the **U.S. Custom House** (Cass Gilbert, 1907) on Bowling Green between State and Whitehall streets.

8 Early Skyscraper (1880–1920)

The invention of the skyscraper can be traced directly to the use of cast iron in the 1840s for storefronts, such as those seen in New York's SoHo. Experimentation with cast and wrought iron in the construction of interior skeletons eventually allowed buildings to rise higher. (Previously, buildings were restricted by the height supportable by their load-bearing walls.) In Chicago, important technical innovations—involving safety elevators, electricity, fireproofing, foundations, plumbing, and telecommunications—combined with advances in skeletal construction to create a new building type, the skyscraper. These buildings were spacious, cost-effective, efficient, and quickly erected—in short, the perfect architectural solution for America's growing downtowns.

Solving the technical problems of the skyscraper did not resolve how the building should look. Most solutions relied on historical precedents, including decoration reminiscent of the Gothic, Romanesque (a style characterized by the use of rounded arches), or beaux arts.

Other features of the early skyscrapers include:

- A rectangular shape with a flat roof
- Tripartite division of the facade, similar to that of a column, with a *base* (usually of two stories), *shaft* (midsection with a repetitive window pattern), and *capital* (typically an elaborate, terra-cotta cornice)
- Exterior expression of the building's interior skeleton through an emphasis on horizontal and vertical elements
- Use of *terra cotta,* a light and fireproof material that could be cast in any shape and attached to the exterior

New York's early skyscrapers relied heavily on historical decoration. A good early example in the beaux arts mode is the **American Surety Company,** at 100 Broadway (Bruce Price, 1895). The triangular **Flatiron Building,** at Fifth Avenue and 23rd Street (Daniel H. Burnham & Co., 1902), has strong tripartite divisions and Renaissance Revival detail. And, finally, the later **Woolworth Building** (Cass Gilbert, 1913), on Broadway at Park Place, dubbed the "Cathedral of Commerce," is a neo-Gothic skyscraper with flying buttresses, spires, sculptured gargoyles, and pointed arches.

9 Art Deco (1925–40)

Art Deco is a decorative style that took its name from a Paris exposition in 1925. The jazzy style embodied the idea of modernity. One of the first widely accepted styles not based on historic precedents, it influenced all areas of design from jewelry and household goods to cars, trains, and ocean liners.

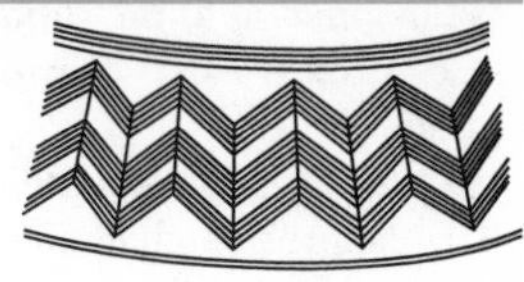

Chevron

Art Deco buildings are characterized by a linear, hard edge, or angular composition often with a vertical emphasis and highlighted with stylized decoration. The New York zoning law of 1916, which required set backs in buildings above a certain height to ensure that light and air could reach the street, gave the style its distinctive profile. Other important features include:

- An emphasis on geometric form
- Strips of windows with decorated *spandrels* (the horizontal panel below a window) that added to the sense of verticality
- Use of hard-edged, low-relief ornamentation around doors and windows
- Frequent use of black and silver tones
- Decorative motifs of parallel straight lines, zigzags, chevrons (see illustration), and stylized florals

Despite the effects of the Depression, several major Art Deco structures were built in New York in the 1930s, often providing crucial jobs. **Rockefeller Center** (1932–40), a complex sprawling from 48th to 50th streets between Fifth and Sixth avenues, includes 30 Rockefeller Plaza, a tour de force of Art Deco style with a soaring, vertical shaft and aluminum details. The **Chrysler Building,** Lexington Avenue at 42nd Street (William Van Alen, 1930), is a towering tribute to the automobile (see illustration). The Chrysler's needlelike spire with zigzag patterns in glass and metal is a distinctive feature on the city's skyline. The famous **Empire State Building,** Fifth Avenue at 34th Street (Shreve, Lamb & Harmon, 1931), contains a black- and silver-toned lobby among its many Art Deco features.

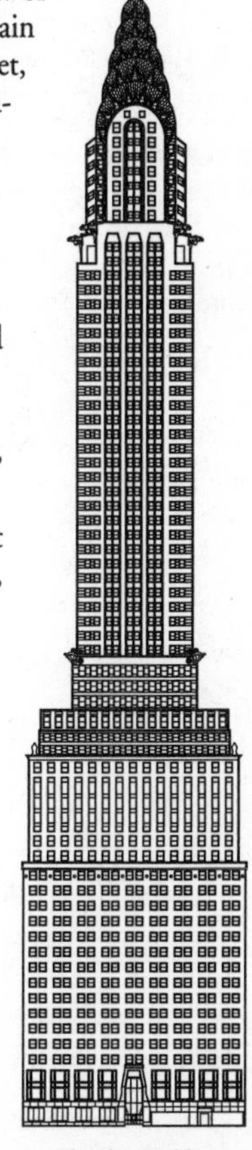

Chrysler Building

10 Art Moderne (1930–45)

Art moderne strove for modernity and an artistic expression for the sleekness of the machine age. Unbroken horizontal lines and smooth curves visually distinguish it from Art Deco and give it a streamlined effect. It was popular with movie theaters and was often applied to cars, trains, and boats to suggest the idea of speed.

The key features of art moderne buildings are:

- A flat roof
- Soft or rounded corners
- Smooth wall finish without surface ornamentation
- Horizontal bands of windows creating a distinctive streamlined or wind-tunneled effect
- Ornamentation of mirrored panels, cement panels, and perhaps low-relief metal panels around doors and windows
- Aluminum and stainless steel for door and window trim, railings, and balusters
- Metal or wood doors may have circular windows or patterns with circular and angular outlines

The **Majestic Apartments,** at 115 Central Park West (Irwin S. Chanin, 1930), has futuristic forms and wide banks of windows that wrap around corners. **Radio City Music Hall,** on Sixth Avenue at 50th Street (Edward Durrell Stone and Donald Deskey, 1932), has a sweeping art moderne marquee.

11 International Style (1920–45)

In 1932, the Museum of Modern Art hosted its first architecture exhibit, titled simply "Modern Architecture." Displays included images of International Style buildings from around the world, many designed by architects from Germany's Bauhaus, a progressive design school. The structures all shared a stark simplicity and vigorous functionalism, a definite break from historically based, decorative styles.

The International Style was popularized in the United States through the teachings and designs of **Ludwig Mies van der Rohe** (1886–1969), a German émigré based in Chicago. Interpretations of the "Miesian" International Style were built in most U.S. cities, including New York, as late as 1980. In the 1950s, erecting an office building in this mode made companies appear progressive. In later decades, after the International Style was a corporate mainstay, the style took on conservative connotations.

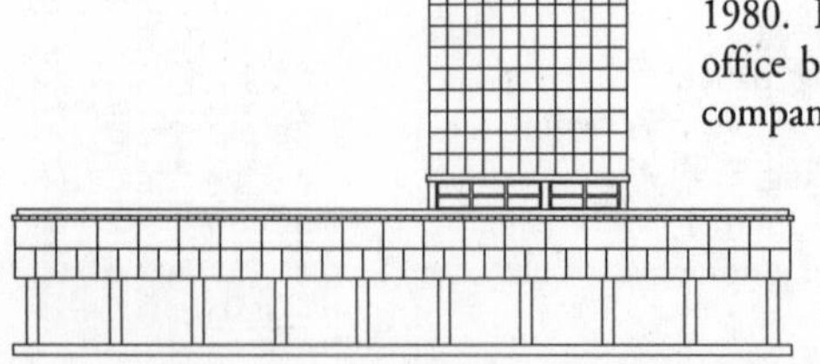

Lever House

Features of the International Style as popularized by Mies include:

- A rectangular shape
- Frequent use of glass
- Balance and regularity, but not symmetry
- Horizontal bands of windows
- Windows meeting at corners
- Absence of ornamentation
- Clear expression of the building's form and function (the interior structure of stacked office floors is clearly visible, as are the locations of mechanical systems, such as elevator shafts and air-conditioning units)
- Placement, or cantilevering, of building on tall piers

Two famous examples of this style in New York are the **Seagram Building,** at 375 Park Ave. (Ludwig Mies van der Rohe, 1958), and **Lever House** (see illustration), 390 Park Ave., between 53rd and 54th streets (Skidmore, Owings & Merrill, 1952). The latter, designed by a firm that made "Miesian" architecture a corporate staple, is credited for popularizing the use of plazas and glass curtain walls. Another well-known example is the Secretariat building in the **United Nations** complex, at First Avenue and 46th Street (1947–53), designed by an international committee of architects.

12 Postmodern (1975–90)

After years of steel-and-glass office towers in the International Style, postmodernism burst on the scene in the 1970s with the reintroduction of historical precedents in architecture. With many feeling that the office towers of the previous style were too cold, postmodernists began to incorporate classical details and recognizable forms into their designs—often applied in outrageous proportions.

Characteristics of postmodern skyscrapers tend to include:

- An overall shape (or incorporation) of a recognizable object, not necessarily associated with architecture
- Classical details, such as columns, domes, or vaults, often oversized and used in inventive ways
- A distinctive profile in the skyline
- A use of stone rather than glass

The **Sony Building,** at 550 Madison Ave. (Philip Johnson/John Burgee, 1984), brings the distinctive shape of a Chippendale cabinet to the New York skyline. The **Morgan Bank Headquarters,** 60 Wall St. (Kevin Roche John Dinkeloo & Assocs., 1988) resembles a classical column, with modern interpretations of a base, shaft, and capital. The base of the column mirrors in style the facade of the 19th-century building across the street.

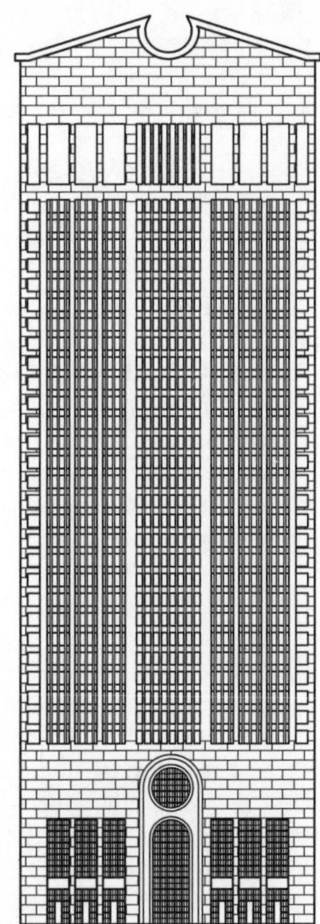

Sony Building

3

Planning Your Trip to New York City

In the pages that follow, you'll find everything you need to know to handle the practical details of planning your trip in advance: airlines and area airports, a calendar of events, resources for those of you with special needs, and much more.

Note that there's no need to rent a car. Driving is a nightmare and parking is ridiculously expensive (or near to impossible in some neighborhoods). It's much easier to get around using public transportation, taxis, and your own two feet. If you're going to visit Aunt Erma on Long Island or you have some other need to travel beyond the five boroughs, call one of the major car-rental companies, such as **National** (✆ **800/227-7368;** www.nationalcar.com), **Hertz** (✆ **800/654-3131;** www.hertz.com), or **Avis** (✆ **800/230-4898;** www.avis.com), all of which have airport and Manhattan locations.

1 Visitor Information

For information before you leave home, your best source (besides this book, of course) is **NYC & Company,** the organization that fronts the New York Convention & Visitors Bureau (NYCVB), 810 Seventh Ave., New York, NY 10019. You can call ✆ **800/NYC-VISIT** or 212/397-8222 to order the **Official NYC Visitor Kit,** which contains the *Official NYC Guide* detailing hotels, restaurants, theaters, attractions, events, and more; a foldout map; a decent newsletter on the latest goings-on in the city; and brochures on attractions and services. It costs $5.95 to receive the packet (payable by credit card) in 7 to 10 days, $9.95 for rush delivery (3–4 business days) to U.S. addresses and international orders. (*Note:* I have received complaints that packages don't always strictly adhere to these time frames.)

You can also find a wealth of free information on the bureau's website, **www.nycvisit.com**. To speak with a travel counselor who can answer specific questions, call ✆ **212/484-1222,** which is staffed daily weekdays from 8:30am to 6pm EST, weekends from 9am to 5pm EST.

For visitor center and information desk locations once you arrive, see "Visitor Information," in chapter 5.

See also the box called "Site Seeing: The Big Apple on the Web" on p. 14. There, you'll find details on the best online resources for planning your trip.

FOR U.K. VISITORS The **NYCVB Visitor Information Center** is at 33–34 Carnaby St., London W1F 7DW (✆ **0207/437-8300**). You can order the Official NYC Visitor Kit by sending an A5-size self-addressed envelope and 72p postage to the above address. For New York–bound travelers in the London area, the center also offers free one-on-one travel-planning assistance.

2 Money

You never have to carry too much cash in New York, and while the city's pretty safe these days, it's best not to overstuff your wallet (although always make sure you have at least $20 in taxi fare on hand).

In most Manhattan neighborhoods, you can find a bank with **ATMs** every couple of blocks. The only places you may have some difficulty are in more far-flung neighborhoods, like the far East Village or far uptown in Harlem. The city's biggest banks are Citibank, Chase, Fleet, and HSBC, which belong to both the **Cirrus** (✆ **800/424-7787;** www.mastercard.com) and **PLUS** (✆ **800/843-7587;** www.visa.com/atms) networks. Expect to pay $1.50 or $2 each time you withdraw money from an ATM, in addition to what your home bank charges. Try to stay away from commercial machines, like those in hotel lobbies and corner delis, which often charge $3 or more per transaction and usually limit the amount of cash you can withdraw. Avoid poorly lit or out-of-the-way ATMs, especially at night. Put your money away discreetly—don't flash it around or count it in a way that could attract the attention of thieves.

Traveler's checks are something of an anachronism from the days before the ATM made cash accessible at any time. But if you want to avoid constant ATM withdrawal charges, and you prefer the security of the tried-and-true, you might be better off with traveler's checks—provided you don't mind showing identification every time you want to cash one. You can get traveler's checks at almost any bank, usually incurring a service charge ranging from 1% to 4%. You can also get **American Express** traveler's checks over the phone by calling ✆ **800/221-7282** or online at **www.americanexpress.com**. Amex gold or platinum cardholders can avoid paying the fee by ordering over the telephone. **American Automobile Association (AAA) members** can obtain checks with no fee at most AAA offices.

Visa offers traveler's checks at Citibank locations nationwide, as well as at several other banks; call ✆ **800/732-1322** for information. **MasterCard** also offers traveler's checks; call ✆ **800/223-9920** for a location near you.

As for credit cards, **American Express, MasterCard,** and **Visa** are accepted virtually everywhere in New York. **Carte Blanche** and **Diner's Club** have made a comeback, especially in hotel circles, and **Discover** is also quite popular (although don't count on it being accepted everywhere). Because New York has such a heavy influx of international visitors, cards like **enRoute, Eurocard,** and **JCB** are also widely accepted, particularly at hotels.

3 When to Go

Summer or winter, rain or shine, there's always great stuff going on in New York City, so there's no real "best" time to go.

Culture hounds might come in fall, winter, and early spring, when the theater and performing arts seasons reach their heights. During summer, many of the top cultural institutions, especially Lincoln Center, offer alfresco entertainment. Those who want to see the biggest hits on Broadway usually have the best luck getting tickets in the slower months of January and February.

Gourmands might find it easiest to land the best tables during July and August, when New Yorkers escape the city on weekends. If you prefer to walk every city block to take in the sights, spring and fall usually offer the mildest and most pleasant weather.

New York is a nonstop holiday party from early December through the start of the new year. Celebrations of the season abound in festive holiday windows and events like the lighting of the Rockefeller Center tree and the Radio City Christmas Spectacular—not to mention those terrific seasonal sales that make New York a holiday shopping bonanza. However, keep in mind that hotel prices go sky high (more on that below), and the crowds are almost intolerable. If you'd rather have more of the city to yourself—better chances at restaurant reservations and show tickets, easier access to museums and other attractions—choose another time of year to visit.

MONEY MATTERS At press time, it was still unclear as to what kinds of lasting effects 9/11 would have on New York City's tourism fortunes. While hotel prices are more flexible than they've been in years, New York hotels are by no means throwing a fire sale. Therefore, if money is a big concern, you might want to follow these rough seasonal guidelines.

Bargain hunters might want to visit in winter, between the first of the year and early April. Sure, you might have to bear some cold weather, but that's when hotels are suffering from the postholiday blues, and rooms often go for a relative song. In the winter of 2002, you could even get a room at the ultra-luxurious Le Parker Meridien for as little as $199 on select nights, and rooms at the truly comfortable Comfort Inn–Central Park West were going for as little as $80 to $90. AAA cardholders could even do better in many cases (generally a 5%–10% savings, if the hotel offers a AAA discount). However, be aware that the occasional convention or event, such as February's annual Fashion Week, can sometimes throw a wrench in your winter savings plans.

Spring and fall are traditionally the busiest, and most expensive, seasons after holiday time. Don't expect hotels to be handing you deals, but you may be able to negotiate a decent rate.

The city is drawing more families these days, and they usually visit in the summer. Still, the prospect of heat and humidity keeps some people away, making July and the first half of August a significantly cheaper time to visit than later in the year; good hotel deals are often available.

At Christmas, all bets are off—expect to pay top dollar for everything. The first 2 weeks of December—the shopping weeks—are the absolute worst when it comes to scoring an affordable hotel room; that's when shoppers from around the world converge on the town to catch the holiday spirit and spend, spend, spend. But Thanksgiving can be a great time to come, believe it or not: Business travelers have gone home for the holiday, and the holiday shoppers haven't yet arrived. It's a little-known secret that most hotels away from the Thanksgiving Day Parade route have empty rooms sitting, and they're usually willing to make great deals to fill them.

WEATHER The worst weather in New York is during that long week or 10 days that arrive each summer between mid-July and mid-August, when temperatures go up to around 100°F with 90% humidity. You feel sticky all day, the streets smell horrible, everyone's cranky, and the concrete canyons become furnaces. It can be no fun walking around in this weather. Don't get put off by this—summer has its compensations, such as wonderful free open-air concerts and other events, as I've already mentioned—but bear it in mind. And you may luck out, as the last few summers have been downright lovely. But if you are at all temperature sensitive, your odds of getting comfortable weather are better in June or September.

Another period when you might not like to stroll around the city is during January or February, when temperatures are commonly in the 20s and those concrete canyons turn into wind tunnels. The city looks gorgeous for about a day after a snowfall, but the streets soon become an ugly, slushy mess. Again, you never know—temperatures have regularly been in the 30s and mild 40s during the past few winters. If you hit the weather jackpot, you could have a bargain bonanza (see "Money Matters," above).

Fall and spring are the best times in New York. From April to June and September to November, temperatures are mild and pleasant, and the light is beautiful. With the leaves changing in Central Park and just the hint of crispness in the air, October is a fabulous time to be here—but expect to pay for the privilege.

If you want to know how to pack just before you go, check the Weather Channel's online 10-day forecast at **www.weather.com**; I like to balance it against CNN's online 5-day forecast at **www.cnn.com/weather**. You can also get the local weather by calling ✆ **212/976-1212.**

New York's Average Temperature & Rainfall

	Jan	Feb	Mar	Apr	May	June	July	Aug	Sept	Oct	Nov	Dec
Daily Temp. (°F)	38	40	48	61	71	80	85	84	77	67	54	42
Daily Temp. (°C)	3	4	9	16	22	27	29	29	25	19	12	6
Days of Precipitation	11	10	11	11	11	10	11	10	8	8	9	10

NEW YORK CITY CALENDAR OF EVENTS

The following information is always subject to change. Always confirm information before you make plans around a specific event. Call the venue or the NYCVB at ✆ **212/484-1222,** go to **www.nycvisit.com,** or pick up a copy of **Time Out New York** once you arrive in the city for the latest details.

January

New York National Boat Show. Slip on your Top-Siders and head to the **Jacob K. Javits Convention Center** for the 93rd edition, which promises a leviathan fleet of boats and marine products from the world's leading manufacturers. Call ✆ **212/922-1212** or 212/216-2000, or point your Web browser to www.boatshows.com or www.javitscenter.com. First or second week in January.

February

Chinese New Year. Every year Chinatown rings in its own New Year (based on a lunar calendar) with 2 weeks of celebrations, including parades with dragon and lion dancers, plus vivid costumes of all kinds. The parade usually winds throughout Chinatown along Mott, Canal, and Bayard streets, and along East Broadway. The year 2003 is the Year of the Goat, and the Chinese New Year falls on February 1. Call the NYCVB hot line at ✆ **212/484-1222** or the Chinese Information and Culture Center at ✆ **212/373-1800.**

Westminster Kennel Club Dog Show. The ultimate purebred pooch fest. Some 30,000 dog fanciers from the world over congregate at **Madison Square Garden** for the 125th "World Series of Dogdom." All 2,500 dogs are American Kennel Club Champions of Record, competing for the Best in Show trophy. Call ✆ **800/455-3647** or visit www.westminsterkennelclub.org for further information. Tickets become available after January 1 through **Ticketmaster** (✆ **212/307-7171;** www.ticketmaster.com). February 10 to 11.

Valentine's Day Weddings atop the Empire State Building. You and your honey can become lifetime members of the **Empire State Building** Wedding Club by getting hitched on the 80th floor observation deck on February 14, 2003. Just 15 lucky couples will be chosen based on their "Why We Want to Get Married at the Empire State Building" essay submissions, which are judged on originality, uniqueness, and style. The deadline for submissions is November 30, 2002; call ✆ **212/736-3100** or visit www.esbnyc.com for details.

March

Triple Pier Antiques Show. The city's largest and most comprehensive antiques show takes place over two consecutive weekends, as more than 600 dealers exhibit their treasures, ranging from jewelry to home furnishings, on three piers along the Hudson River between 48th and 51st streets. **Pier 88** features 20th-century modern collectibles; **Pier 90** has all manner of Americana, including country rustic, folk art, and Arts and Crafts; and **Pier 92** houses 18th- and 19th-century formal European antiques. Call ✆ **212/255-0020** or visit www.antiqnet.com/Stella for this year's dates, plus a calendar of additional shows. Usually mid-March, and again in mid-November.

St. Patrick's Day Parade. More than 150,000 marchers join in the world's largest civilian parade, as Fifth Avenue from 44th to 86th streets rings with the sounds of bands and bagpipes. The parade usually starts at 11am, but go extra early if you want a good spot. Call ✆ **212/484-1222.** March 17.

New York International Auto Show. Hot wheels from all over the world whirl into the **Jacob K. Javits Convention Center** for the largest auto show in the United States. Many concept cars show up that will never roll off the assembly line but are fun to dream about nonetheless. Call ✆ **800/282-3336** or 212/216-2000, or point your browser to www.autoshowny.com or www.javitscenter.com. Late March through early April.

April

Easter Parade. This isn't a traditional parade, per se: There are no marching bands, no baton twirlers, no protesters. Once upon a time, New York's gentry came out to show off their tasteful but discreet toppings. Today, if you were planning to slip on a tasteful little number—say something delicately woven in straw with a simple flower or two that matches your gloves—you will *not* be the grandest lady in this springtime hike along Fifth Avenue from 48th to 57th streets. It's more about flamboyant exhibitionism, with hats and costumes that get more outrageous every year—and anybody can join right in for free. The parade generally runs Easter Sunday from about 10am to 3 or 4pm. Call ✆ **212/484-1222.** April 20.

May

Bike New York: The Great Five Boro Bike Tour. The largest mass-participation cycling event in the United States attracts about 30,000 cyclists from all over the world. After a 42-mile (68km) ride through the five boroughs, finalists are greeted with a traditional New York–style celebration of food and music. Call ✆ **212/932-BIKE** (2453) or visit www.bikenewyork.org to register. First or second Sunday in May.

Ninth Avenue International Food Festival. Cancel dinner reservations and spend the day sampling sizzling Italian sausages, homemade pierogi, spicy curries, and an assortment of other ethnic dishes. Street musicians, bands, and vendors add to the festive atmosphere at one of the city's best street fairs, stretching along Ninth Avenue from 37th to 57th streets. Call ✆ **212/484-1222** or visit 9th-ave.com/9thAveFestival.htm. One weekend in mid-May.

Fleet Week. About 10,000 navy and Coast Guard personnel are "at liberty" in New York for the annual Fleet Week at the end of May. Usually from 1 to 4pm daily, you can watch the ships and aircraft carriers as they dock at the piers on the west side of Manhattan, tour them with on-duty personnel, and watch some dramatic exhibitions by the U.S. Marines. Even if you don't take in any of the events, you'll know it's Fleet Week, because those 10,000 sailors invade Midtown in their starched white uniforms. It's simply wonderful—just like *On the Town* come to life. Call ✆ **212/245-0072,** or visit www.fleetweek.com (your best source for a full list of events) or www.uss-intrepid.com. Late May.

June

Belmont Stakes. The third jewel in the Triple Crown is held at the **Belmont Park Race Track** in Elmont, Long Island. If a Triple Crown winner is to be named, it will happen here. For information, call ✆ **516/488-6000,** or visit www.nyracing.com/belmont. Early June.

Museum Mile Festival. Fifth Avenue from 82nd to 104th streets is closed to cars from 6 to 9pm as 20,000-plus strollers enjoy live music from Broadway tunes to string quartets, street entertainers from juggling to giant puppets, and free admission to nine Museum Mile institutions, including the Metropolitan Museum of Art and the Guggenheim. Call ✆ **212/606-2296** or any of the participating institutions for details. Usually the second Tuesday in June.

Lesbian and Gay Pride Week and March. A week of cheerful happenings, from simple parties to major political fund-raisers, precedes a zany parade commemorating the Stonewall Riot of June 27, 1969, which for many marks the beginning of the gay liberation movement. Fifth Avenue goes wild as the gay/lesbian community celebrates with bands, marching groups, floats, and plenty of panache. The parade starts on upper Fifth Avenue around 52nd Street and continues into the Village, where a street festival and a waterfront dance party with fireworks cap the day. Call ✆ **212/807-7433** or check www.nycpride.org. Mid- to late June.

SummerStage. A summer-long festival of outdoor performances in **Central Park,** featuring world music, pop, folk, and jazz artists ranging from Steve Earle to Craig David to Basement Jaxx to the New York Grand Opera (always performing Verdi) to the Chinese Golden Dragon Acrobats. Performances are often free, but certain events require purchased tickets (usually less than $30). Call ✆ **212/360-2777** or visit www.summerstage.org. June through August.

Shakespeare in the Park. The Delacorte Theater in **Central Park** is the setting for first-rate free performances under the stars—including at least one Shakespeare production each season—often with stars on the stage. For details, see "Park It! Shakespeare, Music & Other Free Fun," in chapter 11.

Call ✆ **212/539-8750,** or point your browser to www.publictheater.org. June through August.

July

Independence Day Harbor Festival and Fourth of July Fireworks Spectacular. Start the day amid the patriotic crowds at the Great July Fourth Festival in Lower Manhattan, and then catch Macy's great fireworks extravaganza (one of the country's most fantastic) over the East River (the best vantage point is from the FDR Dr., which closes to traffic several hours before sunset). Call ✆ **212/484-1222,** or Macy's Visitor Center at 212/494-2922. July 4th.

Lincoln Center Festival 2003. This festival celebrates the best of the performing arts from all over the world—theater, ballet, contemporary dance, opera, nouveau circus performances, even puppet and media-based art. Recent editions have featured performances by Ornette Coleman, the Royal Opera, the Royal Ballet, and the New York Philharmonic. Schedules are usually available in mid-March, and tickets go on sale in late May or early June. Call ✆ **212/546-2656,** or visit www.lincolncenter.org. Throughout July.

Midsummer Night's Swing. Dancing duos head to the **Lincoln Center Fountain Plaza** for romantic evenings of big-band swing, salsa, and tango under the stars to the sounds of top-flight bands. Dance lessons are offered with the purchase of a ticket. Call ✆ **212/875-5766,** or visit www.lincolncenter.org. July and August.

Mostly Mozart. World-renowned ensembles and soloists (Alicia de Larrocha and André Watts have performed in the past) are featured at this month-long series at **Avery Fisher Hall.** Schedules are usually available in mid-April and tickets in early May. Call ✆ **212/875-5030** or 212/546-2656 for information, 212/721-6500 to order tickets, or visit www.lincolncenter.org. Late July through August.

August

Lincoln Center Out of Doors. This series of free music and dance performances is held outdoors on the plazas of **Lincoln Center.** Call ✆ **212/875-5108** or 212/546-2656, or visit www.lincolncenter.org for this year's schedule (usually available in mid-July). Throughout August.

New York Fringe Festival. Held in a variety of tiny Lower East Side venues and park spaces for a mainly hipster crowd, this arts festival presents alternative as well as traditional theater, musicals, dance, comedy, and all manner of performance art, including new media. Literally hundreds of events are held at all hours over about 10 days in late August. The quality can vary wildly (lots of performers use Fringe as a workshop to develop their acts and shows), and some performances really push the envelope. Nonetheless, you'd be surprised at how many shows are actually *good.* Call ✆ **888/FRINGE-NYC** or 212/420-8777, or visit www.fringenyc.org. Throughout August.

Harlem Week. The world's largest black and Hispanic cultural festival actually spans almost the whole month to include the Black Film Festival, the Harlem Jazz and Music Festival, and the Taste of Harlem Food Festival. Expect a full slate of music, from gospel to hip-hop, and lots of other festivities. Call ✆ **212/484-1222** or visit www.discoverharlem.com or for this year's schedule of events and locations. Throughout August.

U.S. Open Tennis Championships. The final Grand Slam event of the tennis season is held at the Arthur Ashe Stadium at the USTA National Tennis Center, the largest public tennis center in the world, at **Flushing Meadows Park** in Queens. Tickets go on sale in May or early June. The event sells out immediately, because many of the tickets are held by corporate sponsors who hand them out to customers. (It's worth it to check the list of sponsors to determine if anyone you know has a connection for getting tickets.) You can usually buy scalped tickets outside the complex (an illegal practice, of course), which is right next to Shea Stadium. The last few matches of the tournament are the most expensive, but you'll see a lot more tennis early on, when your ticket allows you to wander the outside courts and view several different matches. Call ✆ **888/OPEN-TIX** or 718/760-6200 well in advance; visit www.usopen.org or www.usta.com for additional information. Two weeks around Labor Day.

September

West Indian–American Day Parade. This annual Brooklyn event is New York's largest street celebration. Come for the extravagant costumes, pulsating rhythms (soca, calypso, reggae), bright colors, folklore, food (jerk chicken, oxtail soup, Caribbean soul food), and 2 million hip-shaking revelers. The route can change from year to year, but it usually runs along Eastern Parkway from Utica Avenue to Grand Army Plaza (at the gateway to Prospect Park). Call ✆ **212/484-1222** or 718/625-1515. Labor Day.

Wigstock. The ultimate drag festival is an annual event in which the Lady Bunny, Hedda Lettuce, Lypsinka, even RuPaul—plus hundreds of other fabulous drag queens—strut their stuff at the self-proclaimed festival of "Peace, Love, and Hairspray." Organizers have threatened to pull the plug on future Wigstocks, citing high expenses. Common wisdom is that this is an empty threat, and the city can expect a Wigstock 2003. However, definitely check to make sure it's on as the date gets closer before you build any travel plans around the event. Call ✆ **800/494-TIXS** or visit www.wigstock.nu for tickets (expect to pay at least $25 a head). You can also usually get Wigstock information from the Lesbian and Gay Community Services Center website at www.gaycenter.org. For a preview—or a nostalgic look, if we have indeed seen the end of Wigstock—see Goldwyn's *Wigstock: The Movie.* Labor Day weekend.

Broadway on Broadway. This free alfresco afternoon show features the songs and casts from virtually every Broadway production performing on a stage erected in the middle of Times Square. This event keeps getting bigger and bigger—it was even broadcast on ABC-TV in 2000—so you can expect the big stars and top production numbers. Call ✆ **212/768-1560,** or visit www.timessquarebid.org and click on "Events." Sunday in mid-September.

Feast of San Gennaro. An atmospheric Little Italy street fair honoring the patron saint of Naples, with great food, traditional music, carnival rides, games, and vendors set up along Mulberry Street north of Canal Street. Expect big crowds. And who knows? You may even spot a godfather or two. Call **212/768-9320** or visit www.sangennaro.org for this year's schedule. Usually 10 days in mid-September.

New York Film Festival. Legendary hits *Pulp Fiction* and *Mean*

Streets both had their U.S. premieres at the Film Society of Lincoln Center's 2-week festival, a major stop on the film fest circuit. Schedules in recent years have included advance looks at *The Sweet Hereafter, Rushmore,* and *All About My Mother.* Screenings are held in various Lincoln Center venues; advance tickets are a good bet always, and a necessity for certain events (especially evening and weekend screenings). Call ✆ **212/875-5600** for information, 212/875-5050 for tickets, or check out www.filmlinc.com. Two weeks from late September to early October.

BAM Next Wave Festival. One of the city's most important cultural events takes place at the **Brooklyn Academy of Music.** The months-long festival showcases experimental new dance, theater, and music works by both renowned and lesser-known international artists. Recent celebrated performances have included Astor Piazzolla's *Maria de Buenos Aires* (featuring Piazzolla disciple Gidon Kremer), the 25th anniversary of the Kronos Quartet, and choreographer Bill T. Jones's *We Set Out Early . . . Visibility Was Poor* (set to the music of Igor Stravinsky, John Cage, and Peteris Vask). Call ✆ **718/636-4100** or visit www.bam.org. September through December.

October

Feast of St. Francis. Animals from goldfish to elephants are blessed as thousands of Homo sapiens look on at the **Cathedral of St. John the Divine.** A magical experience—pets, of course, are welcome. A festive fair follows the blessing and music events. Buy tickets in advance because they can be hard to come by. Call ✆ **212/316-7540** or 212/662-7133 for tickets, or visit www.stjohndivine.org. First Sunday in October.

Ice-Skating. Show off your skating style in the limelight at the diminutive **Rockefeller Center** rink (✆ **212/332-7654;** www.rockefellercenter.com), open from mid-October to mid-March or early April (you'll skate under the magnificent Christmas tree for the month of Dec), or at the larger **Wollman Rink** in Central Park, on the east side of the park between 62nd and 63rd streets (✆ **212/439-6900;** www.wollmanskatingrink.com), which usually closes in early April.

Greenwich Village Halloween Parade. This is Halloween at its most outrageous. You may have heard Lou Reed singing about it on his classic album *New York*—he wasn't exaggerating. Drag queens and assorted other flamboyant types parade through the Village in wildly creative costumes. The parade route has changed over the years, but most recently it has started after sunset at Spring Street and marched up Sixth Avenue to 23rd Street or Union Square. Call the *Village Voice* Parade hot line at ✆ **212/475-3333, ext. 4044,** point your Web browser to www.halloween-nyc.com, or check the papers for the exact route so you can watch—or participate, if you have the threads and the imagination. October 31.

November

New York City Marathon. Some 30,000 hopefuls from around the world participate in the largest U.S. marathon, and more than a million fans will cheer them on as they follow a route that touches on all five New York boroughs and finishes at Central Park. Call ✆ **212/423-2249,** or 212/860-4455, or point your Web browser to www.nyrrc.org, where you can find applications to run. November 3 in 2002, November 2 in 2003.

Radio City Music Hall Christmas Spectacular. A rather gaudy extravaganza, but lots of fun nonetheless. Starring the Radio City Rockettes and a cast that includes live animals (just try to picture the camels sauntering in the Sixth Ave. entrance!). After undergoing an extensive restoration, spectacular Radio City itself is a sight to see. For information, call ✆ **212/247-4777** or visit www.radiocity.com; buy tickets at the box office or via Ticketmaster's **Radio City Hot Line** (✆ **212/307-1000**), or visit www.ticketmaster.com. Throughout November and December.

Triple Pier Antiques Show. The city's largest antiques show takes place over 2 consecutive weekends, usually just before Thanksgiving; for details, see March, above. Call ✆ **212/255-0020** or visit www.antiqnet.com/Stella for this year's dates.

Macy's Thanksgiving Day Parade. The procession from Central Park West and 77th Street and down Broadway to Herald Square at 34th Street continues to be a national tradition. Huge hot-air balloons in the forms of Rocky and Bullwinkle, Snoopy, Underdog, the Pink Panther, Bart Simpson, and other cartoon favorites are the best part of the fun. The night before, you can usually see the big blow-up on Central Park West at 79th Street; call in advance to see if it will be open to the public again this year. Call ✆ **212/484-1222,** or Macy's Visitor Center at 212/494-2922. November 28 in 2002, November 27 in 2003.

Big Apple Circus. New York City's homegrown, not-for-profit performing-arts circus is a favorite with children and everyone who's young at heart. Big Apple is committed to maintaining the classical circus tradition with sensitivity, and only features animals that have a traditional working relationship with humans. A tent is pitched in **Damrosch Park** at **Lincoln Center.** Call ✆ **212/268-2500,** or visit www.bigapplecircus.org. November through January.

The Nutcracker. Tchaikovsky's holiday favorite is performed by the New York City Ballet at **Lincoln Center.** The annual schedule is available from mid-July, and tickets usually go on sale in early October. Call ✆ **212/870-5570,** or go online to www.nycballet.com. Late November through early January.

Lighting of the Rockefeller Center Christmas Tree. The annual lighting ceremony is accompanied by an ice-skating show, singing, entertainment, and a huge crowd. The tree stays lit around the clock until after the new year. Call ✆ **212/332-6868** or visit www.rockefellercenter.com for this year's date. Late November or early December.

December

Holiday Trimmings. Stroll down festive Fifth Avenue, and you'll see doormen dressed as wooden soldiers at **FAO Schwarz,** a 27-foot (8m) sparkling snowflake floating over the intersection outside **Tiffany's,** the **Cartier** building ribboned and bowed in red, wreaths warming the necks of the **New York Public Library**'s lions, and fanciful figurines in the windows of **Saks Fifth Avenue** and **Lord & Taylor.** Madison Avenue between 55th and 60th streets is also a good bet; **Sony Plaza** usually boasts some fabulous windows (Martha Stewart did 'em in 2000), as does **Barney's New York.** Throughout December.

Christmas Traditions. In addition to the **Radio City Music Hall Christmas Spectacular** and the

New York City Ballet's staging of ***The Nutcracker*** (see "November," above), traditional holiday events include ***A Christmas Carol*** at **The Theater at Madison Square Garden** (© **212/465-6741** or www.thegarden.com, © 212/307-7171 or www.ticketmaster.com for tickets), usually featuring a big name to draw in the crowds (Roger Daltrey even did it back in 1998). At **Avery Fisher Hall** is the National Chorale's singalong performances of Handel's ***Messiah*** (© **212/875-5030;** www.lincolncenter.org) for a week before Christmas. Don't worry if the only words you know are "Alleluia, Alleluia!"—a lyrics sheet is given to ticket holders. Throughout December

Lighting of the Hanukkah Menorah. Everything is done on a grand scale in New York, so it's no surprise that the world's largest menorah (32 ft./9.5m high) is at Manhattan's **Grand Army Plaza,** Fifth Avenue and 59th Street. Hanukkah celebrations begin at sunset, with the lighting of the first of the giant electric candles. November 29 in 2002, December 19 in 2003.

New Year's Eve. The biggest party of them all happens in **Times Square,** where hundreds of thousands of raucous revelers count down in unison the year's final seconds until the new lighted ball drops at midnight at 1 Times Square. I personally don't understand it, since it's always a crowded, cold, boozy madhouse, but hey! Call © **212/768-1560,** 212/484-1222, or visit www.timessquarebid.org. December 31.

Runner's World **Midnight Run.** Enjoy **fireworks** followed by the New York Road Runner's Club's annual run in **Central Park,** which is fun for runners and spectators alike; call © **212/860-4455** or visit www.nyrrc.org. December 31.

Brooklyn's fireworks celebration. Head to Brooklyn for the city's largest New Year's Eve **fireworks** celebration at Prospect Park; call **718/965-8999** or visit www.prospectpark.org. December 31.

New Year's Eve Concert for Peace. The Cathedral of St. John the Divine is known for its annual concert, whose past performers have included the Manhattan School of Music Chamber Sinfonia, Tony award–winning composer Jason Robert Brown (*Parade*), American soprano Lauren Flanigan, and the Forces of Nature Dance Company. Call © **212/316-7540** for information, 212/662-2133 for tickets, or go online to www.stjohndivine.org. December 31.

4 Health & Insurance

WHAT TO DO IF YOU GET SICK AWAY FROM HOME

If you suffer from a chronic illness, consult your doctor before your departure. For conditions like epilepsy, diabetes, or heart problems, wear a **Medic Alert Identification Tag** (© **800/825-3785;** www.medicalert.org), which will immediately alert doctors to your condition and give them access to your records through Medic Alert's 24-hour hot line.

Pack **prescription medications** in their original containers in your carry-on luggage. Also bring along copies of your prescriptions in case you lose your pills or run out. If you do get sick, ask the concierge at your hotel to recommend a local doctor, even his or her own. This will probably yield a better recommendation than any 800 number would. There are also several walk-in medical centers, like **DOCS**

at New York Healthcare, 55 E. 34th St., between Park and Madison avenues (✆ **212/252-6001**), for non-emergency illnesses. The clinic, affiliated with Beth Israel Medical Center, is open Monday through Thursday from 8am to 8pm, Friday from 8am to 7pm, Saturday from 9am to 3pm, and Sunday from 9am to 2pm. The **NYU Downtown Hospital** offers physician referrals at ✆ **888/698-3362.**

If you have dental problems, a nationwide referral service known as **1-800-DENTIST** (✆ **800/336-8478**) will provide the name of a nearby dentist or clinic.

If you can't find a doctor who can help you right away, try the emergency room at the local hospital. For a list of local hospitals, see "Fast Facts: New York City," in chapter 5.

Most health insurance policies cover you if you get sick away from home—but check, particularly if you're insured by an HMO.

TRAVEL INSURANCE

Check your existing insurance policies before you buy travel insurance to cover trip cancellation, lost luggage, medical expenses, or car rentals. You're likely to have partial or complete coverage. But if you need some, ask your travel agent about a comprehensive package. The cost of travel insurance varies widely, depending on the cost and length of your trip, your age and overall health, and the type of trip you're taking. For information, contact one of these popular insurers:

- **Access America** (✆ 800/284-8300; www.accessamerica.com)
- **Travel Guard International** (✆ 800/826-1300; www.travelguard.com)
- **Travel Insured International** (✆ 800/243-3174; www.travelinsured.com)
- **Travelex Insurance Services** (✆ 800/228-9792; www.travelex-insurance.com)

There are three major types of **trip-cancellation insurance** (TCI)—one, in the event that you pre-pay a tour or package that gets cancelled, and you can't get your money back; a second, when you or someone in your family gets sick or dies, and you can't travel (but beware that you may not be covered for a pre-existing condition); and a third, when bad weather makes travel impossible. Some insurers provide coverage for events like jury duty; natural disasters close to home, like floods or fire; even the loss of a job. A few have added provisions for cancellations due to terrorist activities. Always check the fine print before signing on, and don't buy trip-cancellation insurance from the tour operator that may be responsible for the cancellation; buy it only from a reputable travel insurance agency. Don't overbuy. You won't be reimbursed for more than the cost of your trip. Your homeowner's or renter's insurance may cover lost luggage; check with your insurer. The airlines are responsible for losses up to $2,500 on domestic flights if they lose your luggage. Be sure to file a claim immediately, as most airlines enforce a 21-day deadline. If you plan to bring anything valuable, keep it in your carry-on bag.

5 Tips for Travelers with Special Needs

FOR FAMILIES

As a result of the startling decrease in crime and the sudden increase in family-oriented entertainment, the city's sidewalks are full of pint-sized visitors. New York boasts hundreds of ways to keep the kids entertained, from kid-oriented museums and theater to theme park–style shopping and restaurants.

For the best places to stay and eat, see "Family-Friendly Hotels," in chapter 6, and "Family-Friendly Restaurants," in chapter 7. For details on sightseeing, check out the section called "Especially for Kids," in chapter 8. For more extensive recommendations, you might want to purchase a copy of ***Frommer's New York City with Kids,*** an entire guidebook dedicated to family visits to the Big Apple.

Good bets for the most timely information include the "Weekend" section of Friday's ***New York Times,*** which has a whole section dedicated to the week's best kid-friendly activities; the weekly ***New York*** magazine, which has a full calendar of children's events in its "Cue" section; and ***Time Out New York,*** which also has a great weekly kids section with a bit of an alternative bent. The *Big Apple Parents' Paper* is usually available for free at children's stores and other locations in Manhattan; you can also find good information from the folks behind the paper at **www.parentsknow.com**.

The Busy Person's Guide to Traveling with Children (http://wz.com/travel/TravelingWithChildren.html) offers a "45-second newsletter" where experts weigh in on the best websites and resources for tips for traveling with children.

The first place to look for **babysitting** is in your hotel (better yet, ask about babysitting when you reserve). Many hotels have babysitting services or will provide you with lists of reliable sitters. If this doesn't pan out, call the **Baby Sitters' Guild** (**© 212/682-0227**; www.babysittersguild.com). The sitters are licensed, insured, and bonded, and can even take your child on outings.

FOR TRAVELERS WITH DISABILITIES

New York is more accessible to disabled travelers than ever before. The city's bus system is wheelchair-friendly, and most of the major sightseeing attractions are easily accessible. Even so, **always call first** to be sure that the places you want to go to are fully accessible.

Most hotels are ADA compliant, with suitable rooms for wheelchair-bound travelers as well as those with other disabilities. But before you book, **ask lots of questions based on your needs.** Many city hotels are housed in older buildings that have had to be modified to meet requirements; still, elevators and bathrooms can both be on the small side, and other impediments may exist. If you have mobility issues, you'll probably do best to book one of the city's newer hotels, which tend to be more spacious and accommodating. At **www.access-able.com** (see below), you'll find links to New York's best accessible accommodations (click on "World Cities"). Some Broadway theaters and other performance venues provide total wheelchair accessibility; others provide partial accessibility. Many also offer lower-priced tickets for disabled theatergoers and their companions, though you'll need to check individual policies and reserve in advance.

GENERAL TRAVEL INFORMATION Moss Rehab ResourceNet (**© 215/456-9900;** www.mossresourcenet.org) is a great Web source for information, tips, and resources relating to accessible travel. You'll find links to a number of travel agents who specialize in planning trips for disabled travelers here and through **Access-Able Travel Source** (**© 303/232-2979;** www.access-able.com), another excellent online source. You'll also find relay and voice numbers for airlines and car-rental companies on Access-Able's user-friendly site, as well as links to New York's best accessible accommodations, attractions, transportation, tours, local medical resources and equipment repair, and much more.

The Society for Accessible Travel and Hospitality (**© 212/447-7284;** www.sath.org) offers a wealth of travel resources for all types of disabilities and informed recommendations on destinations, access guides, travel agents, tour operators, vehicle rentals, and companion services. Annual membership costs $45 for adults, $30 for seniors and students.

CITY-SPECIFIC INFORMATION **Hospital Audiences, Inc.** (© **212/575-7676;** www.hospitalaudiences.org), arranges attendance and provides details about accessibility at cultural institutions as well as cultural events adapted for people with disabilities. Services include "Describe!," which allows visually impaired theatergoers to enjoy theater events; and the invaluable **HAI Hot Line** (© **212/575-7676**), which offers accessibility information for hotels, restaurants, attractions, cultural venues, and much more. This nonprofit organization also publishes ***Access for All,*** a guidebook on accessibility, available by calling © **212/575-7663** or by sending a $5 check to 548 Broadway, 3rd floor, New York, NY 10012-3950.

Another terrific source for disabled travelers coming to New York City is **Big Apple Greeter** (© **212/669-8159;** www.bigapplegreeter.org). All of its employees are extremely well versed in accessibility issues. They can provide a resource list of agencies that serve the city's disabled community, and sometimes have special discounts available to theater and music performances. Big Apple Greeter even offers one-to-one tours that pair volunteers with disabled visitors; they can even introduce you to the public transportation system if you like. Reserve at least 1 week ahead.

GETTING AROUND **Gray Line Air Shuttle** (© **800/451-0455** or 212/315-3006; www.graylinenewyork.com) operates minibuses with lifts from JFK, LaGuardia, and Newark airports to Midtown hotels by reservation; arrange pickup 3 or 4 days in advance. **Olympia Trails** (© **877/894-9155** or 212/964-6233; www.olympiabus.com) provides service from Newark Airport, with half-price fares for disabled travelers (be sure to pre-purchase your tickets to guarantee the discount fare, as drivers can't sell discounted tickets). Not all buses are appropriately equipped, so call ahead for the daily schedule of accessible buses (press "0" to reach a real person).

A licensed ambulate company, **Upward Mobility Limousine** (© **718/645-7774;** www.brainlink.com/~phil) is a wheelchair-accessible car service that can provide door-to-door airport shuttle service as well as taxi service anywhere in the metropolitan area. Arrange airport pickups with as much advance notice as possible.

Taxis are required to carry people who have folding wheelchairs and guide or therapy dogs. However, don't be surprised if they don't run each other down trying to get to you; even though you shouldn't have to, you may have to wait a bit for a friendly (or fare-desperate) driver to come along.

Public buses are an inexpensive and easy way to get around New York. All buses' back doors are supposed to be equipped with wheelchair lifts (though the city has had complaints that not all are in working order). Buses also "kneel," lowering their front steps for people who have difficulty boarding. Passengers with disabilities pay half-price fares (75¢). The **subway** isn't yet fully wheelchair accessible, but a list of about 30 accessible subway stations and a guide to wheelchair-accessible subway itineraries is on the MTA website. Call © **718/596-8585** for bus and subway transit info or go online to www.mta.nyc.ny.us/nyct and click on "Accessibility."

You're better off not trying to rent your own car to get around the city. But if you consider it the best mode of transportation for you, **Wheelchair**

Getaways (© **800/379-3750** or 800/344-5005; www.wheelchair-getaways.com) rents specialized vans with wheelchair lifts and other features for travelers with disabilities throughout the New York metropolitan area.

FOR SENIOR TRAVELERS

Mention your senior status when you first make your travel reservations, since all major airlines and many hotels offer discounts for seniors. Major airlines also offer coupons for domestic travel for seniors over age 60. Typically, a book of four coupons costs less than $700, which means you can fly anywhere in the continental U.S. for under $350 round-trip.

New York subway and bus fares are half price (75¢) for people 65 and older. Many museums and sights (and some theaters and performance halls) offer discounted entrance and tickets to seniors, so don't be shy about asking. Always bring an ID card, especially if you've kept your youthful glow.

Many hotels offer senior discounts; **Choice Hotels** (which include Comfort Inns, some of my favorite affordable Midtown hotels; see chapter 6, "Where to Stay"), for example, gives 30% off their published rates to anyone over 50, provided you book your room through their nationwide toll-free reservations number (that is, not directly with the hotels or through a travel agent). For a complete list of Choice Hotels, visit **www.hotelchoice.com**.

Members of **AARP** (formerly known as the American Association of Retired Persons; © **800/424-3410** or 202/434-2277; www.aarp.org), get discounts on hotels, airfares, and car rentals, as well as other wide-ranging benefits. Anyone over 50 can join. The **Alliance for Retired Americans** (© **301/578-8422;** www.retiredamericans.org) also offers members discounts on hotel and auto rentals. *Note:* Members of the former National Council of Senior Citizens receive automatic membership in the Alliance.

FOR GAY & LESBIAN TRAVELERS

Gay and lesbian culture is as much a part of New York's basic identity as yellow cabs, high-rises, and Broadway theater. Indeed, in a city with one of the world's largest, loudest, and most powerful gay and lesbian populations, homosexuality is squarely in the urban mainstream. So city hotels tend to be neutral on the issue, and gay couples shouldn't have a problem; for particularly gay-friendly accommodations, see "Best for Gay & Lesbian Travelers" under "Best Hotel Bets," in chapter 1. You'll want to see "The Gay & Lesbian Scene," in chapter 11 for nightlife suggestions.

The **International Gay & Lesbian Travel Association** (**IGLTA;** © **800/448-8550** or 954/776-2626; www.iglta.org), links travelers up with additional gay-friendly hoteliers as well as tour operators and airline representatives. **Now, Voyager** (© **800/255-6951;** www.nowvoyager.com), a San Francisco–based gay-owned and operated travel service, is another excellent source for those who want assistance with trip planning.

All over Manhattan, but especially in neighborhoods like the **West Village** (particularly Christopher St., famous the world over as the main drag of New York gay male life) and **Chelsea** (especially Eighth Ave. from 16th to 23rd sts. and West 17th to 19th sts. from Fifth to Eighth aves.), shops, services, and restaurants have a lesbian and gay flavor. The **Oscar Wilde Bookshop,** 15 Christopher St. (© **212/255-8097;** www.oscarwildebooks.com), is the city's best gay and lesbian bookstore, and a good source for information on the city's gay community.

Moments **Stonewall Remembered**

Many gay visitors will want to visit the **Stonewall Bar,** 53 Christopher St., east of Seventh Avenue (✆ **212/463-0950**), in nearly the same location as where the famed Stonewall Inn once stood. On the night of June 27, 1969, customers at the original Stonewall, tired of constant police harassment, decided to fight back. That milestone marked the beginnings of the contemporary gay liberation movement. The usually celebratory, always engaging Lesbian and Gay Pride March is held in late June to commemorate the Stonewall "Riots"—see the "Calendar of Events," earlier in this chapter.

The **Lesbian and Gay Community Services Center** is at 208 W. 13th St., between Seventh and Eighth avenues (✆ **212/620-7310;** www.gaycenter.org). The center is the meeting place for more than 400 lesbian, gay, and bisexual organizations. You can check the online events calendar, which lists hundreds of happenings—lectures, dances, concerts, readings, films—or call for the latest. Their site offers links to additional gay-friendly hotels and guesthouses in and around New York, plus tons of other information; the staff is also exceedingly friendly and helpful in person or over the phone.

Other good sources for lesbian and gay events are ***HX*** (www.hx.com), ***New York Blade*** (www.nyblade.com), ***Next*** (www.nextnyc.com), ***LGNY*** (www.lgny.com); and the ***Village Voice*** (www.villagevoice.com)—all free weeklies that you can pick up in appropriate bars, clubs, stores, and sidewalk boxes throughout town. You'll also find lots of information on their corresponding websites. The glossy weekly ***Time Out New York*** (www.timeoutny.com) boasts a terrific gay and lesbian section. The Lesbian and Gay Community Services Center (see above) publishes a monthly guide listing dozens of events (also listed on its website).

In addition, there are lesbian and gay musical events, such as performances by the **New York City Gay Men's Chorus** (✆ **212/242-1777;** www.nycgmc.org); health programs sponsored by the **Gay Men's Health Crisis (GMHC;** ✆ **800/AIDS-NYC** or 212/807-6655; www.gmhc.org); the **Gay & Lesbian National Hot Line** (✆ **212/989-0999;** www.glnh.org), offering peer counseling and information on upcoming events; and many other organizations.

6 Getting There

BY PLANE

Three major airports serve New York City: **John F. Kennedy International Airport** (✆ **718/244-4444**) in Queens, about 15 miles (24km; 1 hr. driving time) from Midtown Manhattan; **LaGuardia Airport** (✆ **718/533-3400**), also in Queens, about 8 miles (13km; 30 min.) from Midtown; and **Newark International Airport** (✆ **973/961-6000**) in nearby New Jersey, about 16 miles (26km; or 45 min.) from Midtown. Information about all three airports is available online at **www.panynj.gov**; click on the "Airports" tab on the left.

Even though LaGuardia is the closest airport to Manhattan, it earned the dubious distinction of being the worst airport in the nation for flight delays—both departures and arrivals—in 2000, according to the

Tips Choosing Your NYC–Area Airport

It's more convenient to fly into Newark than Kennedy if your destination is Manhattan, and consider that fares to Newark are often cheaper than those to the other airports. Newark is particularly convenient if your hotel is in Midtown West or downtown. Taxi fare into Manhattan from Newark is roughly equivalent to the fare from JFK—and now, with the new Air-Train in place (see "Transportation to & from the New York–Area Airports," below), Newark has the quickest and easiest-to-use public transportation link with Manhattan.

FAA. What's more, LaGuardia has a hideous reputation for terminal chaos, in both ticket-desk lines and baggage claim. It is hoped airport officials will have rectified the problems by the time you fly, but you may want to use JFK or Newark instead. (JFK has the best reputation for timeliness among New York–area airports.)

Almost every major domestic carrier serves at least one of the New York–area airports; most serve two or all three. Among them are **America West** (© 800/235-9292; www.americawest.com), **American** (© 800/433-7300; www.aa.com), **Continental** (© 800/525-0280; www.continental.com), **Delta** (© 800/221-1212; www.delta.com), **Northwest** (© 800/225-2525; www.nwa.com), **US Airways** (© 800/428-4322; www.usairways.com), and **United** (© 800/241-6522; www.united.com).

In recent years, there has been rapid growth in the number of start-up, no-frills airlines serving New York. You might check out Atlanta-based **Air-Tran** (© 800/247-8726; www.airtran.com); Chicago-based **ATA** (© 800/435-9282; www.ata.com); Denver-based **Frontier** (© 800/432-1359; www.flyfrontier.com); Raleigh/Durham-based **Midway Airlines** (© 800/446-4392; www.midwayair.com); Milwaukee- and Omaha-based **Midwest Express** (© 800/452-2022; www.midwestexpress.com); Las Vegas–based **National Airlines** (© 888/757-5387; www.nationalairlines.com); Detroit-based **Spirit Airlines** (© 800/772-7117; www.spiritair.com); and Kansas City-based **Vanguard Airlines** (© 800/VAN-GUARD; www.flyvanguard.com). The JFK-based cheap-chic airline **jet-Blue** ★ (© 800/JETBLUE; www.jetblue.com) has taken New York by storm with its low fares and classy service to cities throughout the nation. The nation's leading discount airline, **Southwest** (© 800/435-9792; www.iflyswa.com), flies into MacArthur (Islip) Airport on Long Island, 50 miles (80km) east of Manhattan.

Most major international carriers also serve New York; see chapter 4, "For International Visitors," for details.

FLY FOR LESS: TIPS FOR GETTING THE BEST AIRFARES

- Airlines periodically lower prices on their most popular routes, which sometimes include New York. Check your newspaper for advertised discounts or call the airlines directly and ask if any **promotional rates or special fares** are available. You'll almost never see a sale during July and August, or during the Thanksgiving or Christmas seasons; in periods of low-volume travel, however, you should pay no more than $500 for a cross-country flight with a 14- or 21-day advance purchase.

Tips New Air Travel Security Measures

In the wake of the terrorist attacks of September 11, 2001, the airline industry began implementing sweeping security measures in airports. Expect a lengthy check-in process and extensive delays, both at New York's area airports and at your home airport. Although regulations vary from airline to airline, you can expedite the process by taking these steps:

- **Arrive early.** Arrive at the airport *at least* 2 hours before your departure time for domestic flights, earlier for international flights, because you'll have to negotiate extensive lines both at the ticket counter and the security gate. E-tickets seldom speed up the check-in process these days, since interacting with a check-in agent is essential to the new security processes.
- **Try not to drive your car to the airport.** Parking and curbside access to the terminal may be limited. Call ahead and check.
- **Realize that curbside check-in is a thing of the past.** While a few offer it on a limited basis, most airlines and airports have stopped curbside check-in altogether. For the latest on this, check with the individual airline.
- **Carry plenty of documentation.** A government-issued photo ID (federal, state, or local) is now required. You may need to show this at various checkpoints. With an E-ticket, you may be required to have with you printed confirmation of purchase, and perhaps even the credit card with which you bought your ticket. This varies from airline to airline, so call ahead to make sure you have the proper documentation. And be sure that your ID is **up to date:** An expired driver's license or passport may keep you from boarding the plane altogether. Be prepared to show it multiple times: at the ticket counter, the security gate, and at boarding.
- **Know what you can carry on—and what you can't.** Travelers in the United States are now limited to one carry-on bag, plus one personal bag (such as a purse or a briefcase). The Transportation Security Administration (TSA) has also issued a list of newly restricted carry-on items that includes knives (including the Swiss Army variety) and metal scissors. For the latest restrictions, visit **www.tsa.gov** and click on "Traveler Tips and Prohibited Items."
- **Prepare to be searched.** Expect spot-checks, both at the security and boarding gates. Electronic items, such as laptops and cellphones, should be readied for additional screening. Limit the metal items you wear on your person.
- **Remember: No ticket, no gate access.** Only ticketed passengers will be allowed beyond the screener checkpoints, except for those travelers with specific medical or parental needs.

Note, however, that the lowest-priced fares are often nonrefundable, require a Saturday-night stay, and carry penalties for changing dates of travel. So, when you're quoted a fare, know exactly what the restrictions are before you commit.

- **Consolidators,** also known as bucket shops, are a good place to find low fares. Consolidators buy seats in bulk from the airlines and then sell them back to the public at prices usually below even the airlines' discounted rates. Their small ads usually run in Sunday newspaper travel sections.

  Before you pay, however, ask for a confirmation number from the consolidator and then call the airline itself to confirm your seat. Be prepared to book your ticket with a different consolidator—there are many to choose from—if the airline can't confirm your reservation. Also be aware that consolidator tickets are usually nonrefundable or come with stiff cancellation penalties. And keep in mind that if an airline sale is going on, or if it's high season, you can often get the same or better rates from the airlines directly, so do some comparison shopping before you buy. Also check out the airline; you may not want to fly on No-Name Airlines, even if you're saving $50.

  I've gotten great deals on many occasions from **Cheap Tickets** (✆ **888/922-8849;** www.cheaptickets.com). **Council Travel** (✆ **800/226-8624;** www.counciltravel.com) and **STA Travel** (✆ **800/781-4040;** www.statravel.com) cater especially to young travelers, but they have discounted fares available to people of all ages. **The TravelHub** (✆ **888/AIR-FARE;** www.travelhub.com) represents nearly 1,000 travel agencies, many of whom offer consolidator and discount fares. Other reliable consolidators include **1-800-FLY-CHEAP** (www.1800flycheap.com); **TFI Tours International** (✆ **800-745-8000** or 212/736-1140; www.lowestairprice.com), which serves as a clearinghouse for unused seats; or "rebators" such as **Travel Avenue** (✆ **800/333-3335;** www.travelavenue.com), which rebate part of their commissions to you.

- Search **the Internet** for cheap fares. Internet users can now tap into the same travel-planning databases that were once accessible only to travel agents via sites such as **Travelocity.com, Expedia.com,** and **Orbitz.com.**

  Additionally, many airlines now offer special "Internet Only" fares through their own websites. (I recently scored a $195 round-trip fare between New York and Phoenix by surfing Continental's website.) You can also sign up for e-mail alerts that notify you about travel specials and last-minute discounts at airline websites. Or check mega-sites that compile comprehensive lists of last-minute specials, most notably **Smarter Living** (www.smarterliving.com) and **WebFlyer** (www.webflyer.com).

TRANSPORTATION TO & FROM THE NEW YORK–AREA AIRPORTS

Since there's no need to rent a car in New York, you're going to have to

Money-Saving Tip

If your schedule is flexible, you can almost always get a cheaper fare by staying over a Saturday night; by flying on Tuesday, Wednesday, or Thursday; by taking the first flight of the day; or by making a connection rather than opting for a direct flight. Many airlines won't volunteer this information, so be sure to ask.

Frommers.com: The Complete Travel Resource

For an excellent travel-planning resource, we highly recommend **Frommers.com** (www.frommers.com). We're a little biased, of course, but we guarantee that you'll find the travel tips, reviews, monthly vacation giveaways, and online-booking capabilities thoroughly indispensable. Among the special features are our popular **Message Boards,** where Frommer's readers post queries and share advice (sometimes even our authors show up to answer questions); **Frommers.com Newsletter,** for the latest travel bargains and inside travel secrets; and Frommer's **Destinations Section,** where you'll get expert travel tips, hotel and dining recommendations, and advice on the sights to see for more than 2,500 destinations around the globe. When your research is done, the **Online Reservation System** (www.frommers.com/booktravelnow) takes you to Frommer's favorite sites for booking your vacation at affordable prices.

figure out how you want to get from the airport to your hotel and back.

For complete transportation information for all three airports (JFK, LaGuardia, and Newark), call **Air-Ride** (✆ **800/247-7433**), which offers recorded details on bus and shuttle companies and private car services registered with the New York and New Jersey Port Authority 24 hours a day. Similar information is available at **www.panynj.gov/airports**; just click on the airport at which you'll be arriving.

On the arrivals level at each airport, the Port Authority also runs staffed Ground Transportation Information counters on the baggage claim level in each terminal at each airport, where you can get information and book on all manner of transport once you land. Most transportation companies also have courtesy phones near the baggage-claim area.

Generally, travel time between the airports and Midtown Manhattan by taxi or car is 45 to 60 minutes for JFK, 20 to 35 minutes for LaGuardia, and 35 to 50 minutes for Newark. Always allow extra time, though, especially during rush hour, peak holiday travel times, and if you're taking a bus.

SUBWAYS & PUBLIC BUSES

For the most part, your best bet is to stay away from the MTA when traveling to and from the airport. You might save a few dollars, but subways and buses that currently serve the airports involve multiple transfers, and you'll have to drag your luggage up and down staircases. On some subways, you'd be traveling through undesirable neighborhoods. Spare yourself the drama.

The only exception to this rule that I feel comfortable with is the subway service to and from JFK—but you should only consider it if money is extremely tight *and* you're already well versed in the ways of New York. It's a huge hassle, and you should expect it to take 90 minutes or more, but you can take the **A train,** which connects to one of two free **shuttle buses** that serve all the JFK terminals. Upon exiting the terminal, pick up the shuttle bus (marked **LONG-TERM PARKING LOT**) out front; it takes you to the **Howard Beach station,** where you pick up the A train to the west side of Manhattan. Service is every 10 to 15 minutes during rush hour and every 20 minutes at midday, and the subway fare is $1.50. If you're traveling to JFK from Manhattan, be sure to take the A train that says **FAR ROCKAWAY** or **ROCKAWAY PARK**—*not* LEFFERTS BOULEVARD. Get off at the Howard

Money-Saving Package Deals

Before you start your search for the lowest airfare, you may want to consider booking your flight as part of a travel package that allows you to buy airfare and accommodations (and sometimes extras like sightseeing tours and hard-to-get theater tickets) at a pay-one-price discount.

Here are a few tips to help you tell one package from another, and figure out which one is right for you:

- **Read this guide.** Do a little homework. Compare the hotel rack rates that we've published to the rates being offered by the packagers. If you're being offered a stay in a hotel that we haven't recommended, do more research to learn about it, especially if it isn't a reliable franchise like Holiday Inn or Hyatt. It's not a deal if you end up at a dump.
- **Read the fine print.** Make sure you know *exactly* what's included in the price you're being quoted, and what's not. Are hotel taxes and airport transfers included, or will you have to pay extra? Conversely, don't pay for a rental car you don't need—and you won't need one in New York. Before you commit to a package, make sure you know how much flexibility you have, say, if your kid gets sick or your boss suddenly asks you to adjust your vacation schedule.
- **Use your best judgment.** Stay away from fly-by-nights and shady packagers. If a deal appears to be too good to be true, it probably is. Go with a reputable firm with a proven track record. This is where your travel agent can come in handy; he or she should be knowledgeable about different packagers.

So how do you find a package deal?

The best place to start your search is the travel section of your local Sunday newspaper. Also check the ads in the back of national travel

Beach/JFK Airport station and connect to the shuttle bus, A or B, that goes to your terminal (they're clearly marked, and there's usually a guide to point you to the right one).

The subway can actually be more reliable than taking a car or taxi at the height of rush hour, but *a few words of warning:* This isn't the right option for you if you're bringing more than a single piece of luggage, since there's a good amount of walking and some stairs involved in the trip, and you'll have nowhere to put it on the subway train. And *do not* use this method if you're traveling to or from the airport after dark or too early in the morning—it's just not safe. For additional subway information, see "Getting Around," in chapter 5.

TAXIS Taxis are a quick and convenient way to travel to and from the airports. They're available at designated taxi stands outside the terminals, with uniformed dispatchers on hand during peak hours at JFK and LaGuardia, around the clock at Newark. Follow the GROUND TRANSPORTATION or TAXI signs. There may be a long line, but it generally moves pretty quickly. Fares, whether fixed or metered, do not include bridge and tunnel tolls ($3.50–$4) or a tip for the cabbie (15%–20% is customary). They do include all passengers in the cab and luggage—never pay more magazines like *Travel Holiday, National Geographic Traveler,* and *Arthur Frommer's Budget Travel.*

A terrific source specifically for Big Apple packages is **New York City Vacation Packages** ★ (✆ **888/692-8701** or 570-714-4692; www.nycvp.com), which can sell you a complete vacation package including hotel stay, theater tickets, and more—usually for significantly less than you can do by booking everything on your own. What's more, NYCVP can often build a package that includes otherwise sold-out tickets to Broadway shows like *The Lion King* and sporting events; they'll even book airport transportation and dining reservations for you, if you wish.

One of the biggest packagers in the Northeast, **Liberty Travel** (✆ **888/271-1584**; www.libertytravel.com) offers great-value 2- to 7-night New York packages that usually include such freebies as a Circle Line cruise or tickets to the Empire State Building observatory, plus lots of good hotels at every price point.

The major airlines offering good-value packages to New York include **Continental Airlines Vacations** (✆ **800/634-5555**; www.coolvacations.com); **Delta Vacations** (✆ **800/872-7786**; www.deltavacations.com); **US Airways Vacations** (✆ **800/455-0123**; www.usairwaysvacations.com); **United Vacations** (✆ **800/328-6877**; www.unitedvacations.com); **American Airlines Vacations** (✆ **800/321-2121**; www.aavacations.com); and **Northwest WorldVacations** (✆ **800/800-1504**; www.nwa.com/vacpkg). You may want to choose the airline that has frequent service to your hometown or the one on which you accumulate frequent-flier miles (you may even be able to pay with your trip using miles).

than the metered or flat rate, except for tolls and a tip (8pm–6am, a 50¢ surcharge also applies on New York yellow cabs). Taxis have a limit of four passengers, so if there are more in your group, you'll have to take more than one cab. For more on taxis, see "Getting Around," in chapter 5.

- **From JFK:** A flat rate of $35 to Manhattan (plus tolls and tip) is charged. The meter will not be turned on and the surcharge will not be added. The flat rate does not apply on trips from Manhattan to the airport.
- **From LaGuardia:** $16 to $26, metered, plus tolls and tip.
- **From Newark:** The dispatcher for New Jersey taxis gives you a slip of paper with a flat rate ranging from $30 to $38 (toll and tip extra), depending on where you're going in Manhattan, so you'll have to be precise about your destination. New York yellow cabs aren't permitted to pick up passengers at Newark. The yellow-cab fare from Manhattan to Newark is the meter amount plus $10 and tolls (about $40–$50, perhaps a few dollars more with tip). New Jersey taxis aren't permitted to take passengers from Manhattan to Newark.

Note that a taxi fare increase was being discussed at press time, so fares may be a few dollars higher by the time you arrive.

PRIVATE CAR & LIMOUSINE SERVICES Private car and limousine companies provide convenient 24-hour door-to-door airport transfers for roughly the same cost of a taxi. The advantage they offer over taking a taxi is that you can arrange your pickup in advance and avoid the hassles of the taxi line. Call at least 24 hours in advance (even earlier on holidays), and a driver will meet you near baggage claim (or at your hotel for a return trip). You'll probably be asked to leave a credit-card number to guarantee your ride. You'll likely be offered the choice of indoor or curbside pickup; indoor pickup is more expensive, but makes it easier to hook up with your driver (who usually waits in baggage claim bearing a sign with your name on it). You can save a few dollars if you arrange for an outside pickup; call the dispatcher as soon as you land, and then take your luggage out to the waiting area, where you'll wait for the driver to come around, which can take anywhere from 10 minutes to a half-hour. Besides the wait, the other disadvantage of this option is that curbside can be chaos during prime deplaning hours.

Vehicles range from sedans to vans to limousines and tend to be relatively clean and comfortable. Prices vary slightly by company and the size of car reserved, but expect a rate roughly equivalent to taxi fare if you request a basic sedan and have only one stop; toll and tip policies are the same. (*Note:* Car services are not subject to the flat-rate rule that taxis have for rides to and from JFK.) Ask when booking what the fare will be and if you can use your credit card to pay for the ride so there are no surprises at drop-off time. There may be waiting charges tacked on if the driver has to wait an excessive amount of time for your plane to land when picking you up, but the car companies will usually check on your flight beforehand to get an accurate landing time.

I've had the best luck with **Carmel** (✆ **800/922-7635** or 212/666-6666) and **Legends** (✆ **888/LEGENDS** or 718/788-1234); **Allstate** (✆ **800/453-4099** or 212/333-3333) and **Tel-Aviv** (✆ **800/222-9888** or 212/777-7777) also have reasonable reputations. (Keep in mind, though, that these services are only as good as the individual drivers—and sometimes there's a lemon in the bunch. If you have a problem, report it immediately to the main office.)

These car services are good for rush hour (no ticking meters in rush-hour traffic), but if you're arriving at a quieter time of day, taxis work fine.

PRIVATE BUSES & SHUTTLES Buses and shuttle services provide a comfortable and less expensive (but usually more time-consuming) option for airport transfers than do taxis and car services.

Gray Line Air Shuttle and **Super Shuttle** serve all three airports; **New York Airport Service** serves JFK and LaGuardia; **Olympia Trails** serves Newark. These services are my favorite option for getting to and from Newark during peak travel times

An Airport Warning

Never accept a car ride from the hustlers who hang out in the terminal halls. They're illegal, don't have proper insurance, and aren't safe. You can tell who they are because they'll approach you with a suspicious conspiratorial air and ask if you need a ride. Not from them, you don't. Sanctioned city cabs and car services wait outside the terminals.

A Fast & Easy Airport Connection: Newark's AirTrain

In 2001, a new rail link revolutionized the process of connecting by public transportation to New York's notoriously underserved airport: the brand-new **AirTrain Newark,** which now connects Newark Airport with Manhattan via a speedy monorail/rail link.

Even though you have to make a connection, the system is fast, pleasant, affordable, and easy to use. Each arrivals terminal at Newark Airport has a boarding station for the AirTrain, so just follow the signs once you collect your bags. All AirTrains head to **Newark International Airport Station,** where you transfer to a **NJ Transit** train. NJ Transit will deliver you directly to New York Penn Station at 33rd Street and Seventh Avenue, where you can pick up a cab to your hotel.

The whole process can have you in Manhattan in 20 minutes, if you catch a quick connection. NJ Transit trains run 2 to 3 times an hour during peak travel times (once an hour during early and late hours); you can check the schedules on monitors before you leave the airport terminal, and again at the train station. Tickets can be purchased from vending machines at both the air terminal and the train station (no ticket is required to board the AirTrain). The one-way fare is $11.15 (children under 5 ride free). (On your return trip to the airport, the AirTrain is far more predictable, timewise, than subjecting yourself to the whims of traffic.)

Note that travelers heading to points beyond the city can also pick up Amtrak and other NJ Transit trains at Newark International Airport Station to their final destination.

A word of warning, however: If you have mobility issues, mountains of luggage that will make connections difficult, or a bevy of small children to keep track of, skip the AirTrain. You'll find it easier to rely on a taxi, car service, or shuttle service that can offer you door-to-door transfers.

For more information on AirTrain Newark, call © **888/EWR-INFO** or go online to **www.airtrainnewark.com**. For connection details, click on the links on the AirTrain website or contact **NJ Transit** (© **800/626-RIDE;** www.njtransit.com) or **Amtrak** (© **800/USA-RAIL;** www.amtrak.com).

because the drivers usually take lesser-known surface streets that make the ride much quicker than if you go with a taxi or car, which will virtually always stick to the traffic-clogged main route.

Gray Line Express Shuttle USA (© **800/451-0455** or 212/315-3006; www.graylinenewyork.com) vans depart JFK, LaGuardia, and Newark every 20 to 30 minutes between 7am and 11:30pm. They will drop you off at most hotels between 21st and 103rd streets in Manhattan. No reservation is required; just go to the ground-transportation desk or dial **24** on the Gray Line courtesy phone in the baggage-claim area. Service from mid-Manhattan to all three airports operates daily from 5am to 9pm; you must call a day in advance to arrange a hotel pickup. The regular one-way fare

If You're Flying into Islip Airport on Southwest

Southwest Airlines flies into the New York area via Long Island's Islip MacArthur Airport, 50 miles (80km) east of Manhattan. If you're on one of these flights, here are your options for getting into the city:

Colonial Transportation (✆ **631/589-3500;** www.colonialtransportation.com), **Classic Transportation** (✆ **631/567-5100;** www.classictrans.com), and **Legends** (✆ **888/LEGENDS** or 718/788-1234; www.legendslimo.com) will pick you up at Islip Airport and deliver you to Manhattan via private sedan, but expect to pay about $125 plus tolls and tip for door-to-door service. Be sure to arrange for it at least 24 hours in advance.

For a fraction of the cost, you can catch a ride aboard a **Hampton Jitney** coach (✆ **631/383-4600;** www.hamptonjitney.com) to various drop-off points on Midtown's east side. The cost is $25 per person, plus a minimal taxi fare from the terminal to the Hampton Jitney stop. Hampton Jitney can explain the details and arrange for taxi transport.

Colonial Transportation (✆ **631/589-3500;** www.colonialtransportation.com) also offers regular shuttle service that traverses the 3 miles (5km) from the airport to the Ronkonkoma Long Island Rail Road Station, where you can pick up an LIRR (Long Island Rail Road) train to Manhattan. The shuttle fare is $5 per person, $1 for each additional family member accompanying a full-fare customer. From Ronkonkoma, it's about a 1½-hour train ride to Manhattan's Penn Station; the one-way fare is $9.50 at peak hours, $6.50 off-peak (half fare for seniors 65 or older and kids 5–11). You can also catch the Suffolk County Transit bus S-57 between the airport and the station daily except Sundays for $1.50. Trains usually leave Ronkonkoma once or twice every hour, depending on the day and time. For more information, call ✆ **718/217-LIRR** or visit **www.mta.nyc.ny.us/lirr**.

For additional options and the latest information, call **631/467-3210** or visit **www.macarthurairport.com**.

to and from JFK is $19, to and from LaGuardia is $16, and to and from Newark is $19, but you can save a few bucks by prepaying your round-trip at the airport ($28 for JFK and Newark, $26 for LaGuardia).

The familiar blue vans of **Super Shuttle** (✆ **800/BLUE-VAN** or 212/258-3826; www.supershuttle.com) serve all three area airports, providing door-to-door service to Manhattan and points on Long Island every 15 to 30 minutes around the clock. As with Gray Line, you don't need to reserve your airport-to-Manhattan ride; just go to the ground-transportation desk or use the courtesy phone in baggage claim and ask for Super Shuttle. Hotel pickups for your return trip require 24 to 48 hours' notice; you can make your reservations online. Fares run $13 to $22 per person, depending on the airport, with discounts available for additional persons in the same party.

New York Airport Service (✆ **718/875-8200;** www.nyairportservice.com) buses travel from JFK and LaGuardia to the Port Authority Bus Terminal (42nd St. and Eighth Ave.), Grand Central Terminal (Park Ave. between 41st and 42nd sts.), and to select Midtown hotels between 27th and 59th streets, plus the Jamaica LIRR Station in Queens, where you can pick up a train for

Getting to the Other Boroughs & 'Burbs

If you're traveling to a borough other than Manhattan, call **ETS Air Service** (✆ **718/221-5341**) for shared door-to-door service. For Long Island service, call **Classic Transportation** (✆ **631/567-5100;** www.classictrans.com) for car service, or **JFK Flyer** (✆ **516/766-6722**) for bus service. For service to Westchester County or Connecticut, contact **Connecticut Limousine** (✆ **800/472-5466** or 203/878-2222; www.ctlimo.com) or **Prime Time Shuttle of Connecticut** (✆ **800/733-8267;** www.primetimeshuttle.com).

If you're traveling to points in New Jersey from Newark Airport, call **Olympic Limousine** (✆ **800/822-9797** or 732/938-4300) for Ocean and Monmouth counties; the **Airporter** (✆ **800/385-4000** or 609/587-6600; www.goairporter.com) to Middlesex and Mercer counties, plus Bucks County, PA; or **State Shuttle** (✆ **800/427-3207** or 973/729-0030; www.stateshuttle.com) for destinations throughout New Jersey.

Additionally, **New York Airport Service** express buses (✆ **718/875-8200;** www.nyairportservice.com) serve the entire New York metropolitan region from JFK and LaGuardia, offering connections to the Long Island Rail Road; the Metro North Rail Road to Westchester County, upstate New York, and Connecticut; and New York's Port Authority, where you can pick up buses to points throughout New Jersey.

Long Island. Follow the GROUND TRANSPORTATION signs to the curbside pickup or look for the uniformed agent. Buses depart the airport every 20 to 70 minutes (depending on your departure point and destination) between 6am and midnight. Buses to JFK and LaGuardia depart the Port Authority and Grand Central Terminal on the Park Avenue side every 15 to 30 minutes, depending on the time of day and the day of the week. To request direct shuttle service from your hotel, call the above number at least 24 hours in advance. One-way fare for JFK is $13, $23 round-trip; to and from LaGuardia, it's $10 one way, $17 round-trip.

Olympia Airport Express (✆ **877/894-9155** or 212/964-6233; www.olympiabus.com) provides service every 5 to 30 minutes (depending on the time of day) from Newark Airport to Penn Station (the pickup point is the northwest corner of 34th St. and Eighth Ave. and the drop-off point is the southwest corner), the Port Authority Bus Terminal (on 42nd St. between Eighth and Ninth aves.), and Grand Central Terminal (on 41st St. between Park and Lexington aves.). Passengers to and from the Grand Central Terminal location can connect to Olympia's Midtown shuttle vans, which service select Midtown hotels. Call for the exact schedule for your return trip to the airport. The fare runs $11 one-way, $21 round-trip; it's $5 more if you connect to the hotel shuttle. Senior and disabled citizens ride for $5.

BY TRAIN

Amtrak (✆ **800/USA-RAIL;** www.amtrak.com) runs frequent service to New York City's **Penn Station,** on Seventh Avenue between 31st and 33rd streets, where you can easily pick up a taxi, subway, or bus to your hotel. To get the best rates, book early (as much as 6 months in advance) and travel on weekends.

If you're traveling to New York from a city along Amtrak's Northeast Corridor—such as Boston, Philadelphia, Baltimore, or Washington,

Before You Leave Home: Big Apple Travel Checklist

- If you have your heart set on seeing a particular Broadway show or attending another event while you're in town, procure tickets or make reservations well in advance.
- Ditto for restaurant reservations for that special-occasion meal. The city's most coveted tables demand advance reservations. See chapter 7 for booking tips.
- If you're planning your sightseeing itinerary around specific attractions, make sure they'll be open while you're in town. While the vast majority of city attractions have devised post-9/11 security plans and settled back into regular hours, public access, open hours, or programming schedules at any attractions can change at any time. You'll save yourself heartache by confirming details over the web or by telephone in advance. This is also a good way to check current programming. See chapter 8, "Exploring New York City."
- Be sure to have your ATM card and credit card PIN numbers at hand so you can access ready cash (you'll go through it faster than you expect on the streets of New York). If you purchased traveler's checks, record the check numbers and store the documentation separately. It's a good idea to leave copies of the check numbers with someone back home, in the unlikely event your luggage is lost.
- Make sure you have a safe, accessible place to store money. It may be decidedly unsexy, but a money belt is a good idea nonetheless. See "Playing It Safe," in chapter 5, for further suggestions.
- Pack the most comfortable walking shoes you own—you'll need them.
- Bring any ID cards that could entitle you to discounts, such as AAA and AARP membership cards and student IDs.
- Don't leave home without a valid photo ID, such as your driver's license or passport.
- Bring extras of anything—such as eyeglasses or contact lenses—that you can't do without. Pack copies of any prescriptions in case you need emergency refills.
- Don't forget your camera. You might also wish to invest in protective pouches to shield your film from airport x-rays.
- Last but not least, always leave a copy of your itinerary, with flight numbers and hotel information, with someone at home.

D.C.—Amtrak may be your best travel bet now that they've rolled out their new high-speed Acela trains, which will have replaced all the old Metroliners by the time you read this. The Acela Express trains cut travel time from D.C. down to 2½ hours, and travel time from Boston to a lightning-quick 3 hours.

BY BUS

Buses arrive at the **Port Authority Terminal,** on Eighth Avenue between 40th and 42nd streets, where you can easily transfer to your hotel by taxi, subway, or bus. I don't suggest taking the bus because the ride is long and uncomfortable, and fares are usually no cheaper than the much quicker and more comfortable train. But if for some reason bus is your preferred mode of transportation, call **Greyhound Bus Lines** (**© 800/229-9424**; www.greyhound.com).

BY CAR

From the **New Jersey Turnpike** (I-95) and points west, there are three Hudson River crossings into the city's west side: the **Holland Tunnel** (lower Manhattan), the **Lincoln Tunnel** (Midtown), and the **George Washington Bridge** (upper Manhattan).

From **upstate New York,** take the **New York State Thruway** (I-87), which crosses the Hudson on the Tappan Zee Bridge and becomes the **Major Deegan Expressway** (I-87) through the Bronx. For the east side, continue to the Triborough Bridge and then down the FDR Drive. For the west side, take the Cross Bronx Expressway (I-95) to the Henry Hudson Parkway or the Taconic State Parkway to the Saw Mill River Parkway to the Henry Hudson Parkway south.

From **New England,** the **New England Thruway** (I-95) connects with the **Bruckner Expressway** (I-278), which leads to the Triborough Bridge and the FDR on the east side. For the west side, take the Bruckner to the Cross Bronx Expressway (I-95) to the Henry Hudson Parkway south.

Note that you'll have to pay tolls along some of these roads and at most crossings.

Once you arrive in Manhattan, park your car in a garage (expect to pay $20–$45 per day) and leave it there. Don't use your car for traveling within the city. Public transportation, taxis, and walking will easily get you where you want to go without the headaches of parking, gridlock, and dodging crazy cabbies.

4

For International Visitors

New York's global media profile might make it appear familiar, but movies and TV, music videos, and news images distort as much as they reflect. The gap between image and reality can make certain situations puzzling for the foreign—or even the domestic—visitor. This chapter will help prepare you for the more common issues or problems that you may encounter.

1 Preparing for Your Trip

ENTRY REQUIREMENTS

Check at any U.S. embassy or consulate for current information and requirements. You can also obtain a visa application and other information online at the **U.S. State Department**'s website, at **www.travel.state.gov**.

VISAS The U.S. State Department has a **Visa Waiver Program** allowing citizens of certain countries to enter the United States without a visa for stays of up to 90 days. At press time these included Andorra, Australia, Austria, Belgium, Brunei, Denmark, Finland, France, Germany, Iceland, Ireland, Italy, Japan, Liechtenstein, Luxembourg, Monaco, the Netherlands, New Zealand, Norway, Portugal, San Marino, Singapore, Slovenia, Spain, Sweden, Switzerland, the United Kingdom, and Uruguay. Citizens of these countries need only a valid passport and a round-trip air or cruise ticket in their possession upon arrival. If they first enter the United States, they may also visit Mexico, Canada, Bermuda, and/or the Caribbean islands and return to the United States without a visa. Further information is available from any U.S. embassy or consulate. *Note:* This list can change at any time—witness the removal of Argentina from the list in February 2002—so never assume. Always check visa requirements well in advance. Canadian citizens may enter the United States without visas; they need only proof of residence.

Citizens of all other countries must have (1) a valid passport that expires at least 6 months later than the scheduled end of their visit to the United States, and (2) a tourist visa, which may be obtained without charge from any U.S. consulate.

To obtain a visa, the traveler must submit a completed application form (either in person or by mail) with a 1½-inch-square photo, and must demonstrate binding ties to a residence abroad. Usually you can obtain a visa at once or within 24 hours, but it may take longer during the summer rush from June through August. If you cannot go in person, contact the nearest U.S. embassy or consulate for directions on applying by mail. Your travel agent or airline office may also be able to provide you with a visa application and instructions. The U.S. consulate or embassy that issues your visa will determine whether you will be issued a multiple- or single-entry visa and any restrictions regarding the length of your stay.

British subjects can obtain up-to-date passport and visa information by calling the **U.S. Embassy Visa**

Information Line (✆ **0891/200-290**) or the **London Passport Office** (✆ **0990/210-410** for recorded information), or they can find the visa information on the U.S. Embassy Great Britain website (**www.passport.gov.uk**).

Irish citizens can obtain up-to-date passport and visa information through the **Embassy of USA Dublin,** 42 Elgin Rd., Dublin 4, Ireland (✆ **353/1-668-8777**) or checking the visa website at **www.gov.ie/iveagh/services/passports/passportforms.htm**.

Australian citizens can obtain up-to-date passport and visa information by calling the **U.S. Embassy Canberra,** Moonah Place, Yarralumla, ACT 2600 (✆ **02/6214-5600**) or checking the website's visa page (**www.usis-australia.gov/consular/niv.html**).

Citizens of **New Zealand** can obtain up-to-date passport and visa information by calling the **U.S. Embassy New Zealand,** 29 Fitzherbert Terr., Thorndon, Wellington, New Zealand (✆ **644/472-2068**) or get the information directly from the website (**http://usembassy.org.nz**).

MEDICAL REQUIREMENTS Unless you're arriving from an area known to be suffering from an **epidemic** (particularly cholera or yellow fever), inoculations or vaccinations are not required for entry into the United States. If you have a medical condition that requires **syringe-administered medications,** carry a valid, signed prescription from your physician—the Federal Aviation Administration (FAA) no longer allows airline passengers to pack syringes in their carry-on baggage without documented proof of medical need. If you have a disease that requires treatment with **narcotics,** you should also carry documented proof with you—smuggling narcotics aboard a plane is a serious offense that carries severe penalties in the U.S.

For **HIV-positive visitors,** requirements for entering the United States are somewhat vague and change frequently. According to the latest publication of *HIV and Immigrants: A Manual for AIDS Service Providers,* the Immigration and Naturalization Service (INS) doesn't require a medical exam for entry into the United States, but INS officials may stop individuals because they look sick or because they are carrying AIDS/HIV medicine.

If an HIV-positive noncitizen applies for a non-immigrant visa, the question on the application regarding communicable diseases is tricky no matter which way it's answered. If the applicant checks "no," INS may deny the visa on the grounds that the applicant committed fraud. If the applicant checks "yes" or if INS suspects the person is HIV-positive, it will deny the visa unless the applicant asks for a special waiver for visitors. This waiver is for people visiting the United States for a short time, to attend a conference, for instance, to visit close relatives, or to receive medical treatment. It can be a confusing situation. For further up-to-the-minute information, contact the Centers for Disease Control's **National Center for HIV** (✆ **404/332-4559;** www.hivatis.org) or the **Gay Men's Health Crisis** (✆ **212/367-1000;** www.gmhc.org).

DRIVER'S LICENSES Foreign driver's licenses are mostly recognized in the U.S., although you may want to get an international driver's license if your home license is not written in English.

PASSPORT INFORMATION

Safeguard your passport in an inconspicuous, inaccessible place like a money belt. Make a copy of the critical pages, including the passport number, and store it in a safe place, separate from the passport itself. If you lose your passport, visit the nearest consulate of your native country as soon as possible for a replacement. Passport applications are downloadable from the Internet sites listed below.

Note that the International Civil Aviation Organization (ICAO) has recommended a policy requiring that *every* individual who travels by air have his or her own passport. In response, many countries are now requiring that children must be issued their own passport to travel internationally, where before those under 16 or so may have been allowed to travel on a parent or guardian's passport.

FOR RESIDENTS OF CANADA

You can pick up a passport application at one of 28 regional passport offices or most travel agencies. As of December 11, 2001, Canadian children who travel will need their own passport. However, if you hold a valid Canadian passport issued before December 11, 2001, that bears the name of your child, the passport remains valid for you and your child until it expires. Passports cost C$85 for those 16 years and older (valid 5 years), C$35 children 3 to 15 (valid 5 years), and C$20, children under 3 (valid 3 years). Applications, which must be accompanied by two identical passport-size photographs and proof of Canadian citizenship, are available at travel agencies throughout Canada or from the central **Passport Office, Department of Foreign Affairs and International Trade,** Ottawa, Ont. K1A 0G3 (✆ **800/567-6868;** www.dfait-maeci.gc.ca/passport). Processing takes 5 to 10 days if you apply in person, or about 3 weeks by mail.

FOR RESIDENTS OF THE UNITED KINGDOM

To pick up an application for a regular 10-year passport (the Visitor's Passport has been abolished), visit your nearest passport office, major post office, or travel agency. You can also contact the **London Passport Office** at ✆ **0171/271-3000** or search its website at www.ukpa.gov.uk. Passports are £21 for adults and £11 for children under 16.

FOR RESIDENTS OF IRELAND

You can apply for a 10-year passport, costing IR£45, at the **Passport Office,** Setanta Centre, Molesworth Street, Dublin 2 (✆ **01/671-1633;** www.irlgov.ie/iveagh/services/passports/passportforms.htm). Those under age 18 and over 65 must apply for a IR£10 3-year passport. You can also apply at 1A South Mall, Cork (✆ **021/272-525**) or over the counter at most main post offices.

FOR RESIDENTS OF AUSTRALIA

Apply at your local post office or passport office or search the government website at **www.dfat.gov.au/passports/**. Passports for adults are A$126 and for those under 18 are A$63.

FOR RESIDENTS OF NEW ZEALAND

You can pick up a passport application at any travel agency or Link Centre. For more info, contact the **Passport Office,** P.O. Box 805, Wellington (✆ **0800/225-050**). Passports for adults are NZ$80 and for those under 16 they're NZ$40.

CUSTOMS

WHAT YOU CAN BRING IN

Every visitor more than 21 years of age may bring in, free of duty, the following: (1) 1 liter of wine or hard liquor; (2) 200 cigarettes, 100 cigars (but not from Cuba), or 3 pounds of smoking tobacco; and (3) $100 worth of gifts. These exemptions are offered to travelers who spend at least 72 hours in the United States and who have not claimed them within the preceding 6 months. It is altogether forbidden to bring into the country foodstuffs (particularly fruit, cooked meats, and canned goods) and plants (vegetables, seeds, tropical plants, and the like). Foreign tourists may bring in or take out up to $10,000 in U.S. or foreign currency with no formalities; larger sums must be declared to U.S. Customs on entering or leaving, which includes filing form CM 4790. For more specific information regarding U.S. Customs, call your nearest U.S. embassy or consulate, or the **U.S. Customs** office at ✆ **202/927-1770** or www.customs.ustreas.gov.

WHAT YOU CAN TAKE HOME

U.K. citizens returning from a non-EU country have a customs allowance of: 200 cigarettes; 50 cigars; 250g of smoking tobacco; 2 liters of still table wine; 1 liter of spirits or strong liqueurs (over 22% volume); 2 liters of fortified wine, sparkling wine or other liqueurs; 60cc (ml) perfume; 250cc (ml) of toilet water; and £145 worth of all other goods, including gifts and souvenirs. People under 17 cannot have the tobacco or alcohol allowance. For more information, contact **HM Customs & Excise,** Passenger Enquiry Point, 2nd Floor Wayfarer House, Great South West Road, Feltham, Middlesex, TW14 8NP (✆ **0181/910-3744;** from outside the U.K. 44/181-910-3744), or consult their website at www.passport.gov.uk.

For a clear summary of **Canadian** rules, write for the booklet *I Declare,* issued by **Revenue Canada,** 2265 St. Laurent Blvd., Ottawa K1G 4KE (✆ **506/636-5064**). Canada allows its citizens a C$750 exemption, and you're allowed to bring back duty-free one carton of cigarettes, 1 can of tobacco, 40 imperial ounces of liquor, and 50 cigars. In addition, you're allowed to mail gifts to Canada valued at less than C$60 a day, provided they're unsolicited and don't contain alcohol or tobacco (write on the package UNSOLICITED GIFT, UNDER C$60 VALUE). All valuables should be declared on the Y-38 form before departure from Canada, including serial numbers of valuables you already own, such as expensive foreign cameras. *Note:* The $750 exemption can only be used once a year and only after an absence of 7 days.

The duty-free allowance in **Australia** is A$400 or, for those under 18, A$200. Personal property mailed back from the U.S. should be marked "Australian goods returned" to avoid payment of duty. Upon returning to Australia, citizens can bring in 250 cigarettes or 250 grams of loose tobacco, and 1,125ml of alcohol. If you're returning with valuable goods you already own, such as foreign-made cameras, you should file form B263. A helpful brochure, available from Australian consulates or Customs offices, is *Know Before You Go.* For more information, contact **Australian Customs Services,** GPO Box 8, Sydney NSW 2001 (✆ **02/9213-2000**).

The duty-free allowance for **New Zealand** is NZ$700. Citizens over 17 can bring in 200 cigarettes, or 50 cigars, or 250 grams of tobacco (or a mixture of all three if their combined weight doesn't exceed 250g); plus 4.5 liters of wine and beer, or 1.125 liters of liquor. New Zealand currency does not carry import or export restrictions. Fill out a certificate of export, listing the valuables you are taking out of the country; that way, you can bring them back without paying duty. Most questions are answered in a free pamphlet available at New Zealand consulates and Customs offices: *New Zealand Customs Guide for Travellers, Notice no. 4.* For more information, contact **New Zealand Customs,** 50 Anzac Ave., P.O. Box 29, Auckland (✆ **09/359-6655**).

HEALTH INSURANCE

Although it's not required of travelers, health insurance is highly recommended. Unlike many European countries, the United States does not usually offer free or low-cost medical care to its citizens or visitors. Doctors and hospitals are expensive, and in most cases will require advance payment or proof of coverage before they render their services. Policies can cover everything from the loss or theft of your baggage and trip cancellation to the guarantee of bail in case you're arrested. Good policies will also cover the costs of an accident, repatriation, or death. See "Health & Insurance," in chapter 3, for more information. Packages such as **Europ Assistance's "Worldwide Healthcare Plan"** are sold by European automobile clubs and travel agencies at attractive rates. **Worldwide Assistance** (✆ **800/821-2828;** www.worldwideassistance.com) is the agent for Europ Assistance in the United States.

Though lack of health insurance may prevent you from being admitted to a hospital in nonemergencies, don't worry about being left on a street corner to die: The American way is to fix you now and bill the living daylights out of you later.

INSURANCE FOR BRITISH TRAVELERS Most big travel agents offer their own insurance, and will probably try to sell you their package when you book a holiday. Think before you sign. **Britain's Consumers' Association** recommends that you insist on seeing the policy and reading the fine print before buying travel insurance. **The Association of British Insurers** (✆ **0171/600-3333;** www.abi.org.uk/) gives advice by phone and publishes *Holiday Insurance,* a free guide to policy provisions and prices. You might also shop around for better deals: Try **Columbus Direct** (✆ **020/7375-0011;** www.columbusdirect.net) or, for students, **Campus Travel** (✆ **020/7730-2101**).

INSURANCE FOR CANADIAN TRAVELERS Canadians should check with their provincial health plan offices or call **Health Canada** (✆ **613/957-2991;** www.hc-sc.gc.ca/) to find out the extent of their coverage and what documentation and receipts they must take home in case they are treated in the United States.

MONEY

CURRENCY The U.S. monetary system is very simple: The most common **bills** are the $1 (colloquially, a "buck"), $5, $10, and $20 denominations. There are also $2 bills (seldom encountered), $50 bills, and $100 bills (the last two are usually not welcome as payment for small purchases). All the paper money was recently redesigned, making the famous faces adorning them disproportionately large. The old-style bills are still legal tender.

There are seven denominations of coins: 1¢ (1 cent, or a penny); 5¢ (5 cents, or a nickel); 10¢ (10 cents, or a dime); 25¢ (25 cents, or a quarter); 50¢ (50 cents, or a half dollar); the new gold "Sacagawea" coin worth $1; and, prized by collectors, the rare, older silver dollar.

CURRENCY EXCHANGE The foreign-exchange bureaus so common in Europe are rare even at airports in the United States and nonexistent outside major cities. You'll find them in New York's prime tourist areas like Times Square, but expect to get extorted on the exchange rate. **American Express** (✆ **800/AXP-TRIP;** www.americanexpress.com) has many offices throughout the city, including 1185 Sixth Ave., at 47th Street (✆ 212/398-8585); at the New York Marriott Marquis hotel, 1535 Broadway, in the 8th-floor lobby (✆ 212/575-6580); on the mezzanine level at

Macy's Herald Square, 34th Street and Broadway (© 212/695-8075); and at 374 Park Ave., at 53rd Street (© 212/421-8240). Visit **http://travel.americanexpress.com** to locate additional travel service offices.

Thomas Cook Currency Services (© **800/CURRENCY;** www.us.thomascook.com) has locations at 1590 Broadway, at 48th Street (© 212/265-6063); 1271 Broadway, at 32nd Street (© 212/679-4877); 317 Madison Ave., at 42nd Street (© 212/883-0401); 29 Broadway, 2 blocks south of Wall Street (© 212/363-6206); and 511 Madison Ave., at 53rd Street (© 212/753-2595).

It's best not to expect to change foreign money (or traveler's checks denominated in a currency other than U.S. dollars) at a small-town bank, or even a bank branch in New York. In fact, it's best to just leave any currency other than U.S. dollars at home—it may prove a greater nuisance to you than it's worth.

You'll actually get the best exchange rate if you withdraw money from an ATM. But keep in mind that many banks impose a fee every time a card is used at an ATM (usually $1–$3, depending on the ATM you choose and what your home bank is), so you may want to factor these fees in when you weigh your options.

TRAVELER'S CHECKS Though traveler's checks are widely accepted, make sure that they're denominated in U.S. dollars, as foreign-currency checks are often difficult to exchange. The three traveler's checks that are most widely recognized—and least likely to be denied—are **Visa, American Express,** and **Thomas Cook.** Be sure to record the numbers of the checks, and keep that information in a separate place in case they get lost or stolen. Most businesses are pretty good about taking traveler's checks, but you're better off cashing them in at a bank (in small amounts, of course) and paying in cash. *Remember:* You'll need identification, such as a driver's license or passport, to change a traveler's check.

CREDIT CARDS & ATMS Credit cards are the most widely used form of payment in the United States: **Visa** (BarclayCard in Britain), **MasterCard** (EuroCard in Europe, Access in Britain, Chargex in Canada), **American Express, Diners Club, Discover,** and **Carte Blanche;** you'll also find that New York vendors may accept international cards like **enRoute, Eurocard,** and **JCB,** but not as universally as Amex, MasterCard, or Visa. There are, however, a handful of stores and restaurants that do not take credit cards, so be sure to ask in advance. And be aware that often businesses require a minimum purchase price, anywhere from $10 or $20, to use a credit card.

It is strongly recommended that you bring at least one major credit card. You must have a credit or charge card to rent a car. Hotels and airlines usually require a credit-card imprint as a deposit against expenses, and in an emergency a credit card can be priceless.

You'll find **automated teller machines (ATMs)** on just about every block in Manhattan. Some ATMs will allow you to draw U.S. currency against your bank and credit cards. Check with your bank before leaving

Travel Tip

Be sure to keep a copy of all your travel papers separate from your wallet or purse, and leave a copy with someone at home should you need it faxed in an emergency.

Size Conversion Chart

Women's Clothing								
American	4	6	8	10	12	14	16	
French	34	36	38	40	42	44	46	
British	6	8	10	12	14	16	18	
Women's Shoes								
American	5	6	7	8	9	10		
French	36	37	38	39	40	41		
British	4	5	6	7	8	9		
Men's Suits								
American	34	36	38	40	42	44	46	48
French	44	46	48	50	52	54	56	58
British	34	36	38	40	42	44	46	48
Men's Shirts								
American	14½	15	15½	16	16½	17	17½	
French	37	38	39	41	42	43	44	
British	14½	15	15½	16	16½	17	17½	
Men's Shoes								
American	7	8	9	10	11	12	13	
French	39½	41	42	43	44½	46	47	
British	6	7	8	9	10	11	12	

home, and remember that you will need your personal identification number (PIN) to do so. Most accept Visa, MasterCard, and American Express, as well as ATM cards from other U.S. banks. Expect to be charged up to $3 per transaction, however, if you're not using your own bank's ATM.

One way around these fees is to ask for cash back at grocery stores that accept ATM cards and don't charge usage fees. Of course, you'll have to purchase something first.

ATM cards with major credit card backing, known as "debit cards," are now a commonly acceptable form of payment in most stores and restaurants. Debit cards draw money directly from your checking account. Some stores enable you to receive "cash back" on your debit-card purchases as well.

SAFETY

GENERAL SAFETY SUGGESTIONS Tourist areas in Manhattan are generally safe, and the city has experienced a dramatic drop in its crime rate in recent years. Still, crime is a national problem, and U.S. urban areas tend to be less safe than those in Europe or Japan. You should always stay alert, use common sense, and trust your instincts. If you're in doubt about which neighborhoods are safe, don't hesitate to make inquiries with the hotel front desk staff or the local tourist office.

Avoid deserted areas, especially at night, and don't go into public parks after dark unless there's a concert or similar occasion that will attract a crowd.

Avoid carrying valuables with you on the street, and keep expensive cameras or electronic equipment bagged up or covered when not in use. If you're using a map, try to consult it inconspicuously—or better yet, study it before you leave your room. Hold onto your pocketbook, and place your billfold in an inside pocket. In theaters, restaurants, and other public places, keep your possessions in sight.

Always lock your room door—don't assume that once you're inside the hotel you are automatically safe and no longer need to be aware of your surroundings. Hotels are open to the public, and in a large hotel, security may not be able to screen everyone who enters.

For more about personal security in Manhattan, see "Playing It Safe," on p. 100.

DRIVING An inviolable rule of thumb for New York: Don't even think of driving within the city. Like many cities, New York has its own arcane rules of the road, confusing one-way streets, incomprehensible street-parking signs, and outrageously expensive parking garages. Public transportation—whether buses, subways, or taxis—will get you anywhere you want to go quickly and easily, and that's where you'll be most comfortable.

If you do drive to New York in a rental car, return it as soon as you arrive and rent another when you're ready to leave the city. Always keep your car doors locked. Never leave any packages or valuables in sight because thieves will break car windows. If someone attempts to rob you or steal your car, don't resist. Report the incident to the police department immediately.

2 Getting to the U.S.

In addition to the domestic airlines listed in chapter 3, "Planning Your Trip to New York City," many international carriers serve John F. Kennedy International and Newark airports. **British Airways** (✆ **0845/77-333-77,** 0870/55-111-55 in the U.K., or 800/AIRWAYS in the U.S.; www.british-airways.com) has daily service from London as well as direct flights from Manchester and Glasgow. **Virgin Atlantic** (✆ **01293/747-747,** 01293/511-581 in the U.K., or 800/862-8621 in the U.S.; www.virgin-atlantic.com) flies from London's Heathrow to New York.

Canadian readers might book flights on **Air Canada** (✆ **888/247-2262;** www.aircanada.ca), which offers direct service from Toronto, Montreal, Ottawa, and other cities.

Aer Lingus flies from Ireland to New York (✆ **0818/365000** in Ireland, or 800/IRISH-AIR in the U.S.; www.aerlingus.ie). The following U.S. airlines fly to New York from most major European cities: **Continental** (✆ **0800/776-464** in the U.K., or 800/231-0856 in the U.S.; www.continental.com); **United** (✆ **0845/844-4777** in the U.K., or 800/538-2929 in the U.S.; www.ual.com); **American** (✆ **0208/572-5555,** 0845/778-9789 in the U.K., or 800/433-7300 in the U.S.; www.aa.com); and **Delta** (✆ **0800/414-767** in the U.K., or 800/241-4141 in the U.S.; www.delta.com).

Qantas (✆ **13-13-13** in Australia, or 800/227-4500 in the U.S.; www.qantas.com.au) and **Air New Zealand** (✆ **0800/737-000** in New Zealand, or 800/262-1234 in the U.S.; www.airnewzealand.co.nz) fly to the West Coast and will book you straight through to New York City on a partner airline.

AIRLINE DISCOUNTS The smart traveler can find numerable ways to reduce the price of a plane ticket simply by taking time to shop around. For example, overseas visitors can take advantage of the APEX (Advance Purchase Excursion) reductions offered by all major U.S. and European carriers. For more money-saving airline advice, see "Getting There," in chapter 3. For the best rates, compare fares and be flexible with the dates and times of travel.

IMMIGRATION AND CUSTOMS CLEARANCE Visitors arriving by air, no matter what the port of entry, should cultivate patience and resignation before setting foot on U.S. soil. Getting through immigration control can take as long as 2 hours on some days, especially on summer weekends, so be sure to carry this guidebook or something else to read. This is especially true in the aftermath of the September 11, 2001, terrorist attacks, when security clearances have been considerably beefed up at U.S. airports.

People traveling by air from Canada, Bermuda, and certain countries in the Caribbean can sometimes clear Customs and Immigration at the point of departure, which is much quicker.

3 Getting Around the U.S.

BY PLANE Some large airlines (for example, Northwest and Delta) offer travelers on their transatlantic or transpacific flights special discount tickets under the name **Visit USA,** allowing mostly one-way travel from one U.S. destination to another at very low prices. These discount tickets are not on sale in the United States and must be purchased abroad in conjunction with your international ticket. This system is the best, easiest, and fastest way to see the United States at low cost. You should obtain information well in advance from your travel agent or the office of the airline concerned, because the conditions attached to these discount tickets can be changed without advance notice.

BY TRAIN International visitors (excluding Canada) can also buy a **USA Railpass,** good for 15 or 30 days of unlimited travel on Amtrak (✆ **800/USA-RAIL;** www.amtrak.com). The pass is available through many foreign travel agents. Prices in 2002 for a 15-day pass were $295 off-peak, $440 peak; a 30-day pass costs $385 off-peak, $550 peak. With a foreign passport, you can also buy passes at some Amtrak offices in the United States, including locations in San Francisco, Los Angeles, Chicago, New York, Miami, Boston, and Washington, D.C. Reservations are generally required and should be made for each part of your trip as early as possible. Regional rail passes are also available.

BY BUS Although bus travel is often the most economical form of public transit for short hops between U.S. cities, it can also be slow and uncomfortable—certainly not an option for everyone (particularly when Amtrak, which is far more luxurious, offers similar rates). **Greyhound/Trailways** (✆ **800/231-2222**), the sole nationwide bus line, offers an **International Ameripass** that must be purchased before coming to the United States or by phone through the Greyhound International Office at the Port Authority Bus Terminal in New York City (✆ **212/971-0492**). The pass can be obtained from foreign travel agents and costs less than the domestic version. 2002 passes cost as follows: 4 days ($135), 7 days ($184), 10 days ($234), 15 days ($274), 21 days ($324), 30 days ($364), 45 days ($404), or 60 days ($494). You can get more info on the pass at www.greyhound.com, or by calling ✆ **212-971-0492** (14:00–21:00 GMT) and ✆ **402-330-8552** (all other times). In addition, special rates are available for senior citizens and students.

BY CAR Unless you plan to spend the bulk of your vacation time in New York City, where walking is the best and easiest way to get around, the most cost-effective, convenient, and comfortable way to travel around the United States is by car. The interstate highway system connects cities and towns all over the country; in addition to these high-speed, limited-access roadways, there's an extensive network of federal, state, and local highways and roads. Some of the national car-rental companies include **Alamo** (✆ 800/327-9633; www.goalamo.com), **Avis** (✆ 800/331-1212; www.avis.com), **Budget** (✆ 800/527-0700; https://rent.drivebudget.com), **Dollar** (✆ 800/800-4000; www.dollar.com), **Hertz** (✆ 800/654-3131; www.hertz.com), **National** (✆ 800/227-7368; www.nationalcar.com), and **Thrifty** (✆ 800/367-2277; www.thrifty.com).

If you plan to rent a car in the United States, you probably won't need the services of an additional automobile organization. If you're planning to buy or borrow a car, automobile-association membership is recommended. The **American Automobile Association** (AAA; ✆ **800/222-4357**), is the country's largest auto club and supplies its members with maps, insurance, and, most important, emergency road service. The cost of joining runs from $63 for singles to $87 for two members, but if you're a member of a foreign auto club with reciprocal arrangements, you can enjoy free AAA service in America. See below for more information.

FAST FACTS: For the International Traveler

Also see "Fast Facts: New York City," in chapter 5, for more New York City–specific information.

Automobile Organizations Auto clubs will supply maps, suggested routes, guidebooks, accident and bail-bond insurance, and emergency road service. The **American Automobile Association (AAA)** is the major auto club in the United States. If you belong to an auto club in your home country, inquire about AAA reciprocity before you leave. You may be able to join AAA even if you're not a member of a reciprocal club; to inquire, call AAA (✆ **800/222-4357**). AAA is actually an organization of regional auto clubs; so look under "AAA Automobile Club" in the White Pages of the telephone directory. AAA has a nationwide emergency road service telephone number (✆ 800/AAA-HELP).

Business Hours Offices are usually open weekdays from 9am to 5pm. Banks are open weekdays from 9am to 3pm or later and sometimes Saturday mornings. Stores typically open between 9 and 10am and close between 5 and 6pm from Monday through Saturday. Stores in shopping complexes or malls tend to stay open late: until about 9pm on weekdays and weekends, and many malls and larger department stores are open on Sundays.

Currency & Currency Exchange See "Entry Requirements" and "Money" under "Preparing for Your Trip," earlier in this chapter.

Drinking Laws The legal age for purchase and consumption of alcoholic beverages is 21; proof of age is required and often requested at bars, nightclubs, and restaurants, so it's always a good idea to bring ID when you go out. Beer and wine often can be purchased in supermarkets, but liquor laws vary from state to state.

Do not carry open containers of alcohol in your car or any public area that isn't zoned for alcohol consumption. The police can fine you on the spot. And nothing will ruin your trip faster than getting a citation for DUI ("driving under the influence"), so don't even think about driving while intoxicated.

Electricity Like Canada, the United States uses 110 to 120 volts AC (60 cycles), compared to 220 to 240 volts AC (50 cycles) in most of Europe, Australia, and New Zealand. If your small appliances use 220 to 240 volts, you'll need a 110-volt transformer and a plug adapter with two flat parallel pins to operate them here. Downward converters that change 220–240 volts to 110–120 volts are difficult to find in the United States, so bring one with you.

Embassies & Consulates All embassies are located in the nation's capital, Washington, D.C. Some consulates are located in major U.S. cities, and most nations have a mission to the United Nations in New York City. If your country isn't listed below, call for directory information in Washington, D.C. (✆ **202/555-1212**), for the number of your national embassy.

The embassy of **Australia** is at 1601 Massachusetts Ave. NW, Washington, DC 20036 (✆ **202/797-3000;** www.austemb.org). There are consulates in New York, Honolulu, Houston, Los Angeles, and San Francisco.

The embassy of **Canada** is at 501 Pennsylvania Ave. NW, Washington, DC 20001 (✆ **202/682-1740;** www.canadianembassy.org). Other Canadian consulates are in Buffalo (N.Y.), Detroit, Los Angeles, New York, and Seattle.

The embassy of **Ireland** is at 2234 Massachusetts Ave. NW, Washington, DC 20008 (✆ **202/462-3939;** www.irelandmb.org/contact.html). Irish consulates are in Boston, Chicago, New York, and San Francisco.

The embassy of **Japan** is at 2520 Massachusetts Ave. NW, Washington, DC 20008 (✆ **202/238-6700;** www.embjapan.org). Japanese consulates are located in Atlanta, Kansas City, San Francisco, and Washington D.C.

The embassy of **New Zealand** is at 37 Observatory Circle NW, Washington, DC 20008 (✆ **202/328-4800;** www.nzemb.org). New Zealand consulates are in Los Angeles, Salt Lake City, San Francisco, and Seattle.

The embassy of the **United Kingdom** is at 3100 Massachusetts Ave. NW, Washington, DC 20008 (✆ **202/462-1340;** www.britainusa.com/consular/embassy/). Other British consulates are in Atlanta, Boston, Chicago, Cleveland, Houston, Los Angeles, New York, San Francisco, and Seattle.

Emergencies Call ✆ **911** to report a fire, call the police, or get an ambulance anywhere in the United States. This is a toll-free call (which means that no coins are required at public telephones.)

If you have a medical emergency that doesn't require an ambulance, you can walk into a hospital's 24-hour emergency room (usually a separate entrance). For a list of hospitals, see "Fast Facts: New York City," in chapter 5. Because emergency rooms are often crowded and waits are long, one of the walk-in medical centers listed under "What to Do If You Get Sick Away From Home" (under "Health & Insurance," in chapter 3) might be a better option.

If you encounter serious problems, contact the **Traveler's Aid International** (✆ **202/546-1127;** www.travelersaid.org) to help direct you to a local branch. This nationwide, nonprofit, social-service organization geared to helping travelers in difficult straits offers services that might include reuniting families separated while traveling, providing food and/or shelter to people stranded without cash, or even emotional counseling. If you're in trouble, seek them out.

Gasoline (Petrol) Petrol is known as gasoline (or simply "gas") in the United States, and petrol stations are known as both gas stations and service stations. Gasoline costs about half as much here as it does in Europe (about $1.65 per gal. at press time), and taxes are already included in the printed price. One U.S. gallon equals 3.8 liters or 0.85 Imperial gallons.

Holidays Banks, government offices, post offices, and many stores, restaurants, and museums are closed on the following legal national holidays: January 1 (New Year's Day), the third Monday in January (Martin Luther King, Jr., Day), the third Monday in February (Presidents' Day, Washington's Birthday), the last Monday in May (Memorial Day), July 4th (Independence Day), the first Monday in September (Labor Day), the second Monday in October (Columbus Day), November 11 (Veterans' Day/Armistice Day), the fourth Thursday in November (Thanksgiving Day), and December 25 (Christmas). Also, the Tuesday following the first Monday in November is Election Day and is a federal government holiday in presidential-election years (held every 4 years, and next in 2004).

Legal Aid If you are "pulled over" for a minor infraction (such as speeding), never attempt to pay the fine directly to a police officer; this could be construed as attempted bribery, a much more serious crime. Pay fines by mail, or directly into the hands of the clerk of the court. If accused of a more serious offense, say and do nothing before consulting a lawyer. Here the burden is on the state to prove a person's guilt beyond a reasonable doubt, and everyone has the right to remain silent, whether he or she is suspected of a crime or actually arrested. Once arrested, a person can make one telephone call to a party of his or her choice. Call your embassy or consulate.

Mail If you aren't sure what your address will be in the United States, mail can be sent to you, in your name, c/o General Delivery at the main post office of the city or region where you expect to be. (Call ✆ **800/275-8777** for information on the nearest post office.) The addressee must pick up mail in person and must produce proof of identity (driver's license, passport, and so on). Most post offices will hold your mail for up to one month, and are open Monday to Friday from 8am to 6pm, and Saturday from 9am to 3pm.

Generally found at intersections, mailboxes are blue with a red-and-white stripe and carry the inscription U.S. Mail. If your mail is addressed to a U.S. destination, don't forget to add the five-digit postal code (or ZIP code), after the two-letter abbreviation of the state to which the mail is addressed. This is essential to prompt delivery.

At press time, domestic postage rates were 22¢ for a postcard and 37¢ for a letter. For international mail, a first-class letter of up to one-half ounce costs 60¢ (46¢ to Canada and 40¢ to Mexico); a first-class postcard costs 50¢ (including Canada and Mexico); and a preprinted postal aerogramme costs 50¢.

Measurements See the chart on the inside front cover of this book for details on converting metric measurements to U.S. equivalents.

Newspapers & Magazines In addition to the *New York Times* and other city papers, many newsstands carry a selection of international newspapers and magazines. For major newspapers and magazines from around the world, visit **Universal News & Magazines,** at 234 W. 42nd St., between Seventh and Eighth avenues (✆ **212/221-1809**), and 977 Eighth Ave., between 57th and 58th streets (✆ **212/459-0932**), or **Hotalings News Agency,** 624 W. 52nd St., between Eleventh and Twelfth avenues (✆ **212/974-9419**). Other good bets include the **Hudson** newsdealers located in Grand Central Terminal, at 42nd Street and Lexington Avenue, and Penn Station, at 34th Street and Seventh Avenue.

Taxes The United States has no value-added tax (VAT) or other indirect tax at the national level. Every state, county, and city has the right to levy its own local tax on all purchases, including hotel and restaurant checks, airline tickets, and so on.

Telephone, Telegraph, Telex & Fax The telephone system in the United States is run by private corporations, so rates, especially for long-distance service and operator-assisted calls, can vary widely. Generally, hotel surcharges on long-distance and local calls are astronomical, so you're usually better off using a **public pay telephone,** which you'll find clearly marked in most public buildings and private establishments as well as on the street. Convenience grocery stores and gas stations always have them. Many convenience groceries and packaging services sell **prepaid calling cards** in denominations up to $50; these can be the least expensive way to call home. Many public phones at airports now accept American Express, MasterCard, and Visa credit cards. **Local calls** made from public pay phones in most locales cost either 25¢ or 35¢. Pay phones do not accept pennies, and few will take anything larger than a quarter.

You may want to look into leasing a cellphone for the duration of your trip.

Most long-distance and international calls can be dialed directly from any phone. **For calls within the United States and to Canada,** dial 1 followed by the area code and the seven-digit number. **For other international calls,** dial 011 followed by the country code, city code, and the telephone number of the person you are calling.

Calls to area codes **800, 888,** and **877** are toll-free. However, calls to numbers in area codes **700** and **900** (chat lines, bulletin boards, "dating" services, and so on) can be very expensive—usually a charge of 95¢ to $3 or more per minute, and they sometimes have minimum charges that can run as high as $15 or more.

For **reversed-charge or collect calls,** and for person-to-person calls, dial 0 (zero, not the letter O) followed by the area code and number you want; an operator will then come on the line, and you should specify that you are calling collect, or person-to-person, or both. If your operator-assisted call is international, ask for the overseas operator.

For **local directory assistance** ("information"), dial 411; for long-distance information, dial 1, then the appropriate area code and 555-1212.

Telegraph and telex services are provided primarily by Western Union. You can bring your telegram into the nearest Western Union office (there are hundreds across the country) or dictate it over the phone (✆ **800/325-6000**). You can also telegraph money, or have it telegraphed to you, very quickly over the Western Union system, but this service can cost as much as 15 to 20 percent of the amount sent.

Most hotels have **fax machines** available for guest use (be sure to ask about the charge to use it). Many hotel rooms are even wired for guests' fax machines. A less expensive way to send and receive faxes may be at stores such as Mail Boxes Etc., a national chain of packing service shops. (Look in the Yellow Pages directory under "Packing Services.")

There are two kinds of telephone directories in the United States. The so-called **White Pages** list private households and business subscribers in alphabetical order. The inside front cover lists emergency numbers for police, fire, ambulance, the Coast Guard, poison-control center, crime-victims hot line, and so on. The first few pages will tell you how to make long-distance and international calls, complete with country codes and area codes. Government numbers are usually printed on blue paper within the White Pages. Printed on yellow paper, the so-called **Yellow Pages** list all local services, businesses, industries, and houses of worship according to activity with an index at the front or back. (Drugstores/pharmacies and restaurants are also listed by geographic location.) The Yellow Pages also include city plans or detailed area maps, postal ZIP codes, and public transportation routes.

Time The continental United States is divided into **four time zones:** eastern standard time (EST), central standard time (CST), mountain standard time (MST), and Pacific standard time (PST). Alaska and Hawaii have their own zones. For example, noon in New York City (EST) is 11am in Chicago (CST), 10am in Denver (MST), 9am in Los Angeles (PST), 8am in Anchorage (AST), and 7am in Honolulu (HST).

Daylight saving time is in effect from 1am on the first Sunday in April through 1am on the last Sunday in October, except in Arizona, Hawaii, part of Indiana, and Puerto Rico. Daylight saving time moves the clock 1 hour ahead of standard time.

For the correct local time in New York, dial ✆ **212/976-1616.**

Tipping Tipping is so ingrained in the American way of life that the annual income tax of tip-earning service personnel is based on how much they should have received in light of their employers' gross revenues. Accordingly, they may have to pay tax on a tip you didn't actually give them.

Here are some rules of thumb:

In hotels, tip **bellhops** at least $1 per bag ($2–$3 if you have a lot of luggage) and tip the **chamber staff** $1 to $2 per day (more if you've left a disaster area for him or her to clean up, or if you're traveling with kids and/or pets). Tip the **doorman** or **concierge** only if he or she has provided you with some specific service (for example, calling a cab for you or obtaining difficult-to-get theater tickets). Tip the **valet-parking attendant** $1 every time you get your car.

In restaurants, bars, and nightclubs, tip **service staff** 15% to 20% of the check, tip **bartenders** 10% to 15%, tip **checkroom attendants** $1 per garment, and tip **valet-parking attendants** $1 per vehicle. Tip the **doorman** only if he has provided you with some specific service (such as calling a cab for you). Tipping is not expected in cafeterias and fast-food restaurants.

Tip **cab drivers** 15% of the fare.

As for other service personnel, tip **skycaps** at airports at least $1 per bag ($2–$3 if you have a lot of luggage) and tip **hairdressers** and **barbers** 15% to 20%.

Tipping ushers at movies and theaters, and gas-station attendants, is not expected.

Toilets You won't find public toilets or "restrooms" on the streets in most U.S. cities, but they can be found in hotel lobbies, bars, restaurants, museums, department stores, railway and bus stations, and service stations. Large hotels and fast-food restaurants are probably the best bet for good, clean facilities. If possible, avoid the toilets at parks and beaches, which tend to be dirty; some may be unsafe. Restaurants and bars in resorts or heavily visited areas may reserve their restrooms for patrons. Some establishments display a notice indicating this. You can ignore this sign or, better yet, avoid arguments by paying for a cup of coffee or a soft drink, which will qualify you as a patron. See "Restrooms" under "Fast Facts: New York City," in chapter 5.

5

Getting to Know New York City

This chapter gives you an insider's take on Manhattan's most distinctive neighborhoods and streets, tells you how to get around town, and serves as a handy reference to everything from personal safety to libraries and liquor.

1 Orientation

VISITOR INFORMATION

INFORMATION OFFICES

- The **Times Square Visitors Center,** 1560 Broadway, between 46th and 47th streets (where Broadway meets Seventh Ave.), across from the TKTS booth on the east side of the street (✆ **212/768-1560;** www.timessquarebid.org), is the city's top info stop. This pleasant and attractive center features a helpful info desk offering loads of citywide information. There's also a tour desk selling tickets for Gray Line bus tours and Circle Line boat tours; a Metropolitan Transportation Authority (MTA) desk staffed to sell MetroCard fare cards, provide public transit maps, and answer all of your questions on the transit system; a Broadway Ticket Center providing show information and selling full-price show tickets; ATMs and currency exchange machines; and computer terminals with free Internet access courtesy of Yahoo! It's open daily from 8am to 8pm.
- The New York Convention and Visitors Bureau runs the **NYCVB Visitor Information Center** at 810 Seventh Ave., between 52nd and 53rd streets. In addition to loads of information on citywide attractions and a multilingual counselor on hand to answer questions, the center also has interactive terminals that provide free touch-screen access to visitor information via Citysearch and sell advance tickets to major attractions, which can save you from standing in long ticket lines once you arrive (you can also buy CityPass using these; see box on p. 243). There's also an ATM, a gift shop, and a bank of phones that connect you directly with American Express card member services. The center is open Monday through Friday from 8:30am to 6pm, Saturday and Sunday from 9am to 5pm. For over-the-phone assistance, call ✆ **212/484-1222.**

PUBLICATIONS

For comprehensive listings of films, concerts, performances, sporting events, museum and gallery exhibits, street fairs, and special events, the following are your best bets:

- The ***New York Times*** (**www.nytimes.com** or www.nytoday.com) features terrific arts and entertainment coverage, particularly in the two-part Friday

"Weekend" section and the Sunday "Arts & Leisure" section. Both days boast full guides to the latest happenings in Broadway and Off-Broadway theater, classical music, dance, pop and jazz, film, and the art world. Friday is particularly good for cabaret, family fun, and general-interest recreational and sightseeing events.

- ***Time Out New York*** (**www.timeoutny.com**) is my favorite weekly magazine. Dedicated to weekly goings-on, it's attractive, well organized, and easy to use. *TONY* features excellent coverage in all categories, from live music, theater, and clubs (gay and straight) to museum shows, dance events, book and poetry readings, and kids' stuff. The regular "Check Out" section, unequaled in any other listings magazine, will fill you in on upcoming sample and closeout sales, crafts and antiques shows, and other shopping-related scoops. A new issue hits newsstands every Thursday.
- The free weekly ***Village Voice*** (**www.villagevoice.com**), the city's legendary alterna-paper, is available late Tuesday downtown and early Wednesday in the rest of the city. From classical music to clubs, the arts and entertainment coverage couldn't be more extensive, and just about every live music venue advertises its shows here. But I find the paper a bit unwieldy to navigate, and the exposé tone of its features can be tiresome.

Other useful weekly rags include the glossy ***New York*** magazine (**www.newyorkmag.com** or www.nymetro.com), which offers valuable restaurant reviews and whose "Cue" section is a selective guide to city arts and entertainment; the ***New Yorker*** (**www.newyorker.com**), which features an artsy "Goings On About Town" section at the front of the magazine; and the ***New York Press*** (**www.nypress.com**), a free left-of-center weekly in the *Village Voice* vein. Monthly ***Paper*** (**www.papermag.com**) is a glossy alterna-mag that serves as good prep for those of you who want to experience the hipper side of the city.

CITY LAYOUT

Open the sheet map that comes free with this book and you'll see the city is comprised of five boroughs: **Manhattan,** where most of the visitor action is; the **Bronx,** the only borough connected to the mainland United States; **Queens,** where Kennedy and LaGuardia airports are located and which borders the Atlantic Ocean and occupies part of Long Island; **Brooklyn,** south of Queens, which is also on Long Island and is famed for its attitude, accent, and Atlantic-front Coney Island; and **Staten Island,** the least populous borough, bordering Upper New York Bay on one side and the Atlantic Ocean on the other.

When most visitors envision New York, they think of Manhattan, the long finger-shaped island pointing southwest off the mainland—surrounded by the Harlem River to the north, the Hudson River to the west, the East River (really an estuary) to the east, and the fabulous expanse of Upper New York Bay to the south. Despite the fact that it's the city's smallest borough (13½ miles/22km long, 2¼ miles/3.5km wide, 22 sq. miles/57 sq. km), Manhattan contains the city's most famous attractions, buildings, and cultural institutions. For that reason, almost all of the accommodations and restaurants suggested in this book are in Manhattan.

In most of Manhattan, finding your way around is a snap because of the logical, well-executed grid system by which the streets are numbered. If you can discern uptown and downtown, and East Side and West Side, you can find your way around pretty easily. In real terms, **uptown** means north of where you happen to be and **downtown** means south, although sometimes these labels have vague psychographical meanings (generally speaking, "uptown" chic vs. "downtown" bohemianism).

Avenues run north–south (uptown and downtown). Most are numbered. **Fifth Avenue** divides the East Side from the West Side of town, and serves as the eastern border of Central Park north of 59th Street. **First Avenue** is all the way east and **Twelfth Avenue** is all the way west. The three most important unnumbered avenues on the East Side you should know are between Third and Fifth avenues: **Madison** (east of Fifth), **Park** (east of Madison), and **Lexington** (east of Park, just west of Third). Important unnumbered avenues on the West Side are **Avenue of the Americas,** which all New Yorkers call Sixth Avenue; **Central Park West,** which is what Eighth Avenue north of 59th Street is called as it borders Central Park on the west (hence the name); **Columbus Avenue,** which is what Ninth Avenue is called north of 59th Street; and **Amsterdam Avenue,** or Tenth Avenue north of 59th.

Broadway is the exception to the rule—it's the only major avenue that doesn't run uptown–downtown. It cuts a diagonal path across the island, from the northwest tip down to the southeast corner. As it crosses most major avenues, it creates **squares** (Times Sq., Herald Sq., Madison Sq., and Union Sq., for example).

Streets run east–west (crosstown) and are numbered consecutively as they proceed uptown from Houston (pronounced *House*-ton) Street. So to go uptown, simply walk north of, or to a higher-numbered street than, where you are. Downtown is south of (or a lower-numbered street than) your current location.

As I've already mentioned, Fifth Avenue is the dividing line between the **East Side** and **West Side** of town (except below Washington Sq., where Broadway serves that function). On the East Side of Fifth Avenue, streets are numbered with the distinction "East"; on the West Side of that avenue they are numbered "West." East 51st Street, for example, begins at Fifth Avenue and runs east to the East River, while West 51st Street begins at Fifth Avenue and runs west to the Hudson River.

If you're looking for a particular address, remember that even-numbered street addresses are on the south side of streets and odd-numbered addresses are on the north. Street addresses increase by about 50 per block starting at Fifth Avenue. For example, nos. 1 to 50 East are just about between Fifth and Madison avenues, while nos. 1 to 50 West are just about between Fifth and Sixth avenues. Traffic generally runs east on even-numbered streets and west on odd-numbered streets, with a few exceptions, like the major east-west thoroughfares—**14th, 23rd, 34th, 42nd, 57th, 72nd, 79th, 86th,** and so on—which have two-way traffic. Therefore 28 W. 23rd St. is a short walk west of Fifth Avenue; 325 E. 35th St. would be a few blocks east of Fifth.

Avenue addresses are irregular. For example, 994 Second Ave. is at East 51st Street, but so is 320 Park Ave. Thus, it's important to know a building's cross street to find it easily. If you don't have the cross street and you want to figure out the exact location using just the address, use the **Manhattan Address Locator,** later in this chapter.

Unfortunately, the rules don't apply to neighborhoods in Lower Manhattan, south of 14th Street—like Wall Street, Chinatown, SoHo, TriBeCa, the Village—since they sprang up before engineers devised this brilliant grid scheme. A good map is essential when exploring these areas.

STREET MAPS You'll find a useful pullout map of Manhattan at the back of this book. There's also a decent one available for free as part of the **Official NYC**

Tips Orientation Tips

I've indicated the cross streets for every destination in this book, but be sure to ask for the cross street (or avenue) if you're ever calling for an address.

When you give a taxi driver an address, always specify the cross streets. New Yorkers, even most cab drivers, probably wouldn't know where to find 994 Second Ave., but they do know where to find 51st and Second. If you're heading to the restaurant Le Bernadin, for example, tell them that it's on 51st Street between Sixth and Seventh avenues. The exact number (in this case, no. 155) is given only as a further precision.

If you have only the numbered address on an avenue and need to figure out the cross street, use the **Manhattan Address Locator** on p. 89.

Visitor Kit if you write ahead for information (see "Visitor Information," in chapter 3); you can also pick it up for free at the visitor centers listed above.

Even with all these freebies at hand, I suggest investing in a map with more features if you really want to zip around the city like a pro. **Hagstrom** maps are my favorites because they feature block-by-block street numbering—so instead of trying to guess the cross street for 125 Prince St., you can see right on your map that it's Greene Street. Hagstrom and other visitor-friendly maps are available at just about any good bookstore, including the Barnes & Noble and Borders branches around town; see chapter 10 for locations. You might also want to look for *The New York Map Guide: The Essential Guide to Manhattan* (Penguin), by Michael Middleditch, a 64-page book that maps the entire city, including attractions, restaurants, and nightlife spots.

Keep in mind that, due to construction and the World Trade Center disaster, certain subway lines will be in flux throughout 2002 and 2003, especially downtown. Therefore, don't rely on any subway map that hasn't been printed by the Metropolitan Transit Authority; more on this in "Getting Around," later in this chapter.

MANHATTAN'S NEIGHBORHOODS IN BRIEF

Because they grew up over the course of hundreds of years, Manhattan neighborhoods have multiple, splintered personalities and fluid boundaries. Still, it's relatively easy to agree upon what they stand for in general terms—so if you stop a New Yorker on the street and ask them to point you to, say, the Upper West Side or the Flatiron District, they'll know where you want to go. From south to north, here is how I've defined Manhattan's neighborhoods throughout this book.

Downtown

Lower Manhattan: South Street Seaport & the Financial District At one time, this was New York—period. Originally established by the Dutch in 1625 (hence the city's original name, Nieuw Amsterdam), New York's first settlements sprung up here, on the southern tip of Manhattan island; everything uptown was farm country and wilderness. While all that's changed, this is still the best place in the city to search for the past.

Lower Manhattan constitutes everything south of Chambers Street. **Battery Park,** the point of departure for the Statue of Liberty, Ellis Island, and Staten Island, is on the very south tip of the island. The

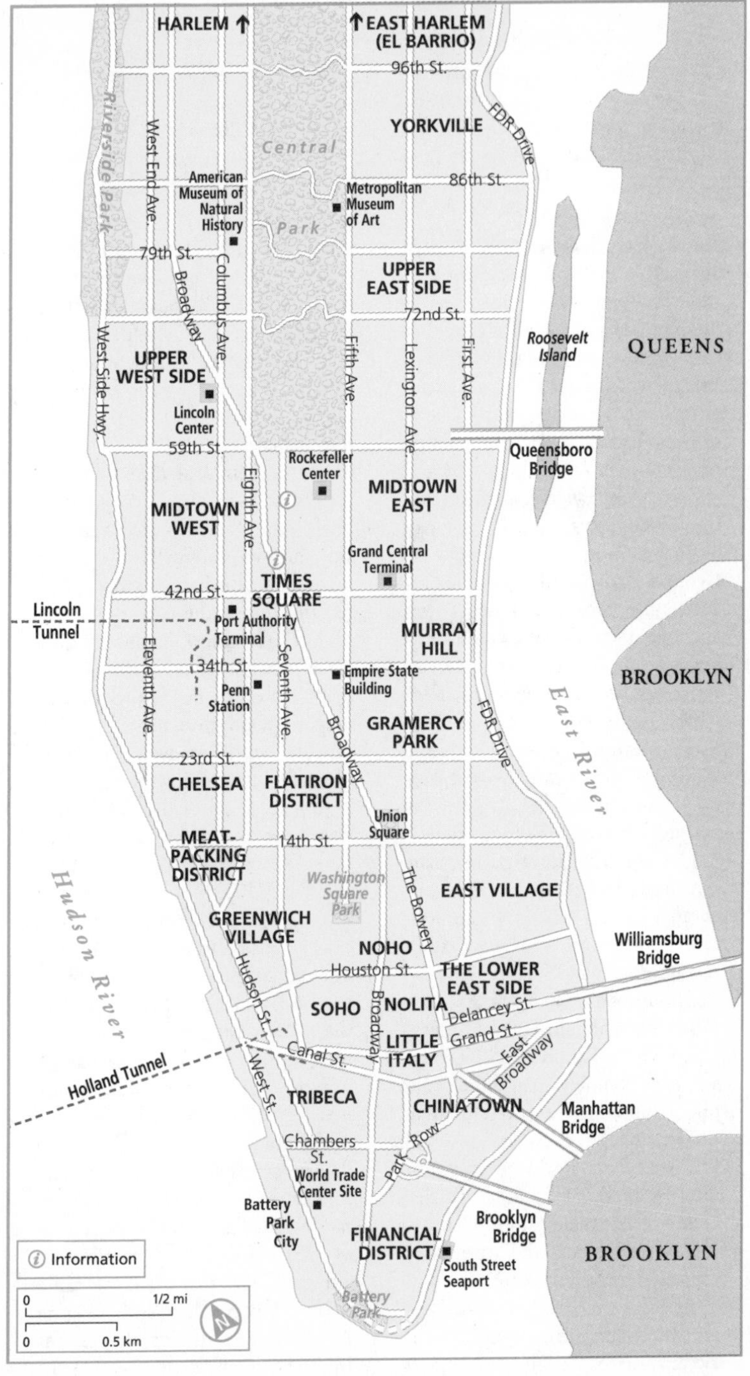
HARLEM
EAST HARLEM (EL BARRIO)
96th St.
YORKVILLE
FDR Drive
Riverside Park
West End Ave.
Central Park
American Museum of Natural History
Metropolitan Museum of Art
86th St.
79th St.
Broadway
Columbus Ave.
UPPER EAST SIDE
72nd St.
West Side Hwy.
UPPER WEST SIDE
Lincoln Center
Fifth Ave.
Lexington Ave.
First Ave.
Roosevelt Island
QUEENS
59th St.
Queensboro Bridge
Rockefeller Center
MIDTOWN EAST
MIDTOWN WEST
Eighth Ave.
Grand Central Terminal
TIMES SQUARE
42nd St.
Lincoln Tunnel
Port Authority Terminal
MURRAY HILL
Eleventh Ave.
34th St.
Penn Station
Seventh Ave.
Empire State Building
BROOKLYN
East River
GRAMERCY PARK
23rd St.
CHELSEA
FLATIRON DISTRICT
Union Square
MEAT-PACKING DISTRICT
14th St.
Hudson River
Washington Square Park
The Bowery
EAST VILLAGE
GREENWICH VILLAGE
NOHO
Williamsburg Bridge
Houston St.
THE LOWER EAST SIDE
Hudson St.
SOHO
NOLITA
Delancey St.
LITTLE ITALY
Grand St.
East Broadway
Canal St.
Holland Tunnel
West St.
TRIBECA
CHINATOWN
Manhattan Bridge
Chambers St.
Park Row
World Trade Center Site
Battery Park City
FINANCIAL DISTRICT
Brooklyn Bridge
South Street Seaport
BROOKLYN
Information
0
1/2 mi
0
0.5 km
Battery Park

Tips **Lower Manhattan Accessibility Update**

Lower Manhattan was almost fully operational at press time, with the exception of the World Trade Center site itself. However, things can change at any time. For the latest, check with **NYC & Company,** New York City's official tourism office, at ✆ **212/484-1222** or visit **www.nycvisit.com**.

South Street Seaport, now touristy but still a reminder of times of when shipping was the lifeblood of the city, lies a bit north on the east coast; it's just south of the Brooklyn Bridge, which stands proudly as the ultimate engineering achievement of New York's 19th-century Industrial Age.

The rest of the area is considered the **Financial District,** but may even be more famous now as **Ground Zero.** Until September 11, 2001, the Financial District was anchored by the **World Trade Center,** with the World Financial Center complex and residential Battery Park City to the west, and **Wall Street** running crosstown a little south and to the east. Now, a gaping hole sits where the Twin Towers and its five sister buildings stood.

Despite the devastation, the Financial District deserves to be celebrated as an incredible story of recovery amongst the ruins. Within six months of the horrific day, the neighborhood was running pretty much normally just about everywhere but the World Trade Center site itself. Some nearby hotels and office buildings remain closed at this writing, but the adjacent World Financial Center was up and running by early 2002, and even discount department store Century 21, directly across the street, had reopened by March 2002.

At press time, the Ground Zero site was still in the clean-up process. Because no redevelopment plan was yet in place, there's no way to speculate what's to come. However, one thing's for sure: The Ground Zero you see will still be a massive construction zone throughout 2003. Whether viewing platforms will remain in place throughout the process is anybody's guess; see chapter 8 for information on how to find the latest.

You can rest assured that the surrounding area—including Wall Street, the South Street Seaport, and Battery Park—will be open and ready for business. **City Hall** remains the northern border of the district, abutting Chambers Street (look for City Hall Park on the map). Most of the streets of this neighborhood are narrow concrete canyons, with Broadway serving as the main uptown-downtown artery.

Just about all of the major subway lines congregate here before they either end or head to Brooklyn (the B, D, F, J, M, Q, V, W, and Z lines being the chief exceptions)—it crosses into Brooklyn from the Lower East Side, over the Manhattan Bridge). At this writing, all but the 1 and 9 lines were up and running again—even the stop named "World Trade Center" on the E line is reopened (it actually lets you out to the north of the site). The 1 and 9 were scheduled to resume their runs to the southern tip of Manhattan, South Ferry (the southern tip of the island), by sometime in autumn 2002. Any event can cause delays, however, so see "Getting Around" later in this chapter for information on where to gather the latest subway information.

TriBeCa Bordered by the Hudson River to the west, the area north of Chambers Street, west of Broadway, and south of Canal Street is the *Tri*angle *Be*low *Ca*nal Street, or TriBeCa. Since the 1980s, as SoHo became saturated with chic, the spillover has been quietly transforming TriBeCa into one of the city's hippest residential neighborhoods, where celebrities and families quietly coexist in cast-iron warehouses converted into spacious, expensive loft apartments. Artists' lofts and galleries as well as hip antiques and design shops pepper the area, as do some of the city's best restaurants. Standing in the north shadow of the World Trade Center, TriBeCa suffered greatly in the wake of the disaster; however, it has recovered beautifully.

Robert DeNiro gave the neighborhood a tremendous boost when he established the TriBeCa Film Center, and Miramax headquarters gave the area further capitalist-chic cachet. Still, historic streets like White (especially the Federal-style building at no. 2) and Harrison (the complete stretch west from Greenwich St.) evoke a bygone, more human-scaled New York, as do a few holdout businesses and old-world pubs. I love this neighborhood because it seems to have brought together the old city and the new without bastardizing either. And because retail spaces are usually a few doors apart rather than right on top of one another, it also manages to be more peaceful than similarly popular neighborhoods.

The main uptown-downtown drag is **West Broadway** (2 blocks to the west of Broadway). Consider the Franklin Street subway station on the 1/9 line to be your gateway to the heart of the action. (Note that 1 and 2 trains will stop there until the 1 and 9 trains are up and running normally again.) Take your map; the streets are a maze.

Chinatown New York City's most famous ethnic enclave is bursting past its traditional boundaries and encroaching on Little Italy. The former marshlands northeast of City Hall and below Canal Street, from Broadway to the Bowery, are where Chinese immigrants arriving from San Francisco were forced to live in the 1870s. This booming neighborhood is now a conglomeration of Asian populations. It offers tasty cheap eats in cuisines from Sichuan to Hunan to Cantonese to Vietnamese to Thai. Exotic shops offer strange foods, herbs, and souvenirs; bargains on clothing and leather are plentiful. The area is also home to sweatshops, however, and doesn't have quite the quaint character you'd find in San Francisco. Still, it's a blast to walk down Canal Street, peering into the myriad electronics and luggage stores and watching crabs cut loose from their handlers at the exotic fish markets.

The Canal Street (J, M, Z, N, R, 6, Q, W) station will get you to the heart of the action. The streets are crowded during the day and empty out after around 9pm; they remain quite safe, but the neighborhood is more enjoyable during the bustle.

Little Italy Near Chinatown is Little Italy, just as ethnic if not quite so vibrant, and compelling for its own

---

Impressions

Can we actually "know" the universe? It's hard enough finding your way around Chinatown.

—Woody Allen

Visiting the Lower East Side

The **Lower East Side Business Improvement District** operates a neighborhood visitor center at 261 Broome St., between Orchard and Allen streets (✆ **888/825-8374** or 212/226-9010), that's open daily from 10am to 4pm (sometimes later). Stop in for an Orchard Street Bargain District shopping guide (which they can also send you in advance), plus other information on this historic yet freshly hip 'hood. You can also find shopping, dining, and nightlife directories online at **www.lowereastsideny.com**.

culinary treats. Traditionally the area east of Broadway between Houston and Canal streets, the community is shrinking today, due to the encroachment of thriving Chinatown. It's now limited mainly to **Mulberry Street,** where you'll find most restaurants, and just a few offshoots. With rents going up in the increasingly trendy Lower East Side, a few chic spots are moving in, further intruding upon the old-world landscape. Because the Grand Street subway station is scheduled to be closed until 2005 (except for one-stop shuttle service from the Broadway-Lafayette St. station), the best way to reach Little Italy is to walk east from the Spring Street station, on the no. 6 line, to Mulberry Street; turn south for Little Italy (you can't miss the year-round red, green, and white street decorations). September, when Mulberry Street comes alive during the Feast of San Gennaro, is a great time to visit.

The Lower East Side The Lower East Side boasts the best of both old and new New York: Witness the stretch of Houston between Forsyth and Allen streets, where Yoneh Shimmel's Knish Shop sits shoulder-to-shoulder with the city's newest art-house cinema—and both are thriving, thank you very much. Some say that the Lower East Side has come full circle: Hipster 20-somethings with Ivy League educations and well-honed senses of entitlement have been drawn back to the neighborhood their immigrant grandparents worked their fingers to the bone to escape.

Of all the successive waves of immigrants and refugees who passed through this densely populated tenement neighborhood from the mid–19th century to the 1920s, Eastern European Jews left the most lasting impression here. The Jewish communities, which first popped up between Houston and Canal streets, east of the Bowery, have been ultimately supplanted by drugs and crime, dragging the Lower East Side into the gutter—until now, that is. The neighborhood has experienced quite a renaissance over the last few years, and makes a fascinating itinerary stop for both nostalgists and nightlife hounds. Still, the blocks well south of Houston can be grungy in spots, so walk them with confidence and care after dark.

There are some remnants of what was once the largest Jewish population in America along **Orchard Street,** where you'll find great bargain hunting in its many old-world fabric and clothing stores still thriving between the club-clothes boutiques and trendy lounges. Keep in mind that the old-world shops close early on Friday afternoon and all day on Saturday (the Jewish Sabbath). The exponentially expanding trendy set can be found in the blocks between Allen and Clinton streets south of Houston and north of Delancey, with more new shops, bars, and restaurants popping up in the blocks to the east every day.

This area is not well served by the subway system (one cause for its years of decline), so your best bet is to take the F train to Second Avenue and walk east on Houston; when you see Katz's Deli, you'll know you've arrived. You can also reach the neighborhood from the Delancey Street station on the F line, and the Essex Street station on the J, M, and Z lines.

SoHo & Nolita No relation to the London neighborhood of the same name, **SoHo** got its moniker as an abbreviation of "*So*uth of *Ho*uston Street." This superfashionable neighborhood extends down to Canal Street, between Sixth Avenue to the west and Lafayette Street (1 block east of Broadway) to the east. It's easily accessible by subway: Take the N or R to the Prince Street Station; the C, E or 6 to Spring Street; or the F or V train to the Broadway-Lafayette stop (note that the B, D, and Q trains will not be serving Broadway-Lafayette during the life of this book due to construction on the Manhattan Bridge).

An industrial zone during the 19th century, SoHo retains the impressive cast-iron architecture of the era, and in many places, cobblestone peeks out from beneath the street's asphalt. In the early 1960s, cutting-edge artists began occupying the drab and deteriorating buildings, soon turning it into the trendiest neighborhood in the city. SoHo is now a prime example of urban gentrification and a major New York attraction thanks to its impeccably restored buildings, fashionable restaurants, and stylish boutiques. On weekends, the cobbled streets and narrow sidewalks are packed with shoppers, with the prime action between Broadway and Sullivan Street north of Grand Street.

Some critics claim that SoHo is becoming a victim of its own popularity—witness the recent departure of art galleries and independent boutiques that fled to TriBeCa and Chelsea as well as the influx of suburban mall-style stores like J. Crew, Victoria's Secret, and Smith & Hawken. However, SoHo is still one of the best shopping neighborhoods in the city, and few are more fun to browse. High-end street peddlers set up along the boutique-lined sidewalks, hawking silver jewelry, coffee-table books, and their own art. At night, the neighborhood is transformed into a terrific, albeit pricey, dining and barhopping neighborhood. You can even stay here now, thanks to the introduction of two supertrendy hotels, the Mercer and the Soho Grand.

In recent years, SoHo has been crawling its way east, taking over Mott and Mulberry streets—and white-hot Elizabeth Street in particular—north of Kenmare Street, an area now known as **Nolita** for its *No*rth of *Li*ttle I*ta*ly location. Nolita is becoming increasingly well known for its hot shopping prospects, which include a number

Impressions

Nobody's going to come from the boondocks anymore and live in SoHo and be an artist. You can't afford to park there, let alone live there.

—Pete Hamill

of pricey antiques and home design stores. Taking the 6 to Spring Street will get you closest by subway, but it's just a short walk east from SoHo proper.

The East Village & NoHo The **East Village,** which extends between 14th Street and Houston Street, from Broadway east to First Avenue and beyond to Alphabet City—avenues A, B, C, and D—is where the city's real bohemia has gone. Once, flower children tripped along St. Marks Place and listened to music at the Fillmore East; now the East Village is a fascinating mix of affordable ethnic and trendy restaurants, upstart clothing designers and kitschy boutiques, punk-rock clubs (yep, still), and folk cafes, all of which give the neighborhood a youthful vibe. A half dozen Off-Broadway theaters also call this place home.

The gentrification that has swept the city has made a huge impact on the East Village, but there's still a seedy element that some of you won't find appealing—and some of you will. Frankly, I love the East Village more than the West Village for its genuine melting-pot vibe. Now yuppies and other ladder-climbing types make their homes alongside old-world Russian immigrants who have lived in the neighborhood forever, and the cross-dressers and squatters who settled here in between. The neighborhood still embraces great ethnic diversity, with strong elements of its Ukrainian and Irish heritage, while more recent immigrants have taken over Sixth Street between First and Second avenues, turning it into a Little India.

The East Village isn't very accessible by subway; unless you're traveling along 14th Street (the L line will drop you off at Third and First aves.), your best bet is to take the 4, 5, 6, N, Q, R, or W to 14th Street/Union Square; the N, R to 8th Street; or the 6 to Astor Place and walk east.

Until 1998 or so, **Alphabet City** resisted gentrification and remained a haven of drug dealers and other unsavory types—no more. Bolstered by a major real estate boom, this way-east area of the East Village has blossomed. French bistros and smart shops have popped up on every corner. Nevertheless, the neighborhood can get deserted late at night, since it's generally the province of locals. It's far off the subway lines, so know where you're going if you venture out here.

The southwestern section of the East Village, around Broadway and Lafayette between Bleecker and 4th streets, is called **NoHo** (for *No*rth of *Ho*uston), and has a completely different character. As you might have guessed from its name, this area has developed much more like its neighbor to the south, SoHo. Here you'll find a crop of trendy lounges, stylish restaurants, cutting-edge designers, and upscale antiques shops. NoHo is fun to browse; the Bleecker Street stop on the no. 6 line will land you in the heart of it, and the Broadway-Lafayette stop on the F/V line will drop you at its southern edge.

Greenwich Village Tree-lined streets crisscross and wind, following ancient streams and cow paths. Each block reveals yet another row of Greek Revival town houses, a well-preserved Federal-style house, or a peaceful courtyard or square. This is "the Village," from Broadway west to the Hudson River, bordered by Houston Street to the south and 14th Street to the north. It defies Manhattan's orderly grid system with streets that predate it, virtually every one chockablock with activity, and unless you live here, it may be impossible to master the lay of the land—so be sure to take a map along as you explore.

The Seventh Avenue line (1, 2, 3, 9) is the area's main subway artery, while the West 4th Street stop (where the A, C, E lines meet the F and V lines) serves as its central hub. (*Note:* Due to rail work, the B, D, and Q subway trains will not be serving W. 4th St. during the life of this book.)

Nineteenth-century artists like Mark Twain, Edgar Allan Poe, Henry James, and Winslow Homer first gave the Village its reputation for embracing the unconventional. Groundbreaking artists like Edward Hopper and Jackson Pollack were drawn in, as were writers like Eugene O'Neill, e.e. cummings, and Dylan Thomas. Radical thinkers from John Reed to Upton Sinclair basked in the neighborhood's liberal ethos, and beatniks Allen Ginsberg, Jack Kerouac, and William Burroughs dug the free-swinging atmosphere. Now the Village is the roost of choice for the young celebrity set, with the likes of Gwyneth Paltrow, the Beastie Boys, and Matthew Broderick and Sarah Jessica Parker drawn by its historic, low-rise, laid-back charms. Gentrification and escalating real-estate values conspire to push out the artistic element, but culture and counterculture still rub shoulders in cafes, internationally renowned jazz clubs, neighborhood bars, Off-Broadway theaters, and an endless variety of tiny shops and restaurants.

The Village is probably the most chameleon-like of Manhattan's neighborhoods. Some of the highest-priced real estate in the city runs along lower Fifth Avenue, which dead-ends at **Washington Square Park.** Serpentine **Bleecker Street** stretches through most of the neighborhood and is emblematic of the area's historical bent. The tolerant anything-goes attitude in the Village has fostered a large gay community, which is still largely in evidence around **Christopher Street** and Sheridan Square. The streets west of Seventh Avenue, an area known as the **West Village,** boast a more relaxed vibe and some of the city's most charming and historic brownstones. Three colleges—New York University, Parsons School of Design, and the New School for Social Research—keep the area thinking young.

Streets are often crowded with weekend warriors and teenagers, especially on Bleecker, West 4th, 8th, and surrounding streets, and have known to become increasingly sketchy west of Seventh Avenue in the very late hours, especially on weekends. Keep an eye on your wallet when navigating the weekend throngs. And Washington Square Park was cleaned up a couple of years back, but it's still best to stay out of the area after dark.

Midtown

Chelsea & the Meat-Packing District Chelsea has come on strong in recent years as a hip address, especially for the gay community. A low-rise composite of town houses, tenements, lofts, and factories, the neighborhood comprises roughly the area west of Sixth Avenue from 14th to 30th streets. (Sixth Ave. itself below 23rd St. is actually considered part of the Flatiron District; see below.) Its main arteries are Seventh and Eighth avenues, and it's primarily served by the C, E and 1, 9 subway lines.

The **Chelsea Piers** sports complex to the far west and a host of shops (both unique boutiques and big names like Williams-Sonoma), well-priced bistros, and thriving bars along the main drags have

Where to Check Your E-mail in the City that Never Sleeps

You don't have to be out of touch just because you don't carry a laptop while you travel. There are a number of ways to get your e-mail on the web, using any computer.

Your **Internet Service Provider (ISP)** may have a Web-based interface that lets you access your e-mail on computers other than your own. Just find out how it works before you leave home.

Or check out **www.mail2web.com**. This amazing free service allows you to type in your regular e-mail address and password and retrieve your e-mail from any web browser, anywhere, so long as your home ISP hasn't blocked it with a firewall.

Or just open a free-mail account with a web-based e-mail provider, such as Microsoft's **Hotmail (hotmail.com)** or **Yahoo! Mail (mail.yahoo.com)**. Your home ISP may be able to forward your home e-mail to the web-based account automatically.

All you'll need to check your e-mail while you're away from home is a Web connection, easily available via your hotel's business center or cash- and credit-card Internet-access machine (which many hotels now feature in the lobby), as well as Internet cafes and copy shops throughout the Big Apple. After logging on, just point the browser to the service you're using. Enter your user name and password, and you'll have access to your mail, for both receiving and sending messages to friends and family back home, usually for just a few dollars an hour.

The **Times Square Visitors Center,** 1560 Broadway, between 46th and 47th streets (✆ **212/768-1560;** open daily 8am–8pm), has computer terminals that you can use to send e-mails courtesy of Yahoo!; you can even send an electronic postcard with a photo of yourself home to Mom.

contributed to the area's rebirth. Even the Hotel Chelsea—the neighborhood's most famous architectural and literary landmark, where Thomas Wolfe and Arthur Miller wrote, Bob Dylan composed "Sad-Eyed Lady of the Low Land," Viva and Edie Sedgwick of Andy Warhol fame lived, and Sid Vicious killed girlfriend Nancy Spungeon—has undergone a renovation. You'll find a number of very popular flea markets set up in parking lots along Sixth Avenue, between 24th and 27th streets, on the weekends.

One of the most influential trends in Chelsea has been the establishment of far **West Chelsea** (from Ninth Ave. west) and the adjacent **Meat-Packing District** (south of West Chelsea, roughly from 17th St. to Little W. 12th St.) as the style-setting neighborhoods for the 21st century. What SoHo was in the '60s, this industrial west world (dubbed "the Lower West Side" by *New York* magazine) is today. New restaurants, cutting-edge shopping, and superhot nightspots pop up daily in the still-beefy Meat-Packing District, while the area from West 22nd to West 29th streets between Tenth and Eleventh avenues is home to the cutting edge of today's New York art scene, with West 26th serving as

Open 24/7 in the heart of Times Square, **easyInternetCafé** ★, 235 W. 42nd St., between Seventh and Eighth avenues (✆ **212/398-0775**; www.easyeverything.com), is the first stateside branch of a worldwide web of Internet cafes. Boasting 15-inch flat-screen monitors and a superfast T-3 connection, this mammoth place makes accessing the Internet cheap through the economy of scale: Access is available for $1, and the length of access time that buck buys you fluctuates depending on the occupancy at the time you log on. This will generally work out to the cheapest Web time you can buy in the city.

CyberCafe (www.cyber-cafe.com)—in Times Square at 250 W. 49th St., between Broadway and Eighth Avenue (✆ **212/333-4109**), and in SoHo at 273 Lafayette St., at Prince Street (✆ **212/334-5140**)—is more expensive at $6.40 per half hour, with a half-hour minimum (you're billed $3.20 for every subsequent 15 min.). But their T1 connectivity gives you much speedier access, and they offer a full range of other cyber, copy, fax, and printing services.

Kinko's (www.kinkos.com) charges 30¢ per minute ($15 per hr.) and is open at 100 Wall St., at Water Street (✆ 212/269-0024); near City Hall at 105 Duane St., between Broadway and Church Street (✆ 212/406-1220); 250 E. Houston St., between avenues A and B (✆ 212/253-9020); 21 Astor Place, between Broadway and Lafayette Street in the Village (✆ 212/228-9511); 245 Seventh Ave., at 24th Street (✆ 212/929-2679); 60 W. 40th St., between Fifth and Sixth avenues (✆ 212/921-1060); 221 W. 72nd St., at Broadway (✆ 212/362-5288); and about a billion other locations around town. If you want to do some advance planning, check the website for the location nearest your hotel before you leave home.

the unofficial "gallery row." The power of art can also be found at the Joyce Theater, New York's principal modern dance venue. This area is still seriously industrial and in the early stages of transition, however, and not for everyone. With galleries and bars tucked away in converted warehouses and former meat lockers, browsing can be frustrating, and the sometimes-desolate streets a tad intimidating. Your best bet is to have a specific destination (and an exact address) in mind, be it a restaurant, gallery, boutique, or nightclub, before you come.

The Flatiron District, Union Square & Gramercy Park These adjoining and at places overlapping neighborhoods are some of the city's most appealing. Their streets have been rediscovered by New Yorkers and visitors alike, largely thanks to the boom-to-bust dot-com revolution of the late 1990s; the Flatiron District served as its geographical heart and earned the nickname "Silicon Alley" in the process. These neighborhoods boast great shopping and dining opportunities and a central-to-everything location that's hard to beat. A number of impressive new hotels have been added to the mix over the last few years. The commercial spaces are often large, loftlike expanses

Tips Touring Tip

If you'd like to tour a specific neighborhood with an expert guide, call **Big Apple Greeter** (✆ **212/669-8159**; www.bigapplegreeter.org) at least 1 week ahead of your arrival. This nonprofit organization has specially trained volunteers who take visitors around town for a free 2- to 4-hour tour of a particular neighborhood. And they say New York isn't friendly!

with witty designs and graceful columns.

The **Flatiron District** lies south of 23rd Street to 14th Street, between Broadway and Sixth Avenue, and centers around the historic Flatiron Building on 23rd (so named for its triangular shape) and Park Avenue South, which has become a sophisticated new Restaurant Row. Below 23rd Street along Sixth Avenue (once known as the Ladies' Mile shopping district), mass-market discounters like Filene's Basement, Bed Bath & Beyond, and others have moved in. The shopping gets classier on Fifth Avenue, where you'll find a mix of national names and hip boutiques. Lined with Oriental carpet dealers and high-end fixture stores, Broadway is becoming the city's home-furnishings alley; its crowning jewel is the justifiably famous ABC Carpet & Home, with eight floors of gorgeous textiles, housewares, and gifts on one side of Broadway, and an equally dazzling display of floor coverings on the other.

Union Square is the hub of the entire area; the N, R, 4, 5, 6, and L trains stop here, as do Q and W trains (until 2004), making it easy to reach from most other city neighborhoods. Long in the shadows of the more bustling (Times and Herald) and high-toned (Washington) city squares, Union Square has experienced a major renaissance in the last decade. Local businesses joined forces with the city to rid the park of drug dealers a few years back, and now it's a delightful place to spend an afternoon. Union Square is best known as the setting for New York's premier green market every Monday, Wednesday, Friday, and Saturday. In-line skaters take over the market space in the after-work hours. A number of hip restaurants rim the square, as do superstores like Toys"R"Us, the city's best Barnes & Noble superstore, and a Virgin Megastore.

From about 16th to 23rd streets, east from Park Avenue South to about Second Avenue, is the leafy, largely residential district known as **Gramercy Park.** The pity of the Gramercy Park district is that so few can enjoy the park: Built by Samuel Ruggles in the 1830s to attract buyers to his property in the area, it is the only private park in the city and is locked to all but those who live on its perimeter (the rule is that your windows have to look over the park for you to have a key). Located at the southern endpoint of Lexington Avenue (at 21st St.), it is one of the most peaceful spots in the city. If you know someone who has a magic key, go there. Or better yet, book a room at the Gramercy Park Hotel, whose guests have park privileges.

At the northern edge of the area, fronting the Flatiron Building on 23rd Street and Fifth Avenue, is another of Manhattan's lovely little parks, **Madison Square.** Across from its northeastern corner once stood Stanford White's original Madison Square Garden (in whose roof garden White was murdered in 1906 by possibly deranged, but definitely jealous, millionaire Harry K. Thaw). It's now majestically presided over by the massive New York Life Insurance Building, the masterful New York State Supreme Court, and the Metropolitan Life Insurance Company, whose tower in 1909 was the tallest building in the world at 700 feet (210m).

Times Square & Midtown West **Midtown West,** the vast area from 34th to 59th streets west of Fifth Avenue to the Hudson River, encompasses several famous names: Madison Square Garden, the Garment District, Rockefeller Center, the Theater District, and Times Square. This is New York's tourism central, where you'll find the bright lights and bustle that draw people from all over the world. As such, this is the city's biggest hotel neighborhood, with choices running the gamut from cheap to chic. Rates can fluctuate dramatically, though, because this is where everybody wants to stay; in periods of high demand, even so-called "budget" hotels often price around the $200 mark.

The 1, 2, 3, 9 subway line serves the massive neon station at the heart of Times Square, at 42nd Street between Broadway and Seventh Avenue, while the F, V line runs up Sixth Avenue to Rockefeller Center (B and D lines also serve Rockefeller Center but travel no farther south than 34th St. until Manhattan Bridge work is complete in 2004). The N, R line cuts diagonally across the neighborhood, following the path of Broadway before heading up Seventh Avenue at 42nd Street (the Q and W trains also use this line until 2004). The A, C, E line serves the west side, running along Eighth Avenue.

If you know New York but haven't been here in a few years, you'll be quite surprised by the "new" **Times Square.** Longtime New Yorkers like to kvetch nostalgic about the glory days of the old peep-show-and-porn-shop Times Square that this cleaned-up, Disney-fied version supplanted, but the truth is that it's a hugely successful regentrification. Grand old theaters have come back to life as Broadway and children's playhouses, and scores of new family-friendly restaurants and shops have opened (including the terrific Virgin Megastore on Broadway as well as Disney and Warner Bros. studio stores). Plenty of businesses have moved in—MTV studios overlook Times Square at 1515 Broadway, and *Good Morning America* has its own street-facing studio at Broadway and 44th Street. The neon lights have never been brighter, and Middle America has never been more welcome. Expect dense crowds, though; it's often tough just to make your way along the sidewalks.

Most of the great Broadway theaters light up the streets just off Times Square, in the West 40s just east and west of Broadway. At the heart of the **Theater District,**

Impressions

I'm opposed to the redevelopment. I think there should be one neighborhood in New York where tourists are afraid to walk.

—Fran Lebowitz on the "new" Times Square

where Broadway meets Seventh Avenue, is the TKTS booth, where crowds line up daily to buy discount tickets for tonight's shows.

To the west of the Theater District, in the 40s and 50s between Eighth and Tenth avenues, is **Hell's Kitchen,** which has become much nicer than it sounds in recent years. The neighborhood resisted gentrification until the mid-'90s, but has grown into a charming, less touristy adjunct to the neighboring Theater District. Ninth Avenue, in particular, has blossomed into one of the city's finest dining avenues; just stroll along and you'll have a world of great dining to choose from, ranging from American diner to sexy Mediterranean to traditional Thai. Stylish boutiques and bars (including not a few gay bars) have also popped up in this area in the last three or so years. Realtors have tried to rename the area Clinton, but locals have held fast to the Hell's Kitchen moniker with delight.

Unlike Times Square, gorgeous **Rockefeller Center** has needed no renovation. Situated between 46th and 50th streets from Sixth Avenue east to Fifth, this Art Deco complex contains some of the city's great architectural gems, which house hundreds of offices, a number of NBC studios (including *Saturday Night Live, Late Night with Conan O'Brien,* and the famous glass-walled *Today* show studio at 48th St.), and some pleasing upscale boutiques (attention, shoppers: Saks Fifth Avenue is just on the other side of Fifth). Holiday time is a great time to be here, as ice-skaters take over the central plaza and the huge Christmas tree twinkles against the night sky.

Along Seventh Avenue south of 42nd Street is the **Garment District,** of little interest to tourists except for its sample sales, where some great new fashions are sold off cheap to serious bargain hunters willing to scour the racks. Other than that, it's a pretty grim commercial area. Between Seventh and Eighth avenues and 31st and 33rd streets, **Penn Station** sits beneath unsightly behemoth **Madison Square Garden,** where the Rangers and the Knicks play. Taking up all of 34th Street between Sixth and Seventh avenues is **Macy's,** the world's largest department store; exit Macy's at the southeast corner and you'll find more famous-label shopping around **Herald Square.** The blocks around 32nd Street just west of Fifth Avenue have developed into a thriving Koreatown, with midprice hotels and bright, bustling Asian restaurants offering some of the best-value stays and eats in Midtown.

Midtown West is also home to some of the city's most revered museums and cultural institutions, including **Carnegie Hall,** the **Museum of Modern Art, Radio City Music Hall,** and the ***Intrepid* Sea-Air-Space Museum,** to name just a few.

Midtown East & Murray Hill **Midtown East,** the area including Fifth Avenue and everything east from 34th to 59th streets, is the more upscale side of the Midtown map. This side of town is short of subway trains, served primarily by the Lexington Avenue 4, 5, 6 line.

Midtown East is where you'll find the city's finest collection of grand hotels, mostly along Lexington Avenue and near the park at the top of Fifth. The stretch of **Fifth Avenue** from Saks at 49th Street extending to FAO Schwarz at 59th is home to the city's most high-profile haute shopping, including Tiffany & Co. and Bergdorf Goodman, but more midprice names like

Manhattan Address Locator

To locate avenue addresses, cancel the last figure, divide by 2, and add (or subtract) the key number below. The answer is the nearest numbered cross street, approximately.

Avenue A: add 3
Avenue B: add 3
Avenue C: add 3
First Avenue: add 3
Second Avenue: add 3
Third Avenue: add 10
Sixth Avenue: subtract 12
Eighth Avenue: add 9
Ninth Avenue: add 13
Tenth Avenue: add 14
11th Avenue: add 15
Amsterdam Avenue: add 59
Columbus Avenue: add 59 or 60
Lexington Avenue: add 22
Madison Avenue: add 27
Park Avenue: add 34
Park Avenue South: add 8
West End Avenue: add 59
York Avenue: add 4

Note special instructions for finding address locations on the following:

Fifth Avenue

63 to 108: add 11
109 to 200: add 13
201 to 400: add 16
401 to 600: add 18
601 to 775: add 20
776 to 1286: cancel last figure of house number and subtract 18 (do not divide house number by 2)
For 1310 to 1494: cancel last figure of house number. For 1310, subtract 20 and for every additional 20 street numbers, increase deduction by 1.

Seventh Avenue

1 to 1800: add 12
above 1800: add 20

Broadway

Anything from 1 to 754 is south of 8th Street, and hence a named street.

756 to 846: subtract 29
847 to 953: subtract 25
above 953: subtract 31

Central Park West

Cancel last figure and add 60.

Riverside Drive

Cancel last figure and
Up to 567: add 72
568 and up: add 78

Banana Republic and Liz Claiborne have moved their superstores in over the last 5 years or so. The stretch of 57th Street between Fifth and Lexington avenues is also known for high-fashion boutiques (Chanel, Hermès) and high-ticket galleries, but change is underway since names like Levi's and Niketown squeezed in. You'll find plenty of spillover along **Madison Avenue,** a great strip for shoe shopping in particular.

Magnificent architectural highlights include the recently repolished **Chrysler Building,** with its stylized gargoyles glaring down on passersby; the beaux-arts tour de force that is **Grand Central Terminal; St. Patrick's Cathedral;**

and the glorious **Empire State Building.**

Far east, swank Sutton and Beekman places are enclaves of beautiful town houses, luxury living, and tiny pocket parks that look out over the East River. Along this river is the **United Nations,** which isn't officially in New York City, or even the United States, but on a parcel of international land belonging to member nations.

Claiming the territory east from Madison Avenue, **Murray Hill** begins somewhere north of 23rd Street (the line between it and Gramercy Park is fuzzy), and is most clearly recognizable north of 30th Street to 42nd Street. This brownstone-lined quarter is largely a quiet residential neighborhood, most notable for its handful of good budget and midprice hotels. The stretch of Lexington Avenue in the high 20s is known as Curry Hill and has usurped the East Village's Little India as the destination for inexpensive, high-quality Indian food.

Uptown

Upper West Side North of 59th Street and encompassing everything west of Central Park, the Upper West Side contains **Lincoln Center,** arguably the world's premier performing arts venue, and the **American Museum of Natural History,** whose renovated Dinosaur Halls and magnificent new Rose Center for Earth and Space garner justifiably rave reviews. A growing number of midprice hotels whose larger-than-Midtown rooms and nice residential location make them some of the best values—and some of my favorite places to stay—in the entire city.

Unlike the more stratified Upper East Side, the Upper West Side is home to an egalitarian mix of middle-class yuppiedom, laid-back wealth (lots of celebs and monied media types call the grand apartments along Central Park West home), and ethnic families who were here before the gentrification.

The neighborhood runs all the way up to Harlem, around 125th Street, and encompasses **Morningside Heights,** where you'll find **Columbia University** and the perennial construction project known as the **Cathedral of St. John the Divine.** But prime Upper West Side—the part you're most likely to explore—is the area running from Columbus Circle at 59th Street into the 80s, between the park and Broadway. North of 59th Street is where Eighth Avenue becomes Central Park West, the eastern border of the neighborhood (and the western border of Central Park); Ninth Avenue becomes Columbus Avenue, lined with attractive boutiques and cafes; and Tenth Avenue becomes Amsterdam Avenue, less charming than Columbus to the east and less trafficked than bustling Broadway (whose highlights are the gourmet megamarts Zabar's and Fairway) to the west; still, Amsterdam has blossomed into quite a happening restaurant and bar strip over the last couple of years. You'll find Lincoln Center in the mid-60s, where Broadway crosscuts Amsterdam.

Two major subway lines service the area: the 1, 2, 3, 9 line runs up Broadway, while the B and C trains run up glamorous Central Park West, stopping right at the historic Dakota apartment building (where John Lennon was shot and Yoko still lives) at 72nd Street, and at the Museum of Natural History at 81st Street.

Upper East Side North of 59th Street and east of Central Park is some of the city's most expensive residential real estate. This is New

York at its most gentrified: Walk along Fifth and Park avenues, especially between 60th and 80th streets, and you're sure to encounter some of the wizened WASPs and Chanel-suited socialites that make up the most rarefied of the city's population. Madison Avenue from 60th Street well into the 80s is the monied crowd's main shopping strip, recently vaunting ahead of Hong Kong's Causeway Bay to become the most expensive retail real estate *in the world*—so bring your platinum card. You can also use it to stay at one of the neighborhood's remarkably luxurious hotels, such as the Carlyle, or to dine at four-star wonders like Le Cirque 2000 and Daniel.

The main attraction of this neighborhood is **Museum Mile,** the stretch of Fifth Avenue fronting Central Park that's home to no fewer than 10 terrific cultural institutions, including Frank Lloyd Wright's **Guggenheim,** and anchored by the mind-boggling **Metropolitan Museum of Art.** But the elegant rows of landmark town houses are worth a look alone: East 70th Street, from Madison east to Lexington, is one of the world's most charming residential streets. If you want to see where real people live, move east to Third Avenue and beyond; that's where affordable restaurants and active street life start popping up.

A second subway line is in the works, but it's still no more than an architect's blueprint. For now, the Upper East Side is served solely by the crowded Lexington Avenue line (4, 5, 6 trains), so wear your walking shoes (or bring taxi fare) if you're heading up here to explore.

Harlem Now that Bill Clinton has moved his post-presidential office—and more than a few Secret Service agents—into this uptown neighborhood, the whole world has heard the good news about Harlem, which has benefited from a dramatic image makeover in the last few years.

Harlem is really two areas. Harlem proper stretches from river to river, beginning at 125th Street on the West Side and 96th Street on the East Side. East of Fifth Avenue, **Spanish Harlem** (El Barrio) runs between East 100th and East 125th streets. Harlem proper, in particular, is benefiting greatly from the revitalization that has swept so much of the city, with national-brand retailers moving in, restaurants and hip nightspots opening everywhere, and visitors arriving to tour historic sites related to the golden age of African-American culture, when great bands like the Count Basie and Duke Ellington orchestras played the Cotton Club and Sugar Cane Club, and literary giants like Langston Hughes and James Baldwin soaked up the scene. Some houses date from a time when the area was something of a country retreat and represent some of the best brownstone mansions in the city. On Sugar Hill (from 143rd to 155th sts., between St. Nicholas and Edgecombe aves.) and Striver's Row (West 139th St. between

---

Finds **Discovering Harlem**

You'll find sightseeing, restaurants, arts, and nightlife information about Harlem in the pages of this book. But if you want to learn more, your best source is the **Harlem Association for Travel & Tourism** website at **www.hatt.org**.

Adam Clayton Powell Jr. and Frederick Douglass blvds.) are a significant number of fine town houses. For cultural visits, there's the Morris-Jumel Mansion, the Schomburg Center, the Studio Museum, and the Apollo Theatre.

By all means, come see Harlem—it's one of the city's most vital, historic neighborhoods, and no other feels quite so energized right now. Your best bet for seeing all the sights is to take a guided tour (see "Organized Sightseeing Tours," in chapter 8); if you head up on your own to sightsee, come in daylight. Don't wander thoughtlessly through Harlem, especially at night. If you head up after dark to a restaurant or nightspot, just be clear and confident about where you're going and stay alert.

Washington Heights & Inwood Located at the northern tip of Manhattan, Washington Heights (the area from 155th St. to Dyckman St., with adjacent Inwood running to the tip) is home to a large segment of Manhattan's Latino community, plus an increasing number of yuppies who don't mind trading a half-hour subway commute to Midtown for much lower rents. **Fort Tryon Park** and **the Cloisters** are the two big reasons for visitors to come up this way. The Cloisters houses the Metropolitan Museum of Art's stunning medieval collection, in a building perched atop a hill, with excellent views across the Hudson to the Palisades. Committed off-the-beaten-path sightseers might also want to visit the **Dyckman Farmhouse,** a historic jewel built in 1783 and the only remaining Dutch Colonial structure in Manhattan.

2 Getting Around

Frankly, Manhattan's transportation systems are a marvel. It's simply miraculous that so many people can gather on this little island and move around it. For the most part, you can get where you're going pretty quickly and easily using some combination of subways, buses, and cabs; this section will tell you how to do just that.

But between traffic gridlock and subway delays, sometimes you just can't get there from here—unless you walk. Walking can be the fastest way to navigate the island. During rush hours, you'll easily beat car traffic while on foot, as taxis and buses stop and groan at gridlocked corners (don't even *try* going crosstown in a cab or bus in Midtown at midday). You'll also just see a whole lot more by walking than you will if you ride beneath the street in the subway or fly by in a cab. So pack your most comfortable shoes and hit the pavement—it's the best, cheapest, and most appealing way to experience the city.

BY SUBWAY

Run by the **Metropolitan Transit Authority (MTA),** the much-maligned subway system is actually the fastest way to travel around New York, especially during rush hours. Some 3.5 million people a day seem to agree with me, as it's their primary mode of transportation. The subway is quick, inexpensive, relatively safe, and pretty efficient, as well as being a genuine New York experience.

The subway runs 24 hours a day, 7 days a week. The rush-hour crushes are roughly from 8 to 9:30am and from 5 to 6:30pm on weekdays; the rest of the time the trains are relatively uncrowded.

On the Sidewalks

What's the primary means New Yorkers use for getting around town? The subway? Buses? Taxis? Nope. Walking. They stride across wide, crowded pavements without any regard for traffic lights, weaving through crowds at high speeds, dodging taxis and buses whose drivers are forced to interrupt the normal flow of traffic to avoid flattening them. **Never take your walking cues from the locals.** Wait for walk signals and always use crosswalks—don't cross in the middle of the block. Do otherwise and you could quickly end up as a flattened statistic.

Always pay attention to the traffic flow. Walk as if you're driving, staying to the right. Pay attention to what's happening in the street, even if you have the right of way. At intersections, keep an eye out for drivers who don't yield, turn without looking, or think a yellow traffic light means "Hurry up!" as you cross. Unfortunately, most bicyclists seem to think that the traffic laws don't apply to them; they'll often blithely fly through red lights and dash the wrong way on one-way streets, so be on your guard.

For more important safety tips, see "Playing It Safe," later in this chapter.

PAYING YOUR WAY

The subway fare is $1.50 (half price for seniors and those with disabilities), and children under 44 inches tall ride free (up to three per adult). *Note:* As of this writing, a fare increase was being discussed, so it's entirely possible that the fare will be higher by the time you visit.

While **tokens** still exist (although they'll soon be phased out altogether), most people pay fares with the **MetroCard,** a magnetically encoded card that debits the fare when swiped through the turnstile (or the fare box on any city bus). Once you're in the system, you can transfer freely to any subway line that you can reach without exiting your station. MetroCards—not tokens—also allow you **free transfers** between the bus and subway within a 2-hour period.

MetroCards can be purchased from each station's staffed token booth, where you can only pay with cash; at the ATM-style vending machines now located in just about every subway station in the city, which accept cash, credit cards, and debit cards; from a MetroCard merchant, such as most Rite Aid drugstores or Hudson News at Penn Station and Grand Central Terminal; or at the MTA information desk at the Times Square Visitor Center, 1560 Broadway, between 46th and 47th streets.

MetroCards come in a few different configurations:

Pay-Per-Ride MetroCards, which can be used for up to four people by swiping up to four times (bring the whole family). You can put any amount from $3 (two rides) to $80 on your card. Every time you put $15 on your Pay-Per-Ride MetroCard, it's automatically credited 10%—that's one free ride for every $15. You can buy Pay-Per-Ride MetroCards in any denomination at any subway station; an increasing number of stations now have automated MetroCard vending machines, which allow you to buy MetroCards using your major credit card. MetroCards are also available from shops and newsstands around town in $15 and $30 values. You can refill your card at any time until the expiration date on the card, usually about a year from the date of purchase, at any subway station.

Unlimited-Ride MetroCards, which can't be used for more than one person at a time or more frequently than 18-minute intervals, are available in four values: the **daily Fun Pass,** which allows you a day's worth of unlimited subway and bus rides for $4; the **7-Day MetroCard,** for $17; and the **30-Day MetroCard,** for $63. Seven- and 30-day Unlimited-Ride MetroCards can be purchased at any subway station or a MetroCard merchant. Fun Passes, however, cannot be purchased at token booths—you can only buy them at a MetroCard vending machine; from a MetroCard merchant; at the MTA information desk at the Times Square Visitor Center; or from www.metrocard.citysearch.com. Unlimited-Ride MetroCards go into effect not at the time you buy them but the first time you use them—so if you buy a card on Monday and don't begin to use it until Wednesday, Wednesday is when the clock starts ticking on your MetroCard. A Fun Pass is good from the first time you use it until 3am the next day, while 7- and 30-day MetroCards run out at midnight on the last day. These MetroCards cannot be refilled; throw them out once they've been used up and buy a new one.

Tips for using your MetroCard: The MetroCard swiping mechanisms at turnstiles are the source of much grousing among subway riders. If you swipe too fast or too slow, the turnstile will ask you to swipe again. If this happens, ***do not move to a different turnstile,*** or you may end up paying twice. If you've tried repeatedly and really can't make your MetroCard work, tell the token booth clerk; chances are good, though, that you'll get the movement down after a couple of uses.

If you're not sure how much money you have left on your MetroCard, or what day it expires, use the station's MetroCard Reader, usually located near the station entrance or the token booth (on buses, the fare box will also provide you with this information).

To locate the nearest MetroCard merchant, or for any other MetroCard questions, call © **800/METROCARD** or 212/METROCARD (212/638-7622) Monday through Friday between 7am and 11pm, Saturday and Sunday from 9am to 5pm. Or go online to **www.mta.nyc.ny.us/metrocard**, which can give you a full rundown of MetroCard merchants in the tristate area.

USING THE SYSTEM

As you can see from the full-color subway map on the inside cover of this book, the subway system basically mimics the lay of the land aboveground, with most lines in Manhattan running north and south, like the avenues, and a few lines east and west, like the streets.

To go up and down the east side of Manhattan (and to the Bronx and Brooklyn), take the 4, 5, or 6 train.

To travel up and down the west side (and also to the Bronx and Brooklyn), take the 1, 2, 3, or 9 line; the A, C, E, or F line; or the B or D line.

The N, R, Q, and W lines first cut diagonally across town from east to west and then snake under Seventh Avenue before shooting out to Queens.

The crosstown S line, the Shuttle, runs back and forth, back and forth, between Times Square and Grand Central Terminal. Farther downtown, across 14th Street, the L line works its own crosstown magic.

Lines have assigned colors on subway maps and trains—red for the 1, 2, 3, 9 line; green for the 4, 5, 6 trains; and so on—but nobody ever refers to them by color. Always refer to them by number or letter when asking questions. Within Manhattan, the distinction between different numbered trains that share the

Subway Service Interruption Notes

Due to two factors—ongoing work by the Metropolitan Transit Authority (MTA) on the Manhattan Bridge into 2004, and the World Trade Center disaster—normal subway service will experience numerous interruptions during the life of this book.

Changes resulting from **Manhattan Bridge work** are clear. So far, the necessary rerouting of the B, D, and Q lines serving Sixth Avenue, Chinatown, Brooklyn, and Queens seems to be working out well. Here's a summary of the changes as it will affect visitors to Manhattan:

- Chinatown's Grand Street subway station is served only by a one-stop shuttle train that runs between SoHo's Broadway–Lafayette Street station and Grand Street. To reach Chinatown, either take the F train to Broadway–Lafayette Street (which is no longer served by the B, D, or Q trains) and change to the new gray S train to Grand Street; or take the N or R train to the Canal Street station instead.
- The 34th Street/Herald Square station is now the southern terminus of the orange-line B and D trains. For Sixth Avenue service below 34th Street, use the F train or the new V train, which makes all F-train (local) stops in Manhattan along the Sixth Avenue line from Second Avenue at the south end to 47th–50th streets/Rockefeller Center before veering east to Queens.
- Q trains now run express along the N and R track (which runs along Broadway) instead of along their normal Sixth Avenue path in Manhattan, as does the new temporary (until 2004) W train. Both the Q and W trains stop at express stops only from 34th Street south.

Kudos to the MTA, because train interruptions resulting from the **World Trade Center disaster** had largely been rectified by this writing. Service interruptions are almost exclusively limited to the 1 and 9 lines, which run local along the west side of Manhattan to the southern tip of the island. At press time, 1 and 2 trains were running local to Chambers Street, where they veered to Brooklyn; 3 trains run express from 14th Street north; and 9 service was suspended altogether.

However, all 1, 2, 3, 9 service was scheduled to return to normal—with 2/3 trains running express and 1/9 trains running local to South Ferry—by sometime in autumn 2002. All stations on the 1/9 line should reopen with the exception of Cortlandt Street (which was the World Trade Center stop on this line).

The subway map featured on the inside back cover of this book was as accurate as possible at press time. However, since reopening of the 1/9 line could be delayed for any reason and service is always subject to change, your best bet is to contact the **Metropolitan Transit Authority (MTA)** for the latest details; call ✆ **718/330-1234,** or visit **www.mta.nyc.ny.us,** where you'll find system updates that are thorough, timely, and clear. Once you're in town, you can also stop at the MTA desk at the **Times Square Visitors Center,** 1560 Broadway, between 46th and 47th streets (where Broadway meets Seventh Ave.) to pick up the latest subway map. (You can also ask for one at any token booth, but they might not always be stocked.)

same line is usually that some are express and others are local. **Express trains** often skip about three stops for each one that they make; express stops are indicated on subway maps with a white (rather than solid) circle. Local stops usually come about 9 blocks apart.

Directions are almost always indicated using "Uptown" (northbound) and "Downtown" (southbound), so be sure to know what direction you want to head in. The outsides of some subway entrances are marked UPTOWN ONLY or DOWNTOWN ONLY; read carefully, as it's easy to head in the wrong direction. Once you're on the platform, check the signs overhead to make sure that the train you're waiting for will be traveling in the right direction. If you do make a mistake, it's a good idea to wait for an express station, like 14th Street or 42nd Street, so you can get off and change for the other direction without paying again.

The days of graffiti-covered cars are gone, but the stations—and an increasing number of trains—are not nearly as clean as they could be. Trains are air-conditioned (move to the next car if yours isn't), though during the dog days of summer the platforms can be sweltering. In theory, all subway cars have PA systems to allow you to hear the conductor's announcements, but they don't always work well. It's a good idea to move to a car with a working PA system in case sudden service changes are announced that you'll want to know about.

For **subway safety tips,** see "Playing It Safe," below.

BY BUS

Less expensive than taxis and more pleasant than subways (they provide a mobile sightseeing window on Manhattan), MTA buses are a good transportation option. Their very big drawback: They can get stuck in traffic, sometimes making it quicker to walk. They also stop every couple of blocks, rather than the 8 or 9 blocks that local subways traverse between stops. So for long distances, the subway is your best bet; but for short distances or traveling crosstown, try the bus.

Tips For More Bus & Subway Information

For additional transit information, call the Metropolitan Transit Authority's **MTA/New York City Transit's Travel Information Center** at ✆ **718/330-1234.** Extensive automated information is available at this number 24 hours a day, and travel agents are on hand to answer your questions and provide directions daily from 6am to 9pm. For online information that's always up-to-the-minute current, visit **www.mta.nyc.ny.us**.

To request system maps, call the Customer Assistance Line at ✆ **718/330-3322** (although realize that recent service changes may not yet be reflected on printed maps). Disabled riders should direct inquiries to ✆ **718/596-8585;** hearing-impaired riders can call ✆ **718/596-8273.** For MetroCard information, call ✆ **212/638-7622** weekdays from 7am to 11am, weekends 9am to 5pm, or go online to **www.mta.nyc.ny.us/metrocard**.

You can get bus and subway maps and additional transit information at most information centers (see "Visitor Information" in "Orientation," earlier in this chapter). A particularly helpful MTA transit information desk is located at the **Times Square Visitor Center,** 1560 Broadway, between 46th and 47th streets, where you can also buy MetroCards. Maps are sometimes available in subway stations (ask at the token booth), but rarely on buses.

PAYING YOUR WAY

Like the subway fare, **bus fare** is $1.50, half price for seniors and riders with disabilities, free for children under 44 inches (up to three per adult). The fare is payable with a **MetroCard,** a **token** (for now, anyway), or **exact change.** Bus drivers don't make change, and fare boxes don't accept dollar bills or pennies. You can't purchase MetroCards or tokens on the bus, so you'll have to have them before you board; for details on where to get them, see "Paying Your Way" under "By Subway," above.

If you pay with a MetroCard, you can transfer to another bus or to the subway for free within 2 hours. If you use a token, you must request a **free transfer** slip that allows you to change to an intersecting bus route only (legal transfer points are listed on the transfer paper) within 1 hour of issue. Transfer slips cannot be used to enter the subway.

USING THE SYSTEM

You can't flag a city bus down—you have to meet it at a bus stop. **Bus stops** are located every 2 or 3 blocks on the right-side corner of the street (facing the direction of traffic flow). They're marked by a curb painted yellow and a blue-and-white sign with a bus emblem and the route number or numbers. Guide-A-Ride boxes at most stops display a route map and a hysterically optimistic schedule.

Almost every major avenue has its own **bus route.** They run either north or south: downtown on Fifth, uptown on Madison, downtown on Lexington, uptown on Third, and so on. There are **crosstown buses** at strategic locations all around town: 8th Street (eastbound); 9th (westbound); 14th, 23rd, 34th, and 42nd (east- and westbound); 49th (eastbound); 50th (westbound); 57th (east- and westbound); 65th (eastbound across the West Side, through the park, and then north on Madison, continuing east on 68th to York Ave.); 67th (westbound on the East Side to Fifth Ave. and then south on Fifth, continuing west on 66th St. through the park and across the West Side to West End Ave.); and 79th, 86th, 96th, 116th, and 125th (east- and westbound). Some bus routes, however, are erratic: The M104, for example, starts at the East River, then turns at Eighth Avenue and goes up Broadway. The buses of the Fifth Avenue line go up Madison or Sixth and follow various routes around the city.

Most routes operate 24 hours a day, but service is infrequent at night. Some say that New York buses have a herding instinct: They come only in groups. During rush hour, main routes have "limited" buses, identifiable by the red card in the front window; they stop only at major cross streets.

To make sure the bus you're boarding goes where you're going, check the maps on the sign that's at every bus stop, get your hands on a route map (see "For More Bus & Subway Information," above), or **just ask.** The drivers are helpful, as long as you don't hold up the line too long.

While traveling, look out the window not only to take in the sights but also to keep track of cross streets so you know when to get off. Signal for a stop by pressing the tape strip above and beside the windows and along the metal straps, about 2 blocks before you want to stop. Exit through the pneumatic back doors (not the front door) by pushing on the yellow tape strip; the doors open automatically (pushing on the handles is useless unless you're as buffed as Hercules). Most city buses are equipped with wheelchair lifts, making buses the preferable mode of public transportation for wheelchair-bound travelers; for more on this topic, see "Tips for Travelers with Special Needs," on p. 41. Buses also "kneel," lowering down to the curb to make boarding easier.

BY TAXI

If you don't want to deal with public transportation, finding an address that might be a few blocks from the subway station, or sharing your ride with 3.5 million other people, then take a taxi. The biggest advantages are, of course, that cabs can be hailed on any street (providing you find an empty one—often simple, yet at other times nearly impossible) and will take you right to your destination. I find they're best used at night when there's little traffic to keep them from speeding you to your destination and when the subway may seem a little daunting. In Midtown at midday, you can usually walk to where you're going more quickly.

Official New York City taxis, licensed by the Taxi and Limousine Commission (TLC), are yellow, with the rates printed on the door and a light with a medallion number on the roof. You can hail a taxi on any street. *Never* accept a ride from any other car except an official city yellow cab (private livery cars are not allowed to pick up fares on the street).

The base fare on entering the cab is $2. The cost is 30¢ for every one-fifth mile (0.32km) or 20¢ per minute in stopped or very slow-moving traffic (or for waiting time). There's no extra charge for each passenger or for luggage. However, you must pay bridge or tunnel tolls (sometimes the driver will front the toll and add it to your bill at the end; most times, however, you pay the driver before the toll). You'll also pay a 50¢ night surcharge after 8pm and before 6am. A 15% to 20% tip is customary.

Note: Taxi drivers were lobbying for a fare increase at press time, and Mayor Bloomberg was supporting it, so don't be surprised if you find higher fares when you arrive.

Forget about hopping into the back seat and having some double-chinned, cigar-chomping, all-knowing driver slowly turn and ask nonchalantly, "Where to, Mac?" Nowadays most taxi drivers speak only an approximation of English and drive in engagingly exotic ways. Always wear your seat belt—taxis are required to provide them.

The TLC has posted a **Taxi Rider's Bill of Rights** sticker in every cab. Drivers are required by law to take you anywhere in the five boroughs, to Nassau or Westchester counties, or to Newark Airport. They are supposed to know how to get you to any address in Manhattan and all major points in the outer boroughs. They are also required to provide air-conditioning and turn off the radio on demand, and they cannot smoke while you're in the cab. They are required to be polite.

You are allowed to dictate the route that is taken. It's a good idea to look at a map before you get in a taxi. Taxi drivers have been known to jack up the fare on visitors who don't know better by taking a circuital route between point A

Tips Taxi-Hailing Tips

When you're waiting on the street for an available taxi, look at the **medallion light** on the top of the coming cabs. If the light is out, the taxi is in use. When the center part (the number) is lit, the taxi is available—this is when you raise your hand to flag the cab. If all the lights are on, the driver is off duty.

A taxi can't take more than four people, so expect to split up if your group is larger.

Impressions

Traffic signals in New York are just rough guidelines.

—David Letterman

and point B. Know enough about where you're going to know that something's wrong if you hop in a cab at Sixth Avenue and 57th Street to go to the Empire State Building (Fifth Ave. and 34th St.), say, and you suddenly find yourself on Ninth Avenue.

On the other hand, listen to drivers who propose an alternate route. These guys spend 8 or 10 hours a day on these streets, and they know them well—where the worst midday traffic is, where Con Ed has dug up an intersection that should be avoided. A knowledgeable driver will know how to get you to your destination quickly and efficiently.

Another important tip: **Always make sure the meter is turned on at the start of the ride.** You'll see the red LED readout register the initial $2 and start calculating the fare as you go. I've witnessed unscrupulous drivers buzzing unsuspecting visitors around the city with the meter off, and then overcharging them at drop-off time.

Always ask for the receipt—it comes in handy if you need to make a complaint or have left something in a cab. In fact, it's a good idea to make a mental note of the driver's four-digit medallion number (usually posted on the divider between the front and back seats) just in case you need it later. You probably won't, but it's a good idea to play it safe.

For driver complaints and lost property, call the 24-hour Consumer Hot Line at © **212/NYC-TAXI.** For details on getting to and from the local airports by taxi, see "By Plane" under "Getting There," in chapter 3. For further taxi information—including a complete rundown of your rights as a taxi rider—point your Web browser to **www.ci.nyc.ny.us/taxi**.

BY CAR

Forget driving yourself around the city. It's not worth the headache. Traffic is horrendous, and you don't know the rules of the road (written or unwritten) or the arcane alternate-side-of-the-street parking regulations (in fact, precious few New Yorkers do). You don't want to find out the monstrous price of parking violations or live the Kafka-esque tragedy of liberating a vehicle from the tow pound. Not to mention the security risks.

If you do arrive in New York City by car, park it in a garage (expect to pay at least $25–$45 per day) and leave it there for the duration of your stay. If you drive a rental car in, return it as soon as you arrive and rent another on the day you leave. Just about all of the major car-rental companies, including **National** (© **800/227-7368;** www.nationalcar.com), **Hertz** (© **800/654-3131;** www.hertz.com), and **Avis** (© **800/230-4898;** www.avis.com), have multiple Manhattan locations.

TRAVELING FROM THE CITY TO THE SUBURBS

The **PATH** (© **800/234-7284;** www.panynj.gov/path) system connects urban communities in New Jersey, including Hoboken and Newark, to Manhattan by subway-style trains. Stops in Manhattan are at Christopher and 9th streets, and along Sixth Avenue at 14th, 23rd, and 33rd streets. A new lower Manhattan station, to replace the one destroyed beneath the World Trade Center, is not expected to be up and running until 2004. The fare is $1.50.

New Jersey Transit (**© 800/626-RIDE;** www.njtransit.com) operates commuter trains from Penn Station, and buses from the Port Authority at Eighth Avenue and 42nd Street, to points throughout New Jersey.

The **Long Island Rail Road** (**© 718/217-LIRR;** www.mta.nyc.ny.us/lirr) runs from Penn Station, at Seventh Avenue between 31st and 33rd streets, to Queens (ocean beaches, Shea Stadium, Belmont Park) and points beyond on Long Island, to even better beaches and summer hot spots like Fire Island and the Hamptons.

Metro North (**© 800/METRO-INFO** or 212/532-4900; www.mta.nyc.ny.us/mnr) departs from Grand Central Terminal, at 42nd Street and Lexington Avenue, for areas north of the city, including Westchester County, the lovely Hudson Valley, and Connecticut.

3 Playing It Safe

Sure, there's crime in New York City, but millions of people spend their lives here without being robbed and assaulted. In fact, New York is safer than any other big American city, and is listed by the FBI as somewhere around 150th in the nation for total crimes. While that's quite encouraging for all of us, it's still important to take precautions. Visitors especially should remain vigilant, as swindlers and criminals are expert at spotting newcomers who appear disoriented or vulnerable.

Men should carry their wallets in their front pockets and women should keep constant hold of their purse straps. Cross camera and purse straps over one shoulder, across your front, and under the other arm. Never hang a purse on the back of a chair or on a hook in a bathroom stall; keep it in your lap or between your feet with one foot through a strap and up against the purse itself. Avoid carrying large amounts of cash. You might carry your money in several pockets so that if one is picked, the others might escape. Skip the flashy jewelry and keep valuables out of sight when you're on the street.

Panhandlers are seldom dangerous and can be ignored (more aggressive pleas can firmly be answered, "Not today"). If a stranger walks up to you on the street with a long sob story ("I live in the suburbs and was just attacked and don't have the money to get home" or whatever), it's likely to be a scam, so don't feel any moral compulsion to help. You have every right to walk away and not feel bad. Be wary of an individual who "accidentally" falls in front of you or causes some other commotion, because he or she may be working with someone else who will take your wallet when you try to help. And remember: You *will* lose if you place a bet on a sidewalk card game or shell game.

Impressions

I like it here in New York. I like the idea of having to keep eyes in the back of your head all the time.

—John Cale

Certain areas should be approached with care late at night. I don't recommend going to the Lower East Side, Alphabet City in the far East Village, or the Meat-Packing District unless you know where you're going. Don't be afraid to go, but head straight for your destination and don't wander onto deserted side streets. The areas above 96th Street aren't the best, either (although they're

Tips The Top Safety Tips

Trust your instincts, because they're usually right. You'll rarely be hassled, but it's always best to walk with a sense of purpose and self-confidence, and don't stop in the middle of the sidewalk to pull out and peruse your map. Anywhere in the city, if you find yourself on a deserted street that feels unsafe, it probably is; leave as quickly as possible. If you do find yourself accosted by someone with or without a weapon, remember to keep your anger in check and that the most reasonable response (maddening though it may be) is not to resist.

improving almost by the day). Times Square has been cleaned up, and there'll be crowds around until midnight, when theater- and moviegoers leave the area. Still, stick to the main streets, such as Broadway or Ninth Avenue, Midtown West's newest restaurant row. The areas south of Times Square are best avoided after dark, as they're largely abandoned once the business day ends. Take a cab or bus when visiting the Jacob Javits Center on 34th Street and the Hudson River. Don't go wandering the parks after dark, unless you're going to a performance; if that's the case, stick with the crowd.

If you plan on visiting the outer boroughs, go during the daylight hours. If the subway doesn't go directly to your destination, your best bet is to take a taxi. Don't wander the side streets; many areas in the outer boroughs are absolutely safe, but neighborhoods change quickly, and it's easy to get lost.

All this having been said, don't panic. New York has experienced a dramatic drop in crime and is generally safe these days, especially in the neighborhoods that visitors are prone to frequent. There's a good police presence on the street, so don't be afraid to stop an officer, or even a friendly-looking New Yorker (trust me—you can tell), if you need help getting your bearings.

SUBWAY SAFETY TIPS In general, the subways are safe, especially in Manhattan. There are panhandlers and questionable characters like anywhere else in the city, but subway crime has gone down to 1960s levels. Still, stay alert and trust your instincts. Always keep a hand on your personal belongings.

When using the subway, **don't wait for trains near the edge of the platform** or on extreme ends of a station. During nonrush hours, wait for the train in view of the token booth clerk or under the yellow DURING OFF HOURS TRAINS STOP HERE signs, and ride in the train operator's or conductor's car (usually in the center of the train; you'll see his or her head stick out of the window when the doors open). Choose crowded cars over empty ones—there's safety in numbers.

Avoid subways late at night, and splurge on a cab after about 10 or 11pm—it's money well spent to avoid a long wait on a deserted platform. Or take the bus.

FAST FACTS: New York City

American Express Travel service offices are at many Manhattan locations, including 1185 Sixth Ave., at 47th Street (© 212/398-8585); at the New York Marriott Marquis, 1535 Broadway, in the 8th-floor lobby (© 212/575-6580); on the mezzanine level at Macy's Herald Square, 34th Street and

Broadway (✆ 212/695-8075); and 374 Park Ave., at 53rd St. (✆ 212/421-8240). Call ✆ **800/AXP-TRIP** or go online to **www.americanexpress.com** for other city locations or general information.

Area Codes There are four area codes in the city: two in Manhattan, the original **212** and the new **646,** and two in the outer boroughs, the original **718** and the new **347.** Also common is the **917** area code, which is assigned to cell phones, pagers, and the like. All calls between these area codes are local calls, but you'll have to dial 1 + the area code + the 7 digits if the number you're calling is not within your area code.

Business Hours In general, **retail stores** are open Monday through Saturday from 10am to 6pm or 7pm, Thursday from 10am to 8:30 or 9pm, and Sunday from noon to 5pm (see chapter 10). **Banks** tend to be open Monday through Friday from 9am to 3pm and sometimes Saturday mornings.

Dentists See "Health & Insurance" in chapter 3.

Doctors For medical emergencies requiring immediate attention, head to the nearest emergency room (see "Hospitals," below). For less urgent health problems, New York has several walk-in medical centers, like **DOCS at New York Healthcare,** 55 E. 34th St., between Park and Madison avenues (✆ **212/252-6001**), for nonemergency illnesses. The clinic, affiliated with Beth Israel Medical Center, is open Monday through Thursday from 8am to 8pm, Friday from 8am to 7pm, Saturday from 9am to 3pm, and Sunday from 9am to 2pm. Tthe **NYU Downtown Hospital** offers physician referrals at ✆ **888/698-3362.**

Embassies & Consulates See "Fast Facts: For the International Traveler" in chapter 4.

Emergencies Dial ✆ **911** for fire, police, and ambulance. The **Poison Control Center** can be reached at ✆ **800/222-1222** toll-free from any phone.

Hospitals The following hospitals have 24-hour emergency rooms. Don't forget your insurance card.

Downtown: New York Downtown Hospital, 170 William St., between Beekman and Spruce streets (✆ 212/312-5063 or 212/312-5000); **St. Vincents Hospital and Medical Center,** 153 W. 11th St., at Seventh Avenue (✆ 212/604-7000); and **Beth Israel Medical Center,** First Avenue and 16th Street (✆ 212/420-2000).

Midtown: Bellevue Hospital Center, 462 First Ave., at 27th Street (✆ 212/562-4141); **New York University Medical Center,** 560 First Ave., at 33rd Street (✆ 212/263-7300); and **Roosevelt Hospital,** 425 W. 59th St., between Ninth and Tenth avenues (✆ 212/523-6800).

Upper West Side: St. Luke's Hospital Center, Amsterdam Avenue and 113th Street (✆ 212/523-3335); and **Columbia Presbyterian Medical Center,** 622 W. 168th St., between Broadway and Fort Washington Avenue (✆ 212/305-2500).

Upper East Side: New York Presbyterian Hospital, 525 E. 68th St., at York Avenue (✆ 212/746-5050); **Lenox Hill Hospital,** 100 E. 77th St., between Park and Lexington avenues (✆ 212/434-2000); and **Mount Sinai Medical Center,** Fifth Avenue at 100th Street (✆ 212/241-6500).

Hot Lines The 24-hour **Rape and Sexual Abuse Hot Line** is ✆ 212/267-7273. The **Bias Crimes Hot Line** is ✆ 212/662-2427. The **LIFENET hot line** for suicide prevention, substance abuse, and other mental health crises is ✆ 800/543-3638. For **Mental Health and Alcoholism Services Crisis Intervention,** call ✆ 212/219-5599. You can reach **Alcoholics Anonymous** at ✆ 212/870-3400 (general office) or 212/647-1680 (intergroup, for alcoholics who need immediate counseling from a sober, recovering alcoholic). The **Domestic Violence Hot Line** is ✆ 800/621-4673. Other useful numbers include the **Crisis Help Line** ✆ 212/532-2400; **Samaritans' Suicide Prevention Line** ✆ 212/673-3000; to locate local **police** precincts ✆ 646/610-5000 or 718/610-5000; **Department of Consumer Affairs** ✆ 212/487-4444; and **taxi complaints** at ✆ 212/NYC-TAXI or 212/676-1000. If you suspect your car may have been towed, call the **Department of Transportation TOWAWAY Help Line** at ✆ 212/869-2929.

Internet Centers See the box called "Where to Check Your E-Mail in the City that Never Sleeps" on p. 84.

Libraries The **New York Public Library** is on Fifth Avenue at 42nd Street (✆ **212/930-0830**). This beaux-arts beauty houses more than 38 million volumes, and the beautiful reading rooms have been restored to their former glory. More efficient and modern, if less charming, is the mid-Manhattan branch at 455 Fifth Ave., at 40th Street, across the street from the main library (✆ **212/340-0833**). There are other branches in almost every neighborhood; you can find a list online at **www.nypl.org**.

Liquor Laws The minimum legal age to purchase and consume alcoholic beverages in New York is 21. Liquor and wine are sold only in licensed stores, which are closed on Sunday, holidays, and election days while the polls are open. Beer can be purchased in grocery stores and delis 24 hours a day, except Sunday before noon. Last call in bars is at 4am, although many close earlier.

Newspapers & Magazines There are three major daily newspapers: the *New York Times,* the *Daily News,* and the *New York Post.* For details on where to find arts and entertainment listings, see "Publications" under "Visitor Information" in "Orientation," earlier in this chapter.

If you want to find your hometown paper, visit **Universal News & Magazines,** at 234 W. 42nd St., between Seventh and Eighth avenues (✆ **212/221-1809**); and 977 Eighth Ave., between 57th and 58th streets (✆ **212/459-0932**), or **Hotalings News Agency,** 624 W. 52nd St., between Eleventh and Twelfth avenues (✆ **212/974-9419**). Other good bets include the **Hudson** newsdealers located in Grand Central Terminal, at 42nd Street and Lexington Avenue, and Penn Station, at 34th Street and Seventh Avenue.

Pharmacies **Duane Reade** (www.duanereade.com) has 24-hour pharmacies in Midtown at 224 W. 57th St., at Broadway (✆ **212/541-9708**); on the Upper West Side at 2465 Broadway, at 91st Street (✆ **212/799-3172**); and on the Upper East Side at 1279 Third Ave., at 74th Street (✆ **212/744-2668**).

Police Dial ✆ **911** in an emergency; otherwise, call ✆ **646/610-5000** or 718/610-5000 (NYPD headquarters) for the number of the nearest precinct.

Restrooms Public restrooms are available at the visitor centers in Midtown (1560 Broadway, between 46th and 47th sts.; and 810 Seventh Ave., between 52nd and 53rd sts.). Grand Central Terminal, at 42nd Street between Park and Lexington avenues, also has clean restrooms. Your best bet on the street is Starbucks or another city java chain—you can't walk more than a few blocks without seeing one. The big chain bookstores are good for this, too. You can also head to hotel lobbies (especially the big Midtown ones) and department stores like Macy's and Bloomingdale's. On the Lower East Side, stop into the Lower East Side BID Visitor Center, 261 Broome St., between Orchard and Allen streets (open Sun–Fri 10am–4pm, sometimes later).

Salon Services Need a haircut or a manicure while you're here in town? Bold, bustling **Warren-Tricomi,** 16 W. 57th St., just west of Fifth Avenue (✆ **212/262-8899;** www.warrentricomi.com), can meet all of your salon needs. For a dash of downtown style (and slightly lower prices), make an appointment at **Arte,** 284 Lafayette St., SoHo (✆ **212/941-5932**). If it's a good manicure or pedicure you need, visit **Pinky,** which has five locations on the Upper West Side, including 2050 Broadway, at 70th St. (✆ **212/362-9466**); 312 Columbus Ave., at 74th St. (✆ **212/787-0390**); and 2240 Broadway, at 80th St. (✆ **212/877-4992**).

Smoking Smoking is prohibited on all public transportation, in the lobbies of hotels and office buildings, in taxis, and in most shops. Smoking also may be restricted or not permitted in restaurants; for more on this, see p. 158.

Taxes **Sales tax** is 8.25% on meals, most goods, and some services, but it is not charged on clothing and footwear items under $110. **Hotel tax** is 13.25% plus $2 per room per night (including sales tax). **Parking garage tax** is 18.25%.

Time For the correct local time, dial ✆ **212/976-1616.**

Transit Information For information on getting to and from the airport, see "Getting There," in chapter 3, or call **Air-Ride** at ✆ **800/247-7433.** For information on subways and buses, call the **MTA** at ✆ **718/330-1234,** or see "Getting Around," earlier in this chapter.

Traveler's Assistance **Travelers Aid (www.travelersaid.org)** helps distressed travelers with all kinds of problems, including accidents, sickness, and lost or stolen luggage. There is an office on the second floor of the International Arrivals Building at JFK Airport (✆ **718/656-4870**), and one in Newark Airport's Terminal B (✆ **973/623-5052**).

Weather For the current temperature and next day's forecast, look in the upper-right corner of the front page of the *New York Times* or call ✆ **212/976-1212.** If you want to know how to pack before you arrive, point your browser to **www.cnn.com/weather** or **www.weather.com.**

6

Where to Stay

In 2001, the average hotel room rate in New York reached a whopping $227, higher than ever before in the city's history, and higher than any other city in the country. (Boston's median daily hotel rate is less than $198, while San Francisco's is just $155.) With rates at these levels—and that's just for an *average* hotel room, mind you—the largest portion of your travel budget is likely to go to accommodations.

Now the good news: There are more hotel bargains to be had these days than there have been in years. A severe dip in average room rates—down to around $168 by early 2002—is largely in response to three factors: A building boom that resulted in a glut of new hotel rooms over the last two years (more than 3,000 new rooms were added to the market in 2000 alone); a severe cutback in corporate travel; and leisure visitors who, in the wake of the less-than-solid economy and stick-close-to-home attitudes that prevailed in the wake of the 9/11 terrorist attacks, were simply less willing to shell out for pricey accommodations.

Don't set your expectations at too low a price point, however. Many hoteliers have held fast to higher rates ("rate integrity," they like to call it) and forsaken deep discounts in an effort to make up for steep financial losses in fourth quarter 2001—or because New York's sky-high real estate costs simply don't allow it. Believe it or not, hotels don't always want to put heads in beds at any cost.

Still, New York's hotel scene is much more of a buyer's market than it was a couple of years back. In the pages that follow, I'll tell you about truly wonderful places to stay that offer value for your money at every price point.

When deciding what you're willing to pay versus what you're willing to put up with, keep in mind that New York is still the land of $200-a-night Holiday Inns—so if you only want to spend 100 bucks a night or less, you're going to have to put up with some inconveniences, such as sharing a hall bathroom with your fellow travelers. (Europeans seem to have a much easier time with this than do Americans.) If you want a room with standard amenities—like a private bathroom or a real closet (rather than just a bar screwed to the wall)—plan on spending at least $150 a night or so. If you do better than that, you've landed a deal.

New York hotel rooms give everybody a whole new perspective on "small." Space is the city's biggest asset, and getting some costs. If you're traveling on a budget, don't be surprised if your room isn't much bigger than the bed that's in it and your cramped bathroom has a sink so small that it looks like it was manufactured for the Keebler elves. Even expensive rooms can be on the small side, or lack closet space, or have smallish bathrooms.

PRICE CATEGORIES & RACK RATES The **rates** quoted in the listings below are "rack rates"—the maximum rates that a hotel charges for rooms. I've used these rack rates to divide the hotels into four price categories, ranging from "Very Expensive" to "Inexpensive," for easy reference. But rack rates are only guidelines, and there are often ways around them; see "Tips for Saving on Your Hotel Room," below.

The hotels listed below have provided us with their best rate estimates for 2003, and all quoted rates were correct at press time. Be aware, however, that **rates can change at any time.** Rates are always subject to availability, seasonal fluctuations, and plain old rate changes. It's smart to expect price shifts in both directions in late 2002 and 2003 as hoteliers adjust to new demand patterns.

PET POLICIES I've indicated in the listings below those hotels that generally accept pets. However, understand that these policies may have limitations, such as weight and breed restrictions; may require a deposit and/or a signed waiver against damages; and may be revoked at any time. Always inquire when booking if you're bringing Bowser, Fluffy, or Spike along—*never* just show up with him or her in tow.

TIPS FOR SAVING ON YOUR HOTEL ROOM

In the listings below, I've tried to give you an idea of the kind of deals that may be available at particular hotels: which ones have the best discounted packages, which ones offer AAA and other discounts, which ones allow kids to stay with Mom and Dad for free, and so on. But there's no way of knowing what the offers will be when you're booking, so also consider these general tips:

- **Choose your season carefully.** Room rates can vary dramatically—by hundreds of dollars in some cases—depending on what time of year you visit. Winter, from January through March, is best for bargains, with summer (especially July and Aug) second best. Fall is the busiest and most expensive season after Christmas, but November tends to be quiet and rather affordable, as long as you're not booking a parade-route hotel on Thanksgiving weekend. All bets are off at Christmastime—expect to pay top dollar for everything. For more on this subject, see "Money Matters" in "When to Go," in chapter 3.
- **Go uptown or downtown.** The advantages of a Midtown location are highly overrated, especially when saving money is your object. The subway can whisk you anywhere you want to go in minutes; even if you stay on the Upper East Side, you can be at the ferry launch for the Statue of Liberty in about a half hour. You'll get the best value for your money by staying outside the Theater District, in the residential neighborhoods where real New Yorkers live, like Greenwich Village, Chelsea, Murray Hill, or—my absolute favorite for space-seekers and bargain hunters—the Upper West Side. These are the neighborhoods where real New Yorkers hang out, too, so you won't want for good eats, nightlife, or Big Apple bustle.
- **Visit over a weekend.** If your trip includes a weekend, you might be able to save big. Business hotels tend to empty out, and rooms that go for $300 or more Monday through Thursday can drop dramatically, as low as $150 or less, once the execs have headed home. These deals are especially prevalent in the Financial District, but they're often available in tourist-friendly Midtown, too. Look in the Travel section of the Sunday *New York Times* for some of the best weekend deals. They're also often advertised on the hotel's website. Or just ask when you call.

Tips More Important Advice on Accommodations

For an easy-to-scan introduction to the best of what the city has to offer, check out "Best Hotel Bets" in chapter 1. For extra help in choosing a location, take a close look at "Manhattan's Neighborhoods in Brief" in chapter 5.

And remember: All hotel rooms are subject to 13.25% tax plus $2 per night.

- **Shop online.** Hotels often offer "Internet only" deals that can save you 10% to 20% over what you'd pay if you booked over the telephone. Also, hotels often advertise all of their available deals on their websites, so you don't have to rely on a reservation agent to fill you in. What's more, some of the discount reservations agencies (see below) have sites that allow you to book online. And consider joining the **Playbill Online Theater Club (www.playbillclub.com)**, a free service that offers some excellent members-only rates at select city hotels in addition to discounts on theater tickets. American Automobile Association members can often score the best discounts by booking at **www.aaa.com**. Travel search sites like **Orbitz (www.orbitz.com)**, **Microsoft Expedia (www.expedia.com)**, and **Travelocity (www.travelocity.com)** offer more discount options.
- **Investigate reservation services.** These outfits usually work as consolidators, buying up or reserving rooms in bulk, and then dealing them out to customers at a profit. You can get 10% to 50% off; but remember, these discounts apply to rack rates—inflated prices that people rarely end up paying. You may get a decent rate, but always call the hotel direct to see if you can do better.

  Quikbook (© **800/789-9887** or 212-779-7666 www.quikbook.com) is probably the best of the bunch. Another good bet is **Hotel ConXions** (© **800/522-9991** or 212/840-8686; www.hotelconxions.com). You might also try the **Hotel Reservations Network,** also known as HotelDiscount!com (© **800/364-0801;** www.180096HOTEL.com or www.hoteldiscount.com), and **Accommodations Express** (© **800/950-4685;** www.accommodations express.com).

  Note: Never just rely on a reservations service or an online booking site. Do a little homework; compare the rack rates to the discounted rates being offered by the service to see what kind of deal they're actually offering. If you're being offered a stay in a hotel I haven't recommended, do more research to learn about it, especially if it isn't a reliable chain name like Holiday Inn or Hyatt. It's not a deal if you end up at a dump.
- **Buy a money-saving package deal.** A travel package that gets your plane tickets and your hotel stay for one price may just be the best bargain of all. In some cases, you'll get airfare, accommodations, transportation to and from the airport, plus extras—maybe an afternoon sightseeing tour, or restaurant and shopping discount coupons—for less than the hotel alone would have cost had you booked it yourself. For more on this, see "Money-Saving Package Deals" in chapter 3.
- **Or rely on a qualified professional.** Certain hotels give travel agents discounts in exchange for steering business their way, so if you're shy about bargaining, an agent may be better equipped to negotiate discounts for you.

- **Consider a B&B accommodation or an apartment.** If Big Apple hotels just seem too expensive, or you'd just like something a little more like home, consider renting a room in a genuine New York apartment—or even an entire apartment. These accommodations can range from spartan to splendid, from a hosted bedroom in a private home to an unhosted, fully equipped apartment with multiple bedrooms. No matter what, you can pretty much guarantee that you'll get more for your money than if you book into a regular hotel. You'll save money on taxes alone, because hotel tax (13¼% plus $2 per night) isn't invoked (you'll usually pay just sales tax [8¼%] for short stays and no tax at all for longer stays, but never assume—always ask when booking.) However, you need to be rather independent-minded to enjoy this option.

  The place to start is with **Manhattan Getaways** (✆ **212/956-2010;** www.manhattangetaways.com). Judith Glynn maintains a beautifully kept and managed network of bed-and-breakfast rooms (from $105 nightly) and unhosted apartments (from $145) around the city. There's a 3-night minimum stay, and credit cards are accepted. Another decent bet is **A Hospitality Company** (✆ **800/987-1235** or 212/965-1102; www.hospitalityco.com), which owns and manages 300 apartments around Manhattan starting at $115 a night, or $795 weekly for a basic studio. These are rather sparsely furnished apartments and the company offers very little in the way of service (it took me five days to get my broken TV fixed when I was displaced from home by renovation), but the apartments are clean and do the trick. There's no minimum stay, and credit cards are accepted. Optional cleaning services are available for longer stays.

  Additional agencies that can book you into a B&B room or a private apartment, with prices starting at $90 nightly, include **As You Like It** (✆ **800/277-0413** or 212/695-0191; www.furnapts.com); **Abode Apartment Rentals** (✆ **800/835-8880** or 212/472-2000; www.abodenyc.com); **City Sonnet** (✆ **212/614-3034;** www.citysonnet.com); **Manhattan Lodgings** (✆ **212/677-7616;** www.manhattanlodgings.com); and **New York Habitat** (✆ **212/255-8018;** www.nyhabitat.com). Be sure to get all details in writing and an exact total up front to avoid disappointments.

1 South Street Seaport & the Financial District

This is it—Ground Zero. These Lower Manhattan neighborhoods were most seriously affected by the events of September 11, 2001. Whether you want to stay away or gravitate towards the reconstruction is entirely up to you. However, keep in mind that this area will continue to be a major construction zone throughout 2003; beyond the emotional aspects, you may find the noise and heavy-equipment traffic to be a bit much. That said, the hotels that I've recommended below are away from the worst of the World Trade Center damage, and all offer easy subway access to the rest of the city.

This area has always been the province of business travelers on weekdays, so don't expect much in the way of services at night or on the weekends. Still, Lower Manhattan offers New York's best luxury-for-dollar hotel values to leisure travelers on weekends and holidays, once corporate travelers have headed home. It's also the heart of pre-Revolutionary New York, and offers easy access to the gorgeous Battery Park waterfront and Lady Liberty.

To locate the hotels in this section, see the map on p. 109.

Downtown Accommodations: The Financial District, TriBeCa, Lower East Side, SoHo & Greenwich Village

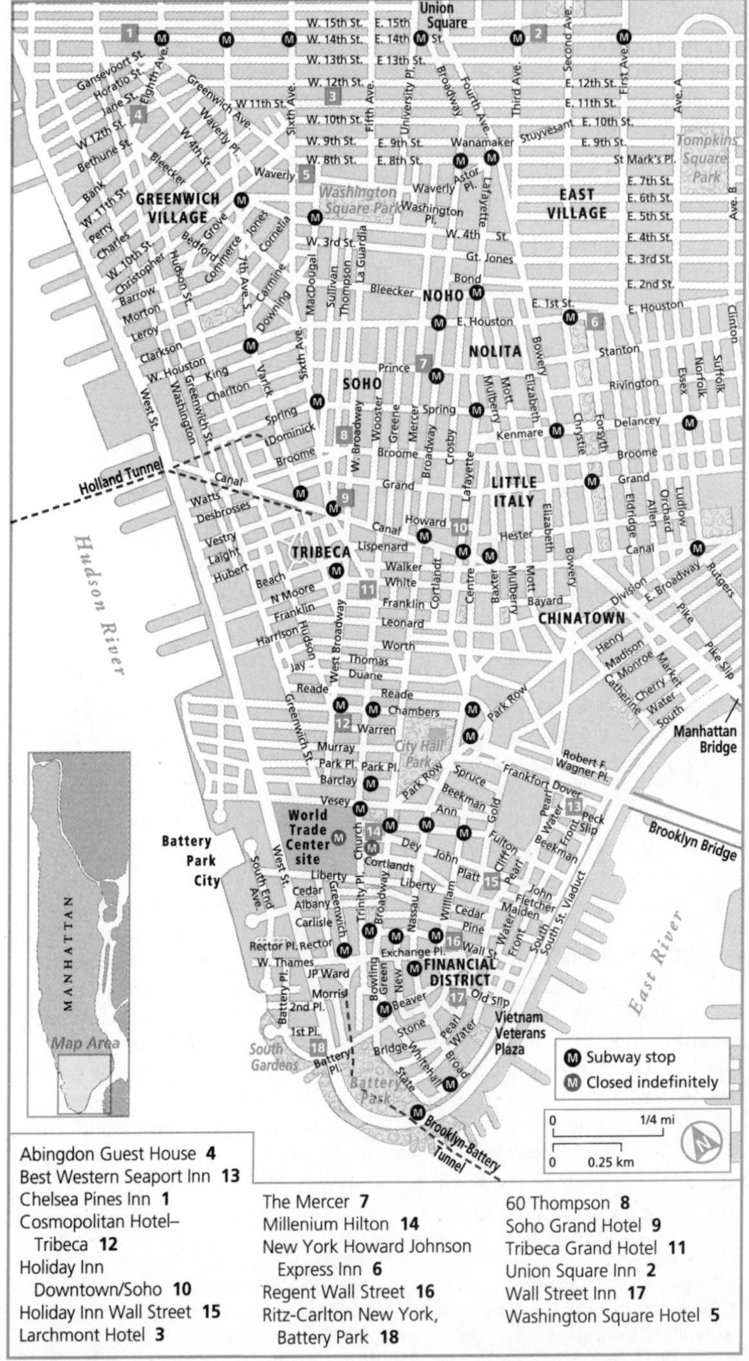

Abingdon Guest House **4**
Best Western Seaport Inn **13**
Chelsea Pines Inn **1**
Cosmopolitan Hotel–Tribeca **12**
Holiday Inn Downtown/Soho **10**
Holiday Inn Wall Street **15**
Larchmont Hotel **3**
The Mercer **7**
Millenium Hilton **14**
New York Howard Johnson Express Inn **6**
Regent Wall Street **16**
Ritz-Carlton New York, Battery Park **18**
60 Thompson **8**
Soho Grand Hotel **9**
Tribeca Grand Hotel **11**
Union Square Inn **2**
Wall Street Inn **17**
Washington Square Hotel **5**

VERY EXPENSIVE

Regent Wall Street ★★★ A stunningly gorgeous 1842 Greek Revival building at 55 Wall Street—which originally served as the New York Mercantile Exchange (there are even jail cells for debtors in the basement) and the U.S. Customs House—now houses the Financial District's finest hotel. The legendary architectural firm McKim, Mead, and White remade the grand interiors in Italian Renaissance style in 1907, extending a neoclassical grandeur that's been preserved and smartly updated by the regal Regent Hotels chain.

Geared to traveling VPs and CEOs, this ultradeluxe hotel sets a new standard for expense-account luxury. The mammoth and supremely comfortable rooms boast refined Italian-inspired decor in soothing natural tones and sumptuous fabrics. But the real story is the amenities, which include 34-inch TVs, large work desks with printer/fax/copier, and even minibars that the attentive staff will stock with your favorite beverages. On site is the excellent Regent Spa, which boasts a serene ambience and stress-relieving treatments. Food service is first rate.

Rack rates are insanely high, but value-seekers looking to splurge can score value-loaded weekend packages; even weekday promotional rates can drop as low as $325 on occasion.

55 Wall St. (at William St.), New York, NY 10005. ✆ **800/545-4000** or 212/845-8600. Fax 212/845-8601. www.regenthotels.com/wallstreet. 144 units. $495–$595 double; from $625 suite. Promotional rates, discounted weekend rates, and value-added packages as low as $245. Rollaway for extra adult $50. AE, DC, DISC, MC, V. Valet parking $50. Subway: 2, 3 to Wall St. **Amenities:** Fine-dining restaurant; cigar lounge serving lighter fare; state-of-the-art health club; first-rate spa with signature treatments; 24-hr. concierge; well-equipped business center with secretarial services; 24-hr. room service; dry cleaning/laundry service; DVD and CD libraries. *In room:* A/C, TV w/pay movies and DVD, CD player, fax/printer/copier, dataport and high-speed connectivity, minibar/fridge, hair dryer, safe.

Ritz-Carlton New York, Battery Park ★★ This brand-new luxury hotel standing at Manhattan's south tip arrived on the scene at exactly the wrong moment, but it debuted graciously nonetheless. Ritz-Carlton's re-entry into the New York market is also Manhattan's first-ever waterside luxury hotel, and it's a gem. Blessedly, the new glass-and-brick tower is designed such that 66% of rooms boast views over New York Harbor; even those that are oriented to the city are largely sheltered from views of Ground Zero, 5 blocks away.

The hotel diverges from the standard Ritz-Carlton English countryside look for a somewhat more contemporary, Art Deco–influenced style that suits the new architecture. The look is lovely, with warm marquetry woods and gorgeous textiles; furnishings include a generous and well-equipped work desk with desk-level inputs. Expect the full slate of Ritz-Carlton comforts and services, from Frette-dressed feather beds to the refined chain's signature Bath Butler, who will draw a scented bath for you (which you choose from an extensive menu) in your own deep soaking tub. Many harbor-view rooms have views of Lady Liberty; all have sweeping views and telescopes with which to enjoy them. Just beyond the front door is beautifully manicured Robert Wagner Park (great for a morning jog) and the Museum of Jewish Heritage. Service is impeccable, of course.

2 West St., New York, NY 10004. ✆ **800/241-3333** or 212/344-0800. Fax 212/344-3804. www.ritzcarlton.com. 298 units. $465–$625 double; from $565 suite. Promotional rates and weekend rates, and value-added packages as low as $199 at press time. Extra person 17 and under $40 ($100 on club level). AE, DC, DISC, MC, V. Valet parking $50. Subway: 4, 5 to Bowling Green. **Amenities:** Fine-dining restaurant; lobby lounge for afternoon tea and cocktails; 14th floor cocktail bar with light dining and outdoor seating; state-of-the-art health club with views; spa treatments; 24-hr. concierge; well-equipped business center with 24-hr. secretarial services; 24-hr. room service; dry cleaning/laundry service; shuttle service within Lower Manhattan;

technology butler and bath butler services; Ritz-Carlton club level with 5 food presentations daily. *In room:* A/C, TV w/pay movies and video games, CD player, dataport and high-speed connectivity, minibar/fridge, hair dryer, safe; DVD with surround sound in suites and club rooms.

EXPENSIVE/MODERATE

Best Western Seaport Inn Catering primarily to business travelers, this well-kept chain hotel is also a good bet for vacationers. It's located in cobblestone South Street Seaport, within walking distance of the ferries to the Statue of Liberty and Ellis Island.

Though housed in an 1852 building with a beautifully restored exterior, the guest rooms are what you'd expect from a Best Western, but they're quite comfortable. Each is equipped with a work desk; some have small dining tables, sleeper sofas, steam baths, whirlpools, and/or terraces with fine views of seaport or skyline. Rooms are constantly kept fresh with new towels, carpeting, wallpaper, and the like. Ask for a corner room for extra space—they boast two queen beds and lots of windows, some with wonderful water views.

33 Peck Slip (2 blocks north of Fulton St., btwn Front and Water sts.), New York, NY 10038. ✆ **800/HOTEL-NY** or 212/766-6600. Fax 212/766-6615. www.bestwestern.com/seaportinn. 72 units. $189–$229 double. Rates include continental breakfast. Corporate rates from $169; family, senior, and weekend discounts may also be available. Extra person $10. Children under 18 stay free in parents' room. AE, DC, DISC, MC, V. Parking $20 nearby. Subway: 2, 3 to Fulton St.; A, C to Broadway–Nassau St. **Amenities:** Exercise room; tour desk; dry cleaning/laundry service; video library. *In room:* A/C, TV/VCR, fax, dataport, fridge, coffeemaker, hair dryer, iron, safe.

Holiday Inn Wall Street ★ This new-in-2000 hotel is Lower Manhattan's most technologically advanced hotel, and a welcome addition to the Financial District landscape. The comfortable queen-bedded rooms are stocked with everything an executive might need, including an 8-foot L-shaped workstation with desk-level inputs, dual-line portable phones, and the kind of office supplies you never bring but always need, like paper clips and tape. About half of the rooms have PCs with Microsoft Word and Office applications and a CD drive. The top floor is dedicated to special SMART rooms, which feature Toshiba Satellite laptop computers (with carrying case), fax/printer/copiers, and other upgraded amenities, plus buffet breakfast. The room decor is chain standard all the way, but fresh, and perfectly comfortable; an easy chair and ottoman expands seating options. Management is always staying on the cutting edge with such techno-toys as a "Pocket Concierge" plug-in in the lobby that allows you to download local information to your PDA; an ATM-style machine for one-touch credit card check-in (similar to a self-serve gas pump); and cellular connection services that allow you to forward your room calls to your cellphone. Guests are well cared for.

15 Gold St. (at Platt St.), New York, NY 10038. ✆ **800/HOLIDAY,** 212/232-7800, or 212/232-7700. Fax 212/425-0330. www.holidayinnwsd.com or www.holiday-inn.com. 138 units. $169–$419 double; from $389 suite. Check for discounts galore (AAA, AARP, corporate, government, military), plus deeply discounted weekend rates (as low as $109 at press time) and other specials. AE, DC, DISC, MC, V. Parking $24. Subway: 2, 3, 4, 5, A, C, J, M, Z to Fulton St./Broadway–Nassau St. Pets up to 25 lb. accepted (dogs only). **Amenities:** Restaurant; bar; exercise room and access to nearby health club; concierge; self-service business center; 24-hr. room service, delivery from 24-hr. deli; dry cleaning/laundry service; executive-level rooms; CD library. *In room:* A/C, TV w/pay movies, Internet access, and Nintendo, CD player, standard dataport and high-speed connectivity, minibar, coffeemaker, hair dryer, iron, safe.

Wall Street Inn ★ *Finds* Housed in an impeccably restored seven-story building, this intimate hotel is an ideal choice for those who want a Lower Manhattan location without corporate blandness. The lovely early American interiors boast a pleasing freshness. The hotel is warm, comforting, and serene, and the professional staff offers the kind of personalized service you won't get from the Marriott or Hilton. Rooms aren't huge, but the bedding is top-quality and all the conveniences are at hand. Rooms ending in "01" are smallest; seventh-floor rooms are best, as the bathrooms have extra counter space and whirlpool tubs.

Vacationers who don't mind the weekend quiet of Wall Street will find amazing deals once the execs go home: Rates can drop as low as $139 on weekend nights, and the staff will assign you the best available room when you check in.

9 S. William St. (at Broad St.), New York, NY 10004. ✆ **212/747-1500.** Fax 212/747-1900. www.thewallstreetinn.com. 46 units. $249–$450 double. Rates include continental breakfast. Ask about corporate, group, and/or deeply discounted weekend rates (as low as $139 at press time). AE, DC, DISC, MC, V. Parking $35–$40 nearby. Subway: 2, 3 to Wall St.; 4, 5 to Bowling Green. **Amenities:** Well-outfitted exercise room with sauna and steam; concierge; business center; babysitting; dry cleaning/laundry service; video library; common guest kitchen with microwave. *In room:* A/C, TV/VCR, dataport, fax, fridge, hair dryer, iron, safe.

2 TriBeCa

The *Tri*angle *Be*low *Ca*nal boasts two of my favorite hotels in the city: one luxury, one budget. It's one of Manhattan's hippest precincts—just ask Robert DeNiro, Harvey Keitel, or Miramax monarch Harvey Weinstein, who put this loft-dominated residential neighborhood on the map. Despite its proximity to Ground Zero, it's bounced back well. It continues to feel very trendy and boast some of the city's finest dining; however, it can feel rather deserted after dark, so it may be a better base for returning visitors and intrepid types than for wide-eyed first-timers.

To locate the hotels in this section, see the map on p. 109.

VERY EXPENSIVE

Tribeca Grand Hotel ★★ This sister to the Soho Grand (see "SoHo" below) is even more triumphant in merging high style, luxury comforts, and a hip downtown location. Set on a triangular plot just south of SoHo, the decidedly retro brick-and-cast-iron exterior blends perfectly with the surrounding neighborhood. The Larry Bogdanow–designed interiors are unabashedly modern, and key to the hotel's runaway success.

The dramatic eight-story atrium lobby, with its soaring proportions, is consumed by the sexy Church Lounge, an upscale bar and restaurant.

Set along open atrium-facing corridors, the streamlined guest rooms boast generous built-in work space (with a Herman Miller Aeron chair) and state-of-the-art technology. A warm gold-and-red palette, interesting textures, and soft, glowing light emphasize luxury in the modern, utilitarian design.

2 Sixth Ave. (at White and Church sts.), New York, NY 10013. ✆ **877/519-6600** or 212/519-6600. Fax 212/519-6700. www.tribecagrand.com. 203 units. $259–$549 double or studio; from $549 suite. Internet-only rates from $279 at press time; ask about corporate rates and value-added packages. AE, DC, DISC, MC, V. Parking $32. Subway: 1, 9 to Franklin St.; A, C, E to Canal St. Pets welcomed. **Amenities:** Oh-so-hip restaurant and lounge; fitness center; well-connected 24-hr. concierge; business center with complete workstations; 24-hr. room service; same-day laundry and dry-cleaning; video and CD libraries; screening room; coffee, tea, and cocoa bar on each floor. *In room:* A/C, TV/VCR with Internet access, CD player, fax/printer/copier, standard dataport and high-speed connectivity, minibar, hair dryer, safe, mini-TV in bathroom.

INEXPENSIVE

Cosmopolitan Hotel–Tribeca ★ *Value* Hiding behind a plain-vanilla TriBeCa awning is one of the best hotel deals in Manhattan for budget travelers who insist on a private bathroom. Everything is strictly budget, but nice: The modern IKEA-ish furniture includes a work desk and an armoire (a few rooms have a dresser and hanging rack instead); for a few extra bucks, you can have a love seat, too. Beds are comfy, and sheets and towels are of good quality. Rooms are small but make the most of the limited space, and the whole place is pristine. The two-level minilofts have lots of character, but expect to duck on the second level. Management does a great job of keeping everything fresh and new. The TriBeCa location is safe, superhip, and subway-convenient. Services are kept at a bare minimum to keep costs down, so you must be a low-maintenance guest to be happy here.

95 W. Broadway (at Chambers St.), New York, NY 10007. ✆ **888/895-9400** or 212/566-1900. Fax 212/566-6909. www.cosmohotel.com. 113 units. $119–$159 double. AE, DC, MC, V. Parking $20, 1 block away. Subway: 1, 2, 3, 9 to Chambers St. *In room:* A/C, TV, dataport, ceiling fan.

3 The Lower East Side

The Lower East Side makes a great base for both nostalgics and nightlife hounds; keep in mind, however, that it's still gritty around the edges, and out of the way by Manhattan standards.

To locate the hotels in this section, see the map on p. 109.

INEXPENSIVE

New York City Howard Johnson Express Inn ★★ *Value* This brand-new construction is a boon to budget-minded travelers looking for quality comforts at a great price, a trendy location, or both. It's the kind of hotel where recent college grads would feel comfortable putting up their parents—*and* where they'd like to stay themselves.

The hotel sits on a wide thoroughfare next to a beautifully renovated Yiddish vaudeville house that now houses a state-of-the-art art-house movie complex. Bars, live-music clubs, affordable restaurants (including Katz's, New York's best Jewish deli), and offbeat shops abound on the surrounding blocks; East Village action is just across Houston (pronounced *how*-ston) Street, and stylish SoHo is to the west. The neighborhood may be on the cutting edge, but this HoJo is wonderfully predictable. Rooms are small, but furnishings and textiles are attractive and of good quality: Mattresses are nice and firm, work desks boast desk-level inputs and an ergonomic chair, and the granite baths are nicer than those in some luxury hotels (some even have Jacuzzis). Those with room numbers ending in 01, 02, or 03 are the largest.

135 E. Houston St. (at Forsyth St.), New York, NY 10002. ✆ **800/406-1411** or 212/358-8844. Fax 212/473-3500. www.hojo.com. 54 units. $119–$149 double. Rates include continental breakfast. Inquire about AAA, AARP, and corporate discounts. AE, DC, DISC, MC, V. Parking $29, 4 blocks away. Subway: F to Second Ave. **Amenities:** Dry cleaning/laundry service. *In room:* A/C, TV, dataport, hairdryer, iron.

4 SoHo

Downtown's gorgeous cast-iron district is the gold-plated heart of hip New York. It makes the ideal base for visiting trend watchers with hard-core shopping in mind. Bring your platinum card, though, because hotel rooms don't come cheap in this Land of the Beautiful People (although an edge-of-Chinatown Holiday Inn offers some relief from SoHo's sky-high rates).

To locate the hotels in this section, see the map on p. 109.

VERY EXPENSIVE

The Mercer ★★ André Balazs, boutique hotelier extraordinaire, opened the Mercer in April 1997, and the beautiful people have been keeping the place booked ever since. The lobby feels like a postmodern library lounge, with design books lining the shelves and a hip staff scurrying about in Isaac Mizrahi finery. The hotel is more service-oriented than competitors like the Royalton, but I found its ultracool, almost frostily exclusive air a little off-putting. Even the entrance, guarded by heavy curtains, feels almost uninviting. Still, the heart-of-SoHo location, almost Zen-like Christian Liaigre interiors, and a celeb-heavy cast of regulars make the Mercer the unrivaled epicenter of downtown chic.

The high-ceilinged guest rooms are more welcoming than the public spaces, with strong, angular custom furnishings in beautiful African wenge and ipe woods. The linens are gorgeous textured cottons; there's comfortable seating, and a large work table easily doubles as a dining table. The austerely beautiful tile-and-marble bathrooms have a steel cart for storage, an oversize shower stall or oversize two-person tub (state your preference when booking). Nice extras include VCRs and CD players, on-screen Web access, and minibars stocked with goodies from Dean & Deluca.

The Kitchen is the French/Asian fusion domain of superstar chef Jean-Georges Vongerichten (of four-star Jean Georges; see chapter 7); the lobby offers more casual dining, drinking, and scene-making space.

147 Mercer St. (at Prince St.), New York, NY 10012. ✆ **888/918-6060** or 212/966-6060. Fax 212/965-3838. www.mercerhotel.com. 75 units. $395–$425 double; $500–$565 studio; from $1,100 suite. AE, DC, DISC, MC, V. Parking $35 nearby. Subway: N, R to Prince St. **Amenities:** Restaurant; cellar lounge; food and drink service in lobby; free access to nearby Crunch fitness center; 24-hr. concierge; secretarial services; 24-hr. room service; dry cleaning/laundry service; video and CD libraries. *In room:* A/C, TV/VCR with Internet access, CD player, dataport and T1 connectivity, minibar, safe, ceiling fan.

Soho Grand Hotel ★★ Built from the ground up in 1996 as a modern ode to SoHo's cast-iron past, this haven for the image conscious was the first hotel to open in the neighborhood in more than a century. Here, the self-conscious modern design that overwhelms at the Mercer is toned down and warmed up with natural hues, textures, and materials. What's more, the scene is a tad more relaxing than that at the Soho's unabashedly modern sister, the Tribeca Grand. Nevertheless, it's huge with an entertainment-industry crowd.

Guest rooms boast retro-reproduction furnishings with an Asian slant. The natural colors are warm and soothing, and William Morris fabrics and soft lighting abound. The beds are fitted with Frette linens, cushioned Naugahyde headboards, and gorgeous coverlets. Decked out in ceramic subway tile, the bathrooms are beautiful but simple.

Awarded two stars by the *New York Times,* Canal House serves sophisticated and satisfying New England–style tavern fare. The retro-clubby Grand Bar is so popular the action often spills out into the lobby's comfy, high-ceilinged living room–like "salon."

310 W. Broadway (at Grand St.), New York, NY 10013. ✆ **800/965-3000** or 212/965-3000. Fax 212/965-3244 (reservations) or 212/965-3200 (guests). www.sohogrand.com. 373 units. $374–$529 double; from $1,399 penthouse suite. Corporate, promotional, and Internet-only rates as low as $209; your travel agent may be able to do even better. AE, DC, DISC, MC, V. Parking $40. Subway: A, C, E, N, R, 1, 9 to Canal St. Pets welcomed. **Amenities:** Fine restaurant; hip bar and lounge; fitness center; concierge; 24-hr. room service; dry cleaning/laundry service; butler's pantry with complimentary coffee, tea, and hot chocolate on every floor. *In room:* A/C, minibar, TV/VCR, CD player, dataport, hair dryer, safe.

MODERATE

Holiday Inn Downtown/SoHo This Holiday Inn is actually on the northern edge of Chinatown, but its just-off-SoHo location is perfect for hipsters who want access to the ultrachic scene without its high price tag. It's everything you'd expect from this good-value chain: clean, well outfitted, reliable, and comfortable. The guest rooms are standard but have everything you need. Doubles are a good-value bet for small families or sharing friends. You'll find Asian touches throughout the hotel—a nod to the brink-of-Chinatown location—and a well-respected Cantonese restaurant. Rack rates are high, but it's easy to snag a discount or score a room on the low end with advance booking.

138 Lafayette St. (at Howard St., 1 block north of Canal St.), New York, NY 10013. © **800/HOLIDAY** or 212/966-8898. Fax 212/966-3933. www.holidayinn-nyc.com. 227 units. $139–$269 double. Check for AAA, AARP, government, corporate, and other discounts. Extra person $20. Children 18 and under stay free in parents' room. AE, DC, DISC, MC, V. Parking $27. Subway: 6, N, R, Q, W, J, M to Canal St. **Amenities:** Restaurant (Cantonese); bar; access to nearby health club; concierge; fax and copy service; room service (6:30am–11pm); dry cleaning/laundry service. *In room:* A/C, TV w/pay movies, CD player, fax (in most junior suites), dataport, coffeemaker, hair dryer, iron.

5 Greenwich Village

The quirky, chameleon-like Village offers an ideal combination of affordability and cachet for those who prefer to experience the "real" New York—in all of its left-of-center, low-rise glory—over tourist magnet Midtown. Its narrow, winding streets can be a maze even to New Yorkers, however, and there are no visitor services, so you may be better off in Midtown or the Upper West Side if the Big Apple is new to you.

To locate the hotels in this section, see the map on p. 109.

MODERATE

Abingdon Guest House ★ *Finds* Steve Austin and his partner, Zachary Stass, run this lovely guesthouse (and its downstairs coffee bar, Brewbar) in a wonderful retail-and-residential West Village neighborhood. All of the rooms are artistically done in bold colors and outfitted with well-chosen art and furnishings; each can be previewed on their website, so choose the one that best fits your personal style and budget. No matter which one you choose, you'll get a superior-quality mattress and linens; cozy bathrobes; a telephone with your own answering machine; and a private bathroom that's en suite (in room) or just outside your room, in the hall (rooms with adjacent hall bathrooms are cheapest). The best (and most expensive) is the Ambassador Room, which has a witty British Raj theme and a kitchenette with microwave, VCR, and sleeper sofa for a third person.

The neighborhood is terrific, with good restaurants and boutiques, but it's a bit off the beaten path if you're planning on lots of Midtown sightseeing. The Abingdon is best for mature, independent-minded travelers, since there's no regular staff on-site. The thoughtful style and privacy make it ideal for an affordable romantic escape, but friends traveling together won't feel out of place (in fact, two rooms feature two twin beds). No smoking.

13 Eighth Ave. (btwn W. 12th and Jane sts.), New York, NY 10014. © **212/243-5384.** Fax 212/807-7473. www.abingdonguesthouse.com. 9 units. $157–$177 double with adjacent bathroom; $177–$222 with en-suite bathroom. Rates are $10 less for single travelers. Extra person $25. 4-night minimum on weekends, 2-night minimum on weekdays. AE, DC, DISC, MC, V. Parking $20 nearby. Subway: A, C, E, L, 1, 2, 3, 9 to 14th St. **Amenities:** Coffee bar. *In room:* A/C, TV, dataport, hair dryer, iron, safe.

INEXPENSIVE

Larchmont Hotel ★★ *Value* Well located on a beautiful tree-lined block in a quiet residential part of the Village, this European-style hotel is simply a gem. If you're willing to share a bathroom, it's hard to do better for the money. The entire place has a wonderful air of warmth and sophistication; the butter-yellow lobby even *smells* good. Each bright guest room is tastefully done in rattan and outfitted with a writing desk, a minilibrary of books, an alarm clock, a washbasin, and a few extras that you normally have to pay a lot more for, such as cotton bathrobes, slippers, and ceiling fans. Every floor has two shared bathrooms (with hair dryers) and a small, simple kitchen. The management is constantly renovating, so everything feels clean and fresh. What's more, those looking for a hip downtown base couldn't be better situated, since some of the city's best shopping, dining, and sightseeing—plus your choice of subway lines—are just a walk away. Book *well* in advance (the management suggests 6–7 weeks' lead time).

27 W. 11th St. (btwn Fifth and Sixth aves.), New York, NY 10011. ✆ **212/989-9333.** Fax 212/989-9496. www.larchmonthotel.com. 58 units (all with shared bathroom). $70–$95 single; $90–$125 double. Rates include continental breakfast. Children under 13 stay free in parents' room. AE, DC, DISC, MC, V. Parking $18 nearby. Subway: A, C, E, F, V to West 4th St. (use 8th St. exit); F to 14th St. **Amenities:** Tour desk; fax service; room service (10am–6pm); common kitchenette. *In room:* A/C, TV, hairdryer, safe, ceiling fan.

Washington Square Hotel Popular with a young international crowd, this affordable hotel sits behind a pretty facade facing Washington Square Park (historically Henry James territory, now the heart of New York University) in the heart of Greenwich Village. A marble-and-brass lobby leads to tiny rooms that benefited from a pleasant freshening in 2000. Each comes with a firm bed, a private bathroom, and a small closet with a pint-size safe. It's worth paying a few extra dollars for a south-facing room on a high floor, since others can be a bit dark. Both the Union Square Inn and Murray Hill's Thirty Thirty offer a bit more space and brand-new everything for a similar price; nevertheless, the heart-of-campus location is ideal for youthful (or youth-minded) travelers who want to be near Village restaurants, bars, and jazz clubs. On site is a very good restaurant and lounge, C3, which even draws locals with its stylish design, well-priced cocktails and international bistro fare, and Sunday jazz brunch. The hotel staff has been known to be terse in the past, but service seems to be on an upswing.

103 Waverly Place (btwn Fifth and Sixth aves.), New York, NY 10011. ✆ **800/222-0418** or 212/777-9515. Fax 212/979-8373. www.wshotel.com. 170 units. $101–$131 single; $118–$151 double; $145–$188 quad. Rates include continental breakfast. Inquire about special rates and jazz packages. Rollaway $20. AE, MC, V. Parking $20 nearby. Subway: A, C, E, F, V to West 4th St. (use 3rd St. exit). **Amenities:** Restaurant and lounge; exercise room; dry cleaning/laundry service. *In room:* A/C, TV, dataport, hair dryer, iron, safe.

6 Chelsea

Straddling the Midtown/downtown border, Chelsea is the center of New York's very out-and-about gay community, so stay elsewhere if that will make you uncomfortable. If it doesn't, you'll find the trendy-funky residential-and-retail neighborhood to have a central location and some of Manhattan's best affordable accommodations.

To find the hotels described in this section, see p. 118.

MODERATE

Hotel Chelsea ★ If you're looking for dependable, predictable comforts, book a room next door at the Chelsea Savoy. But if it's Warhol's New York you're here to discover—or Sarah Bernhardt's or Eugene O'Neill's or Lenny Bruce's—the Hotel Chelsea is the only place to stay. Thomas Wolfe wrote *You Can't Go Home Again* at the Chelsea; Arthur Miller penned *After the Fall* here; William Burroughs moved in to work on *Naked Lunch;* and in a defining moment of punk history, Sid Vicious killed screechy girlfriend Nancy Spungeon here. No other hotel boasts so much genuine atmosphere. Currently, most of the 400 rooms are inhabited by long-term residents of the creative bent, so the bohemian spirit and sense of community are as strong as ever.

The landmark 1884 redbrick Victorian boasts graceful cast-iron balconies and a bustling lobby filled with museum-quality works by prominent current and former residents. A recent renovation has taken the seediness out of the allure—these days, the hotel is looking very nice. It's still very quirky, mind you, and not for everybody: I'm told that all of the individually decorated rooms and suites now have air-conditioning, but otherwise it's a crapshoot. Accommodations tend to be sparsely furnished, but they're almost universally large and virtually soundproof (you can see how this would be a plus for unbridled creation). I loved no. 520, a pretty purple-painted junior suite with two double beds, a ceiling fan, a sofa, and a pantry kitchenette. Everything is clean, but don't expect new. The hotel is service-oriented, but in an appropriately fluid way: There's no room or valet service, but the bellmen will be happy to deliver takeout to your room or run your dirty clothes to the cleaners. Adjacent is budget-chic El Quijote for Spanish eats and margaritas, and the basement-dwelling Serena is *très* hip for cocktails (see chapter 11).

222 W. 23rd St. (btwn Seventh and Eighth aves.), New York, NY 10011. ✆ **212/243-3700.** Fax 212/675-5531. www.hotelchelsea.com. 400 units, about 100 available to travelers. $135–$250 single; $165–$300 double or junior suite; $300–$350 suite. Ask about long-stay discounts. AE, MC, V. Parking $20 nearby. Subway: C, E, 1, 9 to 23rd St. **Amenities:** Restaurant; lounge; bellman service. *In room:* A/C, TV.

The Inn on 23rd ★★ *Finds* Friendly innkeepers Annette and Barry Fisherman have launched one of Manhattan's few—and one of its finest—full-service bed-and-breakfast inns. The Inn on 23rd is a marvelous find for those who love individualized accommodations and a personal touch.

All guest rooms are spacious. Each has a king or queen bed outfitted with a supremely comfy pillow-top mattress and top-quality linens; a satellite TV; a new private bathroom with thick Turkish towels; a roomy closet; two-line phones; and a wonderfully homey vibe. The gorgeous mix of antiques, family heirlooms, and contemporary art is the product of Annette's impeccable eye. I love the coolly sophisticated Rosewood Room, with gorgeous '60s built-ins; the Bamboo Room, peacefully quiet and elegantly Asian; the '40s Room, a Heywood-Wakefield lover's dream come true; and Ken's Cabin, a large, lodgey room with cushy, well-worn leather furnishings and wonderful Americana relics. The suite has a skylight with ultra romantic Empire State Building views.

An elevator means you don't have to cart your luggage up multiple flights of stairs, and a number of rooms have pullout sofas or Murphy beds to accommodate more than two travelers. The New School now holds culinary classes daily in Annette's kitchen, so even if you don't want to join in you may still benefit from the gourmet leftovers. This place is a real gem!

131 W. 23rd St. (btwn Sixth and Seventh aves.), New York, NY 10011. ✆ **877/387-2323** or 212/463-0330. Fax 212/463-0302. www.bbonline.com/ny/innon23rd. 11 units. $175–$250 double; from $250 suite. Rates include generous continental breakfast. Extra person $20. Children under 12 stay free in parents' room. AE, DC, MC, V. Parking $20 nearby. Subway: F, 1, 9 to 23rd St. **Amenities:** Fax and copy service; cozy library with stereo and VCR. *In room:* A/C, TV, dataport, hair dryer, iron.

INEXPENSIVE

Another excellent choice is the very charming **Chelsea Pines Inn,** 317 W. 14th St. (✆ **212/929-1023;** www.chelseapinesinn.com), which caters largely to gay travelers but offers excellent value to all open-minded adult travelers.

Midtown, Chelsea & Gramercy Park Accommodations

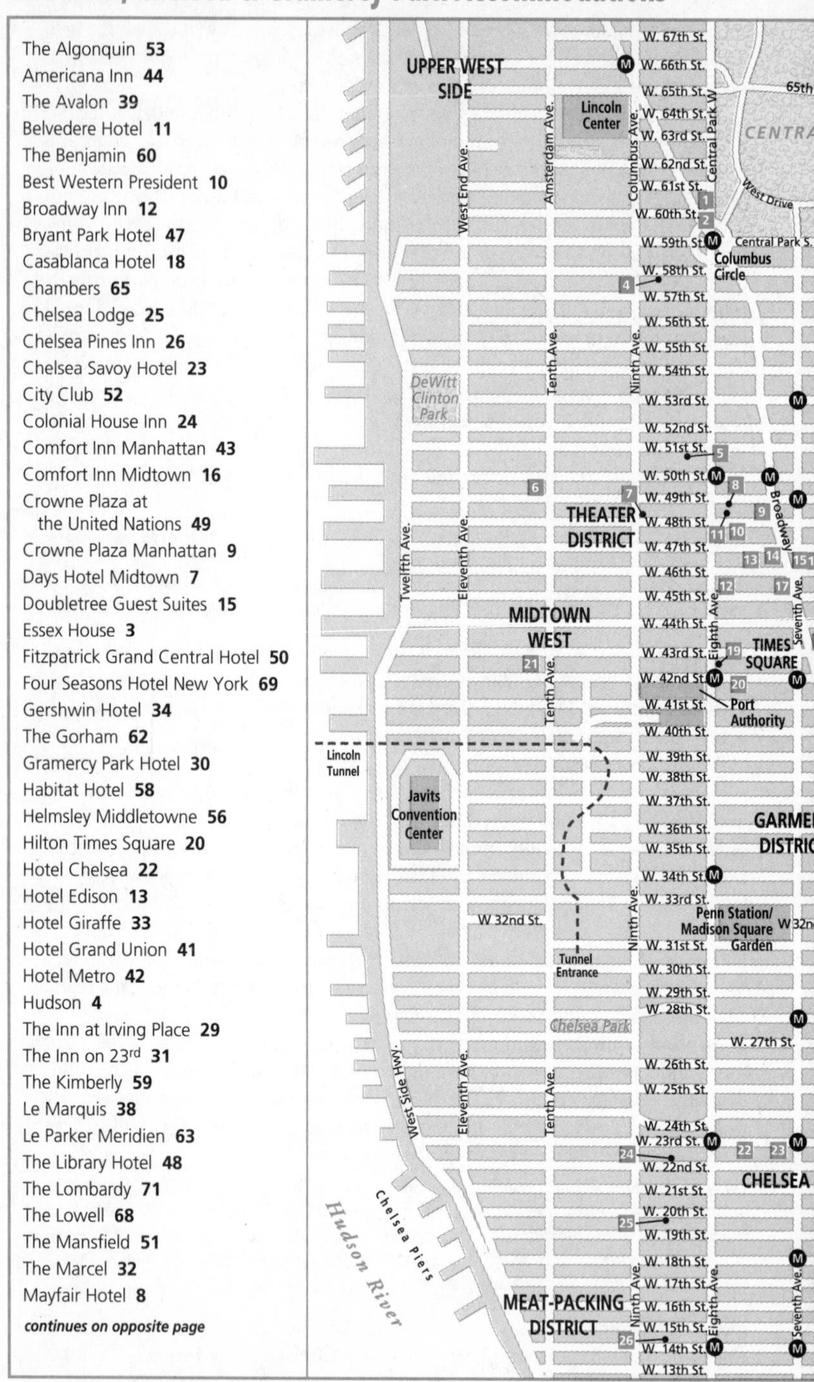

America Online Keyword: Travel
Booked seat 6A, open return.
Rented red 4-wheel drive.
Reserved cabin, no running water.
Discovered space.

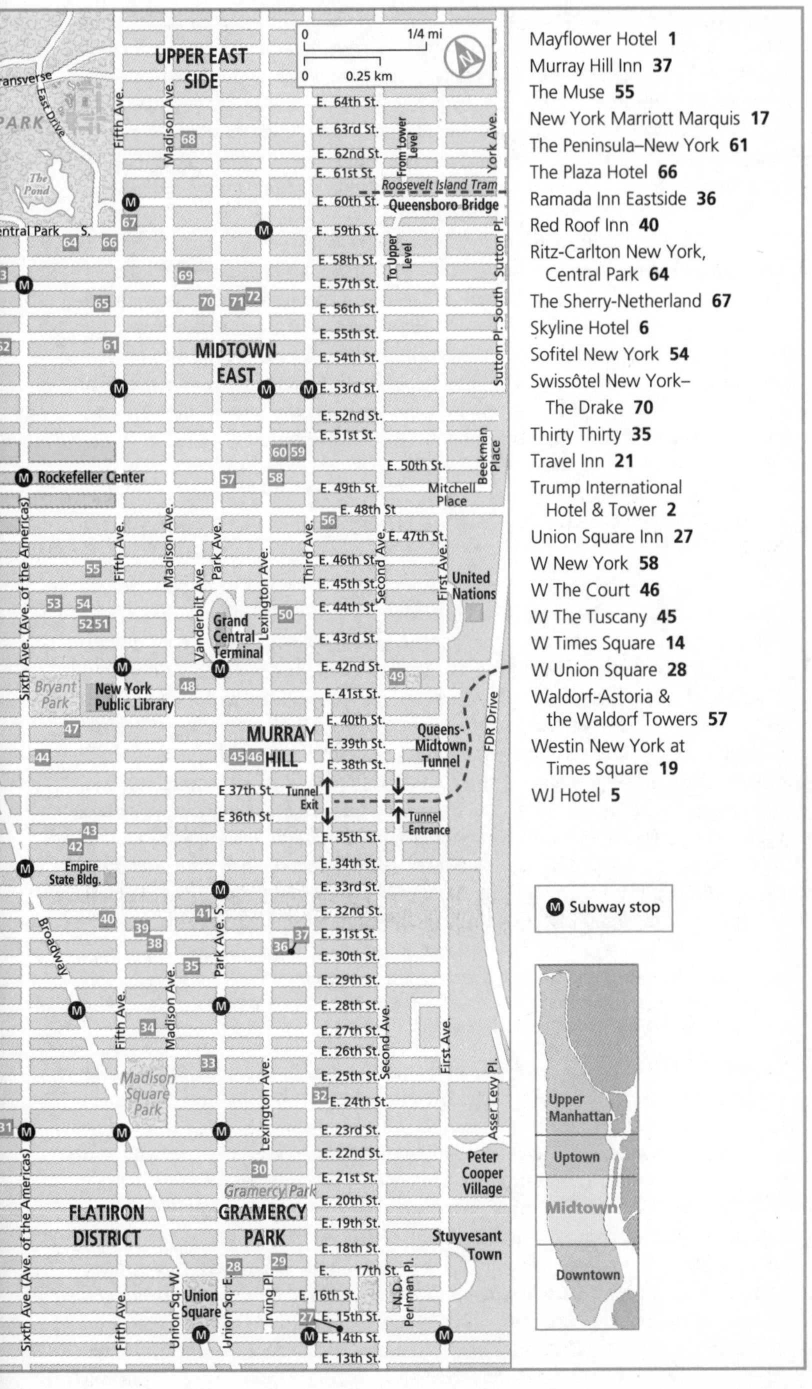

Mayflower Hotel 1
Murray Hill Inn 37
The Muse 55
New York Marriott Marquis 17
The Peninsula–New York 61
The Plaza Hotel 66
Ramada Inn Eastside 36
Red Roof Inn 40
Ritz-Carlton New York, Central Park 64
The Sherry-Netherland 67
Skyline Hotel 6
Sofitel New York 54
Swissôtel New York–The Drake 70
Thirty Thirty 35
Travel Inn 21
Trump International Hotel & Tower 2
Union Square Inn 27
W New York 58
W The Court 46
W The Tuscany 45
W Times Square 14
W Union Square 28
Waldorf-Astoria & the Waldorf Towers 57
Westin New York at Times Square 19
WJ Hotel 5
Subway stop
UPPER EAST SIDE
MIDTOWN EAST
MURRAY HILL
FLATIRON DISTRICT
GRAMERCY PARK
0 1/4 mi
0 0.25 km
Rockefeller Center
Grand Central Terminal
New York Public Library
Bryant Park
Empire State Bldg.
Madison Square Park
Gramercy Park
Union Square
United Nations
Queens-Midtown Tunnel
Tunnel Exit
Tunnel Entrance
Queensboro Bridge
Roosevelt Island Tram
From Lower Level
To Upper Level
Peter Cooper Village
Stuyvesant Town
Beekman Place
Mitchell Place
FDR Drive
Fifth Ave.
Madison Ave.
Park Ave.
Vanderbilt Ave.
Lexington Ave.
Third Ave.
Second Ave.
First Ave.
York Ave.
Sutton Pl.
Sutton Pl. South
Sixth Ave. (Ave. of the Americas)
Broadway
Park Ave. S.
Irving Pl.
Union Sq. W.
Union Sq. E.
N.D. Perlman Pl.
Asser Levy Pl.
Upper Manhattan
Uptown
Midtown
Downtown

Chelsea Lodge ★★ *Value* Housed in a lovely brownstone on a landmarked block, this small hotel is utterly charming and a terrific value—arguably the best in the city for budget-minded travelers. The young, friendly husband-and-wife owners, Paul and GG Weisenfeld, have put in an incredible effort: Impeccable renovations have restored original woodwork to mint condition and created a homey, country-in-the-city vibe. The beds are the finest and best outfitted I've seen in this price category. Ongoing renovations include newly redecorated common areas and bathrooms at this writing.

The only place with a similar grown-up sensibility for the same money is Greenwich Village's Larchmont (p. 115), but there, all bathroom facilities are shared; at Chelsea Lodge, each room has its own sink and in-room shower stall, so you only have to share a cute toilet room with your neighbors. I won't kid you—rooms are petite, the open closets are small, and beds are full-size (queens wouldn't cut it). But considering the stylishness, the amenities, and the great neighborhood, you'd be hard-pressed to do better for the money. Best for couples rather than shares. *Tip:* Try to book 2A, which is bigger than most, or one of the first-floor rooms, whose high ceilings make them feel more spacious.

318 W. 20th St. (btwn Eighth and Ninth aves.), New York, NY 10011. ✆ **800/373-1116** or 212/243-4499. Fax 212/243-7852. www.chelsealodge.com. 24 units (all with semiprivate bathroom). $90 single; $105 double. AE, DC, DISC, MC, V. Parking about $20 nearby. Subway: 1, 9 to 18th St.; C, E to 23rd St. *In room:* A/C, TV, ceiling fan.

Chelsea Savoy Hotel ★ *Value* This newish hotel (built in 1995) has been a welcome addition to Chelsea, a neighborhood abloom with art galleries, restaurants, nightclubs, and weekend flea markets but formerly devoid of comfortable, affordable hotels. The generic but cheery rooms are good size and have big closets and roomy, immaculate bathrooms with tons of counter space. Creature comforts abound: The rooms boast mattresses, furniture, and linens of high quality, plus the kinds of amenities you usually have to pay more for, like minifridges and in-room safes; free continental breakfast makes an already-good value even better. Most rooms are street-facing and sunny; corner rooms tend to be brightest but noisiest. Ask for a darker, back-facing room if you crave total silence. A plain but pleasant sitting room off the lobby makes an excellent place to enjoy your morning coffee over a selection of newspapers and magazines.

204 W. 23rd St. (at Seventh Ave.), New York, NY 10011. ✆ **866/929-9353** or 212/929-9353. Fax 212/741-6309. www.chelseasavoy.qpg.com or www.chelseasavoynyc.com. 90 units. $99–$115 single; $125–$175 double; $145–$195 quad. Rates include continental breakfast. Children stay free in parents' room. AE, MC, V. Parking $25 nearby. Subway: 1, 9 to 23rd St. *In room:* A/C, TV, dataport, fridge, hair dryer, iron, safe.

Colonial House Inn ★ *Finds* This charming 1850 brownstone, on a pretty residential block in the heart of gay-friendly Chelsea, was the first permanent home of the Gay Men's Health Crisis. The four-story walk-up caters to a largely gay and lesbian clientele, but the friendly staff welcomes everybody equally, and straight couples are a common sight. The whole place is beautifully maintained and professionally run. Rooms are small and basic but clean; those that share a hall bathroom (at a ratio of about three rooms per bathroom) have in-room sinks. Deluxe rooms—those with private bathrooms—also have minifridges, and a few have fireplaces that accommodate Duraflame logs. Both private and shared bathrooms are basic but nice. A terrific, mostly abstract art collection brightens the public spaces. Book at least a month in advance for weekend stays. At parlor level is a cute breakfast room where a continental spread is put out from 8am to noon daily; coffee and tea are available all day. Rooms don't have hairdryers and irons, but the front desk will lend them out with a smile. There's a nice roof deck split by a privacy fence; the area behind the fence is clothing optional. The neighborhood is chock-full of great restaurants and shopping, and offers easy access to the rest of the city.

318 W. 22nd St. (btwn Eighth and Ninth aves.), New York, NY 10011. ✆ **800/689-3779** or 212/243-9669. Fax 212/633-1612. www.colonialhouseinn.com. 20 units (12 with shared bathroom). $80–$99 single or double with shared bathroom; $125–$140 with private bathroom. Rates include expanded continental breakfast. 2-night minimum on weekends. Extra person $15. Weekly rates available. MC, V. Parking $20 nearby. Subway: C, E to 23rd St. **Amenities:** Fax service; Internet-access PC in lounge. *In room:* A/C, TV, dataport.

7 Union Square, the Flatiron District & Gramercy Park

These appealing, retail-and-restaurant-rich neighborhoods, which really flowered with the rise of the new Internet economy, now feature a terrific range of hotels in all price categories. They're ideal for visitors who want a home base that's outside the tourist districts but not *too* far off the beaten path. This area is even more central-to-everything than Chelsea, especially if you choose a hotel close to Union Square's multiple subway lines.

To find the hotels described in this section, see p. 118.

EXPENSIVE

In addition to the choices below, hipsters looking for both cutting-edge design and predictable comforts might also consider the new **W Union Square** (✆ **877/W-HOTELS** or 212/253-9119; www.whotels.com); see the box called "The Wonderful World of W" on p. 140.

Hotel Giraffe ★★ This all-new-in-2000 boutique hotel dominates the Flatiron hotel scene with its smart accommodations and 1930s Moderne-inspired grace. Juliet balconies, French windows, and graceful dormers lend the Giraffe a wonderful—and entirely neighborhood-appropriate—streamline feel. Soothing, low-lit halls lead to guest rooms that brim with style, comfort, and high-tech functionality.

The contemporary interiors star a rich palette—Bordeaux, champagne, and platinum textiles, honey-hued woods—that bespeaks luxury. Even the smallest room doesn't feel cramped thanks to soaring 10-foot ceilings and the smartest built-ins I've seen, including huge granite-topped work desks, good armoires and closets, and lots of drawer space. Oversize fluted-glass doors lead to gorgeous granite bathrooms with better-than-average counter space. Suites have living rooms with long-legged coffee tables that serve nicely for in-room dining or as additional work space.

Those who book early have a good chance at scoring a king or double/double (the most spacious configurations) in the "deluxe" category, which have French doors (with bedside-controlled blackout drapes) leading to a small balcony. But even the "superior" rooms have good windows that open to let fresh air in and almost magically shut out the street noise when closed.

365 Park Ave. South (at 26th St.), New York, NY 10016. ✆ **877-296-0009** or 212/685-7700. Fax 212/685-7701. www.hotelgiraffe.com. 73 units. $325–$425 double; from $425 1- or 2-bedroom suite; from $2,500 penthouse suite. Rates include continental breakfast and weekday wine and cheese accompanied by piano music. Check website or ask about reduced rates (as low as $259 at press time). AE, DC, MC, V. Parking $24. Subway: 6 to 23rd St. **Amenities:** Restaurant (undergoing renovation at press time); 2 bars; free access to Duomo Gym; concierge; business services; limited room service; dry cleaning/laundry service; rooftop garden; video and CD libraries. *In room:* A/C, TV/VCR, CD player, dataport and high-speed connectivity, minibar, hair dryer, iron, safe.

Inn at Irving Place ★★ *Finds* Tucked away on a quiet, brownstone-lined street in adjoining 1834 Greek Revival town houses, this hidden jewel offers the city's ultimate romantic getaway. The decor is lavishly late Victorian—pure *Age of Innocence*—yet comforts are wholly modern. Each impeccable room boasts a nonworking fireplace, antiques and art, Oriental rugs and kilims, luxuriant fabrics, and a spacious, like-new cream-and-white bathroom with a pedestal sink and a period vibe. Standard rooms feature queen beds, while deluxe rooms add a small seating area; larger than most city apartments, suites are ultra luxurious. Every accommodation has its own distinct personality and detailing: the O' Henry is a gorgeous standard with a big bathroom and a pretty brass bed and the Elsie deWolf suite has an extra anteroom with a daybed that makes it perfect for small families and shares.

With its roaring fireplace, the cozy parlor is the ideal spot to leaf through an Edith Wharton novel or the Sunday *Times*. Lady Mendl's Tea Salon serves the city's finest high tea (see chapter 7); drinks and cheese-and-caviar plates are also available evenings at chic Cibar, while less urbane all-day meals are served at the pleasing Irving on Irving bistro next door. The extremely professional staff will go the extra mile at your behest, whether it be serving you breakfast in bed, arranging for an in-room massage, or even doing a bit of shopping for you.

56 Irving Place (btwn 17th and 18th sts.), New York, NY 10003. ✆ **800/685-1447** or 212/533-4600. Fax 212/533-4611. www.innatirving.com. 12 units. $325–$415 double; $475–$525 suite. Rates include continental breakfast. Extra person $25. 2-night minimum on weekends. AE, DC, MC, V. Parking $25–$30 nearby. Subway: N, R, 4, 5, 6 to 14th St./Union Sq. Children under 12 not accepted. **Amenities:** 2 restaurants (tea and dessert salon, American bistro); martini lounge; access to nearby health club; concierge; 24-hr. room service; in-room massage; dry cleaning/laundry service; video and CD libraries. *In room:* A/C, TV/VCR, CD player, dataport, minibar, hair dryer; laptops and fax machines on request.

MODERATE

Gramercy Park Hotel *Kids* Opened in 1924, this old-world hotel has one of the best settings in the city. It's in one of New York's loveliest neighborhoods, ideally located on the edge of the private park—restricted to just a few area residents and to hotel guests, who can also get a key—that gives Gramercy Park the air of a quiet London square.

Management has this dowager looking very good these days. You'll still have to overlook the finer details, including ancient TVs and mix-and-match bathrooms that have been updated haphazardly. But rooms are huge by city standards, decently furnished, and comfortable, and the hotel has a surprisingly appealing old New York feel, due in large part to an incredibly loyal staff, many of whom have worked here since the Nixon administration. Standard doubles have a king bed or two doubles, and some suites have pullout sofas that make them large enough to sleep six; all have big closets and fluffy towels in the roomy bathrooms. Request a park-facing room, which costs no more but features a great view and a small kitchenette (most suites have kitchenettes, too). Off the bustling lobby are a continental restaurant (renovated in 2001) and a divey piano lounge with nightly entertainment that draws a young, retro-obsessed crowd.

2 Lexington Ave. (at 21st St.), New York, NY 10010. ✆ **800/221-4083** or 212/475-4320. Fax 212/505-0535. www.gramercyparkhotel.com. 509 units. $150–$160 single; $160–$170 double; $200–$220 suite. Extra person $10. Children under 12 stay free in parents' room. AE, DC, DISC, MC, V. Parking $28 nearby. Subway: 6 to 23rd St. Pets accepted. **Amenities:** Restaurant; lounge; salon; limited room service; in-room massage; dry cleaning/laundry service. *In room:* A/C, TV, fridge, hair dryer.

INEXPENSIVE

Gershwin Hotel ★ *Kids* If you see glowing horns protruding from a lipstick-red facade, you're in the right place. This creative-minded, Warhol-esque hotel caters to up-and-coming artistic types—and well-established names with an eye for good value—with its bold modern art collection and wild style. The lobby is a colorful postmodern cartoon of kitschy furniture and pop art. The standard rooms are clean and bright, with Picasso-style wall murals and Phillippe Starck-ish takes on motel furnishings. Superior rooms are best, as they're newly renovated, and well worth the extra $10; all have either a queen bed, two twins, or two doubles, plus a newish private bathroom with cute, colorful tile. Families and groups of friends on the lookout for value will love the family room, a two-room suite that nicely accommodates four with a queen bed in one room, two twins in the other.

There's always something going on at the Gershwin, whether it's live jazz, alt rock, or stand-up comedy in the Living Room, nightly happy hour (7–9pm) in the Red Room beer bar, summer film screenings in the rooftop garden, or a show at the hotel's own art gallery. The hotel is more service-oriented than you usually see at this price level, and the staff is very professional.

7 E. 27th St. (btwn Fifth and Madison aves.), New York, NY 10016. © **212/545-8000.** Fax 212/684-5546. www.gershwinhotel.com. 121 units. $99–$189 double (usually less than $150); $189–$219 family room. Check website for discounts, third-night-free specials, or other value-added packages. Extra person $10. AE, MC, V. Parking $25 3 blocks away. Subway: N, R, 6 to 28th St. **Amenities:** Cafe (breakfast only); beer bar; tour desk; dry cleaning/laundry service; Internet-access PC. *In room:* A/C, TV, dataport, hair dryer, iron.

The Marcel ★ *Finds* Being budget-challenged doesn't mean you have to settle for boring. This Gramercy Park hotel offers high style and a super-hip scene at low, low prices. Thanks to designers Goodman Charlton, who love to infuse retro styles with futuristic freshness, the Marcel sits on the cutting edge style-wise. Fab faux *Mod Squad*–era Scandinavian stylings in the lobby lead to guest rooms boasting gorgeous blond-would built-ins that make clever use of limited space, and a bold geometric cushioned headboard adds a downright luxurious flair. The designer furnishings and textiles look and feel expensive, even if the somewhat lumpy beds don't; still, budget travelers will be thrilled. Even if the service isn't fabulous or the little details aren't perfect, you should feel like you're getting a great deal here.

One of the strongest appeals of the Marcel is Spread (www.spreadnyc.com), a sexy restaurant/lounge hybrid offering a creative small plates menu, a first-rate sushi bar, terrific cocktails, and a blast of an after-dark scene. The subterranean lounge Coal is an even more seductive space.

201 E. 24th St. (at Third Ave.), New York, NY 10011. © **888/66-HOTEL** or 212-696-3800. Fax 212/696-0077. www.nychotels.com. 97 units. $125–$175 double. AE, DISC, MC, V. Parking: $24. Subway: 6 to 28th St. **Amenities:** Terrific fusion and sushi restaurant; stylish lounge; all-day coffee and cappuccino bar; limited room service; dry cleaning/laundry service. *In room:* A/C, TV w/pay movies, CD player, dataport, hairdryer, iron.

Union Square Inn ★ *Value* Situated a stone's throw east of Union Square, on the fringe of the energetic East Village, this unassuming little hotel is a welcome addition to the budget hotel scene. Rooms here aren't quite as cheap as those at its sister hotel, the Murray Hill Inn, but comforts are better quality; every room has a private bathroom, and everything feels fresh and new. Four standard rooms are tiny twins with trundle beds, and a handful in the deluxe category are spacious rooms with two double beds that can accommodate more than two if necessary. Most fall in the moderate category, with one double bed and little room to spare. All rooms boast quality mattresses and bedding and pretty all-new Italian-tile bathrooms. On the downside, all rooms lack views, open wall racks substitute for closets, most bathrooms have showers only, halls are narrow, and there's no elevator—but those are minimal sacrifices considering the low prices. Services are virtually nonexistent in order to keep costs down, but everything you'll need—from restaurants to dry cleaners to a slate of subway lines—is right at hand in the hip, central-to-everything location.

209 E. 14th St. (btwn Second and Third aves.), New York, NY 10003. © **212/614-0500.** Fax 212/614-0512. www.unionsquareinn.com. 40 units. $99–$169 double. Rates include basic continental breakfast. Extra person $20. AE, MC, V. Parking $25 nearby. Subway: L to Third Ave., or 4, 5, 6, N, R to 14th St./Union Sq. **Amenities:** Coffee bar serving light meals. *In room:* A/C, TV, dataport.

8 Times Square & Midtown West

This is where most visitors want to stay, and for good reason. You'll be at the neon-lit hub of the Big Apple action—there's absolutely no better base for theatergoers, and kids will love the bright lights and bustle. Expect to pay for the privilege of a Midtown West location, though, especially in autumn and at holiday time. Budget travelers looking for good value should choose another neighborhood, as should anybody who's turned off by constant crowds and tires easily of tourist schlock.

Keep in mind that hotel prices fluctuate wildly in Midtown West—sometimes by more than $200—based on the season. Many hotels listed as Moderate, or even Expensive, can be downright cheap much of the year; conversely, many of the hotels listed under "Inexpensive" inflate their rates beyond proportion during the busiest fall and Christmas seasons. Your best bet is to shop around; you also may be able to score a lower rate by using one of the discount reservations services mentioned on p. 107. Otherwise, try a different neighborhood; even Midtown East rates tend to be significantly more stable from month to month.

To find the hotels described in this section, see page 118.

VERY EXPENSIVE

In addition to the choices below, you might also wish to consider the new **Ritz-Carlton New York, Central Park,** 50 Central Park S. (© **800/241-3333** or 212/308-9100; www.ritz-carlton.com), which will be open on the site of the former St. Moritz by the time you arrive. Unlike the more contemporary Ritz-Carlton New York, Battery Park (p. 110), this one is more in keeping with Ritz-Carlton style; expect all of the traditional trappings and Ritz-Carlton's signature impeccable service.

Also consider the **Essex House,** 160 Central Park South (© **800/937-8461** or 212/247-0300; www.westin.com), more Central Park–glamorous than ever now that it's operated under the Westin flag and boasts New York's newest four-star restaurant, the wildly expensive Alain Ducasse. For the ultimate in stuffy luxury, book a room in the exclusive St. Regis Club, where you'll enjoy private butler-style concierge service.

Le Parker Meridien ★★★ This formerly stuffy French luxury hotel has shed its Biedermeier-meets-the-1980s style in favor of a decidedly more up-to-date, laid-back approach that's epitomized in its slogan: "Uptown. Not Uptight." The airy neoclassical lobby now boasts a fresh, hip look that incorporates classic modern furnishings, cool Damien Hirst art, and a staff fashionably outfitted in black and ecru.

The spacious guest rooms have been redone in a sleek yet comfortable Scandinavian-modern style, with clean-lined, blond-wood platform beds with featherbeds; warm blue and ecru fabrics; built-ins that include large work desks with desk-level inputs and stylish Aeron chairs; terrific task lighting; oversized TVs with DVD/CD players; and slate-and-limestone bathrooms. The beautifully configured junior suites boast a clever swivel entertainment center that caters to both sitting area and bedroom and serves as an attractive room divider.

But it's the top-notch facilities that elevate the Parker to a higher level, drawing international CEOs and celebs who could afford to stay anywhere. It has one of the city's best hotel dining scenes: Norma's is a soaring, ultramodern ode to breakfast food (see chapter 7), while ultra-charming Seppi's is the uptown version of Prince Street's Raoul's, a classic French bistro. Jack's is a post-modern lobby bar with a cool vibe and a fun cocktail menu. The excellent (if unfortunately named) Gravity is a mammoth 17,000-square-foot, state-of-the-art health club with a full slate of classes, a jogging track, racquetball, personal trainers, a full-service spa, and a fabulous 42nd-floor pool with skyline views.

Despite the high rates, there's no arguing with the value you get for your money here, especially if you catch one of the Parker's great package deals.

118 W. 57th St. (btwn Sixth and Seventh aves.), New York, NY 10019. ✆ **800/543-4300** or 212/245-5000. Fax 212/307-1776. www.parkermeridien.com. 731 units. $370–$680 double; from $480 suite. Excellent packages and weekend rates often available (as low as $199 at press time). Extra person $30. AE, DC, DISC, MC, V. Parking $40. Subway: N, R, B, Q to 57th St. Pets accepted. **Amenities**: 2 restaurants (American, French); 2 bars; fantastic fitness center and spa; concierge (2 with Clefs d'Or distinction); full-service business center; 24-hr. room service; dry cleaning/laundry service; courtesy car to/from Wall St. *In room:* A/C, 32-inch TV, DVD/CD player, fax, dataport, minibar, hair dryer, iron, safe.

EXPENSIVE

In addition to the choices below, the Times Square area is home to a number of big convention hotels, most notably the 50-story **New York Marriott Marquis,** 1535 Broadway (✆ **800/236-2427** or 212/398-1900; www.nycmarriott.com), which boasts a whopping 1,946 surprisingly large and well-outfitted rooms (pets accepted). There's also the smaller and more inviting **Crowne Plaza Manhattan,** 1605 Broadway (✆ **800/243-6969** or 212/977-4000; www.crowneplaza.com), the international flagship of Holiday Inn's upscale arm, and a perfectly fine hotel; noted designer Adam Tihany gave the public spaces new zest in 1999. Both properties regularly offer a fleet of discounts and special deals, and make great perches for Thanksgiving Day parade watching and the New Year's ball drop (forget about deals at these prime times, though). Expect zilch in the way of style or personal attention, however.

Hipsters looking for a Times Square–central location and chic cutting-edge design might also want to look into the new **W Times Square** (✆ **877/W-HOTELS** or 212/407-2975; www.whotels.com); for details, see the box called "The Wonderful World of W" on p. 140.

Set to debut in November 2002 is the new **Westin New York at Times Square,** 255 W. 42nd St., at Eighth Avenue (✆ **800/228-3000** or 212/921-9575; www.westinny.com). This brand-new tower will boast 863 rooms, all outfitted with Westin's truly celestial Heavenly Bed—a custom Simmons Beautyrest® pillow-top mattress set dressed in layer upon layer of fluffy down and crisp white linen—and the signature Heavenly Bath, with plush velour robes and oversized bath sheets. Heavenly Cribs will even be on hand for the kids.

Boutique Hotels a Bust?

The independent boutique movement of 2000 and 2001, which saw a whole crop of fashion-first independents debut with the pomp and circumstance of an Upper East Side sweet 16, are in the midst of a serious sophomore slump. I've excised many from this chapter, since there have been questions about service, management, and their ability to hold their own against hotels with worldwide reservations networks and proven track records with clients. But if you're willing to take the risk to end up in an ultra-stylish roost, you might also consider the best of the bunch, the **Bryant Park Hotel,** 40 West 40th St. (✆ **877/640-9300;** www.bryantparkhotel.com), housed in the majestic 1924 American Radiator Building overlooking the city's most lovely pocket park; the loftlike, David Rockwell-designed **Chambers,** 15 W. 56 St. (✆ **800/337-4685;** www.chambershotel.com); and the exclusive, society-snooty **City Club,** 55 W. 44th St. (✆ **212/921-5500;** www.cityclubhotel.com), which claims they emphasize service over style (they all do). For chic SoHo residential style, consider **60 Thompson,** 60 Thompson St. (✆ **877/431-0400;** www.60thompson.com).

The Algonquin ★★ This 1902 hotel is one of the Theater District's best-known landmarks: This is where the *New Yorker* was born, where Lerner and Loewe wrote *My Fair Lady,* and—most famously—where some of the biggest names in 1920s literati, among them Dorothy Parker, met to trade boozy quips at the celebrated Algonquin Round Table. Thankfully, the past isn't just a memory here anymore—a complete 1998 restoration returned this venerable place to its full Arts-and-Crafts splendor, transforming it into one of my absolute favorite hotels. Considering the history and comforts here, it also happens to be an excellent value.

True to its tradition, the Algonquin is a very social hotel: The splendid oak-paneled lobby is the comfiest and most welcoming in the city, made to linger over afternoon tea or an elegant cocktail. While posher than ever, the small rooms are comfortable but on the cramped side—fine for tourists out on the town all day, but not suitable for business travelers who may need to spread out and get some work done. Extras include stocked candy jars (a nice touch). The freshened bathrooms boast short but deep soaking tubs, terry robes, and an appealing period feel. Twins are the roomiest doubles. For the ultimate New York vibe, opt for one of the surprisingly affordable literary-themed suites.

Meals are served in the atmospheric Rose Room, while the fabulous Oak Room is one of the city's top cabaret rooms, featuring such esteemed talents as Andrea Marcovicci and Julie Wilson (see chapter 11). The publike Blue Bar is home to a rotating collection of Hirschfeld drawings that's well worth a browse.

59 W. 44th St. (btwn Fifth and Sixth aves.), New York, NY 10036. ✆ **800/555-8000** or 212/840-6800. Fax 212/944-1419. www.algonquinhotel.com. 165 units. $199–$369 double; from $299 suite. Check website or inquire about discounted rates or special package deals. AE, DC, DISC, MC, V. Parking $28 across street. Subway: B, D, F, V to 42nd St. **Amenities:** 2 restaurants (American/Continental, pub); lounge; bar; well-outfitted exercise room; concierge; limited room service; dry cleaning/laundry service. *In room:* A/C, TV w/pay movies, dataport, hair dryer, iron, safe.

Doubletree Guest Suites ★ *Kids* For less than the cost of a standard room in many hotels, you can have a very nice suite in this 43-story glass monolith, situated right in the heart of the bustling Times Square action. Each spacious suite has a separate bedroom, a dining/work area, and a living room with a pull-out sofa, a wet bar with microwave and coffeemaker, two TVs with Sony PlayStation, and multiple dual-line phones. For business travelers, conference suites are large enough for small meetings and feature good workstations. What's more, this is also an exceedingly family friendly hotel, with a floor of childproof family size suites and special amenities for kids, such as the Kids Club, designed by Philadelphia's Please Touch Museum for children ages 3 to 12, featuring a playroom, an arts-and-crafts center, and computer and video games. Cribs and strollers are available, and there's even a kids' room-service menu.

1568 Broadway (at 47th St. and Seventh Ave.), New York, NY 10036. ✆ **800/222-TREE** or 212/719-1600. Fax 212/921-5212. www.doubletree.com. 400 units. $249–$659 suite. Ask about senior, corporate, and AAA discounts and special promotions. Extra person $20. Children under 12 stay free in parents' suite. AE, DC, DISC, MC, V. Parking $35. Subway: N, R to 49th St. **Amenities:** Restaurant (hotel-standard American); pleasant Broadway-themed lounge; fitness center; children's playroom; concierge; business center with secretarial services; 24-hr. room service; babysitting; dry cleaning/laundry service; coin-op laundry. *In room:* A/C, 2 TVs w/pay movies and video games, dataport and high-speed connectivity, minibar, wet bar with coffeemaker and microwave, hair dryer, iron, safe.

Hilton Times Square ★ *Kids* This shiny new high-rise, opened in May 2000, is a prime symbol of the Times Square renaissance. It's at once family friendly, chain-reliable, and surprisingly sophisticated, thanks to a few co-opted airs from the boutique hotel movement, including sleek contemporary interiors, an open lobby with a stylish bar and a chic New American restaurant, and contemporary art from David Hockney and other notables. Despite its central location as part of Times Square's newest development (next door to the new Madame Tussaud's Wax Museum and 25 AMC movie theaters), the hotel is quiet and serene. An elevator whisks you up to the "Sky Lobby," and guest rooms don't begin until the 23rd floor.

The beige room decor is less than exciting, but it's better quality than most in this category, and larger-than-average room configurations allow for king beds or two doubles (great for families who don't mind sharing), an easy chair with ottoman, a generous work desk. Everything is spanking new, and bathrooms have generous marble counters. Twenty-first-century technology reigns, from desk-level inputs to TVs with on-screen web access. With upgraded decor, original art, a pullout sofa, and extra space, the well-outfitted suites are an excellent value if you're visiting in the right season. Views are superb from the 35th floor up; pricing is run of house, so request a high floor at check-in.

234 W. 42nd St. (btwn Broadway and Eighth Ave.), New York, NY 10036. ✆ **800/HILTONS** or 212/840-8222. Fax 212/840-5516. www.timessquare.hilton.com. 444 units. $179–$500 double (usually less than $300); from $375 suite. Check for AARP, AAA, government, corporate discounts as well as value-added packages. Children under 18 stay free in parents' room. AE, DC, DISC, MC, V. Parking $34. Subway: 1, 2, 3, 7, 9, N, R, S to 42nd St./Times Sq.; A, C, E to 42nd St. Pets accepted. **Amenities:** 1 notable restaurant; bar; trainer-staffed exercise room; access to nearby health club; children's program; concierge; business center; 24-hr. room service; babysitting; dry cleaning/laundry service. *In room:* A/C, TV/VCR w/pay movies, video games, and wireless Internet access, CD, dataport and high-speed connectivity; minibar, coffeemaker, hair dryer, iron, laptop-size safe.

The Mansfield ★ Built in 1905 as a well-heeled bachelor's residence, this is one of Midtown's most charming midprice hotels. The Mansfield (part of the hotel group that also includes the Upper East Side's Wales and Murray Hill's Roger Williams), is a bit pricier than it should be, but it's impeccably kept, discount deals are common, and freebies like all-day cappuccino and cookies and bottled water soften the blow, as does the heart-of-theater-and-sightseeing location. The building is rich with history (W. B. Yeats's dad lived here in 1909), perpetuated by rich architectural details and an evocative collection of 1920s portraits in pencil (supposedly discovered rolled up in the basement).

Rooms are smallish, but they boast a welcoming blend of period style and modern comforts. Nice design touches include ebony-stained floors covered with natural-fiber rugs, wood Venetian blinds, and well-made beds with gorgeous Belgian linens and metal-mesh headboards that recall Victorian sleigh beds. The nicely renovated, generally good-size marble-and-stainless steel bathrooms sport limestone counters and Frette robes. About 50% of rooms lack closets, but brilliant built-in solutions conceal the wall racks that most hotels don't bother to hide. The tiny standards are best for only a night or two, so try to upgrade if you're staying longer.

Off the lobby is a romantic lounge with a wood-burning fireplace and a slate of international newspapers. M Bar is a swanky library-style lounge that's an attraction in its own right, with a first-rate cocktail bar and a very popular weekly Wednesday jazz night (see chapter 11).

12 W. 44th St. (btwn Fifth and Sixth aves.), New York, NY 10036. ✆ **877/847-4444** or 212/944-6050. Fax 212/764-4477. www.mansfieldhotel.com. 124 units. $235–$400 double; $395–$995 suite (most less than $500). Rates include all-day cappuccino, coffee, and tea. Special promotions as low as $129 (suites as low as $279) may be available. Extra person $20. Children under 18 stay free in parents' room. AE, DC, DISC, MC, V. Parking $28 nearby. Subway: B, D, F, V to 42nd St. Pets accepted with deposit. **Amenities:** Excellent bar/lounge; access to nearby health club; concierge; business center; 24-hr. room service; dry cleaning/laundry service; video and CD libraries. *In room:* A/C, TV/VCR, CD player, dataport, hair dryer, safe, complimentary bottled water.

The Muse ★★ *Finds* Here's a boutique hotel for travelers who desire the tone and service a boutique hotel can offer, but find no appeal in the often hard-edged modern design that usually goes hand-in-hand with the concept. Whereas places like the Hudson (below) are all about attitude, the Muse has anything but.

You'll know that the Muse is something different the moment you step beyond the avowedly modern exterior into the warmly contemporary, mahogany-paneled lobby. Management has done away with the traditional front desk in favor of sit-down concierge service that makes everyone feel like an extra-special, warmly welcomed guest. An attentive bellman will familiarize you with your well-equipped room. Each one features attractive classic-meets-contemporary decor rich with warm woods and soft pastel tones; a hand-screened duvet adds an unique and arty touch. In keeping with the hotel's emphasis on "anticipatory service," everything is designed with comfort and functionality in mind. Plusses include plump featherbeds, CD players, cordless phones, business cards personalized with your name and in-house direct-dial line, and handsome, well-outfitted baths.

Off the lobby is District, one of Broadway's best new restaurants, with stellar New American cuisine from celebrity chef Sam DeMarco (First) and warm, comfortable interiors by David Rockwell (Nobu). A star on every front.

130 W. 46th St. (btwn Fifth and Sixth aves.), New York, NY 10036. ✆ **877/THE-MUSE** or 212/485-2400. Fax 212/485-2900. www.themusehotel.com. 200 units. $199–$365 double; from $395 suite. Extra person $20. AE, DC, DISC, MC, V. Parking $43. Subway: B, D, F, V to 42nd St. Pets welcomed. **Amenities:** Noted restaurant; good fitness room; concierge; business services; limited room service with overnight "midnight pantry" access; in-room massage; dry cleaning/laundry service. *In room:* A/C, TV w/pay movies, CD player, dataport and high-speed connectivity, coffeemaker, hair dryer, iron, safe.

Sofitel New York ★★ *Finds* This *très français* hotel is ideal for travelers who want it all: sophisticated style, luxury comforts, and a prime Theater District location. Rates are quite reasonable considering the high quality of the comforts, amenities, and service. The curvaceous 30-story glass tower is a brand-new construction, so there's no compromising comfort to the constrictions of a dated building. The drama begins from the moment you enter the lobby, with its soaring ceilings and streamlined European Art Moderne style. The check-in desk is tucked to the side, with adds to the lobby's sexy, loungey feel.

Public spaces lined with gallery-quality New York– and Paris-themed art leads to guest rooms that are both gorgeously outfitted and supremely comfortable. Champagne and gold tones, Art Deco-meets-modern lines, rich bird's-eye maple set an elegant vibe, while dashes of red add sex appeal. Lighting is soft and flattering, walls and windows are soundproofed. The honey-marble bathrooms are spacious and gorgeous, and appointments are 21st century all the way. The attentive management seems to have thought of everything; they've even done away with maid carts so as not to clutter the halls. The only misstep is the shortage of king beds, which occupy suites only; despite their general spaciousness, most rooms are equipped with queens.

The bilingual staff is efficient and attentive, the straight-outta-St. Germain brasserie is a thoroughly enjoyable place to dine, and the wonderful one-of-a-kind gift shop—filled with treats from both sides of the Atlantic—boasts some of Midtown's most delightful souvenirs.

45 W. 44th St. (btwn Fifth and Sixth aves.), New York, NY 10036. ✆ **800/SOFITEL** or 212/354-8844. Fax 212/354-2480. www.sofitelnewyork.com or www.sofitel.com. 398 units. $189–$329 double; from $299 suite. One child stays free in parents' room. AE, DC, MC, V. Parking $39. Subway: B, D, F, V to 42nd St. Pets accepted. **Amenities:** French brasserie with bar; exercise room; concierge; business center; 24-hr. room service; dry cleaning/laundry service. *In room:* A/C, TV w/pay movies and Internet access, CD player, dataport and high-speed connectivity, minibar, hair dryer, iron, safe.

MODERATE

Belvedere Hotel ★ *Kids* Here's another excellent choice from the Empire Hotel Group, the people behind the Upper West Side's Lucerne and Newton. Done with a sharp retro-modern-deco flair, the impressively stylish public spaces lead to sizable, comfortable, freshly renovated, and attractive rooms. Beds are nice and firm, the cherrywood furnishings and fabrics are of high quality, bathrooms are smallish but very nice, and every room has a work desk and a pantry kitchenette with minifridge, sink, and microwave (BYO utensils or go plastic). Double/doubles are big enough for friends and small families who don't mind sharing, and your kids will love you for booking a room with Nintendo and on-screen Web access. Executive-level rooms and suites boast duvet-dressed down comforters, workstations with ergonomic chairs and task lighting, CD players, and plush robes. Whether or not you go executive, ask for a high floor (eight and above) for great views, which usually cost no more (ask when booking).

On-site are a cute cafe and the festive Churrascaria Plataforma, an all-you-can-eat Brazilian steakhouse (see chapter 7). The neighborhood is the Theater District's trendiest, boasting a wealth of fantastic restaurants along Ninth Avenue and nearby Restaurant Row. Overall, the Belvedere is a great bargain if you can snare a room for less than $160 in winter, $175 or so in high season (which you usually can).

319 W. 48th St. (btwn Eighth and Ninth aves.), New York, NY 10036. ✆ **888/HOTEL58** or 212/245-7000. Fax 212/245-4455. www.newyorkhotel.com. 400 units. $135–$300 double. AAA discounts available; check website for special Internet deals (as low as $139 with breakfast at press time). AE, DC, DISC, MC, V. Parking $22.50 nearby. Subway: C, E to 50th St. **Amenities:** Notable Brazilian steakhouse; breakfast cafe; lounge; concierge; car-rental desk; self-service business center; dry cleaning/laundry service; coin-op laundry; executive-level

rooms. *In room:* A/C, TV w/pay movies, video games, and Internet access; dataport; wet bar with microwave, fridge, and coffeemaker; hair dryer; iron; safe.

Broadway Inn ★★ *Finds* More like a San Francisco B&B than a Theater District hotel, this lovely, welcoming inn is a real charmer. The second-floor lobby sets the homey, easygoing tone with stocked bookcases, cushy seating, and cafe tables where breakfast is served. The rooms are basic but comfy, outfitted in an appealing neo-deco style with firm beds, good-quality linens and textiles, and nice bathrooms (about half have showers only). The whole place is impeccably kept—neatniks won't have a quibble. Two rooms have king beds and whirlpool tubs, but the standard doubles are just fine for two if you're looking to save some dough. If there are more than two of you, or you're looking to stay a while, the suites—with pullout sofa, microwave, minifridge, and lots of closet space—are a great deal. The location can be noisy, but double-paned windows keep the rooms surprisingly peaceful; still, ask for a back-facing one if you're extra sensitive.

The inn's biggest asset is its terrific staff, who go above and beyond the call to make guests happy; they'll even give you a hot line number upon check-in so you can call while you're on the town for directions, advice, and other assistance. Service just doesn't get any better in this price range. This nicely gentrified corner of the Theater District makes a great home base, especially for theatergoers. The inn has inspired a loyal following, so reserve early. However, there's no elevator in the four-story building, so overpackers and travelers with limited mobility should book elsewhere.

264 W. 46th St. (at Eighth Ave.), New York, NY 10036. ✆ **800/826-6300** or 212/997-9200. Fax 212/768-2807. www.broadwayinn.com. 41 units. $99–$139 single; $135–$225 double; $199–$299 suite. Rates include continental breakfast. Check the website for special deals (as low as $79 single, $99 double at press time). Extra person $10. Children under 12 stay free in parents' room. AE, DC, DISC, MC, V. Parking $20 3 blocks away. Subway: A, C, E to 42nd St. **Amenities:** 2 neighboring restaurant where inn guests have special discounts; concierge; fax and copy service. *In room:* A/C, TV, dataport, fridge, hair dryer, iron.

Casablanca Hotel ★ *Value* A wealth of freebies—including breakfast; coffee, tea, and cookies all day; wine and cheese most evenings; free passes to a nearby health club with pool and sauna; and use of Internet-access PCs—make this stylish Moroccan-themed boutique hotel an excellent value. With vibrant mosaic tiles, warm woods and rattan, potted palms, and North African–themed art gracing the public spaces and guest rooms, the ambience is just right—the only thing missing is Bogart and Bergman.

The rooms aren't big, but they're nicely outfitted with comfortable platform beds, ceiling fans, two-line phones, bathrobes, and double-paned windows for quiet. The bathrooms are done in gorgeous Andalusian tile, and even the smallest is spacious enough for an oversize shower (request a tub when booking if you want one). Suites have pullout sofas that convert to single beds, but they're really too small to accommodate families. Everything is high quality, and beautiful touches like Murano glass sconces and framed Moroccan carpets in the halls add an extra flair.

Rick's Cafe is one of the city's finest hotel guest lounges, boasting a serve-yourself cappuccino machine, a fireplace, a big-screen TV, and PCs with T1 connectivity. A tiled second-floor courtyard is also ideal for summer lounging, and the rooftop deck is a perfect vantage for watching the New Year's ball drop. The staff is attentive, and the ambitious manager is constantly at work improving the property. With a sterling Theater District location as the icing on the cake, who could ask for anything more? Book well ahead, as an increasing number of happy repeat guests and corporate clients fill this place up fast.

147 W. 43rd St. (just east of Broadway), New York, NY 10036. ✆ **888/922-7225** or 212/869-1212. Fax 212/391-7585. www.casablancahotel.com. 48 units. $215–$265 double; from $295 suite. Rates include continental breakfast, all-day cappuccino, and weekday wine and cheese. Check website for Internet rates and other special deals (as low as $179 at press time). AE, DC, MC, V. Parking $25 next door. Subway: N, R, 1, 2, 3, 9 to 42nd St./Times Sq. **Amenities:** Cyber lounge; free access to New York Sports Club; concierge; business center; limited room service; dry cleaning/laundry service; video library. *In room:* A/C, TV/VCR, CD player, dataport, minibar, hair dryer, ceiling fan.

The Gorham ★ *Kids* Well located in the best section of Midtown West—close enough to the Broadway action, yet far enough from the bustle and grime that can go along with it—the Gorham is a wonderful, well-priced choice. The hotel isn't exactly stylish, but the caring management is committed to maintaining the fresh feel and excellent value. The hotel caters to business travelers and families alike, and attracts lots of return guests. All of the large, pleasingly contemporary rooms have fully equipped kitchenettes and marble bathrooms. The suites feature a separate sitting room with a pullout sofa and an extra TV, plus a whirlpool tub.

There may not be a better hotel in the city for families, especially at this price. Parlor Suites boast a separate alcove-style sitting area that's perfect for a crib, while the pullout sofa in the same area suits caregivers or children. Notify your hotel that you're coming with a little one and the "Baby Concierge" will outfit your room with a crib and a stroller, and greet you with a welcome diaper bag filled with such goodies as no-tears shampoo and baby wipes. The Baby Concierge can also supply toys, books, and stuffed animals; older kids have Nintendo and a "pillow fight" pillow menu to occupy them. Available rollaways help expand the options for families.

The Gorham regularly offers theater packages and discounts to city cultural attractions, which only add to the thoughtful service and good value. You're also unlikely to find a better-connected concierge at this price—a real boon if you're in the market for hard-to-get theater tickets.

136 W. 55th St. (btwn Sixth and Seventh aves.), New York, NY 10019. ✆ **800/735-0710** or 212/245-1800. Fax 212/582-8332. www.gorhamhotel.com. 115 units. $189–$285 double; from $219 suite. Packages usually on offer (as low as $179 double, $209 suite at press time). Extra person $20. Children under 16 stay free in parents' room. AE, DC, MC, V. Parking $33. Subway: N, R, Q, W to 57th St./Seventh Ave.; F to 57th St. **Amenities:** Restaurant/bar (Northern Italian); breakfast room; exercise room; concierge; secretarial services; limited room service; babysitting; dry cleaning/laundry service. *In room:* A/C, TV/VCR and video games, fax/copier, dataport and high-speed connectivity; kitchenette with fridge, coffeemaker, and microwave, hair dryer, iron, safe.

Hotel Edison This Theater District dowager no longer qualifies as the neighborhood's best hotel value, but it's still a reasonably good deal. A grand, block-long Art Deco–style lobby leads to rooms that have been pretty nicely renovated in recent years. Don't expect much more than the basics, but you will find a firm bed, motel decor that's more attractive than most in this category, and a clean, perfectly adequate tile bathroom. Most double rooms feature two twins or a full bed, but there are some queens; request one at booking and show up early in the day for your best chance at one. Quad rooms are larger, with two doubles. The hotel fills up with tour groups from the world over, but since it has nearly 900 rooms, you can carve out some space if you call early enough.

Off the attractive deco-style lobby is the Cafe Edison, a hoot of an old-style Polish deli that's a favorite among ladder-climbing theater types and down-market ladies who lunch; Sofia's, a just-fine Continental restaurant; and the Rum House for cocktails and live entertainment most nights.

228 W. 47th St. (btwn Broadway and Eighth Ave.), New York, NY 10036. ✆ **800/637-7070** or 212/840-5000. Fax 212/596-6850. www.edisonhotelnyc.com. 850 units. $150–$170 single; $170–$200 double; $185–$230 triple or quad; $225–$275 suite. Extra person $15. AE, DC, DISC, MC, V. Parking $35. Subway: N, R to 49th St.; 1, 9 to 50th St. **Amenities:** 2 restaurants (Polish deli, Continental); cocktail lounge; exercise room; tour desk; dry cleaning/laundry service. *In room:* A/C, TV, dataport.

Hotel Metro ★★ *Kids* The Metro is the hands-down best choice in Midtown for those who don't want to sacrifice either style or comfort for affordability. This lovely Art Deco–style jewel has larger rooms than you'd expect for the price. They're outfitted with smart retro furnishings, playful fabrics, fluffy pillows, and smallish but beautifully appointed marble bathrooms, and alarm clocks. Only about half the bathrooms have tubs, but the others have shower stalls big enough for two (junior suites have whirlpool tubs). The family room is an ingenious invention: A two-room suite that has a second bedroom in lieu of a sitting area; families on tighter budgets can opt for a roomy double/double.

The neo-deco design gives the whole place an air of New York glamour that I've not otherwise seen in this price range. A great collection of black-and-white photos, from Man Ray classics to Garbo and Dietrich portraits, adds to the vibe. The comfy, fire-lit library/lounge area off the lobby, where complimentary buffet breakfast is laid out and the coffeepot's on all day, is a popular hangout. Service is attentive, and the well-furnished rooftop terrace boasts a breathtaking view of the Empire State Building, and makes a great place to order up room service from the stylish—and very good—Metro Grill. One of my all-time favorites—highly recommendable.

45 W. 35th St. (btwn Fifth and Sixth aves.), New York, NY 10001. ✆ **800/356-3870** or 212/947-2500. Fax 212/279-1310. www.hotelmetronyc.com. 179 units. $150–$250 double; $165–$300 triple or quad; $200–$350 family room; $225–$400 suite. Rates include continental breakfast. Check with airlines and other package operators for great-value package deals. Extra person $25. One child under 14 stays free in parents' room. AE, DC, MC, V. Parking $17 nearby. Subway: B, D, F, V, N, R to 34th St. **Amenities:** 1 recommended restaurant (New American); alfresco rooftop bar in summer; good fitness room; salon; limited room service; dry cleaning/laundry service. *In room:* A/C, TV, dataport, fridge, hair dryer, iron.

Hudson ★ Unveiled in October 2000, the newest hotel from celebrity hotelier Ian Schrager instantly became the white-hot center of the style universe—two years later, it still is. Schrager has managed to transform a decidedly unattractive plain-vanilla structure on a decidedly unhip block into Scene Central, attracting an adoring crowd and star-studded events (including Hillary Clinton's birthday bash) to its wild Philippe Starck–designed digs. If you're looking for a scene, book now, because you've found it.

The vibrant, eye-popping hotel boasts a postmodern Ivy League–on-acid plan that radiates youthful energy. The ivy-draped lobby and the second-level "Private Park" deck—the best outdoor space in any Big Apple hotel—serve as the quad from which everything radiates, including the red-hot Hudson Bar (see chapter 11), the classic-goes-Warhol Library, and the love-it-or-hate-it cafeteria-style restaurant. A riotous Louis XV–meets-*Barbarella* design sensibility makes every space a delightful surprise.

Good thing about the great public spaces, because many of the guest rooms are woefully petite (think budget cabin on a Carnival cruise and you'll get the picture). There's no arguing with their beauty, though: They were designed on the retro-romantic ocean liner model, with rich African Makore paneling, hardwood floors, beautifully made white-on-white beds, clever bedside lamps featuring translucent art by Francesco Clemente, a petite steel desk, and studded white-leather steamer trunk upholstery. Ultra efficient appointments make even the smallest feel like a treat. Word is that the service is less than attentive, however, so don't expect much. A style hound's delight, but anybody who needs space or service should book elsewhere.

356 W. 58th St. (btwn Eighth and Ninth aves.), New York, NY 10019. © **800/444-4786** or 212/554-6000. Fax 212/554-6001. www.ianschragerhotels.com. 1,000 units. $95–$295 double; $350–$450 studio. AE, DC, DISC, MC, V. Parking $46. Subway: 1, 9, A, B, C, D to 59th St./Columbus Circle. **Amenities:** Restaurant; 2 ultra-chic bars; 24-hr. state-of-the-art fitness center; 24-hr. concierge; business center; room service (6:30am–midnight); dry cleaning/laundry service; CD library. *In room:* A/C, TV w/pay movies, CD player, dataport and high-speed connectivity, minibar, hair dryer, safe.

WJ Hotel Situated in the heart of a lovely bistro-lined block, this newly renovated hotel emphasizes the hipness in its newly gentrified Hell's Kitchen neighborhood, which has come a long way in recent years. Nearby Ninth Avenue has evolved into one of Manhattan's best affordable dining strips, and the Theater District is a walk away.

Anyone who stayed here when the WJ was the Washington Jefferson won't recognize the joint. The lobby has tripled in size and taken on a warm and welcoming ambience, with a friendly, snappily attired staff and more than a dash of designer style. Snazzy red-carpeted halls lead to rooms that are *small*—don't say I didn't warn you—but very attractively outfitted in a palette of soft grays. Nice touches include platform beds with generous cushioned headboards and fluffy goose-down comforters. The gorgeous limestone-and-slate bathrooms are stylish and relatively spacious, although some have showers only. Score one of the 18 king rooms if you can; they're roomy and boast a pullout love seat as well as a Jacuzzi tub in the bathroom.

All in all, a perfectly decent bet if you want all-new comforts and an affordable base in the heart of the action. Ask for a back room if you crave quiet.

318 W. 51st St. (btwn Eighth and Ninth aves.), New York, NY 10019. © **888/567-7550** or 212/246-7550. Fax 212/246-7622. www.wjhotel.com. 132 units. $119 single; $159–$295 double. Rates include continental breakfast with Krispy Kreme doughnuts (subject to change at any time, so call before you count on it). Ask about special deals (from $99 at press time). AE, DC, DISC, MC, V. Parking $25 nearby. Subway: C, E to 50th St. **Amenities:** Exercise room; limited room service; restaurant in the works at press time. *In room:* A/C, TV w/pay movies, video games, and Internet access, dataport, hair dryer, iron, safe.

INEXPENSIVE

In addition to the choices below, you might also consider the **Comfort Inn Manhattan,** 42 W. 35th St. (© **800/228-5150** or 212/947-0200; www.comfortinnmanhattan.com or www.comfortinn.com), a characterless but comfortable member of the reliable chain that includes free continental breakfast in its daily rates. The **Best Western President,** 234 W. 48th St., between Broadway and Eighth Avenue (© **800/826-4667** or 212/246-8800; www.bestnyhotels.com or www.bestwestern.com), is also reliably comfortable if nothing special; executive-level rooms have extra space and verve. Another chain hotel worth trying is the **Days Hotel Midtown,** 790 Eighth Ave., at 48th Street (© **800/544-8313** or 212/581-7000; www.daysinn.com). The new French bistro Pigalle (see chapter 7) gives the hotel a better-than-budget flair, and the motel-like rooms are well worth the $105 to $130 rate you might be able to snare at the last minute or in slower seasons. Be sure to ask about senior, AAA, corporate, and promotional rates at all three hotels, and check for online booking discounts.

Americana Inn ★ *Value* The cheapest hotel from the Empire Hotel Group—the people behind the Belvedere, the Lucerne, and the Newton among other top-notch properties—is a star in the budget-basic category. Linoleum floors give the rooms a somewhat unfortunate institutional quality, but the hotel is professionally run and immaculately kept. Rooms are mostly spacious, with good-size closets, private sinks, and an alarm built into the TV; the beds are the most comfortable I've found at this price. Most rooms come with a double bed or two twins; a few can accommodate three guests in two twin beds and a pullout sofa or in three twins. One hall bathroom accommodates every three rooms or so; all are spacious and spotless. Every floor has a common kitchenette with microwave, stove, and fridge (BYO cooking tools and utensils, or go plastic). The five-story building has an elevator and four rooms are accessible for travelers with disabilities. The Garment District location is convenient for Midtown sightseeing and shopping; ask for a back-facing room away from the street noise.

69 W. 38th St. (at Sixth Ave.), New York, NY 10018. ✆ **888/HOTEL-58** or 212/840-6700. Fax 212/840-1830. www.newyorkhotel.com. 50 units (all with shared bathroom). $65–$75 single; $75–$115 double. Check website for specials (winter rates as low as $60 double). Extra person $10. AE, MC, V. Parking $25–$35 nearby. Subway: B, D, F, V to 34th St. Common kitchen. *In room:* A/C, TV, hair dryer (ask reception).

Comfort Inn Midtown *Finds* A major renovation turned the formerly dour Hotel Remington into a agreeably value-oriented Comfort Inn back in 1998. Rates can climb to ridiculous highs in autumn or at Christmastime, but low-season rates often make the rooms one of Midtown's best bargains. The petite but comfortable and nicely outfitted guest rooms boast neo-Shaker furnishings, blackout drapes, and good marble-and-tile bathrooms; a few have showers only, so request a tub if it matters to you. Rollaways aren't available, so families are better off elsewhere. Don't expect much in the way of service, but the location is excellent—just steps from Times Square, Rockefeller Center, Broadway theaters, and a wealth of dining options.

Note: As of August 2001, the Comfort Inn Midtown has taken a bold step forward by declaring itself a non-smoking hotel. Every room previously in the "smoking allowed" category has been thoroughly disinfected to remove remaining cigarette odors.

129 W. 46th St. (btwn Sixth Ave. and Broadway), New York, NY 10036. ✆ **800/567-7720** or 212/221-2600. Fax 212/790-2760. www.applecorehotels.com or www.comfortinn.com. 79 units. $89–$329 double. Rates include continental breakfast. Ask about senior, AAA, corporate, and promotional discounts; check www.comfortinn.com for online booking discounts. Extra person $10. Children under 14 stay free in parents' room. AE, DC, DISC, MC, V. Parking $20 nearby. Subway: 1, 2, 3, 9 to 42nd St./Times Sq.; N, R to 49th St.; B, D, F, V to 47–50th sts./Rockefeller Center. **Amenities:** Small but satisfying fitness room; self-serve business center; dry cleaning/laundry service. *In room:* A/C, TV, dataport, coffeemaker, hair dryer, iron.

Mayfair Hotel Be prepared—the rooms here are *tiny.* The elevator is, too. That's it for the bad news. Now the good: The Mayfair is one of the Theater District's friendliest and best-kept budget hotels, and the location couldn't be better. Each room boasts a smallish but nice black-and-white tile bathroom (all but a few singles have tub/shower combos) and unstylish but perfectly nice decor. The wood-paneled lobby is more elegant than most in this price range; just off it is the cute French bistro Le Garrick, an attraction in its own right. A super-nice staff is merely the icing on the cake. Don't be frightened off by the rack-rate range; while prices can soar in peak seasons, rates generally stay well below $200 (which they should—if you're quoted more, stay elsewhere).

242 W. 49th St. (btwn Broadway and Eighth Ave.), New York, NY 10019. ✆ **800/55-MAYFAIR** or 212/586-0300. Fax 212/307-5226. www.mayfairnewyork.com. 78 units. $90–$250 single or double ($100–$150 in

most seasons). Corporate rates $10–$20 less; also check for low-season specials. AE, DC, DISC, MC, V. Parking $18 nearby. Subway: 1, 9, C, E to 50th St. **Amenities:** Restaurant (adorable and well-regarded French bistro); concierge. *In room:* A/C, TV, dataport, hair dryer, iron, safe.

Red Roof Inn ★★ *Value* Manhattan's first Red Roof Inn opened in mid-2000, and it offers welcome relief from Midtown's high-priced hotel scene. The hotel occupies a former office building that was gutted and laid out fresh, allowing for more spacious rooms and bathrooms than you'll usually find in this price category. The high-ceilinged lobby feels smarter than most in this price category, and elevators are quiet and efficient. What's more, in-room amenities are better than most competitors', and furnishings are fresh, brand-new, and comfortable. The location—on a bright, bustling block lined with nice hotels and affordable Korean restaurants, just a stone's throw from the Empire State Building and Herald Square—is excellent. It's usually easy to score a room for less than $150 if you book well in advance; be sure to compare the rates offered by Apple Core Hotel's reservation line (the management company) and those quoted on Red Roof's national reservation line and website, as they can vary significantly. Complimentary continental breakfast adds to the good value.

6 W. 32nd St. (btwn Broadway and Fifth Ave.), New York, NY 10001. ✆ **800/567-7720,** 800/RED-ROOF, or 212/643-7100. Fax 212/643-7101. www.applecorehotels.com or www.redroof.com. 171 units. $89–$329 double (usually less than $159). Rates include continental breakfast. Children 13 and under stay free in parents' room. AE, DC, DISC, MC, V. Parking $22. Subway: B, D, F, V, N, R to 34th St. **Amenities:** Pleasant breakfast room; mezzanine-level wine and beer lounge; modern exercise room; concierge; business center; dry cleaning/laundry service. *In room:* A/C; TV w/pay movies, video games, and Internet access, dataport, fridge, coffeemaker, hair dryer, iron.

Skyline Hotel *Kids* This nice, newly renovated motor hotel offers predictable comforts and some uncommon extras—free storage parking (easily worth $25 or more a day) and a lovely indoor pool—that make it a very good value. A pleasant lobby leads to motel-standard rooms that are a far cry from stylish, but are bigger than most in this price range. They boast decent-size closets, small work desks (in most), and double-paned windows that open to let fresh air in, and shut out a surprising amount of street noise when closed. Some rooms have brand-new bathrooms, but the older ones are still fine. The junior suites are basically one large room with a pullout sofa bed, but the full suites have a sitting room with a pullout sofa and a big separate room with two double beds and an extra TV, making them great for families. Everything is very well kept. The pool has a nicely tiled deck and plush deck chairs, but it's only open limited hours, so call ahead if it matters.

725 Tenth Ave. (at 49th St.), New York, NY 10019. ✆ **800/433-1982** or 212/586-3400. Fax 212/582-4604. www.skylinehotelny.com. 230 units. $109–$209 double or suite. Check website or inquire about special rates (as low as $89 at press time). Extra person $15. Children 14 and under stay free in parents' room. AE, DC, DISC, MC, V. Free storage parking (charge for in/out privileges). Subway: A, C, E to 50th St. Pets accepted with $200 deposit. **Amenities:** Restaurant (American/Italian); bar with extensive beer list, big-screen TV, and live entertainment; indoor pool; Gray Line tour desk; Internet-access machine in lobby. *In room:* A/C, TV w/pay movies, video games, and Internet access, hair dryer (on request), iron (on request), safe.

Travel Inn *Kids* Extras like a huge outdoor pool and sundeck, a sunny and up-to-date fitness room, and absolutely free parking (with in and out privileges!) make the Travel Inn another terrific deal, similar to the one offered by the Skyline Hotel (see above). Like the Skyline, the Travel Inn may not be loaded with personality, but it does offer the clean, bright regularity of a good chain hotel—an attractive trait in a city where "quirky" is the catchword at most affordable hotels. Rooms are oversized and comfortably furnished, with extra firm beds and

Family-Friendly Hotels

Doubletree Guest Suites (p. 126) Your young ones will have their very own Kids Club (for ages 3–12), with a playroom, an arts-and-crafts center, and computer and video games. For after playtime, there's an entire floor of childproof suites, complete with kitchenettes and living rooms, for just about the same price you'd pay for a regular room in another Theater District hotel of this high quality.

Gershwin Hotel (p. 123) This funky Flatiron District hotel looks like the exclusive domain of the artsy crowd at first glance, but it actually suits wallet-watching families extremely well. Parents in search of a high space-to-dollar ratio will love the family room, a two-room suite that nicely accommodates Mom and Dad in a queen bed in one bedroom, two kids in two twins in the adjacent one.

The Gorham (p. 131) This well-located Midtown choice is another good deal for families, since the large rooms are big enough for two queen beds, and the well-priced parlor suites feature crib alcoves and pullout sofas to accommodate the kids. A Baby Concierge will make sure Mom and Dad want for nothing—they'll make sure your room comes with its own stroller (no need to tote one from home) and even stock the fully equipped kitchenette with formula upon request. Nintendo on the TV and an honest-to-goodness "pillow fight" pillow menu will keep Junior occupied for hours.

Gramercy Park Hotel (p. 122) There are no special amenities that make this moderately priced, old-world hotel particularly kid-friendly, but you'll see a lot of youngsters cruising the wood-paneled lobby nonetheless. That's because parents end up with a lot of space for their money here: Standard doubles are big enough for two double beds, still with play space to spare, and some suites have pullout sofas that make them large enough to sleep six.

Helmsley Middletowne (p. 147) This affordable Midtown East hotel isn't exactly overloaded with amenities, but it can offer families one thing that's consistently hard to come by in this city: space. Check out the prices on the 1- and 2-bedroom suites, a welcome relief from cramming a family of four into a single hotel room.

work desks; even the smallest double is sizable and has a roomy bathroom, and double/doubles make great affordable shares for families. A total renovation over the last couple of years has made everything feel like new, even the nicely tiled bathrooms. The neighborhood has gentrified nicely and isn't as far-flung as you might think: Off-Broadway theaters and great affordable restaurants are at hand, and it's just a 10-minute walk to the Theater District.

515 W. 42nd St. (just west of Tenth Ave.), New York, NY 10036. ✆ **888/HOTEL58**, 800/869-4630, or 212/695-7171. Fax 212/967-5025. www.newyorkhotel.com. 160 units. $125–$200 double. AAA discounts available; check website for special Internet deals (as low as $105 at press time). Extra person $10. Children under 16 stay free in parents' room. AE, DC, DISC, MC, V. Free self-parking. Subway: A, C, E to 42nd St./Port Authority. **Amenities:** Coffee shop; terrific outdoor pool with deck chairs and lifeguard in season; fitness center; Gray Line tour desk; 24-hr. room service. *In room:* A/C, TV, dataport, hair dryer, iron.

Hilton Times Square (p. 127) This brand-new hotel is located in the heart of newly gentrified Times Square. Your kids will love the easy access to Madame Tussaud's Wax Museum (next door), the state-of-the-art Broadway City arcade (across the street), and two 25-screen movieplexes (next door and across the street)—not to mention the proximity to the rest of Times Square's neon-lit attractions. Connector rooms and suites with pullout sofas are great for families, but even standard rooms with two doubles are large enough to accommodate you and the kids.

Hotel Beacon (p. 152) Ideally located in one of the city's most kid-friendly neighborhoods, the Beacon is one of the best deals in town for families. Fitted with two double beds, virtually all of the spacious standard rooms are big enough for wallet-watching families. The well-outfitted 1- and 2-bedroom suites are great bargains that give families room to spread out. Every room features a fully equipped kitchenette that makes breakfast and snack time a cinch, and there's a laundromat on site to make life easier.

Hotel Metro (p. 132) This lovely and affordable Art Deco–inspired Midtown hotel is an excellent choice for families, thanks to the hotel's own creation, the family room: a two-room suite with a second bedroom in lieu of a sitting area. This configuration gives parents their privacy, and kids get their own real beds instead of a sleeper sofa. Families on tighter budgets can opt instead for a roomy and well-priced room with two double beds.

The Milburn (p. 155) This neighbor to the Beacon also offers rooms and suites with kitchenettes, but for even less. The Milburn may not be quite as nice as the Beacon, but it offers equal value for your dollar, and the one-bedroom suites with a pullout queen sofa are a great bargain for families.

Skyline Hotel and **Travel Inn** (p. 135) Hauling the kids to town in the minivan? You can take advantage of the free parking at these two nice, newly renovated motor hotels. Even if you're not sporting your own wheels, you'll like the family-size rooms, and the kids will love the pools at playtime (a rarity in affordable hotels).

9 Midtown East & Murray Hill

Midtown East offers a central location that's more sophisticated, more attractive, and less touristy than Midtown West; some of the city's finest and most historic luxury hotels are here (including the Plaza and the Waldorf). Quiet, residential Murray Hill offers wallet-watching visitors relief from the wild price fluctuations of Times Square. Beware, though, because traveling across town for dining and theater can be a drag at rush hour.

To find the hotels described in this section, see p. 118.

VERY EXPENSIVE

Four Seasons Hotel New York ★★ Hollywood meets Manhattan in the grand but frosty lobby of this ultraluxury, ultramodern, multiple-award-winning hotel. Designed by überarchitect I. M. Pei in 1993, the modernist tower of honey-hued limestone rises 52 stories, making it the city's tallest hotel and providing hundreds of rooms with a view. As soon as you enter the soaring lobby, with its marble floors and backlit onyx ceiling, you'll immediately know this place is special—even in superluxe New York, where anything goes.

The completely soundproofed guest rooms are among the city's largest, averaging 600 square feet. Each is beautifully furnished in an understated but plush contemporary style and has an entrance foyer, a sitting area, an oversize oval desk with two leather chairs, custom built-ins, coffered ceilings, and massive windows (50% of which boast Central Park views). About 2 dozen of the priciest rooms also have terraces. The mammoth Florentine marble bathrooms have soaking tubs that fill in 60 seconds, and separate showers with pressure controls. Other special touches include goose-down pillows, Frette-made beds, oversize bath towels, and cushy robes, plus multidisk CD players in suites. You'd expect less? For this much money, you deserve *more.*

Awarded three stars by the *New York Times,* first-rate, Mediterranean-tinged Fifty-Seven, Fifty-Seven is a favorite among the city's elite for power-breakfasting and lunching, while there's hardly a more chic place in town for a martini than the bar.

57 E. 57th St. (btwn Park and Madison aves.), New York, NY 10022. ✆ **800/819-5053,** 800/487-3769, or 212/758-5700. Fax 212/758-5711. www.fourseasons.com. 368 units. $585–$865 double; from $1,350 suite. Weekend rates from $435; also check for value-added packages and other deals. Extra person $50. AE, DC, DISC, MC, V. Parking $42. Subway: N, R, 4, 5, 6 to 60th St. **Amenities:** Restaurant (an excellent and expensive New American grill); martini bar with evening entertainment; lobby lounge for afternoon tea and light fare; 5,000-sq.-ft. spa and fitness center with whirlpool, steam, and sauna; children's program; 24-hr. concierge; business center with secretarial services; 24-hr. room service; in-room massage; babysitting; dry cleaning/laundry service with 1-hr. pressing; courtesy limo. *In room:* A/C, TV w/pay movies, dataport and high-speed connectivity; minibar, hair dryer, safe.

The Peninsula–New York ★★★ After a $45 million renovation, the Peninsula reopened in November 1998 as a state-of-the-art stunner. Inside, all that's left of the beaux arts past is the marvelous wedding-cake ceiling in the lobby. Work your way past the redecorated public floors and everything's brand new; the guest room floors were totally gutted and laid out afresh, allowing for high-speed wiring, better room configurations, and what may be the most fabulous bathrooms in the city.

The decor is a rich mix of Art Nouveau, vibrant Asian elements (including gorgeous silk bedcovers), and contemporary art. Every room boasts lots of storage and counter space, plus fabulous linens that include the cushiest bathrobes I've seen. But the real news is the technology, which includes a room-wide speaker system and mood lighting; an executive workstation with desk-level inputs, fax, and dual-line speakerphones; a bedside panel for everything, from climate controls to the DO NOT DISTURB sign; even a door-side weather display. But wait, there's more: In the huge marble bathrooms, a tub-level panel allows you to control the speaker system, answer the phone, and, if you're in any room above the lowest (superior) level, control the bathroom TV. Simply marvelous—but why go this far and put VCRs and CD players in the suites only? First-rate food service and a faultless concierge desk ("We'll do anything guests ask, as long as it's legal") round out the fabulousness. The tri-level rooftop Peninsula Spa is one of the biggest (35,500 sq. ft.) and best spa-and-health clubs in town.

700 Fifth Ave. (at 55th St.), New York, NY 10019. ✆ **800/262-9467** or 212/956-2888. Fax 212/903-3949. www.peninsula.com. 241 units. $550–$690 double; from $770 suite. Winter weekend package rates from

$350 at press time. Extra person $50. Children under 12 stay free in parents' room. AE, DC, DISC, MC, V. Valet parking $45. Subway: E, F to Fifth Ave. Pets accepted. **Amenities:** 2 restaurants (Modern French, casual bistro); library-style lounge for afternoon tea and cocktails; spectacular rooftop bar; trilevel rooftop health club and spa with heated pool, exercise classes, whirlpool, sauna, and sundeck; 24-hr. concierge; business center; 24-hr. room service; in-room massage; babysitting; dry cleaning/laundry service. *In room:* A/C, TV w/pay movies, fax/copier/printer, dataport and T1 connectivity, minibar, hair dryer, laptop-size safe, complimentary "water bar" with 5 choices of bottled water.

The Sherry-Netherland ★★★ *Finds* For a taste of genteel New York apartment living, come to the Sherry-Netherland. Housed in a wonderful 1927 neo-Romanesque building overlooking Fifth Avenue and Central Park, the Sherry is one of a kind: It's both a first-class hotel and a quietly elegant residential building where the guest rooms are privately owned co-ops. As a result, the rooms vary greatly in style, but each is grandly proportioned with high ceilings, big bathrooms, and walk-in closets. These are the largest rooms I've seen, and every one features high-quality furnishings and art. About half are suites with kitchenettes that have a cook top or microwave, often both. The hotel is expensive, but at least you get a lot for your dollar here; what's more, it's in top-notch form after an $18 million refurbishment in 2000.

The most wonderful thing about the Sherry is its homeyness—even the standard doubles have a residential feel. You'll pay more for a lighter, park- or street-facing room; the views are stunning, but the lower floors can be noisy for light sleepers. Interior-facing rooms are darker and quieter but no less fabulous, and a lot cheaper; one of my favorites is no. 814, an Art Deco–contemporary one-bedroom with a gorgeous marble bathroom, a terrific kitchen with bar, and a wealth of luxurious space. If you'd prefer a more traditionally styled room, let the excellent staff know. The hotel is old-world formal but not the least bit stuffy.

Packed with Armani-suited moguls, million-dollar models, and East Side denizens, Cipriani's is the ultimate power spot; the wildly expensive food is excellent (especially the pappardelle with in-season mushrooms), as is the tuxedoed service.

781 Fifth Ave. (at 59th St.), New York, NY 10022. ✆ **800/247-4377** or 212/355-2800. Fax 212/319-4306. www.sherrynetherland.com. 77 units. $295–$525 double; from $595 1- and 2-bedroom suite. Rates include continental breakfast at Cipriani's. Children stay free in parents' room. AE, DC, DISC, MC, V. Parking $40. Subway: N, R to Fifth Ave. Pets accepted. **Amenities:** Acclaimed, expensive restaurant; fitness room; concierge; business center; salon; 18-hr. room service; in-room massage; babysitting; dry cleaning/laundry service; video library. *In room:* A/C, TV/VCR, fax, fridge with free soft drinks.

EXPENSIVE

In addition to the choices below, consider the **Sheraton Russell,** 45 Park Ave., at 37th Street in tranquil, residential Murray Hill (✆ **800/325-3535** or 212/685-7676; www.sheraton.com). This intimate, old-world hotel is Sheraton's finest entry in the Manhattan market; it's also far more civilized and distinctive than you might expect from the brand. With its very own crackling fireplace, the mahogany-paneled sitting room off the lobby will feel like your very own elegant library. Rooms are very well outfitted, and service is faultless.

You might also check out this stylish matching twin set: **W The Court/W The Tuscany** (✆ **877/W-HOTELS,** 212/685-1100, or 212/685-1600; www.whotels.com). Midtown East also boasts the very first of Starwood's chic chain of corporate boutique hotels, **W New York** (✆ **877/W-HOTELS** or 212/755-1200). For details on all three hotels, see the box called "The Wonderful World of W" on p. 140.

The Wonderful World of W

With it fledgling chain of W Hotels, Starwood Hotels & Resorts—the folks behind Westin, Sheraton, St. Regis, and other big-name brands—has managed to blend the best of boutique hotels—intimacy, individualism, and attention-getting restaurants and bars—with the best of what a chain hotel can offer: namely, functionality, reliability, and attentive service that meets the needs of business and leisure travelers alike.

New York is home to five non-conforming members of the chain that nevertheless share common traits. Guest rooms boast bold angular furnishings, vibrant color accents, and luxury comforts that include celestial copies of sister chain Westin's Heavenly Bed; technology galore, including a 27-inch TV with web access and an oversized work desk with high-speed connectivity for laptop-toters; and one of the best minibars in the business. Each W has a front-and-center restaurant that's garnered raves, plus a sizzling bar scene crafted by cocktail-hour impresario Rande Gerber (Mr. Cindy Crawford).

The first-ever W hotel, **W New York,** 541 Lexington Ave., between 49th and 50th streets (✆ 212/755-1200), was conceived as a nature-inspired oasis in the urban jungle. At its heart is a living room–style lobby overflowing with warmth and light. You'll need it, because guest rooms are *small*—too small. Still, there's no denying the lasting fabulousness of celebrity restaurateur Drew Nieporent's healthy-gourmet Heartbeat, Gerber's ultra-popular Whiskey Blue, and the heavenly Away Spa, with its Zen-serene ambience and extensive treatment menu.

I prefer the rooms at **W The Court** and **W The Tuscany** ★, a W twin set at 120–130 E. 39th St., at Lexington Avenue (✆ 212/685-1100 or 212/685-1600). W's designers rid themselves of the previous hotel's high-minded nature concept and just went glam here; the results are big rooms bursting with sex appeal. The Court boasts Nieporent's sleek Icon restaurant, while Gerber's new Cherry—the first of his lounges to serve food—has made a splash over at The Tuscany.

Überarchitect David Rockwell has transformed the magnificent 1911 Guardian Life building overlooking leafy Union Square into the **W Union Square** ★, 201 Park Ave. South (✆ 212/253-9119), where he has successfully fused original beaux arts detailing with bold, clean-lined modernism and a relaxing, grown-up air. Rooms boast distinctive touches like luminous mother-of-pearl counters in the baths. Star chef Todd English's Mediterranean-accented Olives is one of the best hotel restaurants in town and Gerber's dark and sultry Underbar is just downstairs.

Newest on the scene is **W Times Square** ★★ in the heart of the Theater District at 1567 Broadway, at 47th Street (✆ 212/407-2975). Conceived as the new W flagship, it's the hippest of the bunch, ultra-sleek and supercool. Everything has been pumped up here; you'll even find a DVD player in every room. Supermod seafooder Blue Fin won two precious *New York Times* stars out of the gate, and the Whiskey is an even better realization than Gerber's original hotspot. Don't be surprised if you see some MTV-familiar faces in the loungey lobby.

To make a reservation at any of the Big Apple's W Hotels, call ✆ **877/W-HOTELS** or visit **www.whotels.com**.

The Avalon ★ *Finds* This mostly suite-filled boutique hotel is one of the city's real hidden gems. This amenity-laden ode to luxury offers one of the finest in-room amenities you'll find in any city hotel: 5-foot body pillows. The George Patero–designed interiors are attractively done in a muted palette and a sophisticated but comfy Americana style. The basic doubles (there are only 20) are on the small side, but they come with good work desks with ergonomically correct chairs, two-line speakerphones with direct-dial number, and desk-level inputs; double-paned windows to block out noise; Egyptian cotton and Irish linens; marble bathrooms; fluffy Frette bathrobes; and even umbrellas. All suites have pullout sofas and two TVs; expect even more in the most expensive ones, such as whirlpool tubs, cordless phones, and Bose radios. The stylish staff is professional, if a little aloof; still, you can expect to have all your desires met. The rates have come down to earth in the past years, making this a good value for travelers looking for luxury, and special rates can be a bona fide steal.

16 E. 32nd St. (btwn Fifth and Madison aves.), New York, NY 10016. ✆ **888/HI-AVALON** or 212/299-7000. Fax 212/299-7001. www.theavalonny.com. 100 units. $200–$350 double; $240–$400 junior suite; $300–$600 deluxe or executive suite. Rates include continental breakfast. Call or check website for money-saving deals (as low as $179 at press time). Extra person $20. Children under 12 stay free in parents' room. AE, DC, MC, V. Parking $35. Subway: B, D, F, V, N, R to 34th St.; 6 to 33rd St. **Amenities:** Restaurant; bar; library-style breakfast room; exercise room, access to nearby health club; business center; room service (7am–midnight); dry cleaning/laundry service; executive-level rooms. *In room:* A/C, TV w/pay movies, dataport and high-speed connectivity, minibar, coffeemaker, hair dryer, iron, laptop-size safe.

The Benjamin ★★★ Brand new in 2000, this sophisticated boutique-style hotel is one of my absolute Big Apple favorites. The Benjamin boasts soothing, beautifully styled neoclassical-meets-21st-century rooms that are some of the best outfitted in town. Serious planning was put into the design and layout, with one eye to comfort and the other to technology; you'd have to book in at the much pricier Peninsula to guarantee similar quality, service, and high-tech amenities.

First, the bed: a custom-designed Serta bed luxuriously dressed in Frette linens and down duvet, with a cushioned headboard. For the waking hours, you'll have one of the city's biggest and best-outfitted workstations, with desk-level inputs. The 27-inch TV has Web TV, Sony PlayStation, and front-access inputs for CD players and VCRs (available on request). The smallish white marble bathrooms are designed to maximum advantage, with good counter and shelf space, ingenious shower caddies with shaving mirrors, and even under-the-counter TV speakers so you can listen to the *Today* show while you shave. But wait—there's more: Every room has a gourmet kitchenette stocked with goodies like popcorn and gummy bears; a Bose Wave radio; Frette robes; and big closets. Upgrading to a studio will simply get you a king bed instead of a queen and some additional floor space, while a suite will garner you a CD stereo and a sitting area with a terrifically cozy sofa and a cocooning mohair chair that you'll never want to leave. Larry Forgione's An American Place is one of the city's best contemporary American restaurants—the devil's food cake is to die for, and you can even have it delivered to your room—and the divine full-service spa is an attraction in its own right. Excellent on every front.

125 E. 50th St. (at Lexington Ave.), New York, NY 10022. ✆ **888/4-BENJAMIN,** 212/320-8002, or 212/715-2500. Fax 212/715-2525. www.thebenjamin.com. 209 units. $295–$420 standard double; $315–$465 studio double; from $480 suite. Call or check website for special weekend-stay offers. AE, DC, DISC, MC, V. Parking $35. Subway: 6 to 51st St.; E, F to Lexington Ave. Pets 35 lb. or less accepted. **Amenities:** Excellent New American restaurant; cocktail lounge; state-of-the-art exercise room; full-service Woodstock Spa and Wellness Center; concierge; business services; 24-hr. room service; dry cleaning/valet service. *In room:* A/C; TV w/pay movies, video games, and Internet access, fax/copier/printer, dataport and high-speed connectivity, kitchenette with minibar, microwave, coffeemaker, china, laptop-size safe.

Crowne Plaza at the United Nations ★ Here's a very nice chain hotel that boasts all the expected comforts, plus a surprising bit of personality. Housed in a lovely neo-Tudor building, the guest rooms have all been renovated within the last couple of years; they're very well done, with excellent-quality linens and fabrics (the towels could be plusher, but the sheets are fabulous) and such extras as two-line phones, good work space, bedside control panels for everything from air to lights, double-paned windows to shut out street noise, trouser presses, and Italian marble bathrooms. Executive rooms and suites also feature whirlpool tubs, bidets, and pullout sofas or love seats; guests in these units have access to the Crowne Plaza Club lounge, with a big-screen TV, Internet access, fax, complimentary continental breakfast, and cocktails. A surprisingly attractive collection of French prints and historic city photos gives the entire hotel a nice sense of style. Some may find the far-east location a bit out of the way (Grand Central is a 5-min. walk away), but visitors interested in a quiet, attractive neighborhood will find it fits the bill.

304 E. 42nd St. (just east of Second Ave.), New York, NY 10017. ✆ **800/879-8836** or 212/986-8800. Fax 212/297-3440. www.unitednations.crowneplaza.com. 300 units. $229–$499 double; $489–$689 suite. Ask about weekend packages and other discounts (as low as $139 at press time), and check online for Internet-only deals. Extra person $25. Children under 17 stay free in parents' room. AE, DC, DISC, MC, V. Parking $40. Subway: 4, 5, 6, 7, S to 42nd St./Grand Central. Small pets accepted with $500 deposit. **Amenities:** Restaurant and bar (under renovation at press time; scheduled to be complete by the time you arrive); very good 24-hr. exercise room with sauna and massage services; Clefs d'Or concierge; staffed business center with secretarial services; limited room service; dry cleaning/laundry service; executive-level rooms. *In room:* A/C, TV w/pay movies, dataport and high-speed connectivity, minibar, coffeemaker, hair dryer, iron, laptop-size safe.

Fitzpatrick Grand Central Hotel ★ This attractive and intimate Irish-themed hotel is from the Dublin-based Fitzpatrick chain, and it's a terrific choice for those who like the creature comforts a chain hotel can offer but detest the generic blandness that's usually part of the package. Kelly green–carpeted hallways lead to guest rooms that are pleasingly modern with traditional European accents. Half-canopies are a unique and sophisticated touch, and three phones, a fridge stocked with Irish spring water, windows that shut out the street noise and open to let fresh air in, a pants press, terry robes, and sharp white- and navy blue–tiled bathrooms with lots of space and makeup mirrors add to the comfort level. The L-shaped junior suites also have VCRs, CD players, and extra TVs (including one in the giant bathroom), but a sitting room sans pullout sofa means they're most suited for couples looking for luxury. The penthouse level is named for Liam Neeson, a close friend of Mr. Fitzpatrick's. The Garden Suites may not boast the Waterford crystal chandelier and other antiques that the main Penthouse Suite does, but outdoor patios and big, beautifully tiled bathrooms make them a worthy splurge. The staff is accustomed to catering to U.N. dignitaries, so you can reasonably expect your needs to be well met. The Wheeltapper Pub is an attractive and comfortable Irish pub serving genuine, affordable pub grub as well as Sunday brunch.

141 E. 44th St. (at Lexington Ave.), New York, NY 10017. ✆ **800/367-7701** or 212/351-6800. Fax 212/818-1747. www.fitzpatrickhotels.com. 155 units. $249–$349 double; from $325junior suite. Ask or check website for special rates (as low as $179 at press time; suites from $250). Extra person $30. Children under 12 stay free in parents' room. AE, DC, DISC, MC, V. Parking $38. Subway: 4, 5, 6, 7, S to 42nd St./Grand Central. **Amenities:** Pub; exercise room and access to nearby health club; concierge; 24-hr. room service; dry cleaning/laundry service; car service. *In room:* A/C, TV w/video games, fax, dataport and high-speed connectivity, fridge, coffeemaker, hair dryer, iron, safe.

The Kimberly ★ *Value* Surprisingly good rates on suites mean that you could be standing on your private balcony overlooking Manhattan for a lot less than you'd pay for a cell-like room in many other Midtown hotels. Most New Yorkers don't have it this good: These are full apartments with dining areas; living rooms with Oriental rugs; full-size, fully equipped kitchens complete with china and cookware; marble bathrooms; tons of closet space; and private unfurnished balconies (in all but eight suites)—it's all part of the package. The executive suites have larger living space, but the standard one-bedrooms are just fine for most. The two-bedroom suites each have two bathrooms; you can choose between a configuration that adjoins the bedrooms or puts them at opposite ends of the apartment (great for couples traveling together). The 21 regular rooms are handsome and comfortable, too, with extra-nice bathrooms with deep tubs. Additional amenities include two-line phones and plush robes. The hotel may not be the most stylish place in town, but it's done in an attractive traditional style that's cozy and comfortable, and everything is in very good condition.

On scene is Olica, where a Michelin two-star chef lords over the French-Mediterranean kitchen; and One51, a chic supper club and late-night dance club. A unique perk is complimentary boarding of a 75-foot yacht for a 3-hour sunset cruise (weekends May–Oct, always weather-dependent).

145 E. 50th St. (btwn Lexington and Third aves.), New York, NY 10022. ✆ **800/683-0400**, 212/755-0400, or 212/702-1600. Fax 212/750-0113. www.kimberlyhotel.com or srs-worldhotels.com. 186 units. $259–$349 double; $299–$1,000 1-bedroom suite (including specialty suites); $459–$689 2-bedroom suite. Check on deeply discounted off-season and weekend rates (as low as $219 at press time) as well as package deals. Extra person $25. Children 17 and under stay free in parents' room. AE, DC, DISC, MC, V. Parking $30. Subway: 6 to 51st St.; E, F to Lexington Ave. **Amenities:** 2 restaurants; 2 bars; free access to fabulous New York Health & Racquet Club, with pool, classes, racquetball courts, and indoor golf; concierge; room service (6am–11pm); in-room massage; babysitting; dry cleaning/laundry service; executive-level rooms. *In room:* A/C, TV w/pay movies and PlayStation, fax/copier, dataport, minibar, fridge, hair dryer, iron, laptop-size safe.

Le Marquis ★ *Finds* I've always loved the hotel interiors created by George Patero (who also did the Avalon, above, and Midtown West's Hotel Metro), but the designer really outdid himself at this brand-new Murray Hill boutique hotel. He's created a comfortable yet distinctively contemporary look throughout the hotel, in both the public and private spaces. The gorgeous lobby elicited a "wow!" from me with its warm cherry woods and sexy blue-glass light fixtures (you'll want to take them home, too). In the back is a wonderful living room–style lounge that you're meant to really enjoy—it boasts a 40-inch flat-screen TV, books, board games, and sofas you can sink in to—plus a breakfast room with a generous morning spread (at a charge).

I won't kid you—the guest rooms are not the biggest in town. But Patero filled the available space beautifully with custom furnishings that include armoires and efficiently sized work desks, all done in the same rich cherry. The predominant color is a deep, warm Americana blue, with geometric patterns—squares on the carpet, stripes in the window treatments—adding a welcome dash of boldness. A smart and dedicated GM who pays attention to every detail has incorporated such luxurious appointments as platform beds dressed in goose-down and Frette linens; DVD/CD/MP3 players; plush terry robes; and Aveda toiletries. I adore the sparkling white-tiled bathrooms with their beveled blue-tile accents. While having bathrooms with showers only is often seen as a liability in a hotel, double-wide stalls and luxurious rainshower heads make these rooms more desirable than those with standard tub/shower combos (which are available, if you prefer).

12 East 31st St. (btwn Fifth and Madison aves.), New York, NY 10016. ✆ **866/MARQUIS** or 212/889-6363. Fax: 212/889-6699. www.lemarquisny.com. 123 units. $225–$275 double. Check for seasonal specials (as low

as $159 at press time). AE, DC, DISC, MC, V. Parking: $35. Subway: B, D, F, V, N, R to 34th St. **Amenities:** Breakfast room serving morning buffet; all-day coffee bar in library lounge; cocktail lounge serving light fare; exercise room with Finnish sauna; concierge; dry cleaning/laundry service; DVD and CD libraries. *In room:* A/C; TV w/pay movies, video games, and Internet access, DVD/CD/MP3 player, dataport, minibar, hairdryer, safe.

The Library Hotel ★★ The new-in-2000 Library is a real gem. This intimate and beautifully outfitted hotel boasts the boutique movement's most clear and consistent unifying theme (inspired by the location, just a block from the New York Public Library), which both emphasizes the residential feel and lends it a joyful sense of discovery. The floors are categorized according to the Dewey Decimal system, and each room is assigned a corresponding subject that is reflected in the art and books within: The Classics, Zoology, Fairy Tales, Religion, Erotic Literature, New Media, and so on. Space-flight buffs might like the Astronomy room (Neil Armstrong did), while more mystical types may prefer the Paranormal room (on the Philosophy floor), where available reading runs the gamut from Shirley MacLaine's spirit-minded tomes to *The Complete Prophecies of Nostradamus.*

No matter which room you choose, you'll enjoy gorgeous classic-goes-contemporary interiors (done by the same winning team behind sibling Hotel Giraffe, reviewed in "Union Square, the Flatiron District & Gramercy Park," earlier in this chapter) with sumptuous fabrics in rich honey and natural hues, mahogany built-ins that give you a wealth of work and spreading-out space, marvelous bathrooms, and extras that include VCRs, CD players, and cordless phones. (Beware, though—the petite rooms really are.) The intimate hotel feels like a classic New York town house, with wonderful salon-like public spaces that you'll actually want to use, including a gorgeous reading lounge where you can enjoy a generous morning spread and all-day self-serve cappuccino; a clubby sitting room with fireplace; and a lovely alfresco terrace. A real jewel of a hotel—and a book-lover's delight!

299 Madison Ave. (at 41st St.), New York, NY 10017. ✆ **877/793-7323** or 212/983-4500. Fax 212/499-9099. www.libraryhotel.com. 60 units. $265–$345 double; $395 Love Room or junior suite; $740 two-room family suite. Rates include continental breakfast buffet, all-day snacks, and weekday wine and cheese. Inquire about corporate, promotional, and weekend rates (as low as $199 at press time). AE, DC, MC, V. Parking $28 nearby. Subway: 4, 5, 6, 7, S to 42nd St./Grand Central. **Amenities:** Restaurant (Italian); free access to nearby health club; business center; limited room service; dry cleaning/laundry service; video library of American Film Institute's Top 100 films. *In room:* TV/VCR, CD, dataport and high-speed connectivity, minibar, hair dryer, iron, laptop-size safe.

The Lombardy ★★ *Finds* If the Sherry-Netherland sounds divine but you just can't afford it, book into the lovely Lombardy instead. This mostly suite hotel was built in the 1920s by William Randolph Hearst for his mistress, silent film star Marion Davies, and it still feels like a grand New York apartment house. In fact, just like at the Sherry, the apartments are individually owned, individually decorated co-ops, which gives you the best of both worlds: Genuine luxury apartment living, plus a full spectrum of hotel services.

While studios are available, the one-bedroom suites are far superior in both size and decor. Decor runs the gamut from classic to contemporary; I adore no. 402, a one-bedroom outfitted in glorious mid-century style. The one-bedrooms average 850 square feet, and almost all have been gorgeously renovated in recent years. Studios often fall short in the style department; still, they offer a lot of space and comfort for your dollar, since they're roughly twice the size of your average hotel room, and owners are required to keep them up to snuff. All apartments have fully outfitted galley kitchens; all have fridges and microwaves, most have coffeemakers, and many have stovetops and/or dishwashers. Bathrooms are usually marble and always very nice, but not large (a vestige of the building's age); closets, on the other hand, are mammoth.

The hotel is beautifully run by a longtime general manager and fabulously attentive white-gloved staff who are fiercely committed to this jewel of a hotel. For an Old New York experience, it's hard to do better.

111 E. 56th St. (btwn Park and Lexington aves.), New York, NY 10022. ✆ **800/223-5254** or 212/753-8600. Fax 212/754-5683. www.lombardyhotel.com. 115 units. $290 double; $415–$575 1- or 2-bedroom suite. AE, DC, MC, V. Parking $21. Subway: 4, 5, 6 to 59th St. Not for children under 12. **Amenities:** Noted Etoile restaurant with bar; exercise room; day spa; 24-hr. concierge; business center; salon; limited room service; dry cleaning/laundry service. *In room:* TV, dataport, fridge, hair dryer.

Plaza Hotel ★ There's no denying the glamour and recognizability of the Plaza, probably the Big Apple's most famous hotel. Remember *North by Northwest*? *Home Alone 2*? The splashy nuptials of Michael Douglas and Catherine Zeta-Jones? This is the place.

The 1907 landmark French Renaissance palace has been beautifully refurbished by the Fairmont chain, who recently renovated the guest rooms and lobby to the tune of $60 million and added a honey of a spa, the 8000-square-foot Plaza Spa. Halls and rooms have been beautifully redone in an opulent traditional style in soft, elegant colors, with nice touches like pillow-top mattresses and big leather-top desks; everything is fresh and immaculately detailed. Even the smallest room is a reasonable size, and the building's U shape means that every one gets a measure of fresh air and sunlight. Some suites still boast lavish, look-how-much-money-I-have red and gold decor; redone park-view ones feature PCs with high-speed Internet access.

There's good news on the dining front: The dusty old Edwardian Room has been reinvented as One CPS, a stylish American brasserie; the Palm Court still serves elegant tea; the Oyster Bar is an authentic pub straight outta the British Isles; and the Oak Bar is still one of Manhattan's most legendary cocktail spots.

I prefer the ambience, substantially larger rooms, and the often-better rates at the equally famous Waldorf (below). Tourist hordes can give the public spaces a theme-park feel here. Still, there's no arguing with a legend like this.

768 Fifth Ave. (at 59th St.), New York, NY 10019. ✆ **800-441-1414** or 212/759-3000. Fax 212/546-5256. www.fairmont.com. 805 units. $250–$584 double; from $549 suite. Some rate plans include continental breakfast. AE, DC, DISC, MC, V. Subway: N, R to Fifth Ave. **Amenities:** 4 restaurants (grill, pub, tearoom, New American); excellent full-service spa and health club with Jacuzzi and sauna; concierge (with Clefs d'Or distinction) and ticket desk; car-rental desk; salon; business center with secretarial services; 24-hr. room service; babysitting; dry cleaning/laundry service, video and CD libraries; executive-level rooms. *In room:* A/C, TV w/pay movies, CD player, fax, dataport, minibar, hair dryer, iron, safe.

Swissôtel New York, The Drake ★★★ This Drake has it all: Classic New York grace, top-notch service, and 21st-century style. This regal hotel has presided over Park Avenue since 1929, but a tip-to-toe renovation, completed in 2001, has it looking more like Prince William than Queen Elizabeth, if you know what I mean.

The grand lobby sets the tone immediately with a fresh, contemporary look blending warm woods, sepia-hued parchment sconces, blown Murano glass vases, and a massive spray of fresh blossoms. Spacious and high-ceilinged, the guest rooms blend classic Regency and contemporary styles with boldness; lines are strong, textures are rich, colors are vibrant. Every room boasts an extra-large workdesk, a club chair or other comfy seating area, and thoughtful touches like plush robes and an umbrella in the closet for rainy days. The large suites also feature a wet bar with mini-fridge; some also have entertainment centers, terraces, or other special features.

Service is assured and gracious throughout your stay, and the facilities are first-rate. Stylish Q56 deserves attention in its own right thanks to a beautifully designed interior, a creative cocktail menu, and executive chef Rhys Rosenblum's stellar globetrotting seafood menu; it's well worth a night out even if you don't stay in the hotel. Parisian chocolatier Fauchon operates a large, elegant boutique featuring a sweet tea salon and sparkling glass cases displaying a gorgeous array of chocolates and sweet treats flown in daily. The Park Avenue Spa & Fitness Center is one of the hotel scene's best.

440 Park Ave. (at 56th St.), New York, NY 10022. ✆ **888/737-9477** or 212/421-0900. www.swissotel.com or www.raffles.com. Fax 212/371-4190. 495 units. $225–$625 double; from $315 suite. Weekend rates as low as $189 at press time; value-added packages may also be available. AE, DC, MC, V. Subway: 4, 5, 6 to 59th St. Pets welcome. **Amenities:** Notable restaurant (global seafood) and cocktail bar; Parisian tea salon; full-service fitness center and spa (with hydrotherapy treatments); concierge; staffed business center with secretarial services; salon; 24-hr. room service; dry cleaning/laundry service. *In room:* A/C, TV w/pay movies, fax, dataport, minibar, coffeemaker, hair dryer, iron, safe.

Waldorf=Astoria and the Waldorf Towers ★★★ For legendary New York glamour, there's hardly a more recognizable address in town than the Waldorf. Only the Plaza is on equal footing, but you'll get lots more space and genuine elegance here. Hilton Hotels spent a fortune renovating this Art Deco landmark, and they're committed to keeping the legend in tip-top shape. No two rooms are exactly alike, but all are high-ceilinged and oversize, boasting attractive traditional decor, excellent quality linens and comfy beds, spacious marble bathrooms and closets, and the luxury amenities befitting an old-world hotel of this level, plus nods to the 21st century such as fax machines and dual-line phones.

Renowned for its excellent butler service and respect for privacy, the exquisite, exclusive, residential-style Waldorf Towers—managed under Hilton's ultra-luxury Conrad banner—occupies floors 27 to 42 and has a separate entrance, away from the pleasant bustle of the main hotel. Many of these big, gorgeous rooms and suites are outfitted with original art and antiques in themed traditional styles like English countryside and French provincial, plus full dining rooms, kitchens, and maid's quarters. The Presidential Suite is aptly named, having cosseted many world leaders.

Although the elegant Peacock Alley now serves Sunday brunch only, the hotel still boasts a notable collection of restaurants. The mahogany-paneled Bull & Bear is ideal for stiff drinks or a well-grilled steak in the adjoining dining room. Serving exquisite Japanese food, Inagiku recently got a stylish face-lift from Adam Tihany, as did affordable Oscar's, a pleasing American brasserie. At the Cocktail Terrace, you can sit down to afternoon tea or coddle an evening cocktail while a pianist tickles the ivories on Cole Porter's very own Steinway Grand, while Sir Harry's Bar overflows with clubby ambience.

301 Park Ave. (btwn 49th and 50th sts.), New York, NY 10022. ✆ **800/WALDORF,** 800/774-1500, or 212/355-3000. Fax 212/872-7272 (Astoria) or 212/872-4799 (Towers). www.waldorfastoria.com or www.waldorf-towers.com. 1,242 units (159 in the Towers). Waldorf-Astoria: $259–$485 double; from $349 suite. Waldorf Towers: $429–$625 double; from $515 suite. Corporate, senior, seasonal, and weekend discounts may be available (as low as $189 at press time), as well as attractive package deals. Extra person $40. Children under 18 stay free in parents' room. AE, DC, DISC, MC, V. Parking $45. Subway: 6 to 51st St. **Amenities:** 4 fine restaurants (Japanese, American, chophouse, Sun brunch); 5 bars and lounges; 3,000-square-foot fitness center with massage and personal training; concierge and theater desk; expansive 24-hr. business center; salon;

24-hr. room service; dry cleaning/laundry service; executive-level rooms. Tower rooms include butler service, Clefs d'Or concierge. *In room:* A/C, TV w/pay movies, fax/copier/printer, dataport (high-speed connectivity in executive-level rooms and suites), minibar, coffeemaker, hair dryer, iron; also kitchenette or wet bar with fridge, safe in Waldorf Towers.

MODERATE

Helmsley Middletowne *Kids* This value-laden member of the Helmsley chain (yes, as in Leona Helmsley) boasts little in the way of style, services, or amenities, but rooms and suites are spacious, comfortable, and well priced, and the location is great. The hotel started life as an apartment building, and still has the feel and the large rooms. The lobby is virtually nonexistent, but the front desk staff—most of whom have worked here for *years*—is brisk and friendly. Room decor is generic and furnishings are older, but beds are firm and everything is well kept. Each room has a refrigerator (usually with a wet bar), multiple-line phones, a dated but just-fine bathroom, and a wealth of closet space. The one- and two-bedroom suites are well priced and big enough to accommodate families. They also boast walk-in kitchenettes (some lack dishware, though, so request it or bring plastic); some have fireplaces and/or balconies as well. Not sexy, but a nice choice in the mid-price range.

148 E. 48th St. (btwn Third and Lexington aves.), New York, NY 10017. ✆ **800/221-4982** or 212/755-3000. Fax 212/832-0261. www.helmsleyhotels.com. 192 units. $195–$205 double; from $235 1- or 2-bedroom suite. Rates include continental breakfast. Ask about weekend packages. Children under 12 stay free in parents' room. AE, DC, MC, V. Parking $30. Subway: 6 to 51st St. **Amenities:** Restaurant (Indian); dry cleaning/laundry service. *In room:* A/C, TV, fax (on request), fridge, hairdryer, iron; suites have kitchenettes.

INEXPENSIVE

Habitat Hotel ★ This new-in-1999 hotel is marketed as "upscale budget," with rooms dressed to appeal to travelers who are short on funds but big on style. They're well designed in a natural palette accented with black-and-white photos. Everything is better quality and more attractive than in most hotels in this price range, from the firm mattresses to the plush towels to the pedestal sinks in every room. The bathrooms are all-new; choose between shared (one for every three to four rooms), private, or a semiprivate "minisuite" (two rooms sharing an adjacent bathroom—great for friends traveling together).

The only downside—and it may be a big one for romance-seeking couples—are the sleeping accommodations. A few queens are available (at the highest end of the price spectrum, of course), but most of the double rooms consist of a twin bed with a pullout trundle, which takes up most of the width of the narrow room when it's open. Despite that drawback, rates are attractive, especially for the rooms with shared bathroom, considering the *Metropolitan Home* mindset and the A-1 location. I prefer the private-bath rooms at sister hotel Thirty Thirty (below), because they don't have the space limitations these have, but this hotel has a more thrilling location and a more exciting vibe thanks to the popular new restaurant and bar, Opus. The four pricey penthouse deluxe rooms have queen beds, private bathrooms, microwaves, and minifridges—but if you're going to spend that much money, stay at the Waldorf instead.

The second-floor lobby is designer-stylish and professionally staffed, the bar scene hops and the neighborhood is safe, chic, and super convenient—especially for shoppers, since Bloomingdale's is just 2 blocks away. You won't even have to put on your shoes to visit Kenneth Cole, whose new boutique is just downstairs.

130 E. 57th St. (at Lexington Ave.), New York, NY 10022. ✆ **800/255-0482** or 212/753-8841. Fax 212/829-9605. www.habitatny.com. 300 units (about 40 with private bathroom). $85–$115 single or double with shared bathroom; $125–$195 single or double with private bathroom; $240–$270 minisuite (two rooms with

shared bathroom); $325–$450 penthouse studio with private bathroom. Rates include continental breakfast. Inquire or check website for student rates and promotions (from $79 at press time). AE, DC, DISC, MC, V. Parking $25. Subway: 4, 5, 6 to 59th St.; E, F to Lexington Ave. **Amenities:** Restaurant/bar; tour desk. *In room:* A/C, TV, dataport.

Hotel Grand Union This centrally located hotel is big with budget-minded international travelers. A pleasant white-on-white lobby leads to clean and spacious rooms with nice extras that are uncommon in this price category, like hair dryers and free HBO. Bad florescent overhead lighting, unattractive colonial-style furniture, and an utter lack of natural light dampen the mood—but considering the roominess, low rates, and excellent central-to-everything location, the Grand Union is a very good deal. A nicely configured quad with two twins and a queen in a separate alcove, no. 309 is a great bet for families. Most bathrooms have been freshly outfitted in granite or tile; ask for a newly renovated one to get the most for your money. The staff is helpful, there's a pleasant sitting room off the lobby, and an adjacent coffee shop is convenient for morning coffee or a quick burger.

34 E. 32nd St. (btwn Madison and Park aves.), New York, NY 10016. ✆ **212/683-5890.** Fax 212/689-7397. www.hotelgrandunion.com. 95 units. $116–$138 single or double; $132–$158 twin or triple; $158–$190 quad. Call or check website for special rates (as low as $90 at press time). AE, DC, DISC, MC, V. Parking $22 nearby. Subway: 6 to 33rd St. **Amenities:** Coffee shop open for breakfast, lunch, and dinner; tour desk; fax service. *In room:* A/C, TV, dataport, fridge, hair dryer.

Murray Hill Inn Housed in a renovated five-story walk-up in a pleasant and quiet residential neighborhood, the Murray Hill Inn is shoestring-basic—but there's no arguing with its cleanliness, which is key when judging accommodations in this price range. Rooms are tiny and outfitted with not much more than either one or two beds with motel-standard bedspread and furnishings, a wall rack, a phone, and a small TV; most rooms with shared bathroom also have private sinks (request one when booking). These Euro-style rooms share the in-hall bathrooms that are new and spotless. Some of the doubles have an alcove that can accommodate a third traveler on a cot if you're on an extra-tight budget. Rooms with private bathrooms are definitely the nicest; they're spacious, with new bathrooms and dataports on the telephones. Most also have pullout sofas that can accommodate an extra traveler or two. Don't expect much in terms of facilities beyond a pleasant (if tiny) lobby, plus a plain downstairs sitting area with a vending machine, an ATM, and a luggage-storage area. Services are kept to a bare minimum to keep costs down, but the staff is personable.

143 E. 30th St. (btwn Lexington and Third aves.), New York, NY 10016. ✆ **888/996-6376** or 212/683-6900. Fax 212/545-0103. www.murrayhillinn.com. 50 units (10 with shared bathroom). $75 double with shared bathroom; $125 double with private bathroom. Extra person $20. Children under 12 stay free in parents' room. Ask about discounts and special rates (as low as $75 double with shared bathroom, $95 with private bathroom at press time). AE, MC, V. Parking about $25 nearby. Subway: 6 to 28th St. *In room:* A/C, TV.

Ramada Inn Eastside The most affordable of the Apple Core Hotels (which also include the Red Roof Inn and the Comfort Inn Midtown; see "Times Square & Midtown West," earlier in this chapter), this former Quality Hotel freshly falls under the Ramada banner in 2002. It's nothing special—just some small, rather basic rooms with older bathrooms—but a complete guest-room renovation has given them a fresh new look in greens and beige. Its other recommendable features are the location, in nice, quiet, residential Murray Hill, which abounds with affordable restaurants; the value-added amenities, which include free continental breakfast, free local phone calls, a business center, and a fitness room; and the usually low rates. Don't expect anything in the way of service, but considering how expensive an average room has become in this city, this hotel is a reasonable value. It's quite easy to score a room for $139 or less for most of the year.

161 Lexington Ave. (at 30th St.), New York, NY 10016. ✆ **800/567-7720** or 212/545-1800. Fax 212/790-2760. www.applecorehotels.com. 96 units. $89–$209 double. Rates include continental breakfast. Inquire about seasonal and weekend discounts (as low as $79 at press time). Children under 13 stay free in parents' room. AE, DC, DISC, MC, V. Parking $20 nearby. Subway: 6 to 33rd St. **Amenities:** Coffee shop; basic exercise room and business center (both under renovation at press time). *In room:* A/C, TV w/pay movies, video games, and Internet access, dataport, coffeemaker, hair dryer, iron.

Thirty Thirty ★★ *Value* This new-in-2001 hotel from the CityLife Hotel Group is not quite so expensive as big brother On the Ave. on the Upper West Side, and doesn't boast the space limitations of budget-minded baby sister Habitat, in Midtown East—which makes Thirty Thirty just right for bargain-hunting travelers looking for a splash of style with an affordable price tag. The building—which formerly housed the well-known Martha Washington women's hotel and the legendary nightclub Danceteria, where Madonna got her start—was gutted, renovated, and redone with brand-new everything.

The design-conscious tone is set in the loft-like industrial-modern lobby. Rooms are mostly on the smallish side, but do the trick for those who intend to spend their days out on the town rather than holed up here. They're done in a natural palette with a creative edge—purplish carpet, khaki bedspread, woven wallpaper—that comes together more attractively than you might expect. Configurations are split between twin/twins (great for friends), queens, and queen/queens (great for triples, budget-minded quads, or shares that want more spreading-out room). Nice features include cushioned headboards, firm mattresses, two-line phones, nice built-in wardrobes, and spacious, nicely tiled bathrooms. No. 1135 is a large L-shaped queen with a nice granite bathroom—worth scoring if you can. A few larger units have kitchenettes, great if you're staying in town for a while, as you'll appreciate the extra room and the fridge. No room service, but delivery is available from nearby restaurants.

30 E. 30th St. (btwn Madison and Park aves.), New York, NY 10016. ✆ **800/497-6028** or 212/689-1900. Fax 212/689-0023. www.thirtythirty-nyc.com. 240 units. $125–$1745 double; $145–$195 double with kitchenette; $185–$245 quad. Call for last-minute deals, or check website for special promotions (as low as $99 at press time). AE, DC, DISC, MC, V. Parking $35 1 block away. Subway: 6 to 28th St. Pets accepted with advance approval. **Amenities:** Concierge; dry cleaning/laundry service; restaurant in the works at press time (inquire when booking if it matters). *In room:* A/C, TV, dataport, hair dryer.

10 The Upper West Side

A residential vibe that's two steps down on the stress scale from Midtown, an excellent collection of midprice hotels with larger-than-average rooms, a terrific selection of affordable restaurants, and easy access to attractions (including the American Museum of Natural History, Central Park, and Lincoln Center, all right in the 'hood), make the Upper West Side one of my favorite home-base neighborhoods. An excellent choice for newcomers and returning visitors alike.

To find the hotels described in this section, see p. 150.

VERY EXPENSIVE

Trump International Hotel & Tower ★★★ Forget all your preconceptions about The Donald—this is a surprisingly cultivated venture from the ultimate 1980s Bad Boy. The hotel is housed on 14 lower floors of a freestanding 52-story mirrored monolith at the southwest corner of Central Park, with unobstructed views on all sides. Rooms are on the small side, but high ceilings and smart

Uptown Accommodations

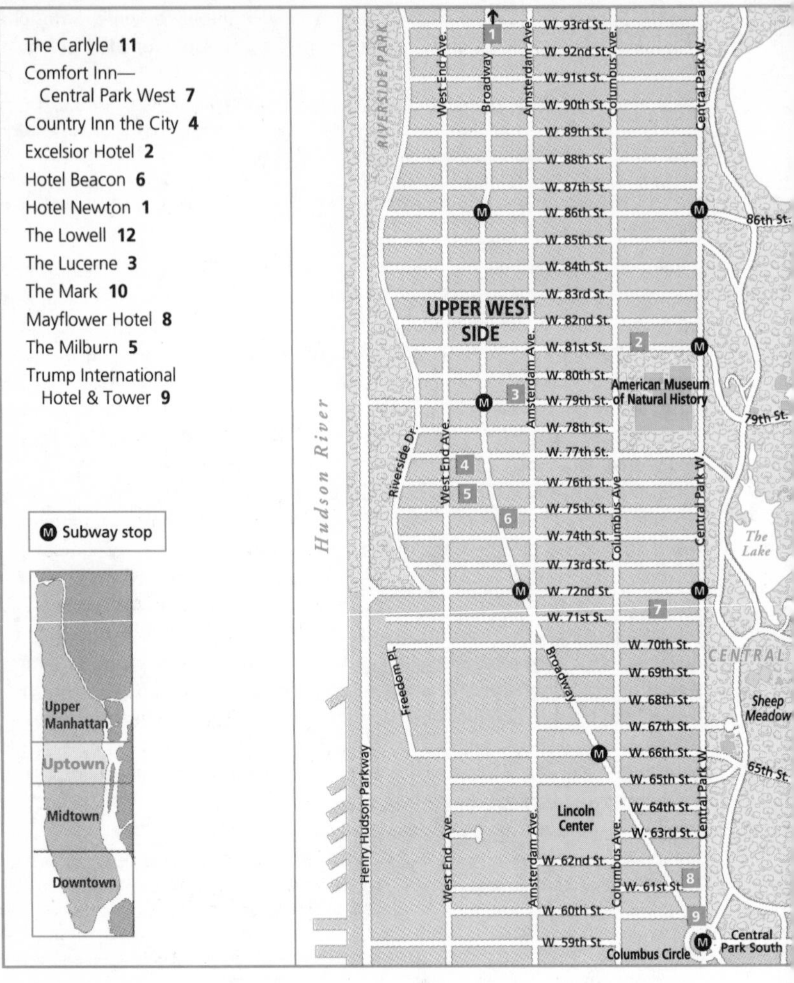

design make them feel uncluttered. They're beautifully done in an understated contemporary style, with clean-lined furniture, beautiful fabrics, and soothing Tuscan tones. Floor-to-ceiling windows maximize the spectacular views, which are especially breathtaking on the park side. Each room boasts a Jacuzzi tub in the marble bathroom, excellent bathrobes (light in summer, warm in winter), umbrellas, and a telescope for taking in the views. Suites also have a European-style kitchen stocked with china and crystal.

The signature services and facilities are what really set the hotel apart. Each guest is assigned a Trump attaché who functions as your own personal concierge, providing comprehensive business and personal services and, following your stay, recording your preferences to have on hand for your next visit. The amazing 6,000-foot spa and fitness center features a 55-foot lap pool, personal trainers, and a full treatment menu. Awarded the coveted four stars by the *New York Times,* Jean Georges serves faultless contemporary French cuisine (see chapter 7); unfortunately, word is that not enough reservations are always set aside for guests, so

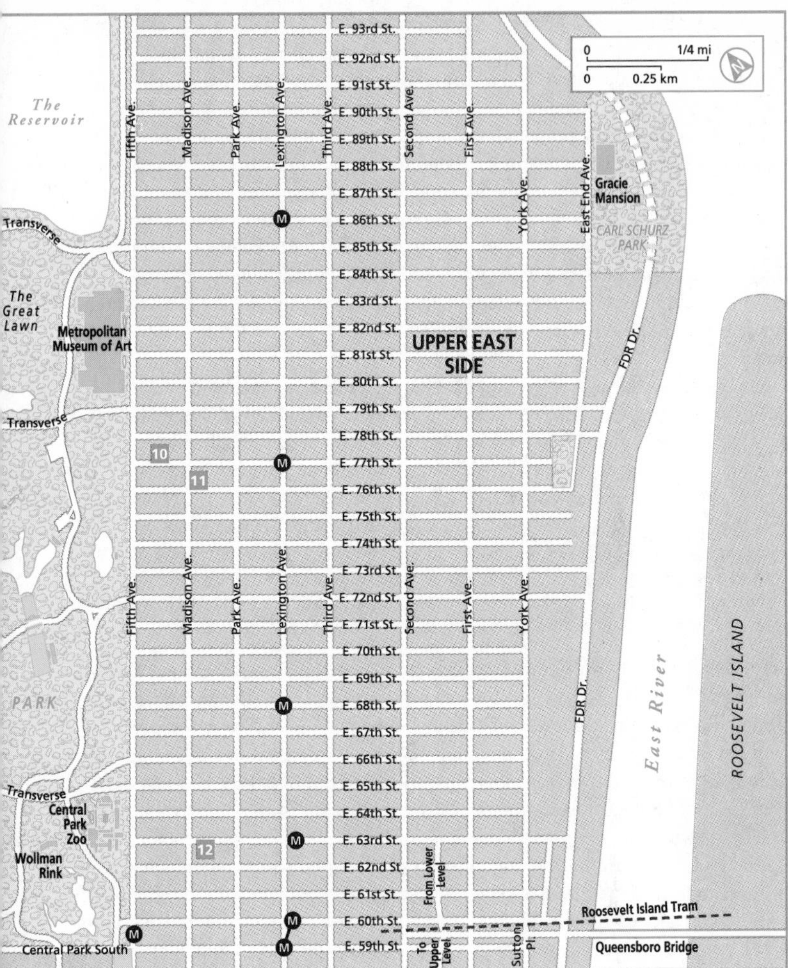

book a table well ahead. For the ultimate in romance and decadence, arrange in advance to have a chef from Jean Georges cook and prepare a multicourse meal right in your suite's own kitchen.

1 Central Park West (at 60th St.), New York, NY 10023. ✆ **888/44-TRUMP** or 212/299-1000. Fax 212/299-1150. www.trumpintl.com. 167 units. $525–$575 double; from $795 1- or 2-bedroom suite. Check website for special rates (as low as $355 at press time) and package deals; also try booking through www.travelweb.com for discounted rates. Children stay free in parents' room. AE, DC, DISC, MC, V. Parking $42. Subway: A, B, C, D, 1, 9 to 59th St./Columbus Circle. **Amenities:** 4-star restaurant (New French); spa and health club with steam, sauna, and pool; Clefs d'Or concierge; staffed business center with secretarial services; 24-hr. room service; in-room massage; babysitting; dry cleaning/laundry service; butler service; CD library. *In room:* A/C, TV/VCR w/pay movies and video games, DVD/CD player, fax/copier/printer, dataport and high-speed connectivity, minibar, coffeemaker, hair dryer, iron, laptop-size safe.

MODERATE

Country Inn the City ★★ *Finds* This charming 1891 town house is rich with original details, impeccable Americana-style decor, and more home-style comforts than you'll find anywhere else for the price. Each immaculate unit is actually a large studio apartment (approximately 550 sq. ft.), with a cozy sofa, table and chairs for two, a private phone with answering machine, an extra phone jack for laptop-toters, and a gorgeous, supremely comfortable queen bed in the large, high-ceilinged bedroom; a big galley kitchenette with everything you'll need to prepare a full meal; and a spacious, pretty bathroom. The whole place is bright and elegant, and the appointments, from the Oriental carpets covering the hardwood floors to the (nonworking) fireplaces that grace every room, couldn't be finer. Wonderful portraits in oil, tasteful collectibles, and brandy and fresh fruit enhance the homey atmosphere. My favorite room is no. 4, done in soft yellow with a high poster bed and whitewashed floorboards. No. 6 is the smallest, with a pretty sleigh bed in the corner, a smaller kitchenette, and a shower only in the bathroom, but its fabulous private terrace more than makes up the difference.

A quiet, peaceful air pervades the house, and the neighborhood couldn't be nicer. An excellent choice in every respect. It's best for travelers of the independent sort, however, since there's no resident innkeeper and a maid only services your unit every few days (you'll need to make your own bed). No smoking, and no walk-ins; call ahead to reserve.

270 W. 77th St. (btwn Broadway and West End Ave.), New York, NY 10024. ✆ **212/580-4183.** Fax 212/874-3981. www.countryinnthecity.com. 4 units. $150–$220 double. Rates include continental breakfast. No sales tax added for stays of 7 nights or more. 3-night minimum. Maximum 2 guests per apt. No credit cards (MC, V for overseas guest deposits only). Parking $30–$35 nearby. Subway: 1, 9 to 79th St. No children under 12. *In room:* A/C, TV, dataport, kitchenette with stocked fridge and coffeemaker, hair dryer, iron, safe.

Excelsior Hotel Now that renovations are complete, the newly elegant Excelsior almost gives the Lucerne (see below) a run for its money. Everything is fresh throughout the hotel, from the richly wood-paneled lobby to the supremely comfy guest rooms to the small but state-of-the-art exercise room. The chic residential location is across from the Museum of Natural History and just steps from Central Park. However, the staff can't quite live up to the Lucerne's impeccable example.

Freshly done in an attractive traditional style, the guest rooms boast high-quality furnishings, commodious closets, two-line phones, thick terry bathrobes, a work desk, free bottled water, and full-length dressing mirrors (a nice touch). The pretty new bathrooms are most impressive. The two-bedded rooms are large enough to accommodate budget-minded families (a few even have two queens), and suites feature pullout sofas, and pants presses. The sunny museum-facing rooms are only worth the extra dough if a park view is really important to you, as all rooms are relatively bright and quiet. Housekeeping is impeccable throughout the hotel. On the second floor is a gorgeous library-style lounge with working fireplace, books, games, gorgeous leather seating, writing desks, and a large flat-screen TV with VCR and DVD player. All in all, a good midprice choice.

45 W. 81st St. (btwn Columbus Ave. and Central Park West), New York, NY 10024. ✆ **800/368-4575** or 212/362-9200. Fax 212/721-2994. www.excelsiorhotelny.com. 198 units. $179–$279 double; $239–$359 1-bedroom suite; $459–$639 2-bedroom suite. Inquire about seasonal rates and specials (winter rates can go as low as $145, $209 for suites). Extra person $20. Children 12 and under stay free in parents' room. AE, DC, DISC, MC, V. Parking $27 nearby. Subway: B, C to 81st St./Museum of Natural History. **Amenities:** Breakfast room with 2 open-air decks and daily breakfast buffet; exercise room; concierge; dry cleaning/laundry service. *In room:* A/C; TV w/pay movies, video games, and Internet access; fax/copier, dataport, hair dryer, iron, safe.

Hotel Beacon ★ *Kids* Ideally located in one of the city's most desirable neighborhoods, only a few blocks from Lincoln Center, Central Park, and the Museum of Natural History, the Beacon is one the best values in town, especially for families. You'll get more style and state-of-the-art comforts at the Excelsior and better service at the Lucerne, but the Beacon will give you *space.* Every generously sized room features a kitchenette, a roomy closet, and a new marble bathroom. The Beacon won't win any personality awards, but management is conscientious and constantly renovating; rooms were freshly done in 1999 with muted florals and plush linens, and hallway redos were being completed at press time. Virtually all standard rooms feature two double beds, and they're plenty big enough to sleep a family on a budget. The large one- and two-bedroom suites are some of the best bargains in the city; each has two closets and a pull-out sofa in the well-furnished living room. The two-bedrooms have a second bathroom, making them well outfitted enough to house a small army. All in all, a great place to stay—and a great value to boot. There's no room service, but with gourmet markets like Zabar's and Fairway nearby, cooking is an attractive alternative, plenty of restaurants are in the immediate area. A self-serve laundromat is another fab family friendly extra.

2130 Broadway (at 75th St.), New York, NY 10023. ✆ **800/572-4969** or 212/787-1100. Fax 212/724-0839. www.beaconhotel.com. 236 units. $180–$225 single or double; from $250 1- or 2-bedroom suite. Check website for special deals (doubles from $145, 1-bedroom suites as low as $195 at press time). Extra person $15. Children under 17 stay free in parents' room. AE, DISC, MC, V. Parking $28 1 block away. Subway: 1, 2, 3, 9 to 72nd St. **Amenities:** Coffee shop adjacent; access to terrific nearby health club; concierge; fax and copy service; dry cleaning/laundry service; coin-op laundry. *In room:* A/C, TV w/pay movies, kitchenette, hair dryer, iron, laptop-size safe.

The Lucerne ★★ *Finds* Want top-notch comforts and service without paying top-dollar prices? Then book into this Mobil four-star, AAA three-diamond hotel. As soon as the suited doorman greets you at the entrance to the 1903 landmark building, you'll know you're getting a lot for your money. The bright marble lobby leads to comfortable guest rooms done in a tasteful Americana style. The standard rooms are big enough for a king, queen, or two doubles (great for those traveling with kids). All rooms have two-line phones with dataport (although not always near the work desk), TVs with Nintendo and on-screen Web access, and an attractive bathroom with spacious travertine counters. A thoughtful GM with an eye for detail makes sure that everything is always fresh and immaculate. The suites also boast very nice kitchenettes with microwave and stocked minifridge, terry robes, and sitting rooms with sofas and extra TVs (and Nintendo sets). The junior suites are a great deal for couples willing to spend a few extra dollars, while the larger suites (with pullout sofas) give families the room they need (although you get more space for their money at the Beacon).

201 W. 79th St. (at Amsterdam Ave.), New York, NY 10024. ✆ **800/492-8122** or 212/875-1000. Fax 212/579-2408. www.newyorkhotel.com. 250 units. $140–$270 double or queen; $160–$290 king or junior suite; $220–$440 1-bedroom suite. Continental breakfast an additional $5 per person. AAA discounts offered; check website for special Internet deals. Extra person $20. Children under 16 stay free in parents' room. AE, DC, DISC, MC, V. Parking $25 nearby. Subway: 1, 9 to 79th St. **Amenities:** Better-than-average fitness center; business center; 24-hr. room service; dry cleaning/laundry service. *In room:* A/C, TV w/Nintendo and Internet access, dataport, coffeemaker, hair dryer, iron.

Mayflower Hotel Set on the edge of Central Park near Lincoln Center, the Mayflower has a spectacular location—on the southern fringe of the Upper West Side, within shouting distance of Lincoln Center, and just a stone's throw from the hustle and bustle of Midtown. The traditionally styled rooms are large (with two doubles, two queens, or a king) and feature walk-in closets and a service pantry with a refrigerator. Bathrooms are fine, although some could use regrouting; still, management keeps the place in fine shape, and a number of the most needy rooms (and all hallways) have recently undergone renovations. All in all, the Mayflower is not the neighborhood's best deal—the Beacon and the Lucerne are better values—but it makes a perfectly fine place to stay, the parkside location is fabulous, and the value-for-dollar ratio is better than what you're likely to find just a few blocks away in Midtown. Nice perks include an ATM, free newspapers, and fax and currency-exchange machines in the lobby, plus free morning coffee for early risers (6–7am). VCRs can be requested, and cellphones are available for rent. You'll pay more for park views, but they're fabulous.

15 Central Park West (at 61st St.), New York, NY 10023. ✆ **800/223-4164** or 212/265-0060. Fax 212/265-0227. www.mayflowerhotel.com. 365 units. $200–$240 single; $225–$265 double; from $290 suite; from $600 penthouse or 2-bedroom suite. Call or check website for specials (from $139 double, $189 suite at press time). Extra person $20. Children under 16 stay free in parents' room. AE, DC, DISC, MC, V. Parking $35. Subway: A, B, C, D, 1, 9 to 59th St./Columbus Circle. Small pets accepted. **Amenities:** Good American restaurant and bar overlooking Central Park; early morning coffee service (6–7am); well-outfitted fitness center; limited room service; babysitting; dry cleaning/laundry service. *In room:* A/C, TV w/pay movies, dataport, pantry with fridge, hair dryer, iron.

INEXPENSIVE

Comfort Inn–Central Park West *Value* This very nice, newly renovated chain hotel is a great place to stay if you can snag a good rate—which you usually can. It's fabulously located, tucked away in the Upper West Side's best residential territory, just steps from the finest areas of Central Park—in fact, the hotel is so understated and attractive that most locals don't even realize it's there. Everything is fresh, new, nicely kept, and professionally done. Rooms aren't huge or stylish, but there's no arguing with the quality. Layout is smart; bedding, fabrics, and window treatments are good; and blackout drapes let you sleep until noon if you so choose. Closets are on the small side, but you'll have a new tiled bathroom, some with hair dryers (which can otherwise be provided upon request). Most rooms have work desks, too. Executive rooms are smartly outfitted in a more modern, less chain-standard style, with nice mahogany built-ins and individual climate controls.

An extended continental breakfast is served in the charming breakfast room (where free newspapers are on hand), which really helps to up the ante on the excellent value. Rates are seasonal, but phenomenally low $80 deals are common in the slowest seasons for AAA cardholders and seniors.

31 W. 71st St. (btwn Columbus Ave. and Central Park West), New York, NY 10023. ✆ **800/228-5150** (worldwide reservations), 877/727-5236 (direct), or 212/721-4770. Fax 212/579-8544. www.comfortinn.com or www.bestnyhotels.com. 96 units. $119–$209 standard double; $179–$299 executive double. Rates include continental breakfast. Ask about senior, AAA, corporate, and promotional discounts; check www.hotelchoice.com for excellent rates (often as low as $80–$90). Extra person $15. Children 12 and under stay free in parents' room. AE, DC, DISC, MC, V. Parking $25 nearby. Subway: B, C to 72nd St. **Amenities:** Small exercise room; concierge; business center; dry cleaning/laundry service; executive-level rooms. *In room:* A/C, TV, dataport, iron.

Hotel Newton *Value* Finally—a genuinely inexpensive hotel that's actually *nice.* Unlike many of its peers, the Newton doesn't scream "budget!" at every turn, or require you to have the carefree attitude of a college student to put up with it. As you enter the pretty lobby, you're greeted by a uniformed staff that's attentive and professional. The rooms are generally large, with good, firm beds, a work desk, and a sizable new bathroom, plus roomy closets in most (a few of the cheapest have wall racks only). Some are big enough to accommodate families with two doubles or two queen beds. The suites feature two queen beds in the bedroom, a sofa in the sitting room, plus niceties like a microwave, minifridge, and iron, making them well worth the few extra dollars. The bigger rooms and suites have been upgraded with cherrywood furnishings, but even the older laminated furniture is much nicer than I usually see in this price range. The AAA-approved hotel is impeccably kept, and there was lots of sprucing up going on—new drapes here, fresh paint there—during my last visit. The 96th Street express subway stop is just a block away, providing convenient access to the rest of the city. A nice bet all the way around. The increasingly gentrified neighborhood boasts lots of affordable restaurants, and a cute diner in the same block provides room service.

2528 Broadway (btwn 94th and 95th sts.), New York, NY 10025. © **888/HOTEL58** or 212/678-6500. Fax 212/678-6758. www.newyorkhotel.com. 110 units. $85–$160 double or junior suite. AAA, corporate, senior, and group rates available; check website for special Internet deals (from $75 double at press time). Extra person $10. Children under 15 stay free in parents' room. AE, DC, DISC, MC, V. Parking $20 nearby. Subway: 1, 2, 3, 9 to 96th St. **Amenities:** 24-hr. room service. *In room:* A/C, TV, hair dryer.

The Milburn ★ *Kids* On a quiet side street a block from the Beacon, the Milburn also offers reasonably priced rooms and suites with equipped kitchenettes in the same great neighborhood—for nearly half the price. These suites might not be quite as nice as the Beacon's, but they're arguably a better value. Every studio-style suite is rife with amenities, including a dining area; a nice newish bathroom and kitchenette (with free coffee!); two-line phones; and more. Junior and one-bedroom suites also boast a pullout queen sofa, an extra TV, a CD player, and a work desk. Don't expect much from the decor (the laminated furniture is clearly a cheaper grade than what you'll get at the Beacon), but everything is attractive and in good shape. The conscientious management keeps the whole place spotless and in good working order. In fact, what makes the Milburn a real find is that it's more service-oriented than most hotels in this price range: The friendly staff will do everything from providing free copy, fax, and e-mail services to picking up your laundry at the dry cleaner next door. All in all, this is a great choice for bargain-hunters—especially families, for whom roll-aways and cribs are on hand.

242 W. 76th St. (btwn Broadway and West End Ave.), New York, NY 10023. © **800/833-9622** or 212/362-1006. Fax 212/721-5476. www.milburnhotel.com. 114 units. $129–$179 studio double; $149–$185 junior suite; $169–$205 1-bedroom suite. Extra person $10. Children 12 and under stay free in parents' room. AE, DC, MC, V. Parking $20–$29. Subway: 1, 9 to 79th St. **Amenities:** Fitness room with personal TVs; access to nearby health club; business services; coin-op laundry; free video library. *In room:* A/C, TV/VCR (Sony PlayStation on request), dataport, kitchenette with fridge and coffeemaker, hair dryer, iron, safe; CD player in suites.

11 The Upper East Side

The city's toniest residential neighborhood boasts Manhattan's most exclusive hotels. If you want to rub shoulders with the society set, prowl haute couture Madison Avenue, or spend all your days wandering the halls of the Met and other Museum Mile institutions, you can't do better in terms of location. Luckily, there's one good hotel choice for midrange travelers, but you'll get more for your money on the Upper West Side.

To find the hotels described in this section, see p. 150.

VERY EXPENSIVE

In addition to the choices below, you might also consider **The Mark,** 25 E. 77th St., at Madison Avenue (© **800/843-6275** or 212/744-4300; www.mandarinoriental.com), a member of the ultra-luxurious—and justifiably world-renowned—Mandarin Oriental hotel group, and the Carlyle's chief rival. It's superbly elegant and somewhat more contemporary in feeling than the Carlyle; which one you'd prefer all depends on your personal style.

The Carlyle ★★★ Countless movie stars and international heads of states (including JFK, who was supposedly once visited by Marilyn here) have lain their heads on the fluffy pillows in this justifiably legendary hotel. Why they choose the Carlyle is clear—it's the hallmark attention to detail. With a staff-to-guest ratio of about two-to-one, the stately service is simply the best. The English manor–style decor is luxurious but not excessive, creating the comfortably elegant ambience of an Upper East Side apartment. Guest rooms range from singles to seven-room suites, some with terraces and full dining rooms. All have marble bathrooms with whirlpool tubs and all the amenities you'd expect from a hotel of this caliber.

Outfitted with the requisite Chinese screens and English hunting prints, the Carlyle Restaurant features formal French dining in the evening as well as lavish breakfast and lunch buffets. Less stuffy but still dressy is the Cafe Carlyle, the supper club where living legend Bobby Short and other big names entertain (see chapter 11). Both rooms serve up a legendary Sunday brunch, a la carte in the restaurant and buffet style in the cafe. Charming Bemelmans Bar (named after children's book illustrator Ludwig Bemelmans, who created the Madeline books and painted the mural here) is a wonderful spot for cocktails; there's live soft jazz Monday through Saturday evenings. Dressed to resemble Turkey's Topkapi Palace, the Gallery serves breakfast, afternoon tea, and cocktails.

35 E. 76th St. (at Madison Ave.), New York, NY 10021. ✆ **800/227-5737** or 212/744-1600. Fax 212/717-4682. 180 units. $495–$750 double; from $750 1- or 2-bedroom suite. AE, DC, MC, V. Parking $50. Subway: 6 to 77th St. Pets accepted. **Amenities:** 3 well-regarded restaurants (including one of the city's best cabaret rooms); tearoom; bar; high-tech fitness room with sauna, Jacuzzi, and spa services; concierge; 24-hr. room service; dry cleaning/laundry service; video library. *In room:* A/C, TV/VCR, CD player, fax/copier/printer, dataport, pantry kitchenette or full kitchen with minibar, hair dryer, safe.

The Lowell ★★ Housed in a historic landmark building on a lovely tree-lined street, this intimate and quietly elegant boutique hotel is a real gem. From the moment you enter the refined deco–French Empire lobby, you know you're in a posh place. The Lowell has a distinct air of exclusivity about it, but without being snobbish. About two-thirds of the rooms are suites. In addition to fine old-world antiques, expect all the luxuries, including ultra luxurious marble-and-brass bathrooms. Each suite has a fully equipped kitchenette but is otherwise unique, with such individual features as wood-burning fireplaces (in most), full dining rooms, garden terrace, or even a private gym (this is the one Madonna chose, natch), so be sure to inquire about the available options. Service is everything it should be.

Wine Spectator has called the Post House one of the 10 best steakhouses in America, but it seems to be resting on its laurels these days. Festooned in English chintz, the Pembroke Room serves breakfast, weekend brunch, and a supremely elegant afternoon tea that's perfect for purists (seasonal, so call ahead).

28 E. 63rd St. (btwn Park and Madison aves.), New York, NY 10021. ✆ **800/221-4444** or 212/838-1400. Fax 212/319-4230. www.lhw.com. 68 units. $385–$635 single or double; from $715 junior, 1-, or 2-bedroom suite. Inquire about special packages and weekend and seasonal rates. Extra person $40. AE, DC, MC, V. Parking $45. Subway: F to Lexington Ave. Pets under 15 lb. accepted. **Amenities:** Steakhouse; tearoom; well-outfitted fitness room with health-snack station, plus access to three health clubs; 24-hr. concierge; limousine service; secretarial services; 24-hr. room service; babysitting; dry cleaning/laundry service; video library. *In room:* A/C, TV/VCR, fax/copier/scanner, dataport, minibar, hair dryer.

7

Where to Dine

Attention, foodies: Welcome to your mecca. Without a doubt, New York is the best restaurant town in the country, and one of the finest in the world. Other cities might have particular specialties, but no other culinary capital spans the globe so successfully as the Big Apple.

That's due in part to New York's vibrant immigrant mix. Let a newcomer arrive and see that his or her native foods aren't represented and *zap!*—there's a new restaurant, cafe, or grocery to fill the void. Yet we New Yorkers can be fickle: One moment a restaurant is hot; the next it's passé. So restaurants close with a frequency we wish applied to the arrival of subway trains—especially these days, in the wake of the softer economy. **Always call ahead.**

But there's one thing we all have to face sooner or later: Eating in New York isn't cheap. The primary cause? The high cost of real estate, which is reflected in what you're charged. Wherever you're from, particularly if you hail from the reasonably priced American heartland, New York's restaurants will seem *expensive.* You can't throw a rock in this town without hitting a restaurant charging $20 to $30 for entrees these days. Yet good value abounds, especially if you're willing to eat ethnic, and venture beyond tourist zones into the neighborhoods where budget-challenged New Yorkers eat, like Chinatown and the East Village. But even if you have no intention of venturing beyond Times Square, don't worry: I've included inexpensive restaurants in every neighborhood, including some of the city's best-kept secrets, so you'll know where to get good value for your money no matter where you are in Manhattan.

RESERVATIONS

Reservations are always a good idea in New York, and a virtual necessity if your party is bigger than two. Do yourself a favor and call ahead as a rule of thumb so you won't be disappointed. If you're booking dinner on a weekend night, it's a good idea to call a few days in advance if you can.

While it's easier than it used to be in the just-say-grow economy of the late 1990s to score the city's top tables, call *far* ahead for any special meal you don't want to miss—a month in advance is a good idea. Most top places start taking reservations exactly 30 days in advance, so if you want to eat at a hot restaurant at a popular hour—Saturday at 8pm, say, at Jean Georges—be sure to mark your calendar and start dialing 30 days prior at 9am. If you're booking a holiday dinner, call even earlier.

Tips **The Best of the Best**

For the best of what the city has to offer, take a moment to check out "Best Dining Bets" in chapter 1.

Tips **OpenTable.com**

OpenTable (www.opentable.com) allows you to book a reservation—and get an instant confirmation—over the Web at about 150 restaurants throughout Manhattan. You'll also find that an increasing number of restaurants, like Veritas, offer online reservations through their own websites.

But if you didn't call well ahead and your heart's set on dinner at Le Cirque 2000 or TanDa, don't despair. Often, early or late hours—between 6 and 7pm, or after 10pm—are available, especially on weeknights. And try calling the day before or first thing in the morning, when you may be able to take advantage of a last-minute cancellation. Or go for lunch, which is usually much easier to book without lots of advance notice. If you're staying at a hotel with a concierge, don't be afraid to use them—they can often get you into hot spots that you couldn't get into on your own.

But What If They Don't *Take* Reservations? Lots of restaurants, especially at the affordable end of the price continuum, don't take reservations at all. One of the ways they keep prices down is by packing people in as quickly as possible. Thus, the best cheap and midpriced restaurants often have a wait. Again, your best bet is to go early. Often you can get in more quickly on a weeknight. Or just go knowing that you're going to have to wait if you head to a popular spot; hunker down with a cocktail at the bar and enjoy the festivities around you.

THE LOWDOWN ON SMOKING

New York City enacted strict no-smoking laws a few years back that made most of the city's dining rooms blessedly smoke-free. However, that doesn't mean that smokers are completely prohibited from lighting up. Here's the deal: Restaurants with more than 35 seats cannot allow smoking in their dining rooms. They can, however, allow smoking in their bar or lounge areas, and most do. Restaurants with fewer than 35 seats—and there are more of those in the city than you'd think—can allow or prohibit smoking as they see fit. This ruling has turned some of the city's small restaurants into particularly smoker-friendly establishments, which might be a turnoff for nonsmokers.

Call ahead and ask about the smoking policy if it matters to you. If you're hell-bent on enjoying an after-dinner cigarette indoors, make sure that the restaurant has a bar or lounge that allows smoking. Some restaurants, like Le Pere Pinard, even offer dinner tables in their lounges where you can puff away all during the meal if you so choose. And smoking is usually allowed in alfresco dining areas, but never assume—always ask. If you're a nonsmoker who doesn't want to be bothered by secondhand smoke, make sure your seat is well away from the bar.

TIPPING

Tipping is easy in New York. The way to do it: Double the 8¼% sales tax and voilà!, happy wait staff. In fancier venues, another 5% is appropriate for the captain. If the wine steward helps, hand him or her 10% of the bottle's price.

Leave $1 per item, no matter how small, for the checkroom attendant.

MORE SOURCES FOR SERIOUS FOODIES

Of course New York has far more fabulous dining than I have room to discuss here—although the listings below are enough to keep you fat and happy for a year, much less the length of a vacation. But if you'd like a wider selection, a few very good sources are available online or from your local bookstore.

Your best online sources are **Citysearch** (**www.citysearch.com**), which runs a great restaurant page that's updated weekly as part of its comprehensive offerings; **New York Metro** (**www.newyorkmetro.com**), the online arm of glossy weekly *New York;* and **New York Today** (**www.nytoday.com**), the *New York Times*'s arts and lifestyle site where you can access a database of the paper's stellar restaurant reviews.

The ***Zagat Survey,*** which has made a name for itself rating restaurants based on extensive diner surveys, maintains a searchable database of city restaurants at **www.zagat.com**, so if you're willing to do your research before you leave home (or if you're toting a laptop), there's no need to acquire a hard copy of the no-frills guide.

If you do want a book reference to have on hand while you're in the city, I suggest the colorful, reviewer-written ***Time Out New York: Eating & Drinking*** guide, which I find to be more comprehensive, candid, and descriptive than Zagat's. If you don't feel the need for a big ol' book, stop at any newsstand for a copy of the slick weekly ***Time Out New York,*** whose "Eat Out" section always includes listings for *TONY*'s 100 Favorite Restaurants in every issue, as well as coverage of new openings and dining trends. Weekly ***New York*** magazine also maintains extensive restaurant listings in the "Cue" section at the back of the magazine.

1 Restaurants by Cuisine

AFTERNOON TEA

Lady Mendl's Tea Salon ★ (Union Square/Gramercy Park, $$, p. 193)
Payard Pâtisserie & Bistro (The Upper East Side, $$, p. 225)
Sarabeth's Kitchen ★★ (The Upper West and East Sides, $$, p. 222)
Tea & Sympathy ★ (Greenwich Village, $, p. 188)

AMERICAN

See also "Contemporary American," below.
Artie's Delicatessen (The Upper West Side, $, p. 223)
Bubby's ★ (TriBeCa, $$, p. 168)
Clove (The Upper East Side, $$$, p. 225)
EJ's Luncheonette (Greenwich Village, $, p. 186)
Empire Diner (Chelsea, $, p. 189)
ESPN Zone (Times Square, $, p. 208)
Guastavino's ★ (Midtown East, $$$, p. 212)
Hard Rock Cafe (Midtown West, $, p. 208)
Jekyll & Hyde Club (Midtown West, $, p. 208)
Joe Allen ★★ (Times Square & Midtown West, $$, p. 203)
Junior's (Midtown East, $, p. 215)
Little Pie Company (Midtown East, $, p. 216)
Mars 2112 (Midtown West, $$, p. 208)
Norma's ★★ (Midtown West, $$, p. 204)
The Odeon (TriBeCa, $$, p. 169)
Old Town Bar & Restaurant (Union Square & the Flatiron District, $, p. 194)

Planet Hollywood (Midtown West, $, p. 208)
Serendipity 3 (The Upper East Side, $, p. 226)
Tavern on the Green ★ (The Upper West Side, $$$, p. 219)
Vynl (Times Square & Midtown West, $, p. 207)
WWE New York (Times Square, $$, p. 208)

ALSATIAN

Brasserie ★★ (Midtown East, $$, p. 214)

AUSTRALIAN

Eight Mile Creek ★★ (SoHo & Nolita, $$, p. 176)

ASIAN FUSION/ PAN-ASIAN/PACIFIC RIM

AZ ★ (Union Square/the Flatiron District, $$$, p. 190)
Rice (SoHo & Nolita, $, p. 178)
Ruby Foo's (Times Square/also Upper West Side, $$, p. 205)
TanDa ★ (Union Square/the Flatiron District, $$$, p. 191)
Zen Palate (Union Square, $, p. 195)

BELGIAN

Steak Frites (Union Square, $$, p. 194)

BRAZILIAN

Brazil Grill ★ (Times Square & Midtown West, $$, p. 202)
Churrascaria Plataforma (Times Square & Midtown West, $$, p. 203)

BREAKFAST & BRUNCH

Artie's Delicatessen (Upper West Side, $, p. 223)
Balthazar (SoHo, $$, p. 174)
Barney Greengrass, the Sturgeon King (The Upper West Side, $, p. 222)
Brasserie ★★ (Midtown East, $$, p. 214)
Bubby's ★ (TriBeCa, $$, p. 168)
D'Artagnan Restaurant & Rotisserie ★★ (Midtown East, $$, p. 214)
EJ's Luncheonette (Greenwich Village, $, p. 186)
Emerald Planet ★ (Greenwich Village/also Midtown West, $, p. 186)
Empire Diner (Chelsea, $, p. 189)
Ess-A-Bagel ★ (Midtown East, $, p. 216)
Florent (Meat-Packing District, $, p. 187)
Home ★★ (Greenwich Village, $$, p. 184)
Jean Georges (in Nougatine cafe) ★★★ (The Upper West Side, $$$$, p. 218)
Katz's Delicatessen ★★ (Lower East Side, $, p. 173)
Le Pain Quotidien ★★ (SoHo/also the Flatiron District, Midtown East and the Upper East and Upper West Sides, $, p. 177)
Le Zinc ★ (TriBeCa, $$, p. 169)
Norma's ★★ (Midtown West, $$, p. 204)
Pastis (Meat-Packing District, $$, p. 186)
Pigalle (Times Square & Midtown West, $$, p. 204)
Sarabeth's Kitchen ★★ (The Upper West and East Sides, $$, p. 222)
Sylvia's (Harlem, $, p. 227)
Veselka ★ (The East Village, $, p. 182)

BRUNCH ONLY (WEEKENDS)

Some of these establishments serve brunch on Sunday only; check listings for specifics.

Acme Bar & Grill (NoHo, $, p. 181)
Aquagrill ★★ (SoHo, $$$, p. 173)
Bayou ★ (Harlem, $$, p. 227)
Blue Water Grill (The Flatiron District, $$, p. 192)
Caffe Grazie (The Upper East Side, $$, p. 225)

Eight Mile Creek ★★ (SoHo & Nolita, $$, p. 176)
First ★ (The East Village, $$, p. 178)
Frank (The East Village, $$, p. 181)
Gabriela's ★★ (The Upper West Side, $, p. 223)
Guastavino's ★ (Midtown East, $$$, p. 212)
Gus' Place (Greenwich Village, $$, p. 184)
Ilo ★★ (Times Square & Midtown West, $$$$, p. 198)
Josie's Restaurant & Juice Bar (The Upper West Side, $$, p. 219)
The Odeon (TriBeCa, $$, p. 169)
Petrossian ★ (Midtown West, $$$, p. 201)
Pipa ★ (Union Square & the Flatiron District, $$, p. 193)
Pisces (The East Village, $, p. 182)
Roettele A.G. (The East Village, $$, p. 180)
Rue des Crepes ★ (Chelsea, $, p. 189)
Russian Tea Room (Midtown West, $$$$, p. 199)
Tavern on the Green (The Upper West Side, $$$, p. 219)
Tea & Sympathy (Greenwich Village, $, p. 188)
Time Cafe ★ (The Upper West Side/also NoHo, $, p. 223)
Tribeca Grill ★ (TriBeCa, $$$, p. 168)
Vynl (Times Square & Midtown West, $, p. 207)

BRITISH

A Salt & Battery (Greenwich Village, $, p. 188)
Christer's (Midtown East, $, p. 216)
Tea & Sympathy (Greenwich Village, $, p. 188)

CHINESE

Canton (Chinatown, $$, p. 170)
Grand Sichuan International ★ (Chelsea, $, p. 189)
Joe's Shanghai ★★ (Chinatown, $, p. 171)
New York Noodletown ★★ (Chinatown, $, p. 172)

CONTEMPORARY AMERICAN

Craft ★★ (Flatiron District, $$$, p. 190)
The Harrison ★ (TriBeCa, $$, p. 168)
Home ★★ (Greenwich Village, $$, p. 184)
Josie's Restaurant & Juice Bar (The Upper West and East Sides, $$, p. 219)
One If By Land, Two If By Sea ★★ (Greenwich Village, $$$, p. 183)
Ouest ★★ (The Upper West Side, $$$, p. 218)
The Red Cat ★ (Chelsea, $$, p. 188)
Sarabeth's Kitchen ★★ (The Upper West and East sides, $$, p. 222)
Tavern Room at Gramercy Tavern ★ (Union Square, $$, p. 194)
The Tasting Room ★★ (East Village, $$, p. 180)
Time Cafe ★ (The Upper West Side/also NoHo, $, p. 223)
Tribeca Grill ★ (TriBeCa, $$$, p. 168)
Veritas ★★★ (The Flatiron District, $$$, p. 191)

CONTINENTAL

Cité ★★ (Midtown West, $$$, p. 200)
Guastavino's ★ (Midtown East, $$$, p. 212)
Petrossian ★ (Midtown West, $$$, p. 201)
Tavern on the Green (The Upper West Side, $$$, p. 219)

CREOLE

Bayou ★ (Harlem, $$, p. 227)

FRENCH

Alain Ducasse at the Essex House ★★★ (Midtown West, $$$$, p. 195)
Balthazar (SoHo, $$, p. 174)
Café Boulud ★ (The Upper East Side, $$$, p. 224)
Chanterelle ★★★ (TriBeCa, $$$$, p. 166)
Daniel ★★ (The Upper East Side, $$$$, p. 224)
D'Artagnan Restaurant & Rotisserie ★★ (Midtown East, $$, p. 214)
Florent (Meat-Packing District, $, p. 187)
Jean Georges ★★★ (The Upper West Side, $$$$, p. 218)
La Grenouille ★★★ (Midtown East, $$$$, p. 209)
Le Bernardin ★★★ (Midtown West, $$$$, p. 198)
Le Cirque 2000 ★ (Midtown East, $$$$, p. 210)
Le Pain Quotidien ★★ (SoHo/also the Flatiron District, Midtown East and on the Upper East and Upper West Sides, $, p. 177)
Le Pere Pinard ★ (The Lower East Side, $$, p. 173)
Le Zinc ★★ (TriBeCa, $$, p. 169)
Pastis (Meat-Packing District, $$, p. 186)
Payard Pâtisserie & Bistro (The Upper East Side, $$, p. 225)
Pigalle (Times Square & Midtown West, $$, p. 204)
Rue des Crepes ★ (Chelsea, $, p. 189)

GERMAN

Knödel (Midtown East, $, p. 216)

GLOBAL

Emerald Planet ★ (Greenwich Village/also Midtown West, $, p. 186)
First ★ (East Village, $$, p. 178)
Ilo ★★ (Times Square & Midtown West, $$$$, p. 198)

GOURMET SANDWICHES/ DELI/TAKEOUT

Barney Greengrass, the Sturgeon King (The Upper West Side, $, p. 222)
Cafe Habana ★ (SoHo & Nolita, $, p. 176)
Carnegie Deli (Midtown West, $, p. 210)
Emerald Planet ★ (Greenwich Village/also Midtown West, $, p. 186)
Ess-A-Bagel ★ (Midtown East, $, p. 216)
Island Burgers & Shakes (Midtown West, $, p. 206)
Katz's Delicatessen ★★ (Lower East Side, $, p. 173)
Le Pain Quotidien ★★ (SoHo/also the Flatiron District, Midtown East and on the Upper East and Upper West Sides, p. 177)
Mangia (The Financial District/also in Midtown West and East, $, p. 166)
Mike's Take-Away (Midtown East, $, p. 216)
Rice (SoHo & Nolita, $, p. 178)
Second Avenue Deli ★ (Lower East Side, $$, p. 210)
Stage Deli (Midtown West, $, p. 210)

GREEK

Gus' Place (Greenwich Village, $$, p. 184)
Molyvos ★ (Midtown West, $$$, p. 201)

INDIAN

Cafe Spice Express (Midtown East, $, p. 216)
Haveli (The East Village, $$, p. 179)
Pongal ★ (Murray Hill, $, p. 216)
Salaam Bombay (TriBeCa, $$, p. 170)

ITALIAN

Babbo ★★★ (Greenwich Village, $$$, p. 183)

Pintaile's Pizza (Greenwich Village; also Upper East Side, $, p. 226)
Two Boots (Midtown East, $, p. 216)

RUSSIAN/UKRAINIAN

Petrossian ★ (Midtown West, $$$, p. 201)
Russian Tea Room ★ (Midtown West, $$$$, p. 199)
Veselka ★ (The East Village, $, p. 182)

SCANDINAVIAN

Aquavit ★ (Midtown West, $$$, p. 200)

SEAFOOD

Aquagrill ★★ (SoHo, $$$, p. 173)
Blue Water Grill (The Flatiron District, $$, p. 192)
City Crab (Union Square, $$, p. 192)
Esca (Midtown West, $$$, p. 183)
Le Bernardin ★★★ (Midtown West, $$$$, p. 198)
Oyster Bar & Restaurant ★ (Midtown East, $$, p. 214)
Pisces (The East Village, $, p. 182)
The Sea Grill ★★ (Midtown West, $$$, p. 202)
Umberto's Clam House (Little Italy, $$, p. 171)

SOUL FOOD

Sylvia's (Harlem, $, p. 227)

SOUTHERN/BARBECUE

Acme Bar & Grill (NoHo, $, p. 181)
Virgil's Real BBQ (Times Square, $$, p. 205)

SPANISH

La Paella (The East Village & NoHo, $$, p. 179)
Pipa ★ (Union Square & the Flatiron District, $$, p. 193)

STEAKS

Cité ★★ (Midtown West, $$$, p. 200)
Dylan Prime (Greenwich Village, $$$, p. 213)
MarkJoseph ★★ (South Street Seaport, $$$, p. 212)
Michael Jordan's–The Steak House ★★ (Midtown East, $$$, p. 212)
Nick & Stef's Steakhouse (Midtown West, $$$, p. 213)
Peter Luger Steakhouse ★ (Brooklyn, $$$, p. 228)
Smith & Wollensky (Midtown East, $$$, p. 213)
Steak Frites (Union Square, $$, p. 194)

SWISS

Roettele A.G. (The East Village, $$, p. 180)

THAI

Siam Inn (Midtown West, $, p. 207)

TURKISH

Pasha (The Upper West Side, $$, p. 219)

VEGETARIAN/ HEALTH-CONSCIOUS

Angelica Kitchen (The East Village, $, p. 181)
Emerald Planet ★ (Greenwich Village/also Midtown West, $, p. 186)
Josie's Restaurant & Juice Bar (The Upper West Side, $$, p. 219)
Pongal ★ (Murray Hill, $, p. 216)
Time Cafe ★ (The Upper West Side/also NoHo, $, p. 223)
Zen Palate (Union Square, $, p. 195)

VIETNAMESE

Nha Trang (Chinatown, $, p. 172)

2 The Financial District & South Street Seaport

If you're sightseeing in the area and in need of nourishment, also consider the restaurants in TriBeCa (p. 166), which are a stone's throw away.

Financial District, TriBeCa, Chinatown & Little Italy Dining

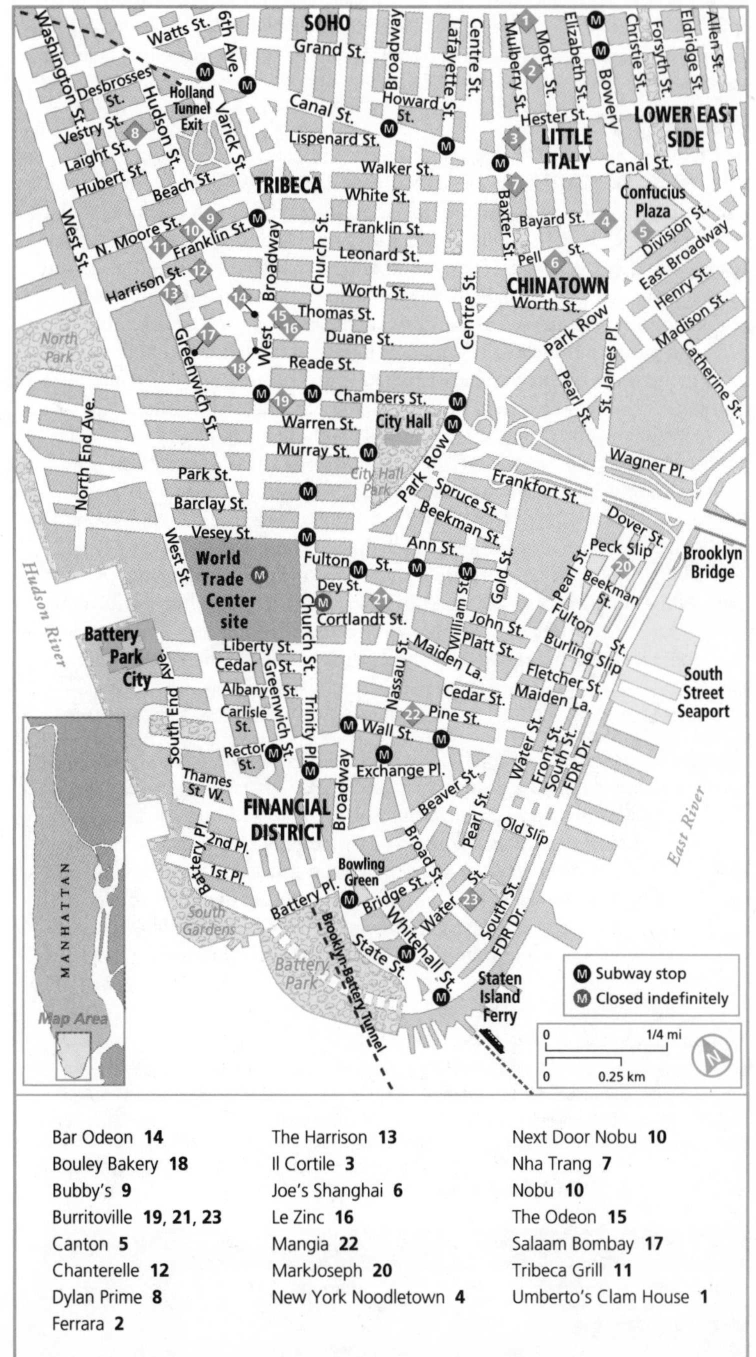

Bar Odeon **14**	The Harrison **13**	Next Door Nobu **10**
Bouley Bakery **18**	Il Cortile **3**	Nha Trang **7**
Bubby's **9**	Joe's Shanghai **6**	Nobu **10**
Burritoville **19, 21, 23**	Le Zinc **16**	The Odeon **15**
Canton **5**	Mangia **22**	Salaam Bombay **17**
Chanterelle **12**	MarkJoseph **20**	Tribeca Grill **11**
Dylan Prime **8**	New York Noodletown **4**	Umberto's Clam House **1**
Ferrara **2**		

EXPENSIVE

If it's a perfect cut of meat you're after, you can't go wrong at **MarkJoseph** ★★, at 261 Water St., at Peck Slip (✆ **212/277-0020;** subway: 2, 3 to Fulton St.), a Seaport-area yearling that scores as Manhattan's best steakhouse. For details, see the box called "The Prime Cut" (p. 212).

INEXPENSIVE

Burritoville *Value* TEX-MEX This bright and cheerful minichain serves up the best "fast food" in the city. In fact, Burritoville fare doesn't deserve to be called fast food. This is forward-thinking Mexican, all prepared with the freshest and healthiest ingredients—including garden-fresh produce, brown rice, and black beans—using no lard, preservatives, or canned goods. Even the tortillas are pressed every day. Options range from well-stuffed tacos and quesadillas to only-at-Burritoville creations such as a spicy white chicken chili with cumin, salad burritos, and a number of choice wraps. The huge menu offers a wealth of options for vegetarians, as well as anyone looking for a quick, healthy bite. Another nice thing about Burritoville is their flexibility—you can make substitutions and special requests without a problem, and usually without an extra charge. *Tip:* The green salsa is hot, the red salsa (made with open-flame-roasted tomatoes) is not.

In addition to this location (a short walk from Battery Park and the Statue of Liberty and Staten Island ferry landings), a second lower Manhattan location is in the Financial District at 20 John St., between Broadway and Nassau (✆ **212/766-2020**). Additionally, there are 11 more Burritovilles throughout the city, most with attractive decor and good table seating that makes Burritoville more attractive and comfortable than your average fast-food joint, too. See "Inexpensive" under each neighborhood section below to see whether there's one near you.

36 Water St. (just north of Broad St.). ✆ **212/747-1100.** www.burritoville.com. Reservations not accepted. Main courses $4.50–$9. AE, DISC, MC, V. Daily 11am–10pm. Subway: 2, 3 to Wall St.; 1, 9 to South Ferry.

Mangia MEDITERRANEAN/GOURMET SANDWICHES This big, bustling gourmet cafeteria is an ideal place to take a break during your day of Financial District sightseeing. Between the giant salad and soup bars, the sandwich and hot entree counters, and an expansive cappuccino-and-pastry counter at the front of the cavernous room, even the most finicky eater will have a hard time deciding what to eat. Everything is freshly prepared and beautifully presented. At press time, Mangia was in the process of adding a sit-down section with waiter service in addition to the self-service cafeteria, in case you don't feel like standing on line.

In addition to the Wall Street location, Mangia has two cafeteria-style cafes in Midtown that offer similar, if not quite such expansive, menus.

40 Wall St. (btwn Nassau and William sts.). ✆ **212/425-4040.** www.mangianet.com. Reservations not accepted. Soups and salads $3.50–$5; sandwiches and main courses $6–$14 (most less than $10). AE, DC, DISC, MC, V. Mon–Fri 7am–5pm (waiter service available 11:30am–4pm). Subway: 2, 3, 4, 5 to Wall St.; J, M, Z to Broad St. Also at 50 W. 57th St., btwn Fifth and Sixth aves. (✆ 212/582-5554; subway: B, Q to 57th St.); open Mon–Fri 7am–8pm, Sat 8:30am–6pm. 16 E. 48th St., btwn Fifth and Madison aves. (✆ 212/754-0637; subway: B, D, F, Q to 47–50th St./Rockefeller Center); open Mon–Fri 7am–6pm.

3 TriBeCa

To find the restaurants reviewed below, see map on p. 165.

VERY EXPENSIVE

Chanterelle ★★★ CONTEMPORARY FRENCH Chanterelle is my absolute favorite special-occasion restaurant. There's no stuffiness here at all;

everyone is encouraged to feel at home and relaxed, and the timing is always perfect. The dining room is simple but beautiful, with a pressed-tin ceiling, widely spaced large tables, comfortable chairs, and gorgeous floral displays; there's also a superb modern art collection.

Your server will know the handwritten menu in depth and can describe preparations in detail and suggest complementary combinations. The artful cuisine is based on traditional French technique, but Pacific and Pan-European notes sneak into the culinary melodies, and lots of dishes are lighter than you'd expect. The seasonal menu changes every few weeks, but one signature dish appears on almost every menu: a marvelous grilled seafood sausage. Cheese lovers should opt for a cheese course—the presentation and selection can't be beat. The wine list is superlative, but I wish there were more affordable options. Still, you don't come to Chanterelle on the cheap—you come to celebrate. Very expensive, but magnificent.

2 Harrison St. (at Hudson St.). ✆ **212/966-6960.** www.chanterellenyc.com. Reservations recommended well in advance. Fixed-price lunch $38; a la carte lunch $19.50–$26.50; 3-course fixed-price dinner $84; tasting menu $95 ($155 with wines). AE, DC, DISC, MC, V. Mon 5:30–11pm; Tues–Sat noon–2:30pm and 5:30–11pm. Subway: 1, 9 to Franklin St.

EXPENSIVE

Nobu/Next Door Nobu ★★★ NEW JAPANESE Deeply rooted in Japanese tradition but heavily influenced by Latin American and Western techniques, Chef Nobuyuki Matsuhisa's cooking bursts with creative spirit. Unusual textures, impulsive combinations, and surprising flavors add up to a first-rate dining adventure that you won't soon forget. Virtually every creation hits its target, whether you opt for the new-style sashimi; light-as-air rock shrimp tempura; or sublime broiled black cod in sweet miso, the best dish in the house. If Kobe beef is available, try this delicacy tataki style (with soy, scallions, and daikon). The knowledgeable staff will be happy to guide you. However, because most dinners are structured as a series of tasting plates, be aware that the bill can soar into the "Very Expensive" category—wallet-watchers should keep a close eye on the tally. The excitement is heightened by the witty modern decor (check out the chopstick-legged chairs at the sushi bar).

But you can't get a reservation at Nobu? Take heart, for there's **Next Door Nobu,** the slightly more casual version that has a firm no-reservations policy. This is great news in this exclusionary town: Just show up, wait your turn, and you get a table. Because waits can be as long as 90 minutes, the secret is to go early: We walked in at 6:30pm on a weeknight and the place was half empty. This isn't cut-rate Nobu—you get the full treatment here, too. The modern room is highly stylized but comfortable, all the house specialties are available, and the service is equal to the main restaurant. There's also a raw bar. Noodle dishes add a moderately priced dimension to the menu, but it takes a lot of willpower to keep the tab low.

One caveat: I adore Nobu, but find the traditional sushi to be merely fine; if you're in the mood for a full sushi meal, consider SoHo's Blue Ribbon instead.

105 Hudson St. (at Franklin St.). ✆ **212/219-0500** for Nobu; ✆ **212/334-4445** for Next Door Nobu. www.myriadrestaurantgroup.com. Reservations required well in advance at Nobu; reservations accepted only for parties of 6 or more at Next Door Nobu. Main courses $8–$23 at lunch; small plates and main courses $8–$32 at dinner; sushi $3–$10 per piece; omakase (chef's choice) from $45 at lunch, from $70 at dinner. AE, DC, MC, V. Nobu: Mon–Fri 11:45am–2:15pm and 5:45–10:15pm; Sat–Sun 5:45–10:15pm. Next Door Nobu: Mon–Thurs 5:45pm–midnight; Fri–Sat 5:45pm–1am; Sun 5:45–11pm. Subway: 1, 9 to Franklin St.

Tribeca Grill ★ CONTEMPORARY AMERICAN If you've come to town to do a bit of stargazing, this decade-old downtown favorite—housed in Robert De Niro's Tribeca Film Center and referred to in *Variety*-reading circles as the "Miramax Cafeteria"—is probably your best bet. While De Niro is a co-owner, investors include Bill Murray, Sean Penn, Ed Harris, and Christopher Walken, and just about every major star has appeared at one time or another. But the Grill's non-elitist attitude as one of its greatest strengths: The staff is warm and welcoming to Oklahoman tourists and Harvey Weinstein alike, and every big, comfortable table is a good one.

The appealing menu offers first-rate New American food. Among the standouts are crisp fried oysters with Asian slaw to start, a divine crab-crusted sea bass accompanied by braised endive and a dab of red-wine sauce, and a beautifully roasted baby chicken with Niçoise potatoes and whole-grain mustard. Yummy desserts and a 1,400-bottle *Wine Spectator* award-winning wine list, too. Come early to cozy up to the gorgeous mahogany-and-brass bar, or feel free to pop in for a drink or a midday nibble after a day of Financial District sightseeing.

375 Greenwich St. (at Franklin St.). ✆ **212/941-3900.** www.myriadrestaurantgroup.com. Reservations recommended. Main courses $12–$22 at lunch, $19–$29 at dinner; 3-course prix-fixe $20 at lunch, $33 at dinner. AE, DC, DISC, MC, V. Mon–Thurs 11:30am–11pm; Fri 11:30am–11:30pm; Sat 5:30–11:30pm; Sun 11:30am–3pm and 5:30–10pm. Subway: 1, 9 to Franklin St.

MODERATE

Bubby's ★ AMERICAN How do I love Bubby's? Let me count the ways. I love Bubby's for the sublime macaroni and cheese, for the divine garlic burger and fries (accompanied by Bubby's own "wup-ass" ketchup), for the homemade meat loaf with warm cider gravy and garlic mashies—better than Ma used to make. I love Bubby's for the roasted rosemary chicken and chipotle-crusted Black Angus steak, and the classic cocktail the bartender will make for me when I'm in the mood. I love Bubby's generous portions and fresh-from-the-field greens. I love Bubby's big home-style breakfasts so much that I don't even mind lining up with the crowds for weekend brunch. I also love Bubby's coziness: The high-ceilinged, brick-walled loftlike space is very homey—very TriBeCa—and I love the candlelight that adds a touch of romance to the evening. I love the friendly wait staff that doesn't neglect me, even when Harvey Keitel is sitting two tables over. Best of all, I love Bubby's pies: the core of Bubby's business, baked fresh daily, a half dozen to choose from (along with another half dozen homemade cakes), and topped with fresh-made whipped cream. (Pumpkin's my favorite.) Yum, yum, Bubby!

120 Hudson St. (at N. Moore St.). ✆ **212/219-0666.** www.bubbys.com. Reservations recommended for dinner (not accepted for brunch). Main courses $2–$16 at breakfast, brunch, and lunch; $10–$22 at dinner. AE, DC, DISC, MC, V. Mon–Thurs 8am–11pm; Fri 8am–midnight; Sat 9am–4:30pm and 6pm–midnight; Sun 9am–10pm. Subway: 1, 9 to Franklin St.

The Harrison ★ CONTEMPORARY AMERICAN This new restaurant from the folks behind the Red Cat (p. 188) arrived at a precarious time and in a precarious place—in Fall 2001 just blocks from Ground Zero. But the newcomer has turned out to be a touchstone for the resilience of TriBeCa: The neighborhood is back in top form, and the Harrison is a hit.

The Harrison seems to be exactly what New Yorkers need these days: A comfortable, valuewise, unpretentious dining experience. A smart update on the classic American bistro, the space is warm and welcoming, lots of warm woods and soft lighting. Prices aren't cheap, but considering the quality of the food and the overall experience, the Harrison offers excellent value. Expect beautifully prepared food that emphasizes comfort but adds an international edge. The rare yellowfin tuna dressed with marinated cucumber and gazpacho sauce is a winning way to start, as is cavatelli with fork-tender veal cheeks and oven-dried tomatoes. I've always loved what chef Jimmy Bradley does with skate; here, citrus accents offer a surprisingly fitting accent. The pan-crisped chicken surpasses the standard with perfect moistness and a zesty lemon and mustard sauce. Whatever your main, the spiced fries make a sublime accompaniment.

Stick with the less fussy desserts, like the addictive chocolate beignets with a side of espresso sauce, for optimal satisfaction. Wines are well chosen and affordable, and beer lovers have some interesting options. A winner on all counts.

355 Greenwich St. (at Harrison St.). ✆ **212/274-9310.** www.theharrison.com. Reservations highly recommended. Main courses $9–$18 at lunch, $18–$24 at dinner. AE, DC, DISC, MC, V. Mon–Thurs noon–2:30pm and 5:30–11:30pm; Fri noon–2:30pm and 5:30–midnight; Sat 5:30–midnight. Subway: 1, 9 to Franklin St.

Le Zinc ★★ *Value* FRENCH BISTRO The second restaurant from David and Karen Waltuck, the husband-and-wife team behind the glorious Chanterelle (see "Very Expensive," above) is this affordable and joyously authentic French bistro. Despite its hip TriBeCa address, Le Zinc is unfussy and unpretentious. Head to Balthazar or Pastis for a beautiful-people scene; come to Le Zinc for genuine warmth and beautifully prepared creative bistro cuisine. The space is open and comfortable, with big, well-spaced tables, comfortable banquette seating, unframed art posters glazed into the walls, and soft, sexy lighting.

The menu features American bistro favorites with gentle David Waltuck accents, some of which reach beyond France to Eastern Europe, Asia, and even New Orleans. Winning choices include a skate wing beautifully browned in butter and capers; Grandma Gaby's hearty Hungarian stuffed cabbage; delectable mussels in snail butter; an excellent duck, foie gras, and pistachio terrine; a tender calf's liver with caramelized onions; classic rib steak and frites; even a thick, juicy bacon cheeseburger. Reservations aren't taken, but any wait you might have is well worth it—just put yourself in the competent hands of the bartenders at the generous mahogany bar. The crowd is grown up and easygoing. A real winner—and reason enough to visit TriBeCa.

139 Duane St. (btwn W. Broadway and Church St.). ✆ **212/513-0001.** www.lezincnyc.com. Reservations not accepted. Main courses $2–$7 at breakfast, $7–$16 at lunch, $10–$21 at dinner. AE, DISC, MC, V. Sun–Thurs 8am–1am; Fri–Sat 8am–3am. Subway: 1, 2, 3, 9 to Chambers St.

The Odeon *Kids* AMERICAN BISTRO The Odeon is always the first place that comes to mind when I crave a late-night meal, but this attractive hot spot is satisfying at any time of day. The striking deco-ish room is perennially trendy but universally welcoming—no velvet ropes here. Sure, De Niro might be a couple of tables away, but it's the food that's the real draw. The restaurant crosses budget and culture lines: It's easy to eat cheap here if you stick to the burgers, vegetarian chili, and sandwiches, or you can spend a little more and go for fresh-off-the-boat Wellfleet oysters, excellent steak frites, roasted free-range chicken, braised lamb shank, and other top-notch brasserie-style dinners. The prices are lower than they have to be for food like this, and the wine list is equally reasonable. With rich wood paneling, Formica-topped tables, leather banquettes, and a sexy bar, the Odeon even manages to be swanky and comfortable at the same time. As proof of its egalitarianism, there's even a kids' menu—and the chocolate pudding is scrumptious.

145 W. Broadway (at Thomas St.). ✆ **212/233-0507.** Reservations recommended. Main courses $9–$25 at lunch, $13.50–$28 at dinner (most less than $21); fixed-price lunch $20. AE, DC, DISC, MC, V. Mon–Thurs noon–2am; Fri noon–2am; Sat–Sun 11:30am–2am. Subway: 1, 2, 3, 9 to Chambers St.

Salaam Bombay PAN-INDIAN Salaam Bombay is much more attractive than most curry houses, and the Pan-Indian cuisine is easily a cut above the standard fare. Dinner is a somewhat pricey affair for Indian, but the room is romantically low-lit and formally outfitted, and service is professional and attentive (although it can be slow on occasion). The kitchen roams the subcontinental map, from Punjabi tandooris to Goan spicy fish; all the dishes are confidently prepared with quality ingredients. In addition to succulent tandooris and other familiar favorites, consider the lesser-known regional specialties, such as *gosht dum pasanda,* a Kasimiri lamb specialty; marinated in yogurt and cooked in a sealed pot, the meat emerges tender and luscious.

Salaam Bombay also makes an great midday choice; it's daily $12.95 all-you-can-eat lunch is a bargain. I know the notion of a buffet can be a turnoff, but this is a freshly prepared, top-quality spread—you'll watch the tandoori chef pulling fresh-baked naan from the clay oven as you fill your plate. There are a dozen or so fresh-made meat and vegetarian dishes to choose from, as well as all the traditional accompaniments.

317 Greenwich St. (btwn Duane and Reade sts.). ✆ **212/226-9400.** www.salaambombay.com. Reservations accepted. Main courses $13–$23; daily all-you-can-eat buffet lunch $12.95. AE, DC, DISC, MC, V. Daily noon–3pm; Sun–Thurs 5–10:30pm. Subway: 1, 2, 3, 9 to Chambers St.

INEXPENSIVE

Burritoville (p. 166) is at 144 Chambers St., at Hudson Street (✆ **212/964-5048**).

4 Chinatown & Little Italy

To find the restaurants reviewed below, see map on p. 175.

MODERATE

Canton CANTONESE Eating in Chinatown doesn't have to mean communicating with hand signals to a non-English–speaking waiter under the glare of florescent lights in a dining room that resembles your high-school cafeteria. Canton may be a bit more expensive than most Chinatown restaurants, but the resulting high quality and comforts are well worth the added expense. The room eschews the standard bustle for a simple, subdued atmosphere where the attentive staff speaks Noo Yawk English, you can have a fork if you want one, and the water glasses stay full—but the Americanization stops there. Canton draws uptowners and monied Chinese with what is probably the best, most authentic Cantonese cuisine in the city. Your waiter can help guide you through the menu and design a family-style meal to your tastes, but I recommend starting with the squab and black-bean sauce in crisp lettuce wraps—and save room for the greaseless Peking duck, which comes with pillow-soft pancakes and does not require an advance order. My only complaint is the fried rice: It's excellent, but $14? Come on. Still, a terrific place to dine, and well worth the dough.

45 Division St. (btwn Bowery and Market St.). ✆ **212/226-4441** or 212/966-7492. Reservations recommended. Main courses $11–$25. No credit cards. Sun and Wed–Thurs noon–19pm; Fri–Sat noon–10pm. Subway: N, R, 6 to Canal St.

Il Cortile CREATIVE ITALIAN The best restaurant in Little Italy stands out on Mulberry Street thanks to its warm, sophisticated demeanor amid the bright lights and trite decor of its lesser neighbors. The interior has a dramatic skylit atrium; I prefer the cozier front room. There's a certain old-world elegance to the menu, which is folded and sealed with gold foil. The second sign that you're out of the Little Italy ordinary arrives with the warm basket of focaccia, crusty small loaves, golden-brown crostini, and crunchy breadsticks. Prepared under the guiding hand of executive chef Michael DeGeorgio, a James Beard award winner, the northern Italian fare is well prepared and pleasing—the greens fresh and crisp, the sauces appropriately seasoned, the pastas perfectly al dente. This is traditional cuisine, but not without a few welcome twists: The filet mignon carpaccio is rolled with onions and parsley, thick cut, and seared; shiitakes give an unexpected flair to the rigatoni. A standout is the polenta with mushrooms in a savory white-wine sauce—an ideal choice for vegetarians. The wait staff, made up of career neighborhood waiters, is attentive and reserved in an appealing old-world style. The extensive wine cellar, hidden at the front of the restaurant behind a beautiful wooden door that looks as if it may have been liberated from a grand European castle, contains a good number of reasonably priced selections.

125 Mulberry St. (btwn Canal and Hester sts.). ✆ **212/226-6060.** www.ilcortile.com. Reservations recommended. Main courses $9.50–$32 (most $12.50–$25); fixed price lunch $14.95. AE, DC, DISC, MC, V. Daily noon–midnight. Subway: N, R, 6 to Canal St.

Umberto's Clam House ITALIAN/SEAFOOD Umberto's has true-crime cachet. It was at the original Mulberry Street location, in 1973, that "reputed" Mafioso Joey Gallo was assassinated while savoring a plate of scungilli. Umberto's moved to this spot a few years back, leaving those famed bullet holes behind, but it still brims with classic Little Italy ambience.

The traditional, seafood-heavy menu is genuinely pleasing. I found the scungilli to be a bit chewy, but the baked clams were divine. You can also expect first-rate raw cherrystones on the half-shell; perfectly al dente linguine with a generous helping of fresh shelled clams in red sauce or extra-virgin olive oil; and excellent lobster ravioli stuffed with whole chunks of lobster (a steal at $14.95). Plenty of meat and pasta dishes are on hand for nonseafood eaters. The wine list is decent and affordable. The atmosphere is unpretentious, vaguely (and a tad cheesily) old-world nautical, with comfortably spaced tables and a small outdoor patio.

386 Broome St. (btwn Mulberry and Mott sts.). ✆ **212/431-7545.** www.umbertosclamhouse.com. Reservations required for Fri–Sat dinner, and for parties of 5 or more. Pastas $10–$19.50; main courses $7–$30 (most $10–$20). AE, DISC, MC, V. Daily 11am–4am. Subway: N, R to Prince St.; 6 to Spring St.

INEXPENSIVE

Joe's Shanghai ★★ SHANGHAI CHINESE Tucked away on a little elbow of a side street just off the Bowery is this Chinatown institution, which serves up authentic cuisine to enthusiastic crowds nightly. The stars of the huge menu are the signature soup dumplings, quivering steamed pockets filled with hot broth and your choice of pork or crab, accompanied by a side of seasoned soy. Listed as "steamed buns" (item numbers 1 and 2), these culinary marvels never disappoint. Neither does the rest of the authentic Shanghai-inspired menu, which boasts such main courses as whole yellowfish bathed in spicy sauce; excellent "mock duck," a saucy bean-curd dish similar to Japanese yuba that's a hit with vegetarians and carnivores alike; and lots of well-prepared staples. The room is set mostly with round tables of 10 or so, and you'll be asked if you're willing to share. I encourage you to do so; it's a great way to watch and learn

Espresso, Anyone?

America's first espresso bar was **Ferrara,** 195 Grand St., between Mott and Mulberry streets (✆ **212/226-6150**), founded in 1892. This big, bright, pleasant Little Italy *pasticceria* is still the place to go for yummy Italian treats such as cannoli (freshly squeezed into the pastry shell as you watch), custard-filled *zeppole, pastiacotti* (Italian cream puffs), *sfogliatelle* (a flaky shell stuffed with baked ricotta, and a *Sopranos* favorite), napoleons, pignolis, macaroons, and much more. Cafe seating is available so you can enjoy instant sweet-tooth gratification. A convenient place to take a break while strolling Chinatown and Little Italy. Open daily 8am to midnight (to 1am on Sat).

from your neighbors (many of whom are Chinese), who are usually more than happy to tell you what they're eating. If you want a private table, expect a wait. *Note:* The Midtown location is geared more to Western diners, and is a couple of dollars more expensive across the board, but it takes major credit cards.

9 Pell St. (btwn Bowery and Mott sts.). ✆ **212/233-8888.** Reservations recommended for 10 or more. Main courses $4.25–$17. No credit cards. Daily 11am–11pm. Subway: N, R, Q, W, 6 to Canal St.; F to Delancey St. Also at 24 W. 56th St., btwn Fifth and Sixth aves. (✆ 212/333-3868; subway: B, Q to 57th St.).

New York Noodletown ★★ CHINESE/SEAFOOD This just may be the best Chinese food in New York City. Among its fans are Ruth Reichl, former restaurant critic for the *New York Times* and now editor-in-chief of *Gourmet* magazine, who constantly puts it at the top of the heap. So what if the fluorescent-lit room has all the ambience of a school cafeteria? The food is fabulous. The mushroom soup is a lunch in itself, thick with earthy chunks of shiitakes, vegetables, and thin noodles. Another appetizer that can serve as a meal is the hacked roast duck in noodle soup. The kitchen excels at seafood preparations, so be sure to try at least one: Looking like a snow-dusted plate of meaty fish, the salt-baked squid is sublime. The quick-woked Chinese broccoli or the crisp sautéed baby bok choy make great accompaniments. Other special dishes are various sandy pot casseroles, hearty, flavorful affairs slow-simmered in clay vessels. Unlike most of its neighbors, New York Noodletown keeps very long hours, which makes it the best late-night bet in the neighborhood, too.

28½ Bowery (at Bayard St.). ✆ **212/349-0923.** Reservations accepted. Main courses $4–$13. No credit cards. Daily 9am–3:30am. Subway: N, R, 6 to Canal St.

Nha Trang *Finds* VIETNAMESE The decor may be standard-issue, no-atmosphere Chinatown (glass-topped tables, linoleum floors, mirrored walls), but this friendly, bustling place serves up the best Vietnamese fare in Chinatown. A plate of six crispy, finger-size spring rolls is a nice way to start; the slightly spicy pork-and-shrimp filling is nicely offset by the wrapping of lettuce, cucumber, and mint. The pho noodle soup comes in a quart-size bowl brimming with bright vegetables and various meats and seafood. But my favorite dish is the simple barbecued pork chops—sliced paper-thin, soaked in a soy/sugar cane marinade, and grilled to utter perfection. Everything is well prepared, though, and your waiter will be glad to help you design a meal to suit your tastes. A recent expansion into an adjacent storefront makes it much easier to get a table these days.

If there's a line, and you don't want to wait, head a couple of blocks over to a second location, **Nha Trang Centre,** which accepts credit cards.

87 Baxter St. (btwn Canal and Bayard sts.). ✆ **212/233-5948.** Reservations accepted. Main courses $4–$12.50. No credit cards (MC, V at Nha Trang Centre). Daily 11am–9:30pm. Subway: N, R, 6 to Canal St. Also at 148 Centre St. (at Walker St.). ✆ 212/941-9292; subway: N, R, 6 to Canal St.

5 The Lower East Side

MODERATE

Le Pere Pinard ★ *Finds* FRENCH BISTRO/WINE BAR This authentic French wine bar and bistro is a charming slice of Le Marais on the gentrifying Lower East Side, with high ceilings, burnished brick walls, well-spaced tables with mix-and-match chairs, and an authentic come-as-you-are air. Everything is well worn in a good, comfortable way. The kitchen specializes in the Gallic version of comfort food: steak frites, shell steak with Roquefort sauce, a delectable shepherd's pie with a delightfully cheesy crust, a terrific brandade, and a generous charcuterie and cheese plate—the perfect match for the sublime crusty-on-the-outside, soft-in-the-middle bread that accompanies every meal. Greens are fresh and well prepared; even a simple mesclun salad wears a just-right vinaigrette. There's a wonderful wine selection by the bottle, carafe, and glass; I like the restaurant's protocol, which allows you to taste first even if you're just ordering by the glass. Service is attentive in a casual, easygoing way. I've eaten here plenty, and both food and service are consistently good. Smoking is allowed in the front (bar) room, while the back room is dedicated to nonsmokers. There's also a pleasant garden in warm weather. (The interior can be uncomfortably warm on the hottest summer days.)

175 Ludlow St. (south of Houston St.). ✆ **212/777-4917.** Reservations recommended. Main courses $11.50–$19.50. AE. Mon–Thurs 5pm–midnight; Fri 5pm–1am; Sat 11am–1am; Sat–Sun 11am–midnight. Subway: F to Second Ave.

INEXPENSIVE

Katz's Delicatessen ★★ *Value* JEWISH DELI Here's the city's best Jewish deli. The motto is, "There's Nothing More New York than Katz's," and it's spot-on. Founded in 1888, this cavernous, brightly lit place is suitably Noo Yawk, with dill pickles, Dr. Brown's cream soda, and old-world attitude to spare.

All of Katz's traditional eats are first-rate: matzo ball and chicken noodle soups, potato knishes, cheese blintzes, egg creams (made with Katz's very own seltzer), and the beloved all-beef hot dogs. There's no faulting the pastrami—smoked to perfection and piled high on rye—or the dry-cured roast beef, either. All of the well-stuffed sandwiches are substantially cheaper than you'll find at any other deli in town. What's more, Katz's is one of the only delis cool enough to let you split one with your travel partner without adding a bogus $2 to $3 "sharing" charge.

205 E. Houston St. (at Ludlow St.). ✆ **212/254-2246.** Reservations not accepted. Sandwiches $2.15–$10; other main courses $5–$17.50. AE, MC, V ($20 minimum). Sun–Tues 8am–10pm; Wed–Thurs 8am–11pm; Fri–Sat 8am–2:30am. Subway: F to Second Ave.

6 SoHo & Nolita

To locate the restaurants reviewed below, see map on p. 175.

EXPENSIVE

Aquagrill ★★ SEAFOOD Attention, seafood lovers: Book now, because this marvelous—and hugely popular—little restaurant serves up some of the city's best fish. The raw bar flies in a phenomenal selection of oysters from around the world daily, usually between 25 and 30 varieties; the Alaskan Canoe Lagoons were some of the creamiest and dreamiest I've ever had. If you like sea urchin, don't pass on the fresh Maine version if it's available; served in the shell with citrus soy and shaved scallions, it was one of New York's most memorable taste sensations. Oddities like Maine periwinkles and abalone sashimi also appear, depending on what's available and in top form. Among the entrees, you can keep it cheap and simple with preparations that let the fish's own fresh, clean flavors sing, like grilled Maine sea scallops or roasted Florida swordfish. Or you can spend a little more and opt for one of the more fanciful preparations, such as Atlantic salmon with a falafel crust, cucumbers, tomatoes, and a tart lemon-coriander vinaigrette; or a shellfish-rich bouillabaisse in a garlic saffron tomato broth. On special during my last visit was meaty escolar—so buttery that it was like the foie gras of fish, bathed in a delicate garlic parsley sauce and accompanied by sautéed broccoli rabe, fresh cranberry beans, roasted garlic cloves, and steamed cockles. Service is knowledgeable and efficient, the award-winning wine list boasts a good number of affordable choices, and there's outdoor seating in warm weather.

210 Spring St. (at Sixth Ave.). ✆ **212/274-0505.** Reservations highly recommended. Main courses $9.50–$23.50 at lunch and brunch, $15–$26 at dinner; $16.50 3-course "Shucker's Special" at lunch (a half dozen oysters, salad, soup). AE, MC, V. Tues–Thurs noon–3pm and 6–10:45pm; Fri noon–3pm and 6–11:45pm; Sat noon–3:45pm and 6–11:45pm; Sun noon–3:45pm and 6–10:30pm. Subway: C, E to Spring St.

Blue Ribbon Sushi ★★ JAPANESE This lovely, almost zenlike closet of a restaurant is the best choice in town for sushi lovers, especially those with adventurous palates. This is hipper-than-thou SoHo, and Blue Ribbon is eternally hot, so don't expect a bargain. But you will get your money's worth here: The fish is very fresh and the top-notch chefs know how to handle it, plus, the selection is marvelous. Almost evenly split between the Pacific and the Atlantic, the dazzling menu offers up the obvious (ruby-red tuna, meaty yellowtail, creamy sea urchin in the shell) and the out there (blue crab roll, Maine lobster, Japanese mountain yam, even jellyfish). There's a changing array of inventive, Nobu-ish appetizers—we had an incredible, almost foie gras–like monkfish liver last time I was there—and an equally impressive sake list, and everything is beautifully presented on gorgeous Japanese ware. The staff is a bit harried, but they're very knowledgeable and do a remarkable job keeping up with demand. The biggest downside is that reservations aren't taken, so come early, come late, or expect a wait. Also, while the booths are very comfortable for two or four, seating can be tight for larger parties.

119 Sullivan St. (btwn Prince and Spring sts.). ✆ **212/343-0404.** Reservations not accepted. A la carte sushi and rolls $4–$15.50 (specials may be higher); sushi combos and main courses $11.50–$25. AE, DC, MC, V. Daily noon–2am. Subway: C, E to Spring St.; N, R to Prince St.

MODERATE

Balthazar *Value* FRENCH BISTRO Balthazar has been one of the hottest scenes in town since its doors opened a few years back (Jerry Seinfeld even popped the question here), and it remains high on the hip list. For good reason: With all the trappings of an authentic Parisian brasserie, the space is simply gorgeous. The classic French bistro fare, ranging from steak frites and grilled calf's liver to a delightful duck shepherd's pie and a wonderful brook trout with honey mustard glaze, is surprisingly affordable and excellently prepared. The expansive raw bar offerings are beautifully displayed and make a worthy splurge.

Lower East Side, SoHo, Nolita & East Village Dining

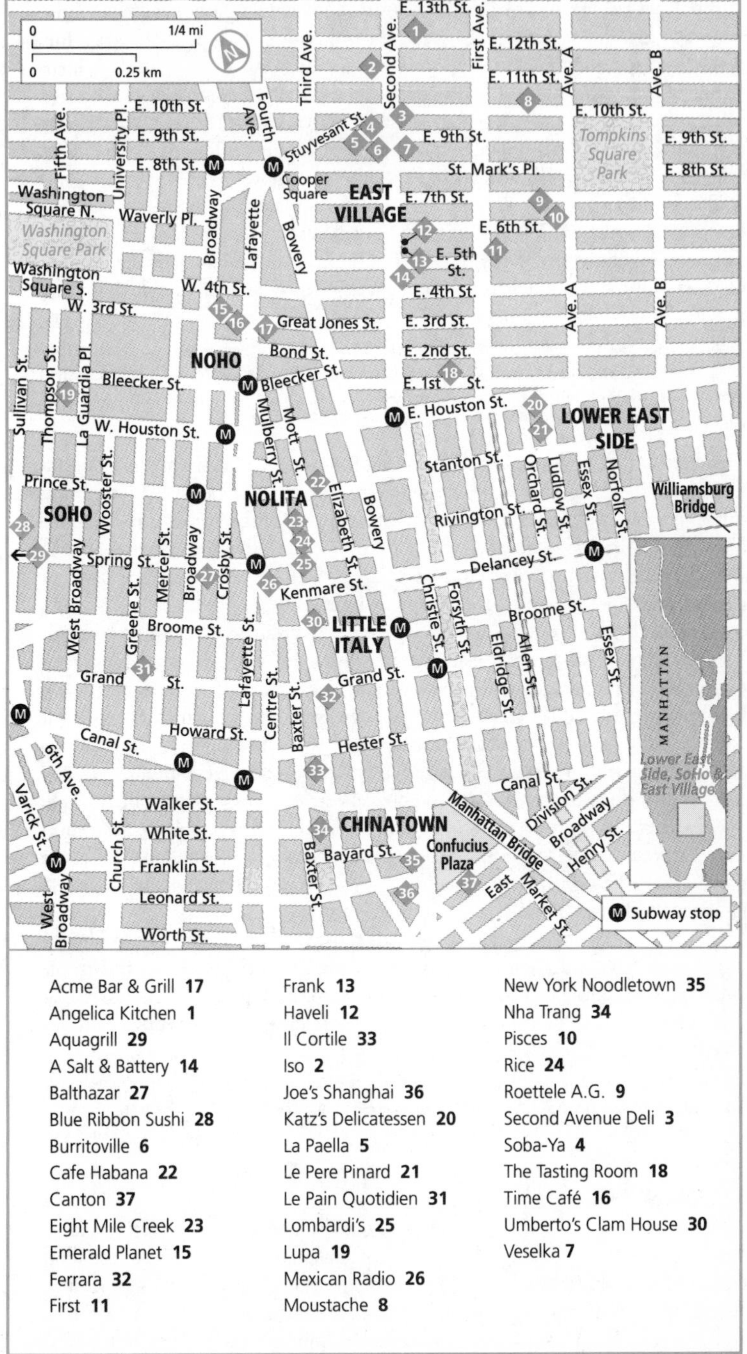

Acme Bar & Grill **17**
Angelica Kitchen **1**
Aquagrill **29**
A Salt & Battery **14**
Balthazar **27**
Blue Ribbon Sushi **28**
Burritoville **6**
Cafe Habana **22**
Canton **37**
Eight Mile Creek **23**
Emerald Planet **15**
Ferrara **32**
First **11**
Frank **13**
Haveli **12**
Il Cortile **33**
Iso **2**
Joe's Shanghai **36**
Katz's Delicatessen **20**
La Paella **5**
Le Pere Pinard **21**
Le Pain Quotidien **31**
Lombardi's **25**
Lupa **19**
Mexican Radio **26**
Moustache **8**
New York Noodletown **35**
Nha Trang **34**
Pisces **10**
Rice **24**
Roettele A.G. **9**
Second Avenue Deli **3**
Soba-Ya **4**
The Tasting Room **18**
Time Café **16**
Umberto's Clam House **30**
Veselka **7**

But I have some complaints: The lofty room is so tightly packed and the tables so uncomfortably close that private conversation is a pipe dream. And this is the loudest restaurant I've ever been in—my husband and I found ourselves yelling at each other across the tiny table (though not every table is subjected to equal volume levels). Still, if you're willing to put up with the discomforts, this is about as exciting as a downtown scene gets. The long mirrored bar is a hopping spot unto itself that attracts beautiful people galore.

The best way to enjoy Balthazar is to come in the off-hours—for breakfast, lunch, or a midday meal—to enjoy the excellent fare in a more relaxing environment. Weekend brunch is busy but enjoyable, but reservations are a must. Or just stop into the adjacent boulangerie, which sells fresh-baked breads, desserts, and sandwiches to go.

80 Spring St. (at Crosby St., 1 block east of Broadway). ✆ **212/965-1414.** Reservations highly recommended (some walk-ins accepted). Main courses $11–$20 at lunch (most less than $16), $12–$32 at dinner (most less than $21). AE, MC, V. Mon–Thurs 7:30am–1:30am; Fri–Sat 7:30am–2:30am; Sun 7:30am–12:30am. Subway: 6 to Spring St.; N, R to Prince St.; F, V to Broadway/Lafayette St.

Eight Mile Creek ★★ *Finds* NEW AUSTRALIAN This simple little Nolita restaurant, the first in New York dedicated to cuisine from Down Under, is a joy for diners in search of a bit of culinary adventure. Outfitted with basic white-linen-clad tables and black-and-white photos of the Outback, the narrow, brick-walled space is warm, cozy, and easygoing; the only downside is a lack of elbowroom, but I've never felt crowded or uncomfortable here.

As far as the food goes, think New American reimagined with antipodal (and, by association, Pan-Asian) twists. Some of my favorite dishes include emu carpaccio with asparagus and enoki mushrooms, delicately dressed in a black truffle vinaigrette; and tender, beautifully seared kangaroo (which tastes like a cross between beef and venison) accompanied by braised endive, green lentils, and whole-grain mustard. For more Northern Hemisphere–minded tastes, there's better-than-dessert King Island blue cheese tarts with a shallot marmalade and balsamic vinaigrette on greens, and a delicious braised Australian lamb shank served over parsnip and chanterelle mushrooms. A wonderful, if a tad pricey, Australian and New Zealand wine list is on hand, and the service is knowledgeable and friendly.

Downstairs is a comfortable lounge, **24/8,** for cocktails and more casual Australian pub fare, including traditional meat pies, beer-battered fish-and-chips, and kangaroo skewers with pepperberry ketchup (only in Oz!), plus Australian beers on tap. I hear they'll even make you a vegemite sandwich, but I've never asked.

240 Mulberry St. (btwn Prince and Spring sts.). ✆ **212/431-4635.** www.eightmilecreek.com. Reservations recommended. Main courses $14–$22 in dining room; $7–$18 (most under $14) in 24/8 lounge. AE, MC, V. Tues–Fri 6–11pm, Sat–Sun 11:30am–11pm. 24/8 lounge, daily 5:30pm–3am. Subway: 6 to Spring St.; B, D, F, Q to Broadway/Lafayette St.

INEXPENSIVE

Cafe Habana ★ HISPANIC I just love this sleek update on a typical Hispanic luncheonette. It's hip without being the least bit pretentious, and what the food may lack in authenticity it more than makes up for in quality and flavor: Shrimps are big and hearty; pork is moist and flavorful; cilantro and other spices are fresh and aromatic. Winning starters include *pozole,* hominy corn stew with shredded chicken or pork in a clear broth that you season to taste with oregano, chile, and lime; and the hugely popular Mexican corn on the cob, which is skewered, coated with lime juice and grated cheese, sprinkled with chile powder, and grilled into a messy but sweet popcorny treat. Main courses include the ultramoist roast pork (perfect with a squeeze of lime) and *camarones al ajillo,* shrimp in spicy garlic sauce. Most everything comes with your choice of red or black beans and rice; go with the yellow rice, as the white rice tends to be a tad anemic. Wine and a handful of Mexican beers are served, but I really enjoyed the not-too-sweet red hibiscus tea.

The room is narrow and tables are petite (especially those for two), but a middle aisle keeps the place from feeling too crowded, and service is easygoing and friendly. Don't be surprised if there's a wait for a table.

If you're strolling Nolita and need a bite, stop into the adjacent storefront sandwich shop around the corner on Elizabeth Street for a pressed sandwich or other takeout treat.

17 Prince St. (at Elizabeth St.). ✆ **212/625-2001.** Reservations not accepted. Main courses $5–$15. AE, MC, V. Daily 9am–midnight. Subway: B, D, F, Q to Broadway/Lafayette St.; 6 to Spring St.

Le Pain Quotidien ★★ FRENCH/BAKERY CAFE This big, airy neoclassical-goes-farmhouse cafe (a Franco-Belgian transplant) is one of my favorites for a sophisticated casual meal at a bargain-basement price. Take a seat at a table for two or cozy up to one of the generous and comfy common tables (the one in the sunlit front room is best). The light menu is made up mostly of beautifully crafted sandwiches and salads. Excellent choices include the open-faced beef carpaccio sandwich dressed with basil, Parmesan, and virgin olive oil on dark country bread; Paris ham with three mustards on crusty French; and a board of fine French cheeses—brie, chavignol, gruyere—and your choice of walnut bread, rye, wheat, or a crusty baguette. All sandwiches are garnished with seasonal greens and fresh herbs. Salads are a particularly good value, because they come piled high and accompanied by generous plate of French bread. Soups are homemade, hearty, and warming. Breads are baked five times daily in small batches to insure freshness. Save room for the divine desserts—fruit tarts, pies, brownies, cookies, brioches—or stop by just for a sweet and a cappuccino; the warm Belgian waffle sprinkled with powdered sugar and fresh blueberries makes a wonderful, light-as-air choice. Tables are waiter-serviced, but an up-front counter serves walk-ins and takeout.

100 Grand St. (between Mercer and Greene sts.). ✆ **212/625-9009.** www.painquotidien.com. Reservations not accepted. Breakfast $3–$7.50; sandwiches and salads $7.50–$18 (most less than $12). No credit cards. Daily 8am–7pm. Subway: N, R to Canal St. Also at ABC Carpet & Home, 38 E. 19th St. (btwn Broadway and Park Ave. S.; ✆ 212/625-9009; subway: 4, 5, 6, N, R, L to 14th St./Union Sq.); 50 W. 72nd St. (btwn Columbus Ave. and Central Park W.; ✆ 212/712-9700; subway: B, C to 72 St.); 833 Lexington Ave. (btwn 63rd and 64th sts.; ✆ 212/755-5810; subway: 4, 5, 6 to 59th St.; N, R to Lexington Ave.); 1336 First Ave. (btwn 71st and 72nd sts.; ✆ 212/717-4800; subway: 6 to 68th St.); 1131 Madison Ave. (btwn 84th and 85th sts.; ✆ 212/327-4900; subway: 4, 5, 6 to 86th St.).

Lombardi's ★★ *Kids* PIZZA Lombardi's makes the best pizza in Manhattan, hands down. It also happens to be a living gem in the annals of the city's culinary history. First opened in 1905, "America's first licensed pizzeria" cooks its delectable pies in its original coal brick oven. The wonderfully smoky crust (a generations-old family recipe that Gennaro Lombardi hand-carried from Naples at the turn of the century) is topped with fresh mozzarella, basil, and pecorino Romano, and San Marzano tomato sauce. From there, the choice is yours. Topping options are suitably old-world (Citterio pancetta, kalamata olives, Esposito sweet Italian sausage, homemade meatballs, beefsteak tomatoes, and the like), but Lombardi's specialty is the fresh clam pie, with hand-shucked clams, oregano, fresh garlic, Romano, extra-virgin olive oil, and fresh-ground pepper (no sauce). The main dining room is narrow but very pleasant, with the usual checkered tablecloths and exposed brick walls. A big draw is the garden out back.

32 Spring St. (btwn Mott and Mulberry sts.). ✆ **212/941-7994.** Reservations accepted for parties of 6 or more. Pies $11.50–$21; extra charge for additional toppings. No credit cards. Mon–Thurs 11:30am–11pm; Fri–Sat 11:30am–midnight; Sun 11:30am–10pm. Subway: 6 to Spring St.; N, R to Prince St.

Mexican Radio MEXICAN The hip SoHo-goes–south of the border decor—deep mango walls, candles, folk art pieces, rough-hewn furniture—creates an artsy-rustic atmosphere in which to dig into surprisingly good Old Mexico fare. The fresh-baked, multicolored corn chips (not free; $2.50) come with a fresh and tangy salsa. Main choices range from excellent, well-stuffed burritos to heaping fajita platters. Fans shouldn't pass on the nutty, chocolately mole (one of the best in the city). Another winner is the carnitas, tender shredded pork soaked in a sweet-citrus marinade of oranges, lemons, limes, and garlic, then grilled with a pepper salsa and served on a heaping plate with freshly made white corn tortillas. The spice meter is turned up pretty high, so ask your young and friendly waiter to point you to the cooler dishes if you shy away from cilantro and other fiery spices. The margaritas are terrific. Beware: The room can get LOUD as weekend evenings wear on.

19 Cleveland Place (just south of intersection of Spring and Lafayette sts.). ✆ **212/343-0140.** Reservations accepted for parties of 6 or more. Main courses $8–$16. AE, MC, V. Sun–Thurs noon–11:30; Fri–Sat noon–midnight. Subway: 6 to Spring St.

Rice *Value* PAN-ASIAN/INDO-CARIBBEAN This sleek, but tiny restaurant has a cool Japanese vibe and a superaffordable seasonal menu built around—you guessed it—rice. You pick your grain from the seven choices, which range from healthy brown to Bhutanese red or Thai black, and pair it with any 1 of 10 toppings. Vietnamese-grilled lemongrass chicken goes well with either short-grain Japanese or sticky rice, while Jamaican jerk chicken wings is an ideal match for yellow rice and peas. Basmati is a must for the warm lentil salad or Indian curry. If you're just not sure, go with the pairing suggestions on the short but appealing menu. Thick Portuguese soup, flavored with potatoes and distinctive caraway-flavored rice, is a vegan's delight; it pairs up well with grilled eggplant maki or rice balls topped with tomato cumin sauce for a complete vegetarian meal for about $10. Rice bowls come small or large to suit your appetite, but all portions tend to be on the daintier side, so big appetites should order accordingly.

A takeout outlet is in the adjacent storefront.

227 Mott St. (btwn Prince and Spring sts.). ✆ **212/226-5775.** Reservations not accepted. Main courses $6–$13. No credit cards. Daily noon–midnight. Subway: 6 to Spring St.

7 The East Village & Noho

To locate the restaurants reviewed below, see map on p. 175.

MODERATE

First ★ CREATIVE GLOBAL CUISINE Native New Yorker Sam DeMarco pioneered quality late-night dining at this East Village spot back in late 1993. Nearly a decade later, First is as hip, and as winning, as ever. The room is big and comfortable, with curved leather banquettes, exposed brick walls, a barrel-vaulted ceiling, and the increasing vibe of a nightclub as the night wears on.

First is all about fun. The best way to open the meal is with one of the bar's "Tiny Tinis," mini martinis that come in a range of silly and seasonal flavors. A large menu of share-able starters offers Sam's haute takes on familiar party foods, including his signature buffalo "lollipop" wings—served on a stick, with blue cheese fondue for dipping—crisp Asian-style oysters with wasabi mayo, shrimp cocktail, and potato skins dressed with smoked salmon, caviar, and crème fraiche. Mains are more straightforward but still have an only-in-New York ethnic flair: witness roast pork loin with sauerkraut and pierogi, crab cakes with peanut noodles and mango salsa, and grilled Mediterranean-style chicken with Greek salad. A small menu of casual bites—including First's famous mini-burgers and a "two-fisted" BLT—rounds out the offerings, making First a worthwhile choice at any time of day.

87 First Ave. (btwn 5th and 6th sts.). ✆ **212/674-3823.** www.first.citysearch.com. Reservations recommended. Starters and share dishes $5–$14; main courses $11–$25; 5-course tasting menu $42 per person ($24 supplement for wine pairings); Sun brunch $13–$15, including unlimited champagne. AE, DC, DISC, MC, V. Sun 11am–4pm and 5pm–1am; Mon–Thurs 6pm–2am; Fri–Sat 6pm–3am. Subway: F to Second Ave.

Haveli INDIAN The stretch of East 6th Street between First and Second avenues in the East Village is known as "Little India" thanks to the dozen or more Indian restaurants that line the block. Around the corner—and a giant step up in quality—from Little India is Haveli, where the authentically prepared dishes, attractively low-lit dining room, and attentive service are far superior to what you'll find on East 6th Street. All of your favorites are here in top form, including well-stuffed samosas (meat or veggie), first-rate tandooris, and mouthwatering nan. Prices are a little steeper than what you'll find in Little India, but the Haveli experience is worth the extra dough. There's sidewalk seating in summer.

100 Second Ave. (btwn 5th and 6th sts.). ✆ **212/982-0533.** www.haveli.citysearch.com. Reservations recommended for weekend dinner and large parties. Main courses $9–$19. AE, DC, DISC, MC, V. Daily noon–midnight. Subway: F to Second Ave.

Iso *Value* JAPANESE Iso is the top choice in town for fresh and beautifully presented sushi at affordable prices. The sushi and sashimi combos make a good-value starting point; supplement with your favorites or a few of the daily special fishes, which may include blue fin toro (tuna belly) or Japanese aji (horse mackerel). The menu also features light, greaseless tempura and entrees like chicken teriyaki and beef negamaki for the sushiphobes in your party. The attractive Keith Haring–themed room is tightly packed but still manages to be relatively comfortable, and service is better than at other sushi joints in this price range. Unless you arrive before 6pm, expect a line—but the high-quality fish and wallet-friendly pricing make Iso worth the wait.

175 Second Ave. (at 11th St.). ✆ **212/777-0361.** Reservations not accepted. A la carte sushi $2.50–$6; sushi rolls $4.50–$12.50; sushi combos and main courses $13.50–$22. AE, MC, V. Mon–Sat 5:15pm–midnight. Subway: 6 to Astor Place.

La Paella *Value* SPANISH Always-consistent La Paella serves up some of the best tapas in town—if not the best, especially for the money—and the paella can hardly be outdone. This is fun eating, the kind of place where patrons return again and again to wash down fish croquettes, chorizos, and green olives with bottles of chilled Negro Modela, a dark Mexican brew that goes well with the flavorful menu of (primarily) grilled delights. There's also a terrific sangria, served in generous pitchers by the frisky wait staff, many of whom seem as though they just blew in from Madrid. Tapas here are more generously apportioned than at many other places; the grilled calamari is a perfectly sized appetizer without being overwhelming. The tapas and paellas are well priced, but it's easy to run up a tab in this festive setting, which tends to attract large parties after 8pm.

214 E. 9th St. (btwn Second and Third aves.). ✆ **212/598-4321.** Reservations accepted Sun–Thurs. Tapas $4.50–$9; paella for 2 $22–$36. MC, V. Daily 5pm–midnight. Subway: 6 to Astor Place; N, R to 8th St.

Roettele A.G. *Finds* SWISS This snug chalet hideaway is New York's only authentic Swiss restaurant, and it's a winner. The cheese fondue, a hearty dinner for two or a generous appetizer for four, is smooth and beautifully presented with crusty bread and fresh vegetables. Build your meal around it by supplementing with other alpine and house specialties, such as air-dried beef, classic raclette and Wiener schnitzel, duck liver mousse, and terrific sautéed wild mushrooms over fresh herbs and polenta—plus spaetzle on the side, of course. The restaurant stocks Swiss and German wines and beers, plus a few French bottles; try the medium-bodied Spatenlager to help wash down all that melted cheese. In keeping with the theme, a wide selection of yummy French and German pastries is available. The formerly harried service is now consistently attentive. A real treat!

126 E. 7th St. (btwn First Ave. and Ave. A). ✆ **212/674-4140.** Reservations recommended, especially on weekends. Main courses $8–$17; fondue for 2 $32–$36. AE, DC, DISC, MC, V. Tues–Thurs 5:30–11pm; Fri 5:30–11:30pm; Sat noon–3pm and 5:30–11:30pm; Sun noon–3pm and 5:30–10pm. Subway: L to First Ave.; 6 to Astor Place.

The Tasting Room ★★ *Finds* REGIONAL NEW AMERICAN Husband-and-wife team Colin and Renée Alevras call their place a wine bar and cafe, but those simple terms don't do justice to this culinary jewel.

The Alevrases haven't exactly reinvented the wheel, but their clever menu is a refreshing change from the standard format. There are always a dozen or so dishes to choose from, each of which comes in two sizes: "taste," akin to a generously portioned appetizer; and "share," about twice that. So, rather than having to commit to an entire roasted John Dory filet (with Brussels sprouts and roasted shallots, from the fall menu) for $25, you can have a taste portion for $13, and also try the braised and roasted Muscovy duck legs (with sweet potatoes and collard greens) for $12. You're free to mix and match dishes as you see fit and dictate the order in which you'd like to enjoy them.

Colin's cooking bursts with clean, fresh flavors, and the changing menu highlights the best of what's in season, from local grown veggies to farmhouse cheeses.

72 E. 1st St. (btwn First and Second aves.). ✆ **212/358-7831.** Reservations necessary. Appetizer-size "taste" plates $6–$15; main-course-size "share" plates $15–$29. AE, DC, DISC, MC, V. Tues–Sat 6pm–1am. Subway: F to Second Ave.

INEXPENSIVE

Also consider the all-kosher **Second Avenue Deli,** 156 Second Ave., at 10th Street (✆ **212/677-0606**), for kosher Jewish deli fare extraordinaire; for details, see "The New York Deli News" box on p. 210.

The original **Time Cafe** is located at 380 Lafayette St., at Great Jones Street (✆ **212/533-7000**); this location also serves breakfast, and I've spotted Michael Stipe here more than once. Subway: 6 to Bleecker St.; B, D, F, Q to Broadway/Lafayette St. There's also **Moustache** (p. 187) at 265 E. 10th St., between First Avenue and Avenue A (✆ **212/228-2022**), for good, affordable Middle Eastern. A second location of authentic chip shop **A Salt & Battery** (p. 188) will be open by the time you arrive, at 80 Second Ave., between 4th and 5th streets, (✆ **212/254 6610**). **Burritoville** (p. 166) is at 141 Second Ave., between St. Mark's Place and 9th Street (✆ **212/260-3300**).

Acme Bar & Grill *Kids* SOUTHERN/BARBECUE Acme's motto is AN OKAY PLACE TO EAT—a witty bit of clear-eyed candor in this best-obsessed town. This easygoing NoHo joint is divey in a pleasing way, with a good-natured staff, a Louisiana roadhouse theme, and the comfortable ambience of a well-worn neighborhood favorite. Acme serves up heaping platters of Southern home cooking and barbecue, including po-boys, boiled crawfish, jambalaya, seafood gumbo, thick-cut pork chops, chicken-fried steak, baby back ribs—not gourmet grub, but good, cheap, filling eats.

9 Great Jones St. (at Lafayette St.). ✆ **212/420-1934.** Reservations accepted for parties of 8 or more. Main courses $6–$14 at lunch, $7–$16 at dinner; fixed-price weekend brunch $10 (includes coffee and tea, plus juice, Bloody Mary, beer, or mimosa). AE, DC, DISC, MC, V. Mon–Thurs 11:30am–midnight; Fri–Sat 11am–1am; Sun 11am–11pm. Subway: 6 to Bleecker St.

Angelica Kitchen ORGANIC VEGETARIAN This cheerful restaurant is serious about vegan cuisine. The kitchen prepares everything fresh daily; they guarantee that at least 95% of all ingredients are organically grown, with sustainable agriculture and responsible business practices additionally required before food can cross the kitchen's threshold. But good-for-you (and good-for-the-environment) doesn't have to mean boring—this is flavorful, beautifully prepared cuisine served in a lovely country kitchen–style setting. Salads spill over with sprouts and all kinds of crisp veggies and are crowned with homemade dressings. The Dragon Bowls, a specialty, are heaping portions of rice, beans, tofu, and steamed vegetables. The daily seasonal specials feature the best of what's fresh and in season in such dishes as fiery three-bean chili; baked tempeh nestled in a sourdough baguette and dressed in mushroom gravy; and lemon-herb baked tofu layered with roasted vegetables and fresh pesto on mixed-grain bread.

300 E. 12th St. (just east of Second Ave.). ✆ **212/228-2909.** www.angelicakitchen.com. Reservations accepted for parties of 6 or more. Main courses $6–$14.50. No credit cards. Daily 11:30am–10:30pm. Subway: L, N, R, 4, 5, 6 to 14th St./Union Sq.

Frank ★★ *Value* HOME-STYLE ITALIAN This home-style restaurant serves genuine, no-nonsense, straight-from-the-boot cuisine that's everything it should be. The menu—like the restaurant itself—is small but satisfying, focusing on what the kitchen knows how to do well: Rigatoni al ragu wears a hearty meat-and-tomato "gravy" that's been slow-cooked to perfection. It appears again on the house specialty, the *polpettone*—literally "the big meatball"—a moist, beautifully seasoned mound of beef accompanied by a cheesy potato-and-pancetta gratin that's better than dessert in my book. The spaghetti with garlic and extra-virgin olive oil is a simple dish, but the pasta is ideally al dente and tossed to perfection with just the right bit of finely grated cheese; anchovy lovers should go with the fishy version for supreme pleasure. There's always homemade gnocchi and ravioli, plus spiced meat loaf and a couple of fish dishes. The wine list is well priced, with a good selection by the glass.

The young wait staff is easygoing and earnest, and the brick-walled room is dimly lit and attractive in a cozy, homey way. On the downside, the tables are so close together that you can't help but overhear your neighbors' conversation; the open kitchen can make the dining room rather smoky at times; and there's often a wait (Vera, Frank's bar, offers a place to relax with a glass of wine). But these are minor inconveniences to bear for the marvelous payoff that is Frank fare.

88 Second Ave. (btwn 5th and 6th sts.). ✆ **212/420-0202.** Reservations accepted only for parties of 8 or more. Main courses $9–$14. No credit cards. Mon–Thurs 10:30am–4pm and 5pm–12:45am; Fri–Sat 10:30am–4pm and 5pm–1:45am; Sun 10:30am–11:45pm. Subway: 6 to Astor Place.

Pisces *Value* SEAFOOD This pleasing fish house serves up the best inexpensive seafood in the city. All the fish is top quality and fresh daily, and all smoked items are prepared in the restaurant's own smoker. The mesquite-smoked whole trout in sherry oyster sauce is better than trout I've had for twice the price; start with the phyllo-fried shrimp or the tuna ceviche with curried potato chips and roasted pepper coulis, and the world is yours. Other winning dishes include flaky pan-fried skate in a burgundy reduction with garlicky mashed potatoes and roasted pearl onions. There are daily specials in addition to the menu; last time we dined here, I feasted on an excellent grilled mako shark with chard in a cockle stew. The creative kitchen shows surprising skill with vegetables as well as fish.

The wine list is appealing and very well priced, the decor suitably nautical without being kitschy, and the service friendly and attentive. For wallet-watchers, the early bird fixed-price makes an already terrific value even better. The Alphabet City locale gives Pisces serious hip, but it's laid-back, ensuring that anyone will be comfortable here. Tables spill out onto the sidewalk on warm evenings, giving you a ringside seat for the funky East Village show.

95 Ave. A (at 6th St.). ✆ **212/260-6660.** Reservations recommended. Main courses $8–$20; 2-course fixed-price dinner (Mon–Thurs 5:30–7pm; Fri–Sun 5:30–6:30pm) $15. AE, DC, MC, V. Mon–Thurs 5:30–11:30pm; Fri 5:30pm–1am; Sat 11:30am–3:30pm and 5:30pm–1am; Sun 11:30am–3:30pm and 5:30–11:30pm. Subway: 6 to Astor Place; F to Second Ave.

Soba-Ya *Finds* JAPANESE NOODLES Shhh—don't tell anybody else about Soba-Ya. It has a loyal following, but the masses haven't discovered it (yet). Good! That makes it easy to walk in and enjoy an affordable, healthy Japanese meal without a wait—the constant bane of Big Apple diners in search of an affordable sit-down meal. Start with one of the special starters, which might be grilled shiitakes or luscious toro (tuna belly) sashimi, and then move on to one of the house specialties: generous, steaming noodle bowls. They come with soba (thin buckwheat) or udon (my favorite, a very thick noodle much like pasta) and in a number of combinations. A menu with descriptions and pictures makes it easy for noodle novices to order. I love the *nabeyaki,* an udon bowl with shrimp tempura, and the excellent-quality una-don, broiled eel over rice. Cold soba dishes topped with your choice of ingredients are also available. Everything is beautifully presented on delicate Japanese dishware, and there's a lengthy list of sakes. The lovely blond-wood dining room is blessed with a soothing, Zen-like vibe and the kind of attentive service for which you usually have to pay much more.

229 E. 9th St. (btwn Second and Third aves.). ✆ **212/533-6966.** Reservations not accepted. Main courses $6.50–$14. AE, DC, DISC, MC, V. Daily noon–4pm and 5:30–10:30pm. Subway: 6 to Astor Place.

Veselka ★ UKRAINIAN DINER Whenever the craving hits for hearty Eastern European fare at old-world prices, Veselka fits the bill with divine *pierogi* (small doughy envelopes filled with potatoes, cheese, or sauerkraut), *kasha varnishkes* (cracked buckwheat and noodles with mushroom sauce), stuffed cabbage, grilled Polish kielbasa, freshly made potato pancakes, and classic soups like a sublime scarlet borscht, voted best in the city by the *New York Times* and *New York* magazine. Try the buckwheat pancakes or cheese blintzes for a perfect breakfast or brunch; the Christmas borscht, which hits the menu in early December and stays through January, is a simple but divine rendering of the Eastern European classic. But if all you want is a burger, don't worry—it's a classic, too.

Despite the authentic fare, the diner is comfortable, modern, and appealing, with an artsy slant and delicious house-made desserts. Regional beers from the Ukraine and Poland and a nice selection of wines from California and South

America add a sophisticated touch. No wonder Veselka surpasses its status as a popular after-hours hangout with club kids and other night owls to be a favorite at any hour.

144 Second Ave. (at 9th St.). ✆ **212/228-9682.** Reservations not accepted. Main courses $5–$13. AE, DC, DISC, MC, V. Daily 24 hours. Subway: 6 to Astor Place.

8 Greenwich Village & the Meat-Packing District

EXPENSIVE

Babbo ★★★ *Value* NORTHERN ITALIAN Chef Mario Batali's zesty, adventurous cooking has attracted a lot of attention since he began appearing on the Food Network. And justifiably so—I consider Babbo to be the best Italian restaurant in the city. *Molto Mario* also runs seafooder **Esca,** 403 W. 43rd St., at Ninth Avenue (✆ **212/564-7272**) as well as Lupa (p. 187), but Babbo is the best forum for enjoying his mind-bogglingly good cuisine.

Tucked away behind an inviting butter-yellow facade, the restaurant is warm and intimate, with well-spaced tables and a relaxed air that makes dining here feel special but comfortable, not formal. The service is smart and friendly—a good thing, because you may need help choosing from the risk-taking menu. Batali has reinvented the notion of antipasti with such starters as fresh anchovies beautifully marinated in lobster oil, and legendary Faicco soppressata accented with roasted beets, shaved fennel, and Macintosh vinegar. The chef has no equal when it comes to creative pastas; ask anyone who's dined here and they'll wax poetic about the spicy lamb sausage in delicate clouds called mint love letters. Frankly, if all you want to eat is pasta—not exactly a sacrifice—you can get out of here quite affordably.

Heavy with offals and game meats, the *secondi* menu features such wonders as tender fennel-dusted sweetbreads; smoky grilled quail in a gamey but heavenly fig and duck liver vinaigrette; and spicy 2-minute calamari, a paragon of culinary simplicity. The knowledgeable sommelier can help you choose from the unusual but excellent wine list, all Italian and well priced. Last-minute diners can eat at four nonreserved cafe tables and 10 bar seats, but you should book ahead—preferably well ahead, before you leave home—to guarantee a comfortable table.

110 Waverly Place (just east of Sixth Ave.). ✆ **212/777-0303.** Reservations highly recommended. Pastas $16–$24 (most under $21); meats and fish $23–$29; 7-course tasting menus $59–$65 ($45 supplement for accompanying wines, $90 for reserves). AE, MC, V. Mon–Sat 5:30–11:30pm; Sun 5–11pm. Subway: A, C, E, F, V to W. 4th St. (use 8th St. exit).

One If By Land, Two If By Sea ★★ CONTEMPORARY AMERICAN Ask just about any New Yorker to point you to the city's most romantic restaurant and you'll end up at this candlelit, rose-filled 18th-century carriage house once owned by Aaron Burr. This beautiful, intimate space has been a haven of lovers (and those who hope to be) for nearly 30 years. The fireplace crackles and a pianist fills the room with melody as you are escorted to your table for two by the tuxedoed maître'd. Given the emphasis on romance, it's no wonder that food has always been secondary here. It's never been bad—just committedly retro in the way that makes food snobs turn up their noses ("Beef Wellington? Ugh!"). But now that Chef Brian Goode has given the kitchen a contemporary shot in the arm, even gourmands are giving One If By Land a second look. It's still has a pleasing continental-classic vibe, but a New American update has given the menu new life. The crisped Magret duck breast in a garlic sauce is greaseless and nicely accompanied with Concord grapes and a hint of lavender, while pistachio-crusted arctic char gets special-occasion pizzazz from morels and an elegant orange butter. And, of course, there's the beef Wellington with bordelaise sauce—still a classic, and outstanding. The formal service is attentive without being intrusive. The wine list boasts no bargains, but does have a number of celebratory champagnes.

17 Barrow St. (btwn W. 4th St. and Seventh Ave. S.). ✆ **212/228-0822.** www.oneifbyland.com. Reservations strongly recommended. Jacket suggested for men; tie optional. 3-course prix fixe $56; 7-course tasting menu $72. AE, DC, DISC, MC, V. Daily 5:30–11:15pm (dinner from 5:15pm). Subway: 1, 9 to Christopher St.; A, E, C, F, S TO W. 4th St. (use W. 3rd St. exit).

MODERATE

Gus' Place GREEK Tucked away on a quiet corner in the heart of the Village, this neighborhood stalwart is easygoing and charming, and the authentic food is consistently terrific. The room is softly lit and comfortably furnished, with a first-date ambience and lovely murals adding a Mediterranean touch, plus a bar in a separate back room that locals love. All of your favorites are on the menu, from octopus to moussaka to baklava. Start off with the puréed salad combination platter, which includes hearty hummus and a delightfully salty taramosalata (caviar purée), plus warm-from-the-oven pita. The spanakopita is dense and flaky, as it should be. The rich and gooey ouzo-soaked sagazaki will salve your disappointment that it doesn't arrive at your table flaming. Gus's Greek salad arrives heavy with feta and accompanied by yummy stuffed grape leaves. Among the mains, the lamb souvlaki is always a better cut than you'd expect for the price, cooked to order, and accompanied with nicely grilled veggies, herbed rice, and creamy tzatziki (a yogurt-and-cucumber chutney). The wine list is reasonably priced and contains some interesting Mediterranean selections; we enjoyed a terrific Macedonian red on our last visit.

149 Waverly Place (just west of Sixth Ave.). ✆ **212/645-8511.** Reservations recommended. Mezes $4–$10.50; main courses $7–$14 at lunch and brunch, $13.50–$23 at dinner (most less than $20); fixed-price Sun brunch $12. AE, DC, DISC, MC, V. Mon–Thurs noon–4pm and 5–11pm; Fri noon–4pm and 5–11:30pm; Sat 5–11:30pm; Sun 10:30am–4pm and 5–11pm. Subway: 1, 9 to Christopher St.

Home ★★ *Finds* CONTEMPORARY AMERICAN HOME COOKING I just love Home. This cozy restaurant is the domain of a husband-and-wife team, Chef David Page and co-owner Barbara Shinn, who have made home-style cooking something to celebrate. Page and Shinn keep things fresh, popularly priced, and welcoming; as a result, their narrow, tin-roofed dining room is always packed. The dinner menu changes regularly, but look for such signature dishes as the rich and creamy blue cheese fondue with rosemary toasts; an excellent cumin-crusted pork chop on a bed of homemade barbecue sauce; a filleted-at-your-table brook trout accompanied by white beans, escarole, and a tangerine sauce for a zesty accent; and perfectly moist roasted chicken with a side of spicy onion rings. Chocolate lovers should save room for the silky-smooth pudding. Breakfast and weekend brunch are great times to visit, too, with fluffy pancakes and excellent egg dishes. The wine list is lovely, boasting a large selection of local bottles from Long Island's North Fork. This is a quintessential Village restaurant, loaded with sophisticated charm, but it is tiny. Seating isn't uncomfortable and you won't feel intruded upon by your neighbors, but the tight room isn't built for large parties or those who want to spread out. Heated year-round, the lovely garden is most charming in warm weather; book an outside table well ahead.

Greenwich Village Dining

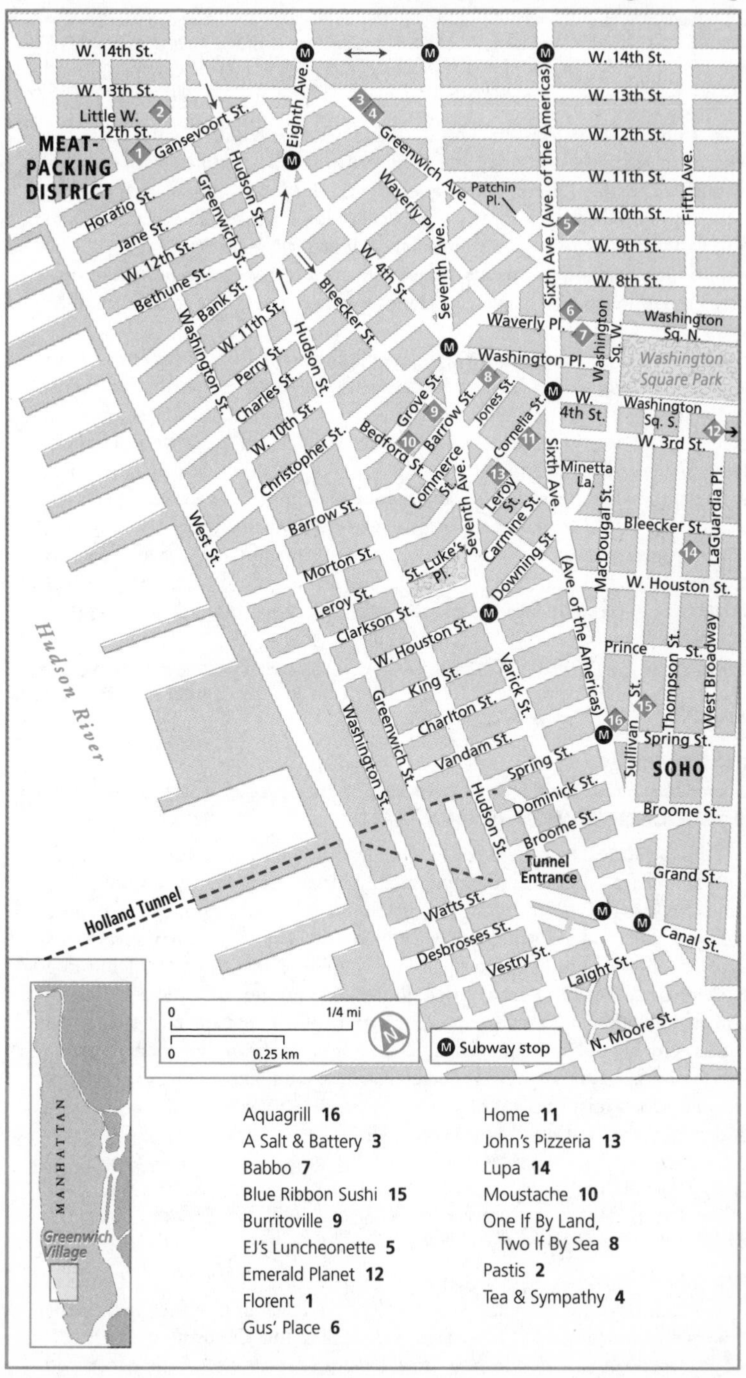

W. 14th St.
W. 13th St.
Little W. 12th St.
MEAT-PACKING DISTRICT
Gansevoort St.
Eighth Ave.
Greenwich Ave.
W. 12th St.
W. 11th St.
W. 10th St.
W. 9th St.
W. 8th St.
Fifth Ave.
Sixth Ave. (Ave. of the Americas)
Patchin Pl.
Waverly Pl.
Seventh Ave.
W. 4th St.
Horatio St.
Jane St.
Bethune St.
Bank St.
Hudson St.
Greenwich St.
Washington St.
Bleecker St.
Perry St.
Charles St.
Christopher St.
Grove St.
Barrow St.
Bedford St.
Commerce St.
Jones St.
Cornelia St.
Washington Pl.
Washington Sq. W.
Washington Sq. N.
Washington Square Park
Washington Sq. S.
W. 3rd St.
Minetta La.
MacDougal St.
LaGuardia Pl.
Leroy St.
Carmine St.
Downing St.
St. Luke's Pl.
Morton St.
Clarkson St.
W. Houston St.
King St.
Charlton St.
Vandam St.
Varick St.
Spring St.
Dominick St.
Broome St.
Prince St.
Sullivan St.
Thompson St.
West Broadway
SOHO
Tunnel Entrance
Grand St.
Watts St.
Desbrosses St.
Vestry St.
Laight St.
Canal St.
N. Moore St.
West St.
Hudson River
Holland Tunnel
0 1/4 mi
0 0.25 km
N
Subway stop
MANHATTAN
Greenwich Village
Aquagrill 16
A Salt & Battery 3
Babbo 7
Blue Ribbon Sushi 15
Burritoville 9
EJ's Luncheonette 5
Emerald Planet 12
Florent 1
Gus' Place 6
Home 11
John's Pizzeria 13
Lupa 14
Moustache 10
One If By Land, Two If By Sea 8
Pastis 2
Tea & Sympathy 4

20 Cornelia St. (btwn Bleecker and W. 4th sts.). ✆ **212/243-9579.** Reservations highly recommended. Main courses $8–$12 at breakfast and lunch, $14–$18 at dinner; fixed-price lunch $13; 3-course dinner $28 ($48 with wines) AE. Mon–Fri 9am–4pm and 5–11pm; Sat 10:30am–4:30pm and 5:30–11pm; Sun 10:30am–4:30pm and 5:30–10pm. Subway: A, C, E, F, V to W. 4th St. (use W. 3rd St. exit).

Pastis FRENCH BISTRO This très-French Meat-Packing District bistro is a spitting image of big-sister hot spot Balthazar (p. 174)—complete with straight-from-the–Left Bank decor, classic bistro fare, ridiculously close tables, and the noise level of a Metallica show—with slightly lower prices. Your best bet is to dine early, or come for weekday breakfast or lunch, when things are quieter. The reward for putting up for the noise level and crowds at weekend brunch or dinner? The fashionable set makes for great people-watching. (I spotted Kevin Kline and Phoebe Cates on my last visit.)

The food is great. The *rillettes fermière,* a thick-cut rabbit paté served with greens and toasts, makes a hearty starter, while the nicely seasoned grilled octopus with white beans is a great choice for lighter tastes. On my last visit, the plat du jour was *poulet à la crème*—a comforting Gallic TV dinner in a Crock-Pot, complete with supermoist roast chicken, veggies, and rice. The steak frites with rich béarnaise is a classic, as it should be in a place like this. There's no massive raw bar as at Balthazar, but the oysters on the half shell are from the same top-quality source. Bottles are pricey, but plenty of good, affordable wines are available by the carafe. (Don't make the mistake we did and order a half carafe, which was only $4 less than the full.) The crêpes Suzettes are an appropriately yummy finish.

9 Ninth Ave. (at Little W. 12th St.). ✆ **212/929-4844.** www.pastisny.com. Reservations recommended. Salads and sandwiches $9–$16; main courses $13–$22. AE, MC, V. Sun–Thurs 9am–5pm and 6pm–1am; Fri–Sat 9am–5pm and 6pm–3am. Subway: A, C, E to 14th St.

INEXPENSIVE

There's also a nice branch of **Burritoville** (p. 166) is at 298 Bleecker St., near Seventh Avenue (✆ **212/633-9249**).

EJ's Luncheonette *Kids* AMERICAN DINER This retro diner is popular with all Village types, including yuppies and their kids, who come for hearty American fare in a 1950s setting—turquoise vinyl booths, Formica tabletops, a soda fountain, and a lunch counter with stools that spin. The menu features a large selection of breakfasts so good you won't be ashamed of indulging in a stack of banana-pecan pancakes for dinner. There's also a terrific selection of burgers (including a great veggie version), well-stuffed sandwiches, hearty green salads, and blue-plate main dishes such as meat loaf with mashed potatoes. Everything is better than you'd expect from a joint like this, and service is friendly. Don't miss the amazing sweet potato fries. Weekend brunch is a big deal at all three locations, but expect a wait.

432 Sixth Ave. (btwn 9th and 10th sts.). ✆ **212/473-5555.** Reservations not accepted. Main courses $4–$12. AE. Sun–Thurs 8:30am–10:30pm; Fri–Sat 8:30am–11pm. Subway: A, B, C, D, E, F, Q to W. 4th St. (use 8th St. exit). Also at 447 Amsterdam Ave., btwn 81st and 82nd sts. (✆ 212/873-3444; subway: 1, 9 to 79th St.). 1271 Third Ave., at 73rd St. (✆ 212/472-0600; subway: 6th–77th sts.).

Emerald Planet ★ GLOBAL/VEGETARIAN/SANDWICHES This San Francisco import led the charge to bury the sandwich and replace it with the wrap, a phenomenon that has reached every mall in America by now. The Emerald Planet ideology is simple: You can eat wraps at every meal, from bacon and eggs (the Omaha) in the morning to fresh grilled veggies with goat cheese (the

Sonoma) at noon to jerk chicken, mango salsa, and jasmine rice (the Kingston) at dinner. All ingredients are fresh, and the emphasis is on healthy.

2 Great Jones St. (at Broadway). ✆ **212/353-9727.** www.emeraldplanet.citysearch.com. Wraps $5–$8; smoothies $4–$5. AE, MC, V. Mon–Fri 9am–10pm; Sat noon–10pm; Sun noon–8pm. Subway: 6 to Bleecker St.; N, R to 8th St. Also at 30 Rockefeller Plaza, lower concourse level (down the hall from the skating rink; ✆ 212/218-1133; subway: B, D, F, Q to 47th–50th sts./Rockefeller Center).

Florent *Kids* DINER/FRENCH BISTRO Located in the Meat-Packing District, Florent, the nearly 24-hour French bistro dressed up as a '50s-style diner, is a perennial hot spot no matter what the time of day; a children's menu makes this the perfect place to bring the kids for lunch or early dinner. But it's after the clubs close when the joint really jumps. Tables are tightly packed, almost uncomfortably so in some cases, but it's all part of the late-night festivities. This place has a real sense of humor (check out the menu boards above the bar) and a CD catalog full of the latest indie sounds, all adding to the hipster fun. The food's good, too: The grilled chicken with herbs and mustard sauce is a winner, moist and flavorful, as is the French onion soup crowned with melted Gruyère. There are always diner faves like burgers and chili in addition to Gallic standards like moules frites, and the comfort food specialties such as chicken potpie make regular appearances. The fries are light, crispy, and addictive.

69 Gansevoort St. (2 blocks south of 14th St. and 1 block west of Ninth Ave., btwn Greenwich and Washington sts.). ✆ **212/989-5779.** www.restaurantflorent.com. Reservations recommended for dinner. Main courses $4.50–$14.50 at brunch and lunch, $8–$20.50 at dinner (most less than $15); 2-course fixed-price lunches $8.25–$11.95; 3-course fixed-price dinner $18.95 before 7:30pm, $20.95 7:30pm–midnight. No credit cards. Mon–Wed 9am–5am; Thurs–Sun 24 hours. Subway: A, C, E, L to 14th St.

Lupa ★★ *Value* CENTRAL ITALIAN God bless Mario Batali, New York's one big-name chef who thinks you shouldn't have to spend a fortune to eat like a king. The man behind Babbo (see earlier in this chapter), the Food Network's *Molto Mario* also operates this winning Roman-style trattoria. Reservations are taken for the back room only, and I strongly advise you to arrange for them if you can, because it's quieter and more civilized. The front room is reserved for walk-ins; it's loud and cramped and you'll probably have to wait for a table unless you come early, but the food is worth it.

Don't be scared off by the all-Italian menu, as a few folks seemed to be on our first visit; the helpful butcher-coated waiter will steer you through the language and preparations. The menu boasts lots of treats. As always with Mario, the pastas stand out: The *bucatini all'amatriciana,* a classic Italian tube pasta in a smoky tomato sauce made from hog jowl (bacon), is divine, as is the creamy ricotta gnocchi with Italian sausage and fennel. Lupa is also a *salumeria,* so don't miss an opportunity to start with the prosciutto di carpegna with roasted figs, an ideal marriage of salt and sweet; in fact, it's easy to build a value-packed meal from the long list of antipasti options. Among the main courses, the classic saltimbocca was a disappointment, but the oven-roasted littleneck clams with sweet soppressata was a joy. Another delight? The wine list is massive and superaffordable.

170 Thompson St. (btwn Houston and Bleecker sts.). ✆ **212/982-5089.** www.luparestaurant.com. Reservations highly recommended. Antipasti $5–$12; main courses $9–$17; 4-course prix fixe $30 at lunch, $45 at dinner (only for parties of 7 or more). AE, DC, MC, V. Daily noon–2:45pm and 5:30–11:30pm. Subway: 1, 9 to Houston St.

Moustache *Value* MIDDLE EASTERN Moustache (pronounced moo-*stah*-sh) is the sort of exotic neighborhood spot that's just right. On a quiet side street in the West Village, this charming hole-in-the-wall boasts a cozy Middle Eastern vibe and authentic fare that's both palate-pleasing and wallet-friendly. Delicately seasoned dishes bear little resemblance to the food at your average falafel joint. Expect subtly flavored hummus, tabbouleh, and spinach-chickpea-tomato salad (or a large plate of all three); excellent oven-roasted "pitzas," thin, matzo-like pita crusts topped with spicy minced lamb and other savory ingredients; and—best of all—fluffy, hot-from-the-oven homemade pita bread, which puts any of those store-bought Frisbees to shame. Moustache is hugely and justifiably popular, so don't be surprised if there's a line—but it's well worth the wait.

90 Bedford St. (btwn Barrow and Grove sts.). ✆ **212/229-2220.** Reservations not accepted. Main courses $5–$12. No credit cards. Daily noon–midnight (last orders at 11pm). Subway: 1, 9 to Christopher St. Also at 265 E. 10th St. (btwn First Ave. and Ave. A). ✆ 212/228-2022; L to First Ave.

Tea & Sympathy ★ AFTERNOON TEA/BRITISH When Londoner Nicky Perry moved to New York, she was disappointed to find no proper British tearoom, so she opened her own in the heart of the West Village. Tea & Sympathy seems as if it was transplanted wholesale from Highgate, complete with an oddball collection of creamers and teapots, a snappy British wait staff, and plenty of old-time charm. Elbowroom is at a minimum and the place is perpetually packed, but it's worth the squeeze for the full afternoon tea, which comes on a tiered tray with crustless finger sandwiches, scones with jam and Devonshire cream, and cakes and cookies for a sugary finish. The menu also features such traditional British comforts as shepherd's pie, bangers and mash, and a savory chicken and leek pie. Anglophiles line up for the Sunday dinner—roast beef and Yorkshire pudding, of course. For dessert, try the treacle pudding, warm ginger cake, or yummy sherry trifle.

In addition to a cute shop selling next door imported English sweets (including genuine Cadbury Wispas, Flake, and Crunchie bars) and trinkets, the newest addition to Nicky's burgeoning pax Brittania is **A Salt & Battery,** 112 Greenwich Ave. (✆ **212/691-2713;** www.asaltandbattery.com), a fish-and-chips shop so genuine that they serve the goods wrapped in newspaper. Stick with the traditional varieties (halibut, cod) and you'll enjoy the real thing—crispy batter outside, flaky and greaseless inside. (Word is that the deep-fried Mars Bar makes a divine dessert, but I'm too chicken to try it.) A second location will be open at 80 Second Ave., between 4th and 5th streets (✆ **212/254-6610**) in the East Village by the time you arrive.

108 Greenwich Ave. (btwn 12th and 13th sts.). ✆ **212/807-8329** or 212/989-9735. www.teaandsympathynewyork.com. Reservations not accepted. Main courses $5.50–$12 at lunch and brunch, $10.50–$17 at dinner; full afternoon tea $19 ($35 for 2). MC, V. Daily 11:30am–10pm. Subway: A, C, E, 1, 2, 3, 9 to 14th St.

9 Chelsea

To locate the restaurants in this section, see map on p. 196.

MODERATE

The Red Cat ★ CONTEMPORARY AMERICAN This pleasing newcomer symbolizes the renaissance that has taken root in West Chelsea. Just a few years back, New Yorkers could've never envisioned a bistro this mature and refined making a home for itself this far west. But things change quickly, and now the Red Cat is right at home in this gentrifying, gallery-rich neighborhood. Outfitted like a chic-but-cozy farmhouse with an urban flair, like something out of the pages of *Metropolitan Home,* the long dining room is a pleasing setting for Chef Jimmy Bradley's flavorful and substantial Mediterranean-accented New

American cooking. Witness the thick-cut, char-grilled pork chop, accompanied by a savory purée of black olives, port wine, and red onion; the simply grilled New York strip, served with yukon golds, fennel, and aioli in a cabernet sauce; or the skate wing, pan-crisped in brown butter with capers, squash, chanterelles, and piquillo peppers. Bradley diversifies his core ingredients, which I like; in addition to skate, a recent menu boasted balsamic- and thyme-basted quail, toasted orzo with steamed mussels, and calf's liver au poivre. Wines are well chosen and affordable, and service is friendly and efficient.

227 Tenth Ave. (btwn 23rd and 24th sts.). ✆ **212/242-1122.** www.theredcat.com. Reservations highly recommended. Main courses $18–$28 (most less than $23). AE, DC, MC, V. Mon–Thurs 5:30–11:30pm; Fri–Sat 5:30pm–midnight; Sun 5–10pm. Subway: C, E to 23rd St.

INEXPENSIVE

In addition to the choices below, **Burritoville** (p. 166) is at 264 W. 23rd St., between Seventh and Eighth avenues (✆ **212/367-9844**).

Empire Diner AMERICAN DINER This throwback shrine to the slicked-up all-American diner looks suspiciously like an Airstream camper plunked down on the corner. This classic joint boasts a timeless Art Deco vibe, honest coffee, and great mashed potatoes. The food is basic diner fare: eggs, omelettes, burgers, overstuffed sandwiches, and a very nice turkey platter. Frankly, I think the Empire Diner is overrated—you'll find better breakfast fare elsewhere—but there's no denying its permanent status as a red-hot fixture on the late-night scene.

210 Tenth Ave. (at 22nd St.). ✆ **212/243-2736.** Reservations not accepted. Main courses $9–$18. AE, DC, DISC, MC, V. Daily 24 hours. Subway: C, E to 23rd St.

Grand Sichuan International ★ *Value* SICHUAN There's no need to head to Chinatown—Grand Sichuan serves up the real thing right here in Chelsea. This comfortable spot has garnered rave reviews for its authentic Sichuan cuisine. Spicy food lovers will be particularly thrilled, as the kitchen excels at dishes that are intensely spiced without being palate-numbing—a brilliant culinary balance that few Chinatown kitchens can achieve. The flavors are complex and strong, especially in such top choices as Sichuan wontons in red oil, Chairman Mao's pork with chestnuts, and my favorite, boneless whole fish with pine nuts in a modified sweet-and-sour sauce. The house bean curd in spicy sauce is another winner, but only for those with a high tolerance for hot. If some in your party shy away from hot and spicy, never fear: The staff will be more than happy to recommend milder dishes.

229 Ninth Ave. (at 24th St.). ✆ **212/620-5200.** Reservations accepted for parties of 3 or more. Main courses $3.25–$14. AE, DC, MC, V. Daily 11:30am–11pm. Subway: C, E to 23rd St. Also at 745 Ninth Ave., btwn 50th and 51st sts. (✆ 212/582-2288; subway: C, E to 50th St.).

Rue des Crepes ★ *Value* FRENCH Seldom do decor, quality, and service come together so well in such an affordable restaurant. Evoking a Parisian sidewalk cafe with muraled walls, tiled floors, Art Nouveau street lamps, and petite cafe tables, the dining room is comfortable and appealingly romantic. Chef Michael Kalajian, a Culinary Institute of America graduate and former student of four-star chef Charlie Palmer, whips up light-as-air buckwheat (and cholesterol-free) crepes and folds them around a whole host of savory fillings, from classics like turkey and brie to spicy Moroccan merguez sausage accompanied by white beans and roasted garlic. Vegetarian options are available, including yummy homemade hummus and roasted veggies. Soups and salads are also served; sandwiches are prepared on fresh baguettes from Amy's Bread, and pre-prepared ones are wrapped and ready to go in the takeout case. Sweet dessert crepes come with your choice of fillings; my favorite is the "Sidewalk," a classic preparation with butter, sugar, lemon, and chocolate. *Money-saving tip:* Check the website for a 10% off coupon.

104 Eighth Ave. (btwn 15th and 16th sts.). ✆ **212/242-9900.** www.ruedescrepes.com. Reservations not accepted. Main courses $6–$9. AE, MC, V. Sun–Thurs 11am–11pm; Fri–Sat 11am–1am. Subway: A, C, E to 14th St.

10 Union Square, the Flatiron District & Gramercy Park

To locate the restaurants in this section, see map on p. 196.

EXPENSIVE

AZ ★ ASIAN FUSION My favorite new restaurant in 2001 is this gorgeous trilevel restaurant, the domain of chef Patricia Yeo, who has finally brought first-class Asian Fusion cuisine to New York. First, the space: three floors outfitted like an urban Zen garden, with a three-story-high trickling waterfall, clean-lined modern decor sexed up with brick-red accents and bold Japanese-inspired lines.

Despite its compactness, the dazzling menu makes it hard to choose. Stars among the starters include a sashimi tasting plate, with a delicate, winning *hijiki* seaweed vinaigrette; and a wonderful salad of hot smoked steelhead trout, warm potatoes, and watercress. The best main at our table was seared diver scallops with rock shrimp hash and sweet-tart *umeboshi* (Japanese plum) sauce—but the miso-braised short ribs with taro gnocchi and Chinese mustard greens weren't far behind, and every dish was delectable. Desserts are all divine, but the simplest one was the standout: Meyer lemon and tangerine ices, attended by citrus vodka–soaked fruits. Portions are not overlarge, which I found to be refreshing, but hearty eaters may be disappointed. Service is earnest and attentive. An excellent selection of wines is available by the glass, which well suits the diversity of the menu.

21 W. 17th St. (btwn Fifth and Sixth aves.). ✆ **212/691-8888.** www.aznyc.com. Reservations highly recommended. A la carte lunch $16–$20; 2-course fixed-price lunch $20; 3-course fixed-price dinner $57; tasting menu $75. AE, DC, DISC, MC, V. Mon–Wed noon–2:30pm and 5:30–11pm; Thurs–Fri noon–2:30pm and 5:30–11:30pm; Sat 5:30–11:30pm; Sun 5:30–10:30pm. Subway: F to 14th St.; 4, 5, 6, N, R to 14th St./Union Sq.

Craft ★★ CONTEMPORARY AMERICAN This stylish but laidback new restaurant from chef Tom Colicchio (the deft hand behind Gramercy Tavern) is one of 2001's best new restaurants, if not the best. The large and lovely craftsman-meets-modern interior sets the perfect tone for Colicchio's true American cooking: Simple, straightforward preparations showcasing the best hand-fed, farm-raised, organically grown bounty the USA has to offer.

Much fuss has been made over Craft's design-your-own-meal concept, but it's actually pretty simple. The menu is divided into major categories—fish, meat, vegetables, potatoes, grains and beans—and subcategories: roasted, braised, sautéed, puréed, and so on. My one complaint is that the descriptions are too spare; I wish "organic chicken" (in the "roasted" column) said more about what seasonings were used, whether bones were involved, and so on. But the solicitous staff was more than happy to help us build a family-style meal that suited our tastes to a T. And the bird that ended up on my plate was chicken beyond perfect: lightly seasoned and crisped on the outside, tender and juicy on the inside. Everything we sampled was gorgeously prepared. I highly recommend any of the unusual mushrooms if you're a fan (we loved the roasted bluefoots), as well as the starchy, purple, potatolike Jerusalem artichokes. *Note:* Some guests may be disappointed by the simple menu; diners looking for extravagant dishes and a special-occasion feel will be happier elsewhere.

For a more casual, affordable take on Colicchio's fare, head to the adjacent **Craftbar,** a full-service restaurant serving up Italian-accented, moderately priced lighter fare—gourmet sandwiches, soups, salads, starters—in a casual, convivial atmosphere. No reservations, but worth the wait.

41 E. 19th St. (btwn Broadway and Park Ave. South). ✆ **212/780-0880.** www.craftrestaurant.com. Reservations highly recommended; not accepted at Craftbar. Main courses $22–$35; tasting menu $72. Main courses $15–$19 at Craftbar. AE, DC, DISC, MC, V. Craft: Tues–Sun 5:30–10pm. Craftbar: Daily noon–1am. Subway: L, N, R, 4, 5, 6 to 14th St./Union Sq.

TanDa ★ SOUTHEAST ASIAN If you're looking to rub elbows with Carrie Bradshaw types, TanDa has your table. This stylish Southeast Asian hotspot has stepped in to fill the void for hypertrendy Moomba, which made news more for its A-list regulars (including Leo DiCaprio in his post-*Titanic* party-animal stage) than its food.

The Moomba folks are behind TanDa, so the formula is roughly the same: Trendy cuisine, ultra-stylish decor, downstairs dining for the masses, upstairs lounge and dining room for the well-connected and beautiful. I like the decor, with its whimsical *Scent of Green Papaya* ambience and servers bedecked jewel-toned nehrus. I also like the food, which doesn't bow to mild palates. German-Chinese executive chef Stanley Wong has fused European technique with the fragrant, complex flavors of Indonesia and environs. The carpaccio-thin charred beef tenderloin is served on a simple but perfect papaya and lime salad, while Maine lobster is bathed in a delicious broth of carrot and ginger tea. Some dishes are so spiced as to be overbearing, though, so ask if it matters, because the staff will not volunteer such information. (My husband ordered a mild-sounding prawn dish that couldn't have been hotter if it was actually on fire.)

TanDa seems like a throwback to the just-say-grow, dot-com years, with too-high entree prices and ridiculously overpriced cocktails ($12?!). Still, there's no denying its star power. And pastry chef Wendy Israel's ethereal desserts are reason enough to come. Her cookies and milk—dense chocolate chips with coconut milk for dipping—is my favorite dessert of the year. I prefer sitting downstairs, but be sure to request an upstairs table at booking if you want one.

331 Park Ave. South (btwn 24th and 25th sts.). ✆ **212/253-8400.** Reservations recommended. Main courses $18–$28. AE, DC, DISC, MC, V. Mon–Sat 11:30am–3pm and 5:30pm–3am; Sun 11:30am–3pm and 5:30pm–3am (dinner until 11pm). Subway: 6 to 23rd St.

Veritas ★★★ CONTEMPORARY AMERICAN This *New York Times* three-star winner (out of a possible four) was my favorite new restaurant of 1999, and it still shines brightly. The simple 65-seat room is the embodiment of clean-lined contemporary style and unpretentious grace—and the ideal showcase for Scott Bryan's straightforward yet sophisticated cooking, itself a perfect foil for the spectacular 1,300-bottle wine collection. Much of the wine cellar is comprised of full-bodied reds, so Mr. Bryan has created a robust cuisine as accompaniment. There's surprisingly little red meat on the compact menu, but even a pan-roasted monkfish, dressed with white beans, smoked bacon, roasted tomato, and picholines, bursts with flavors that can stand up to a big, bold red. The menu changes seasonally, but expect such lovely starters as Peekytoe crab ravioli with fines herbes, tomato, and lemon in a delicate shellfish emulsion. Sweetbreads are sublimely roasted and given an Asian slant with marinated shiitakes, a soy glaze, and a peel of ginger. Despite the gravity of the wine list, there are many well-priced choices; the first-rate sommelier will be glad to help you choose, no matter what your budget. Serious oenophiles who want to plan ahead can download the full list in advance, and have their choice opened and waiting at reservation time. Wine tastings are a regular part of the calendar. Service is mature and attentive.

43 E. 20th St. (btwn Fifth Ave. and Park Ave. South). ✆ **212/353-3700.** www.veritas-nyc.com. Reservations recommended. 3-course fixed-price dinner $68. AE, DC, MC, V. Mon–Sat 5:30–10:30pm; Sun 5–10pm. Subway: N, R, 6 to 23rd St.

MODERATE

Also consider **Craftbar,** 47 E. 19th St., between Broadway and Park Ave. South, (✆ **212/780-0880**), for a casual, more affordable alternative to the gorgeous American cooking at pricey Craft (see "Expensive," above).

Zarela Martínez, the owner of first-rate Mexican restaurant Zarela (p. 215), opened a second spot: **Danzón,** 126 East 28th St., between Park and Lexington avenues (✆ **212/252-1345**), an attractive two-story restaurant that specializes in the seafood-heavy cuisine of Veracruz, on the Gulf of Mexico.

Blue Water Grill SEAFOOD This stylish seafooder serves up good-quality fish to an energetic crowd. The high-ceilinged, casually sophisticated room is beautifully lit and perfect for romancing couples and celebratory groups alike. I prefer the creativity at Aquagrill (see "SoHo & Nolita," earlier in this chapter), but you won't be disappointed by the more predictable fare here; besides, it's much easier to score a table at Blue Water, and you'll have more elbowroom. In warm weather, there are few better outdoor patios than Blue Water's.

You can put together a platter of oysters and littlenecks on the half shell from the extensive raw bar, order lobster by the pound (steamed, grilled, or broiled), or go with one of the prepared catches of the day. (Sushi platters are available as well, but you're better off at a sushi restaurant if that's what you crave.) Look for both Asian and Mediterranean influences on the menu, which makes the most of what's fresh. The best selections—often Atlantic salmon, wild striped bass, and Pacific mahi—come from the kitchen's wood-burning grill. There's pasta, chicken, and filet mignon for the nonseafooders in your group.

A live jazz combo entertains in the Art Deco–influenced downstairs dining room nightly, while everybody swings at Sunday brunch.

31 Union Sq. West (at 16th St.). ✆ **212/675-9500.** Reservations recommended. Main courses $12.50–$25 (most less than $20); Sun jazz brunch $10–$26 (most less than $19), including cocktail and coffee/tea. AE, MC, V. Sun–Tues 11:30am–midnight; Wed–Thurs 11:30am–12:30am; Fri–Sat 11:30am–1am. Subway: L, N, R, 4, 5, 6 to 14th St./Union Sq.

Bondí Ristorante SICILIAN This unassuming and charmingly authentic Italian cafe serves Sicilian delicacies with skill and care. The dedication of the Settepani brothers, who own and run the place, shows at every level, from the quality of the food to the friendliness of the staff. You might start with the *conca d'oro,* a lively salad of oranges, fennel, black olives, and red onions in an oil-and-vinegar dressing. The fish soup is from an 11th-century Saracen recipe: sole, grouper, mussels, clams, and shrimp in a sauce of capers, saffron, garlic, pine nuts, and laurel leaves. Among the notable entrees are the shellfish-stuffed brioche (lobster, shrimp, clams, mussels) seasoned with a delicate curry, and an excellent veal scallopini. The biggest reason to dine here, though, is the rear garden, which is one of the most delightful alfresco spots in the city.

7 W. 20th St. (btwn Fifth and Sixth aves.). ✆ **212/691-8136.** www.bondi-ny.com. Reservations recommended. Pastas $9–$15; meat and fish main courses $16–$25; 5-course fixed-price dinner $39. AE, DC, MC, V. Mon–Sat 11:30am–11pm; Sun 5pm–10:30pm. Subway: N, R, F to 23rd St.

City Crab SEAFOOD This big, bustling, nautical-themed bi-level restaurant is a good choice for affordable top-quality seafood. The ambience is more roll-up-your-sleeves casual and the prices cheaper than at nearby Blue Water Grill (above). The menu is huge, and preparations are always satisfying. It's easy to eat as simply or as decadently as you like: Choices run the gamut from simple but hearty bowls of clam chowder to grilled whole Maine lobsters. Always-reliable choices include fresh-off-the-boat oysters (usually a half dozen varieties to choose from); very good Maryland crab cakes; sautéed jumbo Gulf shrimp; an honest-to-goodness New England lobster club; whole steamed Dungeness crabs; and jumbo-sized Florida stone crab claws. (They don't call this place City Crab for nothing.) The yummy desserts tend toward comfort foods: Oreo ice-cream cake, a warm brownie, New York cheesecake, Key lime pie. The service can be slow, but don't let that keep you from coming.

235 Park Ave. South (at 19th St.). ✆ **212/529-3800.** Reservations recommended. $7–$17 lunch; 3-course "express lunch" $15 (Mon–Fri 11:30am–3:30pm); $14–$30 dinner (most under $20). AE, MC, V. Mon–Fri 11:30am–11:30pm; Sat noon–11:30pm; Sun noon–11pm. Subway: 4, 5, 6, N, R, L to 14th St./Union Sq.

Lady Mendl's Tea Salon ★ *Finds* AFTERNOON TEA Even if you don't stay at the ultraromantic Inn at Irving Place (see chapter 6), you can enjoy the city's finest afternoon tea service in the high Victorian parlor of the gorgeous 1834 Greek Revival town house. Named for 19th-century society decorator Elsie deWolfe (Mendl was her married name), the tearoom is a bastion of period civility, with impeccable antiques arranged in ladylike groupings, vintage lamps illuminating the rich textiles and soft colors, and two fireplaces casting a warm glow. The refined staff serves a graceful and delicious five-course afternoon tea that includes a selection of delicate finger sandwiches (sans crusts, of course), home-baked scones with Devonshire cream and homemade strawberry jam, and two dessert courses, including a cookie course (with light-as-air palmiers) and a cake course (don't pass on anything chocolate). The lovely thing about Lady Mendl's is that it's supremely elegant without being the least bit stuffy or formal; anyone with a modicum of manners will feel very comfortable here. A real hidden jewel!

At the Inn at Irving Place, 56 Irving Place (btwn 17th and 18th sts.). ✆ **212/533-4600.** Afternoon tea $30. AE, DC, MC, V. Wed–Fri at 3 and 5pm; Sat–Sun at 2 and 4:30pm. Subway: N, R, 4, 5, 6 to 14th St./Union Sq.

Pipa ★ LATIN AMERICAN/TAPAS Chef Douglas Rodriguez, who first put Nuevo Latino cuisine on the Manhattan map at Patria, is turning the Flatiron into a Pan-Latin dining mecca. Ceviches take center stage at his festive **Chicama,** 32 E. 18th St. (✆ **212/505-2233**), but I prefer this more affordable space, where he's given tapas the Latin treatment. The big, sexy, theatrically decorated room feels like it was outfitted by stylish gypsies, with brocade-covered banquettes, an eclectic mix of chandeliers and oversized mirrors, and flickering candlelight; there's a festive, order-another-pitcher-of-sangria vibe.

The big menu of small plates is well suited to larger parties, but even duos can assemble a pleasing and diverse meal. Flat breads come piled high with fixings; my favorite features porcini mushrooms, smoked San Simeon cheese, figs, toasted almonds, and sliced Serrano ham, crowned with a spritz of truffle oil. If you love pork, don't pass on the charcuterie plate; you may even find yourself opting for seconds on the salt-cured *jamón serrano* instead of dessert, as we did. Seafood has a strong presence on the menu; among the top choices are delightfully crispy anchovies wrapped in sage leaves, and head-on shrimp seared in olive oil and garlic. The seafood-rich paella is a scrumptious recent addition to the menu. The cheese course is a divine way to finish; your waiter will gladly help you choose among the dozen Spanish and Portuguese varieties. My only (minor) complaint is that the tables are too small to accommodate the multitude of dishes—but for food this good, I'll live.

38 E. 19th St. (btwn Broadway and Park Ave. S.), adjacent to ABC Carpet & Home. ✆ **212/677-2233.** Reservations recommended. Tapas plates $7–$15; main courses $19–$24. AE, MC, V. Mon–Thurs noon–3pm and 6pm–11pm; Fri noon–3pm and 5:30pm–midnight; Sat 11am–3:30pm and 5:30pm–midnight; Sun 11am–3pm and 5:30–10pm. Subway: N, R to 23rd St.

Steak Frites BELGIAN/STEAKS A restaurant that names itself for its signature dish better do it right—and Steak Frites does. The certified Black Angus arrives at your table faultlessly grilled and juicy—pink inside, blackened outside. The mussels are an equal draw; they come in a number of presentations, the best of which are the white wine and fresh herbs or the hearty Belgian beer. The delicately crispy frites are addictive, and you can have good ol' American ketchup on the side as well as Euro-style mayo. Brasserie-style entrees like spit-roasted chicken and pan-roasted monkfish round out the selection, and all of the food is well priced and well prepared.

The big room is loud and the service could be more attentive, but I love the bustling slice-of-St-Germain atmosphere, complete with mahogany-and-brass bar and Toulouse Lautrec-style murals on the walls. There's wonderful sidewalk dining at Parisian-style cafe tables in warm weather. A good selection of wines and Belgian beers are on hand, as you'd expect. Don't be surprised if you have to wait for your table on busy nights, even with a reservation.

9 E. 16th St. (between Fifth Ave. and Union Sq. W.). ✆ **212/463-7101.** www.steakfritesnyc.com. Reservations recommended. Main courses $9–$18 at lunch, $16–$23 at dinner. AE, MC, V. Daily 11:30am–midnight. Subway: L, N, R, 4, 5, 6 to 14th St./Union Sq.

Tavern Room at Gramercy Tavern ★ *Value* CONTEMPORARY AMERICAN Unquestionably, Gramercy Tavern's main dining room remains one of New York's finest. However, if you want to spend big bucks on chef Tom Colicchio's creative New American cooking, you're better off these days at Craft, his smashing new venture (see "Expensive," above). But if you want to sample his first-class fare at fire-sale prices, go to the Tavern Room, a friendly, informal bistro-style alternative where you can decide to eat at the last minute and still dine on some of the best food in town—without breaking the bank in the process.

The compact but immensely appealing menu offers a lighter, more casual take on Colicchio's excellent regional American fare. I love the perfectly roasted baby chicken with butternut squash succotash; nobody in town does chicken better. And where else are you going to get a filet mignon this good for 20 bucks? There's also a good selection of salads, a terrific tomato garlic-bread soup, and a handful of fish dishes and sandwiches for lighter eaters, plus the restaurant's signature selection of farmhouse cheeses and homestyle, yet elegant desserts. The room is very comfortable, with well-spaced tables and a pleasant energy that still allows for conversation; owner Danny Meyer's blanket no-smoking policy prevents any second-hand smoke from interfering with your meal. Service is top-notch, too.

42 E. 20th St. (btwn Broadway and Park Ave. S.). ✆ **212/477-0777.** Reservations not accepted. Main courses $14–$20. AE, DC, DISC, MC, V. Sun–Thurs noon–11pm; Fri–Sat noon–midnight. Subway: N, R, 6 to 23rd St.

INEXPENSIVE

For celestial baked goods and gourmet sandwiches and salads, try **Le Pain Quotidien** (p. 177) at ABC Carpet & Home, 38 E. 19th St. (between Broadway and Park Ave. S.; ✆ **212/625-9009**).

Old Town Bar & Restaurant AMERICAN If you've watched TV at all over the last couple of decades, this place should look familiar: It was featured nightly in the old *Late Night with David Letterman* intro, starred as Riff's Bar in *Mad About You,* and appeared in too many commercials to count, as well as in such movies as *The Devil's Own,* Woody Allen's *Bullets Over Broadway,* and Whit Stillman's *The Last Days of Disco.* But this is no stage set—it's a genuine tin-ceilinged 19th-century bar serving up good pub grub, lots of beers on tap, and a real sense of New York history. Sure, there are healthy salads on the menu, but everybody comes for the burgers. Whether you go low-fat turkey or bacon-chili-cheddar, they're great every time. You have your choice of sides, but go with the shoestring fries. Other good choices include spicy Buffalo wings with blue cheese, fiery bowls of chili sprinkled with cheddar cheese and dolloped with sour cream, and a Herculean Caesar salad slathered with mayo and topped with anchovies. Food comes up from the basement kitchen courtesy of ancient dumbwaiters behind the bar, where equally crusty bartenders would rather *not* make you a Cosmopolitan, thank you very much. If you want to escape the cigarette smoke and the predatory singles scene that pulls in after work and on weekends, head upstairs to the blissfully smoke-free dining room.

45 E. 18th St. (btwn Broadway and Park Ave. S.). ✆ **212/529-6732.** Reservations not accepted. Main courses $6–$12. AE, MC, V. Mon–Fri 11:30am–midnight; Sat–Sun 12:30pm–midnight. Subway: L, N, R, 4, 5, 6 to 14th St./Union Sq.

Zen Palate PAN-ASIAN/VEGETARIAN Zen Palate has adopted the healthy, less-is-more approach to Asian cuisine. Each location shares the same Japanese-influenced postmodern decor, with teak and patinaed copper governing the aesthetic; the Union Square flagship is a standout, with a long counter downstairs for on-the-run eaters and a warren of spare but attractive dining rooms upstairs, including some with Japanese-style seating.

Tofu is king here, but you're not limited to it. Stars on the wide-ranging menu include taro spring rolls and basil moo-shu rolls for something creative, as well as steamed veggie dumplings and buns for a more traditional Asian choice. Despite the good-for-you approach, main courses such as Rose Petals (homemade soy pasta in a sweet rice ginger sauce with garden vegetables) and Curry Supreme (with tofu, potatoes, and carrots) are very flavorful, and some will particularly appeal to spicy food lovers. Even more affordable casual grazing dishes are served in the all-day gourmet shop downstairs. All in all, a good bet for health-minded diners.

Lest it all sound too good for you, you're welcome to BYOB with no corkage fee in the upstairs dining room at this location.

34 Union Square East (at 16th St.). ✆ **212/614-9345.** www.zenpalate.com. Reservations accepted. Main courses $7–$17.50 ($3–$8 in gourmet shop). AE, MC, V. Mon–Sat 11am–10:45pm; Sun noon–10:45pm. Subway: L, N, R, 4, 5, 6 to 14th St./Union Sq. Also at 663 Ninth Ave., at 46th St. (✆ 212/582-1669; subway: A, C, E to 42nd St.). 2170 Broadway, btwn 76th and 77th sts. (✆ 212/501-7768; subway: 1, 9 to 79th St.).

11 Times Square & Midtown West

VERY EXPENSIVE

Alain Ducasse at the Essex House ★★★ CLASSIC FRENCH When Europe's most famous Michelen three-star chef debuted his first New York restaurant in 2000, it seemed like he may have even pushed we'll-pay-anything New Yorkers too far. Initial reviews said nothing to justify the price tags, and rituals like presenting a selection of pens like they were fine cigars at bill-signing time just seemed silly. In the subsequent year, however, Ducasse set aside some of the initial imperiousness and put his staff to the grindstone, and ultimately

Midtown, Chelsea, Flatiron District & Gramercy Park Dining

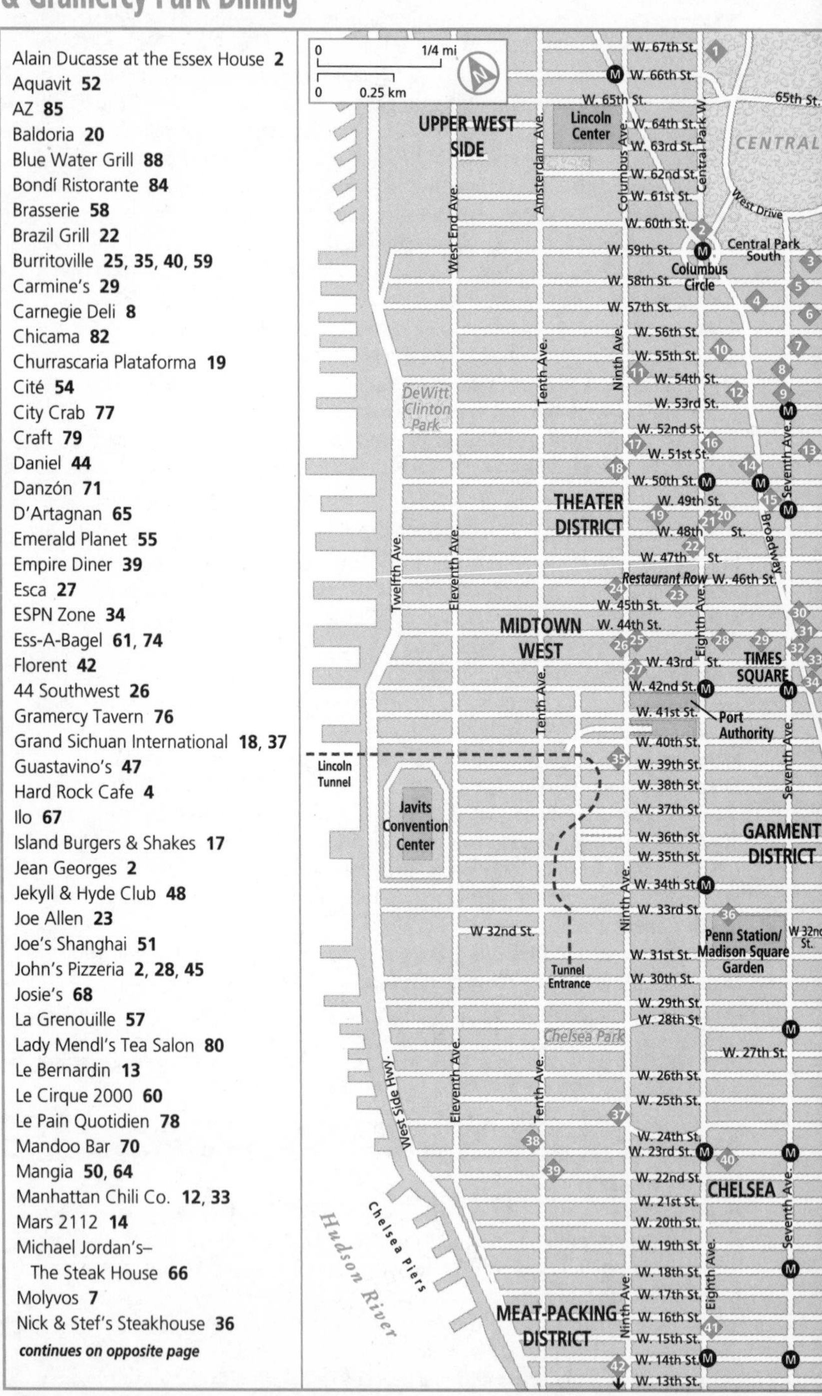

continues on opposite page

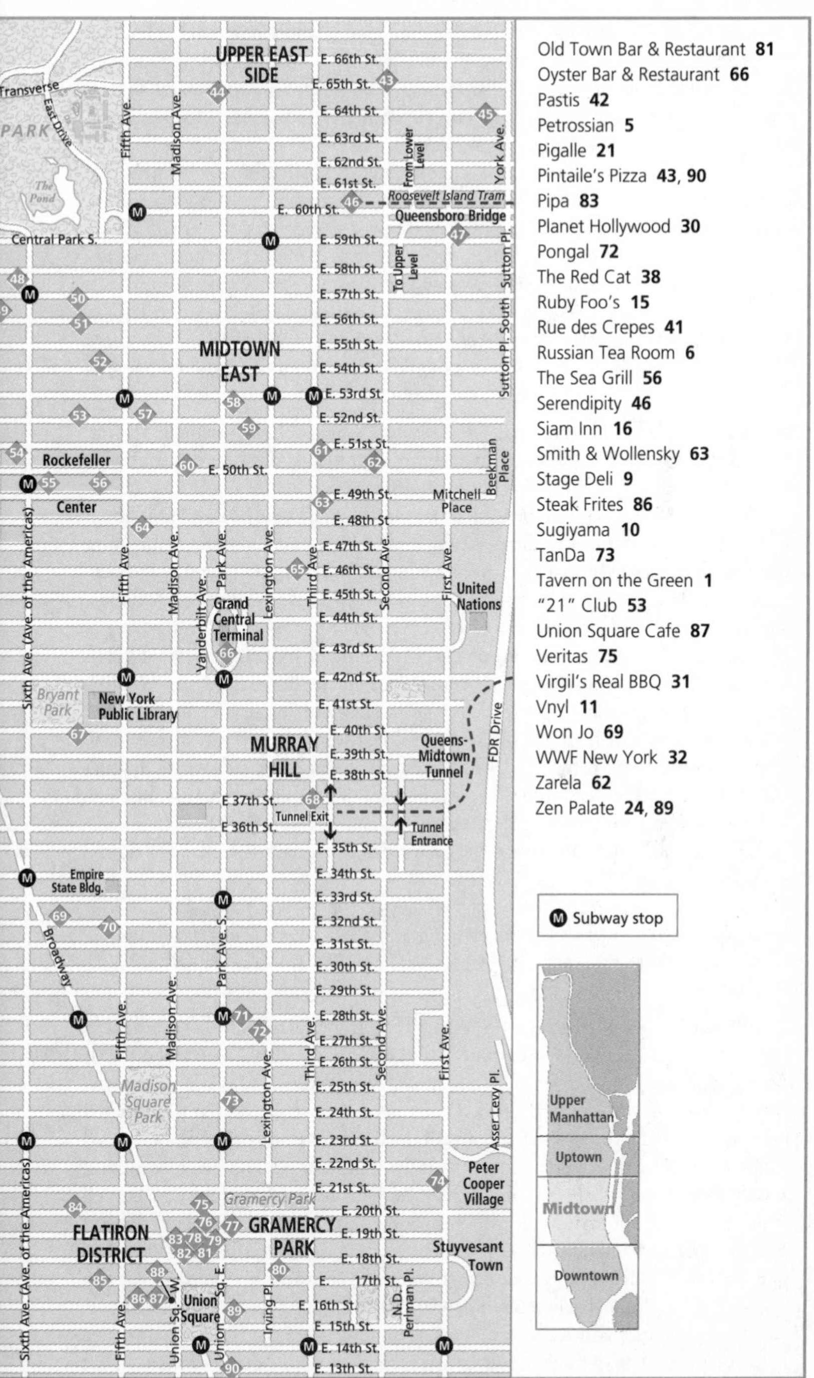
Old Town Bar & Restaurant 81
Oyster Bar & Restaurant 66
Pastis 42
Petrossian 5
Pigalle 21
Pintaile's Pizza 43, 90
Pipa 83
Planet Hollywood 30
Pongal 72
The Red Cat 38
Ruby Foo's 15
Rue des Crepes 41
Russian Tea Room 6
The Sea Grill 56
Serendipity 46
Siam Inn 16
Smith & Wollensky 63
Stage Deli 9
Steak Frites 86
Sugiyama 10
TanDa 73
Tavern on the Green 1
"21" Club 53
Union Square Cafe 87
Veritas 75
Virgil's Real BBQ 31
Vnyl 11
Won Jo 69
WWF New York 32
Zarela 62
Zen Palate 24, 89
Subway stop
UPPER EAST SIDE
MIDTOWN EAST
MURRAY HILL
GRAMERCY PARK
FLATIRON DISTRICT
Rockefeller Center
Grand Central Terminal
New York Public Library
Bryant Park
Empire State Bldg.
Madison Square Park
Gramercy Park
Union Square
United Nations
Mitchell Place
Beekman Place
Peter Cooper Village
Stuyvesant Town
Queensboro Bridge
Roosevelt Island Tram
Queens-Midtown Tunnel
Tunnel Exit
Tunnel Entrance
From Lower Level
To Upper Level
FDR Drive
Sutton Pl. South
Sutton Pl.
York Ave.
First Ave.
Second Ave.
Third Ave.
Lexington Ave.
Park Ave.
Park Ave. S.
Vanderbilt Ave.
Madison Ave.
Fifth Ave.
Sixth Ave. (Ave. of the Americas)
Broadway
Irving Pl.
Union Sq. E.
Union Sq. W.
N.D. Perlman Pl.
Asser Levy Pl.
Central Park S.
Transverse
East Drive
PARK
The Pond
Upper Manhattan
Uptown
Midtown
Downtown

mellowed the restaurant into the city's newest *New York Times* four-star winner. The sky-high prices are still in place, but Ducasse is earning them now.

Ducasse has elevated special-occasion dining to a whole new level. The intimate, antique-filled dining rooms are bold, colorful, and richly formal; unlike so many other "fine" dining establishments, this is a place worth dressing up for. Expect ultra-elegant haute French cuisine with the occasional Mediterranean flair. Each dish is a symphony of bold flavors, and claims that preparations were uneven early on have disappeared. The standard $160 prix-fixe features five courses, the $145 version only four. If it's truffle season, beware your wallet, because truffle supplements are in the $70 range—or delight if you can afford it, because it doesn't get any better than this. The wine list is phenomenally expensive but fabulous. Service is smooth and elegant, exactly as it should be.

158 W. 58th St. (btwn Sixth and Seventh aves.). ✆ **212/265-7300.** www.alain-ducasse.com. Reservations required. Jacket and tie required for men. 3-course lunch $65; 3- to 4-course dinner $145–$160; tasting menus $160–$280. AE, DC, DISC, MC, V. Tues–Wed and Sat 6:30–9pm; Thurs–Fri noon–2pm and 6:30–9pm. Subway:B, D, F, V to 42nd St.

Ilo ★★ GLOBAL In Finnish, "Ilo" means "a place of joy"—and is it ever. Chef Rick Laakonen has devised a restaurant that blends ultra-modernism with classic extravagance, and it's a winning combination.

The dining room is set at the back of the lobby of the new Bryant Park Hotel, in the glorious American Radiator Building; be sure to take a minute to admire the gilt-edged facade from across the street before you rush in to meet your reservation. Inside, the room is magnificently modern, with clean lines, high ceilings, and a rich palette of red and chocolate. Table spacing is generous and seating is comfortable; if you can, score one of the plush leather banquettes (best for four).

In his cuisine, Laakonen puts an exotic spin on the familiar—from sashimi-quality tuna to grilled sturgeon to rack of lamb—and the results are thrilling. Dishes are lush with fragrances, flavors, and textures, but never overwhelming. The star of the menu is the "Tidal Pool" starter, a clear broth rich with Olympia oysters and such shellfish exotics as percebes, sea urchin, and silver ears. But you won't go wrong with anything here. A real joy!

Tip: Make plans to start or end the evening in the romantic Cellar Bar downstairs (see chapter 11).

In the Bryant Park Hotel, 40 W. 40th St. (btwn Fifth and Sixth aves.). ✆ **212/642-2255.** www.ilorestaurant.com. Reservations required. Main courses $27–$41; tasting menu $110 ($55 supplement for wines). AE, DC, DISC, MC, V. Mon–Fri noon–3pm and 5:30–11pm; Sat–Sun 11am–2:30pm and 5:30–11pm. Subway:B, D, F, V to 42nd St.

Le Bernardin ★★★ FRENCH/SEAFOOD If forced to choose, I'd probably peg Le Bernardin as my favorite splurge restaurant in the city. The seafood at this *New York Times* four-star winner (one of only six in the city) is the best in the Big Apple, if not the world. Food doesn't get better than the flash-marinated black bass ceviche, the freshest fish awash in cilantro, mint, jalapeños, and diced tomatoes. Chef Eric Ripert's tuna tartare always exhilarates, its Asian seasoning a welcome exotic touch. Among lightly cooked dishes that shine are herbed crabmeat in saffron ravioli and shellfish-tarragon reduction; roast baby lobster tail on asparagus-and-cèpe risotto; and an extravagant mix of sea scallops, foie gras, and truffles from the Périgord, wrapped and steamed in a cabbage leaf and splashed with truffle vinaigrette. The crusted cod, served on a bed of haricots verts with potatoes and diced tomatoes, is another favorite. The formal service is impeccable, as is the outrageously pricey wine list, and the room is uptown gorgeous, if a little generic. The fixed-price lunch is a bargain, given the master in the kitchen. The desserts—especially the frozen rum-scented chestnut soufflé or chocolate dome with crème brûlée on a macaroon—end the meal with a flourish.

155 W. 51st St. (btwn Sixth and Seventh aves.). ✆ **212/489-1515.** www.le-bernardin.com. Reservations required. Jacket required/tie optional. Fixed-price lunch $47; fixed-price dinner $79; tasting menus $95–$130. AE, DC, DISC, MC, V. Mon–Thurs noon–2:30pm and 5:30–10:30pm; Fri noon–2:30pm and 5:30–11pm; Sat 5:30–11pm. Subway: N, R to 49th St.; 1, 9 to 50th St.

Russian Tea Room ★ RUSSIAN One of the city's most glamorous restaurants since 1927, the Russian Tea Room has been reborn for the new millennium. The new RTR is a mixed bag, but I prefer it to sister restaurant Tavern on the Green (p. 219). The decor can't really be called elegant: The gold is too shiny, the reds too bright. Still, anyone who remembers the garishness of the original will consider this subtle in comparison, and there's no denying the special-occasion appeal.

The menu is comprised of traditional Russian dishes, including a decadent tenderloin beef Stroganoff in a mustard cream sauce. The *shashlik Caucasian*—lamb loin skewered, seasoned with Georgian spices (coriander, fenugreek, savory, and the like), and open-flame grilled—is another winning dish. The borscht is a great way to start, but if you're really celebrating, don't miss the caviar show, presented on silver with buckwheat blinis, melted butter, and a flourish. Ask the sommelier to recommend a flight of iced vodkas for you to taste as the perfect accompaniment. Very touristy, but a worthwhile dining experience if you're set on experiencing a legend.

150 W. 57th St. (between Sixth and Seventh aves.). ✆ **212/974-2111.** www.russiantearoom.com. Reservations highly recommended. Main courses $15–$34 at lunch and brunch, $22nd]$39 at dinner; 3-course fixed-price pre-theater dinner (Mon–Fri 5–6:15pm) $32. AE, DC, DISC, MC, V. Mon–Fri 11:30am–3pm and 5pm–midnight; Sat 11am–3pm and 5pm–midnight; Sun 11am–3pm and 5–11pm. Subway: B, N, R, Q to 57th St.

Sugiyama ★★ *Finds* JAPANESE KAISEKI Tucked among Midtown's high-rises, this little-known jewel is a worthy splurge for fans of elegant Japanese food. Nao Sugiyama is a modern master of the artful kaiseki tradition, in which each delicate dish is more sensational than the last. The warm, honey-wood-paneled room is Zen-simple, with clean-lined tables and cocooning booths. Between 6 and 14 courses, all gorgeously arranged in bento-style boxes and on delicate Japanese dishes, arrive at an easy pace. Highlights include creamy monkfish liver, Japan's version of foie gras; rich, velvety sashimi that may just be the best you'll ever have; and sweet lobster, beef tenderloin, and other delicacies, which you grill yourself on your very own smooth, glowing hot stone. You can watch chef Nao and his minions prepare each dish in the open, sushi bar–style kitchen. Service is quietly friendly and faultless, and servers are pleased to explain anything you wish. The atmosphere is serene without being uncomfortably so; expect your fellow diners to be expense-account Japanese businessmen and other adventurous *gaijin* like you. The $45 meal is an excellent choice for pre-theater dining. A vegetarian menu is available; be sure to request it when you book.

251 W. 55th St. (btwn Broadway and Eighth Ave.). ✆ **212/956-0670.** Reservations recommended. 6- to 12-course fixed-price meals $45, $60, $80, and $100. AE, DC, MC, V. Tues–Sat 5:45–10:30pm. Subway: A, B, C, D, 1, 9 to 59th St./Columbus Circle.

EXPENSIVE

Steak lovers might also consider **Nick & Stef's Steakhouse,** 9 Penn Plaza, at Eighth Avenue and 33rd Street (✆ **212/563-4444;** www.nickandstefs.com); see "The Prime Cut" on p. 212.

Aquavit ★ *Value* SCANDINAVIAN When Aquavit opened in a refined pocket of Midtown nearly 15 years ago, it opened the eyes of New Yorkers to what fine Scandinavian food could be. The main dining room is soaring and Scandinavian-sleek, with birch trees and an indoor waterfall; the more casual and affordable upstairs cafe, another sophisticated Scandinavian-modern space, is one of New York's best dining bargains. Both dining rooms focus on good-value fixed-price meals.

Some of my favorite selections are well-prepared Scandinavian standards, such as the smorgasbord plate, an assortment of delicacies including smoky herring and zesty hot-mustard glazed salmon (which also comes as a full-size entree), and the venison meatballs, a perfect realization of this traditional Swedish dish, accompanied by parsley root purée, Brussels sprouts, and lingonberry sauce (beats IKEA by a mile!). The hot smoked Arctic char on the main a la carte menu, served with quail egg risotto and wild mushroom consommé, is another lovely choice. The bar offers a wide selection of aquavits, distilled liquors not unlike vodka flavored with fruit and spices and served Arctic cold, which have a smooth finish and are best accompanied by a full-bodied European brew like Carlsberg. Most fixed-price menus offer a well-chosen beverage accompaniment option, which lets you enjoy the beautifully prepared food and confident setting and service without a worry.

13 W. 54th St. (btwn Fifth and Sixth aves.). ✆ **212/307-7311.** www.aquavit.org. Reservations recommended. Cafe: Main courses $9–$20; 3-course fixed-price meal $20 at lunch, $32 at dinner. Main dining room: Fixed-price meal $35 at lunch, $65 at dinner ($39 for vegetarians); 3-course pre-theater dinner (5:30–6:15pm) $39. Tasting menus $48 at lunch, $85 at dinner ($58 for vegetarians); supplement for paired wines $25 at lunch, $35 at dinner. AE, DC, MC, V. Daily noon–2:30pm and 5:30–10:30pm. Subway: E, F to Fifth Ave.

Baldoria ★★ ITALIAN Baldoria is like a scene out of the Sopranos; in fact, don't be surprised if the guys at the next table look like they know Uncle Junior or Paulie Walnuts personally. Baldoria drips with atmosphere—the place looks like Sinatra would've stopped by after a show for a Chivas and steak—so it comes as a surprise that it's a fairly recent addition to the Theater District dining scene. But the proprietor, Frank Pellegrino, Jr., knows a thing or two about atmosphere, since his dad is the force behind the legendary East Harlem hangout Rao's (where Sinatra really did swill Chivas).

The handsome main dining room is exactly as you'd expect: dark walnut paneling, tin ceiling, white tablecloths, and big round booths. Servers go about their business in a pleasingly old-school way—no cozy chitchat here, but you'll do without nothing. The food is classic Italian, generously portioned, and beautifully prepared, from the perfect Caesar to the veal scallopini to the pastas in thick, zesty tomato sauce. The mostly-Italian wine list is pricey—we found only two reds under $40, but the one we chose was excellent. Cocktails are perfect, of course—this crowd wouldn't stand for anything else.

249 W. 49th St. (btwn Broadway and Eighth Ave.). ✆ **212/582-0460.** Reservations recommended. Pastas $17.50–$25; main courses $19–$32. AE, MC, V. Mon–Tues noon–3pm and 6–9:30pm; Wed–Thurs noon–3pm and 6–10:45pm; Fri noon–3pm and 6–11pm; Sat 6–11pm; Sun 6–9:30pm (closing hour indicates last reservation). Subway: N, R to 49th St.

Cité ★★ *Value* CONTINENTAL/STEAKS This pleasing Art Deco steakhouse has the air of a refined Parisian brasserie, making it a sophisticated—and value-wise—choice for a fine Theater District dinner. The standard pre-theater fixed-price is a good value unto itself, offering a pleasing number of choices, including the filet mignon steak frites, a mammoth cut that arrives impeccably grilled. But the real deal comes after 8pm (5pm on Sun), with Cité's fabulous Wine Dinner: Choose any appetizer, main course, and dessert from the full dinner menu for $60, and enjoy unlimited quantities of the night's four featured wines *at no extra charge.* This isn't the cheap stuff—the sommelier takes this program seriously and has chosen well. Among the wines on recent offer were a Burgess Cellars cabernet, an Acacia chardonnay, a Chalone Vineyard reserve Pinot Noir, and a Nicolas Feuillate brut for celebrating. The full menu features an excellent selection of chops and steaks plus a fine spit-roasted garlic chicken and a stellar swordfish steak au poivre. Consider launching your meal with the creamy sweet-corn chowder and wrapping up with the classic Floating Island. The professional wait staff is brisk and attentive, and the overall ambience is much friendlier than at clubbier, more masculine steakhouses; rescued iron grillwork from the old Bon Marché department stores in Paris lend the room genuine Art-Deco grace. The Grill Room is slightly more casual, serving somewhat lighter but still classic fare. In addition to my own great Cité experiences, I get lots of positive feedback on readers from this one.

120 W. 51st St. (btwn Sixth and Seventh aves.). ✆ **212/956-7100.** www.citerestaurant.com. Reservations recommended. Main courses $20–$30; pre-theater (5–7:30pm) 3-course fixed-price $48; 3-course Wine Dinner $60 with wine (Mon–Sat from 8pm; Sun from 5pm). AE, DC, DISC, MC, V. Mon–Fri noon–2:30pm and 5–11:30pm; Sat–Sun 5–11:30pm. Cité Grill: Mon–Sat 11:30am–11:30pm; Sun 11:30am–5pm. Subway: N, R to 49th St.; B, D, E to Seventh Ave.

Molyvos ★ GREEK Ruth Reichl, then of the *New York Times,* was so thrilled by the high quality and authenticity of this cozy upscale taverna that she awarded Molyvos three stars (out of a possible four) a few years ago. She's absolutely right—it's terrific. The menu boasts beautifully prepared favorites (including superb taramasalata, tzatziki, and other traditional spreads), plus a few dishes with contemporary twists. The Greek country salad is generously portioned and as fresh as can be, while the baby octopus starter is grilled over fruitwood to tender, charred perfection. Among the main courses, the lemon- and garlic-seasoned roasted free-range chicken is right on the mark: juicy, tender, and dressed with oven-dried tomatoes, olives, and rustic potatoes. More traditional tastes can opt for excellent moussaka; rosemary-skewered souvlaki; or the day's catch, wood-grilled whole with lemon, oregano, and olive oil in traditional Greek style. Baklava fans shouldn't miss the restaurant's moist, nutty version, which is big enough to share. The room is spacious and comfortable, with a warm Mediterranean appeal that doesn't go overboard on the Hellenic themes, and service that's attentive without being intrusive. The sommelier can help you choose from the surprisingly good list of Greek wines, making Molyvos a winner on all counts.

871 Seventh Ave. (btwn 55th and 56th sts.). ✆ **212/582-7500.** Reservations recommended. Main courses $13–$24.50 at lunch (most less than $20), $19.50–$29.50 at dinner (most less than $25); fixed-price lunch $22.50; pre-theater 3-course dinner $34.50 (5:30–6:45pm). AE, DC, DISC, MC, V. Daily noon–midnight. Subway: N, R to 57th St.; B, D, E to Seventh Ave.

Petrossian ★ CONTINENTAL/RUSSIAN Petrossian is North America's (and France's) largest importer of Caspian caviar, so they're able to serve high-quality Sevruga, Osetra, and Beluga for no more than you'd pay if you picked it up at the deli counter down at Balducci's. Oh, but this is no deli counter—nowhere in New York is caviar more exquisitely served. Available all evening, the three-course fixed-price dinner is almost an unbelievable deal, and definitely the way to go: For $63.50 (even less pre-and post-theater; see below), you can start with more than an ounce of high-quality Sevruga (elegantly served in silver with toast points), and follow with a full entree, the best of which is the plate of Petrossian Teasers, a gourmand's delight of smoked eel, trout, cod, salmon, and sturgeon, accompanied by excellent foie gras and marinated herring. Champagne by the glass ups the tally, but it's the perfect accompaniment. The Art Deco room may not live up to the promise of the gorgeous beaux arts exterior, but it's impressive nonetheless, and you're bound to be surrounded by big-haired high-society mavens who are a hoot to ogle. Service is aloof but attentive, just as it should be.

182 W. 58th St. (at Seventh Ave.). ✆ **212/245-2214.** www.petrossian.com. Reservations highly recommended. Jacket and tie preferred for men. Main courses $21–$28 at lunch, $26–$34 at dinner; fixed-price meals $28 at lunch and brunch, $34 or $42 at dinner ($34 option offered 5:30–6:30pm and 10:30–11:30pm); $21.50 supplement for caviar. Individual caviar presentations from $39 (for 30g). AE, DC, DISC, MC, V. Mon–Sat 11:30am–3pm and 5:30–11:30pm; Sun 11:30am–3pm and 5:30–10:30pm. Subway: B, D, E to Seventh Ave.; N, R to 57th St.

The Sea Grill ★★ SEAFOOD Oddly set below street level, this top-quality seafooder actually has one of the best views in the city, overlooking the Rockefeller Center ice rink in winter, and with a prime view of gold-plated *Prometheus* year-round. Despite the tourist-targeted setting, the food—from Chef Ed Brown, recently hailed as "the dean of the American fish cooks" in the pages of *Gourmet*—is wonderful. While not on grand display, the restaurant nevertheless boasts an impressive raw bar, usually featuring a half dozen choices of clams and oysters, depending on what's fresh, plus perfect jumbo shrimp for a divine shrimp cocktail. Winning hot appetizers include rich house-made raviolis of diver scallops and foie gras, bathed in a light butter sauce; and a wonderful cured salmon belly tartar with fresh dill and black salt. Among the mains, the specialty of the house are your choice of filets (usually halibut, mahimahi, king salmon, or arctic char), *plancha* grilled on a flat iron skillet to sear in the flavors, then served with a stir-fry of watercress, sweet garlic, and parsley—an ideal way to eat well and healthy at the same time. The crab cakes, served with grainy mustard and parsley sauce and nearly 100% crab, are another great choice. The Adam Tihany–designed room is cool, clean, and contemporary, with big tables and comfortable banquettes. Service is top-grade, too; don't miss the minipopsicles for dessert.

At Rockefeller Center, 19 W. 49th St. (btwn Fifth and Sixth aves.). ✆ **212/332-7610.** www.restaurantassociates.com. Reservations recommended. Main courses $18–$29 at lunch, $24–$32 at dinner. AE, DC, DISC, MC, V. Mon–Fri 11:15am–2:15pm and 5–10pm; Sat 5–10pm. Subway: B, D, F, V to 47–50th sts./Rockefeller Center.

MODERATE

In addition to the choices below, also consider **Aquavit** (p. 200), which offers elegant but wonderfully value-priced Scandinavian meals in its lovely cafe.

Brazil Grill ★ *Value* BRAZILIAN The Theater District is loaded with overpriced tourist traps, and many of its affordable restaurants feel dowdy or downscale. So where can you go for a special pre- or post-theater dinner that won't break the bank? Make a beeline for Brazil Grill, where the tables are spacious, the staff is charming, and cobalt-blue accents add a touch of elegance and sophistication to the decor. There's a festive soundtrack, but the noise level—unlike the also-pleasing but significantly rowdier Churrascaria Plataforma (below)—is reasonable.

Sip a tropical *caipirinha* while perusing the menu, which showcases the sunny flavors of Brazil. There's lots of simple country cooking to satisfy the meat-and-potatoes crowd (such as sizzling beef skewers with peppers and onions), while diners with more adventurous palates might try dishes like the spicy *camarao baiana* (shrimp sautéed with palm oil and served in a sauce of coconut milk, tomatoes, and garlic). Portions are generous, and main courses come with ample sides of rice and beans. Don't miss the incredible *doce de leite* for dessert—if you've never tasted this rich and creamy caramel confection of the gods, you'll thank me.

The prix fixe is an incredible deal—three filling courses for a mere $19.95—and the wine list offers affordable choices, including an array of wines by the glass for only $5–$6.

787 Eighth Ave. (at 48th St.). ✆ **212/307-9449.** www.brazilgrill.citysearch.com. Reservations recommended, especially pre-theater. Main courses $10.95–$21.95; 3-course prix-fixe dinner $19.95. AE, DC, MC, V. Daily noon–midnight. Subway: 1, 2 to 50th St.; C, E to 50th St.

Carmine's *Kids* FAMILY-STYLE SOUTHERN ITALIAN Everything is B-I-G at this rollicking, family style Times Square mainstay. The dining room is vast enough to deserve its own zip code, massive platters of pasta hold Brady Bunch–size portions, and large groups wait to join in the rambunctious atmosphere at this sibling of the original Upper West Sider. This is a value-priced restaurant where the bang for your buck increases for every person you add to your party—but so does the wait, so come early or late to avoid the crowds. Caesar salad and a mound of fried calamari are a perfect beginning, followed by heaping portions of pasta topped with red or white clam sauce, mixed seafood, zesty marinara, or meatballs. The meat entrees include veal parmigiana, broiled porterhouse steak, chicken marsala, and shrimp scampi. The tiramisu is pie-size, thick and creamy, bathed in Kahlúa and marsala. Order half of what you think you'll need.

200 W. 44th St. (btwn Broadway and Eighth Ave.). ✆ **212/221-3800.** www.carminesnyc.com. Reservations recommended before 6pm; accepted for 6 or more after 6pm. Family style main courses $15–$49 (most $23 or less). AE, DC, DISC, MC, V. Tues–Sat 11:30am–midnight; Sun–Mon 11:30am–11pm. Subway: A, C, E, N, R, S, 1, 2, 3, 7, 9 to 42nd St./Times Sq. Also at 2450 Broadway, btwn 90th and 91st sts. (✆ 212/362-2200; subway: 1, 2, 3, 9 to 96th St.).

Churrascaria Plataforma *Kids* BRAZILIAN It's a carnival for carnivores at this colorful, upscale, all-you-can-eat Brazilian rotisserie. A large selection of teasers like octopus stew, paella, and carpaccio at the phenomenal salad bar may tempt you to fill up too quickly, but hold out for the never-ending parade of meat. Roving servers deliver beef (too many cuts to mention), ham, chicken (the chicken hearts are great, trust me), lamb, and sausage—more than 15 delectable varieties—and traditional sides like fried yucca, plantains, and rice until you cannot eat another bite. The food is excellent, the service friendly and generous, and the cavernous room *loud*—this is not the place for romance. Instead, it's a fun, festive affair. That terrific salad bar even makes this a good choice for the vegetarians in your party. The ideal accompaniment to the meal is a pitcher of Brazil's signature cocktail, the *caipirinha,* a margarita-like blend of limes, sugar, crushed ice, and raw sugarcane liquor; Plataforma's are the best in town.

316 W. 49th St. (btwn Eighth and Ninth aves.). ✆ **212/245-0505.** www.churrascariaplataforma.com. Reservations recommended. All-you-can-eat fixed-price $28 at lunch, $39 at dinner; half-price for children 5–10. AE, DC, DISC, MC, V. Daily noon–midnight. Subway: C, E to 50th St.

Joe Allen ★★ AMERICAN PUB This upscale Restaurant Row pub is a glorious throwback to the Broadway of yesteryear, when theater types went to places like Sardi's and Lüchow's—and yep, Joe Allen—to toss back a few after the curtain. The good news is that Joe Allen is still going strong; in fact, don't be surprised if you spot a stage star or two among the clientele. The uncomplicated American pub food is reliable and well priced, and served at big, comfortable tables (the kind that restaurant managers don't order anymore because they take up too much real estate) covered with red-checked cloths. The meat loaf, in particular, is terrific, but you can't go wrong with the chili, the decent Greek salad, the great burgers, or anything that comes with mashed potatoes. More than 30 beers are available, and some good wines by the glass. The staff is a congenial, and entirely neighborhood-appropriate, mix of career waiters and aspiring thespians. You'll thoroughly enjoy perusing the walls covered with posters and other memorabilia from legendary Broadway flops.

326 W. 46th St. (btwn Eighth and Ninth aves.). ✆ **212/581-6464.** Reservations recommended (a must for pre-theater dining). Main courses $9–$22 (most less than $17). MC, V. Mon–Tues and Thurs–Fri noon–11:45pm; Wed and Sat–Sun 11:30am–11:45pm. Subway: A, C, E to 42nd St./Port Authority.

Norma's ★★ *Finds* CREATIVE AMERICAN BREAKFAST Nowhere is breakfast treated with such reverence, and decadence, than at Norma's, a soaring, ultramodern ode to the ultimate comfort food. The room is a highly stylized version of an ocean liner, with warm woods, sleek designer lines, soaring ceilings, formal place settings, and professional service. But don't expect stiff; just take a look at the menu. What's a Waz-Za? "Waffle—Fruit inside, fruit outside, crackly brûlée top!"

But that's where the funny business ends, because the kitchen takes breakfast food seriously. There's something for everyone on the huge menu. Classics come in styles both simple and haute: Blueberry pancakes come piled high with fresh Maine berries and Devonshire cream, while buttermilks are topped with fresh Georgia peaches and chopped walnuts. The asparagus and seared rock lobster omelette is silly with seafood, while brioche French toast gets the ultimate decadent twist from foie gras and wild mushrooms. Even oatmeal is special: genuine Irish McCann's, dressed with sautéed green apples and red pears and brûléed for a flash of sugary sweetness. Don't pass on the applewood-smoked bacon, so good that it's worth blowing any diet for. Norma's can even win over breakfast foes with creative sandwiches, a generous Cobb with seared ahi, and a terrific chicken potpie. A genuine delight!

At Le Parker Meridien hotel, 118 W. 57th St. (btwn Sixth and Seventh aves.). ✆ **212/708-7460.** www.leparkermeridien.com. Reservations accepted. Main courses $8–$23 (most $13–$18). AE, DC, DISC, MC, V. Mon–Fri 6:30am–3pm; Sat–Sun 7am–3pm. Subway: B, N,Q, R, W, N, R to 57th St.

Pigalle FRENCH BRASSERIE This new French brasserie has been struggling a bit to find an audience, but it deserves one. It's a wonderful addition to the Theater District, thanks to its winning combination of high quality fare, low prices, and convenient-to-Broadway location—not to mention 24-hour service that makes it the best place to satisfy post-anything munchies. The beautifully designed room by Nancy Mah boasts all the trimmings of a traditional brasserie—zinc-topped bar, colorful rattan, soft ochre lighting—with a designer edge. The room is big, airy, and comfortable, great for couples and larger parties alike. The menu offers true-to-form versions of classic brasserie fare, including onion soup gratinée, *classique* cassoulet, duck confit, and steak au poivre. The food isn't groundbreaking, but it's very satisfying, especially for the price; stick to the classics and you'll enjoy yourself.

I especially love the inspired cocktail menu, which is reason enough to come in. The Violet Martini is perfectly shaken with Grey Goose and a hint of violet essence, then dressed with a single purple petal. The New Yorker is my husband's new favorite: gin, dry vermouth, dill pickle, and garlic, served straight up. The only downside was the shaky service on our last visit; if you're going pre-theater, make it clear from the moment you sit.

790 Eighth Ave. (at 48th St.), adjacent to the Days Hotel. ✆ **212/489-2233.** Reservations recommended. Main courses $6.50–$14 at breakfast and lunch, $8–$18 at dinner. AE, DC, DISC, MC, V. Daily 24 hours. Subway: A, C, E to 50th St.

Ruby Foo's PAN-ASIAN Cross a sushi bar with a dim sum palace, shake with some fanciful modern design and toss in a high-concept cocktail menu, and what do you get? Ruby Foo's. This mammoth, ultra-sexy space is filled to the brim nightly with high-spirited folks who just can't get enough of the big menu, eye-popping Asian-bordello decor, and super-fun vibe. The place is gorgeous, and the sound level is surprisingly tolerable considering the bustle.

And the food is better than you'd expect from a party scene like this. I find the dim sum to be the most pleasing part of the menu: The shrimp and vegetable dumplings were delectably crispy, Malaysian chicken pot stickers were flavorfully curried, and the succulent tamarind-glazed baby-back ribs were a true delight. The sushi is fresh and just fine, although I advise staying away from the more creative preparations—there's a reason the Japanese never rolled filet mignon, lobster, or mango in seaweed before. I also recommend diverging from traditional ordering patterns and mixing one or two main courses in as part of a family-style meal.

1626 Broadway at 49th St. ✆ **212/489-5600.** www.rubyfoos.com. Reservations highly recommended for dinner. Dim sum and sushi rolls $5–$10; main courses $11–$25 (most less than $20); sushi platters $22–$36. AE, MC, V. Sun–Thurs 11:30am–midnight; Fri–Sat 11:30am–1am. Subway: N, R to 49th St. Also at 2182 Broadway, at 77th St. (✆ 212/724-6700; subway: 1, 9 to 79th St.).

Virgil's Real BBQ *Kids* BARBECUE/SOUTHERN Virgil's may look like a comfy theme-park version of a down-home barbecue joint, but this place takes its barbecue seriously. The meat is house-smoked with a blend of hickory, oak, and fruitwood chips, and most every regional school is represented, from Carolina pulled pork to Texas beef brisket to Memphis ribs. You may not consider this contest-winning chow if you're from barbecue country, but we less-savvy Yankees are thrilled to have Virgil's in the 'hood. I love to start with the barbecued shrimp, accompanied by yummy mustard slaw, and a plate of buttermilk onion rings with blue cheese for dipping. The ribs are lip-smackin' good, but the chicken is moist and tender—go for a combo if you just can't choose. Burgers, sandwiches, and other entrees (chicken-fried steak, anyone?) are also available if you can't face up to all that meat 'n' sauce. And cast that cornbread aside for a full order of buttermilk biscuits, which come with maple butter so good it's like dessert. So hunker down, pig out, and don't worry about making a mess; when you're through eating, you get a hot towel for washing up. The bar offers a huge selection of on-tap and bottled brews.

152 W. 44th St. (btwn Sixth and Seventh aves.). ✆ **212/921-9494.** www.virgilsbbq.com. Reservations recommended. Sandwiches $6–$11; main courses and barbecue platters $13–$26 (most less than $19). AE, DC, DISC, MC, V. Sun–Mon 11:30am–11pm; Tues–Sat 11:30am–midnight. Subway: 1, 2, 3, 7, 9, N, R to 42nd St./ Times Sq.

INEXPENSIVE

A second outpost of **Grand Sichuan International** (p. 189) dishes up killer Sichuan Chinese fare at a new outpost at 745 Ninth Ave., between 50th and

51st streets (✆ **212/582-2288**). A branch of **Joe's Shanghai** (p. 171), 24 W. 56th St., just west of Fifth Avenue (✆ **212/333-3868**), offers straight-from-Chinatown soup dumplings and other Shanghai dishes. Check out stylish **Zen Palate** (p. 195), at 663 Ninth Ave., at 46th Street (✆ **212/582-1669**), for Asian-nouvelle vegetarian cuisine.

There's cafeteria-style **Mangia** (p. 166) at 50 W. 57th St., between Fifth and Sixth avenues (✆ **212/582-5882**). Two nice new branches of **Burritoville** (p. 166) are at 352 W. 39th St., at Ninth Avenue (✆ **212/563-9088**), and 625 Ninth Ave., at 44th Street (✆ **212/333-5352**).

If you're looking for the quintessential New York Jewish deli, you have your choice between the **Stage Deli,** 834 Seventh Ave., between 53rd and 54th streets (✆ **212/245-7850;** www.stagedeli.com), known for its jaw-distending celebrity sandwiches; and the **Carnegie Deli,** 854 Seventh Ave., at 55th Street (✆ **212/757-2245;** www.carnegiedeli.com), for the best pastrami, corned beef, and cheesecake in town. For more, see "The New York Deli News" box on p. 210.

Also consider **Emerald Planet** (p. 186), on the lower concourse level at 30 Rockefeller Plaza, down the hall from the skating rink (✆ **212/218-1133**); their freshly made wraps and smoothies make for a healthy, yummy lunch on the go for ambitious sightseers.

44 Southwest ★ *Finds* ITALIAN This mom-and-pop restaurant serves up the best Italian food in Midtown for the money. It's simple but charming, with an original tin ceiling, red-checkered tablecloths, and soft lighting; the result is a romantic first-date ambience (very *Lady and the Tramp* sharing spaghetti, if you know what I mean). The dishes are generously portioned and very satisfying. Pastas are perfectly al dente; I especially love the thick and hearty meat sauce on the linguine bolognese. The chicken Parmesean is classically yummy, and personal pizzas arrive with wonderfully chewy crusts. The wine list is affordable and the service attentive, making 44 Southwest a winner on all fronts for wallet-watching visitors.

621 Ninth Ave. (at 44th St.) ✆ **212/315-4582** or 212/315-4681. Reservations accepted (recommended for pre-theater dining). Main courses $8–$14. AE, DC, DISC, MC, V. Sun–Thurs noon–11pm; Fri–Sat noon–midnight. Subway: A, C, E to 42nd St.

Island Burgers & Shakes GOURMET BURGERS/SANDWICHES This aisle-size diner glows with the wild colors of a California surf shop. Service is minimal and tables are tiny, but the food is top-notch. A small selection of sandwiches and salads are on hand, but as the name implies, folks come here for the Goliath-size burgers—either beef hamburgers or, the specialty of the house, *churrascos* (flattened grilled chicken breasts). Innovation strikes with the more than 40 topping combinations. Though Island Burgers also serves fries, you're meant to eat these fellows with their tasty dirty potato chips.

766 Ninth Ave. (btwn 51st and 52nd sts.). ✆ **212/307-7934.** www.island.citysearch.com. Reservations not accepted. Sandwiches and salads $6.50–$9. No credit cards. Sun–Thurs noon–10:30pm; Fri–Sat noon–11:30pm. Subway: C, E to 50th St.

John's Pizzeria ★ *Kids* PIZZA Thin-crusted, properly sauced, and fresh, the pizza at John's has long been one of New York's best—some even consider these *the* best pies New York has to offer. Housed in the century-old Gospel Tabernacle Church, the split-level dining room is vast and pretty, featuring a gorgeous stained-glass ceiling and chefs working at classic brick ovens right in the room. More important, it's big enough to hold pre-theater crowds, so the wait's never too long despite the place's popularity. At John's you order a whole made-to-order pie rather than ordering by the slice as at most New York pizzerias, so come with friends or family. There's also a good selection of traditional pastas, such as baked ziti and well-stuffed calzones.

This Theater District location is my favorite, but the original Bleecker Street location is loaded with old-world atmosphere, and the Lincoln Center outpost makes for a good and affordable pre-theater meal.

260 W. 44th St. (btwn Broadway and Eighth Ave.). ✆ **212/391-7560.** Reservations accepted for 10 or more. Pizzas $11–$16 (plus toppings); pastas $7–$13. AE, DISC, MC, V. Daily 11:30am–11:30pm. Subway: A, C, E to 42nd St.; N, R, S, 1, 2, 3, 7, 9 to 42nd St./Times Sq. Also at 278 Bleecker St., btwn Sixth and Seventh aves. (✆ 212/243-1680; subway: 1, 9 to Houston St.). 48 W. 65th St., btwn Broadway and Central Park West (✆ 212/721-7001; subway: 1, 9 to 66th St.). 408 E. 64th St., btwn First and York aves. (✆ 212/935-2895; subway: 6 to 68th St.).

Manhattan Chili Co. *Kids* AMERICAN SOUTHWESTERN This big, cartoonish, festive Theater District restaurant adjacent to Dave Letterman's Ed Sullivan Theater is a great choice for a casual and affordable meal, especially if you have the kids in tow. The big, hearty chili bowls are geared to young palates, which tend to be suspicious of anything unfamiliar. The extensive list of chili choices is clearly marked by spice level, from the traditional Abilene with ground beef, tomatoes, basil, and red wine (mild enough for tenderfeet) to the Texas Chain Gang, which adds jalapeños to the mix for those who prefer hot. In addition, expect familiar favorites like nachos, chicken wings, big salads, and generous burritos and burgers. It's really hard to go wrong here—even vegetarians have lots to choose from. A fun place to eat!

1697 Broadway (53rd and 54th sts.). ✆ **212/246-6555.** www.manhattanchilico.com. Reservations accepted. Chili bowls $10; main courses $11–$16; Sat–Sun brunch $10.95. AE, DISC, MC, V. Sun–Mon 11:30am–11pm; Tues–Sat 11:30am–midnight. Subway: B, D, E to Seventh Ave.; 1, 9 to 50th St. Also at 1500 Broadway (entrance on 43rd St.). ✆ 212/730-8666; subway: N, R, S, 1, 2, 3, 7, 9 to 42nd St./Times Sq.

Siam Inn THAI Situated on an unremarkable stretch of Eighth Avenue, Siam Inn is an attractive outpost of very good Thai food. All of your Thai favorites are here, well prepared and served by a brightly attired and courteous wait staff. *Tom kah gai soup* (with chicken, mushrooms, and coconut milk), chicken satay with yummy peanut sauce, and light, flaky curry puffs all make good starters. Among noteworthy entrees are the masaman and red curries (the former rich and peanuty, the latter quite spicy), spicy sautéed squid with fresh basil and chiles, and perfect pad Thai. And unlike many of the drab restaurants in this neighborhood, the decor is pretty and pleasing—black deco tables and chairs, cushy rugs underfoot, and soft lighting.

854 Eighth Ave. (btwn 51st and 52nd sts.). ✆ **212/757-4006.** www.siaminn.com. Reservations suggested. Main courses $8–$12 at lunch, $8–$16 at dinner. AE, DC, MC, V. Mon–Fri noon–11:30pm; Sat–Sun 4–11:30pm. Subway: C, E to 50th St.

Vynl *Value* AMERICAN DINER Vynl adds a hip quotient to the traditional diner formula with groovy Lucite and Bakelite decor, a wonderful collection of action figures through the ages behind the bar (from Captain and Tenille to Tyson Beckford), a hip 1970s-to-now soundtrack, and an affordable menu presented in a memory-inducing gatefold album cover (ours were from Lionel Richie and Three Dog Night). But Vynl isn't just veneer—the food is terrific. The brioche French toast topped with sautéed apples and warm caramel sauce is a great way to launch a weekend day. For daytime and evening, the satisfying fare runs the gamut from classic diner fare to creative Asian-accented dishes

Theme Restaurant Thrills!

I may not know the difference between Stone Cold Steve Austin and the Rock, but I do know that **WWE New York** ★★, 1501 Broadway, at 43rd Street (✆ **212/398-2563;** http://newyork.wwe.com), is one cool place. It's more than just a theme restaurant; rather, it's the World Wrestling Entertainment's 47,000-square-foot (4,366-sq.-m) flagship entertainment complex, with entertainment options galore for wrestling fans and non-fans alike. But you can always stop by for above-average eats with a side of WWE's signature raucousness (more than 100 monitors broadcast WWE action nonstop).

Boasting broader appeal is **ESPN Zone** ★, 1472 Broadway, at 42nd Street (✆ **212/921-3776;** www.espnzone.com). This almost-equally mammoth space houses the Studio Grill, with nonstop ESPN programming; the Screening Room, with two giant screens surrounded by a dozen 36-inchers, and reclining leather chairs with built-in speakers (the perfect place to watch the big game); the Sports Arena, a full floor of sports-related arcade games; set replicas from ESPN's hit shows (including *Sportscenter* and *NBA 2night*); and much more. A sports fan's dream come true.

New York's **Hard Rock Cafe,** 221 W. 57th St., between Broadway and Seventh Avenue (✆ **212/489-6565;** www.hardrockcafe.com), is actually one of the originals of the monster chain, and a wonderful realization of the concept. The memorabilia collection is terrific, with lots of great Lennon collectibles. The comfortable bar mixes up great cocktails.

The subterranean red planet–themed **Mars 2112,** 1633 Broadway, at 51st Street (✆ **212/582-2112;** www.mars2112.com), is a hoot, from the simulated red-rock rooms to the Martian-costumed wait staff to the silly "Man Eats on Mars!" newspaper-style menu. The food is better than you might expect, but skip the Star Tours–style simulated spacecraft ride at the entrance if you don't want to lose your appetite before you get to your table. The kids won't mind, though—they'll love it, along with the extensive video arcade.

Something to scare you with, my dear? You'll enter the **Jekyll & Hyde Club,** 1409 Sixth Ave., between 57th and 58th streets (✆ **212/541-9505;** www.eerie.com), through a small, dark room with a sinking ceiling, where a corpse warns you of the oddities to come. There are five floors—grand salon, library, laboratory, mausoleum, observatory—of bizarre artifacts, wall hangings that come to life, and other interactive bone chillers. Kids love it.

Flagging **Planet Hollywood,** 1540 Broadway, at 45th Street (✆ **212/333-7827;** www.planethollywood.com), got a jolt of much-needed energy in 2000, thanks to a new circle of celebrity investors that includes *NSYNC. JC and Justin do not stop in for Cap'n Crunch fried chicken, and the movie memorabilia doesn't hold the same excitement as the genuine rock-and-roll goods over at the Hard Rock (didn't I see the R2D2 and C3PO robots at three *other* PHs?).

including Thai curries, a veggie stir-fry, and a very good Chinese chicken salad. Service is friendly and attentive. Be sure to pay with a credit card, so you can sign the bill with the coolest pen in town (yours to purchase, if you wish).

824 Ninth Ave. (at 54th St.). ✆ **212/974-2003.** Reservations not accepted. Main courses $4.50–$11. AE, MC, V. Mon–Tues 11:30am–11pm; Wed–Fri 11:30am–midnight; Sat 9:30am–midnight; Sun 9:30am–11pm. Subway: C, E to 50th St.

Won Jo ★ KOREAN BARBECUE/JAPANESE This round-the-clock authentic Korean barbecue is a good bet for first-timers and purists alike. The menu at this brightly lit restaurant is massive, but barbecue is the way to go. All the cuts of meat are high quality (shrimp is available too), and the table barbecues come with six side dishes (including good kimchee), plus rice, dipping sauce, and lettuce leaves for wrapping barbecued meats. This is an interactive meal; you'll cook everything to your taste at your table's built-in grill. Unlike some of the neighboring joints, the food here isn't blazingly spiced, but it's still plenty piquant. The friendly staff may not speak the best English, but they're happy to walk novices through all of the steps. It's a feast that's particularly fun with a crowd—Asian pop blares through the speakers, and groups keep the place hopping all night, especially on weekends—but couples will be well contented, too. The sushi, teriyaki, and *bi bim bop* (Korean hot pot dishes) are well prepared too, if you'd rather forego the cook-your-own option.

23 W. 32nd St. (btwn Broadway and Fifth Ave.). ✆ **212/695-5815.** Reservations not accepted. Full barbecue dinners $17–$20; main courses $8–$27 (most less than $12). AE, MC, V. Daily 24 hours. Subway: B, D, F, Q, N, R to 34th St.

12 Midtown East & Murray Hill

To locate the restaurants in this section, see map on p. 196.

VERY EXPENSIVE

La Grenouille ★★★ CLASSIC FRENCH What a gem! They don't come more old school than this jewel of a restaurant, which has been serving New Yorkers in classic French style since 1962. Formerly the domain of the blue-hair-and-blue-blazer set, La Grenouille is now being discovered by a younger crowd. It's quite a find—so utterly retro that it feels like a breath of fresh air. This is a place that's really worth getting dressed up for.

La Grenouille may be classic, but it doesn't feel the least bit stuffy. You'll know it the instant you walk into the elegant dining room, with its gold silk walls, red velvet banquettes, lavish floral arrangements, and tuxedoed waiters. The wait staff is one of the warmest and most attentive in the city, second only to Chanterelle's—and it's a very close second. There's a rare confidence here, in both the food and the service, that sets a tone of comfort and ease.

Nothing comes out of the kitchen that isn't flawlessly prepared and presented. The foie gras is sautéed to perfection and boasts a delicate hint of vanilla; the black truffle–marinated sea scallops roasted in lobster butter are another winningly decadent starter. The spice-rubbed duckling breast with braised salsify was the best duck I've ever had, while the port-glazed veal sweetbreads were fork-tender, not crispy, and beautifully accompanied by a chestnut and walnut cocotte. Order what strikes your fancy—you can't go wrong with any dish here. The wine list is pricey but excellent; your waiter will be happy to point you to the best values. Save room for the soufflé, the ultimate realization of this classic dessert.

The New York Deli News

There's nothing more Noo Yawk than hunkering down over a mammoth pastrami on rye at an authentic Jewish deli, where anything you order comes with a bowl of lip-smacking sour dills and a side of attitude. All of the following are the real deal—you gotta problem wid'dat?

Opened in 1937, the **Stage Deli,** 834 Seventh Ave., between 53rd and 54th streets (✆ **212/245-7850;** www.stagedeli.com), is noisy and crowded and packed with tourists, but it's still as authentic as they come. Connoisseurs line up to sample the 36 famous specialty sandwiches named after many of the stars whose photos adorn the walls. The celebrity sandwiches, ostensibly created by the personalities themselves, are jaw-distending mountains of top-quality fixings: The Tom Hanks is roast beef, chopped liver, onion, and chicken fat, while the Dolly Parton is (drumroll, please) twin rolls of corned beef and pastrami.

For the quintessential New York experience, head to the **Carnegie Deli,** 854 Seventh Ave., at 55th Street (✆ **800/334-5606** or 212/757-2245; www.carnegiedeli.com), where it's worth subjecting yourself to surly service, tourist-targeted overpricing, and elbow-to-elbow seating for some of the best pastrami and corned beef in town. Even big eaters may be challenged by mammoth sandwiches with names like "Fifty Ways to Love Your Liver" (chopped liver, hard-boiled egg, lettuce, tomato, and onion). Main courses range from goulash to roasted chicken, and the heavenly blintzes come stuffed with cheese or fruit. Real New York cheesecake doesn't get more divine, so save room!

The **Second Avenue Deli,** 156 Second Ave., at 10th Street (✆ **800/NYC-DELI** or 212/677-0606), is the best kosher choice in town (for all you goyim out there, that means no milk, butter, or cheese is served). There's no bowing to tourism here—this is the real deal. The service is brusque, the decor is nondescript, and the sandwiches don't have cute names, but the dishes are true New York classics: gefilte fish, matzo ball soup, chicken livers, potato knishes, nova lox and eggs. The monster

3 E. 52nd St. (just east of Fifth Ave.). ✆ **212/752-1495.** Reservations required (2–3 weeks in advance suggested). Jacket and tie required for men. 3-course fixed-price $45 at lunch, $85 at dinner. AE, DC, MC, V. Tues–Sat noon–2:30pm and 5:30–11:15pm. Subway: E to Fifth Ave.

Le Cirque 2000 ★ MODERN FRENCH Fine dining goes the way of the big top at Le Cirque 2000, and it's a hit. Iconic restaurateur Sirio Maccioni made a bold move when he relocated his legendary Le Cirque a few years back, but it turned out to be a masterstroke. Designer Adam Tihany festooned the gilded-age mansion's almost rococo interiors with jewel-toned circus colors, bright lights, and outrageous furniture.

The food is excellently prepared if not innovative: lobster roasted with young artichokes and wild mushrooms; paupiette of black sea bass in crispy potatoes with braised leeks; Black Angus tenderloin in red wine sauce; and roasted rack of lamb. The starters are almost as pricey as the entrees, but we were won over by the flawlessly sautéed foie gras, and seared sea scallops with wild mushrooms triple-deckers (try wrapping your gums around the corned beef, tongue, and salami) come with a side of fries. The crunchy dills are to die for. Keep an ear tuned to the Catskills-quality banter among crusty wait staff.

Overall, New York's best deli—especially for those of us who want cheese on our pastrami or sour cream with our latkes (or simply cream in our coffee)—is **Katz's Delicatessen** ★★, which remains fabulously old-world despite its hipster-hot Lower East Side location at 205 E. Houston St., at Ludlow Street (✆ **212/254-2246**). For more on Katz's, see p. 173.

Uptown, it's hard to get more authentic than **Barney Greengrass, the Sturgeon King,** 541 Amsterdam Ave., between 86th and 87th streets on the Upper West Side (✆ **212/724-4707**). This unassuming, daytime-only deli has become legend for its high-quality salmon (sable, gravlax, Nova Scotia, kippered, lox, pastrami—you choose), whitefish, and sturgeon (of course). The terrific chicken liver inspired nothing less than a raging, months-long debate among city restaurant critics a few years back; purists won't be disappointed.

The Upper West Side also boasts a newer kid on the block, **Artie's New York Delicatessen,** 2290 Broadway, between 82nd and 83rd streets (✆ **212/579-5959;** www.arties.com), that can hold its own on the playground with the big boys, thank you very much, especially in the wiener department. For more on Arties, see p. 223.

Sandwiches are priced about the same at all these delis, anywhere from $10 to $19, depending on the filling you choose (Midtown delis tend to be most expensive, with downtown delis being most old-world–priced). You'll get your money's worth, however: They come so stuffed with meat that they're more than most average mortals can consume in one sitting. But be prepared to pay a $2 to $3 sharing charge if you want to split one with your travel partner (only Katz's, Artie's, and Barney Greengrass are cool enough to let you share gratis).

and mesclun in a delicate Parmesan basket. Dessert is Le Cirque's finest course: The crème brûlée is a perfect realization of the classic dessert, but go with the chocolate stove for a truly memorable finish. The wine list is remarkable, and there's spectacular courtyard dining in season.

On the downside, service can be patronizing on occasion. Request your room of preference when booking. The Blue Room is an opulent mix of bright and baroque—and where the action is—while the mahogany-and-royal red Hunt Room is more intimate and subdued. I prefer the Hunt (I've dined next to Whoopi Goldberg here), but you're paying too much if you're seated near the kitchen, so ask for a better table if you're led in that direction.

In the Villard Houses, 455 Madison Ave. (at 50th St.). ✆ **212/303-7788.** www.lecirque.com. Reservations required well in advance. Jacket and tie required for men. Main courses $16–$40 (most $30 or higher); 3-course fixed-price lunch $44 ($25 in lounge); 5-course fixed-price dinner $90. AE, DC, MC, V. Mon–Sat 11:45am–2:30pm and 5:30–10:30pm; Sun 5:30–10:30pm. Subway: E, V to Fifth Ave.; 6 to 51st St.

The Prime Cut

Much to the delight of carnivores, this city of great steaks has undergone a big, bold chophouse explosion over the last year or so, virtually doubling the number of prime-cut palaces. The best in town is still Brooklyn's unrivaled **Peter Luger** (p. 228). **Cité** (p. 200) also offers first-rate steakhouse fare, and **Steak Frites** (p. 194) is ideal for carnivores with slightly less cash on hand. The city also boasts a few other standouts you may want to consider.

Don't expect an overpriced burger factory with waiters in Bulls jerseys and basketball-shaped plates from **Michael Jordan's–The Steak House** ★★, on the mezzanine level overlooking the main concourse at Grand Central Terminal (✆ **212/655-2300;** www.theglaziergroup.com). Bursting with beaux arts–meets–Art Deco grandeur, Michael Jordan's is wholly for grown-ups. And with a perfect view of the legendary sky ceiling, this is more than just the city's best-looking steakhouse—it's an incredible only-in–New York dining experience. Many folks consider this Manhattan's best steakhouse too; surely, no other spot offers such a well-rounded experience, and the drop-dead-gorgeous setting is one of a kind. The star of the classic steakhouse menu is the porterhouse for two, a whopping 44 ounces of top-quality cow, served suitably charred and salty on the outside.

MarkJoseph ★★, 261 Water St., at Peck Slip, South Street Seaport (✆ **212/277-0020**), is Michael Jordan's rival for best beef in Manhattan. In fact, MarkJoseph is the brainchild of Peter Luger alumni; the dry-aged steaks are as terrific as those at the legendary Brooklyn joint, but the warm and well-outfitted restaurant is more comfortable, the atmosphere is more relaxing, the service is friendlier, and there are no throngs of tourists (yet). Great for an extra-long lunchtime break after Financial District sightseeing.

EXPENSIVE

Guastavino's ★ AMERICAN BRASSERIE/MODERN CONTINENTAL Kudos to Sir Terence Conran—of Conran's design stores and half the hip restaurants in London—for taking an abandoned but architecturally glorious space under the 59th Street Bridge and turning it into a restaurant of real note. (It was named "America's Best New Restaurant" for 2000 by *Esquire* magazine.) Named for 19th-century architect Rafael Guastavino, the genius responsible for the soaring tiled vaults that define the interior, the grand space is actually two restaurants in one: At street level is the **Restaurant** (sometimes just referred to, confusingly, as Guastavino's), a 300-seat brasserie dominated by a sleek bar, often peopled by Prada-clad singles on the make; and, on the mezzanine level, the 100-seat **Club Guastavino,** a more intimate and refined space that allows you to enjoy the best of the architecture, service, and food.

Downstairs you'll find classic brasserie fare, including oysters on the half-shell, escargot with roasted garlic, smoked salmon and trout plates, a nice lamb shank with braised string beans, and an even better rotisserie half-chicken served

The best of the traditional old-world steakhouses is **Smith & Wollensky,** 797 Third Ave., at 49th Street (© **212/753-1530;** www.smithandwollensky.com), a macho holdover from old New York boasting perfect martinis, big round cabernets, a divinely smoky split pea soup, and top-tier cuts of beef, all served by career waiters with an abundance of attitude.

Nick & Stef's Steakhouse, adjacent to Madison Square Garden at 9 Penn Plaza, at Eighth Avenue and 33rd Street (© **212/563-4444**), is a comfortable contemporary steakhouse from top L.A. toque Joachim Splichal (of Patina fame), who's finally given sports fans somewhere to eat well before the Knicks or Rangers game. The clear choice is the New York strip, dry-aged on the premises and grilled to perfection.

The next generation now has its own carnivorous comfort zone in **Dylan Prime,** 62 Laight St., between Greenwich and Hudson streets (3 blocks south of Canal), in TriBeCa (© **212/334-2274;** www.dylanprime.com), where the traditional steakhouse has been gloriously reinvented for the hipster crowd. Twenty-something Mina Newman rules the kitchen, a clean-lined modern design supplants the dark, clubby standard, and a decidedly female-friendly ambience breaks with New York's misogynist steakhouse tradition. But all the earmarks of classic conspicuous consumption are here, including faultless martinis and first-rate dry-aged cuts.

At these and all other city steakhouses, expect most entrees to fall in the $22 to $38 range. Always book ahead and inquire about dress code, especially at the old-school spots.

with escarole. Daniel Orr's nouveau Continental cuisine shines on the Club level. There are a few stumbles on the menu, but excellent main courses include a roasted Scottish pheasant with braised endive in a whiskey reduction, and a beautiful Dover sole in a rough salt crust; and perfect lamb chops. The sommelier turned us on to a good under-$40 bottle, and service was attentive and courteous across the board. Caviar service (for a supplement) is ideal for elegant special occasions, and suits the grand setting perfectly. Try to snare a table along the railing if you can; they're bigger and offer a majestic view of the architecture as well as the goings-on downstairs.

New for 2002 is **Guastavino Bar & Terrace,** offering warm-weather alfresco dining from the brasserie menu on a gorgeous garden patio.

409 E. 59th St. (btwn First and York aves.). © **212/421-6644** for Club Guastavino, © **212/980-2455** for the restaurant. www.guastavinos.com. Reservations recommended. At Club Guastavino, 3-course fixed-price dinner $65; tasting menus $95–$110. At restaurant, main courses $15–$28; 2-course fixed-price lunch $20. AE, DC, DISC, MC, V. Club Guastavino: Tues–Wed 5:30–10:15pm; Thurs–Sat 5:30–11pm. Restaurant: Mon–Wed 11:30am–2:30pm and 5:30–10:15pm; Thurs–Fri 11:30am–2:30pm and 5:30–11pm; Sat 11:30am–3:30pm and 5:30–11pm; Sun 11:30am–2:30pm and 5:30–10:15pm. Subway: N, R, 4, 5, 6 to 59th St.

MODERATE

In addition to the choices below, also consider the Midtown East outpost of Upper West Side favorite **Josie's** (p. 219), 565 Third Ave., at 37th St. (✆ **212/490-1558**), serving the same delightfully health-conscious New American cooking.

Brasserie ★★ ALSATIAN BRASSERIE This impressive reincarnation of the original Brasserie—a New York legend from 1959 to 1995—boasts a futuristic makeover and the wonderful cooking of Alsace native Luc Dimnet (formerly of Les Célébrités). Although the setting is mod-designed to within an inch of its life (you expect Twiggy, or a twentysomething Mick Jagger with Marianne Faithfull on his arm, to waltz in at any moment), the food is surprisingly classic brasserie fare. Robust Provençale fish soup gets an extra leg up from pastis, Gruyère, and rouille; even a mixed-green salad is elevated above the norm with a delicate vinaigrette, a pleasing mix of lettuces, and crunchy-fresh French beans. The menu runs the gamut from classic bistro burgers to coq au vin, making it easy to eat casually or more elaborately. Steamed mussels are prepared meunière or picante style (with a side of frites, of course), and the divine chicken is slow-roasted until it falls off the bone. The roasted monkfish with dried figs and fennel is a showstopper, and anything with spaetzle is a good idea. There's a small but lovely raw selection, too. Bread comes as a fresh-baked baguette wrapped in paper—a pleasingly authentic touch in an ultramodern space that design could overwhelm, but doesn't.

100 E. 53rd St. (btwn Park and Lexington aves.). ✆ **212/751-4840.** www.restaurantassociates.com/brasserie. Reservations recommended for lunch and dinner. Main courses $8.50–$29 at brunch and lunch (most less than $22), $15–$29 at dinner (most less than $25). AE, DC, DISC, MC, V. Mon–Fri 7am–1am; Sat 11am–1am; Sun 5pm–10pm. Subway: 6 to 51st St.

D'Artagnan Restaurant & Rotisserie ★★ FRENCH No more compelling evidence of New Yorkers' commitment to high living in the post-boom days exists than this relatively new restaurant, devoted to the cuisine of Gascony—which means all the foie gras, duck, and armagnac you can consume in a sitting. The food is outstanding, and relatively affordable considering the decadence level. That may be because the folks behind the restaurant have an inside connection: D'Artagnan is the nation's largest purveyor of paté and foie gras.

The old-world interiors and folk-costumed servers offer a refreshing change from the new hip standard. The restaurant (and downstairs shop) is housed in a converted townhouse, which only adds to the wonderful character. Tables are large and well spaced, and the ambience is warm and conversational. Wear loose pants, because this ain't diet food. Foie gras is available at every course; in fact, two in our party indulged in a six-course foie gras tasting menu with an armagnac course. *L'Assiette des 3 Foie Gras* makes an ideal starter, with three creative preparations; there's also a wonderful charcuterie plate with paté and cornichons. Duck leg confit makes a nice follow-up, as does the fabulously authentic, duck-rich cassoulet. The chicken is free-range and beautifully rotisseried, if you're in the mood for something lighter. Vegetarians might as well stay home.

152 E. 46th St. (btwn Lexington and Third aves.). ✆ **212/687-0300.** www.dartagnan.com. Reservations recommended. Main courses $2–$9 at breakfast, $16.50–$26 at dinner; 2-course fixed-price lunch $20. AE, DC, DISC, MC, V. Daily 7:30am–11pm. Subway: 4, 5, 6 to 42nd St.

Oyster Bar & Restaurant ★ SEAFOOD Here's one New York institution housed within another: The city's most famous seafood joint lies in the world's greatest train station, beautifully renovated Grand Central Terminal. The restaurant is looking spiffy, too, with a main dining room sitting under an impressive curved and tiled ceiling, a more casual luncheonette-style section for walk-ins, and a wood-paneled saloon-style room for smokers.

Upstarts like Aquagrill have surpassed Oyster Bar on the culinary front in recent years, but it's still a terrific place to dine, especially if you want a classic New York experience. A new menu is prepared every day, because only the freshest fish is served. The oysters are irresistible: Kumomoto, Bluepoint, Malepeque, Belon—the list goes on and on. The list of daily catches, which can range from Arctic char to mako shark to ono (Hawaiian wahoo), is equally impressive. Most dinners cost between $20 and $25, though it's easy to jack up the tab by ordering live Maine lobster or one of the rarer daily specialties. But it's just as easy to keep the tab down by sticking with hearty fare like one of the excellent stews and pan roasts (from about $10 for oyster stew to $20 for a combo pan roast rich with oysters, clams, shrimp, lobster, and scallops) or by pairing the New England clam chowder (at $5, an unbeatable lunch) with a smoked starter to make a great meal.

In Grand Central Terminal (lower level), 23 Vanderbilt Ave. (at 42nd St.). ✆ **212/490-6650.** www.oysterbarny.com. Reservations recommended. Main courses $10–$35. AE, DC, MC, V. Mon–Fri 11:30am–9:30pm (last seating); Sat noon–9:30pm. Subway: 4, 5, 6, 7, S to 42nd St./Grand Central.

Zarela ★ MEXICAN Owner and cookbook author Zarela Martínez (*Food from My Heart: The Food and Life of Oaxaca*) draws lively, dedicated crowds with her unsurpassed Mexican food, Manhattan's best margaritas, and a wealth of charm. (Zarela herself often greets patrons at the door.) Zarela's authentic cooking features the richly flavored specialties of Oaxaca and Veracruz, so don't come expecting standard tacos and combo plates—this food is not for gringo palates. The *salpicón de pescado,* a snapper hash with tomatoes, scallions, jalapeños, and aromatic spices, is a great way to start, followed by the shrimp braised with poblanos, onions, and queso blanco. The fajitas, grilled marinated skirt steak served with chunky house-made guacamole and flour tortillas, melt in your mouth. Zarela is one Mexican restaurant that prides itself on great desserts, so check out the day's specials. Don't come, however, expecting a relaxing meal; Zarela's has a relentlessly colorful, festive vibe. Don't be surprised if you have to wait for a table, even with reservations.

You might also wish to consider Zarela's newest restaurant, **Danzón,** 126 East 28th St., between Park and Lexington avenues (✆ **212/252-1345**). The attractive two-story restaurant specializes in the seafood-heavy cuisine of the state of Veracruz, on the Gulf of Mexico (entrees $18–$22).

953 Second Ave. (btwn 50th and 51st sts.). ✆ **212/644-6740.** www.zarela.com. Reservations recommended. Main courses $12–$17 at lunch, $15–$18 at dinner; 3-course fixed-price dinner $40. AE, DC, MC, V. Mon–Thurs noon–3pm and 5–11pm; Fri noon–3pm and 5–11:30pm; Sat 5–11:30pm; Sun 5–10pm. Subway: E, F to Lexington Ave.; 6 to 51st St.

INEXPENSIVE

The lower concourse of **Grand Central Terminal** ★★, 42nd Street at Park Avenue, has developed into a quick-bite bonanza that makes it an ideal choice for lunch—and the setting is an architecture-lover's delight. Head downstairs from the main concourse and choose among the many outlets, offering everything from bratwurst to sushi. Standouts among the bounty include **Junior's,** an adorable offshoot of the Brooklyn stalwart, serving deli sandwiches, terrific steakburgers, and their world-famous cheesecake in their own waiter-serviced dining area. (With a few exceptions, most of the other outlets are takeout counters;

diners can then avail themselves of the abundant and comfortable seating at the center of the concourse.) **Mike's Take-Away,** serves up gourmet soups, salads, and sandwiches, including a warming mushroom stew in winter. **Little Pie Company** serves up the Big Apple's best pies, hands down, plus fresh-baked morning muffins and the concourse's best coffee. **Cafe Spice Express,** serves up terrific Indian fare, while countermates **Christer's** and **Knödel,** specialize, respectively, in traditional batter-dipped fish 'n' chips and terrific German-style brats, wieners, and sausages. There's also an outpost of popular pizzeria **Two Boots.** If you want beer or wine to accompany your meal, visit one of the two **bar cars,** which sit near tracks 105 and 112. For a complete list of vendors, check out **www.grandcentralterminal.com**.

In addition to the listings below, there's also a cafeteria-style branch of **Mangia** (p. 166) at 16 E. 48th St., just east of Fifth Avenue (✆ **212/754-0637**); and a **Burritoville** (p. 166), at 866 Third Ave. (actually on 52nd St. between Lexington and Third aves.; ✆ **212/980-4111**).

Ess-A-Bagel ★ BAGEL SANDWICHES Ess-A-Bagel turns out the city's best bagel, edging out rival H&H, which won't make you a sandwich. Baked daily on-site, the giant hand-rolled delicacies come in 12 flavors—plain, sesame, poppy, onion, garlic, salt, whole wheat, pumpernickel, pumpernickel raisin, cinnamon raisin, oat bran, and everything. They're so plump, chewy, and satisfying that it's hard to believe they contain no fat, cholesterol, or preservatives. Head to the back counter for a baker's dozen or line up for a sandwich overstuffed with scrumptious salads and spreads. Fillings can range from a generous schmear of cream cheese to smoked Nova salmon or chopped herring salad (both have received national acclaim) to sun-dried tomato tofu spread. There also are lots of deli-style meats to choose from, plus a wide range of cheeses, salads (egg, chicken, light tuna, and so on), and vegetarian items. Homemade soups and salads round out the menu. The cheerful dining room has plenty of bistro-style tables.

831 Third Ave. (at 51st St.). ✆ **212/980-1010.** Reservations not accepted. Sandwiches $1.50–$8.50. AE, DC, DISC, MC, V. Mon–Fri 6am–10pm; Sat–Sun 7am–5pm. Subway: E, F to Lexington Ave.; 6 to 51st St. Also at 359 First Ave. (at 21st St.). ✆ 212/260-2252; subway: L to First Ave., 6 to 23rd St.

Pongal ★ *Finds* VEGETARIAN INDIAN My favorite Indian food is served at this standout on Curry Hill, the stretch of Lexington in the high 20s that's home to a number of Indian restaurants. Pongal specializes in the vegetarian cuisine of southern India, and also happens to be kosher (only in New York!). Trust me, you don't have to be a vegetarian to love this place. The hearty dishes are always freshly prepared to order by the conscientious kitchen (no vats of saag paneer sitting around getting stale in this joint). Ingredients are always top-quality, vegetables and legume dishes are never overcooked, and the well-spiced sauces are outstanding. The specialty of the house is *dosai,* a large golden crepe filled with onions, potatoes, and other goodies, accompanied by coconut chutney and flavorful sauce. The food is very cheap, with nothing priced over $10, but that doesn't mean you have to put up with a crusty cafeteria to get such a bargain: The restaurant is low-lit and attractive, with a pleasing ambience, making it a nice choice for a special night on the town. Service can be slow on occasion, so have patience and don't be shy about waiving down your waiter.

110 Lexington Ave. (btwn 27th and 28th sts.). ✆ **212/696-9458.** www.pongal.org. Reservations not accepted. Main courses $6–$11 (most less than $9). DC, DISC, MC, V. Mon–Fri noon–3pm and 5–10pm; Sat–Sun noon–10pm. Subway: 6 to 28th St.

Kids Family-Friendly Restaurants

While it's always smart to call ahead to make sure a restaurant has kids' menus and high chairs, you can count on the following to be especially accommodating. Additionally, you and the kids might also consider **Acme Bar & Grill** (p. 181); **Lombardi's** (p. 177) for pizza; **Florent** (p. 187); **Artie's Delicatessen** (p. 211); and **Churrascaria Plataforma** (p. 203) for a Brazilian-style party.

Among the city's theme restaurants, young sci-fi fans shouldn't miss **Mars 2112,** which boasts its very own theme-park ride and a video arcade that can keep the kids busy for hours (or until you run out of quarters). Little groovy ghoulies will love the thrills and chills of the **Jekyll & Hyde Club,** while sports-minded kids can drag their baseball dads and soccer moms to the **ESPN Zone.** For details on these other choices, see the box called "Theme Restaurant Thrills!" on p. 208.

Carmine's (p. 203) This rollicking family style Italian restaurant was created with kids in mind. Expect Brady Bunch–size portions of all the favorites, including Caesar salad, veal parmigiana, and pasta topped with zesty marinara and little fist-size meatballs. The bigger the group, the better the bargain.

EJ's Luncheonette (p. 186) These pleasing retro-1950s diners do what they're supposed to do best: serve up great burgers, fries, and blue-plate specials. There's even a kids' menu featuring peanut-butter-and-jelly sandwiches along with downsized versions of the classics. Order up a milk shake on the side, and your kid will be in hog heaven.

John's Pizzeria (p. 206) What kid doesn't love pizza? The Times Square location is particularly well located and kid-friendly, with family-size tables, chefs cooking up pies in brick ovens right before your eyes, and a bustling atmosphere where kids can be kids.

Manhattan Chili Co. (p. 207) These fun Theater District restaurants are geared for all-American tastes and palates—just what a kid wants, right? Expect kid-friendly nachos, chicken wings, not-too-hot bowls of thick and meaty chili, and other faves like burritos and burgers.

Serendipity 3 (p. 226) Kids will love this whimsical restaurant and ice-cream shop, which serves up a huge menu of American favorites, followed up by colossal ice-cream treats. This irony-free charmer even makes grown-ups feel like kids again.

Tavern on the Green (p. 219) If you want to take the entire family out for a special-occasion or holiday meal, this Central Park classic is an excellent choice. Your kids will be wowed by the setting, and a children's menu makes them easy and affordable to feed. What's more, if the little ones get rambunctious, you just have to take them outdoors to blow off a little steam.

Virgil's Real BBQ (p. 205) This pleasing Times Square barbecue joint welcomes kids with open arms—and Junior will be more than happy, I'm sure, to be *allowed* to eat with his hands.

13 Upper West Side

VERY EXPENSIVE

Jean Georges ★★★ FRENCH The recipient of universally rave reviews since its 1997 debut, Jean-Georges Vongerichten's *New York Times* four-star winner is the city's best restaurant, hands down. Dining in the warmly lit and elegantly modern Adam Tihany–designed room is a sublime experience. The menu is the best of Vongerichten's past successes (Vong, JoJo) taken one step further: French and Asian touches mingle with a new passion for offbeat harvests, like lamb's quarters, sorrel, yarrow, quince, and chicory. Young garlic soup with thyme and a plate of sautéed frogs' legs makes a great beginning. Muscovy duck steak with Asian spices and sweet-and-sour jus is carved table-side, while the lobster tartine with lemongrass, pea shoots, and a broth of fenugreek (one of Jean-Georges's signature aromatic plants) receives a final dash of spices seconds before you dig in. If the chestnut soup is on the menu, don't miss it. The wine list is also excellent, with a number of unusual choices in every price range.

The food is equally excellent but more affordably priced in the **Nougatine** cafe; don't expect equally comfy chairs or as much elbow room, however. The professional service doesn't miss a beat in the main restaurant, and still attentive if not quite as well paced in the cafe. Still, Nougatine may be your best bet for a pre-theater dinner or for a four-star lunch without the three-hour break in sightseeing. If you're visiting in the warm weather, try for a table on the lovely outdoor terrace. *One qualification:* They have a tendency to really jack up the prices for holiday meals, so be on your guard. Book any meal before you leave home to guarantee a table.

In the Trump International Hotel & Tower, 1 Central Park West (at 60th St./Columbus Circle). ✆ **212/299-3900.** www.jean-georges.com. Reservations required well in advance. Jacket required for men; tie optional. Main courses $26–$42; 3- or 4-course fixed-price lunch $35–$45; 3- or 7-course fixed-price dinner $85–$115. AE, DC, MC, V. Dining room: Mon–Fri noon–2:30pm and 5:30–11pm; Sat 5:30–11pm. Nougatine: Mon–Sat 7am–10:30am, noon–3pm, and 5:30–11pm; Sun 8am–3pm and 5:30–10pm. Subway: A, B, C, D, 1, 9 to 59th St./Columbus Circle.

EXPENSIVE

Ouest ★★ CONTEMPORARY AMERICAN Finally—a fabulous, sophisticated new restaurant in the heart of the Upper West Side, a neighborhood usually known for mediocre Italian joints. Ouest (pronounced WEST) is a sleek, sexy brasserie, the brainchild of chef-owner Tom Valenti, who presides over the open kitchen. Sink into one of the round red leather booths, martini in hand, and you'll feel that you're in your own private world.

Among the show-stopping appetizers, we enjoyed Valenti's signature: a rich Parmesan custard topped with a chilled sweet-pea broth. The main courses take hearty comfort-food dishes in sophisticated new directions, with bold flavors and inventive twists. My unbelievably tender braised short ribs, nestled on a bed of polenta and surrounded by assorted mushrooms and fresh fava beans, were the envy of my table. For dessert, chocolate lovers should throw self-restraint to the winds and choose between the classic chocolate malt-ball sundae or the devilish chocolate cake with banana ice cream and peanut brittle.

I've heard a complaint or two about the service, but our waiter was charming and knowledgeable. The well-chosen wine list includes a fair number of moderately priced options, with 10 selections available by the glass.

2315 Broadway (at 84th St.). ✆ **212/580-8700.** Reservations required well in advance. Main courses $17–$27. AE, DC, DISC, MC, V. Tues–Thurs 5–11pm; Fri–Sat 5pm–midnight; Sun 5–10pm. Subway: 1, 2 to 86th St.

Tavern on the Green ★ *Kids* AMERICAN/CONTINENTAL This legendary Central Park restaurant is one of a kind. The late Warner LeRoy's fantasy palace has one of the city's best settings. Antiques and Tiffany glass fill the space, crystal chandeliers cast a romantic light, tiny twinkling lights glimmer on nearby trees, and the views over the park are wonderful. A festive spirit enlivens the Crystal Room, where you should ask to be seated, especially at Christmas. (A couple of the other dining rooms are so overdone they're a bit tacky, though.) The garden, with its Japanese lanterns and whimsical topiary shrubs, is a lovely place for a drink in summer.

When it comes to the food, it's hard to be completely consistent in an operation this mammoth. Generally speaking, the seasonal menus are surprisingly good, particularly if you stick with classic fare. The seared duck foie gras, served with a pear-and-pecan sticky bun and a balsamic-port syrup, is a wonderful beginning to any meal. The superb *al dente* pastas are house-made, and the grilled pork porterhouse is delicious and thick. Despite its big reputation, the Tavern is known for its down-to-earth manner. It can, however, be plagued by uneven service, especially during hectic holiday periods. Book well ahead. A kids' menu is available, so this is a good place to take them at holiday time.

In Central Park, Central Park West and W. 67th St. ✆ **212/873-3200.** www.tavernonthegreen.com. Reservations highly recommended, necessary well in advance on holidays. Main courses $17–$29 at lunch and brunch, $20–$40 at dinner; 3-course lunch $20–$26; 3-course pre-theater fixed-price (Sun–Fri 5–6:30pm) $36–$42; children's complete meals $14–$19. AE, DC, DISC, MC, V. Mon–Thurs noon–3pm and 5–10:30pm; Fri noon–3pm and 5–11:30pm; Sat 10am–3:30pm and 5–11:30pm; Sun 10am–3:30pm and 5–10:30pm. Subway: 1, 9 to 66th St./Lincoln Center.

MODERATE

For fun family-style Italian, there's also the original **Carmine's** (p. 203) at 2450 Broadway, between 90th and 91st streets (✆ **212/362-2200**), in addition to the choices below. And the original branch of **Ruby Foo's** (p. 205) is at 2182 Broadway, at 77th St. (✆ **212/724-7700**), which serves the same creative dim sum and sushi fare as the Times Square location in another fanciful space.

Josie's Restaurant & Juice Bar HEALTH-CONSCIOUS/CONTEMPORARY AMERICAN You have to admire the sincerity of an organic restaurant that uses chemical-free milk paint on its walls. Chef/owner Louis Lanza doesn't stop there: His adventurous menu shuns dairy, preservatives, and concentrated fats. Free-range and farm-raised meats and poultry augment vegetarian choices like baked sweet potato with tamari brown rice, broccoli, roasted beets, and tahini sauce; eggless Caesar salad; and a great three-grain vegetable burger with homemade ketchup and caramelized onions. The yellowfin tuna wasabi burger with pickled ginger is another signature. Everything is made with organic grains, beans, and flour as well as organic produce when possible. You don't have to be a health nut to enjoy Josie's; Lanza's eclectic cuisine really satisfies. And nobody's gonna actually make you do without: If wheat grass isn't your thing, a full wine and beer list is served in this pleasing modern space, which boasts enough colorful Jetsons-style touches to give the room a playful, relaxed feel.

300 Amsterdam Ave. (at 74th St.). ✆ **212/769-1212.** www.josiesnyc.com. Reservations recommended. Main courses $9–$18. AE, DC, MC, V. Mon–Wed noon–11pm; Thurs–Fri noon–midnight; Sat 11:30am–midnight; Sun 11am–11pm. Subway: 1, 2, 3, 9 to 72nd St. Also at 565 Third Ave., at 37th St. (✆ 212/490-1558; subway: 6 to 33rd St.).

Pasha *Finds* TURKISH This sexy red-walled restaurant feels posh without being pricey—hence the reason so many Upper West Siders have pegged this as

Uptown Dining

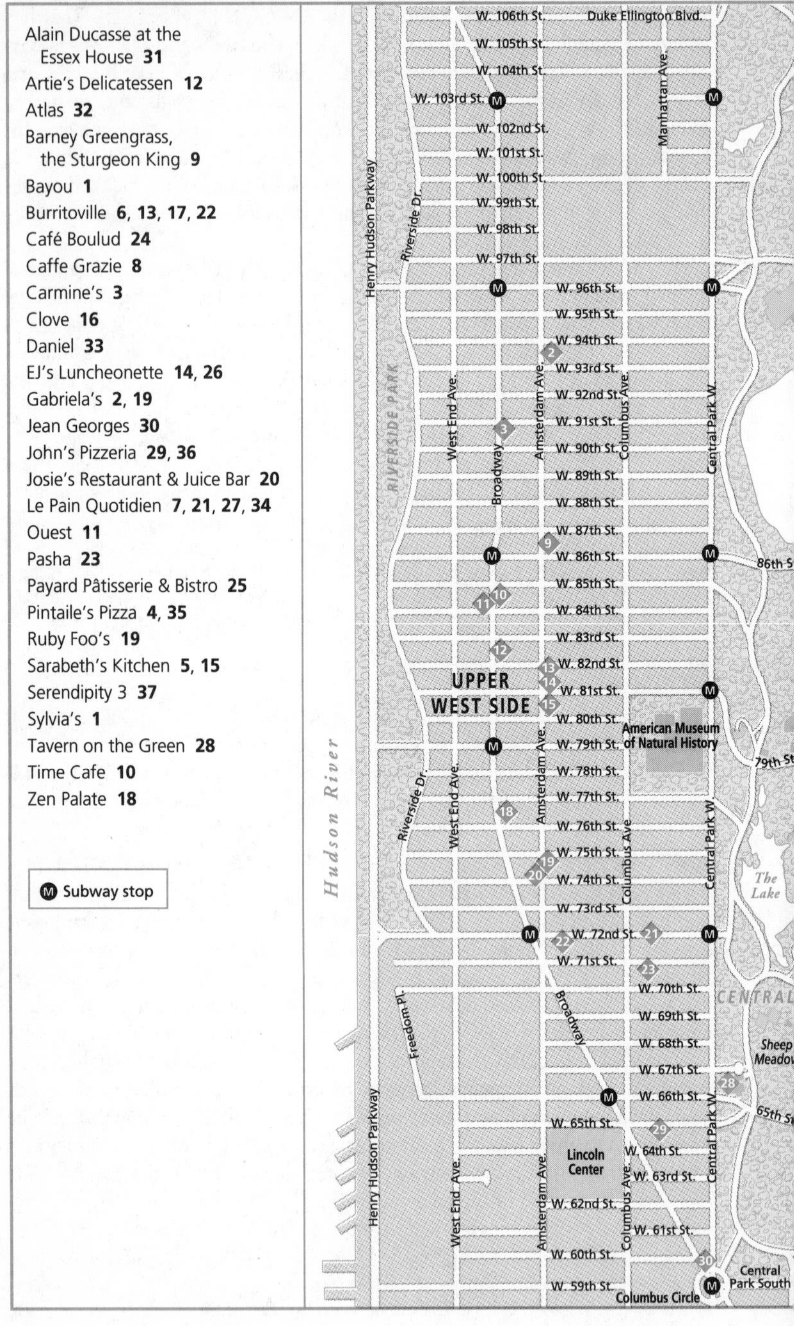

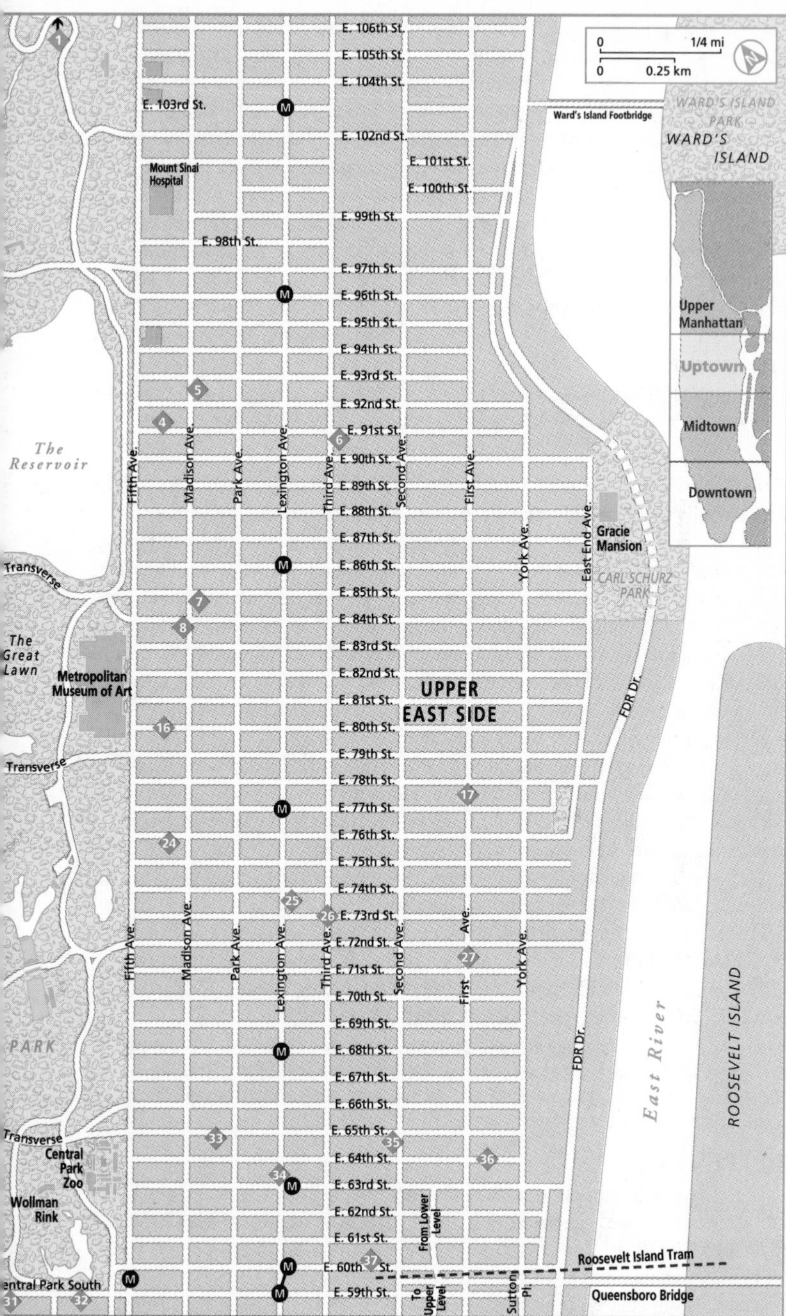
E. 106th St.
E. 105th St.
E. 104th St.
E. 103rd St.
E. 102nd St.
E. 101st St.
E. 100th St.
E. 99th St.
E. 98th St.
E. 97th St.
E. 96th St.
E. 95th St.
E. 94th St.
E. 93rd St.
E. 92nd St.
E. 91st St.
E. 90th St.
E. 89th St.
E. 88th St.
E. 87th St.
E. 86th St.
E. 85th St.
E. 84th St.
E. 83rd St.
E. 82nd St.
E. 81st St.
E. 80th St.
E. 79th St.
E. 78th St.
E. 77th St.
E. 76th St.
E. 75th St.
E. 74th St.
E. 73rd St.
E. 72nd St.
E. 71st St.
E. 70th St.
E. 69th St.
E. 68th St.
E. 67th St.
E. 66th St.
E. 65th St.
E. 64th St.
E. 63rd St.
E. 62nd St.
E. 61st St.
E. 60th St.
E. 59th St.
0 1/4 mi
0 0.25 km
Ward's Island Footbridge
WARD'S ISLAND PARK
WARD'S ISLAND
Mount Sinai Hospital
Upper Manhattan
Uptown
Midtown
Downtown
The Reservoir
Fifth Ave.
Madison Ave.
Park Ave.
Lexington Ave.
Third Ave.
Second Ave.
First Ave.
York Ave.
East End Ave.
Gracie Mansion
CARL SCHURZ PARK
Transverse
The Great Lawn
Metropolitan Museum of Art
UPPER EAST SIDE
FDR Dr.
East River
ROOSEVELT ISLAND
PARK
Central Park Zoo
Wollman Rink
Central Park South
From Lower Level
To Upper Level
Sutton Pl.
Roosevelt Island Tram
Queensboro Bridge
1
4
5
6
7
8
16
17
24
25
26
27
31
32
33
34
35
36
37
M

a favorite secret they'd rather not let out of the bag. (Sorry, guys.) The menu may seem exotic at first glance, but anyone familiar with Middle Eastern and Mediterranean fare will recognize the commonalities instantly: lots of lamb (minced, grilled, kebab), eggplant, marinated chicken, and stuffed grape leaves. The meats are excellent cuts, and everything is beautifully prepared. Consider starting with the *manti,* tender steamed dumplings stuffed with ground lamb and mint, and lightly drizzled with a piquant yogurt sauce; or the *patlican salatasi,* eggplant that has been charcoal-grilled and then mashed and tossed with garlic, lemon, and extra-virgin olive oil into a yummy purée. Most impressive among the main courses was the *kagit kabob,* cubed baby lamb delicately cooked in parchment with fresh veggies, potatoes, and herbs. The service is attentive, and the wine list affordable. I dare you to resist a second basket of the soft, grilled pitalike Turkish bread.

70 W. 71st St. (btwn Columbus Ave. and Central Park W.). © **212/579-8751.** Reservations recommended. Main courses $12–$19; Mon–Sat 5–7pm, fixed-price dinner $23. AE, MC, V. Mon–Thurs 5–11pm; Fri–Sat 5–11:30pm; Sun 5–10:30pm. Subway: B, C to 72nd St.

Sarabeth's Kitchen ★★ CONTEMPORARY AMERICAN Sarabeth's fresh-baked goods, award-winning preserves, and creative American cooking with a European touch keep a loyal following. This charming country restaurant with a distinct Hamptons feel is best known for its breakfast and weekend brunch, when the menu features such treats as porridge with wheat berries, fresh cream, butter, and brown sugar; pumpkin waffles topped with sour cream, raisins, pumpkin seeds, and honey (a sweet tooth's delight); and a whole host of farm-fresh omelettes. Expect a *long* wait for weekend brunch; weekday breakfast and lunch and dinner on any day are just as good, and a lot less crowded. Lunch might be a generous Caesar salad with aged Parmesan, brioche croutons, and a tangy anchovy dressing, accompanied by an amazingly good cream of tomato soup; a beautifully built country-style sandwich; or a good old-fashioned chicken pot pie. Dinner is more sophisticated, with such specialties as hazelnut-crusted halibut in an aromatic seven-vegetable broth and oven-roasted lamb crusted in black mushrooms, with grilled leeks and Vidalia onion rings on the side. Leave room for the scrumptious desserts.

There's another full-service location at 1295 Madison Ave., at 92nd Street (© **212/410-7335**); a cafe inside the Whitney Museum, 945 Madison Ave., at 75th Street (© **212/570-3670**); and a bakery at Chelsea Market, 75 Ninth Ave., between 15th and 16th streets (© **212/989-2424**).

423 Amsterdam Ave. (btwn 80th and 81st sts.). © **212/496-6280.** Reservations accepted for dinner only. Main courses $4.50–$13 at breakfast and brunch, $10.50–$17.50 at lunch, $10.50–$15.50 afternoon tea (Mon–Fri 3:30–5:30pm), $13–$26 at dinner. AE, DC, DISC, MC, V. Mon–Sat 8am–10:30pm; Sun 8am–9:30pm. Subway: 1, 9 to 79th St.

INEXPENSIVE

For breakfast or lunch, also consider **Barney Greengrass, the Sturgeon King,** 541 Amsterdam Ave., between 86th and 87th streets (© **212/724-4707**), one of the best Jewish delis in town; see "The New York Deli News" box on p. 210 for further details.

Near Lincoln Center, **John's Pizzeria,** 48 W. 65th St., between Broadway and Central Park West (© **212/721-7001**), serves up one of the city's best pies in a nice brick-walled dining room (p. 206). For good burgers and diner fare, visit **EJ's Luncheonette** (p. 186), 447 Amsterdam Ave., between 81st and 82nd streets (© **212/873-3444**).

For French baked goods, sandwiches, and salads of a divine order, also consider **Le Pain Quotidien** (p. 177), at 50 W. 72nd St., between Columbus Ave. and Central Park West (✆ **212/712-9700**).

And what would the Upper West Side be without its own **Burritoville** (p. 166)—or two? There's one at 166 W. 72nd St., near Broadway (✆ **212/580-7700**), and a second at 451 Amsterdam Ave., between 81st and 82nd streets (✆ **212/787-8181**).

Vegetarians and health-minded diners might also like to consider **Zen Palate** (p. 195), which has an outpost at 2170 Broadway, between 76th and 77th streets (✆ **212/501-7768**).

Artie's Delicatessen *Kids* JEWISH DELI Just opened in 1999, Artie's has the wonderful vibe of a well-established institution. What's more, it's as good as many of the best delis in Manhattan (I actually prefer it over tourist traps like the Carnegie and the Stage), and far more cheery (no grumpy old men expecting you to know the difference between nova and gravlax here). It's tourist-friendly, but in a good way; even New Yorkers like it here.

All of your Jewish deli favorites are here—from corned beef to chopped liver to tongue on rye—and arrive at your table in top form. The pastrami is everything it should be, and the chicken soup with kreplach is a sore throat's worst nightmare. Artie's chili dogs deserve special note, as they just may be the best in town. Burgers, omelets, and salads are also on hand for middle-market palettes. Nostalgia-inducing desserts include Jello, baked apple, genuine New York black-and-white cookies, very good homemade rugelach, and sliced birthday cake every day ("No birthday necessary—song not included").

2290 Broadway (btwn 82nd and 83rd sts.). ✆ **212/579-5959.** www.arties.com. Reservations not accepted. Main courses $6–$12 at breakfast, $6–$17 at lunch and dinner. AE, DISC, MC, V. Sun–Thurs 9am–11pm; Fri–Sat 9am–11:30pm. Subway: 1, 9 to 86th St.

Gabriela's ★★ *Value* MEXICAN If you love roast chicken, trust me: Gabriela's bird is the best. A blend of Yucatán spices and a slow-roasting rotisserie results in some of the tenderest, juiciest chicken in town—and at $7 for a half chicken with two sides (plenty for all but the biggest eaters) and $13 for a whole, it's one of the city's best bargains, too. All of the authentic Mexican specialties on the extensive menu are well prepared, generously portioned, and satisfying, from the monster tacos to the well-sauced enchiladas. The fresh, chunky, perfectly limed guacamole should please even Southwest natives. The dining room at both locations is large, bright, and pretty, with a pleasing south-of-the-border flair, and the service is quick and attentive. Try one of Gabriela's yummy fruit shakes (both mango and papaya are good bets) or tall *agua frescas* (fresh fruit drinks), which come in a variety of tropical flavors; beer, wine, and margaritas are served, too. A real winner!

315 Amsterdam Ave. (at 75th St.). ✆ **212/875-8532.** www.gabrielas.com. Reservations accepted for parties of 6 or more. Main courses $5–$9 at lunch, $7–$20 at brunch and dinner (most less than $15); early dinner specials $9.95, includes glass of wine or frozen margarita (Mon–Fri 4–7pm; Sat–Sun 3:30–6:30pm). AE, DC, MC, V. Mon–Thurs 11:30am–11pm; Fri–Sat 11:30am–midnight; Sun 11:30am–10pm. Subway: 1, 2, 3, 9 to 96th St. Also at 685 Amsterdam Ave., at 93rd St. (✆ 212/961-0574; subway: 1, 2, 3, 9 to 96th St.).

Time Cafe ★ CONTEMPORARY AMERICAN/HEALTH-CONSCIOUS This easygoing, attractive, and comfortable spot can provide a night's entertainment, the perfect brunch, or anything in between. The menu features a large selection of contemporary fare with a healthy bent, such as a very good arugula salad with red Bartlett pears, blue cheese, walnuts, and a tart raspberry vinaigrette; an appetizer menu that ranges from yummy homemade hummus to smoked Scottish salmon rolls; seared yellowfin tuna with wild mushrooms and barley risotto; herb-roasted free-range chicken with potato gratin and steamed veggies; a very good burger; and a host of creative thin-crust pizzas and entree-sized salads. The food is perfectly satisfying (I enjoyed a hearty mixed-green salad with a blue corn–crusted chicken breast and zesty buttermilk dressing on my last visit) and I like the health-minded preparations, the friendly service, and the casual, laid-back vibe. The lunch special, which includes a full-size bowl of soup (a yummy chicken noodle or the daily variety) and the day's special sandwich or entree-sized salad, is a steal at $10. The well-stacked magazine rack offers a good selection of diversions for solo diners. Both branches have a wonderful Moroccan lounge called Fez (see chapter 11), with the downtown location showcasing cutting-edge performances, too.

2330 Broadway (at 85th St.). ✆ **212/579-5100.** www.timecafenyc.com. Reservations recommended on weekends. Main courses $7–$16 at lunch (most less than $13), $9.50–$22 at dinner (most less than $16); 2-course lunch special (soup and main-course salad or sandwich) $10. AE, MC, V. Mon–Thurs 11:30am–midnight; Fri 11:30am–1am; Sat 10am–1am; Sun 10am–midnight. Subway: 1, 9 to 86th St. Also at 380 Lafayette St., at Great Jones St. (✆ 212/533-7000; subway: 6 to Bleecker St.; B, D, F, Q to Broadway/Lafayette St.).

14 The Upper East Side

To locate the restaurants in this section, map on p. 220.

VERY EXPENSIVE

Daniel ★★ FRENCH COUNTRY If Le Cirque 2000 sounds too over the top for your taste, and Jean Georges just too modern, Daniel Boulud's *New York Times* four-star winner is the place for you. Gorgeous neo-Renaissance features—rich mahogany doors, sensuous arches, elegant Corinthian columns, and soaring terra cotta–tiled ceilings—beautifully accented with a rich autumn color palette make an ideal setting for Boulud's faultless classic-goes-country French cooking.

The menu is heavy with game dishes in elegant but unfussy preparations, plus Daniel signatures like black sea bass in a crisp potato shell, with tender leeks and a light Barolo sauce. Excellent starters include a frisée salad with crisp braised sweetbreads, pistachios, and black truffle. Don't neglect the specials menu; I was the envy of the table with my warm rabbit confit salad with foie gras. Sublime entrees may include braised Chatham cod with cockles and caviar, or chestnut-crusted venison with sweet potato purée. But you can't really go wrong with anything—the kitchen doesn't take a false turn. The wine list is terrific and, divided between seasonal fruits and chocolates, the desserts are uniformly excellent. On the downside, the staff is more formal than I would like, and I've heard the same complaint from others; service at equally classic La Grenouille also stands on ceremony, but I've found it to be much warmer.

Dining in the pleasing lounge is a great way to sample the master's marvelous cuisine without laborious advance planning or succumbing to formality, since the jacket-and-tie dress code for men is not enforced.

60 E. 65th St. (btwn Madison and Park aves.). ✆ **212/288-0033.** www.danielnyc.com. Reservations required. Jacket and tie required for men in main dining room. 3-course fixed-price dinner $82; tasting menus $110–$145. Main courses $34–$38 in bar and lounge. AE, MC, V. Mon–Sat 5:45–11pm (lounge until 11:30pm). Subway: 6 to 68th St.

EXPENSIVE

Café Boulud ★ *Value* FRENCH Dying to try the stellar cuisine of Daniel Boulud, New York's best French chef, but can't get into Daniel? Or the prospect of the bill there makes your wallet tremble with trepidation? Or does it just sound too darn formal for you? Then head instead to Café Boulud, Boulud's more casual playground for new ideas and culinary cross-pollinations. "More casual" is a relative term, mind you—this space is still Upper East Side chic, and very popular with the society ladies who lunch. But Daniel's high style has been pleasingly laid back and toned down here. With the food, Boulud has gone eclectic, offering four menus: *La Tradition,* featuring Boulud's signature French-country classics; *Le Potager,* a vegetarian menu; *La Saison,* seasonal dishes; and *Le Voyage,* a monthly globe-hopping menu highlighting Tuscany, Thailand, or somewhere in between. The experimental nature of the wide-ranging menu makes choosing a thrill, and even the most inventive dishes tend to dazzle the palate. But in true Boulud tradition, *La Tradition* and *La Saison* are where the kitchen really excels. At $29, the two-course prix-fixe lunch is a true bargain; I was thrilled with both my gnocchi starter, delicately seasoned with pumpkin and sage, and the rich, uniquely flavorful braised veal cheeks on soft polenta that followed in perfect juxtaposition. All in all, a first-rate dining experience at more palatable prices than cuisine this memorable usually costs. Don't be in a rush, though, especially at lunch.

20 E. 76th St. (btwn Madison and Fifth aves.). ✆ **212/772-2600.** www.danielnyc.com. Reservations recommended. Main courses $26–$30 at lunch, $26–$37 at dinner; 2- or 3-course fixed-price lunch $29–$36. Sun–Mon 5:45–11pm; Tues–Sat noon–2:30pm and 5:45–11pm (no Sat lunch in July and Aug). Subway: 6 to 77th St.

MODERATE

If it's a well-prepared contemporary meal or a sweet treat you're after, also consider **Sarabeth's Kitchen** (p. 222), which has a pleasing full-service location at 1295 Madison Ave., at 92nd Street (✆ **212/410-7335**), plus a cafe inside the Whitney Museum, 945 Madison Ave., at 75th Street (✆ **212/606-0218**).

Caffe Grazie PAN-ITALIAN This cheery, unpretentious Italian cafe is most notable for its convenient location near the Metropolitan Museum of Art, a neighborhood short on moderately priced, recommendable eats. It's perfect for sipping espresso between museum hops or lingering over an elegant dinner. Appetizers like the bruschetta assortment served with a small salad and the warm white-bean salad over prosciutto are generous enough to be a light meal in themselves. The pasta selection mixes staples (satisfying penne pomodoro and linguine pesto) with standouts (lasagna layered with grilled chicken, fresh tomatoes, cheese, and pesto). The entrees, like veal stuffed with prosciutto and spinach and jumbo shrimp with lemon-caper sauce, are fresh and flavorful. All in all, a hidden treasure in a needy neighborhood.

If you're in the neighborhood but not in the mood for Italian, consider Grazie's new sister restaurant, **Clove,** 24 E. 80th St., between Fifth and Madison avenues (✆ **212/643-1222**), a warm and friendly neighborhood restaurant serving sophisticated takes on classic American comfort foods, including meatloaf and fried chicken (main courses $14–$32).

26 E. 84th St. (at Madison Ave.). ✆ **212/717-4407.** Reservations recommended. Main courses $10.50–$22.50 at lunch (most under $17), $15.50–$26.50 at dinner (most under $23). AE, DC, MC, V. Mon–Fri 11am–11pm; Sat 10:30am–11pm; Sun 10:30am–10pm. Subway: 4, 5, 6 to 86th St.

Payard Pâtisserie & Bistro FRENCH BISTRO/DESSERTS/AFTERNOON TEA Sure, the bistro fare at this grand turn-of-the-century, Parisian-style cafe is good. But the decadent desserts—New York's best—are the reason

Pizza! Pizza!

Beyond classically old-world, brick-oven **John's Pizzeria** (p. 206), which has a branch at 408 E. 64th St., between First and York avenues (✆ **212/935-2895**), the chichi Upper East Side tends to specialize in designer pizza. **Pintaile's Pizza,** at 26 E. 91st St., between Fifth and Madison avenues (✆ **212/722-1967;** www.pintailespizza.com; open daily 11am–9:30pm), dresses their daintily crisp organic crusts with layers of plum tomatoes, extra-virgin olive oil, and other fabulously fresh ingredients. Pintaile's is also at 1237 Second Ave., between 64th and 65th streets (✆ **212/752-6222;** open daily 11am–10:30pm).

to come. There's no need to indulge in a full meal to enjoy Payard; feel free to come for afternoon tea or just dessert (my preference, which is why I've classified Payard as moderately priced rather than expensive).

The biggest problem? Choosing among the fabulous, beautifully presented sweet treats. Displayed like the jewels they are, elegant cakes, tempting pastries, and handmade chocolates fill the gleaming glass cases up front. Everything is house-made, from the signature cakes, breads, and pastries to the delicate candies. Whether you go with the classic crème brûlée or something more decadent (anything chocolate is to die for), you're sure to be wowed. Afternoon tea is a real treat—especially after a day spent on Museum Mile—with petite sandwiches, madeleines, and scones with Chantilly cream and Payard's own jam, and a tasting plate of mini pastries (a great way to avoid choosing just one!).

Served in the back dining salon, the predessert menu is unabashedly classic, with thick slabs of foie gras terrine, crispy pig's feet, a classic pepper steak frites, and a fragrant bouillabaisse. The pre-theater meal is a good value for early diners.

1032 Lexington Ave. (btwn 73rd and 74th sts.). ✆ **212/717-5252.** www.payard.com. Reservations recommended. Main courses $12–$25 at lunch, $24–$33 at dinner; afternoon tea $19–$24; 3-course pre-theater dinner $34 (5:45–6pm seating); desserts $7–$9. AE, DC, MC, V. Mon–Thurs noon–3pm, 3:30–5pm, and 5:45–10:30pm; Fri noon–3pm, 3:30–5pm, and 5:45–11pm; Sat noon–3pm, 3:30–4:30pm, and 5:45–11pm. Subway: 6 to 77th St.

INEXPENSIVE

There's also a branch of **EJ's Luncheonette** (p. 186), the retro all-American diner, at 1271 Third Ave., at 73rd Street (✆ **212/472-0600**). **Burritoville** (p. 166) is at 1489 First Ave., between 77th and 78th streets (✆ **212/472-8800**), and 1606 Third Ave., between 90th and 91st streets (✆ **212/410-2255**).

For divine baked goods and gourmet sandwiches and salads, also consider Franco-Brussels import **Le Pain Quotidien** (p. 177), which has three Upper East Side locations: 833 Lexington Ave., between 63rd and 64th streets (✆ **212/755-5810**); 1336 First Ave., between 71st and 72nd streets (✆ **212/717-4800**); an easy walk from Museum Mile at 1131 Madison Ave., between 84th and 85th streets (✆ **212/327-4900**).

Serendipity 3 *Kids* AMERICAN You'd never guess that this whimsical place was once a top stop on Andy Warhol's agenda. Wonders never cease—and neither does the confection at this delightful restaurant and sweet shop. Tucked into a cozy brownstone a few steps from Bloomingdale's, Serendipity's small front-room curiosity shop overflows with odd objects, from jigsaw puzzles to silly jewelry. But the real action is behind the shop, where the quintessential American soda fountain still reigns supreme. Remember Farrell's? This is the better version (complete with candy to tempt the kids on the way out), and it's still going strong. Happy people gather at marble-topped ice-cream parlor tables for burgers and foot-long hot dogs, country meat loaf with mashed potatoes and gravy, and salads and sandwiches with cute names like "The Catcher in the Rye" (their own twist on the BLT, with chicken and Russian dressing—on rye, of course). The food isn't great, but the main courses aren't the point—they're just an excuse to get to the desserts. The restaurant's signature is Frozen Hot Chocolate, a slushie version of everybody's cold-weather favorite, but other crowd pleasers include dark double devil mousse, celestial carrot cake, lemon icebox pie, and anything with hot fudge. So cast that willpower aside and come on in—Serendipity is an irony-free charmer to be appreciated by adults and kids alike.

225 E. 60th St. (btwn Second and Third aves.). ✆ **212/838-3531.** www.serendipity3.com. Reservations accepted for lunch and dinner (not just dessert). Main courses $7–$18; sweets and sundaes $5–$17 (most under $10). AE, DC, DISC, MC, V. Sun–Thurs 11:30am–midnight; Fri 11:30am–1am; Sat 11:30am–2am. Subway: N, R to Lexington Ave.; 4, 5, 6 to 59th St.

15 Harlem

To locate these two restaurants, see map on p. 220.

MODERATE

Bayou ★ CREOLE This intimate, casually sophisticated Creole restaurant is a prime symbol of Harlem's renaissance. The room is stylish in a trend-defying way, with burnished yellow walls, big oak tables, a long mahogany bar, and dim lighting. The well-prepared food is pure New Orleans: shrimp and okra gumbo, cornmeal-fried oysters, sautéed chicken livers, and shrimp rémoulade with deviled eggs. Shrimp Creole or crawfish etouffeé are both served in their own piquant sauces over rice. Farm-raised catfish is marinated and sliced thin, then deep-fried in cornmeal until the outside is perfectly crisp, while the inside stays moist and flaky. Salads are crisp and bounteous. The only disappointments are the shiitake-and-collard green enchiladas, a half-hearted attempt at a vegetarian option. Service is extremely attentive and professional. An affordable wine list and well-priced desserts and starters make Bayou a good value, to boot. The fine glass of Pinot Noir I had would've been $8 anywhere below 96th Street; here, it was just $6. Desserts, are divine; don't pass up the bread pudding, made with fresh peaches and a scrumptious bourbon sauce.

308 Lenox Ave. (btwn 125th and 126th sts.). ✆ **212/426-3800.** Reservations recommended for dinner. Main courses $7–$13 at lunch, $13–$22 at dinner (most less than $18); Sun brunch $14–$21 (includes starter and Mimosa or Bloody Mary). AE, MC, V. Mon–Thurs 11:30am–4pm and 6–10pm; Fri 11:30am–4pm and 6–11pm; Sat 6–11pm; Sun noon–8pm. Subway: 2, 3 to 125th St.

INEXPENSIVE

Sylvia's SOUL FOOD South Carolina–born Sylvia Woods is the last word in New York soul food. Despite the utter lack of decor, this bustling place is so popular with both locals and visitors alike that the dining room has spilled into the building next door. Don't be surprised if you have a wait for a table, especially on weekend nights, but the reward is worth it. Since 1962, this Harlem institution has dished up authentic, finger-lickin' southern-fried goods: turkey with down-home stuffing; smothered chicken and pork chops; fried chicken and baked ham; collard greens and candied yams; and cavity-inducing sweet tea. And then, of course there's "Sylvia's World Famous, Talked About, Bar-B-Que Ribs Special"—the sauce is sweet, with a potent afterburn. This Harlem landmark is still presided over by 74-year-old Sylvia, who's likely to greet you at the door herself. Chowing down here is still a one-of-a-kind New York experience. Sunday gospel brunch is a joyous time to go.

328 Lenox Ave. (btwn 126th and 127th sts.). ✆ **212/996-0660.** www.sylviassoulfood.com. Reservations only accepted for parties of 10 or more. Main courses $2.50–$8.25 at breakfast, $8–$19 at lunch and dinner; lunch special Mon–Fri 11am–3pm $3.75–$9.25; Sun gospel brunch $17 (includes a cocktail). AE, DISC, MC, V. Mon–Thurs 8am–10:30pm; Fri–Sat 7:30am–10:30pm; Sun 11am–8pm. Subway: 2, 3 to 125th St.

16 Brooklyn

EXPENSIVE

Peter Luger Steakhouse ★ STEAKS If you love steak, then book a table here and hop a cab to Williamsburg. Expect loads of attitude and nothing in the way of decor or atmosphere (beer hall is the theme)—but this century-old institution is porterhouse heaven. The first-rate cuts—the only ones this 113-year-old institution serves—are dry-aged on the premises and come off the grill dripping with fat and butter, crusty on the outside and tender pink within. It's the best steak in the five boroughs, bar none. Nonbelievers can order sole or lamb chops, but don't bother if you're not coming for the cow. As sides go, the German fried potatoes are crisp and delicious, and the creamed spinach is everything it should be. Bring wads of cash because this place is expensive, but doesn't take credit cards (other than their own house account).

178 Broadway (at Driggs Ave.), Williamsburg, Brooklyn. ✆ **718/387-7400.** www.peterluger.com. Reservations essential; call a month in advance for weekend bookings. Main courses $5–$20 at lunch, $20–$32 at dinner. No credit cards (Peter Luger accounts only). Mon–Thurs 11:45am–9:45pm; Fri–Sat 11:45am–10:45pm; Sun 12:45–9:45pm. Subway: J, M, Z to Marcy Ave. (Or take a cab.)

INEXPENSIVE

Grimaldi's Pizzeria ★ PIZZA Here's New York's best pizza; only Lombardi's (p. 228) can claim to be Grimaldi's rival in taste and quality. You don't have to take it from me—just check Zagat's, which gives this Brooklyn classic a whopping 26 (out of 30) for food, a rating usually reserved for the likes of Le Cirque. Thin coal-oven crust, crisp and smoky, is topped with perfectly seasoned red sauce, leafy basil, and only the freshest, whitest mozzarella. Crown this perfect pie with your choice of traditional toppings, including meaty pepperoni and house-roasted red peppers. And you don't have to suffer a greasy pizza joint to enjoy this sublime pizza: Grimaldi's is a surprisingly pleasant place, with red-checked tablecloths, photos of Sinatra covering the walls, and the Chairman of the Board himself crooning from the jukebox. Patsy Grimaldi is likely to greet you himself, warmly, with stogie in hand (despite the no-smoking signs). Otherwise, the service can be gruff, but that's how you'll know you've arrived—in Brooklyn, that is. The best time to come is in summer, when sidewalk tables offer the kind of spectacular views of the Brooklyn Bridge and twinkling lower Manhattan that usually only big money buys.

19 Old Fulton St. (btwn Front and Water sts.), Brooklyn Heights. ✆ **718/858-4300.** Reservations not accepted. Pies $14 and up, depending on toppings. No credit cards. Sun–Thurs 11:30am–11pm; Fri–Sat 11:30am–midnight. Subway: A, C to High St.; 2, 3 to Clark St. (use Henry St. exit). Walk downslope, toward the water; it will be on your right in the last block, across from the Eagle Warehouse.

8

Exploring New York City

If this is your first trip to New York, face the facts: It will be impossible to take in the entire city. Because New York is almost unfathomably big and constantly changing, you could live your whole life here and still make fascinating daily discoveries—we New Yorkers do. This chapter is designed to give you an overview of what's available in this multifaceted place so you can narrow your choices to an itinerary that's digestible for the amount of time you'll be here—be it a day, a week, or something in between.

So don't try to tame New York—you can't. Decide on a few must-see attractions, and then let the city take you on its own ride. Inevitably, as you make your way around the city, you'll be blown off course by unplanned diversions that are just as much fun as what you meant to see. After all, the true New York is in the details. As you dash from sight to sight, take time to admire a lovely cornice on a prewar building, linger over a cup of coffee at a sidewalk cafe, or just idle away a few minutes on a bench watching New Yorkers parade through their daily lives.

1 Sights & Attractions by Neighborhood

MANHATTAN

CHELSEA

Chelsea Piers Sports & Entertainment Complex (p. 290)
Dia Center for the Arts (p. 260)
Spirit Cruises (p. 292)

EAST VILLAGE & NOHO

Merchant's House Museum (p. 277)

THE FLATIRON DISTRICT/UNION SQUARE

Center for Jewish History (p. 258)
Flatiron Building (p. 276)
Theodore Roosevelt Birthplace (p. 273)
Union Square Park (p. 288)

GREENWICH VILLAGE

Forbes Magazine Galleries (p. 261)
Washington Square Park (p. 289)

HARLEM

Abyssinian Baptist Church (p. 278)
Astor Row Houses (p. 275)
Jumel Terrace Historic District (p. 275)
Morris-Jumel Mansion (p. 275)
Mother A.M.E. Zion Church (p. 279)
Schomburg Center for Research in Black Culture (p. 272)
Strivers' Row (p. 275)
Studio Museum in Harlem (p. 273)
Sylvan Terrace (p. 275)
Sugar Hill (p. 275)

LOWER EAST SIDE

Lower East Side Tenement Museum (p. 263)

LOWER MANHATTAN/ THE FINANCIAL DISTRICT/ NEW YORK HARBOR

Battery Park (p. 287)
Bowling Green Park (p. 288)
Brooklyn Bridge (p. 243)

Downtown Attractions

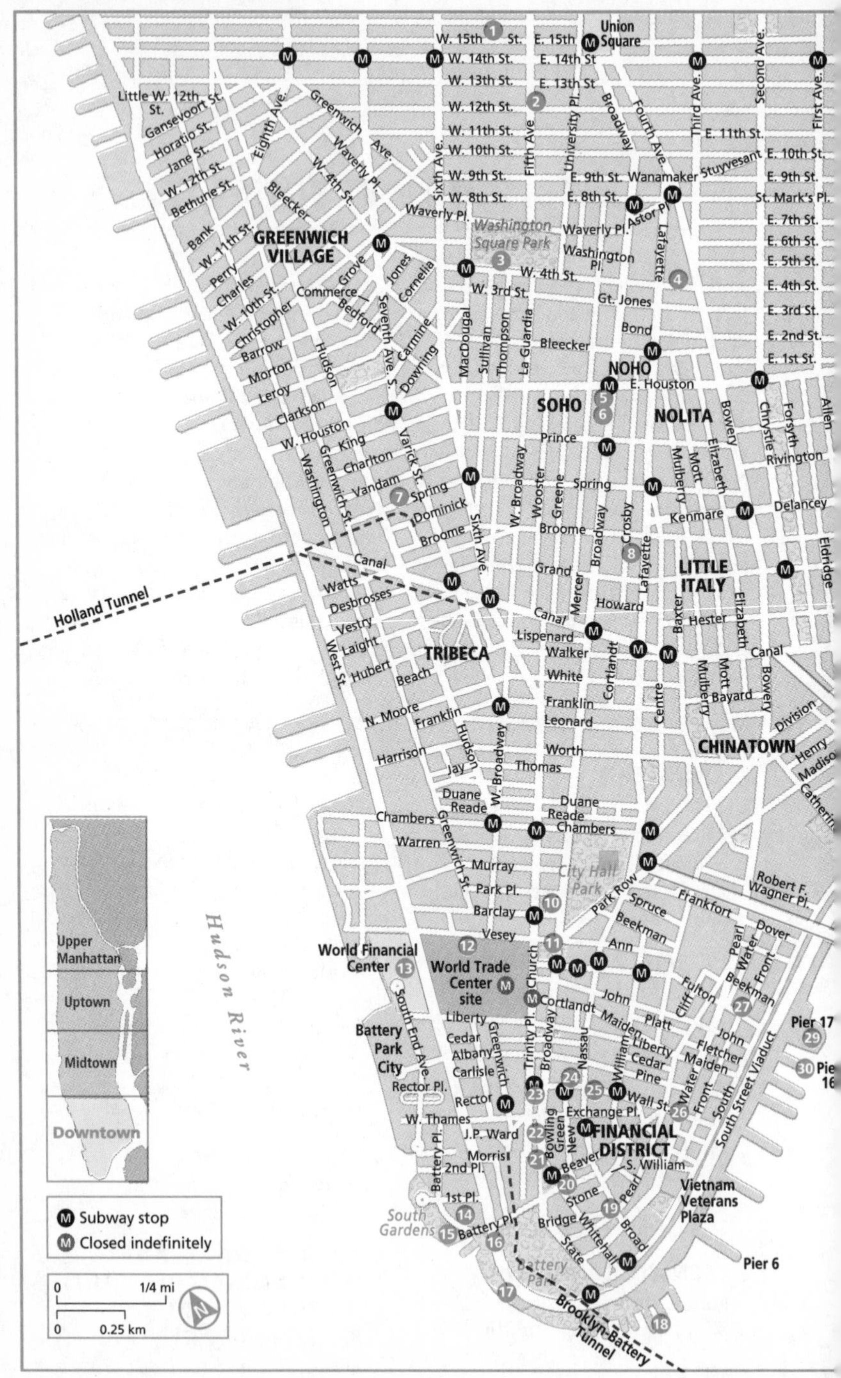

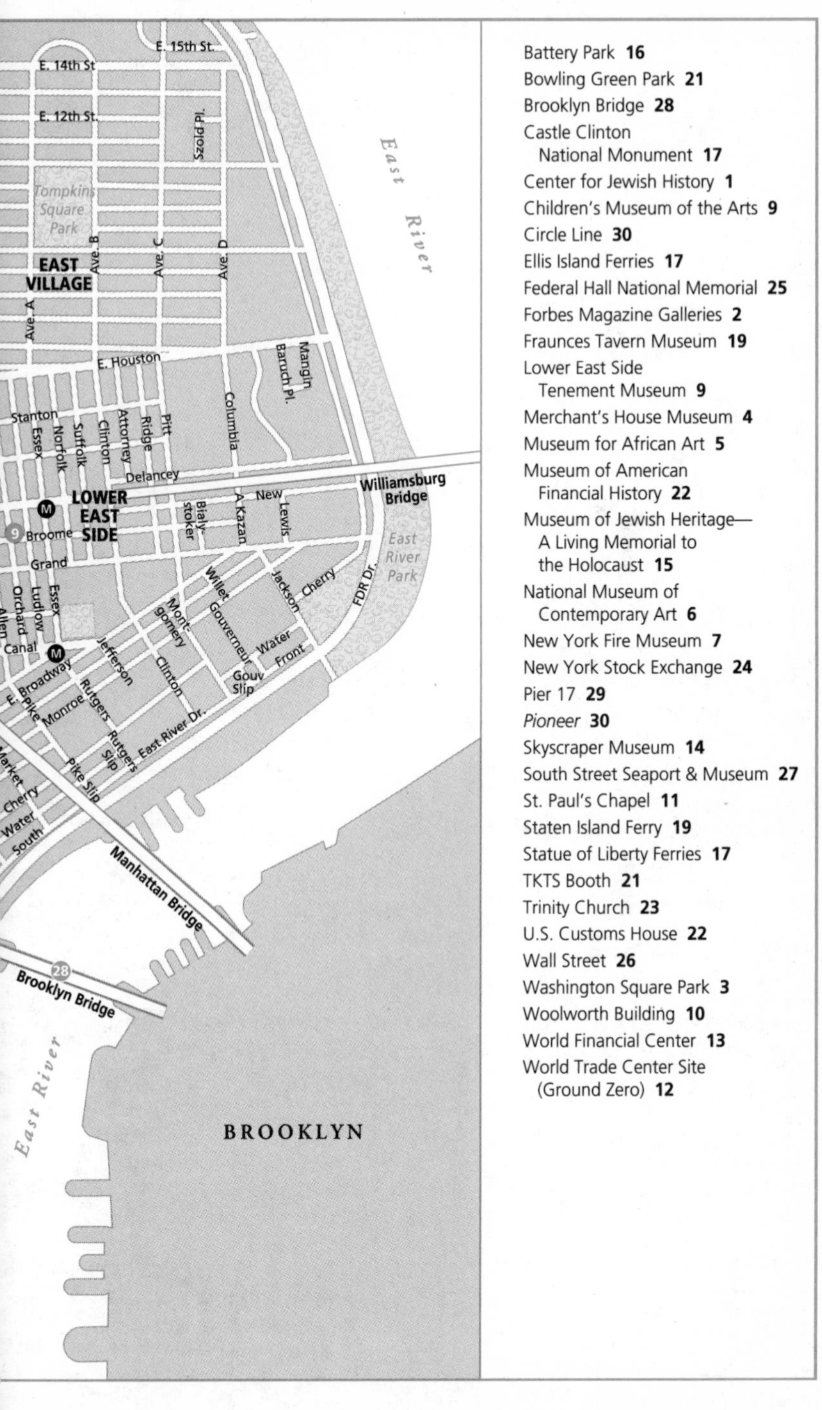

Battery Park **16**
Bowling Green Park **21**
Brooklyn Bridge **28**
Castle Clinton National Monument **17**
Center for Jewish History **1**
Children's Museum of the Arts **9**
Circle Line **30**
Ellis Island Ferries **17**
Federal Hall National Memorial **25**
Forbes Magazine Galleries **2**
Fraunces Tavern Museum **19**
Lower East Side Tenement Museum **9**
Merchant's House Museum **4**
Museum for African Art **5**
Museum of American Financial History **22**
Museum of Jewish Heritage—A Living Memorial to the Holocaust **15**
National Museum of Contemporary Art **6**
New York Fire Museum **7**
New York Stock Exchange **24**
Pier 17 **29**
Pioneer **30**
Skyscraper Museum **14**
South Street Seaport & Museum **27**
St. Paul's Chapel **11**
Staten Island Ferry **19**
Statue of Liberty Ferries **17**
TKTS Booth **21**
Trinity Church **23**
U.S. Customs House **22**
Wall Street **26**
Washington Square Park **3**
Woolworth Building **10**
World Financial Center **13**
World Trade Center Site (Ground Zero) **12**

Midtown Attractions

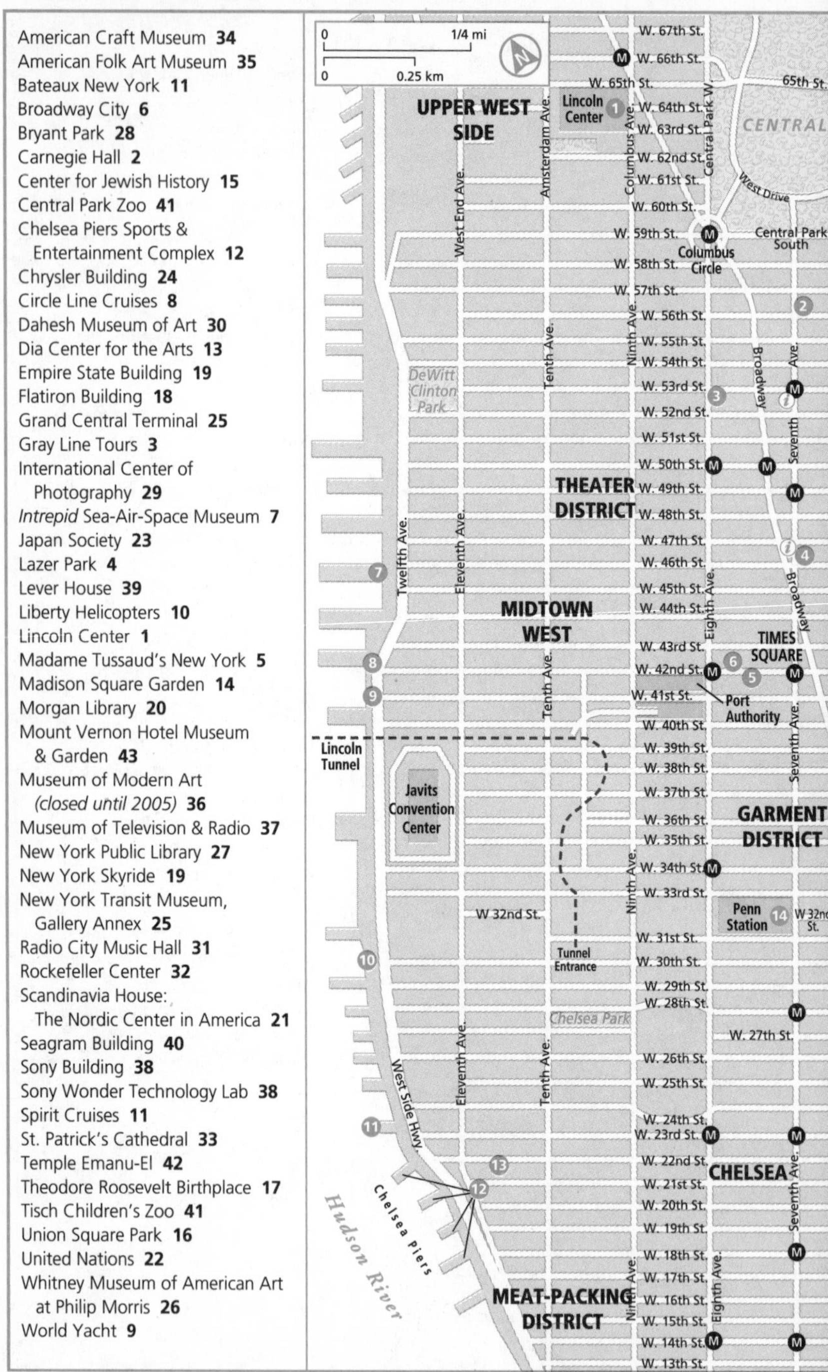

UPPER EAST SIDE
MIDTOWN EAST
MURRAY HILL
FLATIRON DISTRICT
GRAMERCY PARK
Rockefeller Center
Grand Central Terminal
New York Public Library
United Nations
Queensboro Bridge
Roosevelt Island Tram
Queens–Midtown Tunnel
East River
ROOSEVELT ISLAND
QUEENS
Peter Cooper Village
Stuyvesant Town
Union Square
Bryant Park
Madison Square Park
Gramercy Park
Information
Subway stop
Upper Manhattan
Uptown
Midtown
Downtown

Uptown Attractions

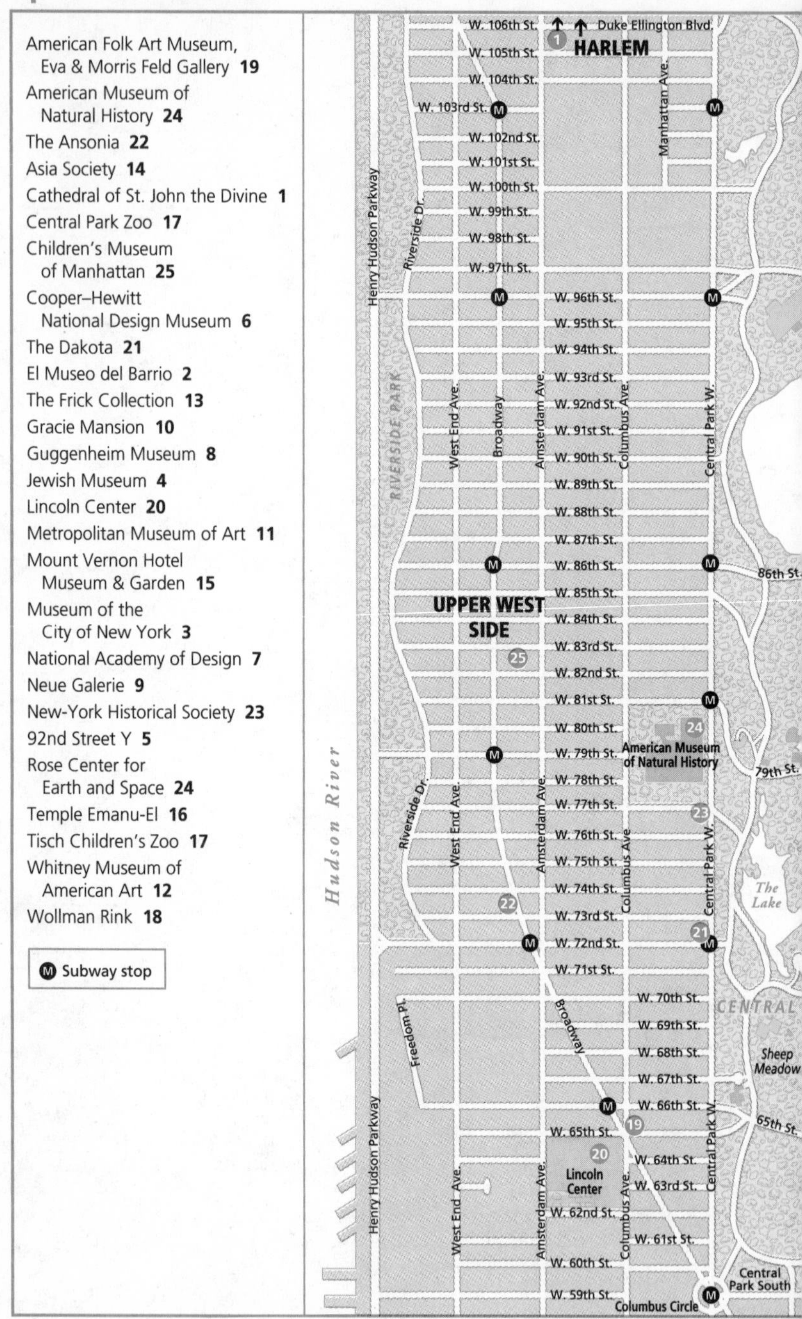

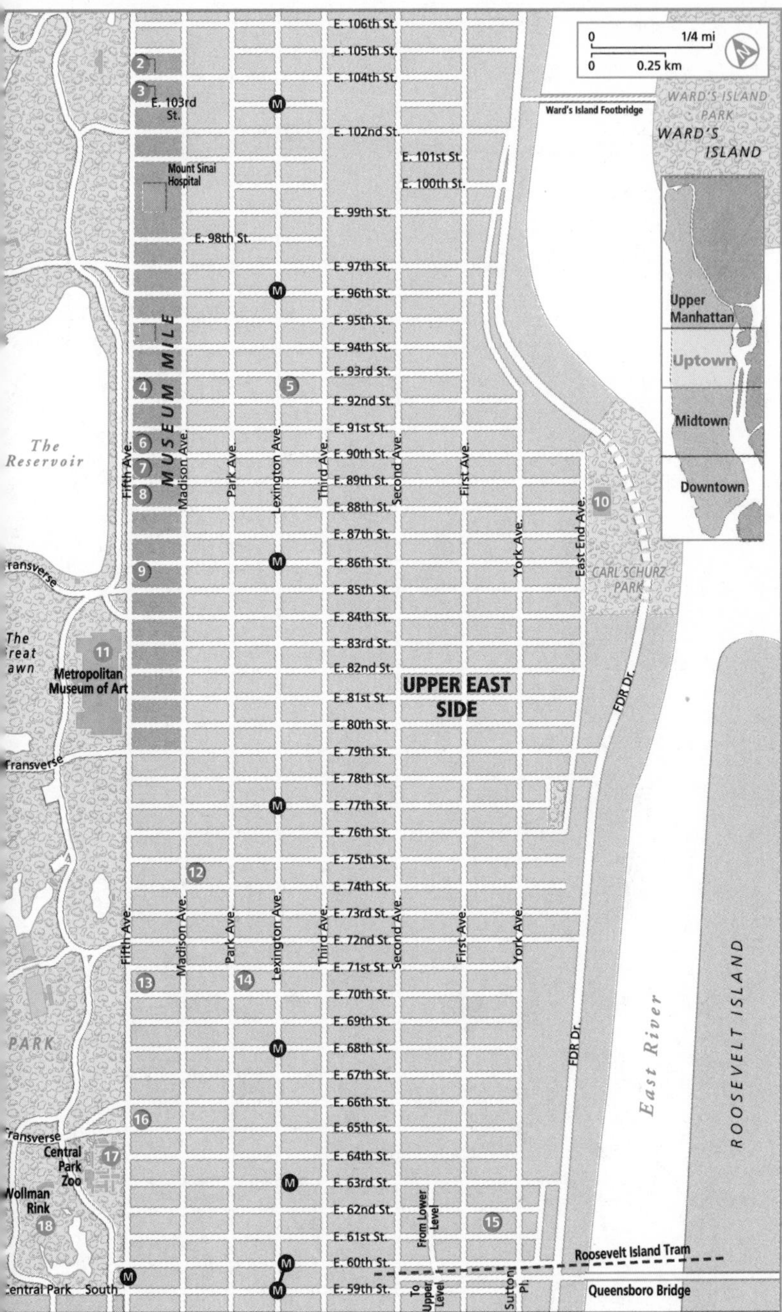

UPPER EAST SIDE
MUSEUM MILE
Mount Sinai Hospital
Metropolitan Museum of Art
Central Park Zoo
Wollman Rink
The Reservoir
The Great Lawn
PARK
Transverse
Central Park South
Fifth Ave.
Madison Ave.
Park Ave.
Lexington Ave.
Third Ave.
Second Ave.
First Ave.
York Ave.
East End Ave.
FDR Dr.
Sutton Pl.
From Lower Level
To Upper Level
E. 106th St.
E. 105th St.
E. 104th St.
E. 103rd St.
E. 102nd St.
E. 101st St.
E. 100th St.
E. 99th St.
E. 98th St.
E. 97th St.
E. 96th St.
E. 95th St.
E. 94th St.
E. 93rd St.
E. 92nd St.
E. 91st St.
E. 90th St.
E. 89th St.
E. 88th St.
E. 87th St.
E. 86th St.
E. 85th St.
E. 84th St.
E. 83rd St.
E. 82nd St.
E. 81st St.
E. 80th St.
E. 79th St.
E. 78th St.
E. 77th St.
E. 76th St.
E. 75th St.
E. 74th St.
E. 73rd St.
E. 72nd St.
E. 71st St.
E. 70th St.
E. 69th St.
E. 68th St.
E. 67th St.
E. 66th St.
E. 65th St.
E. 64th St.
E. 63rd St.
E. 62nd St.
E. 61st St.
E. 60th St.
E. 59th St.
Ward's Island Footbridge
WARD'S ISLAND PARK
WARD'S ISLAND
CARL SCHURZ PARK
East River
ROOSEVELT ISLAND
Roosevelt Island Tram
Queensboro Bridge
0 1/4 mi
0 0.25 km
Upper Manhattan
Uptown
Midtown
Downtown

Harlem & Upper Manhattan

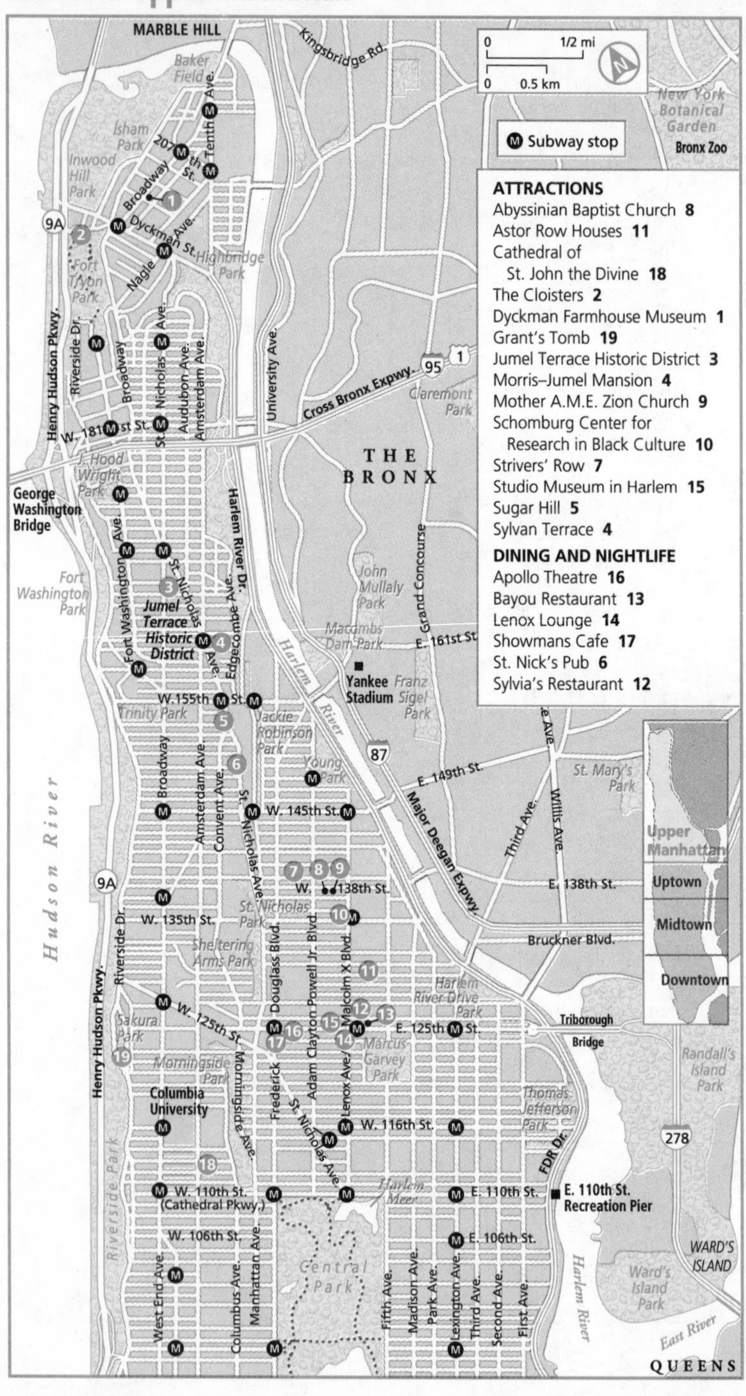

Alert: Lower Manhattan Subway Access Update

At this writing, Lower Manhattan subway access had largely been restored, with local service on the **1/9 line** south of Chambers Street to South Ferry being the chief exception. (At press time, 1 trains were following the 2/3 express line to Brooklyn south of Chambers St., and 9 service was suspended.)

We have maintained all traditional references to 1/9 local service to South Ferry throughout this chapter, however, since 1/9 service is scheduled to be fully restored (with the exception of the Cortlandt St. station) at the same time this edition hits bookshelves, in autumn 2002. But anything can happen in the interim, so I strongly recommend you check with the **Metropolitan Transit Authority** at ✆ **718/330-1234** or **www.mta.nyc.ny.us** before you plan your travel routes; your hotel concierge or any token booth clerk should also be able to assist you.

MIDTOWN EAST

SOHO

TIMES SQUARE & MIDTOWN WEST

UPPER EAST SIDE

UPPER WEST SIDE

UPPER MANHATTAN

OUTER BOROUGHS

THE BRONX

BROOKLYN

QUEENS

SUGGESTED ITINERARIES

If you're a first-time visitor and you'd like a blueprint with which to begin planning your time, consider the following game plan.

Day 1 Start your day off just like the city itself did: At Manhattan's southern tip, New York's oldest and most historic precincts. Leave early to catch the morning's first ferry to the **Statue of Liberty** and **Ellis Island.** This will occupy your morning.

Once you're back on the mainland, if you didn't arrange for tickets before you left home, pop over to the new downtown **TKTS booth** at Bowling Green Park (the line is usually shorter here than it is at the Times Sq. location) to pick up some discounted tickets for a **Broadway** or **Off-Broadway show** (something's always available for the evening or for tomorrow afternoon if you prefer a matinee; see chapter 11).

By then, you're sure to need lunch, if you haven't succumbed to your hunger already. If you're in the mood for a leisurely meal, consider dining at the **Fraunces Tavern Museum,** just like George Washington did way back in 1783 (p. 261). (If a sit-down lunch is a more involved endeavor than you'd like, the gourmet cafeteria **Mangia** is a great place to rub elbows with Wall Street bulls and bears; see chapter 7.)

Afterwards, you might want to see what you can of **Ground Zero.** (Whether or not the temporary viewing platform at Broadway at Fulton St. will still be up while you're in town was up in the air at press time; call the NYCVB at ✆ 212/484-1222 or visit www.nycvisit.com for the latest). You can also pay your respects to the victims of the World Trade Center attack in beautiful waterfront **Battery Park,** where the bronze sphere that once stood on the World Trade Center plaza between the Twin Towers now stands, bearing its war wounds, as a temporary memorial to the victims of 9/11 until a permanent one can be erected.

Or hop the subway over to Brooklyn (the A/C line will whisk you from Lower Manhattan over to the High St. stop in minutes) and stroll back to the 212 area code over the gloriously Gothic **Brooklyn Bridge,** which offers my favorite view of the Manhattan skyline.

Or, if you prefer, use the time to enjoy one of Lower Manhattan's many historic or cultural attractions, such as the insightful and moving **Museum of Jewish Heritage—a Living Memorial to the Holocaust;** surprisingly diminutive **Wall Street;** or the **National Museum of the American Indian,** housed in the stunning, Cass Gilbert–designed 1907 beaux arts **U.S. Customs House,** which is worth a visit for the architecture alone.

Head back to your hotel to freshen up so you can enjoy a leisurely pretheater dinner. If you've chosen a Broadway show, make time before or afterwards to feel the pulse of nighttime in **Times Square.**

Day 2 Spend the bulk of your day at one of the big museums: Either the **Metropolitan Museum of Art** or the **American Museum of Natural History.** Both of these museums can easily fill a week of browsing, so you might want to begin with a Highlights Tour. Don't miss the terrific, new-in-2002 Harrison Ford–narrated Space Show at the Natural History Museum's **Rose Center for Earth and Space.**

After you've had enough of the museum (you'll give out before you e collections), head into tral Park to see some of ghlights; both museums its fringe. If you still have energy left, you might stroll out of the south end of the park to do a bit of shopping along famous **Fifth Avenue.**

Since you've spent lots of time on your feet over the last two days, plan on a leisurely dinner at one of the city's fabulous restaurants (see chapter 7 for recommendations, and be sure to book ahead).

Day 3 Start your morning with the 3-hour **Circle Line Sightseeing Cruise,** which circumnavigates Manhattan and offers a fascinating perspective on the island. Spend the afternoon exploring one or two of the city's downtown neighborhoods—perhaps the cast-iron canyons of **SoHo** (bring your credit card, shoppers!), the winding 19th-century streets of **Greenwich Village,** or exotic **Chinatown.** Walk the prime thoroughfares, poke your head into shops, or park yourself at a street-side cafe and just watch the world go by. If you prefer to have a knowledgeable guide as you explore, schedule a **guided walking tour** (see "Organized Sightseeing Tours," on p. 291).

Stay downtown for the evening, catching dinner in a stylish (or authentically old-world) restaurant and following up with some out-on-the-town time, perhaps in a live music or comedy venue, a cutting-edge dance club, or a hipper-than-thou cocktail lounge (see chapter 11 for recommendations). Or, if you've had enough of downtown, head back to your hotel and freshen up, then head up to Harlem to catch a soul-food dinner and some smooth jazz at the **Lenox Lounge.**

Day 4 Head to **Rockefeller Center** early to start your day with Matt and Katie outside the *Today* studio or to score standby tickets for Conan O'Brien's late-night talkfest. Then make your way to the **Empire State Building** to see the view from the 86th-floor observation deck of New York's tallest building and ultimate landmark skyscraper.

Once you're done, head to **Grand Central Terminal** (the walk is a pleasant one on a nice day) to admire that marvelous beaux arts monument to modern transportation and have lunch. You can cut into a prime cut of beef at **Michael Jordan's–The Steak House;** enjoy first-rate seafood at the legendary, old-world **Oyster Bar & Restaurant;** or plunder the terrific subterranean **food concourse,** with both sit-down and casual, find-a-table options (see chapter 7).

Spend the afternoon browsing one or two of the Big Apple's brilliant smaller museums—maybe the **Morgan Library,** the ***Intrepid*** **Sea-Air-Space Museum,** the **Frick Collection,** or the **Whitney.** Or, if you prefer, use the afternoon to exercise your credit line and shop!

Enjoy another evening at the theater, or catch a performance at **Lincoln Center** or one of the city's other terrific performing-arts institutions; the **Brooklyn Academy of Music** makes an excellent choice for those looking for a left-of-center cultural experience. Or, if it's a lovely summer evening, consider catching a **baseball game;** either the Yankees

---

Impressions

If you're bored in New York, it's your own fault.

—Myrna Loy

---

or the Mets are likely to be in residence (sometimes both), and cheap seats aren't usually hard to score.

Day 5 Use the morning to explore one of the major attractions you've missed thus far. If you spent day 2 at the Met, spend today at the **American Museum of Natural History.** Or go see Frank Lloyd Wright's iconic **Guggenheim Museum.** Tour that nerve center of international relations, the **United Nations.** Or, if you haven't seen **Central Park** yet, go now.

After lunch, take stock: What haven't you done yet that you don't want to miss? What did you do that you want to do more of? Perhaps a bit more shopping, or a visit to a museum that focuses on your interests, such as the **International Center of Photography,** the **American Craft Museum,** or the **Museum of Television & Radio.** You're becoming a pro at exploring the city by now, so take the bull by the horns and make the most of your afternoon.

In the evening, celebrate the end of a great vacation with some live music. A night of jazz at one of the Big Apple's legendary clubs, like the **Village Vanguard** or the **Blue Note,** makes a very festive close, as does a night of laughs at one of the city's legendary comedy clubs, such as **Carolines** or the **Comedy Cellar.** Or, for the ultimate in New York elegance, dress to the nines and opt for a night of champagne and cabaret at the venerable **Cafe Carlyle** or **Oak Room,** or a newer landmark-in-the-making, **Feinstein's at the Regency.**

If you're the party type instead, don your glad rags and dance the night away at one of the city's outrageous club scenes: **Centro-Fly** is techno-chic; **Vinyl** is a pretension-free zone; Latin lovers can kick up their heels at zesty **SOB's;** while baby boomers might shake their groove thangs at **Decade.** No matter what you choose, make it a New York night to remember!

2 The Top Attractions

In addition to the choices below, don't forget about **Central Park** ★★★, the great green swath that is, just by virtue of its existence, New York City's greatest marvel. Central Park is so big and multifaceted that it earns its own dedicated section, starting on p. 281.

American Museum of Natural History ★★★ This is one of the hottest museum tickets in town, thanks to the $210 million **Rose Center for Earth and Space** ★, whose four-story-tall planetarium sphere hosts the new Harrison Ford–narrated Space Show, "Are We Alone?", the most technologically advanced sky show on the planet. Prepare to be blown away. The show is short—less than a half hour from start to finish—but phenomenal. (*New York* magazine has called it "the world's largest, most powerful virtual-reality simulator.")

Buy your tickets in advance for the Space Show in order to guarantee admission (they're available online); you can also buy tickets in advance for a specific IMAX film or special exhibition, such as the Butterfly Conservatory (see below), which I recommend, especially during peak seasons (summer, autumn, holidaytime) and for weekend visits; otherwise, you might miss out.

Start your tour of the museum at the Rose Center with the Space Show. Afterwards, follow the wondrous interactive Cosmic Pathway, which spirals around the sphere and down to the main level, chronicling the 15-billion-year evolution.

(The sphere itself is even used to create a point-of-reference scale that puts the universe into better perspective than the entire semester I spent in undergrad astronomy.) Other must-sees include the Big Bang Theater, which re-creates the theoretical birth of the universe; the main Hall of the Universe, with its very own 15½-ton meteorite; and the terrific Hall of Planet Earth, which focuses on the geologic processes of our home planet (great volcano display!). All in all, you'll need a minimum of 2 hours to fully explore the Rose Center. *Tip:* Friday night is a great time to plan your visit, as the center isn't overcrowded, live jazz and food fills the Hall of the Universe, and, bathed in blue light, the sphere looks magical.

The rest of the 4-square-block museum is nothing to sneeze at, either. Founded in 1869, it houses the world's greatest natural science collection in a square-block group of buildings made of towers and turrets, pink granite and red brick—a mishmash of architectural styles, but overflowing with neo-Gothic charm. The diversity of the holdings is astounding: some 36 million specimens ranging from microscopic organisms to the world's largest cut gem, the Brazilian Princess Topaz (21,005 carats). Rose Center aside, it would take you all day to see the entire museum, and then you *still* wouldn't get to everything. If you don't have a lot of time, you can see the best of the best on free **highlights tours** offered daily every hour at 15 minutes after the hour from 10:15am to 3:15pm. Free daily **spotlight tours,** thematic tours that change monthly, are also offered; stop by an information desk for the day's schedule. **Audio Expeditions,** high-tech audio tours that allow you to access narration in the order you choose, are also available to help you make sense of it all.

If you only see one exhibit, see the **dinosaurs** ★, which take up the entire fourth floor. Start in the **Orientation Room,** where a short video gives an overview of the 500 million years of evolutionary history that led to you. Continue to the **Vertebrate Origins Room,** where huge models of ancient fish and turtles hang overhead, with plenty of interactive exhibits and kid-level displays on hand to keep young minds fascinated. Next come the great **dinosaur halls,** with mammoth, spectacularly reconstructed skeletons, and more interactive displays. **Mammals and Their Extinct Relatives** brings what you've learned in the previous halls home, showing how yesterday's prehistoric monsters have evolved into today's modern animals. Simply marvelous—you could spend hours in these halls alone.

The **Hall of Biodiversity** is an impressive multimedia exhibit, but its doom-and-gloom story about the future of rain forests and other natural habitats might be too much for the little ones. Kids 5 and up should head to the **Discovery Room,** with lots of hands-on exhibits and experiments. (Parents, be prepared: There seems to be a gift shop overflowing with fuzzy stuffed animals at every turn.)

I'm thrilled to report that the outmoded **Hall of Ocean Life** is getting a much-needed face-lift, and should reopen in 2003. In the meantime, the **animal habitat dioramas** and **halls of peoples** seem dated but still have something to teach (that's especially true of the Native American halls); these may also be in the process of piecemeal renovation while you're in town. The **IMAX Theater** also was getting an overhaul at press time but will reopen well before you arrive; it shows neat films such as *Shackleton's Arctic Adventure* and *Africa's Elephant Kingdom* on a four-story screen that puts you right in the heart of the action.

The museum excels at **special exhibitions,** so check to see what will be on while you're in town in case any advance planning is required. The magical **Butterfly Conservatory** ★, a walk-in enclosure housing nearly 500 free-flying

Value Money- & Time-Saving Tip

CityPass just may be New York's best sightseeing deal. Pay one price ($38, or $31 for kids 12–17) for admission to seven major Big Apple attractions: The American Museum of Natural History (admission only; does not include Space Show); the Solomon R. Guggenheim Museum; the Empire State Building; the *Intrepid* Sea-Air-Space Museum; the Whitney Museum of American Art; MoMA QNS (the Museum of Modern Art's temporary home while it undergoes renovation); and a 2-hour Circle Line harbor cruise. If you purchased admission ticket by ticket, you'd spend more than twice as much.

More important, CityPass is not a coupon book. It contains actual admission tickets, so you can bypass lengthy ticket lines. This can literally save you hours of time-wasting, since popular sights such as the Empire State Building often have ticket lines of an hour or more.

CityPass is good for 9 days from the first time you use it. It's sold at all participating attractions and online at **www.citypass.net**. To avoid online service and shipping fees, you may buy the pass at your first attraction (start at an attraction that's likely to have the shortest admission line, like the Guggenheim or the Whitney, or arrive before opening to avoid a wait at such spots as the Empire State). However, if you begin your sightseeing on a weekend or during holiday time, when lines are longest, online purchase may be worthwhile.

For more information call CityPass at ✆ **707/256-0490** (note, however, that CityPass is not sold over the phone). Pricing and attraction list confirmed through March 2003; call or check the website for updated information if your visit falls later in the year.

tropical butterflies, has developed into a can't-miss fixture from October through May; check to see if it's in the house while you're in town.

Central Park West (btwn 77th and 81st sts.) ✆ **212/769-5100** for information, or 212/769-5200 for tickets (tickets can also be ordered online). www.amnh.org. Suggested admission $10 adults, $7.50 seniors and students, $6 children 2–12. Space Show and museum admission $19 adults, $14 seniors and students, $11.50 children under 12. Additional charges for IMAX movies and some special exhibitions. Daily 10am–5:45pm; Rose Center open Fri to 8:45pm. Subway: B, C to 81st St.; 1, 9 to 79th St.

Brooklyn Bridge ★★ *Moments* Its Gothic-inspired stone pylons and intricate steel-cable webs have moved poets like Walt Whitman and Hart Crane to sing the praises of this great span, the first to cross the East River and connect Manhattan to Brooklyn. Begun in 1867 and ultimately completed in 1883, the beautiful Brooklyn Bridge is now the city's best-known symbol of the age of growth that seized the city during the late 19th century. Walk across the bridge and imagine the awe that New Yorkers of that age felt at seeing two boroughs joined by this monumental span. It's still astounding.

Designed by John Roebling, this massive engineering feat was plagued by death and disaster at its birth. Roebling was fatally injured in 1869 when a ferry rammed a waterfront piling on which he stood. His son, Washington, who was subsequently put in charge, contracted the bends in 1872 while working underwater to construct the bridge's towers, and oversaw the rest of the construction with a telescope from his bed at the edge of the East River in Brooklyn Heights (his wife relayed his instructions to the workers). Washington refused to attend the 1883 opening ceremonies, having had a bitter disagreement with the company that financed the construction. Though it was declared the "eighth wonder of the world" upon its completion, the bridge's troubles were not over: Twelve pedestrians were killed in a stampede when panic about its imminent collapse spread like wildfire on the day it opened to the public. Things are usually calmer now.

Walking the Bridge: Walking the Brooklyn Bridge is one of my all-time favorite New York activities, although there's no doubt that the Lower Manhattan views from the bridge now have a painful resonance as well as a joyous spirit. A wide wood-plank pedestrian walkway is elevated above the traffic, making it a relatively peaceful, and popular, walk. It's a great vantage point from which to contemplate the New York skyline and the East River.

There's a sidewalk entrance on Park Row, just across from City Hall Park (take the 4, 5, or 6 train to Brooklyn Bridge/City Hall). But why do this walk *away* from Manhattan, toward the far less impressive Brooklyn skyline? Instead, for Manhattan skyline views, take an A or C train to High Street, one stop into Brooklyn. From there, you'll be on the bridge in no time: Come above ground, then walk through the little park to Cadman Plaza East and head downslope (left) to the stairwell that will take you up to the footpath. (Following Prospect Place under the bridge, turning right onto Cadman Plaza E., will also take you directly to the stairwell.) It's a 20- to 40-minute stroll over the bridge to Manhattan, depending on your pace, the amount of foot traffic, and the number of stops you make to contemplate the spectacular views (there are benches along the way). The footpath will deposit you right at City Hall Park.

If you'd like to extend this walk a bit, I highly recommend pairing it with a quick tour of Brooklyn Heights and its wonderful Promenade; see "Highlights of the Outer Boroughs," later in this chapter, for exact directions.

Subway: A, C to High St.; 4, 5, 6 to Brooklyn Bridge–City Hall.

Ellis Island ★★ One of New York's most moving sights, the restored Ellis Island opened in 1990, slightly north of Liberty Island. Roughly 40% of Americans (myself included) can trace their heritage back to an ancestor who came through here. For the 62 years when it was America's main entry point for immigrants (1892–1954), Ellis Island processed some 12 million people. The greeting was often brusque—especially in the early years of the century, until 1924, when as many as 12,000 came through in a single day. The statistics can be overwhelming, but the **Immigration Museum** skillfully relates the story of Ellis Island and immigration in America by placing the emphasis on personal experience.

It's difficult to leave the museum unmoved. Today you enter the Main Building's baggage room, just as the immigrants did, and then climb the stairs to the **Registry Room,** with its dramatic vaulted tiled ceiling, where millions waited anxiously for medical and legal processing. A step-by-step account of the immigrants' voyage is detailed in the exhibit, with haunting photos and touching oral histories. What might be the most poignant exhibit is **"Treasures from Home,"** 1,000 objects and photos donated by descendants of immigrants, including family heirlooms, religious articles, and rare clothing and jewelry. Outside, the **American Immigrant Wall of Honor** commemorates the names of more than 500,000 immigrants and their families, from Myles Standish and George Washington's great-grandfather to the forefathers of John F. Kennedy, Jay Leno, and

Barbra Streisand. You can even research your own family's history at the interactive **American Family Immigration History Center.** You might also make time to see the award-winning short film ***Island of Hope, Island of Tears,*** which plays on a continuous loop in two theaters. Short live theatrical performances depicting the immigrant experience are also often part of the day's events.

Touring tips: Ferries run daily to Ellis Island and Liberty Island from Battery Park and Liberty State Park at frequent intervals; see the Statue of Liberty listing (p. 252) for details.

In New York Harbor. ✆ **212/363-3200** (general info), or 212/269-5755 (ticket/ferry info). www.nps.gov/elis or www.ellisisland.org. Free admission (ferry ticket charge). Daily 9:30am–5pm (last ferry departs around 3:30pm). For subway and ferry details, see the Statue of Liberty listing on p. 252 (ferry trip includes stops at both sights).

Empire State Building ★★★ It took 60,000 tons of steel, 10 million bricks, 2.5 million feet (750,000m) of electrical wire, 120 miles (193km) of pipe, and 7 million man-hours to build. King Kong climbed it in 1933. A plane slammed into it in 1945. The World Trade Center superseded it in 1970 as the island's tallest building. And in 1997, a gunman ascended it to stage a deadly shooting. On that horrific day of September 11, 2001, it once again regained its status as New York City's tallest building, after 31 years of taking second place. And through it all, the Empire State Building has remained one of the city's favorite landmarks, and its signature high-rise. Completed in 1931, the limestone-and–stainless steel streamline deco dazzler climbs 102 stories (1,454 ft./436m) and now harbors the offices of fashion firms, and, in its upper reaches, a jumble of high-tech broadcast equipment.

Always a conversation piece, the Empire State Building glows every night, bathed in colored floodlights to commemorate events of significance—red, white, and blue for Independence Day; green for St. Patrick's Day; red, black, and green for Martin Luther King Day; blue and white for Hanukkah; even lavender and white for Gay Pride Day (you can find a complete lighting schedule online). The familiar silver spire can be seen from all over the city. My favorite view of the building is from 23rd Street, where Fifth Avenue and Broadway converge. On a lovely day, stand at the base of the Flatiron Building (p. 276) and gaze up Fifth; the crisp, gleaming deco tower jumps out, soaring above the sooty office buildings that surround it.

Impressions

It's the nearest thing to heaven we have in New York.

—Deborah Kerr to Cary Grant in *An Affair to Remember,* on the Empire State Building

But the views that keep nearly 3 million visitors coming every year are the ones from the 86th- and 102nd-floor **observatories.** The lower one is best—you can walk out on a windy deck and look through coin-operated viewers (bring quarters!) over what, on a clear day, can be as much as an 80-mile (129km) visible radius. The citywide panorama is magnificent. One surprise is the flurry of rooftop activity, an aspect of city life that thrives unnoticed from our everyday sidewalk vantage point. The higher observation deck is glass-enclosed and cramped.

Light fog can create an admirably moody effect, but it goes without saying that a clear day is best. Dusk brings the most remarkable views and the biggest crowds. Consider going in the morning, when the light is still low on the horizon, keeping glare to a minimum. Starry nights are pure magic.

Tips Empire State Building Ticket-Buying Tip

Lines can be horrible at the concourse-level ticket booth, so be prepared to wait—or consider purchasing **advance tickets** online using a credit card at **www.esbnyc.org**. You'll pay slightly more—tickets were priced $1 higher on the website at press time—but it's well worth it, especially if you're visiting during busy seasons, when the line can be shockingly long. You're not required to choose a time or date for your tickets in advance; they can be used on any regular open day. However, order them well before you leave home, because only regular mail is free. Expect them to take 7 to 10 days to reach you (longer if you live out of the country). Overnight delivery adds $15 to your total order. With tickets in hand, you're allowed to proceed directly to the second floor—past everyone who didn't plan as well as you did!

In your haste to go up, don't rush through the beautiful three-story-high marble **lobby** without pausing to admire its features, which include a wonderful streamline mural.

350 Fifth Ave. (at 34th St.). ✆ **212/736-3100.** www.esbnyc.com. Observatory admission $10 adults, $9 seniors and children 12–17, $4 children 6–11, free for children under 5. Mon–Fri 10am–midnight, Sat–Sun 9:30am–midnight; tickets sold until 11:25pm. Subway: B, D, F, N, R, V, Q, W to 34th St.; 6 to 33rd St.

Grand Central Terminal ★★ After more than 2 years and $175 million, Grand Central Terminal has come out from under the tarps and scaffolding. Rededicated with all the appropriate pomp and circumstance on October 1, 1998, the 1913 landmark (originally designed by Warren & Wetmore with Reed & Stem) has been reborn as one of the most magnificent public spaces in the country. The restoration, by the New York firm of Beyer Blinder Belle, is an utter triumph. Their work has reanimated the genius of the station's original intent: to inspire those who pass through this urban meeting point with lofty feelings of civic pride and appreciation for Western architectural traditions. In short, they've put the "grand" back into Grand Central.

By all means, come and visit, even if you're not catching one of the subway lines or Metro North commuter trains that rumble through the bowels of this great place. And even if you arrive and leave by subway, be sure to exit the station, walking a couple of blocks south, to about 40th Street, before you turn around to admire Jules-Alexis Coutan's neoclassical sculpture *Transportation* hovering over the south entrance, with a majestically buff Mercury, the Roman god of commerce and travel, as its central figure.

The greatest visual impact comes when you enter the vast **main concourse.** Cleaned of decades of grime and cheesy advertisements, it boasts renewed majesty. The high windows once again allow sunlight to penetrate the space, glinting off the half-acre Tennessee marble floor. The brass clock over the central kiosk gleams, as do the gold- and nickel-plated chandeliers piercing the side archways. The masterful **sky ceiling,** again a brilliant greenish blue, depicts the constellations of the winter sky above New York. They're lit with 59 stars, surrounded by dazzling 24-carat gold and emitting light fed through fiber-optic cables, their intensities roughly replicating the magnitude of the actual stars as seen from Earth. Look carefully and you'll see a patch near one corner left unrestored as a reminder of the neglect once visited on this splendid overhead masterpiece. On the east end of the main concourse is a grand **marble staircase** where there had never been one before, but as the original plans had always intended.

This dramatic beaux arts splendor serves as a hub of social activity as well. Excellent-quality retail shops and restaurants have taken over the mezzanine and lower levels. The highlights of the west mezzanine are **Michael Jordan's–The Steak House,** a gorgeous Art Deco space that allows you to dine within view of the sky ceiling (see chapter 7) as well as the gorgeously restored **Campbell Apartment** which serves cocktails (see chapter 11). Off the main concourse at street level, there's a nice mix of specialty shops and national retailers, as well as the truly grand **Grand Central Market** for gourmet foods (see chapter 10). The **New York Transit Museum Store,** in the shuttle passage, houses city transit-related exhibitions and a terrific gift shop that's worth a look for transit buffs (chapter 10). The **lower dining concourse** ★ houses a stellar food court and the famous **Oyster Bar & Restaurant** (see chapter 7 for details on both).

The **Municipal Art Society** (✆ **212/935-3960;** www.mas.org) offers a free walking tour of Grand Central Terminal on Wednesday at 12:30pm, which meets at the information booth on the Grand Concourse. The **Grand Central Partnership** (✆ **212/697-1245**) runs its own free tour every Friday at 12:30pm, which meets outside the station in front of the Whitney Museum at Phillip Morris gallery, at 42nd Street and Park Avenue. Call to confirm before you set out to meet either tour.

42nd St. at Park Ave. ✆ **212/340-2210** (events hot line). www.grandcentralterminal.com. Subway: S, 4, 5, 6, 7 to 42nd St./Grand Central.

Metropolitan Museum of Art ★★★ Home of blockbuster after blockbuster exhibition, the Metropolitan Museum of Art attracts some 5 million people a year, more than any other spot in New York City. And it's no wonder—this place is magnificent. At 1.6 million square feet (150,000 sq. m), this is the largest museum in the western hemisphere. Nearly all the world's cultures are on display through the ages—from Egyptian mummies to ancient Greek statuary to Islamic carvings to Renaissance paintings to Native American masks to 20th-century decorative arts—and masterpieces are the rule. You could go once a week for a lifetime and still find something new on each visit.

So unless you plan on spending your entire vacation in the museum (some people do), you cannot see the entire collection. My recommendation is to give it a good day—or better yet, 2 half days so you don't burn out. One good way to get an overview is to take advantage of the little-known **Museum Highlights Tour,** offered everyday at various times throughout the day (usually between 10:15am and 3:15pm). Even some New Yorkers who've spent many hours in the

Moments **Evening Events at the Met**

On **Friday and Saturday evenings,** the Met remains open late not only for art viewing but also for cocktails in the Great Hall Balcony Bar (5–8pm) and classical music from a string quintet or trio. A slate of after-hours programs (gallery talks, walking tours, family programs) changes by the week; call for this week's schedule. The restaurant stays open until 10pm (last reservation at 8:30pm), and dinner is usually accompanied by piano music.

museum could profit from this once-over. Visit the museum's website for a schedule of this and subject-specific walking tours (Old Master Paintings, American Period Rooms, Arts of China, Islamic Art, and so on); you can also get a schedule of the day's tours at the Visitor Services desk when you arrive. A daily schedule of **Gallery Talks** is available as well.

The least overwhelming way to see the Met on your own is to pick up a map at the round desk in the entry hall and choose to concentrate on what you like, whether it's 17th-century paintings, American furniture, or the art of the South Pacific. Highlights include the American Wing's **Garden Court,** with its 19th-century sculpture; the terrific ground-level **Costume Hall;** and the **Frank Lloyd Wright room.** The beautifully renovated **Roman and Greek galleries** are overwhelming, but in a marvelous way, as is the collections of **Byzantine Art** and later **Chinese art.** The highlight of the astounding **Egyptian collection** is the **Temple of Dendur,** in a dramatic, specially built glass-walled gallery with Central Park views. The **Greek Galleries,** which at last fully realize McKim, Mead & White's grand neoclassical plans of 1917, and the **Ancient Near East Galleries** are particularly of note. But it all depends on what your interests are. Don't forget the marvelous **special exhibitions,** which can range from "Orazio and Artemisia Gentileschi: Father and Daughter Painters in Baroque Italy" to "Earthly Bodies: Irving Penn's Nudes, 1949–50."

To purchase tickets for concerts and lectures, call © **212/570-3949** (Mon–Sat 9:30am–5pm). The museum contains several dining facilities, including a **full-service restaurant** serving Continental cuisine (© **212/570-3964** for reservations). The roof garden is worth visiting if you're here from spring to autumn, offering peaceful views over Central Park and the city.

The Met's medieval collections are housed in Upper Manhattan at the **Cloisters;** see the full listing on p. 258.

Fifth Ave. at 82nd St. © **212/535-7710.** www.metmuseum.org. Admission (includes same-day entrance to the Cloisters) $10 adults, $5 seniors and students, free for children under 12 when accompanied by an adult. Sun and Tues–Thurs 9:30am–5:30pm; Fri–Sat 9:30am–9pm. No strollers allowed Sun (back carriers available at 81st St. entrance coat-check area). Subway: 4, 5, 6 to 86th St.

Museum of Modern Art/MoMA QNS ★ The Museum of Modern Art (or MoMA, as it's usually called) boasts the world's greatest collection of painting and sculpture from the late 19th century to the present, including everything from Monet's *Water Lilies* and Klimt's *The Kiss* to later masterworks by Frida Kahlo, Edward Hopper, Andy Warhol, Robert Rauschenberg, and many others. Top that off with an extensive collection of modern drawings, photography, architectural models and modern furniture, iconic design objects ranging from tableware to sports cars, and film and video (including the world's largest collection of D. W. Griffith films), and you have quite a museum. If you're into modernism, this is the place to be.

Here's the bad news: MoMA will be closed while you're in town. The museum is undergoing a monster $650 million renovation of its West 53rd Street building under the guidance of Japanese architect Yoshio Taniguchi that will double the exhibit space when the project is complete, which won't be until 2005.

Here's the good news: The museum has opened temporary exhibit space called **MoMA QNS** in an old Swingline stapler factory in Long Island City, Queens. This is no flimsy venture: The 45,000-square-foot (4,181-sq.-m) gallery will exhibit highlights of the museum's collection, including some of its

Tips **Museum-Going Tip**

Many of the city's top museums—including the Natural History Museum, the Met, the Guggenheim, and the Whitney—have late hours on Friday and/or Saturday nights. Take advantage of them. Most visitors run out of steam by dinnertime, so even on jam-packed weekends you'll largely have the place to yourself by 5 or 6pm—which, in most cases, leaves you hours left to explore, unfettered by crowds or screaming kids.

biggest draws, among them van Gogh's *Starry Night,* Picasso's early *Les Demoiselles d'Avignon,* and Warhol's *Gold Marilyn Monroe.* Workshops, a limited program schedule, and special exhibitions will also be part of the fun: Spring 2003 will showcase masterworks by Matisse and Picasso, while summer visitors can expect an installation of Ansel Adams photographs.

Yes—it's definitely worth a short subway ride to Queens. Getting there is quick and easy; in fact, from Midtown, you can be here quicker than you can get to the Village. While you're here, also consider visiting the MoMA affiliate **P.S. 1 Contemporary Art Center,** also in Long Island City (p. 309). In fact, consider making a day of it: The **Queens Artlink** (**www.moma.org/qal**) is a free weekend arts shuttle, running Saturday and Sunday from 11:30am to 5:30pm and linking five top-flight art institutions in the area, including MoMA QNS, P.S. 1, the **Isamu Noguchi Garden Museum** (p. 309), the **American Museum of the Moving Image** (p. 308), and the **Socrates Sculpture Park** (p. 310).

45–20 33rd St., Long Island City, Queens. © **212/708-9400.** www.moma.org. Admission $12 adults, $8.50 seniors and students, free for children under 16 accompanied by an adult; pay what you wish Fri 4:30–8:15pm. Sat–Tues and Thurs 10:30am–5:45pm; Fri 10:30am–8:15pm. Subway: 7 to 33rd St. (MoMA QNS is across the street).

Rockefeller Center ★★ *Moments* A streamline moderne masterpiece, Rockefeller Center is one of New York's central gathering spots for visitors and New Yorkers alike. A prime example of the city's skyscraper spirit and historic sense of optimism, it was erected mainly in the 1930s, when the city was deep in the Depression as well as its most passionate Art Deco phase. Designated a National Historic Landmark in 1988, it's now the world's largest privately owned business-and-entertainment center, with 18 buildings on 21 acres.

For a dramatic approach to the entire complex, start at Fifth Avenue between 49th and 50th streets. The builders purposely created the gentle slope of the Promenade, known here as the **Channel Gardens** because it's flanked to the south by La Maison Française and to the north by the British Building (the Channel, get it?). You'll also find a number of attractive shops along here, including a big branch of the **Metropolitan Museum of Art Store,** a good stop for elegant gifts. The Promenade leads to the **Lower Plaza,** home to the famous ice-skating rink in winter (see next paragraph) and alfresco dining in summer in the shadow of Paul Manship's freshly gilded bronze statue *Prometheus,* more notable for its setting than its magnificence as an artwork. All around, the flags of the United Nations' member countries flap in the breeze. Just behind *Prometheus,* in December and early January, towers the city's official and majestic Christmas tree.

The **Rink at Rockefeller Center** ★ (© **212/332-7654;** www.rockefeller center.com) is tiny but positively romantic, especially during the holidays, when the giant Christmas tree's multicolored lights twinkle from above. It's open from mid-October to mid-March, and you'll skate under the magnificent tree for the month of December. Overlooking the rink, and with a terrific view of *Prometheus,* is the excellent **Sea Grill** restaurant (p. 202).

The focal point of this "city within a city" is the **GE Building** ★, at 30 Rockefeller Plaza, a 70-story showpiece towering over the plaza. It's still one of the city's most impressive buildings; walk through for a look at the granite and marble lobby, lined with monumental sepia-toned murals by José Maria Sert. You can pick up a walking tour brochure highlighting the center's art and architecture at the main information desk in this building. On the 65th floor, the legendary **Rainbow Room** is once again open to the public on a limited basis (see chapter 11).

NBC television maintains studios throughout the complex. *Saturday Night Live* and *Late Night with Conan O'Brien* originate in the GE Building (see "Talk of the Town: TV Tapings," on p. 296, for tips on getting tickets). NBC's ***Today*** show is broadcast live on weekdays from 7 to 10am from the glass-enclosed studio on the southwest corner of 49th Street and Rockefeller Plaza; come early if you want a visible spot, and bring your HI MOM! sign.

The 70-minute **NBC Studio Tour** (✆ **212/664-3700;** www.nbcsuperstore.com) will take you behind the scenes at the Peacock network. The tour changes daily, but may include the *Today* show, *NBC Nightly News, Dateline NBC,* and/or *Saturday Night Live* sets. Who knows? You may even run into Tom Brokaw or Stone Phillips in the hall. Tours run every 15 minutes Monday through Saturday from 8:30am to 5:30pm, Sunday from 9:30am to 4:30pm (later on certain summer days); of course, you'll have a better chance of encountering some real live action on a weekday. Tickets are $17.50 for adults, $15 for seniors and children 6 to 16. You can reserve your tickets for either tour in advance (reservations are recommended) or buy them right up to tour time at the **NBC Experience** store, on Rockefeller Plaza at 49th Street (see chapter 10 for details). They also offer a 75-minute **Rockefeller Center Tour,** which is offered hourly every day between 10am and 4pm. $10 for adults, $8 for seniors and children 6 to 16; two-tour combination packages are available for $21.

Other notable buildings throughout the complex include the **International Building,** on Fifth Avenue between 50th and 51st streets, worth a look for its Atlas statue out front; and the **McGraw-Hill Building,** on Sixth Avenue between 48th and 49th streets, with its 50-foot (15m) sun triangle on the plaza.

The newly restored **Radio City Music Hall** ★, 1260 Sixth Ave., at 50th Street (✆ **212/247-4777;** www.radiocity.com), is perhaps the most impressive architectural feat of the complex. Designed by Donald Deskey and opened in 1932, it's one of the largest indoor theaters, with 6,200 seats. But its true grandeur derives from its magnificent Art Deco appointments. The crowning touch is the stage's great proscenium arch, which from the distant seats evokes a faraway sun setting on the horizon of the sea. The men's and women's lounges are also splendid. The theater hosts the annual **Christmas Spectacular,** starring the Rockettes. The illuminating 1-hour **Stage Door Tour** is offered Monday through Saturday from 10am to 5pm, Sunday from 11am to 5pm; tickets are $16 for adults, $10 for children under 12.

Between 48th and 50th sts., from Fifth to Sixth aves. ✆ **212/332-6868.** www.rockefellercenter.com. Subway: B, D, F, V to 47th–50th sts./Rockefeller Center.

Solomon R. Guggenheim Museum ★ It's been called a bun, a snail, a concrete tornado, and even a giant wedding cake; bring your kids, and they'll probably see it as New York's coolest opportunity for skateboarding. Whatever description you choose to apply, Frank Lloyd Wright's only New York building, completed in 1959, is best summed up as a brilliant work of architecture—so consistently brilliant that it competes with the art for your attention. If you're looking for the city's best modern art, head to MoMA or the Whitney first; come to the Guggenheim to see the house.

It's easy to see the bulk of what's on display in 2 to 4 hours. Inside, a spiraling rotunda circles over a slowly inclined ramp that leads you past changing exhibits that, in the past, have ranged from "The Art of the Motorcycle" to "Norman Rockwell: Pictures for the American People," said to be the most comprehensive exhibit ever of the beloved painter's works. Usually the progression is counterintuitive: from the first floor up, rather than from the sixth floor down. If you're not sure, ask a guard before you begin. Permanent exhibits of 19th- and 20th-century art, including strong holdings of Kandinsky, Klee, Picasso, and French Impressionists, occupy a stark annex called the **Tower Galleries,** an addition accessible at every level that some critics claimed made the original look like a toilet bowl backed by a water tank (judge for yourself—I think there may be something to that view).

The Guggenheim runs some interesting special programs, including free docent tours daily, a limited schedule of lectures, free family films, avant-garde screenings for grown-ups, curator-led guided gallery tours on select Friday afternoons, and the **World Beat Jazz Series,** which resounds through the rotunda on Friday and Saturday from 5 to 8pm.

1071 Fifth Ave. (at 88th St.). ✆ **212/423-3500.** www.guggenheim.org. Admission $12 adults, $8 seniors and students, free for children under 12; pay as you wish Fri 6–8pm. Sun–Wed 9am–6pm; Fri–Sat 9am–8pm. Subway: 4, 5, 6 to 86th St.

Staten Island Ferry ★ *Value* Here's New York's best freebie—especially if you just want to glimpse the Statue of Liberty and not climb her steps. You get an enthralling hour-long excursion (round-trip) into the world's biggest harbor. This is not strictly a sightseeing ride but commuter transportation to and from Staten Island (remember Melanie Griffith, in big hair and sneakers, heading to the office in *Working Girl?*). As a result, during business hours, you'll share the boat with working stiffs reading papers and drinking coffee inside, blissfully unaware of the sights outside.

You, however, should go on deck and enjoy the busy harbor traffic. The old orange-and-green boats usually have open decks along the sides or at the bow and stern; try to catch one of these boats if you can, since the newer white boats don't have decks. Grab a seat on the right side of the boat for the best view. On the way out of Manhattan, you'll pass the Statue of Liberty (the boat comes closest to Lady Liberty on the way to Staten Island), Ellis Island, and from the left side of the boat, Governor's Island; you'll see the Verranzano Narrows Bridge spanning the distance from Brooklyn to Staten Island in the distance.

When the boat arrives at St. George, Staten Island, if you are required to disembark, follow the boat-loading sign on your right as you get off; you'll circle around to the next loading dock, where there's usually another boat waiting to depart for Manhattan. The skyline views are simply awesome on the return trip. Well worth the time spent.

Departs from the Whitehall Ferry Terminal at the southern tip of Manhattan. ✆ **718/815-BOAT.** www.ci.nyc.ny.us/html/dot. Free admission ($3 for car transport on select ferries). 24 hours; every 20–30 min. weekdays, less frequently on off-peak and weekend hours. Subway: N, R to Whitehall St.; 4, 5 to Bowling Green; 1, 9 to South Ferry (ride in the first 5 cars).

Statue of Liberty ★★★ Kids For the millions who first came by ship to America in the last century—either as privileged tourists or needy, hopeful immigrants—Lady Liberty, standing in the Upper Bay, was their first glimpse of America. No monument so embodies the nation's, and the world's, notion of political freedom and economic potential. Even if you don't make it out to Liberty Island, you can get a spine-tingling glimpse from Battery Park, from the New Jersey side of the bay, or during a free ride on the Staten Island Ferry (see above). It's always reassuring to see her torch lighting the way.

Proposed by French statesman Edouard de Laboulaye as a gift from France to the United States, commemorating the two nations' friendship and joint notions of liberty, the statue was designed by sculptor Frédéric-Auguste Bartholdi with the engineering help of Alexandre-Gustave Eiffel (who was responsible for the famed Paris tower) and unveiled on October 28, 1886. Despite the fact that Joseph Pulitzer had to make a mighty effort to attract donations on this side of the Atlantic for her pedestal (designed by American Richard Morris Hunt), more than a million people watched as the French tricolor veil was pulled away. After nearly 100 years of wind, rain, and exposure to the harsh sea air, Lady Liberty received a resoundingly successful $150-million face-lift (including the relandscaping of Liberty Island and the replacement of the torch's flame) in time for its centennial celebration on July 4, 1986. Feted in fireworks, Miss Liberty became more of a city icon than ever before.

Touring tips: Ferries leave daily every half hour to 45 minutes from 9am to about 3:30pm (their clock), with more frequent ferries in the morning and extended hours in summer. Try to go early on a weekday to avoid the crowds that swarm in the afternoon, on weekends, and on holidays.

A stop at **Ellis Island** (p. 244) is included in the fare, but if you catch the last ferry, you can only visit the statue or Ellis Island, not both.

Note that you can **buy ferry tickets in advance** via **www.statueofliberty ferry.com**, which will allow you to board the boat without standing in the sometimes-long ticket line; however, there is an additional service charge attached. Even if you've already purchased tickets, arrive as much as 30 minutes before

---

Lady Liberty Touring Updates

At press time, **only the grounds of Liberty Island were open to the public,** pending additional security arrangements. Whether and when the pedestal, museum, and/or the body of the statue itself will reopen to the public was unknown at this writing, but the close-up view from the grounds alone is breathtaking enough to make the journey worthwhile.

If the statue does reopen, be sure to arrive by noon if your heart's set on experiencing everything. And keep in mind that, for the last few years, the National Park Service has instituted a special "crown" policy during the peak **summer** season: Visitors who want to walk up to the crown must be on one of the **first two ferries of the day** in order to do so. At other times of year, you must be in line to climb to the crown by 2pm; otherwise, you will not be allowed up.

All policies regarding access to the Statue of Liberty and Ellis Island are subject to change at any time. I cannot recommend strongly enough that you call or check the official website (**www.nps.gov/stli**) for the latest access information.

---

your desired ferry time to allow for increased security procedures prior to boarding the ferry. The ferry ride takes about 20 minutes.

Once on Liberty Island, you'll start to get an idea of the statue's immensity: She weighs 225 tons and measures 152 feet (46m) from foot to flame. Her nose alone is 4½ feet (1.25m) long, and her index finger is 8 feet (2.5m) long.

Note: Access to the statue itself was severely restricted at this writing; be sure to read "Lady Liberty Touring Updates," above, for details.

If the statue does reopen to the public, you may have to wait as long as 3 hours to walk up into the crown. If it's summer, or if you're just not in shape for it, you may want to skip it: It's a grueling 354 steps (the equivalent of 22 stories) to the crown, or you can cheat and take the elevator the first 10 stories up (a shortcut I wholeheartedly endorse). But even if you take the elevator to get started, the interior is stifling once the temperature starts to climb. However, you don't have to go all the way up to the crown; there are a number of **observation decks** at different levels, including one at the top of the pedestal that's reachable by elevator. Even if you don't go inside, a stroll around the base is a terrific experience, and the views of the Manhattan skyline are stellar.

On Liberty Island in New York Harbor. ✆ **212/363-3200** (general info), or 212/269-5755 (ticket/ferry info). www.nps.gov/stli or www.statueoflibertyferry.com. Free admission; ferry ticket to Statue of Liberty and Ellis Island $8 adults, $6 seniors, $3 children 3–17. Daily 9am–5pm (last ferry departs around 3:30pm); extended hours in summer. Subway: 4, 5 to Bowling Green; 1, 9 to South Ferry (note that 1, 9 had not resumed service to Lower Manhattan at press time). Walk south through Battery Park to Castle Clinton, the fort housing the ferry ticket booth.

Wall Street & the New York Stock Exchange Wall Street—it's an iconic name, and the world's prime hub for bulls and bears everywhere. This narrow 18th-century lane (you'll be surprised at how little it is) is appropriately monumental, lined with neoclassical towers that reach as far skyward as the dreams and greed of investors who built it into the world's most famous financial market.

At the heart of the action is the **New York Stock Exchange (NYSE),** the world's largest securities trader, where you can watch the billions change hands and get a fleeting idea of how the money merchants work. NYSE came into being in 1792, when merchants met daily under a nearby buttonwood tree to try and pass off to each other the U.S. bonds that had been sold to fund the Revolutionary War. By 1903, they were trading stocks of publicly held companies in this Corinthian-columned beaux arts "temple" designed by George Post. About 3,000 companies are now listed on the exchange, trading nearly 314 billion shares valued at about $16 trillion.

Until September 11, 2001, visitors could acquire free tickets to tour a small interactive museum and watch the action on the trading floor from the glass-lined, mezzanine-level observation gallery. However, the facility has been closed to the public since the terrorist attack for security reasons as well as an ongoing renovation project. It was scheduled to reopen to the public sometime in 2002, but no date could be confirmed at this writing. Your best bet is to call to check the status—as well as the updated ticket procedure—before you come to town.

20 Broad St. (between Wall St. and Exchange Place). ✆ **212/656-5165.** www.nyse.com. Free admission. Mon–Fri 9am–4:30pm (ticket booth opens at 8:45am). *Note:* Information may change when the facility reopens to the public in 2002. Subway: J, M, Z to Broad St.; 2, 3, 4, 5 to Wall St.

Whitney Museum of American Art ★★ What is arguably the finest collection of 20th-century American art in the world belongs to the Whitney thanks to the efforts of Gertrude Vanderbilt Whitney. A sculptor herself, she

What's Happening in Times Square

The writer O. Henry once observed that, "New York City will be a great place if they ever finish it." Indeed, no other city is so darn good at reinventing itself: Witness the "new" Times Square. The dust has finally settled on the epic renewal where Broadway meets 42nd Street, and what was once the city's gritty heart is now the hub of its tourist-friendly rebirth.

The neon lights of Broadway are more dazzling than ever, now that ABC's ***Good Morning America*** has set up a street-facing studio with state-of-the-art video and news ribbons at Broadway and 44th Street (just across from **MTV**'s own); **Nasdaq**'s eight-story billboard—the world's largest video screen, at Broadway and 43rd—has joined the landscape, and the World Wrestling Entertainment spent a mint restoring the landmark Paramount Building to its original splendor and installing a 47,500-square-foot (4413-sq.-m) entertainment complex, **WWE New York.** (Take note of the WWE's marquee: Between the impeccably restored historic scrollwork is a full-color sign that incorporates the latest in LED and fiber-optic technology, and boasts the best resolution in Times Sq.) Corporate America has even moved in; among the big-name headquarters that have relocated to prime Times Square real estate are Condé Nast, Morgan Stanley, and Reuters, all adding to the increased cachet of this formerly seedy crossroads. What's more, a handful of upper-end new hotels right in the heart of the action—including the terrific **Hilton Times Square** and designer-hip **W Times Square,** both already open, and the new **Westin New York,** slated for fall 2002 (see chapter 6)—means that thousands more visitors can stay right on (or just off) the Great White Way.

organized exhibitions by American artists shunned by traditional academies, assembled a sizable personal collection, and founded the museum in 1930 in Greenwich Village.

Today's museum is an imposing presence on Madison Avenue—an inverted three-tiered pyramid of concrete and gray granite with seven seemingly random windows designed by Marcel Breuer, a leader of the Bauhaus movement. The rotating permanent collection consists of an intelligent selection of major works by Edward Hopper, George Bellows, Georgia O'Keeffe, Roy Lichtenstein, Jasper Johns, and other significant artists. A pleasing second-floor exhibit space is devoted exclusively to works from its permanent collection from 1900 to 1950, while the rest of the space is dedicated to rotating exhibits.

Shows are usually all well curated and more edgy than what you'd see at MoMA or the Guggenheim (though not as left-of-mainstream as what you'll find at the New Museum). Topics range from topical surveys, such as "American Art in the Age of Technology" and "The Warhol Look: Glamour Style Fashion" to in-depth retrospectives of famous or lesser-known movements (such as Fluxus, the movement that spawned Yoko Ono, among others) and artists (Mark Rothko, Keith Haring, Duane Hanson, Bob Thompson). Unfortunately for 2003 visitors, the next **Whitney Biennial** is scheduled for spring 2004; a

Along with WWE New York, **ESPN Zone,** the freshly *NSync-funded **Planet Hollywood,** and **B.B. King's Blues Club & Grill** all joined the Times Square pack in the 21st century, thus reinvigorating the whole notion of themed dining and nightlife (see "Theme Restaurant Thrills!" in chapter 7, and chapter 11 for B.B. King's). The rockin' **Virgin Megastore** has a major presence on the square (see chapter 10), as does **MTV,** which draws busloads of exuberant *Total Request Live* fans to Broadway and 45th Street every weekday afternoon, giving the entire square a welcome shot of youth appeal.

Forty-second Street between Seventh and Eighth avenues, the former porn peddler's paradise, has been rebuilt from scratch into a family-oriented entertainment mecca. In addition to a spate of beautifully renovated theaters—including the **New Victory** (see "Kids Take the Stage: Family-Friendly Theater," in chapter 11), the **New Amsterdam** (home to *The Lion King*), and the former Selwyn, reinvented as the **American Airlines Theatre** and now the permanent home of the Roundabout Theater Club—the neon-bright block is chock-full with retail and amusements, including **Madame Tussaud's New York,** a six-floor fully interactive new-world version of London's famous wax museum (p. 264); the multilevel, state-of-the-art **Broadway City** video arcade; two 20-plus-screen movie complexes; and plenty of mall-familiar shopping and dining, including the **Museum Company,** a **Yankees Clubhouse Shop** (where you can purchase home game tix), and **Chevy's Fresh Mex** and **Applebee's** restaurants. (Don't leave home without it, right?)

To quote the great Bart Simpson: "Ay, carumba!"

major event on the national museum calendar, the Biennials serve as the premier launching pad for new American artists working on the vanguard in every media.

Free **gallery tours** are offered daily, and music, screenings, and lectures fill the calendar. The Whitney is also notable for having the best museum restaurant in town: **Sarabeth's at the Whitney,** worth a visit in its own right (see the listing for Sarabeth's Kitchen, in chapter 7).

For details on the **Whitney Museum of American Art at Philip Morris,** the petite Midtown annex, see p. 274.

945 Madison Ave. (at 75th St.). ✆ **877/WHITNEY** or 212/570-3676. www.whitney.org. Admission $10 adults, $8 seniors and students, free for children under 12; pay as you wish Fri 6–9pm. Tues–Thurs and Sat–Sun 11am–6pm; Fri 1–9pm. Subway: 6 to 77th St.

World Trade Center site (Ground Zero) *Moments* The World Trade Center dominated lower Manhattan. The record-breaking complex occupied 16 acres, and its 12 million square feet (1.25 million sq. m) of rentable office space housed more than 350 firms and organizations. About 50,000 people worked in its precincts, and some 70,000 others (tourists and businesspeople) visited each day. The vast complex included, in addition to two 110-story towers—one of which awarded visitors with breathtaking views from the Top of the World observation deck, more than 1,350 feet (405m) in the air—five additional buildings (including a Marriott hotel), a plaza the size of four football fields rich with outdoor sculpture, a vast underground shopping mall with retailers running the gamut from Radio Shack to Coach, and a full slate of restaurants, including the spectacular Windows on the World, the city's ultimate special-occasion restaurant.

Then the first plane hit the north tower, Tower 1, at 8:45am on Tuesday, September 11, 2001. By 10:30am, it was all gone, along with nearly 3,000 innocent victims.

We've all seen the photos. The former Trade Center is now a vast crater; at this writing, it is still being removed of debris, combed for remains, and shored up for what's to come. Clean-up and recovery efforts officially ended in May 2002; at press time, no decisions had yet been finalized as to what would replace it. The likelihood is a combination of victim memorial and commercial real estate—but at this stage, anything can happen.

What will be left to see when you arrive is anybody's guess. At press time, a **temporary viewing platform** was in place at Broadway and Fulton streets, open daily from 9am to 8pm; it is scheduled to remain in place through summer 2002, but its fate thereafter is yet unknown. Free tickets are available at the South Street Museum's ticket booth at Fulton and South streets, open daily from 11am to 6pm (morning viewing tickets are distributed the previous afternoon). Please check the sources listed below for the latest viewing and access information.

As of March 11, 2002, a temporary victim's memorial was in place at **Battery Park** (p. 287): The bronze sphere that once stood on the World Trade Center plaza between the Twin Towers now stands witness, bearing its war wounds, until a permanent one can be erected. Additionally, I expect that the gates of **Trinity Church** (p. 280) will continue to serve as an impromptu memorial, brimming with tokens of remembrance and blessing left by visitors from around the world.

Bounded by Church, Barclay, Liberty, and West sts. ✆ **212/484-1222.** www.nycvisit.com or www.southstseaport.org for viewing information; www.downtownny.com for Lower Manhattan area information and rebuilding updates. Subway: C, E to World Trade Center; N, R to Cortlandt St.

3 More Manhattan Museums

In 1978, New York's finest cultural institutions located on Fifth Avenue from 82nd to 104th streets formed a consortium called **Museum Mile,** the name New York City officially gave to the stretch several years later. The "mile" begins at the **Metropolitan Museum of Art** (p. 247) and moves north to **El Museo del Barrio.** However, even the smallest museums along this stretch require some time, so don't plan on just popping into a few as you stroll along, or you'll be sorely disappointed by what you're able to see. Your best bet is to head directly to the museum that's tops on your list first, and then proceed to your second choice along the mile if you have time. If you're heading to the Metropolitan, forget trying to squeeze in anything else—as it is, you'll only see a portion of the collection there in a full day.

For the **Brooklyn Museum of Art,** the **New York Transit Museum,** the **American Museum of the Moving Image,** the **Queens Museum of Art,** the **Isamu Noguchi Garden Museum,** and the **P.S. 1 Contemporary Art Center,** see "Highlights of the Outer Boroughs," later in this chapter.

If you're traveling with the kids, also consider the museums listed u "Especially for Kids," on p. 277, which include the **Children's Museum** **Manhattan,** the **Sony Wonder Technology Lab,** and the **New York Hall of Science.**

If you're interested in historic house museums, see the box called "In Search of Historic Homes" on p. 277.

Also, don't forget to see what's on at the monumental **New York Public Library,** which regularly holds excellent exhibitions; see p. 276.

American Craft Museum ★ *Finds* This small but aesthetically pleasing museum is the nation's top showcase for contemporary crafts. The collection focuses on objects that are prime examples of form and function, ranging from jewelry to baskets to vessels to furniture. You'll see a strong emphasis on material as well as craft, whether it be fiber, ceramics, or metal. Special exhibitions can range from expressionist clay sculpture to fine bookbinding, and can celebrate movements (such as "Memories of Murano: American Glass Artists in Venice") or single artisans ("Elegant Fantasy: The Jewelry of Arline Fisch," Sept 20, 2002–Jan 5, 2003). Or just take your chances and stop in—you're unlikely to be disappointed. Stop into the gorgeous shop even if you don't make it into the museum (see chapter 10).

40 W. 53rd St. (btwn Fifth and Sixth aves.). ✆ **212/956-3535.** www.americancraftmuseum.org. Admission $7.50 adults, $4 students and seniors, free for children under 12; pay as you wish Thurs 6–8pm. Tues–Wed and Fri–Sun 10am–6pm; Thurs 10am–8pm. Subway: E, V to Fifth Ave.

American Folk Art Museum ★★ New Yorkers can't stop raving about the brand-new home of the American Folk Art Museum, now located on the same block as the under-renovation Museum of Modern Art. Designed by Tod Williams Billie Tsien Architects this gorgeous, ultra-modern boutique museum has been called by *House & Garden* no less than the city's greatest new museum and best work of architecture since Frank Lloyd Wright built the Guggenheim in 1959 while *New York* magazine called it "brilliant" and "a tour de force." Not only is it a stunning structure, but it also heralds American folk art into the top echelon of museum-worthy art.

The new building quadruples the museum's exhibit space to 30,000 square feet (2787 sq. m). The modified open-plan interior features an extraordinary collection of traditional works from the 18th century to the self-taught artists and craftspeople of the present, reflecting the breadth and vitality of the American folk-art tradition. A splendid variety of quilts, in particular, makes the textiles collection the museum's most popular. Look for "American Anthem Part II: Masterworks from the Permanent Collection," the largest installation of its kind that the museum has ever mounted, through December 2002. The book- and gift shop is outstanding, filled with one-of-a-kind objects.

The original Lincoln Center location is now the **Eva and Morris Feld Gallery,** which displays art from the permanent collection, including new acquisitions. There's also a second gift gallery here.

45 W. 53rd St. (btwn Fifth and Sixth aves.). ✆ **212/265-1040.** www.folkartmuseum.org. Admission $9 adults, $5 seniors and students, free for children under 12, free to all Fri 6–8pm. Tues–Thurs and Sat–Sun 10am–6pm; Fri 10am–8pm. Eva and Morris Feld Gallery: 2 Lincoln Sq. (Columbus Ave. between 65th and 66th sts., across from Lincoln Center). ✆ 212/595-9533. Free admission. Tues–Sun 11am–7:30pm; Mon 11am–6pm. Subway: 1, 9 to 66th St.

Asia Society The Asia Society was founded in 1956 by John D. Rockefeller III with the goal of increasing understanding between Americans and Asians

ts, lectures, films, performances, and international confer-
s a leader in presenting contemporary Asian and Asian Amer-
r a $30 million renovation that doubled the exhibition space
2001, the society's headquarters is bigger, smarter, and better
as so much of the core collection, comprised of Rockefeller's
ions dating from 2000 B.C. to the 19th century, been on display before. Well-curated temporary exhibits run the gamut from "The New Way of Tea," exploring Japan's elaborate tea ceremony, to "Through Afghan Eyes: A Culture in Conflict, 1987-1995," a study in photographs and video. Additionally, the mammoth calendar of events ranges from film screenings to arts lectures to discussion panels featuring experts in pan-Asian and global politics, business, and more; call or check the website for a current schedule.

725 Park Ave. (at 70th St.). ✆ **212/288-6400.** www.asiasociety.org. Gallery admission $7 adults, $5 seniors and students; free for children under 16; free to all Fri 6–9pm. Tues–Sun 11am–6pm (Fri to 9pm). Subway: 6 to 68th St./Hunter College.

Center for Jewish History *Finds* Brand-new in late 2000, this 125,000-square-foot (11,613-sq.-m) complex is the largest repository of Jewish history, art, and literature in the Diaspora. It unites five of America's leading institutions of Jewish scholarship: the **American Jewish Historical Society** (www.ajhs.org), the national archives of the Jewish people in the Americas; the **Leo Baeck Institute** (www.lbi.org), documenting the robust history of German-speaking Jewry from the 17th century until annihilation under the Nazis; the **Yeshiva University Museum** (www.yu.edu/museum), general-interest exhibits, plus a renowned collection of Judaica objects confiscated by the Nazis; the **YIVO Institute for Jewish Research** (www.yivoinstitute.org), focusing on exhibits exploring the diversity of the Jewish experience; and the **American Sephardi Federation** (www.asfonline.org), representing the spiritual, cultural, and social traditions of the American Sephardic communities (Jews from Southern Europe, North Africa, and the Middle East). Together, this union represents about 100 million archival documents, 500,000 books, and tens of thousands of objects of art and ephemera, ranging from Thomas Jefferson's letter denouncing anti-Semitism to memorabilia of famous Jewish athletes.

The main gallery space is the Yeshiva Museum, which comprises four galleries, an outdoor sculpture garden, and a children's workshop; a range of exhibits also showcase various holdings belonging to the other institutions as well. A central feature is the **Reading Room,** home to open stacks accessible by serious researchers and lay historians like, as well as the **Center Genealogy Institute,** which offers assistance in family history research. Another huge component of the Center is its 250-seat state-of-the-art auditorium, home to a packed schedule of lectures, music, and film presentations. If you get hungry, a kosher cafe is on site.

15 W. 16th St. (btwn Fifth and Sixth aves.). ✆ **212/294-8301.** www.cjh.org. Admission to Yeshiva University Museum, $6 adults, $4 seniors and students; free admission to all other facilities. Yeshiva University Museum Sun and Tues–Wed 11am–5pm; Thurs 11am–8pm. Reading Room and Genealogy Institute Mon–Thurs 9:30am–4:30pm; Fri by appt. All other exhibition galleries Mon–Thurs 9am–5pm; Fri 9am–4pm. Subway: L, N, R, 4, 5, 6 to 14th St./Union Sq.; F, V to 14th St.

The Cloisters ★★ If it weren't for this branch of the Metropolitan Museum of Art, many New Yorkers would never get to this northernmost point in Manhattan. This remote yet lovely spot is devoted to the art and architecture of medieval Europe. Atop a magnificent cliff overlooking the Hudson River, you'll find a 12th-century chapter house, parts of five cloisters from medieval monasteries, a Romanesque chapel, and a 12th-century Spanish apse brought intact from Europe. Surrounded by peaceful gardens, this is the one place on the island that can even approximate the kind of solitude suitable to such a collection. Inside you'll find extraordinary works that include the famed Unicorn tapestries, sculpture, illuminated manuscripts, stained glass, ivory, and precious metal work.

Despite its remoteness, the Cloisters are extremely popular, especially in fine weather, so try to schedule your visit during the week rather than on a crowded weekend afternoon. A free guided **Highlights Tour** is offered Tuesday through Friday at 3pm and Sunday at noon; gallery talks are also a regular feature. Additionally, **Garden Tours** are offered Tuesdays through Sundays at 1pm in May, June, September, and October; lectures and other special programming is always on Sundays from noon to 2pm; and medieval music concerts are regularly held in the stunning 12th-century Spanish chapel. For an extra-special experience, you may want to plan your visit around one.

At the north end of Fort Tryon Park. © **212/923-3700.** www.metmuseum.org. Suggested admission (includes same-day entrance to the Metropolitan Museum of Art) $10 adults, $5 seniors and students, free for children under 12. Nov–Feb Tues–Sun 9:30am–4:45pm; Mar–Oct Tues–Sun 9:30am–5:15pm. Subway: A to 190th St., then a 10-min. walk north along Margaret Corbin Dr., or pick up the M4 bus at the station (1 stop to Cloisters). Bus: M4 Madison Ave. (Fort Tryon Park–The Cloisters).

Cooper-Hewitt National Design Museum ★ Part of the Smithsonian Institution, the Cooper-Hewitt is housed in the Carnegie Mansion, built by steel magnate Andrew Carnegie in 1901 and renovated to the tune of $20 million in 1996. Some 11,000 square feet (1,022 sq. m) of gallery space is devoted to changing exhibits that are invariably well conceived, engaging, and educational. Shows are both historic and contemporary in nature, and topics range from "The Work of Charles and Ray Eames: A Legacy of Invention" to "Russell Wright: Creating American Lifestyle" to "The Architecture of Reassurance: Designing the Disney Theme Parks." Many installations are drawn from the museum's own vast collection of industrial design, drawings, textiles, wall coverings, books, and prints. Exhibitions scheduled for late 2002–early 2003 include "New Hotels for Global Nomads."

On your way in, note the fabulous Art Nouveau–style copper-and-glass canopy above the entrance. And be sure to visit the garden, ringed with Central Park benches from various eras.

2 E. 91st St. (at Fifth Ave.). © **212/849-8400.** www.si.edu/ndm. Admission $8 adults, $5 seniors and students, free for children under 12; free to all Tues 5–9pm. Tues 10am–9pm; Wed–Sat 10am–5pm; Sun noon–5pm. Subway: 4, 5, 6 to 86th St.

Dahesh Museum of Art If you consider yourself a classicist, this small museum is for you. It's dedicated to 19th- and early-20th-century European academic art, a continuation of Renaissance, baroque, and rococo traditions that were overshadowed by the arrival of Impressionism on the art scene. (If you're not familiar with this academic school, expect lots of painstaking renditions of historical subjects and pastoral life.) Artists represented include Jean-Léon Gérôme, Lord Leighton, and Edwin Long, whose *Love's Labour Lost* is a cornerstone of the permanent collection. Look for "Against the Modern: Dagnan-Bouveret and the Transformation of the Academic Tradition" through December 7, 2002.

601 Fifth Ave. (btwn 48th and 49th sts.), 2nd floor. © **212/759-0606.** www.daheshmuseum.org. Free admission. Tues–Sat 11am–6pm. Subway: B, D, F, V to 47–50th sts./Rockefeller Center.

Dia Center for the Arts Housed in a series of renovated warehouse buildings on the artsy fringe of Chelsea, this contemporary art institution focuses on interdisciplinary art and criticism through a rotating calendar of large-scale, single-artist exhibitions by forward-thinking modern artists with big ideas. Basically, if you think the mainstream museums are too conventional, predictable, and just, well, *small,* this is the place for you. The main space is the four-story warehouse at 548 West 22nd, where exhibits are housed on four floors. The exhibition schedule for late 2002–03 had not been announced at press time, but expect the unexpected, such as these recent shows: *Knots + Surfaces,* a multiprojection video installation by L.A. artist Diana Thater that ran in 2002 and had something intriguing to do with the intersection of mathematics and the dance of the honeybee; Alfred Jensen's heavily geometrical paintings based on his cosmological theories, modern physics, and the ancient Chinese and Maya calendars; or Bruce Neumann's *Mapping the Studio I (Fat Chance John Cage),* another multiprojection exhibit chronicling the nocturnal activities of the artist's cat with various mice.

Call or check the website for the current exhibition schedule, as well as commissioned-artist Web projects, lectures, poetry readings, screenings, and other events of an avant-garde nature. If you like what you see, inquire about additional exhibition spaces in SoHo and TriBeCa that may be open.

545–548 W. 22nd St. (btwn Tenth and Eleventh aves.). ✆ **212/989-5566.** www.diacenter.org. Admission $6 adults, $3 students and seniors. Wed–Sat noon–6pm (hours may vary, so call ahead). Subway: C, E to 23rd St.

El Museo del Barrio What started in 1969 with a small display in a local school classroom in East Harlem is today the only museum in America dedicated to Puerto Rican, Caribbean, and Latin American art. The northernmost Museum Mile institution has a permanent exhibit ranging from pre-Columbian artifacts to photographic art and video. The display of *santos de palo,* wood-carved religious figurines, is especially worth noting, as is "Taíno, Ancient Voyagers of the Caribbean," dedicated to the active, highly developed cultures that Columbus encountered when he landed in the "New World." The well-curated changing exhibitions tend to focus on 20th-century artists and contemporary subjects.

1230 Fifth Ave. (at 104th St.). ✆ **212/831-7272.** www.elmuseo.org. Suggested admission $5 adults, $3 seniors and students, free for children under 12. Wed–Sun 11am–5pm. Subway: 6 to 103rd St.

Federal Hall National Memorial Fronted by 32-foot (9.5m) fluted marble Doric columns, this imposing 1842 neoclassical temple is most famous for what happened here while the site was occupied by the 18th-century City Hall, later called Federal Hall and the seat of New York's colonial government. Peter Zenger, publisher of the outspoken *Weekly Journal,* stood trial in 1735 for "seditious libel" against Royal Governor William Cosby. Defended brilliantly by Alexander Hamilton, Zenger was eventually acquitted, based on the grounds that anything you printed that was true, even if it wasn't very nice, couldn't be construed as libel. The case set the precedent for freedom of the press, later guaranteed in the Bill of Rights, which was drafted and signed inside this building. New York's first major rebellion against British authority also occurred here, when the Stamp Act Congress met in 1765 to protest King George III's policy of "taxation without representation." J.Q.A. Ward's 1883 statue of George Washington on the steps commemorates the spot of the first presidential inauguration, in 1789. Congress met here after the revolution, when New York was briefly the nation's capital.

Exhibits within elucidate these events and other aspects of American history. Call ahead if you'd like to hook up with one of the 20- to 30-minute guided tours (I recommend it), which usually take place between 12:30 and 3:30pm.

26 Wall St. (at Nassau St.). ✆ **212/825-6888.** www.nps.gov/feha. Free admission. Mon–Fri 9am–5pm. Subway: 4, 5 to Wall St.

Forbes Magazine Galleries *Kids* The late publishing magnate Malcolm Forbes may have been a self-described "capitalist tool," but he had esoteric, almost childish, tastes. He also had the altruism to share what he collected with the public for free. With its model boats, toy soldiers, old Monopoly game sets, quirky collection of trophies, miniature rooms, presidential memorabilia, and jewel-encrusted Fabergé eggs, this is a great little museum for both you and the kids. Personal anecdotes explain why certain objects attracted Forbes's attention and turn the collection into an oddly interesting biographical portrait. The Picture and Autograph Galleries, where the exhibits include Abraham Lincoln's Emancipation Proclamation, is also intriguing.

62 Fifth Ave. (at 12th St.). ✆ **212/206-5548.** www.forbes.com/forbescollection. Free admission. Tues–Wed and Fri–Sat 10am–4pm (hours vary, so call ahead). Subway: L, N, R, 4, 5, 6 to 14th St./Union Sq.

Fraunces Tavern Museum This petite museum of early American history and culture is most famous for the Long Room, in which George Washington made his historic farewell to his soldiers at the end of the American Revolution, but it also houses rotating exhibits such as "Colonists, Revolutionaries, Builders: Freemasons in America." Built in 1907, this exact replica of the original 1717 tavern is nevertheless a wonderful example of New York's pre-Revolutionary architectural style.

One of the best ways to experience Fraunces Tavern is to dine there, just like George Washington did. After a million-dollar renovation, the restaurant reopened in 2001, and serves lunch and dinner daily except Sunday. The tavern has been painstakingly recreated and the fare significantly upscaled since the Revolutionary War days—as have entree prices (lunch $18–$20, dinner $18–$30). The fare is mainly American, of course, but the menu includes some West Indian dishes in honor of 18th-century restaurateur Samuel Fraunces. You can also stop by to soak in the historic ambience over a cocktail in the bar.

54 Pearl St. (near Broad St.). ✆ **212/425-1778,** or 212/968-1776 for restaurant reservations. www.fraunces tavernmuseum.org. Admission $3 adults, $2 students and seniors, free for children under 6. Mon–Fri 10am–4:45pm. Restaurant open Mon–Fri 6:30am–9:30pm (last seating); Sat noon–5pm (tavern/bar area only) and 5–9:30pm (dining room). Subway: N, R to Whitehall St.; 2, 3 to Wall St.; 4, 5 to Bowling Green.

The Frick Collection ★★ Henry Clay Frick could afford to be an avid collector of European art after amassing a fortune as a pioneer in the coke and steel industries at the turn of the 20th century. To house his treasures and himself, he hired architects Carrère & Hastings to build this 18th-century French-style mansion (1914), one of the most beautiful remaining on Fifth Avenue.

Most appealing about the Frick is its intimate size and setting. This is a living testament to New York's vanished Gilded Age—the interior still feels like a private home (albeit a really, really rich guy's home) graced with beautiful paintings, rather than a museum. Come here to see the classics by some of the world's most famous painters: Titian, Bellini, Rembrandt, Turner, Vermeer, El Greco, and Goya, to name only a few. A highlight of the collection is the **Fragonard Room,** graced with the sensual rococo series *The Progress of Love.* The portrait of Montesquieu by Whistler is also stunning. Sculpture, furniture, Chinese vases, and

French enamels complement the paintings and round out the collection. Included in the price of admission, the AcousticGuide audio tour is particularly useful because it allows you to follow your own path rather than a proscribed route. A free 22-minute video presentation is screened in the Music Room every half hour from 10am to 4:30pm (from 1:30 on Sun); starting with this helps to set the tone for what you'll see.

In addition to the permanent collection, the Frick regularly mounts small, well-focused temporary exhibitions. Fall 2002 visitors can enjoy "Poussin, Claude, and Their World: 17th-Century French Drawings from the Ecole Nationale des Beaux-Arts, Paris" through November 2002. Additionally, Andrea Mantegna's *Descent into Limbo* (1468), a magnificent example of Italian Renaissance painting, will be on display in the Enamel Room through August 1, 2003.

Free **chamber music concerts** are held twice a month, generally every other Sunday at 5pm in fall and winter, select Thursdays at 5:45pm in warm weather, as well as once-a-month **lectures,** select Wednesdays at 5:30pm; call or visit the website for the current schedule and ticket information.

1 E. 70th St. (at Fifth Ave.). ✆ **212/288-0700.** www.frick.org. Admission $10 adults, $5 seniors and students. Children under 10 not admitted; children under 16 must be accompanied by an adult. Tues–Sat 10am–6pm; Sun 1–6pm. Closed all major holidays. Subway: 6 to 68th St./Hunter College.

International Center of Photography ★ *Finds* In late 2000, the ICP—one of the world's premier educators, collectors, and exhibitors of photographic art—relocated its museum galleries from its original Museum Mile location to this expanded Midtown facility. The state-of-the-art gallery space is ideal for viewing rotating exhibitions of the museum's 50,000-plus prints as well as visiting shows. The emphasis is on contemporary photographic works, but historically important photographers aren't ignored. A must on any photography buff's list.

1133 Sixth Ave. (at 43rd St.). ✆ **212/857-0000.** www.icp.org. Admission $9 adults, $6 seniors and students. Tues–Thurs 10am–5pm; Fri 10am–8pm; Sat–Sun 10am–6pm. Subway: B, D, F, V to 42nd St.

***Intrepid* Sea-Air-Space Museum** ★★ *Kids* The most astonishing thing about the aircraft carrier USS *Intrepid* is how it can be simultaneously so big and so small. It's a few football fields long, weights 40,000 tons, holds 40 aircraft, and sometimes doubles as a ballroom for society functions. But stand there and think about landing an A-12 jet on the deck and suddenly it's minuscule. Furthermore, in the narrow passageways below, you'll find it isn't quite the roomiest of vessels. Now a National Historic Landmark, the exhibit also includes the naval destroyer USS *Edson,* and the submarine USS *Growler,* the only intact strategic missile submarine open to the public anywhere in the world, as well as a collection of vintage and modern aircraft, including the A-12 Blackbird, the world's fastest spy plane.

Kids just love this place. They, and you, can climb inside a replica Revolutionary War submarine, sit in an A-6 Intruder cockpit, and follow the progress of America's astronauts as they work in space. There are even navy flight simulators—including a "Fly with the Blue Angels" program—for educational thrill rides in the Technologies Hall. Look for family-oriented activities and events at least one Saturday a month.

New in 2002 is "All Hands on Deck," which teaches both children and adults how things work on ships, plus a new AH-1 Cobra attack helicopter. The action-packed *Intrepid Wings* shows aircraft carrier take-offs and recoveries in the new Allison and Howard Lutnick Theater; the film runs continuously throughout the day. The exhibit "Remembering 9-11" recalls those lost, both civilians and rescuers. The grand $5.5 million visitor center, which opened in 2000, makes for an impressive entrance, and the massive museum store is well stocked; goods include NYPD and FDNY logo gear. But dress warmly for a winter visit—it's almost impossible to heat an aircraft carrier.

Pier 86 (W. 46th St. at Twelfth Ave.). ✆ **212/245-0072.** www.intrepidmuseum.org. Admission $13 adults, $9 veterans, seniors, and students, $6 children 6–11, $2 children 2–5. $5 extra for flight simulator rides. Apr–Sept Mon–Fri 10am–5pm, Sat–Sun 10am–7pm; Oct–Mar Tues–Sun 10am–5pm. Last admission 1 hr. before closing. Subway: A, C, E to 42nd St./Port Authority. Bus: M42 crosstown.

Japan Society The Japan Society was founded in 1907 to foster mutual cultural understanding and enlightened relations between east and west, and does so admirably. The society's U.S. headquarters, housed in a striking modern building by Junzo Yoshimuro (1971), mounts highly regarded exhibits of Japanese art in a serene gallery. Changing displays have included "Japanese Theater in the World" and "Frank Lloyd Wright and the Art of Japan: The Architect's Other Passion"; upcoming in spring 2003 is "Early Buddhist Art from Korea and Japan, 6th–9th Centuries." The tranquil, elegant building also features a bamboo pond garden as well as a 278-seat auditorium that hosts a wide variety of performances, from contemporary Japanese dance and music to *butoh* dance and kabuki. The extensive program schedule also features lectures, gallery talks, films, and classes throughout the year; call or check the website for current programming.

333 E. 47th St. (btwn First and Second aves.). ✆ **212/832-1155.** www.japansociety.org. Admission $5 adults, $3 seniors and students. Gallery: Tues–Fri 11am–6pm; Sat–Sun 11am–5pm. Subway: E, V to Lexington Ave.; 6 to 51st St.

The Jewish Museum Housed in a Gothic-style mansion renovated in 1993 by AIA Gold Medal winner Kevin Roche, this wonderful museum now has the world-class space it deserves to showcase its remarkable collections, which chronicle 4,000 years of Jewish history. The two-floor permanent exhibit, "Culture and Continuity: The Jewish Journey," tells the story of the Jewish experience from ancient times through today, and is the museum's centerpiece. Artifacts include daily objects that might have served the authors of the books of Genesis, Psalms, and Job, and a great assemblage of intricate Torahs. A wonderful collection of classic TV and radio programs is available for viewing through the Goodkind Resource Center (as any fan of television's Golden Age knows, its finest comic moments were Jewish comedy). The scope of the exhibit is phenomenal, and its story an enlightening—and intense—one. A new random-access audio guide is geared to families (free with admission). In addition to the in-house shop, don't miss the Jewish Museum Design Shop, housed in the adjacent brownstone.

1109 Fifth Ave. (at 92nd St.). ✆ **212/423-3200.** www.thejewishmuseum.org. Admission $8 adults, $5.50 seniors and students, free for children under 12; pay what you wish Thurs 5–8pm. Check website for special online admission discounts (50% off at press time). Sun 10am–5:45pm; Mon–Wed 11am–5:45pm; Thurs 11am–8pm; Fri 11am–3pm. Subway: 4, 5 to 86th St.; 6 to 96th St.

Lower East Side Tenement Museum ★ This museum is the first-ever National Trust for Historic Preservation site that was not the home of someone rich or famous. It's something quite different: A five-story tenement that 10,000 people from 25 countries called home between 1863 and 1935—people who had come to the United States looking for the American dream and made 97 Orchard St. their first stop. The tenement museum tells the story of the great immigration boom of the late 19th and early 20th centuries, when the Lower East Side was considered the "Gateway to America." A visit here makes a good follow-up to an Ellis Island trip—what happened to all the people who passed through that famous way station?

The only way to see the museum is by guided tour. Two primary tenement tours, held on all open days and lasting an hour, offer a satisfying exploration of the museum: **Piecing It Together: Immigrants in the Garment Industry,** which focuses on the restored apartment and the lives of its turn-of-the-century tenants, an immigrant Jewish family named Levine from Poland; and **Getting By: Weathering the Great Depressions of 1873 and 1929,** featuring the homes of the German-Jewish Gumpertz family and the Sicilian-Catholic Baldizzi family, respectively. A knowledgeable guide leads you into each dingy urban time capsule, where several apartments have been faithfully restored to their lived-in condition, and recounts the real-life stories of the families who occupied them in fascinating detail. You can pair them for an in-depth look at the museum, since the apartments and stories are so different; however, one tour serves as an excellent introduction if you don't want to invest an entire afternoon here.

These tours are not really for kids, however, who won't enjoy the serious tone and "don't touch" policy. Much better for them is the 45-minute, weekends-only **Confino Family Apartment** tour, an interactive living history program geared to families, which allows kids to converse with an interpreter who plays teenage immigrant Victoria Confino (ca. 1916); kids can also handle whatever they like in the apartment and even try on period clothes.

The hour-long **Streets Where We Lived** neighborhood heritage walking tour is also offered on weekends from April through December. Small permanent and rotating exhibits, including photos, videos, and a model tenement, are housed in the Visitors' Center and exhibition space in the tenement building at 97 Orchard St. Special tours and programs are sometimes on the schedule.

Tours are limited in number and sell out quickly, so it pays to buy tickets in advance, which you can do online, or over the phone by calling Ticketweb at ✆ **800/965-4827.** Note that the potential acquisition of a neighboring tenement at 99 Orchard St. may change programming, so confirm schedules.

Visitors' Center at 90 Orchard St. (at Broome St.). ✆ **212/431-0233.** www.tenement.org. Tenement and walking tours $9 adults, $7 seniors and students; Confino Apartment $8 adults, $6 seniors and students. Tenement tours depart every 40 minutes Tues–Fri 1–4pm; Sat–Sun every half hour 11am–4:45pm. Confino Apartment tour Sat–Sun hourly noon–3pm. Walking tour Apr–Dec Sat–Sun 1 and 2:30pm. Subway: F to Delancey St.; J, M, Z to Essex St.

Madame Tussaud's New York *Overrated* A branch of the famously garish London institution, this brand-new wax museum is just plain *overpriced.* Considering that you can still get into the Met for 10 bucks, admission to Madame Tussaud's should be $6 or $7, not $20—especially since you'll be in and out of here inside of 2 hours. Museum folks tout the five floors and 85,000 square feet (7,897 sq. m) of space, but there's not a heckuva lot here; the collection of high-profile wax figures is relatively small, numbering less than 200.

That said, not everybody wants to go to the Met, and if you don't mind shelling out, you'll likely enjoy yourself. Don't forget your camera, because fully half the fun is having yourself photographed along eerily lifelike replicas of famous figures ranging from Joan Rivers to Gandhi. (Whoopi Goldberg has deadpanned, "My wax portrait is so close to the real me that one of my husbands asked it for alimony.") Best is the "Opening Night Party," the first room you'll enter, in which a wide range of contemporary stars are arranged in such candid poses that it's sometimes hard to distinguish the real folks from the fakes; in fact, it's almost creepy. While most of the figures are excellent likenesses, a few are clearly off target (the wax Beatles win the "What Were They Thinking?" award). Despite the wealth of John Travoltas and Lenny Kravitzes and Woody Allens and Michael Jordans, I found my favorite figure to be a surprisingly handsome Napoléon; the rest of the bloody "Madame Tussaud's Story" exhibit is downright gruesome, however (she was a French Revolution–era death-mask sculptor), so skip it if you have little ones in tow.

An extra $2 buys you admission to a ridiculous 10-minute virtual-reality movie in a domed theater that's not even entertaining—the best thing about it is a fake "snowfall" at the end (actually some foamy shaving cream-like substance). I recommend taking a pass on it.

234 W. 42nd St. (btwn Seventh and Eighth aves.). ✆ **212/512-9600.** www.madame-tussauds.com. Admission $19.95 adults, $17.95 seniors, $15.95 children 4–12; $2 extra for "New York, New York" screening. Daily 10am–6pm (last ticket sales). Subway: 1, 2, 3, 7, 9, N, R, S to 42nd St./Times Sq.

Morgan Library ★★ *Finds* Here's an undiscovered New York treasure, boasting one of the world's most important collections of original manuscripts, rare books and bindings, master drawings, and personal writings. Among the remarkable artifacts on display under glass are stunning illuminated manuscripts (including Gutenberg bibles), a working draft of the U.S. Constitution bearing copious handwritten notes, Voltaire's personal household account books, and handwritten scores by the likes of Beethoven, Mozart, and Puccini. The collection of mostly 19th-century drawings—featuring works by Seurat, Degas, Rubens, and other great masters—have an excitement of immediacy about them that the artists' more well-known paintings often lack.

This rich repository originated as the private collection of turn-of-the-20th-century financier J. Pierpont Morgan and is housed in a landmark Renaissance-style palazzo building (1906) he commissioned from McKim, Mead & White to hold his masterpieces. Morgan's library and study are preserved virtually intact and are worth a look unto themselves for their landmarked architecture (particularly the rotunda) and richly detailed fittings.

The special exhibitions are particularly well chosen and curated; subjects can range from medieval bookbinding techniques to the literary genesis of the mystery novel and pulp fiction to a display of treasures from the royal tombs of Ur. A reading room is available by appointment, and an exceptional calendar of concerts, lectures, film screenings, gallery talks, and family tours can be found online.

29 E. 36th St. (at Madison Ave.). ✆ **212/685-0610.** www.morganlibrary.org. Admission $8 adults, $6 students and seniors, free for children 12 and under. Tues–Thurs 10:30am–5pm; Fri 10:30am–8pm; Sat 10:30am–6pm; Sun noon–6pm. Subway: 6 to 33rd St.

Mount Vernon Hotel Museum & Garden *Finds* It's a shock, a very pleasant one, to find such a little-known jewel on this otherwise thoroughly modern block. This rare survivor from the early American republic was built as a carriage house for Abigail Adams Smith, daughter of President John Adams, and her husband, William Stephens Smith, in 1799. It's been painstakingly restored by the Colonial Dames of America to its early 19th-century condition, when the house served as the Mount Vernon Hotel—a country hotel for bucolic overnights away from the city, if you can believe it. On a guide-led tour you can explore nine period rooms, outfitted in authentic Federal style, as well as the grounds, planted as a late 18th-century garden would be. An orientation center offers a scale model of the building as it looked in 1799 and screens a video on New York City in the early 19th century. Special events take place throughout the year.

421 E. 61st St. (btwn First and York aves.). ✆ **212/838-6878.** Admission $4 adults, $3 seniors, free for children under 12. Tues–Sun 11am–4pm (last tour 3:15pm). Closed Aug. Subway: N, R to Lexington Ave.; 4, 5, 6 to 59th St.

Museum of American Financial History Real money buffs (and who among us isn't?) may want to make a brief stop here. The exhibits housed in this petite Smithsonian-affiliate museum include numismatic and vintage ticker-tape displays; murals and photos depicting historic Wall Street scenes; and interactive financial news terminals, in partnership with CNNfn, so little bulls and bears can learn how to keep up with the market. Temporary installations have run the gamut from "Morgan," a chronicle of the lasting influence of J. Pierpont Morgan to "High Notes," an oddly compelling exhibit of high-denomination currency.

The **World of Finance Walking Tour** of the Financial District is offered Fridays at 10am; tickets are $15 for adults, $10 for students and seniors. Reservations are only required for parties of 6 or more, but call ahead and confirm to avoid disappointment. (The tour was suspended at press time but scheduled to resume in mid-2002.)

28 Broadway (just north of Bowling Green Park). ✆ **877/98-FINANCE,** 212/908-4110, or 212/908-4519. www.financialhistory.org. Admission $2. Tues–Sat 10am–4pm. Subway: 4, 5 to Bowling Green; J, M to Broad St.; 2, 3 to Wall St.

Museum of the City of New York A wide variety of objects—costumes, photographs, prints, maps, dioramas, and memorabilia—trace the history of New York City from its beginnings as a humble Dutch colony in the 16th century to its present-day prominence. Two outstanding permanent exhibits are the re-creation of John D. Rockefeller's master bedroom and dressing room, and the space devoted to "Broadway!" a history of New York theater. Kids will love "New York Toy Stories," a permanent exhibit showcasing toys and dolls owned and adored by centuries of New York children. The permanent "Painting the Town: Cityscapes of New York" explores the changing cityscape from 1809 to 1997, and carries new profundity in the wake of 9/11. Check for a schedule of other exhibits relating to the terrorist attack, curated as part of the museum's Project September 11.

1220 Fifth Ave. (at 103rd St.). ✆ **212/534-1672.** www.mcny.org. Suggested admission $7 adults, $4 seniors, students, and children, $12 families. Wed–Sat 10am–5pm; Sun noon–5pm. Subway: 6 to 103rd St.

Museum of Jewish Heritage—A Living Memorial to the Holocaust ★ Located in the south end of Battery Park City, the Museum of Jewish Heritage occupies a strikingly spare six-sided building designed by award-winning architect Kevin Roche, with a six-tier roof alluding to the Star of David and the 6 million murdered in the Holocaust. The permanent exhibits—"Jewish Life a Century Ago," "The War Against the Jews," and "Jewish Renewal"—recount the daily prewar lives, the unforgettable horror that destroyed them, and the tenacious renewal experienced by European and immigrant Jews in the years from the late 19th century to the present. The museum's power derives from the way it tells that story: through the objects, photographs, documents, and, most poignantly, through the videotaped testimonies of Holocaust victims, survivors, and their families, all chronicled by Steven Spielberg's Survivors of the Shoah Visual History Foundation. Thursday evenings are dedicated to panel discussions, performances, and music, while Sundays are dedicated to family programs and workshops; a film series is also a regular part of the calendar. A new East

Wing that will triple the exhibition and events space and add a Family History Center is slated for completion in fall 2003.

While advance tickets are not usually necessary, you may want to purchase them to guarantee admission; call ✆ **212/945-0039.** Audio tours narrated by Meryl Streep and Itzhak Perlman are available at the museum for an additional $5.

18 First Place (at Battery Place), Battery Park City. ✆ **212/509-6130.** www.mjhnyc.org. Admission $7 adults, $5 seniors and students, free for children under 5. Check website for $2-off admission coupon (available at press time). Sun–Wed 10am–5:45pm; Thurs 9am–8pm; Fri and eves of Jewish holidays 10am–3pm. Subway: 4, 5 to Bowling Green.

Museum of Television & Radio If you can resist the allure of this museum, I'd wager you've spent the last 70 years in a bubble. You can watch and hear all the great personalities of TV and radio—from Uncle Miltie to Johnny Carson to Jerry Seinfeld—at a private console (available for 2 hr.). And you can also conduct computer searches to pick out the great moments of history, viewing almost anything that made its way onto the airwaves, from the Beatles' first appearance on *The Ed Sullivan Show* to the crumbling of the Berlin Wall (the collection consists of 75,000 programs and commercials). Selected programs are also presented in two theaters and two screening rooms, which can range from "Barbra Streisand: The Television Performances" to little-seen Monty Python episodes.

25 W. 52nd St. (btwn Fifth and Sixth aves.). ✆ **212/621-6800** or 212/621-6600. www.mtr.org. Admission $6 adults, $4 seniors and students, $3 children under 13. Tues–Sun noon–6pm (Thurs until 8pm, Fri theater programs until 9pm). Subway: B, D, F, V to 47–50th sts./Rockefeller Center; E, V to 53rd St.

National Academy of Design Founded in 1825 and housed in a landmarked beaux arts town house, the National Academy is one of the oldest art institutions in the country and is dedicated to preserving the academic tradition. There are three components: a fine arts school; an honorary professional association of artists; and a museum, which mounts regular exhibits drawn from its large collection on such themes as "Art in the Age of Queen Victoria" and "The Watercolors of Charles Hawthorne." The Annual Exhibition is the nation's oldest continuing juried show.

1083 Fifth Ave. (btwn 89th and 90th sts.). ✆ **212/369-4880.** www.nationalacademy.org. Admission $8 adults, $4.50 seniors, $5 students. Wed–Thurs noon–5pm; Fri 10am–6pm; Sat–Sun 10am–5pm. Subway: 4, 5, 6, to 86th St.

National Museum of the American Indian, George Gustav Heye Center This impressive collection represents the Smithsonian Institution's Native People holdings, the oldest collection of its kind in the country. It's housed in New York only until its new home on the Mall in Washington, D.C., is completed in 2004. Until then, enjoy items spanning more than 10,000 years of native heritage, collected a century ago mainly by New York banking millionaire George Gustav Heye. About 70% of the collection is dedicated to the natives of North America and Hawaii; the rest represents the cultures of Mexico and Central and South America. There's a wealth of material here, but it's not as well organized as it could be. The museum also hosts temporary themed exhibitions and interpretive programs plus free storytelling, music, and dance presentations.

The museum is housed in the beautiful 1907 beaux arts **U.S. Customs House** ★, designed by Cass Gilbert and a National Historic Landmark that's worth a look in its own right. The giant statues lining the front of this granite 1907 structure personify *Asia* (pondering philosophically), *America* (bright-eyed and bushy-tailed), *Europe* (decadent, whose time has passed), and *Africa* (sleeping), and were carved by Daniel Chester French (of Lincoln Memorial fame).

Art for Art's Sake: The Gallery Scene

Manhattan has more than 500 private art galleries, selling everything from old masters to tomorrow's news. Galleries are open free to the public, generally Tuesday through Saturday from 10am to 6pm. Saturday afternoon gallery hopping, in particular, is a favorite pastime—nobody will expect you to buy, so don't worry.

The best way to winnow down your choices is by perusing the "Art Guide" in the Friday weekend section of the ***New York Times,*** or in the back of the Sunday "Arts & Leisure" section; the "Cue" section at the back of the weekly ***New York*** magazine, which I find to be particularly descriptive and user-friendly; the Art section in the weekly ***Time Out New York;*** or the ***New Yorker***'s weekly "Goings on About Town" section. You can also find the latest exhibition listings online at **www.nymetro.com**, whose "Arts" page gives you full access to *New York* magazine's Cue listings; **www.newyork.citysearch.com** (click on "Arts"), **www.artnet.com**, and **www.galleryguide.org**. An excellent source—more for practicals on the galleries and the artists and genres they represent rather than current shows—is **www.artincontext.org**. The ***Gallery Guide*** is available at most galleries around town.

I suggest picking a gallery or a show in a neighborhood that seems to suit your taste, and just start browsing from there. Be aware that my list below doesn't even begin to scratch the surface. There are many, many more galleries in each neighborhood, as well as smaller concentrations of galleries in areas like the East Village, TriBeCa, and Brooklyn (check the Art in Context site).

Keep in mind that uptown galleries tend to be more traditional and exclusive-feeling, downtown galleries more high-ticket contemporary, and far west Chelsea galleries the most cutting edge. Museum-quality works dominate uptown, while raw talent and emerging artists are most common in west Chelsea. But there are constant surprises in all neighborhoods.

UPTOWN Uptown galleries are clustered in and around the glamorous crossroads of Fifth Avenue and 57th Street as well as on and off stylish Madison Avenue in the 60s, 70s, and 80s. Unlike their upstart Chelsea and SoHo counterparts, these blue-chip galleries maintain a quiet white-glove demeanor. They include **Hirschl & Adler,** 21 E. 70th St. (© 212/535-8810; www.hirschlandadler.com), for 18th- to 20th-century European and American painting and decorative arts; art-world powerhouses **Gagosian Gallery,** 980 Madison Ave. (© 212/744-2313; www.gagosian.com), and **PaceWildenstein,** 32 E. 57th St. (© 212/421-3292), whose focus is on classic modernism, representing such artists as Jim Dine, Barbara Hepworth, and Claes Oldenburg; **Richard Gray Gallery,** 1018 Madison Ave., 4th floor (© 212/472-8787; www.richardgraygallery.com), featuring American and European contemporary works, with artists ranging from Joan Miró to David Hockney; **Knoedler & Company,** 19 E. 70th St. (© 212/794-0550; www.knoedlergallery.com), specializing in the New York school and representing such contemporary artists as Helen Frankenthaler, Nancy Graves, and Frank Stella; the

Margo Feiden Galleries, 699 Madison Ave. (© 212/677-5330; www.alhirschfeld.com), the sole authorized representative of the works of master ink caricaturist Al Hirschfeld; **James Cohan Gallery,** 41 W. 57th St. (© 212/755-7171; www.jamescohan.com), particularly strong in modern photography; **Mary Boone Gallery,** 745 Fifth Ave. (© 212/752-2929), known for success with such artists as Ross Bleckner and Nancy Ellison; and **Richard L. Feigen & Co.,** 34 E. 69th St. (© 212/628-0700; www.rlfeigen.com), and **Wildenstein,** the classical big brother of PaceWildenstein, 19 E. 64th St. (© 212/879-0500; www.wildenstein.com), both specializing in big-ticket works: old masters, Impressionism, and Renaissance paintings and drawings.

CHELSEA The area in the West 20s between Tenth and Eleventh avenues is home to the avant-garde of today's New York art scene, with West 26th serving as the unofficial "gallery row." Most galleries are not in storefronts but in the large spaces of multistory former garages and warehouses. Galleries worth seeking out include **Paula Cooper,** 534 W. 21st St. (© 212/255-1105), a heavyweight in the modern art world specializing in conceptual and minimal art; **George Billis Gallery,** 526 W. 26th St., 9F (© 212/645-2621; www.georgebillis.com), who shows works by talented emerging artists **Barbara Gladstone Gallery,** 515 W. 24th St. (© 212/206-9300; www.gladstonegallery.com); uptown powerhouse **Gagosian Gallery,** 555 W. 24th St. (© 212/741-1111; www.gagosian.com), which shows such major modern artists as Richard Serra and Julian Schnabel; **Feigen Contemporary,** 535 W. 20th St. (© 212/929-0500), the modern counterpart to the uptown Old Masters gallery; **Cheim & Read,** 547 W. 25th St. (© 212/242-7727), which often shows works by such high-profile pop artists as Diane Arbus and Robert Mapplethorpe; **DCA Gallery,** 525 W. 22nd St. (© 212/255-5511; www.dcagallery. com), specializing in contemporary Danish artists; and **Alexander and Bonin,** 132 Tenth Ave. (© 212/367-7474; www.alexanderandbonin. com), which mounts excellent solo exhibitions.

DOWNTOWN SoHo remains colorful, if less edgy than it used to be, with the action centered around West Broadway and encroaching onto the edge of Chinatown of late. Start with **Bronwyn Keenan,** 3 Crosby St. (© 212/431-5083), who's known for a keen eye for spotting emerging talent; **Peter Blum Gallery,** 99 Wooster St. (© 212/343-0441), who showcased the divine Kim Sooja, a Korean artist who uses traditional Korean bedcovers to comment on the promise of wedded bliss, in early 2002; **Lehmann Maupin,** 39 Greene St. (© 212/965-0753), whose exhibitions run the gamut from young unknowns to contemporary masters like Ross Bleckner; **O. K. Harris,** 383 W. Broadway (© 212/431-3600; www.okharris.com), which shows a wide and fascinating variety of contemporary painting, sculpture, and photography; and **Louis K. Meisel,** 141 Prince St. (© 212/677-1340; www.meiselgallery.com), specializing in photorealism and American pinup art (yep, Petty and Vargas girls). In TriBeCa, try **Cheryl Hazan Arts Gallery,** 35 N. Moore St. (© 212/343-8964; www.cherylhazanarts.com), or **DFN Gallery,** 176 Franklin St. (© 212/334-3400; www.dfngallery.com), both of which focus on fresh and distinctive contemporary art.

The most interesting, if unintentional, sculptural statement—keeping in mind the building's current purpose—is the giant seated woman to the left of the entrance representing America and surrounded by references to Native America: Mayan pictographs adorning her throne, Quetzalcoatl under her foot, a shock of corn in her lap, and the generic plains Indian scouting out from over her shoulder. Inside, the airy oval rotunda designed by Spanish engineer Raphael Guastavino (see the listing for Guastavino's, in chapter 7) was frescoed by Reginald Marsh to glorify the shipping industry (and, by extension, the Customs office once housed here).

1 Bowling Green (btwn State and Whitehall sts.). ✆ **212/514-3700.** www.nmai.si.edu. Free admission. Daily 10am–5pm. Subway: 4, 5 to Bowling Green; N, R to Whitehall.

Neue Gallerie New York *Finds* This new museum is dedicated to German and Austrian art and design, with a particular focus on the early 20th century. Displayed on two floors, the collection features painting, works on paper, decorative arts, and other media from such artists as Klimt, Kokoschka, Kandinsky, Klee, and leaders of the Wiener Werkstätte decorative arts and Bauhaus applied arts movements such as Adolf Loos and Mies van der Rohe, respectively. Once occupied by Mrs. Cornelius Vanderbilt III, the impeccably restored, landmark-designated 1914 Carrèrre & Hastings building (they built the New York Public Library as well) is worth a look in itself. Cafe Sabarsky is modeled on a Viennese cafe, so museumgoers in need of a snack break can expect a fine linzer torte.

1048 Fifth Ave. (at 86th St.). ✆ **212/628-6200.** www.neuegalerie.org. Admission $10. Fri–Mon 11am–7pm. Subway: 4, 5, 6 to 86th St.

New Museum of Contemporary Art ★ With 33,000 square feet (3,066 sq. m) of space and the former curator of contemporary art at the Whitney as its director, the New Museum is now a prime contender on the museum scene. This contemporary arts museum has moved closer to the mainstream in recent years, but it's only a safety margin in from the edge as far as most of us are concerned. Expect adventurous and well-curated exhibitions. The 2003 exhibition calendar had not been announced at press time, but previous schedules have included "Portrait of the Lost Boys," New Zealander Jacqueline Fraser's moving narrative made of sumptuous fabric and fragile wire sculptures that examines the high incidence of suicide among teenage boys in New Zealand; the experimental film and slide projections of Brazilian artist Hélio Oiticica; Belgian artist Wim Devoye's *Cloaca,* a fascinating sculptural installation using an array of laboratory glassware, electric pumps, computer monitors, and plastic tubing to both scientifically and artistically replicate the organic function of the human digestive system. The **Zenith Media Lounge,** a digital and media arts technology space housing rotating installations, is free to the public.

583 Broadway (btwn Houston and Prince sts.). ✆ **212/219-1222.** www.newmuseum.org. Admission $6; $3 Thurs 6–8pm; free to visitors 18 and under. Tues–Wed and Fri–Sun noon–6pm (Zenith Media Lounge to 6:30pm); Thurs noon–8pm. Subway: N, R to Prince St.; F, S to Broadway/Lafayette St.

New York City Fire Museum ★ *Kids* Housed in a real three-story 1904 firehouse, the former quarters of FDNY Engine Co. 30, this museum houses one of the country's most extensive collections of fire-service memorabilia from the 18th century to the present. It is also the best place to pay tribute to the 343 heroic firefighters who lost their lives just blocks away in the World Trade Center disaster. Expect ongoing changing exhibits relating to the 9/11 disaster.

Other displays range from vintage fire marks to fire trucks (including the last-known example of a 1921 pumper) to the gear and tools of modern firefighters. Also look for the leather hoses, fireboats, and Currier & Ives prints, plus a new exhibit on fire safety and burn prevention especially geared to families. Best of all, real firefighters are almost always on hand to share stories and fire-safety information with kids. The retail store sells authorized FDNY logo wear and souvenirs. Call ahead for details on scheduling a guided tour.

278 Spring St. (btwn Varick and Hudson sts.). ✆ **212/691-1303.** www.nycfiremuseum.org. Admission $4 adults, $2 seniors and students, $1 children under 12. Tues–Sat 10am–5pm; Sun 10am–4pm. Subway: C, E to Spring St.

New-York Historical Society ★ Launched in 1804, the New-York Historical Society is a major repository of American history, culture, and art, with a special focus on New York and its broader cultural significance. The grand neoclassical edifice near the Museum of Natural History is finally emerged from the renovation tent. Now open on the fourth floor is the Henry Luce III Center for the Study of American Culture, a state-of-the-art study facility and gallery of fine and decorative arts, which displays more than 40,000 objects amassed over 200 years—including paintings, sculpture, Tiffany lamps, textiles, furniture, even carriages—that had previously been in storage for decades. Also look for paintings from Hudson River School artists Thomas Cole, Asher Durand, and Frederic Church, including Cole's five-part masterpiece, *The Course of Empire.* Of particular interest to scholars and ephemera buffs are the extensive Library Collections, which include books, manuscripts, maps, newspapers, photographs, and more documents chronicling the American experience. (An appointment may be necessary to view some or all of the Library Collections, so call ahead.)

Also of note are the society's wide-ranging temporary exhibits; a 2002 series of exhibits called "History Responds" were some of the best in the city dealing with the 9/11 terrorist attack and its aftermath. World Trade Center–related exhibits are likely to continue, so interested visitors should be sure to check the exhibition schedule.

An extensive, top-quality calendar of public programs runs the gamut from family story hours to Irving Berlin music nights to lectures by such luminaries as Ric Burns and Susan Sontag to expert-led walks through various Manhattan neighborhoods; call or check the website for the schedule.

2 W. 77th St. (at Central Park W.). ✆ **212/873-3400.** www.nyhistory.org. Admission $5 adults, $3 seniors and students, free for children 12 and under. Tues–Sun 10am–5pm. Subway: B, C to 81st St.; 1, 9 to 79th St.

Scandinavia House: The Nordic Center in America *Finds* Opened in October 2000, this brand-new center is dedicated to both the shared and unique cultures of Denmark, Finland, Iceland, Norway, and Sweden. Two floors of galleries and an outdoor sculpture terrace display rotating art and design exhibits that can range from "Scandia: Important Early Maps of the Northern Regions" to "Strictly Swedish: An Exhibition of Contemporary Design." The rest of the space, including the 168-seat Victor Borge Hall, is dedicated to a chock-full calendar of lectures, film screenings, music and drama performances, and scholarly presentations, all of a Nordic ilk. The exquisite modern building—sleekly designed to showcase Scandinavian materials and aesthetics—is worth a look in itself, especially if you're a modern architecture buff. Guided tours are offered Tuesdays and Thursdays at 2pm, and last a half hour; they're free, but reservations are recommended.

The shop is a riot of fine Scandinavian design, and the excellent AQ Cafe—an offshoot of the terrific Midtown restaurant Aquavit (see chapter 7)—serves up Swedish meatballs and other Scandinavian delicacies.

58 Park Ave. (btwn 37th and 38th sts.). ✆ **212/879-9779.** www.scandinaviahouse.org. Suggested admission to 3rd- and 4th-floor galleries $3, $2 seniors and students; free admission to other spaces. Exhibitions Tues–Sun noon–6pm; cafe Mon–Sat 10am–5pm; store Mon–Sat 10am–6pm. Subway: 6 to 33rd St.; 4, 5, 6, 7, S to 42nd St./Grand Central.

Schomburg Center for Research in Black Culture Arturo Alfonso Schomburg, a black Puerto Rican, set himself to accumulating materials about blacks in America, and his massive collection—one of the largest collections of African-American materials in the world—is now housed and preserved at this research branch of the New York Public Library. The Exhibition Hall, the Latimer/Edison Gallery, and the Reading Room host changing exhibits related to black culture, such as "Lest We Forget: The Triumph over Slavery" and "Masterpieces of African Motherhood." A rich calendar of talks and performing arts events is also part of the continuing program. Make an appointment for a guided tour so you can see the 1930s murals by Harlem Renaissance artist Aaron Douglas; it'll be worth your while. Academics and others interested in a more complete look at the center's holding can preview what's available online. Call to inquire about current exhibitions and information on tours and public programs.

515 Malcolm X Blvd. (Lenox Ave., btwn 135th and 136th sts.). ✆ **212/491-2200.** www.nypl.org. Free admission. Gallery: Mon–Sat 10am–6pm; Sun 1–5pm. Subway: 2, 3 to 135th St.

Skyscraper Museum Wowed by the sheer verticality in this town? Awed by the architectural marvel that is the high-rise? You're not alone. If you'd like to learn more about the technology, culture, and sheer muscle behind it all, seek out this formerly itinerant museum, moving into its first permanent home sometime in 2002 in a brand-new 38-story Skidmore, Owings & Merrill tower that also houses the brand-new Ritz-Carlton New York, Battery Park hotel. The new space comprises two galleries, one housing a permanent exhibition dedication to the evolution of Manhattan's commercial skyline, the other for changing shows. Committed to telling the multifaceted story of the multistory high-rise, the museum has always done a bang-up job, so you can expect them to shine once they settle in. Not all details were in place at this writing—including admission fees or an exact opening date—so call or check the website before you go.

2 West St., Battery Park City. ✆ **212/968-1961.** www.skyscraper.org. Subway: 4, 5 to Bowling Green.

South Street Seaport & Museum *Kids* Dating back to the 17th century, this landmark historic district on the East River encompasses 11 square blocks of historic buildings, a maritime museum, several piers, shops, and restaurants.

You can explore most of the Seaport on your own. It's a beautiful but somewhat odd place. The mainly 18th- and 19th-century buildings lining the cobbled streets and alleyways are impeccably restored but nevertheless have a theme-park air about them, no doubt due to the mall-familiar shops housed within. The Seaport's biggest tourist attraction is Pier 17, a historic barge converted into a mall, complete with food court and cheap jewelry kiosks.

Despite its rampant commercialism, the Seaport is well worth a look. There's a good amount of history to be discovered here, most of it around the **South Street Seaport Museum,** a fitting tribute to the sea commerce that once thrived here.

In addition to the galleries—which house paintings and prints, ship models, scrimshaw, and nautical designs, as well as frequently changing exhibitions—there are a number of historic ships berthed at the pier to explore, including the 1911 four-masted *Peking* and the 1893 Gloucester fishing schooner *Lettie G. Howard.* A few of the boats are living museums and restoration works in progress; the 1885 cargo schooner ***Pioneer*** (© **212/748-8786**) offers 2-hour public sails daily from early May through September. Tickets are $25 for adults, $15 for children 12 and under. If you'd rather keep those sea legs on dry land, the museum offers a number of guided walking tours; call or check **www.southstseaport.org** for details.

Even **Pier 17** has its merits. Head up to the third-level deck overlooking the East River, where the long wooden chairs will have you thinking about what it was like to cross the Atlantic on the *Normandie.* From this level you can see south to the Statue of Liberty, north to the Gothic majesty of the Brooklyn Bridge, and Brooklyn Heights on the opposite shore.

At the gateway to the Seaport, at Fulton and Water streets, is the ***Titanic* Memorial Lighthouse,** a monument to those who lost their lives when the ocean liner sank on April 15, 1912. It was erected overlooking the East River in 1913 and moved to this spot in 1968, just after the historic district was so designated.

A variety of events take place year-round, ranging from street performers to concerts to fireworks; check the website or dial © **212/SEA-PORT.**

At press time, the ticket booth at the Seaport corner of Fulton and South streets was the place to pick up free tickets to climb the **Ground Zero viewing platform,** at Broadway and Fulton streets. Whether this process will still be in place when you come to town was anybody's guess at this writing. For more on this process, see the World Trade Center site listing on p. 255.

At Water and South sts.; museum Visitors Center is at 12 Fulton St. © **212/748-8600** or 212/SEA-PORT. www.southstseaport.org or www.southstreetseaport.com. Museum admission $6 adults, $5 seniors, $4 students, $3 children. Museum: Apr–Sept Fri–Wed 10am–6pm, Thurs 10am–8pm; Oct–Mar Wed–Mon 10am–5pm. Subway: 2, 3, 4, 5 to Fulton St. (walk east, or downslope, on Fulton St. to Water St.).

Studio Museum in Harlem The small but lovely museum is devoted to presenting 19th- and 20th-century African-American art as well as 20th-century African and Caribbean art and traditional African art and artifacts. Rotating exhibitions are a big part of the museum's focus, such as "Smithsonian African-American Photography: The First 100 Years, 1842–1942;" the silkscreens and lithographs of Jacob Lawrence; and an annual exhibition of works by emerging artists as part of its Artists-in-Residence program. There's also a small sculpture garden, a good gift shop, and a full calendar of special events. A just-complete renovation and expansion has added 2,500 feet (750m) of gallery space, a cafe, and an auditorium, and also gave the much-needed face-lift to the formerly dour facade.

144 W. 125th St. (btwn Lenox Ave. and Adam Clayton Powell Blvd.). © **212/864-4500.** www.studiomuseuminharlem.org. Admission $5 adults, $3 seniors, $1 children under 12. Free to all first Sat of the month. Sun and Wed–Fri noon–6pm; Sat 10am–6pm. Subway: 2, 3 to 125th St.

Theodore Roosevelt Birthplace The designated National Historic Site is a faithful reconstruction, inside and out, on the same site of the brownstone where Theodore Roosevelt was born on October 27, 1858, and lived for his first

14 years. Period rooms appear as they did in Teddy's youth. The powder-blue parlor is in the rococo revival style popular at the time, the stately green dining room boasts horsehair-covered chairs, and the children's nursery has a window that leads to a small gymnasium built to help the frail young Teddy become more "bully." About 40% of the furniture is original (another 20% belonged to family members). There's also a collection of Roosevelt memorabilia.

28 E. 20th St. (btwn Broadway and Park Ave. S.). ✆ **212/260-1616.** www.nps.gov/thrb. Admission $3; free for visitors under 18 and National Park Passport holders. Hourly tours Mon–Fri 9am–5pm (tours 10am–4pm). Subway: N, R to Broadway/23rd St.; 6 to 23rd St.

Whitney Museum of American Art at Philip Morris This Midtown branch of the Whitney Museum of American Art (p. 253) features an airy sculpture court and a petite gallery that hosts changing exhibits, usually the works of living contemporary artists. Well worth peeking into if you happen to be in the neighborhood; I popped in recently and found a wonderful exhibition that juxtaposed the organic-inspired sculptures and drawings of Isamu Noguchi and Ellsworth Kelly. Free gallery talks are offered Wednesdays and Fridays at 1pm.

120 Park Ave. (at 42nd St., opposite Grand Central Terminal). ✆ **917/663-2453.** www.whitney.org. Free admission. Gallery: Mon–Wed and Fri 11am–6pm; Thurs 11am–7:30pm. Sculpture Court: Mon–Sat 7:30am–9:30pm; Sun 11am–7pm. Subway: S, 4, 5, 6, 7 to 42nd St./Grand Central.

4 Skyscrapers & Other Architectural Highlights

For details on the **Empire State Building,** see p. 245; **Grand Central Terminal,** p. 246; **Rockefeller Center,** p. 249; the **U.S. Customs House,** p. 267; and the **Brooklyn Bridge,** p. 243. You might also wish to check out "Places of Worship," later in this chapter, for treasures like **St. Patrick's Cathedral, Temple Emanu-El,** and the **Cathedral of St. John the Divine.**

In addition to checking out the landmarks below, architecture buffs may also want to seek out these notable buildings: The **Lever House,** built in 1952 at 390 Park Ave., between 53rd and 54th streets, and the neighboring **Seagram Building** (1958), at 375 Park Ave., are the city's best examples of the form-follows-function, glass-and-steel International style, with the latter designed by master architect Mies van der Rohe himself. Also in Midtown East is the **Sony Building,** at 550 Madison Ave., designed in 1984 by Philip Johnson with a pretty rose-granite facade and a playful Chippendale-style top that puts it a cut above the rest on the block.

The Upper West Side is home to two of the city's prime examples of residential architecture. On Broadway, taking up the block between 73rd and 74th streets, is the **Ansonia,** looking for all the world like a flamboyant architectural wedding cake. This splendid beaux arts building has been home to the likes of Stravinsky, Toscanini, and Caruso, thanks to its virtually soundproof apartments. (It was also the spot where members of the Chicago White Sox plotted to throw the 1919 World Series, a year before Babe Ruth moved in after donning the New York Yankees' pinstripes.) Even more notable is the **Dakota,** at 72nd Street and Central Park West. Legend has it that the angular 1884 apartment house—accented with gables, dormers, and oriel windows that give it a brooding appeal—earned its name when its forward-thinking developer, Edward S. Clark, was teased by friends that he was building so far north of the city that he might as well be building in the Dakotas. The building's most famous resident, John Lennon, was gunned down outside the 72nd Street entrance on December 8, 1980; Yoko Ono still lives inside.

Harlem's Architectural Treasures

Originally conceived as a bucolic suburbia for 19th-century Manhattan's monied set, Harlem has always had more than its share of historic treasures. To find them, pay a call on the **Astor Row Houses,** 130th Street between Fifth and Lenox avenues, a fabulous series of 28 redbrick town houses built in the early 1880s by the Astor family and graced with wooden porches, generous yards, and ornamental ironwork.

Equally impressive is **Strivers' Row,** West 139th Street between Adam Clayton Powell Jr. and Frederick Douglass boulevards, where hardly a brick has changed among the gorgeous McKim, Mead & White neo-Italian Renaissance town houses since they were built in 1890. Once the original white owners had moved out, these lovely houses attracted the cream of Harlem, "strivers" like Eubie Blake and W. C. Handy.

Handsome brownstones, limestone townhouses, and row houses are sprinkled atop **Sugar Hill,** 145th to 155th streets, between St. Nicholas and Edgecombe avenues, named for the "sweet life" enjoyed by its residents. In the early 20th century, such prominent blacks as W. E. B. DuBois, Thurgood Marshall, and Roy Wilkins lived in the now-landmarked building at 409 Edgecombe Ave.

And if you're venturing uptown this far, don't miss the **Jumel Terrace Historic District,** west of St. Nicholas Avenue between 160th and 162nd streets. Of particular note is **Sylvan Terrace,** which feels more like an upstate Hudson River town than a part of Harlem—well worth seeking out for architecture lovers. A walk along it will lead you directly to the grand **Morris-Jumel Mansion,** which is open to the public for tours (see the "In Search of Historic Homes" box, below).

Chrysler Building ★★ Built as Chrysler Corporation headquarters in 1930 (they moved out decades ago), this is perhaps the 20th century's most romantic architectural achievement, especially at night, when the lights in its triangular openings play off its steely crown. As you admire its facade, be sure to note the gargoyles reaching out from the upper floors, looking for all the world like streamline–Gothic hood ornaments.

There's a fascinating tale behind this building. While it was under construction, its architect, William Van Alen, hid his final plans for the spire that now tops it. Working at a furious pace in the last days of construction, the workers assembled in secrecy the elegant pointy top—and then they raised it right through what people had assumed was going to be the roof, and for a brief moment it was the world's tallest building (a distinction stolen by the Empire State Building only a few months later). Its exterior chrome sculptures are magnificent and spooky. The observation deck closed long ago, but you can visit its lavish ground-floor interior, which is Art Deco to the max. The ceiling mural depicting airplanes and other early marvels of the first decades of the 20th century evince the bright promise of technology. The elevators are works of art, masterfully covered in exotic woods (especially note the lotus-shaped marquetry on the doors).

405 Lexington Ave. (at 42nd St.). Subway: S, 4, 5, 6, 7 to 42nd St./Grand Central.

Flatiron Building This triangular masterpiece was one of the first skyscrapers. Its knife-blade wedge shape is the only way the building could fill the triangular property created by the intersection of Fifth Avenue and Broadway, and that happy coincidence created one of the city's most distinctive buildings. Built in 1902 and fronted with limestone and terra cotta (not iron), the Flatiron measures only 6 feet (2m) across at its narrow end. So called for its resemblance to the laundry appliance, it was originally named the Fuller Building, then later "Burnham's Folly" (since folks were certain that architect Daniel Burnham's 21-story structure would fall down). It didn't. There's no observation deck, and the building mainly houses publishing offices, but there are a few shops on the ground floor. The building's existence has served to name the neighborhood around it—the Flatiron District, home to a bevy of smart restaurants and shops.
175 Fifth Ave. (at 23rd St.). Subway: R to 23rd St.

New York Public Library ★★ The New York Public Library, adjacent to Bryant Park (p. 288) and designed by Carrère & Hastings (1911), is one of the country's finest examples of beaux arts architecture, a majestic structure of white Vermont marble with Corinthian columns and allegorical statues. Before climbing the broad flight of steps to the Fifth Avenue entrance, take note of the famous lion sculptures—*Fortitude* on the right, and *Patience* on the left—so dubbed by whip-smart former mayor Fiorello LaGuardia. At Christmastime they don natty wreaths to keep warm.

This library is actually the **Humanities and Social Sciences Library,** only one of the research libraries in the New York Public Library system. The interior is one of the finest in the city and features **Astor Hall,** with high arched marble ceilings and grand staircases. The stupendous **Main Reading Rooms** have now reopened after a massive restoration and modernization that both brought them back to their stately glory and moved them into the computer age (goodbye, card catalogs!).

Even if you don't stop in to peruse the periodicals, you may want to check out one of the excellent rotating **exhibitions;** look for "Drawings by Charles Addams: The Unnatural," "Urban Neighbors: Images of New York City Wildlife," and "New York Eats Out," tracing the history of the Big Apple as the world's ultimate restaurant city, among other exhibitions in late 2002–03. Call or check the site to see what's on while you're in town. There's also a full calendar of **lecture programs,** with past speakers ranging from Tom Stoppard to Cokie Roberts; popular speakers often sell out, so it's a good idea to purchase tickets in advance.
Fifth Ave. and 42nd St. ✆ **212/869-8089** (exhibits and events), or 212/661-7220 (library hours). www.nypl.org. Free admission to all exhibitions. Mon and Thurs–Sat 10am–6pm; Tues–Wed 11am–7:30pm. Subway: B, D, F, V to 42nd St.; S, 4, 5, 6, 7 to Grand Central/42nd St.

United Nations In the midst of New York City is this working monument to world peace. The U.N. headquarters occupies 18 acres of international territory—neither the city nor the United States has jurisdiction here—along the East River from 42nd to 48th streets. Designed by an international team of architects (led by American Wallace K. Harrison and including Le Corbusier) and finished in 1952, the complex along the East River weds the 39-story glass slab Secretariat with the free-form General Assembly on beautifully landscaped grounds donated by John D. Rockefeller Jr. One hundred eighty nations use the facilities to arbitrate worldwide disputes.

In Search of Historic Homes

The **Historic House Trust of New York City** preserves 19 houses, located in city parks in all five boroughs. Those particularly worth seeking out include the **Morris-Jumel Mansion** ★, in Harlem at 65 Jumel Terrace (at 160th St. east of St. Nicholas Ave.; ✆ **212/923-8008;** open Wed–Sun 10am–4pm), a grand colonial mansion built in the Palladian style (ca. 1765) and now Manhattan's oldest surviving house.

Built around 1764, the **Dyckman Farmhouse Museum,** farther uptown at 4881 Broadway (at 204th St.; ✆ **212/304-9422;** www.dyckman.org; Tues–Sun 11am–4pm), is the only Dutch Colonial farmhouse remaining in Manhattan, stoically and stylishly surviving the urban development that grew up around it.

The simple **Edgar Allan Poe Cottage,** 2460 Grand Concourse, at East Kingsbridge Road in the Bronx (✆ **718/881-8900;** www.bronxhistorical society.org; open Sat 10am–4pm, Sun 1–5pm), was the last home (1846–49) of the brilliant but troubled poet and author, who moved his wife here because he thought the "country air" would be good for her tuberculosis. The house is outfitted as a memorial to the writer, with period furnishings and exhibits on his life and times.

The **Merchant's House Museum** ★, 29 E. 4th St. between Lafayette Street and Bowery in NoHo (✆ **212/777-1089;** www.merchantshouse.com; open Thurs–Mon 1–5pm), is a rare jewel: a perfectly preserved 19th-century home, complete with intact interiors, whose last resident is said to be the inspiration for Catherine Sloper in Henry James's *Washington Square.*

Each of the 15 others also has its own fascinating story to tell, too. Admission to each house is generally no more than $3 ($5 at Merchant's House). A brochure listing the locations and touring details of all 19 of the historic homes is available by calling ✆ **212/360-8282;** recorded information is available at ✆ **212/360-3448.** You'll also find information online at **www.preserve.org/hht** or **nycparks.completeinet.net** (click on "Things to Do," then "Attractions").

Guided tours leave every half hour or so and last 45 minutes to an hour. Your guide will take you to the General Assembly Hall and the Security Council Chamber and introduce the history and activities of the United Nations and its related organizations. Along the tour you'll see donated objects and artwork, including charred artifacts that survived the atomic bombs at Hiroshima and Nagasaki, stained-glass windows by Chagall, a replica of the first *Sputnik,* and a colorful mosaic called *The Golden Rule,* based on a Norman Rockwell drawing, which was a gift from the United States in 1985.

If you take the time to wander the beautifully landscaped **grounds,** you'll be rewarded with lovely views and some surprises. The mammoth monument *Good Defeats Evil,* donated by the Soviet Union in 1990, fashioned a contemporary St. George slaying a dragon from parts of a Russian ballistic missile and an American Pershing missile.

At press time, the **Delegates' Dining Room** was closed to the public; feel free to call ✆ **212/963-7625** to see if it has reopened to visitors.

At First Ave. and 46th St. ✆ **212/963-8687.** www.un.org/tours. Guided tours $8.50 adults, $7 seniors, $6 high school and college students, $5 children 5–14 (children under 5 not permitted). Daily tours every half hour 9:30am–4:45pm; closed weekends Jan–Feb; a limited schedule may be in effect during the general debate (late Sept to mid-Oct). Subway: S, 4, 5, 6, 7 to 42nd St./Grand Central.

Woolworth Building ★ This soaring "Cathedral of Commerce" cost Frank W. Woolworth $13.5 million worth of nickels and dimes in 1913. Designed by Cass Gilbert, it was the world's tallest edifice until 1930, when it was surpassed by the Chrysler Building. At its opening, Pres. Woodrow Wilson pressed a button from the White House that illuminated the building's 80,000 electric light bulbs. The neo-Gothic architecture is rife with spires, gargoyles, flying buttresses, vaulted ceilings, 16th-century-style stone-as-lace traceries, castlelike turrets, and a churchlike interior. Housing financial institutions and high-tech companies, the grand tower is still dedicated to the almighty dollar.

Step into the lofty marble entrance arcade to view the gleaming mosaic Byzantine-style ceiling and gold-leafed neo-Gothic cornices. The corbels (carved figures under the crossbeams) in the lobby include whimsical portraits of the building's engineer Gunwald Aus measuring a girder (above the staircase to the left of the main door), Gilbert holding a miniature model of the building, and Woolworth counting coins (both above the left-hand corridor of elevators). Stand near the security guard's central podium and crane your neck for a glimpse at Paul Jennewein's murals of *Commerce* and *Labor,* half hidden up on the mezzanine. Cross Broadway for the best overview of the exterior.

233 Broadway (at Park Place, near City Hall Park). Subway: 2, 3 to Park Place; N, R to City Hall.

5 Places of Worship

New York has an incredible range of renowned religious institutions, notable for their history, architecture, and/or inspirational music. I've listed two of Harlem's premier gospel institutions below; if you would rather go to one of these gospel services in the company of a knowledgeable guide, see "Organized Sightseeing Tours," on p. 291 of this chapter. Additionally, if you would like to hear the rousing gospel of the four-time Grammy Award–winning **Brooklyn Tabernacle Choir** ★, see p. 305.

If you do plan to attend a gospel service, be prepared to stay for the entire 1½- to 2-hour service. It is impolite to exit early. (Services are extremely popular, so you'll find it just plain difficult to leave before the end, anyway.)

Abyssinian Baptist Church ★ The most famous of Harlem's more than 400 houses of worship is this Baptist church, founded downtown in 1808 by African-American and Ethiopian merchants. It was moved uptown to Harlem back in the 1920s by Adam Clayton Powell Sr., who built it into the largest Protestant congregation—white or black—in America. His son, Adam Clayton Powell Jr. (for whom the adjoining boulevard was named), carried on his tradition, and also became the first-ever black U.S. congressman. Abyssinian is now the domain of the fiery, activist-minded Rev. Calvin O. Butts, whom the chamber of commerce has declared a "Living Treasure." The Sunday-morning services—at 9 and 11am—offer a wonderful opportunity to experience the Harlem gospel tradition.

132 Odell Clark Place (W. 138th St., btwn Adam Clayton Powell Blvd. and Lenox Ave.). ✆ **212/862-7474.** www.abyssinian.org. Subway: 2, 3, B, C to 135th St.

Cathedral of St. John the Divine ★ The world's largest Gothic cathedral, St. John the Divine has been a work in progress since 1892. Its sheer size is amazing enough—a nave that stretches two football fields and a seating capacity of 5,000—but keep in mind that there is no steel structural support. The church is being built using traditional Gothic engineering; blocks of granite and limestone are carved out by master masons and their apprentices—which may explain why construction is still ongoing, more than 100 years after it began, with no end in sight. In fact, a December 2001 fire destroyed the north transept, which housed the gift shop. But this phoenix rose from the ashes quickly; the cathedral was reopened to visitors within a month, even though the scent of charred wood was still in the air and restoration will not be complete for months to come. That's precisely what makes this place so wonderful: Finishing isn't necessarily the point.

Though the seat of the Episcopal Diocese of New York, St. John's embraces an interfaith tradition. Internationalism is a theme found throughout the cathedral's iconography. Each chapel is dedicated to a different national, ethnic, or social group. The genocide memorial in the Missionary chapel—dedicated to the victims of the Ottoman Empire in Armenia (1915–23), of the Holocaust (1939–45), and in Bosnia-Herzegovina since 1992—moved me to tears, as did the FDNY memorial in the Labor chapel. Although it was originally conceived to honor 12 firefighters killed in 1966, hundreds of personal notecards and trinkets of remembrance have evolved it into a moving tribute to the 343 firefighting heroes killed on September 11, 2001.

You can explore the cathedral on your own, or on the **Public Tour,** offered 6 days a week; also inquire about periodic (usually twice-monthly) **Vertical Tours,** which takes you on a hike up the 11-flight circular staircase to the top, for spectacular views. St. John the Divine is also known for presenting outstanding workshops, musical events, and important speakers. The free **New Year's Eve concert** draws thousands of New Yorkers; so, too, does its annual **Feast of St. Francis** (Blessing of the Animals), held in early October (see the "New York City Calendar of Events" in chapter 3). Call for event information and tickets. To hear the incredible pipe organ in action, attend the weekly **Choral Evensong and Organ Meditation** service, which highlights one of the nation's most treasured pipe organs, Sundays at 6pm.

1047 Amsterdam Ave. (at 112th St.). ✆ **212/316-7540,** 212/932-7347 for tour information and reservations, 212/662-2133 for event information and tickets. www.stjohndivine.org. Suggested admission $2; tour $3; vertical tour $10. Mon–Sat 7am–6pm; Sun 7am–8pm. Tours offered Tues–Sat 11am; Sun 1pm. Worship services Mon–Sat 8 and 8:30am (morning prayer and holy Eucharist), 12:15pm, and 5:30pm (1st Thurs service 7:15am); Sun 8, 9, and 11am and 6pm; AIDS memorial service 4th Sat of the month at 1pm. Subway: B, C, 1, 9 to Cathedral Pkwy.

Mother A.M.E. Zion Church Another of Harlem's great gospel churches is this African Methodist Episcopal house of worship, the first black church to be founded in New York state. Established on John Street in Lower Manhattan in 1796, Mother A.M.E. was known as the "Freedom Church" for the central role it played in the Underground Railroad. Among the escaped slaves the church hid was Frederick Douglass; other famous congregants have included Sojurner Truth and Paul Robeson. Mother A.M.E. relocated to Harlem in 1914, and moved into this grand edifice in 1925. Rousing Sunday services are at 11am.

140–7 W. 137th St. (btwn Adam Clayton Powell Blvd. and Lenox Ave.). ✆ **212/234-1544.** www.motherafricanmethodistezchurch.com. Subway: 2, 3 or B, C to 135th St.

St. Patrick's Cathedral This incredible Gothic white-marble-and-stone structure is the largest Roman Catholic cathedral in the United States, as well as the seat of the Archdiocese of New York. Designed by James Renwick, begun in 1859, and consecrated in 1879, St. Patrick's wasn't completed until 1906. Strangely, Irish Catholics picked one of the city's WASPiest neighborhoods for St. Patrick's. After the death of the beloved John Cardinal O'Connor in 2000, the pope installed Bishop Edward Egan, whom he elevated to cardinal in 2001. The vast cathedral sits a congregation of 2,200; if you don't want to come for Mass, you can pop in between services to get a look at the impressive interior. The St. Michael and St. Louis altar came from Tiffany and Co. (also located here on Fifth Ave.), while the St. Elizabeth altar—honoring Mother Elizabeth Seton, the first American-born saint—was designed by Paolo Medici of Rome.

Fifth Ave. (btwn 50th and 51st sts.). © **212/753-2261.** www.ny-archdiocese.org/pastoral/cathedral_about.html. Free admission. Sun–Fri 7am–8:30pm; Sat 8am–8:30pm. Mass: Mon–Fri 7, 7:30, 8, and 8:30am, noon, and 12:30, 1, and 5:30pm; Sat 8 and 8:30am, noon, and 12:30 and 5:30pm; Sun 7, 8, 9, and 10:15am (Cardinal's mass), noon, and 1, 4, and 5:30pm; holy days 7, 7:30, 8, 8:30, 9, 11, and 11:30am, noon, and 12:30, 1, and 5:30 and 6:30pm. Subway: B, D, F, V to 47–50th sts./Rockefeller Center.

Temple Emanu-El Many of New York's most prominent and wealthy families are members of this Reform congregation—the first to be established in New York City—housed in the city's most famous synagogue. The largest house of Jewish worship in the world is a majestic blend of Moorish and Romanesque styles, symbolizing the mingling of Eastern and Western cultures. The temple houses a small but remarkable collection of Judaica in Herbert & Eileen Bernard Museum, including a collection of Hanukkah lamps with examples ranging from the 14th to the 20th centuries. Three galleries also tell the story of the congregation Emanu-El from 1845 to the present. Tours are given after morning services Saturdays at noon. Inquire for a schedule of lectures, films, music, symposiums, and other events.

1 E. 65th St. (at Fifth Ave.). © **212/744-1400.** www.emanuelnyc.org. Free admission. Daily 10am–5pm. Services: Sun–Thurs 5:30pm; Fri 5:15pm; Sat 10:30am. Subway: N, R to Fifth Ave.; 6 to 68th St.

Trinity Church Serving God and Mammon, this Wall Street house of worship—with neo-Gothic flying buttresses, beautiful stained-glass windows, and vaulted ceilings—was designed by Richard Upjohn and consecrated in 1846. At that time, its 280-foot spire dominated the skyline. Its main doors, embellished with biblical scenes, were inspired in part by Ghiberti's famed doors on Florence's Baptistery. The historic Episcopal church stood strong while office towers crumbled around it on September 11, 2001; however, an electronic organ has temporarily replaced the historic pipe organ, which was severely damaged by dust and debris. The gates to the historic church currently serve as an impromptu memorial to the victims of 9/11, with countless tokens of remembrance left by both locals and visitors alike.

The church runs a brief tour daily at 2pm (a second Sun tour follows the 11:15am Eucharist); groups of five or more should call © **212/602-0872** to reserve. There's a small museum at the end of the left aisle displaying documents (including the 1697 church charter from King William III), photographs, replicas of the Hamilton-Burr duel pistols, and other items. Surrounding the church is a churchyard whose monuments read like an American history book: a tribute to martyrs of the American Revolution, Alexander Hamilton, Robert Fulton, and many more. Lined with benches, this makes a wonderful picnic spot on warm days.

Also part of Trinity Church is **St. Paul's Chapel,** at Broadway and Fulton Street, New York's only surviving pre-Revolutionary church, and a transition shelter for homeless men until it was transformed into a relief center after September 11; it returned to its former duties in mid-2002. Built by Thomas McBean, with a temple-like portico and fluted Ionic columns supporting a massive pediment, the chapel resembles London's St. Martin-in-the-Fields. In the small graveyard 18th- and early-19th-century notables rest in peace and modern businesspeople sit for lunch.

Trinity holds its renowned **Noonday Concert series** of chamber music and orchestral concerts Mondays and Thursdays at 1pm; call ✆ **212/602-0747** or visit the website for the full schedule, and also to see if concert programming had resumed at St. Paul's.

At Broadway and Wall St. ✆ **212/602-0800**, 212/602-0872, or 212/602-0747 for concert information. www.trinitywallstreet.org. Admission and tours free; $2 suggested donation for noonday concerts. Museum: Mon–Fri 9–11:45am and 1–3:45pm; Sat 10am–3:45pm; Sun 1–3:45pm. Services Mon–Fri 8:15am, 12:05, and 5:15pm (additional Healing Service Thurs at 12:30pm); Sat 8:45am; Sun 9 and 11:15am (also 8am Eucharist service at St. Paul's Chapel, between Vesey and Fulton sts.). Subway: 4, 5 to Wall St.

6 Central Park & Other Places to Play

CENTRAL PARK

Without the miracle of civic planning that is **Central Park** ★★★, Manhattan would be a virtual unbroken block of buildings. Instead, smack in the middle of Gotham, an 843-acre natural retreat provides a daily escape valve and tranquilizer for millions of New Yorkers.

While you're in the city, be sure to take advantage of the park's many charms—not the least of which is its sublime layout. Frederick Law Olmsted and Calvert Vaux won a competition with a plan that marries flowing paths with sinewy bridges, integrating them into the natural rolling landscape with its rocky outcroppings, man-made lakes, and wooded pockets. The park's construction, between 1859 and 1870, provided much-needed employment during an economic depression and drew the city's population into the upper reaches of the island, which at that time were still quite rural. Nevertheless, designers predicted the hustle and bustle to come, and tactfully hid traffic from the eyes and ears of park-goers by building roads that are largely hidden from the bucolic view.

On just about any day, Central Park is crowded with New Yorkers and visitors alike. On nice days, especially weekend days, it's the city's party central. Families come to play in the snow or the sun, depending on the season; in-line skaters come to fly through the crisp air and twirl in front of the band shell; couples come to stroll or paddle the lake; dog owners come to hike and throw Frisbees to Bowser; and just about everybody comes to sunbathe at the first sign of summer. On beautiful days, the crowds are part of the appeal—folks come here to peel off their urban armor and relax, and the common goal puts a general feeling of camaraderie in the air. On these days, the people-watching is more compelling than anywhere else in the city. But even on the most crowded days, there's always somewhere to get away from it all, if you just want a little peace and quiet, and a moment to commune with nature.

ORIENTATION & GETTING THERE Look at your map—that great green swath in the center of Manhattan is Central Park. It runs from 59th Street (also known as Central Park S.) at the south end to 110th Street at the north end, and from Fifth Avenue on the east side to Central Park West (the equivalent of Eighth Ave.) on the west side. A 6-mile (9.5km) rolling road, **Central Park Drive,** circles the park, and has a lane set aside for bikers, joggers, and in-line skaters. A number of **transverse** (crosstown) **roads** cross the park at major points—at 65th, 79th, 86th, and 97th streets—but they're built down a level, largely out of view, to minimize intrusion on the bucolic nature of the park.

A number of subway stops and lines serve the park, and which one you take depends on where you want to go. To reach the southernmost entrance on the west side, take an A, B, C, D, 1, or 9 to 59th Street/Columbus Circle. To reach the southeast corner entrance, take the N, R to Fifth Avenue; from this stop, it's an easy walk into the park to the Information Center in the **Dairy** (✆ **212/794-6564;** open daily 11am–5pm, to 4pm in winter), midpark at about 65th Street. Here you can ask questions, pick up park information, and purchase a good park map.

If your time for exploring is limited, I suggest entering the park at 72nd or 79th streets for maximum exposure (subway: B, C to 72nd St. or 81st St. Museum of Natural History). From here, you can pick up park information at the visitor center at **Belvedere Castle** (✆ **212/772-0210;** open Tues–Sun 10am–5pm, to 4pm in winter), midpark at 79th Street. There's also a third visitor center at the **Charles A. Dana Discovery Center** (✆ **212/860-1370;** open daily 11am–5pm, to 4pm in winter), at the northeast corner of the park at Harlem Meer, at 110th Street between Fifth and Lenox avenues (subway: 2, 3 to Central Park N./110th St.). The Dana Center is also an environmental education center hosting workshops, exhibits, music programs, and park tours, and lends fishing poles for fishing in Harlem Meer (park policy is catch-and-release).

Food carts and vendors are set up at all of the park's main gathering points, selling hot dogs, pretzels, and ice cream, so finding a bite to eat is never a problem. You'll also find a fixed food counter at the **Conservatory,** on the east side of the park north of the 72nd Street entrance, and both casual snacks and more sophisticated New American dining at **The Boat House,** on the lake near 72nd Street and Park Drive North (✆ **212/517-2233**). (For **Tavern on the Green,** see p. 219).

GUIDED WALKS The **Central Park Conservancy** offers a slate of free walking tours of the park; call ✆ **212/360-2726** or check **www.centralparknyc.org** for the current schedule (click on the "Walking Tours" button on the left). The Dana Center hosts ranger-guided tours on occasion (call ✆ **212/860-1370** or 800/201-PARK for schedule). Also consider a private walking tour; many of the companies listed in "Organized Sightseeing Tours," later in this chapter, offer guided tours of the park.

FOR FURTHER INFORMATION Call the main number at ✆ **212/360-3444** for recorded information, or 212/310-6600 or 212/628-1036 to speak to a live person. Call ✆ **888/NY-PARKS** for special events information. The park also has two comprehensive websites that are worth checking out before you go: The city parks department's site at **www.centralpark.org**, and the Central Park Conservancy's site at **www.centralparknyc.org**, both of which feature excellent maps and a far more complete rundown of park attractions and activities than I have room to include here. If you have an **emergency** in the park, dial ✆ **800/201-PARK,** which will link you directly to the park rangers.

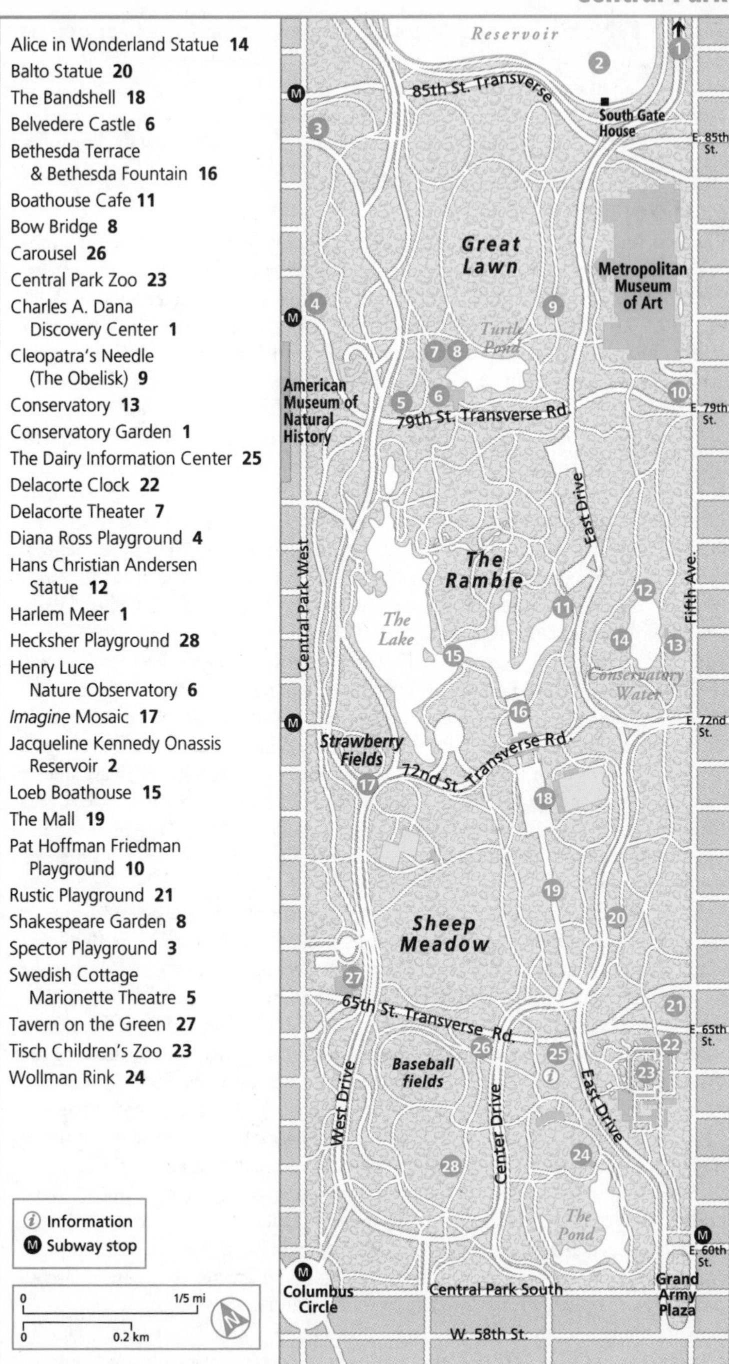
Alice in Wonderland Statue 14
Balto Statue 20
The Bandshell 18
Belvedere Castle 6
Bethesda Terrace & Bethesda Fountain 16
Boathouse Cafe 11
Bow Bridge 8
Carousel 26
Central Park Zoo 23
Charles A. Dana Discovery Center 1
Cleopatra's Needle (The Obelisk) 9
Conservatory 13
Conservatory Garden 1
The Dairy Information Center 25
Delacorte Clock 22
Delacorte Theater 7
Diana Ross Playground 4
Hans Christian Andersen Statue 12
Harlem Meer 1
Heckshер Playground 28
Henry Luce Nature Observatory 6
Imagine Mosaic 17
Jacqueline Kennedy Onassis Reservoir 2
Loeb Boathouse 15
The Mall 19
Pat Hoffman Friedman Playground 10
Rustic Playground 21
Shakespeare Garden 8
Spector Playground 3
Swedish Cottage Marionette Theatre 5
Tavern on the Green 27
Tisch Children's Zoo 23
Wollman Rink 24
Information
Subway stop
0
1/5 mi
0
0.2 km
Reservoir
85th St. Transverse
South Gate House
E. 85th St.
Great Lawn
Metropolitan Museum of Art
Turtle Pond
American Museum of Natural History
79th St. Transverse Rd.
E. 79th St.
East Drive
The Ramble
Central Park West
Fifth Ave.
The Lake
Conservatory Water
E. 72nd St.
Strawberry Fields
72nd St. Transverse Rd.
Sheep Meadow
65th St. Transverse Rd.
E. 65th St.
Baseball fields
West Drive
Center Drive
East Drive
The Pond
E. 60th St.
Columbus Circle
Central Park South
Grand Army Plaza
W. 58th St.

SAFETY TIP Even though the park has the lowest crime rate of any of the city's precincts, keep your wits about you, especially in the more remote northern end. It's a good idea to avoid the park entirely after dark, unless you're heading to one of the restaurants for dinner or to a Summerstage or Shakespeare in the Park event (see chapter 11), when you should stick with the crowds. For more safety tips, see "Playing It Safe," in chapter 5.

EXPLORING THE PARK

The best way to see Central Park is to wander along the park's 58 miles of winding pedestrian paths, keeping in mind the following highlights.

Before starting your stroll, stop by the **Information Center** in the Dairy (✆ **212/794-6464;** open daily 11am to 5pm, to 4pm in winter), midpark in a 19th-century-style building overlooking Wollman Rink at about 65th Street, to get a good park map and other information on sights and events, and to peruse the kid-friendly exhibit on the park's history and design.

The southern part of Central Park is more formally designed and heavily visited than the relatively rugged and remote northern end. Not far from the Dairy is the **Carousel** with 58 hand-carved horses (✆ **212/879-0244;** open daily 10:30am to 6pm, to 5pm in winter; rides are 90¢); the zoo (see the listing below); and the Wollman Rink for roller- or ice-skating (see "Activities," below).

The **Mall,** a long formal walkway lined with elms shading benches and sculptures of sometimes forgotten writers, leads to the focal point of Central Park, **Bethesda Fountain** ★ (along the 72nd St. transverse road). **Bethesda Terrace** and its grandly sculpted entryway border a large **lake** where dogs fetch sticks, rowboaters glide by, and dedicated early morning anglers try their luck at catching carp, perch, catfish, and bass. You can rent a rowboat at or take a gondola ride from **Loeb Boathouse,** on the eastern end of the lake (see "Activities," below). Boats of another kind are at **Conservatory Water** (on the east side at 73rd St.), a stone-walled pond flanked by statues of both **Hans Christian Andersen** and **Alice in Wonderland.** On Saturday at 10am, die-hard yachtsmen race remote-controlled sailboats in fierce competitions following Olympic regulations. (Sorry, model boats aren't for rent.)

If the action there is too intense, **Sheep Meadow** on the southwestern side of the park is a designated quiet zone, where Frisbee throwing and kite flying are as energetic as things get. Another respite is **Strawberry Fields** ★, at 72nd Street on the West Side. This memorial to John Lennon, who was murdered across the street at the Dakota apartment building (72nd St. and Central Park W., northwest corner), is a gorgeous garden centered around an Italian mosaic bearing the title of the lead Beatle's most famous solo song, and his lifelong message: IMAGINE. In keeping with its goal of promoting world peace, the garden has 161 varieties of plants, donated by each of the 161 nations in existence when it was designed in 1985. This is a wonderful place for peaceful contemplation.

Bow Bridge, a graceful lacework of cast iron, designed by Calvert Vaux, crosses over the lake and leads to the most bucolic area of Central Park, the **Ramble.** This dense 38-acre woodland with spiraling paths, rocky outcroppings, and a stream is the best spot for bird-watching and feeling as if you've discovered an unimaginably leafy forest right in the middle of the city.

North of the Ramble, **Belvedere Castle** is home to the **Henry Luce Nature Observatory** (✆ **212/772-0210**), worth a visit if you're with children. From the castle, set on Vista Rock (the park's highest point at 135 ft./40.5m), you can look down on the **Great Lawn,** which has emerged lush and green from renovations, and the **Delacorte Theater,** home to Shakespeare in the Park (see chapter 11). The small **Shakespeare Garden** south of the theater is scruffy, but it does have plants, herbs, trees, and other bits of greenery mentioned by the playwright. Behind the Belvedere Castle is the **Swedish Cottage Marionette Theatre** ★ (✆ **212/988-9093**), hosting various marionette plays for children throughout the year; call to see what's on.

Continue north along the east side of the Great Lawn, parallel to East Drive. Near the glass-enclosed back of the **Metropolitan Museum of Art** (p. 247) is **Cleopatra's Needle,** a 69-foot (21m) obelisk originally erected in Heliopolis around 1475 B.C. It was given to the city as a gift from the khedive of Egypt in 1880. (The khedive bestowed a similar obelisk to the city of London, which now sits on the Embankment of the Thames.)

North of the 86th Street Transverse Road is the **Jacqueline Kennedy Onassis Reservoir,** so named after the death of the beloved first lady, who lived nearby and often enjoyed a run along the 1½-mile (2.5km) jogging track that circles the reservoir.

At the northeast end of the park is the **Conservatory Garden** ★ (at 105th St. and Fifth Ave.), Central Park's only formal garden, with a magnificent display of flowers and trees reflected in calm pools of water. (The gates to the garden once fronted the Fifth Ave. mansion of Cornelius Vanderbilt II.) **Harlem Meer** and its boathouse were recently renovated and look beautiful. The boathouse now berths the **Charles A. Dana Discovery Center,** near 110th Street between Fifth and Lenox avenues (✆ **212/860-1370**), where children learn about the environment and borrow fishing poles for catch-and-release at no charge.

GOING TO THE ZOO

Central Park Zoo/Tisch Children's Zoo ★ *Kids* It has been a decade since the zoo in Central Park was renovated, making it in the process both more human and more humane. Lithe sea lions frolic in the central pool area with beguiling style. The gigantic but graceful polar bears (one of whom, by the way, made himself a true New Yorker when he began regular visits with a shrink) glide back and forth across a watery pool that has glass walls through which you can observe very large paws doing very smooth strokes. The monkeys seem to regard those on the other side of the fence with knowing disdain. In the hot and humid Tropic Zone, large colorful birds swoop around in freedom, sometimes landing next to nonplused visitors.

Because of its small size, the zoo is at its best with its displays of smaller animals. The indoor multilevel Tropic Zone is a real highlight, its steamy rain forest home to everything from black-and-white Colobus monkeys to Emerald tree boa constrictors to a leaf-cutter ant farm; look for the new dart poison frog exhibit, which is very cool. So is the large penguin enclosure in the Polar Circle, which is better than the one at San Diego's Sea World. In the Temperate Territory, look for the Asian red pandas (cousins to the big black-and-white ones), which look like the world's most beautiful raccoons. Despite their pool and piles of ice, however, the polar bears still look sad.

Fun Fact **Where's Balto?**

The people at Central Park say that the question they're asked almost more than any other these days is "Where is the statue of Balto?" The heroic dog is just northwest of the zoo, midpark just above 66th Street.

The entire zoo is good for short attention spans; you can cover the whole thing in 1½ to 3 hours, depending on the size of the crowds and how long you like to linger. It's also very kid-friendly, with lots of well-written and -illustrated placards that older kids can understand. For the littlest ones, there's the $6 million **Tisch Children's Zoo.** With pigs, llamas, potbellied pigs, and more, this petting zoo and playground is a real blast for the 5-and-under set.

830 Fifth Ave. (at 64th St., just inside Central Park). ✆ **212/861-6030.** www.wcs.org/zoos. Admission $3.50 adults, $1.25 seniors, 50¢ children 3–12, free for children under 3. Apr–Oct Mon–Fri 10am–5pm, Sat–Sun 10am–5:30pm; Nov–Mar daily 10am–4:30pm. Subway: N, R to Fifth Ave.

ACTIVITIES

The 6-mile (9.5km) rolling road circling the park, **Central Park Drive,** has a lane set aside for bikers, joggers, and in-line skaters. The best time to use it is when the park is closed to traffic: Monday to Friday 10am to 3pm (except Thanksgiving–New Year's) and 7 to 10pm. It's also closed from 7pm Friday to 6am Monday, but when the weather is nice, the crowds can be hellish.

BIKING Off-road mountain biking isn't permitted; stay on Central Park Drive or your bike may be confiscated by park police.

You can rent 3- and 10-speed bikes as well as tandems in Central Park at the **Loeb Boathouse,** midpark near 72nd Street and Park Drive North, just in from Fifth Avenue (✆ **212/517-2233** or 212/517-3623), for $9 to $20 an hour, with a complete selection of kids' bikes, cruisers, tandems, and the like ($200 deposit required); at **Metro Bicycles,** 1311 Lexington Ave., at 88th Street (✆ **212/427-4450**), for about $7 an hour, or $35 a day; and at **Toga Bike Shop,** 110 West End Ave., at 64th Street (✆ **212/799-9625;** www.togabikes.com), for $30 a day. No matter where you rent, be prepared to leave a credit-card deposit.

BOATING From March through November, gondola rides and rowboat rentals are available at the **Loeb Boathouse,** midpark near 74th Street and Park Drive North, just in from Fifth Avenue (✆ **212/517-2233** or 212/517-3623). Rowboats are $10 for the first hour, $2.50 every 15 minutes thereafter, and a $30 deposit is required; reservations are accepted. (Note that rates were not set for the summer season at press time, so these may change.)

HORSE-DRAWN CARRIAGE RIDES At the entrance to the park at 59th Street and Central Park South, you'll see a line of **horse-drawn carriages** waiting to take passengers on a ride through the park or along certain of the city's streets. Horses belong on city streets as much as chamber pots belong in our homes. You won't need me to tell you how forlorn most of these horses look; if you insist, a ride is about $50 for two for a half hour, but I suggest skipping it.

ICE-SKATING Central Park's **Wollman Rink** ★, on the east side of the park between 62nd and 63rd streets (✆ **212/439-6900;** www.wollmanskatingrink.com), is the city's best outdoor skating spot, more spacious than the tiny rink at Rockefeller Center. It's open for skating generally from mid-October to mid-April, depending on the weather. Rates are $7 for adults, $3.50 for seniors and kids under 12, and skate rental is $3.50; lockers are available (locks are $6.75).

IN-LINE SKATING Central Park is the city's most popular place for blading. See the beginning of this section for details on Central Park Drive, the main drag for skaters. On weekends, head to West Drive at 67th Street, behind Tavern on the Green, where you'll find trick skaters weaving through an NYRSA slalom course at full speed, or the Mall in front of the band shell (above Bethesda

Fountain) for twirling to tunes. In summer, **Wollman Rink** converts to a hot-shot roller rink, with half-pipes and lessons available (see "Ice-Skating," above).

You can rent skates for $20 a day from **Blades Board and Skate,** 120 W. 72nd St., between Broadway and Columbus Avenue (✆ **212/787-3911;** www.blades.com). Wollman Rink (above) also rents in-line skates for park use at similar rates.

PLAYGROUNDS Nineteen Adventure Playgrounds are scattered throughout the park, perfect for jumping, sliding, tottering, swinging, and digging. At Central Park West and 81st Street is the **Diana Ross Playground** ★, voted the city's best by *New York* magazine. Also on the west side is the **Spector Playground,** at 85th Street and Central Park West, and, a little farther north, the **Wild West Playground** at 93rd Street. On the east side is the **Rustic Playground,** at 67th Street and Fifth Avenue, a delightfully landscaped space rife with islands, bridges, and big slides; and the **Pat Hoffman Friedman Playground,** right behind the Metropolitan Museum of Art at East 79th Street, is geared toward older toddlers.

RUNNING Marathoners and wannabes regularly run in Central Park along the 6-mile **Central Park Drive,** which circles the park (run toward traffic to avoid being mowed down by wayward cyclists and in-line skaters). For a shorter loop, try the midpark 1.58-mile (2.5km) track around the **Jacqueline Kennedy Onassis Reservoir** (keep your eyes ready for spotting Madonna and other famous bodies). It's safest to jog only during daylight hours and where everybody else does. Avoid the small walks in the Ramble and at the north end of the park.

OTHER PARKS

For parks in Brooklyn and Queens, see "Highlights of the Outer Boroughs," later in this chapter. For more information on these and other city parks, go online to **nycparks.completeinet.net**.

Battery Park ★★ As you traverse Manhattan's concrete canyons, it's sometimes easy to forget you're actually on an island. But here, at Manhattan's southernmost tip, you get the very real sense that just out past Liberty, Ellis, and Staten islands is the vast Atlantic Ocean.

The 21-acre park is named for the cannons built to defend residents after the American Revolution. **Castle Clinton National Monument** (the place to purchase tickets for the Statue of Liberty and Ellis Island ferry; see listings earlier in this chapter) was built as a fort before the War of 1812, though it was never used as such. The 22-ton **bronze sphere** by Fritz Koenig that was recovered from the rubble of the World Trade Center, where it stood on the plaza between the two Twin Towers as a symbol of global peace, now stands—severely damaged but still whole—in the park as a temporary memorial to the nearly 3,000 victims of the World Trade Center terrorist attack. This may be the finest place in the city to pay tribute to those who were lost.

You'll most likely recognize Battery Park for the prominent role it played in *Desperately Seeking Susan,* Madonna's first movie. Besides the requisite T-shirt vendors and hot-dog carts, you'll find several statues and memorials scattered throughout the park. This is quite the civilized park, with lots of STAY OFF THE GRASS! signs and Wall Streeters eating deli sandwiches on the many park benches. Pull up your own bench for a good view out across the harbor.

From State Street to New York Harbor. Subway: N, R to Whitehall St.; 1, 9 to South Ferry; 4, 5 to Bowling Green.

Bowling Green Park This patch of green at the end of Broadway is most notable for the early history it has seen. This is most likely the spot where, in 1626, Dutchman Peter Minuit gave glass beads and other trinkets worth about 60 guilders ($24) to a group of Indians, and then claimed he had thereby bought Manhattan. The local Indians didn't think they owned this island (not because they didn't believe in property, a colonial myth) because Manhattan was considered communal hunting ground, so it isn't clear what the Indians thought the trinkets meant. Either (a) they just thought the exchange was a formal way of closing an agreement to extend the shared hunting use to this funny-looking group of pale people with yellow beards; or (b) they were knowingly selling land that they didn't own in the first place, thus, performing the first shrewd real-estate deal of the Financial District.

When King George III repealed the hated Stamp Act in 1770, New Yorkers magnanimously raised a statue of him here, although today it's just another lunch spot for stockbrokers. The statue lasted 5 years, until the day the Declaration of Independence was read to the public in front of City Hall (now Federal Hall) and a crowd rushed down Broadway to topple the statue, chop it up, melt it down, and transform it into 42,000 bullets, which they later used to shoot the British.

With the demise of the World Trade Center, the lower Manhattan **TKTS booth,** officially named the **Downtown Theatre Centre,** has relocated at Bowling Green Park Plaza. This is the place to pick up same-day discounted tickets for a Broadway or Off-Broadway show; the line is usually shorter here than it is at the Times Square location. For details, see p. 288.

On the fringe of the park is the stunning, Cass Gilbert–designed 1907 beaux arts **U.S. Customs House,** currently housing the National Museum of the American Indian (p. 267).

From State Street to New York Harbor. Subway:4, 5 to Bowling Green; N, R to Whitehall St.

Bryant Park ★ Another success story in the push for urban redevelopment, Bryant Park is the latest incarnation of a 4-acre site that was, at various times in its history, a graveyard and a reservoir. Named for poet and *New York Evening Post* editor William Cullen Bryant (look for his statue on the east end), the park actually rests atop the New York Public Library's many miles of underground stacks. Another statue is also notable: a squat and evocative stone portrait of Gertrude Stein, one of the few outdoor sculptures of women in the city.

This simple green swath, just east of Times Square, is welcome relief from Midtown's concrete, taxi-choked jungle, and good weather attracts brown-baggers from neighboring office buildings. Just behind the library is **Bryant Park Grill** (✆ **212/840-6500;** www.bryantparkgrill.com), a gorgeous, airy bistro with spectacular views but merely decent New American food. Still, brunch is a good bet, and the grill's two summer alfresco restaurants—**The Terrace,** on the Grill's roof; and the casual **Cafe,** with small tables beneath a canopy of trees—are extremely pleasant on a nice day.

Additionally, the park plays host to New York's **Seventh on Sixth** fashion shows, set up in billowy white tents (open to the trade only) in the spring and fall.

Behind the New York Public Library, at Sixth Ave. between 40th and 42nd sts. Subway: B, D, F, Q to 42nd St.; 7 to Fifth Ave.

Union Square Park Here's a delightful place to spend an afternoon. Reclaimed from drug dealers and abject ruin in the late '80s, Union Square Park is now one of the city's best assets. The seemingly endless subway work should no longer be disturbing the peace by the time you're here. This patch of green

We Can Work It Out

So your hotel doesn't have a gym, and walking around New York just isn't enough of a workout for you? Never fear: The city has a number of health clubs that are open to out-of-towners on a day-to-day basis.

A down-to-earth iron-pumping crowd can be found at **Crunch Fitness,** 404 Lafayette St., between East 4th Street and Astor Place in NoHo (✆ **212/614-0120**); 162 W. 83rd St., between Columbus and Amsterdam avenues on the Upper West Side (✆ **212/875-1902**); 144 W. 38th St., between Broadway and Seventh Avenue (✆ **212/869-7788**); and at seven other locations throughout Manhattan (check **www.crunch.com** or the Yellow Pages). Crunch charges a per-day drop-in fee of $24, and the Lafayette Street location is open 24 hours on weekdays (Sat to 9pm, Sun 8am–9pm, reopening Mon at 5am).

In Midtown, the **New York Sports Club** has an extensive facility with a 50-foot (15m) lap pool and sauna at the Crowne Plaza Manhattan hotel, 1605 Broadway, between 48th and 49th streets (✆ **212/977-8232**); day passes are $25. **Gravity,** the excellent 15,000-square-foot (1,394-sq.-m) facility at Le Parker Meridien hotel, 118 W. 57th St., between Sixth and Seventh avenues (✆ **212/708-7340**), allows day guests access for $25, $50 if you want access to the glass-enclosed 42nd-floor pool.

And don't forget about the fabulous **Sports Center at Chelsea Piers** (below), the best health club in the city, available to day guests for $50.

remains, with or without the construction, the focal point of the newly fashionable Flatiron and Gramercy Park neighborhoods. Don't miss the grand equestrian statue of George Washington at the south end or the bronze statue (by Bartholdi, the sculptor of the Statue of Liberty) of the marquis de Lafayette at the eastern end, gracefully glancing toward France.

This charming square is now best known as the site of New York's premier **Greenmarket.** Every Monday, Wednesday, Friday, and Saturday, vendors hawk fresh veggies and fruits, organic baked goods, cider, wine, and even fresh fish and lobsters in booths that flank the north and west sides of the square. Fresh-cut flowers and plants are also for sale, as are books and postcards. During summer and fall, you can graze the bazaar and easily assemble a cheap and healthy lunch to munch under the trees or at the picnic tables at the park's north end. Musical acts regularly play the small pavilion at the north end of the park, and in-line skaters take over the market space in the after-work hours. A **cafe** is open at the north end of the park in warm weather.

From 14th to 17th sts., btwn Park Ave. South and Broadway. Subway: 4, 5, 6, L, N, R to 14th St./Union Sq.

Washington Square Park You'll be hard-pressed to find much "park" in this mainly concrete square—a burial ground in the late 18th century—but it's undeniably the focal point of Greenwich Village. Chess players, skateboarders, street musicians, New York University students, gay and straight couples, the occasional film crew, and not a few homeless people compete for attention throughout the day and most of the night. (If anyone issues a friendly challenge to play you in the ancient and complex Chinese game of Go, don't take them up on it—you'll lose money.)

The lively scene belies a macabre past. Once marshland traversed by Minetta Brook, it became in 1797 a potter's field (most green and fertile downtown parks were originally graveyards), and the remains of some 10,000 bodies are buried here. In the early 1800s, the square, or more specifically the infamous Hanging Elm in the northwest corner where MacDougal Street meets the park, was used for public executions. It wasn't until the 1830s that the elegant Greek Revival town houses on **Washington Square North** known as "The Row" (note especially nos. 21–26) attracted the elite. Stanford White designed Washington Arch (1891–92) to commemorate the centenary of George Washington's inauguration as first president. While in the neighborhood, peek down charming MacDougal Alley and Washington Mews, both lined with delightful old carriage houses.

At the southern end of Fifth Ave. (where it intersects Waverly Place btwn MacDougal and Wooster sts.). Subway: A, C, E, F, V to W. 4th St. (use 3rd St. exit).

CHELSEA PIERS

One of the city's biggest—and most successful—private urban development projects of the last few years has been the 30-acre **Chelsea Piers Sports & Entertainment Complex** (© **212/336-6666;** www.chelseapiers.com). Jutting out into the Hudson River on four huge piers between 17th and 23rd streets, it's a terrific multifunctional recreational facility.

The **Sports Center** (© **212/336-6000**), a three-football-fields-long megafacility, does health clubs one better. It offers not only the usual cardiovascular training, weights, and aerobics but also a four-lane quarter-mile indoor running track, a boxing ring, basketball courts, a sand volleyball court, a gorgeous 25-yard indoor pool with a whirlpool and sundeck, the world's most challenging rock-climbing wall plus a bouldering wall, and the **Origins Feel-Good Spa** (© **212/336-6780;** www.origins.com/spa/spa-newyork.tmpl), which offers massage, reflexology, facials, and the like. Day passes to the Sports Center are $50 for nonmembers; spa treatments are extra, of course.

The **Golf Club** (© **212/336-6400**) has 52 all-weather fully automated hitting stalls on four levels and a 200-yard net-enclosed artificial-turf fairway jutting out over the water, making it the best place in the city to hit a few. Prices start at $15 for 60 balls (89 balls during off-peak hours), and club rentals are available.

The **Sky Rink** (© **212/336-6100**) has twin around-the-clock indoor rinks for recreational skating and pickup hockey games with Hudson River views. General skating is $12 for adults, $8.50 for seniors and kids 12 and under; skate rental is $5.50. Due to organized skating activities, general skating is limited, so call ahead to find out schedules of availability.

If wheels are your thing, there are two outdoor **Roller Rinks** (© **212/336-6200**) for seasonal in-line skating and roller hockey games. Expect to pay about $7 for adults, $6 for kids for general skating; equipment rentals are available. The general skating schedule can change from month to month and is sometimes limited to weekends, so call ahead. The **Skating School** offers instruction if you would like to learn.

The **Field House** (© **212/336-6500**) is mainly for team sports, but young rock climbers will enjoy the 30-foot indoor **climbing wall,** designed for kids as well as grown-ups. Open climbs are $17, with climbs limited to 2½ hours on weekdays, 90 minutes on weekends; they start taking same-day climb reservations at 9am, and weekends can book up quickly. Children's lessons are available. **Batting cages** are $1 per 10 pitches.

Feeling like a little 10-pin tonight? State-of-the-art **AMF Chelsea Piers Lanes** (✆ **212/835-BOWL;** www.chelseapiersbowl.com) offers 40 lanes of fun. Games are $7 to $8 per person, and shoe rental is $4.50.

Beyond its athletics, the complex is a destination in and of itself. The 1.2-mile esplanade has benches and picnic tables with terrific river views; they serve as the perfect vantage point for watching the *QEII* head out to sea, or the navy and Coast Guard ships sailing in for Fleet Week each May. For waterfront dining there's New York's largest microbrewery/restaurant, the **Chelsea Brewing Company** (✆ **212/336-6440;** www.chelseabrewingco.com), on Pier 61, serving up very good brews and okay food on a terrific waterfront terrace.

Getting there: Chelsea Piers is accessible by taxi and the M23 or M14 crosstown buses. The nearest subway is the C and E at 23rd Street and Eighth Avenue, then pick up the M23 and walk 4 long blocks west. Another option is to take the A, C, E to 14th Street or the L train to Eighth Avenue, walk to the river, then follow the walking/riding/running path along the river north.

7 Organized Sightseeing Tours

Reservations are required on some of the tours listed below, but even if they're not, it's always best to call ahead to confirm prices, times, and meeting places.

DOUBLE-DECKER BUS TOURS

Taking a narrated bus tour is one of the best ways to see and learn quickly about New York's major sights and neighborhoods. However, keep in mind that the commentary is only as good as the guide, who is seldom an expert. Tour guides tend toward hyperbole and might get a few of the facts wrong. The *New York Times* once found tour-bus guides spouting the following inaccuracies: New York has the oldest subway system in the world (third, behind London's—41 years before New York—and Boston's, which was the first in the U.S.); Frank Sinatra was born in Jersey City (it was Hoboken); and Herald Square was named after the founder of the *New York Herald Tribune* (there was no Mr. Herald). But the idea is to see the highlights, not write a dissertation from this stuff. So enjoy the ride—and take the "facts" you hear along the way with a grain of salt.

Gray Line New York Tours Gray Line offers just about every sightseeing tour option and combination you could want. There are bus tours by day and by night that run uptown, downtown, and all around the town, as well as bus combos with Circle Line cruises, helicopter flights, museum entrances, and guided visits of sights. There's no real point to purchasing some combination tours—you don't need a guide to take you to the Statue of Liberty, and you don't save any money on admission by buying the combo ticket. I've found Gray Line to put a higher premium on accuracy than the other big tour-bus operators, so this is your best bet among the biggies.

777 Eighth Ave. (btwn 47th and 48th sts.). Tours depart from additional Manhattan locations. ✆ **800/669-0051** or 212/445-0848. www.graylinenewyork.com. Hop-on, hop-off bus tours from $30 adults, $20 children 5–11.

HARBOR CRUISES

If you'd like to sail the New York Harbor aboard the 1885 cargo schooner ***Pioneer,*** see the listing for South Street Seaport & Museum on p. 272.

Note that some of the lines below may have limited schedules in winter, especially for evening cruises. Call ahead or check the web for current offerings.

Bateaux New York The most elegant and romantic of New York's evening dinner cruises. Cruises are aboard the *Celestial,* designed to accommodate 300 guests with two suites, one dance floor, two outdoor strolling decks, a state-of-the-art sound system, and windows galore. Dinner is a three-course sit-down affair, with jackets and ties suggested for men, evening dresses for women. The food isn't what you'd get at Le Cirque, but Bateaux (sister to egalitarian Spirit Cruises, below) offers a very nice supper club-style night on the town, and the views are fabulous. A live quartet entertains with jazz standard and pop vocal tunes.

Departing from Pier 61, Chelsea Piers, W. 23rd St. and Twelfth Ave. ✆ **212/352-1366.** www.bateauxnewyork.com. 2-hr. lunch cruises $46; 3-hr. dinner cruises $103–$117. Subway: C, E to 23rd St.

Circle Line Sightseeing Cruises ★★ Circle Line is the only tour company that circumnavigates the entire 35 miles around Manhattan, and I love this ride. The **Full Island** cruise takes 3 hours and passes by the Statue of Liberty, Ellis Island, the Brooklyn Bridge, the United Nations, Yankee Stadium, the George Washington Bridge, and more, including Manhattan's wild northern tip. The panorama is riveting, and the commentary isn't bad. The big boats are basic but fine, with lots of deck room for everybody to enjoy the view. Snacks, soft drinks, coffee, and beer are available onboard for purchase.

If 3 hours is more than you or the kids can handle, go for either the 1½-hour **Semi-Circle** or **Sunset/Harbor Lights** cruise, both of which show you the highlights of the skyline. There's also a 1-hour **Seaport Liberty** version that sticks close to the south end of the island. But of all the tours, the kids might like **The Beast** best, a thrill-a-minute speedboat ride offered in summer only.

In addition, a number of adults-only **Live Music and DJ Cruises** sail regularly from the seaport from May through September ($20–$40 per person). Depending on the night of the week, you can groove to the sounds of jazz, Latin, gospel, dance tunes, or blues as you sail along the skyline.

Departing from Pier 83, at W. 42nd St. and Twelfth Ave. Also departing from Pier 16 at South St. Seaport, 207 Front St. ✆ **212/563-3200.** www.circleline.com, www.ridethebeast.com, and www.seaportmusiccruises.com. Sightseeing cruises $13–$25 adults, $11–$20 seniors, $7–$12 children 12 and under. Subway to Pier 83: A, C, E to 42nd St. Subway to Pier 16: J, M, Z, 2, 3, 4, 5 to Fulton St.

Spirit Cruises Spirit Cruises' modern ships are floating cabarets that combine sightseeing in New York Harbor with freshly prepared meals, musical revues, and dancing to live bands. The atmosphere is festive and fun, and a touch more relaxed than aboard World Yacht (below). The buffet meals are nothing special, but they're fine.

Departing from Pier 61, at Chelsea Piers, W. 23rd St. and Twelfth Ave. ✆ **212/727-2789.** www.spiritcruises.com. 2-hr. lunch cruises $30–$44; 3-hr. dinner cruises $53–$84. Inquire about children's rates. Subway: C, E to 23rd St.

World Yacht If you want a more elegant cruise than what Spirit offers, but a slightly more affordable affair than Bateaux's, go with World Yacht. They offer dressy, high-quality, oh-so-romantic cruises with a touch of class and fair-to-middling Continental cuisine. There's a 2-hour Sunday brunch cruise with live piano music, and a 3-hour dinner cruise featuring a four-course meal, live entertainment, dancing, and spectacular views. A great way to celebrate a special occasion. You can buy yourself a higher level of food, seating, and service with Ambassador Service ($35 extra per person). A jacket is required at dinner, and sneakers and jeans aren't permitted at any time.

Departing from Pier 81, at W. 41st St. and Twelfth Ave. ✆ **800/498-4270** or 212/630-8100. www.world yacht.com. 3-hr. dinner cruises $70–$79; 2-hr. Sun brunch cruise $42. Daily sails Apr–Dec; Fri–Sun Jan–Mar. Subway: A, C, E to 42nd St.

AIR TOURS

Liberty Helicopters How about a bird's-eye view of Manhattan? These flight-seeing trips offer a quick thrill—literally. Five-minute tours from Midtown's take in the USS *Intrepid,* Midtown skyscrapers, and Central Park, while longer tours last 10 or 15 minutes and take in a wider view that includes Lower Manhattan and the Statue of Liberty. If you opt for the longest tour, you'll also fly far enough uptown to take in the George Washington Bridge and Yankee Stadium. Flights leave every 15 minutes daily from 9am to 9pm, but note that reservations are required for two or more.

Departing 1 block north of VIP Heliport, W. 30th St. and Twelfth Ave. ✆ **212/967-6464.** www.liberty helicopters.com. Pilot-narrated tours $56nd]$162. Subway: A, C, E, to 34th St.

SPECIALTY TOURS

In addition to the choices below, those interested in touring the Financial District with a knowledgeable guide should also consider the **World of Finance Walking Tour** offered Fridays at 10am by the Museum of American Financial History; see p. 266. Also, both the Municipal Art Society (directly below) and the Grand Central Partnership offer free walking tours of **Grand Central Terminal,** Wednesdays at 12:30pm and Fridays at 12:30pm, respectively; see p. 246.

Additionally the Alliance for Downtown New York, the amazing Business Improvement District in charge of Lower Manhattan, offers a free, 90-minute **Wall Street Walking Tour** ★ every Thursday and Saturday at noon, rain or shine. This guided tour explores the vivid history and amazing architecture of the nation's first capital and the world center of finance. Stops include the New York Stock Exchange, Trinity Church, Federal Hall National Monument, and many other sites of historic and cultural importance. Tours meet on the steps of the Cass Gilbert's gorgeous U.S. Customs House (p. 267), at 1 Bowling Green (subway: 4, 5 to Bowling Green). Reservations are not required (unless you're a group), but you can call ✆ **212/606-4064** or visit **www.downtownny.com** to confirm the schedule.

CULTURAL ORGANIZATIONS

The **Municipal Art Society** ★ (✆ **212/439-1049** or 212/935-3960; www.mas.org) offers excellent historical and architectural walking tours aimed at intelligent, individualistic travelers, not the mass market. Each is led by a highly qualified guide who gives insights into the significance of buildings, neighborhoods, and history. Topics range from the urban history of Greenwich Village to "Mies and the Moderns," examining the architectural legacy of Mies van der Rohe, to an examination of the "new" Times Square. Weekday walking tours are $12, weekend tours are $15. Reservations may be required depending on the tour, so it's always best to call ahead. A full schedule is available online or by calling ✆ **212/439-1049.**

The **92nd Street Y** ★ (✆ **212/415-5500** or 212/415-5628; www. 92ndsty.org) offers a wonderful variety of walking and bus tours, many featuring funky themes or behind-the-scenes visits. Subjects can range from "Diplomat for a Day at the U.N." to "Secrets of the Chelsea Hotel," from "Artists of the

Meat-Packing District" to "Jewish Harlem." Prices range from $20 to $60 (sometimes more for bus tours), but many include ferry rides, afternoon tea, dinner, or whatever suits the program. Guides are well-chosen experts on their subjects, ranging from highly respected historians to an East Village poet, mystic, and art critic (for "Allen Ginsberg's New York" and "East Village Night Spots"), and many routes travel into the outer boroughs; some day trips even reach beyond the city. Advance registration is required for all walking and bus tours. Schedules are planned a few months in advance, so check the website for tours that might interest you.

INDEPENDENT OPERATORS

One of the most highly praised sightseeing organizations in New York is **Big Onion Walking Tours** ★ (© **212/439-1090;** www.bigonion.com). Enthusiastic Big Onion guides (all hold an advanced degree in American history from Columbia or New York universities) peel back the layers of history to reveal the city's inner secrets. The 2-hour tours are offered mostly on weekends, and subjects include the "The Bowery," "Presidential New York," "Irish New York," and the ever-popular "Multiethnic Eating Tour" of the Lower East Side, where you munch on everything from dim sum and dill pickles to fresh mozzarella. Tour prices range from $12 to $18 for adults, $10 to $16 for students and seniors. No reservations are necessary, but Big Onion *strongly recommends that you call to verify schedules.*

NYC Discovery Tours (© **212/465-3331**) offers more than 70 tours of the Big Apple divided into five categories: neighborhood (including "Central Park" and "Brooklyn Bridge and Heights"); theme (such as "Gotham City Ghost Tour" and "Art History NYC"), biography ("John Lennon's New York"), tavern/food tasting, and American history and literature ("The Charles Dickens Tours"). Tours are about 2 hours long and cost $12 per person (more for food tastings).

All tours from **Joyce Gold History Tours of New York** ★★ (© **212/242-5762;** www.nyctours.com) are offered by Joyce Gold herself, an instructor of Manhattan history at New York University and the New School for Social Research, who has been conducting history walks around New York since 1975. Her tours can really cut to the core of this town; Joyce is full of fascinating stories about Manhattan and its people. Tours are arranged around themes like "The Colonial Settlers of Wall Street," "The Genius and Elegance of Gramercy Park," "Downtown Graveyards," "The Old Jewish Lower East Side," "Historic Harlem," and "TriBeCa: The Creative Explosion." Tours are offered most weekends March to December and last from 2 to 4 hours, and the price is $12 per person; no reservations are required. Private tours can be arranged year-round, either for individuals or groups.

For food lovers, **Savory Sojourns** (© **888/9-SAVORY** or 212/691-7314; www.savorysojourns.com), operated by Addie Tomei (Oscar-winning actress Marisa's mom) and Sally Ingraham, offer guided walking tours that are 5- to 6-hour events that give an insider's view of the culinary wonderland that is New York and hands-on experience with its bounty. The tasty adventures include Chinatown, Little Italy, Greenwich Village, and more. Tour prices are all-inclusive and range from $90 to $155. Reservations should be made 3 to 6 months in advance when possible.

Harlem Spirituals (© **800/660-2166** or 212/391-0900; www.harlemspirituals.com) specializes in gospel and jazz tours of Harlem that can be combined

Would you like to cruise by Monica and Chandler's apartment building? How about the courthouse where the prosecutors of *Law & Order* fight the good fight? **On Location Tours** (© **212/334-0492** or 212/935-0168; www.sceneontv.com) offers narrated minibus tours through TV history on their Manhattan TV Tour; tickets are $20 adults, $10 for kids 6 to 9. Or, if you want to see Carrie Bradshaw's Big Apple, cut right to the chase and take the company's 2½-hour ***Sex in the City* Tour** ★, which includes over 40 show-related sights; tickets are $25. Most tours take place on Saturdays and depart from the Times Square Visitor Center (see chapter 5), usually at noon and 2:30pm respectively. There's also a 3-hour ***Sopranos* Tour** that will take you over to New Jersey for an afternoon of sights that range from Satriale's Pork Store to the Bada-Bing! club; this tour leaves from Bryant Park on Sundays at 2pm and costs $30. Reservations are strongly suggested for all tours, as most sell out in advance; it also makes sense to confirm days and times and check for any additional offerings (a brunch program with Joyce Randolph, Trixie from *The Honeymooners,* was in the works at press time).

Now that Seinfeld lives only in syndication, Kenny Kramer, former across-the-hall neighbor of *Seinfeld* co-creator Larry David and the real-life inspiration for Cosmo Kramer ("Giddy-up!"), hopes his 3-hour **Kramer's Reality Tour** for *Seinfeld* fans (© 800/KRAMERS or 212/268-5525; www.kennykramer.com) can fill the void. The tour, which leaves from the Pulse Theater, 432 W. 42nd St., starts out kind of hokey but really gets going once you board the van (equipped with TV monitors for seeing clips of the show) and hit the road. Among the stops are the real Monk's, Tom's Restaurant; the office building where Elaine worked, Kramer had his coffee-table book published, and George had sex with the cleaning lady on his desk; and the vegetable stand where Kramer was banned for squeezing fruit. Tours are offered Saturday and Sunday at noon, and tickets are $37.50—a little pricey, but fun for die-hard fans and casual viewers alike. Reservations are required.

with a traditional soul-food meal. A variety of options are available, including a tour of Harlem sights with gospel service, and a soul-food lunch or brunch as an optional add-on. The Harlem jazz tour includes a neighborhood tour, dinner at a family-style soul-food restaurant, and a visit to a local jazz club; there's also an Apollo Theatre variation on this tour. Additional options include evening tours of Harlem paired with a "behind-the-scenes" gospel choir rehearsal and extended weekday walking tours; Bronx and Brooklyn tours are also an option for those who want a taste of the outer boroughs. Prices start at $30, $22.50 for children, for a Harlem Heritage tour, and go up from there based on length and inclusions (tours that include food and entertainment are pay-one-price). All tours leave from Harlem Spirituals' Midtown office (690 Eighth Ave., between 43rd and 44th sts.), and transportation is included.

Recommended by the Harlem Travel and Tourism Association, **A La Carte New York Tours** (✆ **212/828-7360;** www.alacartecity.com) also offers a slate of walking, bus, architecture, jazz, Apollo Theatre, and gospel tours of everybody's new favorite Upper Manhattan neighborhood. Prices run from $15 to $75, depending on the options you choose. All guides are licensed and extremely knowledgeable.

New York Like a Native ★ (✆ **718/393-7537;** www.nylikeanative.com) offers the city's best guided introduction to Brooklyn. The tours focus mainly on the best of brownstone Brooklyn, and you can choose from a 2½-hour version ($13), or an extended 4½-hour version ($35); the longer tour includes lunch, but you must cover your own bus and subway fares. Tours are generally offered on Saturdays from April through December, and meet at the Brooklyn Library on Grand Army Plaza (subway: 2, 3 to Grand Army Plaza). *Prepaid reservations are required;* visit the website or call ✆ **212/239-1124** to order.

Active visitors with an adventurous spirit can hook up with **Bike the Big Apple** (✆ **877/865-0078;** www.toursbybike.com). Tours by Bike offers guided half-day, full-day, and customized tours through a variety of city neighborhoods, including the fascinating but little-explored Upper Manhattan and Harlem; an ethnic tour that takes you over the legendary Brooklyn Bridge, through Chinatown and Little Italy, and to Ground Zero; and around Flushing, Queens, where you'll feel like you're biking around Hong Kong. You don't have to be an Ironman candidate to participate; tours are designed for the average rider with an emphasis on safety and fun; shorter (approximately 2½ hr.) and longer versions (around 5 hr.) are available. Tours are offered year-round; prices run $49 to $79, and include all gear.

8 Talk of the Town: TV Tapings

The trick to getting tickets for TV tapings in this city is to be from out of town. You visitors have a much better chance than we New Yorkers; producers are gun-shy about filling their audiences with obnoxious locals and see everybody who's not from New York as being from the heartland—and therefore their target TV audience.

If your heart's set on getting tickets to a show, request them as early as possible—6 months ahead isn't too early, and even earlier is better for the most popular shows. You're usually asked to send a postcard. Always include the number of tickets you want, your preferred dates of attendance (be as flexible as you can), and your address *and* phone number. Tickets are always free. The shows tend to be pretty good about trying to meet your specific date requests, but don't be surprised if Ricki or Montel are far more responsive than, say, Dave. And even if you send in your request early, don't be surprised if tickets don't arrive at your house until 1 or 2 weeks before tape date.

If you come to town without any tickets, all hope is not lost. Because they know that every ticket holder won't make it, many studios give out a limited number of standby tickets on the day of taping. If you can just get up a little early and don't mind standing in line for a couple (or a few) hours, you have a good chance of getting one. Now, the bad news: Only one standby ticket per person is allowed, so everybody who wants to get in has to get up at the crack of dawn and stand in line. And even if you get your hands on a standby ticket, it doesn't guarantee admission; they usually only start seating standbys after the regular ticket holders are in. Still, chances are good.

For additional information on getting tickets to tapings, call the NYCVB at ✆ **212/484-1222.** And remember—you don't need a ticket to be on the *Today* show.

If you do attend a taping, be sure to bring a sweater, even in summer. As anybody who watches Letterman knows, it's an icebox in those studios. And bring ID, as proof of age may be required.

The Daily Show with Jon Stewart Comedy Central's boldly irreverent, often hilarious mock newscast tapes every Monday through Thursday at 5:45pm, at 513 W. 54th St. Make your advance ticket requests by phone at ✆ **212/586-2477,** or check with them for any cancellation tickets for the upcoming week; the line is open Monday through Thursday from 10:30am to 4pm for tickets.

Last Call with Carson Daly Tapings of the MTV heartthrob's new NBC late-night gabfest is much like a grown-up TRL, without the countdown or screaming sweet 16s. Tapings are on select weeknights at 7 and/or 9pm. You can reserve up to four tickets in advance by calling ✆ **212/664-3056.** Standby tickets are distributed on the day of taping at 9am outside 30 Rockefeller Plaza, on the 49th Street side of the building, on a first-come, first-served basis (read: come early if you actually want to get one). Note that a standby ticket does not guarantee admission.

Late Night with Conan O'Brien Conan tix might not quite have the cachet of a Dave ticket, but they're a very hot commodity nevertheless—so start planning now. Tapings are Tuesday through Friday at 5:30pm (plan on arriving by 4:45pm if you have tickets), and you must be 16 or older to attend. You can reserve up to four tickets in advance by calling ✆ **212/664-3056.** Standby tickets are distributed on the day of taping at 9am outside 30 Rockefeller Plaza, on the 49th Street side of the building (under the NBC Studios awning), on a first-come, first-served basis (read: come early if you actually want to get one).

The Late Show with David Letterman Here's the most in-demand TV ticket in town. Tapings are Monday through Thursday at 5:30pm (arrive by 4:15pm), with a second taping Thursday at 8pm (arrive by 6:45pm). You must be 18 or older to attend. Send your postcard at least 6 to 9 months in advance (two tickets max; one request only, or all will be disregarded), to *Late Show* Tickets, Ed Sullivan Theater, 1697 Broadway, New York, NY 10019. You can also register at **www.cbs.com/latenight/lateshow** (click on "Get Tickets") to be notified of tickets that may become available for specific dates you select over the next 3 months. On tape days, there are no standby lines anymore; call ✆ **212/247-6497** at 11am for up to 2 standby tickets; start dialing early, because the machine will kick in as soon as all standbys are gone. If you do get through, you may have to answer a trivia question about the show to score tickets.

Live! with Regis and Kelly Tapings with Regis Philbin and Kathie-Lee-replacement Kelly Ripa are Monday through Friday at 9am at the ABC Studios at 7 Lincoln Square (Columbus Ave. and West 67th St.) on the Upper West Side. You must be 10 or older to attend (under 18s must be accompanied by a parent). Send your postcard (four tickets max) at least a *full year* in advance to *Live!* Tickets, Ansonia Station, P.O. Box 230777, New York, NY 10023-0777 (✆ **212/456-3054**). Standby tickets are sometimes available. Arrive at the studio no later than 7am and request a standby number; standby tickets are handed out on a first-come, first-served basis, so earlier is better.

Montel Williams Show Order tickets by calling ✆ **212/989-8101.** Shows typically tape on Wednesday and Thursday at 11:30am, 1:30pm, and 3:30pm. You must be 18 or older to attend.

The Ricki Lake Show Tickets can be requested by calling ✆ **800/GO-RICKI,** or filling out the online form at **www.ricki.com**. You can also use this line, or register on the website, to volunteer yourself as a guest for shows such as "I'm a 30-Year-Old Virgin—Will You Be My First?" or "Stop Being Naked Around My Man!" You must be 18 or older to attend.

The Rosie O'Donnell Show Rosie and her audience giveaways are so popular that her show was not even accepting ticket requests at press time. However, all is not lost. The schedule varies, but in general Rosie tapings are Monday through Thursday at 10am, and Thursday again at 1:30pm. Your best bet is to try standby. Standby tickets, if available, are distributed Monday through Thursday at 7:30am outside 30 Rockefeller Plaza, on the 49th Street side of the building; it's a random lottery system, so it doesn't help to show up too early. You must be present to claim your own ticket. No children under 5 are allowed, and under 18s must be accompanied by an adult.

If you want to try your luck with advanced tickets, call ✆ **212/506-3288** or 212/664-3056 *as far in advance of your arrival in New York as possible* to determine the current ticket-request procedure. Note that comedienne **Caroline Rhea** will be taking over Rosie's desk in 2003; whether or not the change will loosen up the demand for tickets is anybody's guess.

Saturday Night Live SNL tapings are Saturday at 11:30pm (arrival time 10pm); there's also a full dress rehearsal at 8pm (arrival time 7pm). You must be 16 or older to attend. Here's the catch: Tickets are so in demand that the lottery system for advance tickets is usually suspended. However, you can try for standby tickets on the day of the taping, which are distributed at 7am outside 30 Rockefeller Plaza, on the 49th Street side of the building (under the NBC Studios awning), on a first-come, first-served basis; only one ticket per person will be issued. If you want to try your luck with advance tickets, call ✆ **212/664-3056** *as far in advance of your arrival in New York as possible* to determine the current ticket-request procedure.

The *Today* Show Anybody can be on TV with Katie, Matt, and cuddly weatherman Al Roker. All you have to do is show up outside *Today*'s glass-walled studio at Rockefeller Center, on the southwest corner of 49th Street and Rockefeller Plaza, with your very own HI, MOM! sign. Tapings are Monday through Friday from 7am to 10am, but come at the crack of dawn if your heart's set on being in front. Who knows? If it's a nice day, you may even get to chat with Katie, Matt, or Al in a segment. Come extra early to attend a Friday Summer Concert Series show.

Total Request Live The countdown show that made Carson Daly a household name is broadcast live from MTV's second-floor glass-walled studio at 1515 Broadway, at 44th Street in Times Square, weekdays at 3:30pm. Crowds start gathering below at all hours, depending on the drawing power of the day's guest. Audience tickets can sometimes be reserved in advance by calling the **TRL Ticket Reservation Hot Line** at ✆ **212/398-8549;** you must be between the ages of 16 and 24 to attend. If you're not able to score reservations, arrive by 2pm (preferably earlier) if you want a prayer of making it into the in-studio audience; a producer usually roams the crowd asking music trivia questions like

“What's Britney Spears's middle name?” and “Who
Park?” giving away standby tickets for correct answer
your WE LOVE YOU, CARSON! signs large enough to b
may also be able to watch or participate in other M
MTV Store on the corner of 44th and Broadway, w
events are sometimes stacked next to the register.

The View ABC's hugely popular girl-power ga
through Friday at 11am (ticket holders must arrive by
should be made 12 to 16 weeks in advance, can be su [illegible] (www.abc.
go.com/theview) or via postcard to Tickets, *The View,* 320 W. 66th St., New York, NY 10023. Since exact date requests are not usually accommodated, try standby: Arrive at the studio before 10am and put your name on the standby list; earlier is better, since tickets are handed out on a first-come, first-served basis. You must be 18 or older to attend.

Who Wants to Be a Millionaire The trivia show is filmed at ABC's Upper West Side studios. To request tickets to be an audience member, send a postcard to *Who Wants to Be a Millionaire,* Columbia University Station, P.O. Box 250225, New York, NY 10025. Ticket requests are limited to four, and you must be 18 or older to attend. You can also request tickets online at **http://abc.abcnews.go.com/primetime/millionaire**; click on “About the Show” to get to the tickets page, where you can check for the latest taping schedules and standby procedures.

9 Especially for Kids

Some of New York's sights and attractions are designed specifically with kids in mind, and I've listed those below. But many of those I've discussed in the rest of this chapter are terrific for kids as well as adults; I've also included cross-references to the best of them.

Probably the best place of all to entertain the kids is in **Central Park** ★★★, which has kid-friendly diversions galore (see the section beginning on p. 281). For kid-friendly theatrical performances, see the “Kids Take the Stage: Family-Friendly Theater” box in chapter 11.

For general tips and additional resources, see “For Families” under “Tips for Travelers with Special Needs,” in chapter 3.

MUSEUMS

In addition to the museums designed specifically for kids below, also consider the following, discussed elsewhere in this chapter: The **American Museum of Natural History** (p.241), whose dinosaur displays are guaranteed to wow both you and the kids; the ***Intrepid* Sea-Air-Space Museum** (p. 262), on a real battleship with an amazing collection of vintage and high-tech airplanes; the **Forbes Magazine Galleries** (p. 261), whose wacky collection includes a number of vintage toys and games; the **New York City Fire Museum** (p. 270), housed in a real firehouse; the **American Museum of the Moving Image** (p. 308), where you and the kids can learn how movies are actually made; the **Lower East Side Tenement Museum** (p. 263), whose weekend living-history program really intrigues school-age kids; the **New York Transit Museum** (p. 306), where kids can explore vintage subway cars and other hands-on exhibits; and the **South Street Seaport & Museum** (p. 272), which little ones will love for its theme park–like atmosphere and old boats bobbing in the harbor.

useum of Manhattan ★ Kids Here's a great place to take the they're tired of being told not to touch. Designed for ages 2 to 12, seum is strictly hands-on. Interactive exhibits and activity centers urage self-discovery—and a recent expansion means that there's now even ore to keep the kids busy and learning. The Time Warner Media Center takes children through the world of animation and helps them produce their own videos. The Body Odyssey is a zany, scientific journey through the human body. This isn't just a museum for the 5-and-up set—there are exhibits especially designed for babies and toddlers, too. The busy schedule also includes daily art classes and storytellers, and a full slate of entertainment on weekends. Look for *Art Inside Out,* an interactive exhibit dedicated to introducing families to art and museums and featuring a video-making installation from photographer and Weimeraner lover William Wegman, among others, to run from October 2002 through the end of 2003.

212 W. 83rd St. (btwn Broadway and Amsterdam Ave.). ✆ **212/721-1234.** www.cmom.org. Admission $6 children and adults, $3 seniors. Wed–Sun and school holidays 10am–5pm. Subway: 1, 9 to 86th St.

Children's Museum of the Arts Kids Interactive workshop programs for children ages 1 to 12 and their families are the attraction here. Kids dabble in puppet making and computer drawing or join in sing-alongs and live performances. Also look for rotating exhibitions of the museum's permanent collection, featuring WPA work; an exhibit by contemporary artist Melissa Stern in early 2003; and the Piccolo Spolete Festival from May through July 2003. Call or check the website for the current exhibition and activities schedule.

182 Lafayette St. (btwn Broome and Grand sts.). ✆ **212/941-9198** or 212/274-0986. www.cmany.org. Admission $5 for everyone 1–65; pay what you wish Thurs 4–6pm. Wed–Sun noon–5pm (Thurs to 6pm). Subway: 6 to Spring St.

New York Hall of Science ★ Kids Children of all ages will love this huge hands-on museum, which bills itself as "New York's Only Science Playground." This place is amazing for school-age kids—it's just like Beakman's World come to life. Exhibits let them be engulfed by a giant soap bubble (shades of Veruca Salt, Mom and Dad?), float on air in an antigravity mirror, compose music by dancing in front of light beams, and explore the more-than-miniature world of microbes. There are even video machines that kids can use to retrieve astronomical images, including pictures taken by the *Galileo* in orbit around Jupiter. There's a Preschool Discovery Place for the really little ones. But probably best of all is the summertime Outdoor Science Playground for kids 6 and older—ostensibly lessons in physics, but really just a great excuse to laugh, jump, and play on jungle gyms, slides, seesaws, spinners, and more.

The museum is located in **Flushing Meadows–Corona Park,** where kids can enjoy even more fun beyond the Hall of Science. Not only are there more than 1,200 acres of park and playgrounds, but there's also a zoo, a carousel, an indoor ice-skating rink, an outdoor pool, and bike and boat rentals. Kids and grown-ups alike will love getting an up-close look at the Unisphere steel globe, which was not really destroyed in *Men in Black.* The park is also home to the **Queens Museum of Art** (p. 310) as well as Shea Stadium and the U.S. Open Tennis Center.

4701 111th St., in Flushing Meadows–Corona Park, Queens. ✆ **718/699-0005.** www.nyhallsci.org. Admission $7.50 adults, $5 seniors and children 4–17; free Thurs–Fri 2–5pm; extra $2 for Science Playground. Mon–Wed 9:30am–2pm (Tues–Wed to 5pm in summer); Thurs–Sun 9:30am–5pm. Subway: 7 to 111th St.

Sony Wonder Technology Lab *Kids* Not as much of an infomercial as you'd expect. Both kids and adults love this four-level high-tech science and technology center, which explores communications and information technology. You can experiment with robotics, explore the human body through medical imaging, edit a music video, mix a hit song, design a video game, and save the day at an environmental command center. The lab also features the first high-definition interactive theater in the United States. Admission is absolutely free; this place is extremely popular, however, so it's wise to make reservations in advance. Reservations can be made up to 2 weeks in advance by calling © **212/833-5414** on Monday, Wednesday, or Friday between 11am and 4pm. Otherwise, you may not get in, or you may get tickets that require you to return at a different time.

Sony Plaza, 550 Madison Ave. (at 56th St.). © **212/833-8100,** or 212/833-5414 for reservations. www.sonywondertechlab.com. Free admission. Sun, Tues–Wed, and Fri–Sat 10am–6pm; Thurs 10am–8pm; last entrance 30 min. before closing. Subway: E, V or N, R to Fifth Ave.; 4, 5, 6 to 59th St.

OTHER KID-FRIENDLY DIVERSIONS

In addition to the choices below, don't forget New York's fabulous theme restaurants, which are playgrounds unto themselves for visiting kids; see the "Theme Restaurant Thrills!" box, in chapter 7.

ARCADES **Lazer Park,** in Times Square at 1560 Broadway (entrance around the corner at 163 W. 46th St.; © **212/398-3060;** www.lazerpark.com), has amusements ranging from good old-fashioned pinball to virtual-reality games and a full-on laser tag arena. Even better is the brand-new **Broadway City** ★, 241 W. 42nd St., between Seventh and Eighth avenues (© **212/997-9797;** www.broadwaycity.com), a neon-bright, multilevel interactive game center designed on a Big Apple theme where you could lose your kids (and a year's supply of quarters) for an entire day.

SHOPPING Everybody loves to shop in New York—even kids. Don't forget to take them to **Books of Wonder,** that temple of sneakerdom **Niketown,** the **NBA Store,** and **FAO Schwarz,** the best toy store in the world—just ask Tom Hanks (remember *Big?*). Actually, the brand-new **Toys"R"Us** flagship is giving it a run for its money, thanks to its very own indoor Ferris wheel. See chapter 10 for details.

SKY-HIGH VIEWS Kids of all ages can't help but turn dizzy with delight at incredible views from atop the **Empire State Building** (p. 245). The Empire State Building also has the **New York Skyride** (© **212/279-9777;** www.skyride.com), which offers a short motion-flight simulation sightseeing tour of New York, just in case the real one isn't enough for your kids. Open daily 10am to 10pm; tickets are $15.50 adults, $12.50 for seniors and kids 4 to 12; combination Empire State observation deck/New York Skyride tickets are available at a discount.

SPECIAL EVENTS Children's eyes grow wide at the yearlong march of **parades** (especially Macy's Thanksgiving Day Parade), **circuses** (Big Apple, and Ringling Bros. and Barnum & Bailey), and **holiday shows** (the Rockettes' Christmas and Easter performances). See the "New York City Calendar of Events," in chapter 3, for details.

ZOOS & AQUARIUMS Bigger kids will love the legendary **Bronx Zoo** (p. 302), while the **Central Park Zoo** with its Tisch Children's Zoo (p. 286) is particularly suitable to younger kids. At the **New York Aquarium** at Coney Island (p. 305), kids can touch starfish and sea urchins and watch bottlenose dolphins and California sea lions stunt-swim in the outdoor aqua theater. Brooklyn's **Prospect Park** (p. 306) also boasts a wonderful little zoo.

10 Highlights of the Outer Boroughs

IN THE BRONX

In addition to the choices below, literary buffs might also want to visit the **Edgar Allan Poe Cottage,** the final home for the brilliant but troubled author of *The Raven, The Tell-Tale Heart,* and other masterworks. See the "In Search of Historic Homes" box on p. 277.

Bronx Zoo Wildlife Conservation Park ★★★ Kids Founded in 1899, the Bronx Zoo is the largest metropolitan animal park in the United States, with more than 4,000 animals living on 265 acres. This is an extremely progressive zoo as zoos go—most of the old-fashioned cages have been replaced by more natural settings, ongoing improvements keep it feeling fresh and up to date, and it's far more bucolic than you might expect. In fact, I think it's one of the city's best attractions.

One of the most impressive exhibits is the **Wild Asia Complex.** This zoo-within-a-zoo comprises the **Wild Asia Plaza** education center; **Jungle World,** an indoor re-creation of Asian forests with birds, lizards, gibbons, and leopards; and the **Bengali Express Monorail** (open May–Oct), which takes you on a narrated ride high above free-roaming Siberian tigers, Asian elephants, Indian rhinoceroses, and other nonnative New Yorkers (keep your eyes peeled—the animals aren't as interested in seeing you). The **Himalayan Highlands** is home to some 17 extremely rare snow leopards, as well as red pandas and white-naped cranes. The 6½-acre **Congo Gorilla Forest** is home to Western lowland gorillas, okapi, red river hogs, and other African rain-forest animals.

The **Children's Zoo** (open Apr–Oct) allows young humans to learn about their wildlife counterparts. Kids can compare their leaps to those of a bullfrog, slide into a turtle shell, climb into a heron's nest, see with the eyes of an owl, and hear with the acute ears of a fox. There's also a petting zoo. Camel rides are another part of the summertime picture, as is the **Butterfly Zone** and the **Skyfari** aerial tram (each an extra $2 charge).

If the natural settings and breeding programs aren't enough to keep zoo residents entertained, they can always choose to ogle the 2 million annual visitors. But there are ways to beat the crowds. Try to visit on a weekday or on a nice winter's day. In summer, come early in the day, before the heat of the day sends the animals back into their enclosures. Expect to spend an entire day here—you'll need it.

Getting there: Liberty Lines' BxM11 express bus, which makes various stops on Madison Avenue, will take you directly to the zoo; call ✆ **718/652-8400.** By subway, take the 2 train to Pelham Parkway and then walk west to the Bronxdale entrance.

Fordham Rd. and Bronx River Pkwy., the Bronx. ✆ **718/367-1010.** www.wcs.org/zoos. Admission $9 adults, $5 seniors and children 2–12; discounted admission Nov–Mar; free Wed year-round. There may be nominal additional charges for some exhibits. Nov–Mar daily 10am–4:30pm (extended hours for Holiday Lights late Nov–early Jan); Apr–Oct Mon–Fri 10am–5pm, Sat–Sun 10am–5:30pm. Transportation: See "Getting There," above.

New York Botanical Garden ★ A National Historic Landmark, the 250-acre New York Botanical Garden was founded in 1891 and today is one of America's foremost public gardens. The setting is spectacular—a natural terrain of rock outcroppings, a river with cascading waterfalls, hills, ponds, and wetlands.

Highlights of the Botanical Garden are the 27 **specialty gardens** (the Peggy Rockefeller formal rose garden, the Nancy Bryan Luce herb garden, and the restored rock garden are my favorites), an exceptional **orchid collection,** and 40 acres of **uncut forest** as close as New York gets to its virgin state before the arrival of Europeans. The **Enid A. Haupt Conservatory,** a stunning series of Victorian glass pavilions that recall London's former Crystal Palace, shelters a rich collection of tropical, subtropical, and desert plants as well as seasonal flower shows. There's also a **Children's Adventure Garden.** Natural exhibits are augmented by year-round educational programs, musical events, bird-watching excursions, lectures, special family programs, and many more activities. Snuff Mill, once used to grind tobacco, has a charming cafe on the banks of the Bronx River. There are so many ways to see the garden—tram, golf cart, walking tours—that it's best to call or check the website for more information.

Getting there: Take Metro North (✆ **800/METRO-INFO** or 212/532-4900; www.mta.nyc.ny.us/mnr) from Grand Central Terminal to the New York Botanical Garden station; the easy ride takes about 20 minutes. By subway, take the D or 4 train to Bedford Park, then take bus Bx26 or walk southeast on Bedford Park Boulevard for 8 long blocks. The garden operates a shuttle to and from Manhattan April through October on Fridays and weekends, Saturdays only in November and December. Round-trip shuttle and garden tickets are $15 for adults, $12 for seniors and students, $9 for children 2 to 12; call ✆ **718/817-8700** for reservations.

200th St. and Southern Blvd., the Bronx. ✆ **718/817-8700.** www.nybg.org. Admission $3 adults, $2 seniors and students, $1 children 2–12. Extra charges for Everett Children's Adventure Garden, Enid A. Haupt Conservatory, T. H. Everett Rock Garden, Native Plant Garden, and narrated tram tour; entire Garden Passport package is $10 adults, $7.50 seniors and students, $4 children 2–12. Apr–Oct Tues–Sun and Mon holidays 10am–6pm; Nov–Mar Tues–Sun and Mon holidays 10am–4pm. Transportation: See "Getting There," above.

Wave Hill ★ *Finds* Formerly a private estate with panoramic views of the Hudson River and the Palisades, Wave Hill has, at various times in its history, been home to a British U.N. ambassador as well as Mark Twain and Theodore Roosevelt. Set in a stunningly bucolic neighborhood that doesn't look anything like you'd expect from the Bronx, its 28 gorgeous acres were bequeathed to the city of New York for use as a public garden that is now one of the most beautiful spots in the city. It's a wonderful place to commune with nature, both along wooded paths and in beautifully manicured herb and flower gardens, where all of the plants are clearly labeled by careful horticulturists. Benches are positioned throughout the property for quiet contemplation and spectacular views. A great spot for taking in the Hudson River vibe without having to rent a car and travel to Westchester to visit the Rockefeller estate. Programs range from horticulture and environmental education, landscape history and forestry to dance performances and concerts. A new Visitor and Horticultural Center designed by Robert A. M. Stern is currently under construction, and should make this hidden jewel shine even brighter.

Getting there: Take the 1 or 9 subway to 231st St., then take the Bx7 or Bx10 bus to the 252nd Street stop; or take the A subway to 207th Street and pick up the Bx7 to 252nd Street. From the 252nd Street stop, walk west across the parkway bridge and turn left; at 249th Street, turn right. Metro North trains (✆ **212/532-4900**) travel from Grand Central to the Riverdale station; from there, it's a pleasant 5-block uphill walk to Wave Hill.

675 W. 252nd St. (at Independence Ave.), the Bronx. ✆ **718/549-3200.** www.wavehill.org. Admission $4 adults, $2 seniors and students; free in winter, and on Sat mornings and Tues in summer. Tues–Sun 9am–4:30pm; extended in summer (check ahead). Transportation: See "Getting There," above.

IN BROOKLYN

For details on walking the **Brooklyn Bridge,** see p. 243.

It's easy to link visits to the Brooklyn Botanic Garden, the Brooklyn Museum of Art, and Prospect Park, since they're all an easy walk from one another, just off **Grand Army Plaza.** Designed by Frederick Law Olmsted and Calvert Vaux as a suitably grand entrance to their Prospect Park, it boasts a grand Civil War memorial arch designed by John H. Duncan (1892–1901) and the main **Brooklyn Public Library,** an Art Deco masterpiece completed in 1941 (the garden and museum are just on the other side of the library, down Eastern Parkway). The entire area is a half-hour subway ride from Midtown Manhattan.

Brooklyn Botanic Garden ★ Just down the street from the Brooklyn Museum of Art (below) is the most popular botanic garden in the city. This peaceful 52-acre sanctuary is at its most spectacular in May, when thousands of deep pink blossoms of cherry trees are abloom. Well worth seeing is the spectacular **Cranford Rose Garden,** one of the largest and finest in the country; the **Shakespeare Garden,** an English garden featuring plants mentioned in his writings; a **Children's Garden;** the **Osborne Garden,** a 3-acre formal garden; the **Fragrance Garden,** designed for the blind but appreciated by all noses; and the extraordinary **Japanese Hill-and-Pond Garden.** The renowned **C. V. Starr Bonsai Museum** is home to the world's oldest and largest collection of bonsai, while the impressive $2.5 million Steinhardt Conservatory holds the garden's extensive indoor plant collection.

1000 Washington Ave. (at Eastern Pkwy.), Brooklyn. ✆ **718/623-7200.** www.bbg.org. Admission $3 adults, $1.50 seniors and students, free for children under 16; free to all Tues and Sat 10am–noon year-round, plus Wed–Fri from mid-Nov to mid-Mar. Apr–Sept Tues–Fri 8am–6pm, Sat–Sun 10am–6pm; Oct–Mar Tues–Fri 8am–4:30pm, Sat–Sun 10am–4:30pm. Subway: Q to Prospect Park; 2, 3 to Eastern Pkwy./Brooklyn Museum.

Brooklyn Museum of Art ★★ One of the nation's premier art institutions, the Brooklyn Museum of Art rocketed back into the public consciousness in 1999 with the hugely controversial "Sensation: Young British Artists from the Saatchi Collection," which drew international media attention and record crowds who came to see just what an artist—and a few conservative politicians—could make out of a little elephant dung.

Indeed, the museum is best known for its consistently remarkable temporary exhibitions—which ranged from "Jewish Life in Ancient Egypt" to "*Star Wars:* The Magic of Myth" in mid-2002 alone—as well as its excellent permanent collection. The museum's grand beaux arts building, designed by McKim, Mead & White (1897), befits its outstanding holdings, most notably the Egyptian,

---

Moments An Arts Party Grows in Brooklyn

First Saturday is the Brooklyn Museum of Art's ambitious and popular program that takes place on, you guessed it, the first Saturday of each month. It runs from 5 to 11pm and includes free admission and a slate of live music, films, dancing, curator talks, and other entertainment that can get pretty esoteric—think karaoke, lesbian poetry, silent film, experimental jazz, and disco. On a recent Saturday, events included a traditional Irish dance performance, a panel discussion on contemporary black photographers, a screening of *Hair,* and a dance party featuring a funk-and-soul DJ from Brooklyn Underground. As only-in–New York events go, First Saturday is a good one—you can always count on a full slate of cool.

Classical, and Ancient Middle Eastern collection of sculpture, wall reliefs, and mummies. The distinguished decorative arts collection includes 28 American period rooms from 1675 to 1928 (the extravagant Moorish-style smoking room from John D. Rockefeller's 54th St. mansion is my favorite). Other highlights are the African and Asian arts galleries, dozens of works by Rodin, a good costumes and textiles collection, and a diverse collection of both American and European painting and sculpture that includes works by Homer, O'Keeffe, Monet, Cézanne, and Degas. Look for more terrific exhibits on the 2002–03 calendar.

200 Eastern Pkwy. (at Washington Ave.), Brooklyn. ✆ **718/638-5000.** www.brooklynmuseum.org. Suggested admission $6 adults, $3 seniors and students, free for children under 12; free first Sat of the month 5–11pm. Wed–Fri 10am–5pm; first Sat of the month 11am–11pm, each Sat thereafter 11am–6pm; Sun 11am–6pm. Subway: 2, 3 to Eastern Pkwy./Brooklyn Museum.

Brooklyn Tabernacle ★ Under the direction of passionate orator Pastor Jim Cymbala and his choral-director wife Carol, this nondenominational Christian revival church has grown into one of the largest—with a congregation of nearly 10,000 from all walks of city life—and most renowned inner-city churches in the nation. Folks come from all over the world to see the 275-voice, four-time Grammy Award–winning **Brooklyn Tabernacle Choir,** one of the nation's most celebrated gospel choirs.

Brooklyn Tabernacle relocated from Flatbush Avenue to 392 Fulton St., on Fulton Mall in the heart of downtown Brooklyn, in mid-2002. The gloriously renovated 1918 building is the fourth-largest theatrical space in the five boroughs, and seats nearly 4,000 for each service. Still, come early for a prime seat, especially when the choir sings (at the noon and 4pm Sun services).

17 Smith St. (btwn Fulton and Livingston sts.), downtown Brooklyn. ✆ **718/783-0942.** www.brooklyntabernacle.org. Services Sun 9am, noon, and 4pm; Tues 7pm. Subway: A, C, F to Jay St./Borough Hall; 2, 3 to Hoyt St.; 4, 5 to Borough Hall; M, N, R to Lawrence St.

New York Aquarium Kids Because of the long subway ride (about an hour from Midtown Manhattan) and its proximity to the Coney Island boardwalk, this one is really for summer. This surprisingly good aquarium is home to hundreds of sea creatures. Taking center stage are Atlantic bottle-nosed dolphins and California sea lions that perform daily during summer at the **Aquatheater.** Also basking in the spotlight are gangly Pacific octopuses, sharks, and a brand-new sea horse exhibit. Black-footed penguins, California sea otters, and a variety of seals live at the **Sea Cliffs exhibit,** a re-creation of a Pacific coastal habitat. But my absolute favorites are the beautiful white Beluga whales, which exude buckets of aquatic charm. Look for a new alien stingers exhibit opening in autumn 2002. Children love the hands-on exhibits at **Discovery Cove.** There's an indoor oceanview cafeteria and an outdoor snack bar, plus picnic tables.

If you've made the trip out, you simply must check out the human exhibits on nearby **Coney Island**'s 2.7-mile-long boardwalk. Not much is left from its heyday, and it can be a little eerie when the crowds aren't around. But you can still use the beach, drop some cash at the boardwalk arcade, and ride the famed wooden **Cyclone** roller coaster (still a terrifying ride, if only because it seems so . . . rickety). You can't leave without treating yourself to a **Nathan's Famous** hot dog, just off the boardwalk at Surf and Stillwell avenues. This is the original—where the term *hot dog* was coined back in 1906.

502 Surf Ave. (at W. 8th St.), Coney Island, Brooklyn. ✆ **718/265-3400.** www.nyaquarium.com. Admission $9.75 adults, $6 seniors and children 2–12. Memorial Day–Labor Day, Mon–Fri 10am–5pm, Sat–Sun 10am–7pm; April–Memorial Day and Labor Day–October, daily 10am–5pm; Nov–Mar, daily 1am–4:30pm. Subway: D, F to W. 8th St., Brooklyn.

New York Transit Museum *Kids* Undergoing renovations at press time, this underground museum is scheduled to reopen in 2003. It's housed in a real (decommissioned) subway station, is a wonderful place to spend an hour or so. The museum is small but very well done, with good multimedia exhibits exploring the history of the subway from the first shovel full of dirt scooped up at groundbreaking (Mar 24, 1900) to the present. Kids and parents alike will enjoy the interactive elements and the vintage subway cars, old wooden turnstiles, and beautiful station mosaics of yesteryear. New at reopening will be "On the Streets: New York's Trolleys and Buses." All in all, a minor but remarkable tribute to an important development in the city's history.

Remaining open throughout renovation and beyond is the **Gallery Annex & Store at Grand Central Station,** which houses rotating exhibitions and a terrific transit-themed gift shop (see "Museum Stores," in chapter 10). A second museum store, along with a travel information kiosk, is at the **Times Square Visitors Center;** see chapter 5.

Boerum Place and Schermerhorn St., Brooklyn. ✆ **718/694-5100.** www.mta.info/museum. Admission $3 adults, $1.50 seniors and children 3–17 (free for seniors Tues noon–4pm). Mon–Fri 10am–4pm; Sat–Sun noon–5pm. Subway: A, C, F to Jay St.; N, R to Court St.; 2, 3, 4, 5 to Borough Hall. Gallery Annex: In Grand Central Terminal, (on the main level, in the shuttle passage next to the Station Masters' office), 42nd Street and Lexington Ave. (✆ 212/878-0106; subway: 4, 5, 6, 7, S to 42nd St./Grand Central).

Prospect Park ★★ Designed by Frederick Law Olmsted and Calvert Vaux after their great success with Central Park, this 562 acres of woodland, meadows, bluffs, and ponds is considered by many to be their masterpiece and the pièce de résistance of Brooklyn.

The best approach is from Grand Army Plaza, presided over by the monumental **Soldiers' and Sailors' Memorial Arch** (1892) honoring Union veterans. For the best view of the lush landscape, follow the path to Meadowport Arch, and proceed through to the Long Meadow, following the path that loops around it (it's about an hour's walk). Other park highlights include the 1857 Italianate mansion **Litchfield Villa** on Prospect Park West; the **Friends' Cemetery** Quaker burial ground (where Montgomery Clift is eternally prone—sorry, it's fenced off to browsers); the wonderful 1906 beaux arts **boathouse;** the 1912 **carousel,** with white wooden horses salvaged from a famous Coney Island merry-go-round (open Apr–Oct; rides 50¢); and **Lefferts Homestead Children's Historic House Museum** (✆ **718/965-6505**), a 1783 Dutch farmhouse with a museum of period furniture and exhibits geared to kids (open Apr–Nov, Fri–Sun 1–4pm). There's a map at the park entrance that you can use to get your bearings.

On the east side of the park is the **Prospect Park Wildlife Conservation Center** (✆ **718/399-7339**). This is a thoroughly modern children's zoo where kids can walk among wallabies, explore a prairie-dog town, and much more. Admission is $2.50 for adults, $1.25 for seniors, 50¢ for children 3 to 12. April through October, open Monday through Friday 10am to 5pm, to 5:30pm weekends and holidays; November through March, open daily from 10am to 4:30pm.

At Grand Army Plaza, bounded by Prospect Park West, Parkside Ave., and Flatbush Ave., Brooklyn. ✆ **718/965-8951,** or 718/965-8999 for events information. www.prospectpark.org. Subway: 2, 3 to Grand Army Plaza (walk down Plaza St. W. 3 blocks to Prospect Park W. and the entrance) or Eastern Pkwy./ Brooklyn Museum.

BROOKLYN HEIGHTS HISTORIC DISTRICT

Just across the Brooklyn Bridge is **Brooklyn Heights** ★, a peaceful neighborhood of tree-lined streets, more than 600 historic houses built before 1860,

Brooklyn Heights Attractions

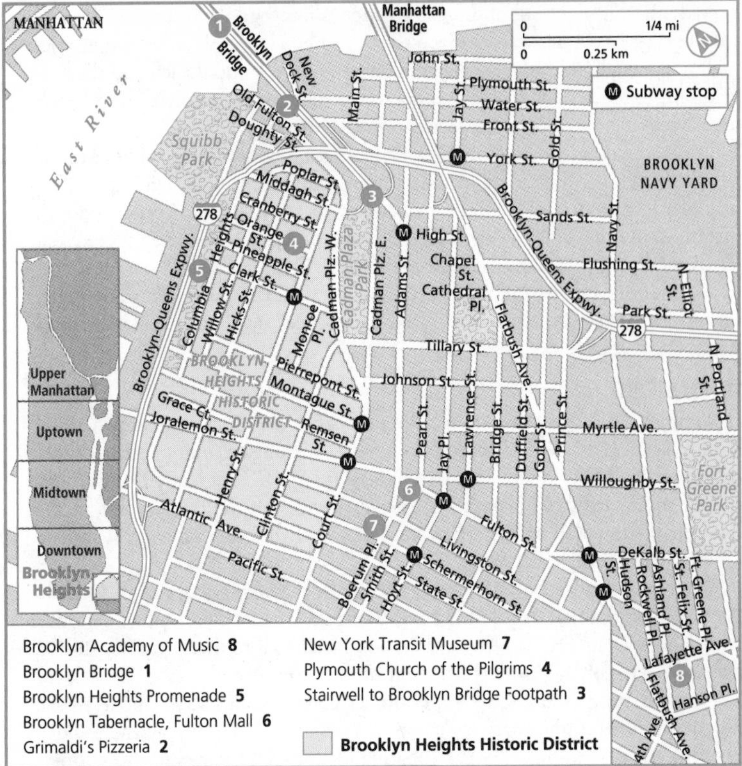

landmark churches, and restaurants. Even with its magnificent promenade providing sweeping views of Lower Manhattan's ragged skyline, it feels more like its own village than part of the larger urban expanse.

This is where Walt Whitman lived and wrote *Leaves of Grass,* one of the great accomplishments in American literature. And in the 19th century, fiery abolitionist Henry Ward Beecher railed against slavery at **Plymouth Church of the Pilgrims** on Orange Street between Henry and Hicks streets (his sister wrote *Uncle Tom's Cabin*). If you walk down **Willow Street** between Clark and Pierrepont, you'll see three houses (nos. 108–112) in the Queen Anne style that was fashionable in the late 19th century, as well as an attractive trio of Federal-style houses (nos. 155–159) built before 1829. Also visit lively **Montague Street,** the main drag of Brooklyn Heights and full of cafes and shops. And don't forget about **Grimaldi's Pizzeria,** near the water on historic Old Fulton Street, serving up the city's best pizza (p. 228).

GETTING THERE Bounded by the East River, Fulton Street, Court Street, and Atlantic Avenue, the Brooklyn Heights Historic District is one of the most outstanding and easily accessible sights beyond Manhattan. The neighborhood is reachable via a number of subway trains: the A, C, F to Jay St.; the 2, 3, 4, 5 to Clark Street or Borough Hall; and the N, R to Court Street.

It's easy to link a walk around Brooklyn Heights and along its Promenade with a walk over the **Brooklyn Bridge** (p. 243), a tour that makes for a lovely afternoon on a nice day. Take a 2 or 3 train to **Clark Street** (the first stop in

Brooklyn). Turn right out of the station and walk toward the water, where you'll see the start of the waterfront **Brooklyn Promenade.** Stroll along the promenade admiring both the stellar views of lower Manhattan to the left and the gorgeous multimillion-dollar brownstones to the right, or park yourself on a bench for a while to contemplate the scene.

The promenade ends at Columbia Heights and Orange Street. To head to the bridge from here, turn left and walk toward the Watchtower Building. Before heading downslope, turn right immediately after the playground onto Middagh Street. After 4 or 5 blocks, you'll reach a busy thoroughfare, Cadman Plaza West. Cross the street and follow the walkway through little **Cadman Plaza Park;** veer left at the fork in the walkway. At Cadman Plaza East, turn left (downslope) toward the underpass, where you'll find the stairwell up to the Brooklyn Bridge footpath on your left.

IN QUEENS

In summer 2002, the **Museum of Modern Art** closed its main midtown Manhattan campus for a 3-year renovation project, opening an interim exhibit space in Long Island City called **MoMA QNS** ★ (p. 248). This 45,000-square-foot (4,181-sq.-m) exhibition space will showcase many of the finest works in the museum's permanent collection, making the quick and easy subway ride out to Queens more than worthwhile.

When you head out to MoMA QNS, consider making a day of it. **Queens Artlink** (**www.moma.org/qal**) is a free weekend arts shuttle, running Saturday and Sunday from 11:30am to 5:30pm and linking all of the institutions listed below (except for the Queens Museum of Art). You can also catch a weekend ride on the **Long Island City Art Loop,** a free shuttle bus service between the Noguchi Museum, the Socrates Sculpture Park, and P.S.1 Saturday and Sunday between noon and 6pm. Any participating institution can answer further questions about either shuttle.

For details on the **New York Hall of Science** and **Flushing Meadows–Corona Park** (also home to the Queens Museum of Art, below), see p. 300.

American Museum of the Moving Image ★ *Kids* Head here if you truly love movies. Unlike Manhattan's Museum of Television & Radio (p. 267), which is more of a library, this is a thought-provoking museum examining how moving images—film, video, and digital—are made, marketed, and shown; it encourages you to consider their impact on society as well. It's housed in part of the Kaufman Astoria Studios, which once were host to W. C. Fields and the Marx Brothers, and more recently have been used by Martin Scorsese (*The Age of Innocence*), Woody Allen (*Radio Days*), Bill Cosby (his *Cosby* TV series), and *Sesame Street.*

The museum's core exhibit, **"Behind the Screen,"** is a thoroughly engaging two-floor installation that takes you step-by-step through the process of making, marketing, and exhibiting moving images. There are more than 1,000 artifacts on hand, from technological gadgetry to costumes, and interactive exhibits where you can try your own hand at sound-effects editing or create your own animated shorts, among other simulations. Special-effects benchmarks from the mechanical mouth of *Jaws* to the blending of past and present in *Forrest Gump* are explored and explained. And in a nod to Hollywood nostalgia, memorabilia that wasn't swept up by the Planet Hollywood chain is displayed, including a Hopalong Cassidy lunch box, an E. T. doll, celebrity coloring books, and Dean Martin and Jerry Lewis hand puppets. Also on display are sets from *Seinfeld.*

Even better are the daily hands-on demonstrations, where you can watch film editors, animators, and the like at work.

"Insiders' Hour" tours are offered every day at 2pm. Additionally, the museum hosts free **film and video screenings,** often accompanied by artist appearances, lectures, or panel discussions. Seminars often feature renowned film and TV pros discussing their craft; past guests have included Spike Lee, Terry Gilliam, Chuck Jones, and Atom Egoyan, so it's definitely worth seeing if someone's on while you're in town.

35th Ave. at 36th St., Astoria, Queens. ✆ **718/784-0077** or 718/784-4777. www.ammi.org. Admission $8.50 adults, $5.50 seniors and college students, $4.50 children 5–18. Tues–Fri noon–5pm; Sat–Sun 11am–6pm (evening screenings Sat–Sun at 6:30pm). Subway: R to Steinway St.; N to Broadway.

Isamu Noguchi Garden Museum ★ *Finds* No place in the city is more Zen than this marvelous indoor/outdoor garden museum showcasing the work of Japanese American sculptor Isamu Noguchi (1904–88). Unfortunately, the original building in Long Island City, built in 1927 and purchased by Noguchi in 1975, will be closed for renovation until spring 2003. The museum has established temporary exhibition space in nearby Sunnyside, Queens. While this temporary space is limited to indoor exhibitions, it's still worth visiting to see a beautifully curated collection of the artist's masterworks in stone, metal, wood, and clay; you'll even see theater sets, furniture, and models for public gardens and playgrounds that Noguchi designed. A free guided tour is offered at 2pm. The museum shop will continue to sell Noguchi's Akari lamps as well as books, cards, posters, and the like.

The museum is set to return home in spring 2003; summer visitors, however, should confirm the return before heading out.

Temporary site: 36-01 43rd Ave. (at 36th St.)., Sunnyside, Queens. Subway: 7 to 33rd St. Walk north to 36th St., turn left and go 1 block to 43rd Ave. Original location, returning spring 2003: 32–37 Vernon Blvd. (at 33rd Rd.), Long Island City, Queens. Subway: N to Broadway. Walk west on Broadway toward Manhattan until Broadway ends at Vernon Blvd.; turn left on Vernon and go 2 blocks. ✆ **718/204-7088.** www.noguchi.org. Suggested admission $4 adults, $2 seniors and students. Wed–Fri 10am–5pm; Sat–Sun 11am–6pm. Subway: 7 to 33rd St. Walk north to 36th St., turn left and go 1 block to 43rd Ave.

Museum for African Art *Finds* This captivating museum is a leading organizer of temporary—and usually excellent—exhibits dedicated to historic and contemporary African art and culture. In September 2002, the museum moved out of its old SoHo space and into a long-term temporary home in Long Island City (the same building where the Isamu Noguchi Museum is temporarily housed), which it will occupy until its new Museum Mile home is ready on Fifth Avenue between 109th and 110th streets. Look for "Facing the Mask," a traditional installation of over 70 of the finest examples of masks from across the African continent, to run through February 2003. Weekend and evening programs include music and dance performances, art-making workshops, family events, and more; call or check the website for the current schedule.

36-01 43rd Ave. (at 36th St.), Long Island City, Queens. ✆ **212/966-1313.** www.africanart.org. Admission $5 adults, $2.50 seniors, students, and children. Tues–Fri 10:30am–5:30pm (to 8:30pm 3rd Thurs of each month); Sat–Sun noon–6pm. Subway: 7 to 33rd St. Walk north to 36th St., turn left and go 1 block to 43rd Ave.

P.S. 1 Contemporary Art Center If you're interested in contemporary art that's too cutting-edge for most museums, don't miss this MoMA affiliate museum. Reinaugurated in 1997 after a 3-year $8.5 million renovation of the Renaissance Revival building that was originally a public school (hence the name), this is the world's largest institution exhibiting contemporary art from

America and abroad. You can expect to see a kaleidoscopic array of works from artists ranging from Jack Smith to Julian Schnabel; the museum is particularly well known for large-scale exhibitions by artists such as James Turrell.

22–25 Jackson Ave. (at 46th Ave.), Long Island City, Queens. ✆ **718/784-2084.** www.ps1.org. Suggested admission $5 adults, $2 seniors and students. Wed–Sun noon–6pm. Subway: E, V to 23rd St./Ely Ave. (walk 2 blocks south on Jackson Ave. to 46th Ave.); 7 to 45th Rd./Court House Sq. (walk 1 block south on Jackson Ave.).

Queens Museum of Art One way to see New York in the shortest time (albeit without the street life) is to visit the Panorama, created for the 1939 World's Fair, an enormous building-for-building architectural model of New York City complete with an airplane that takes off from LaGuardia Airport. The 9,335-square-foot (867-sq.-m) Gotham City is the largest model of its kind in the world, with 895,000 individual structures built on a scale of 1 inch = 100 feet. A red-white-and-blue ribbon is draped mournfully over the Twin Towers, which still stand in this Big Apple.

Also on permanent display is a collection of Tiffany glass manufactured at Tiffany Studios in Queens between 1893 and 1938. The *Contemporary Currents* series features rotating exhibits focusing on the works of a single artist, often with an international theme (suitable to New York's most diverse borough). History buffs should take note of the museum's NYC Building, which housed the United Nation's General Assembly from 1946 to 1952. Rotating art exhibitions, tours, lectures, films, and performances are part of the program, making this a very strong museum on all fronts.

Next to the Unisphere in Flushing Meadows–Corona Park, Queens. ✆ **718/592-9700.** www.queensmuse.org. Suggested admission $5 adults, $2.50 seniors and students, free for children under 5. Tues–Fri 10am–5pm; Sat–Sun noon–5pm. Subway: 7 to Willets Point/Shea Stadium (follow the yellow signs for the 10-min. walk through the park to the museum, which sits next to the Unisphere).

Socrates Sculpture Park This former riverside landfill is now the best exhibition space for large-scale outdoor sculpture in the city. No velvet ropes and motion sensors here—interaction with the artwork is encouraged. Well worth a look, especially on a lovely day. Check the website for the current exhibition schedule—or just let yourself be happily surprised.

Broadway at Vernon Blvd., Long Island City, Queens. ✆ **718/956-1819.** www.socratessculpturepark.org. Free admission. Daily 10am–sunset. Subway: N or W to Broadway; walk 8 blocks along Broadway toward the East River.

11 Spectator Sports

For details on the **New York City Marathon** and the **U.S. Open Tennis Championships,** see the "New York City Calendar of Events," in chapter 3.

BASEBALL With two baseball teams in town, you can catch a game almost any day from opening day in April to beginning of playoffs in October. (Don't bother trying to get subway series tix, though—they're the hottest seats in town. Ditto for Opening Day or any playoff game.)

Star catcher Mike Piazza and the Amazin' **Mets** play at **Shea Stadium** in Queens (subway: 7 to Willets Point/Shea Stadium); even though they lost out to the Yanks in 2000, they're still an exciting team to watch. For tickets (which ran $12–$43 for regular-season games in the 2002 season) and information, call the **Mets Ticket Office** at ✆ **718/507-TIXX,** or visit **www.mets.com**. Also keep in mind that you can buy game tickets (as well as logo wear and souvenirs, if you want to dress appropriately for the big game) at the **Mets Clubhouse Shop,** which has two midtown Manhattan locations; see p. 374.

Moments Year-Round Yankee Tour

For a taste of Yankee glory at any time of year, take the **Insider's Tour of Yankee Stadium** (✆ **718/579-4531**). This official tour of the House That Ruth Built will take you onto the field, to Monument Park, into the dugout. You'll even visit the press box and take a peek inside the clubhouse. The guide peppers the tour with lots of Yankee history and anecdotes as you go. And who knows? You might even spot a certain gorgeous green-eyed multimillionaire shortstop as you make the rounds.

Tours are offered daily at noon except New Year's Day and during Opening Day preparations (usually the 3 weeks prior); plan to arrive by 11:40am. Tickets for the 1-hour basic **Babe Ruth Tour** are $12 for adults, $5 for kids 14 and under. No reservations are required; all you need to do is show up at the ballpark's press gate just before tour time, but it's still a good idea to call and confirm. (Groups of 12 or more require reservations and can book the 80-min. **Champions Tour,** which includes a short film on Yankee history screened in the Adidas Hall of Fame Suite, on a more varied schedule; prices are $17 for adults, $12 for seniors and kids. The **Champions Plus Tour** adds a 15 minutes tour of the club level; $25 adults, $15 kids.) More information is available on the Yankee website (**www.yankees.com**; click on "Yankee Stadium").

Never mind that the **Yankees** lost to the upstart Diamondbacks in 2001—let's see them build a franchise like this one. The Yanks, who won a mind-blowing 26th World Championship in 2000, play at the House That Ruth Built, otherwise known as Yankee Stadium (subway: C, D, 4 to 161st St./Yankee Stadium). For tickets ($8–$65 in 2002), call **Ticketmaster** (✆ **212/307-1212** or 212/307-7171; www.ticketmaster.com) or **Yankee Stadium** (✆ **718/293-6000;** www.yankees.com). Serious baseball fans might check the schedule well in advance and try to catch **Old Timers' Day,** usually held in July, when pinstriped stars of years past return to the stadium to take a bow.

At Yankee Stadium, upper tier box seats (which run about $33), especially those behind home plate, give you a great view of all the action. Upper tier reserve seats are directly behind the box seats and are significantly cheaper ($17). Bleacher seats are even cheaper, and the rowdy commentary from that section's roughneck bleacher creatures is absolutely free. Most of the expensive seats (field boxes) are sold out in advance to season ticket holders. You can often purchase these very same seats from scalpers, but you'll pay a premium for them. Tickets can be purchased at the team's **clubhouse shop** in Manhattan; see p. 375.

Minor-league baseball ★ made a Big Apple splash in summer 2001 when the **Brooklyn Cyclones,** the New York Mets' A-level farm team, and the **Staten Island Yankees,** the Yanks' junior leaguers, came to town. Boasting their very own waterfront stadium, the Brooklyn Cyclones have been a major factor in the revitalization of Coney Island; spanking-new Keyspan Park sits right off the legendary boardwalk (subway: F, N, Q, W to Stillwell Ave./Coney Island). The SI Yanks also have their own shiny new playing field, the Richmond County Bank Ballpark, just a five-minute walk from the Staten Island Ferry terminal (subway: N, R to Whitehall St.; 4, 5 to Bowling Green; 1, 9 to South Ferry). What's more, with bargain-basement ticket prices (which topped out at $8 for the Cyclones, $10 for the Yanks in the 2002 season), this is a great way to experience baseball in the city for a fraction of the major-league hassle and cost. Both teams have already developed a rabidly loyal fan base, so it's a good idea to buy your tickets for the 2003 summer season—which will run from June through September—in advance. For the Cyclones, call ✆ **718/449-8497** or visit **www.brooklyn cyclones.com**; to reach the SI Yanks, call ✆ **718/720-9200** or go online to **www.siyanks.com**.

BASKETBALL Two pro teams call **Madison Square Garden,** Seventh Avenue between 31st and 33rd streets (✆ **212/465-6741** or www.thegarden.com; **212/307-7171** or www.ticketmaster.com for tickets; subway: A, C, E, 1, 2, 3, 9 to 34th St.), home court: Latrell Sprewell, Allen Houston, Marcus Camby, and the rest of the **New York Knicks** (✆ **877/NYK-DUNK** or 212/465-JUMP; www.nyknicks.com); and the **New York Liberty** (✆ **212/564-WNBA;** www.wnba.com/liberty), who electrify fans with their tough-playing defense and star players like Rebecca Lobo and Teresa Weatherspoon. Knicks tickets are hard to come by, so plan ahead if you want a front-row seat near first fan Spike Lee.

ICE HOCKEY The **New York Rangers** play at Madison Square Garden, Seventh Avenue between 31st and 33rd streets (✆ **212/465-6741;** www.newyorkrangers.com or www.thegarden.com; subway: A, C, E, 1, 2, 3, 9 to 34th St.). The memories of the Mark Messier–led 1994 Stanley Cup team linger on, much to the chagrin of the present underachieving team, which suffered another serious blow when Wayne Gretzky retired in April 1999. Tickets are hard to get nevertheless, so plan well ahead; call ✆ **212/307-7171,** or visit www.ticket master.com for online orders.

9

City Strolls

by Reid Bramblett

WALKING TOUR 1 GREENWICH VILLAGE LITERARY TOUR

Start:	**Bleecker Street between La Guardia Place and Thompson Street.**
Subway:	**Take the 6 to Bleecker Street, which lets you out at Bleecker and Lafayette Streets. Walk west on Bleecker.**
Finish:	**14 West 10th St.**
Time:	**Approximately 4 to 5 hours.**
Best Time:	**If you plan to do the whole tour, start fairly early in the day (there's a breakfast break near the start).**

The Village has always attracted rebels, radicals, and creative types, from earnest 18th-century revolutionary Thomas Paine, to early 20th-century radicals, such as John Reed and Mabel Dodge, to the Stonewall rioters who gave birth to the gay liberation movement in 1969. Much of Village life centers around Washington Square Park, the site of hippie rallies and counterculture demonstrations, as well as the former stomping ground of Henry James and Edith Wharton.

Many other American writers have at some time made their homes in the Village. As early as the 19th century, it was New York's literary hub and a venue for salons and other intellectual gatherings. Both the Metropolitan Museum of Art and the Whitney Museum of American Art came into being here, albeit some 60 years apart.

The 20th century saw Greenwich Village transformed from a bastion of old New York families to a bohemian enclave of struggling writers and artists. Though skyrocketing rents made the Village less accessible to aspiring artists after the late 1920s, it remained a mecca for creative people—so much so that almost every building is a literary landmark—though I promise not to take you to every one. Nonetheless, this tour is a long one, and you may want to break it up into two visits.

Begin on Bleecker Street, named for a writer, Anthony Bleecker, whose friends included Washington Irving and William Cullen Bryant, at:

1 145 Bleecker St.

James Fenimore Cooper, author of 32 novels, plus a dozen works of nonfiction, lived here in 1833. Though he is primarily remembered for romantic adventure stories of American frontier—especially *Leatherstocking Tales,* the epic of frontiersman Natty Bumppo (written over a period of 19 years)—Cooper also wrote political commentary, naval history, sea stories, and a group of novels about the Middle Ages.

Greenwich Village Literary Tour

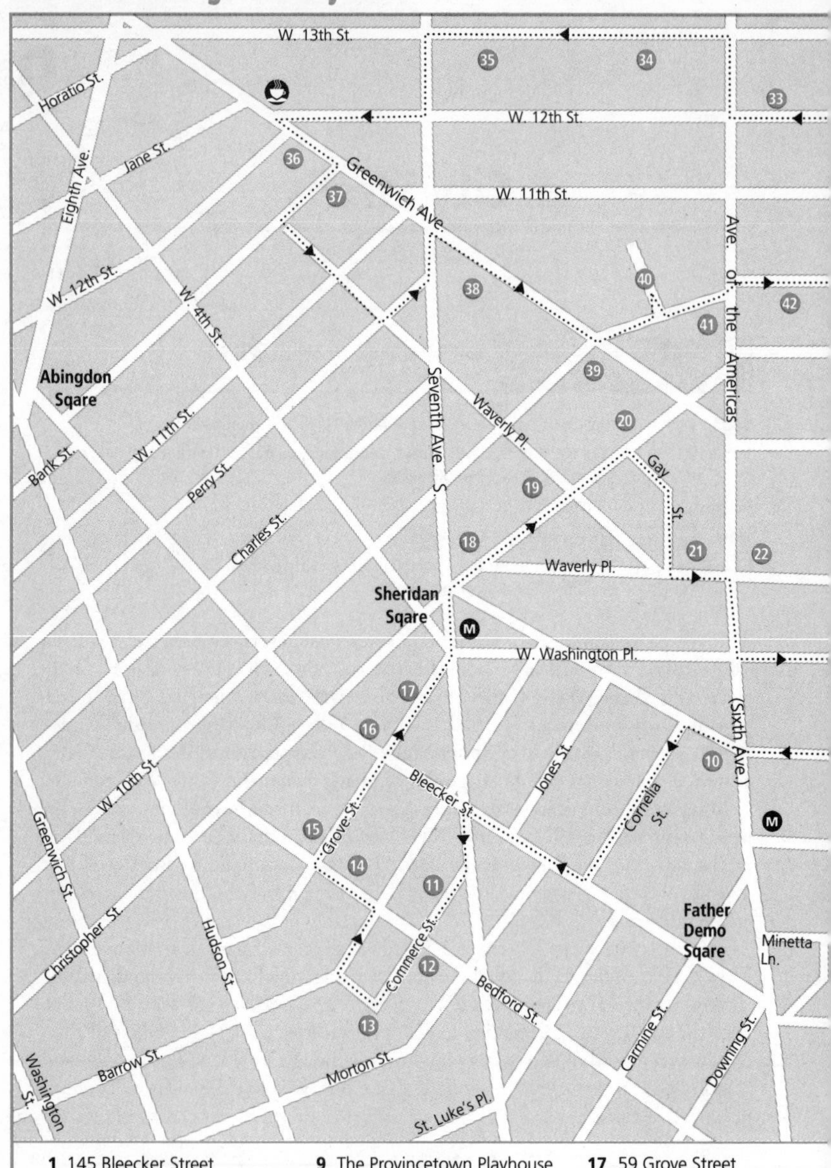

1 145 Bleecker Street
2 Circle in the Square Theater
3 The Atrium
4 172 Bleecker Street
5 189 Bleecker Street
6 Minetta Tavern
7 130-132 MacDougal Street
8 85 West 3rd Street
9 The Provincetown Playhouse
10 Sixth Avenue and West 4th Street
11 11 Commerce Street
12 75 1/2 Bedford Street
13 The Cherry Lane Theatre
14 Chumley's
15 17 Grove Street
16 45 Grove Street
17 59 Grove Street
18 The Stonewall
19 Waverly Place & Christopher Street
20 Gay Street
21 139 Waverly Place
22 116 Waverly Place
23 82 Washington Place
24 Washington Square Park

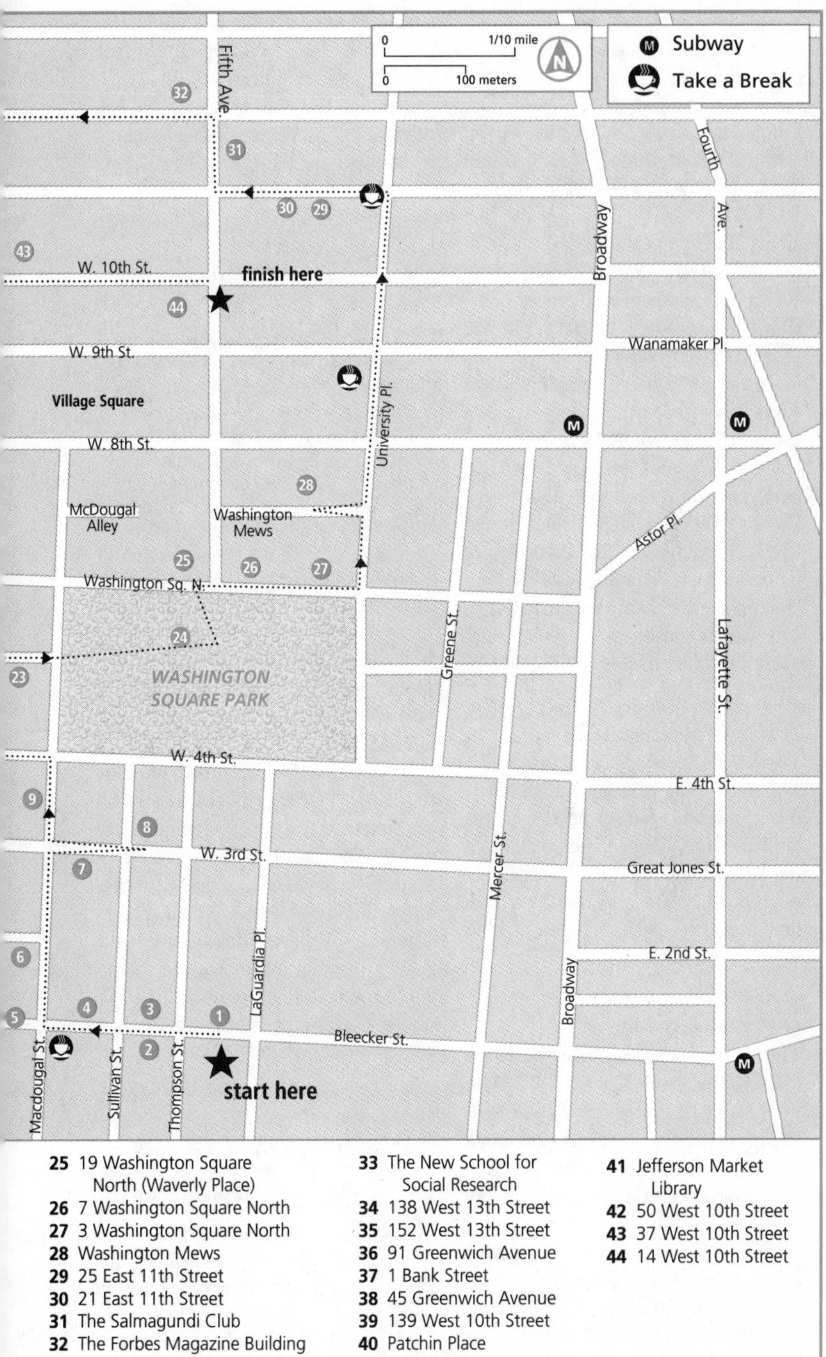

25 19 Washington Square North (Waverly Place)
26 7 Washington Square North
27 3 Washington Square North
28 Washington Mews
29 25 East 11th Street
30 21 East 11th Street
31 The Salmagundi Club
32 The Forbes Magazine Building
33 The New School for Social Research
34 138 West 13th Street
35 152 West 13th Street
36 91 Greenwich Avenue
37 1 Bank Street
38 45 Greenwich Avenue
39 139 West 10th Street
40 Patchin Place
41 Jefferson Market Library
42 50 West 10th Street
43 37 West 10th Street
44 14 West 10th Street

Continue west (walk right) to:

2 Circle in the Square Theater (159 Bleecker St.)

Founded by Ted Mann and Jose Quintero in 1951 at the site of an abandoned nightclub on Sheridan Square, the theater moved to Bleecker Street in 1959. It was one of the first arena, or "in-the-round," theaters in the United States. Tennessee Williams's *Summer and Smoke* (starring Geraldine Page), Eugene O'Neill's *The Iceman Cometh* (starring Jason Robards, Jr.), Thorton Wilder's *Plays for Bleecker Street,* Truman Capote's *The Grass Harp,* and Jean Genet's *The Balcony* all premiered here. Actors Colleen Dewhurst, Dustin Hoffman, James Earl Jones, Cicely Tyson, Jason Robards, George C. Scott, and Peter Falk honed their craft on the Circle in the Square stage. The theater continues to present high-quality productions.

Across the street is:

3 The Atrium (no. 160)

This 19th-century beaux arts building by Ernest Flagg is today a posh apartment building. Before becoming the sadly defunct Village Gate jazz club in the late 1950s, this former flophouse was Theodore Dreiser's first New York residence (in 1895, he paid 25¢ a night for a cell-like room).

Further west is:

4 172 Bleecker St.

This is where James Agee lived in a top-floor railroad flat from 1941 to 1951, after he completed *Let Us Now Praise Famous Men.* Though the book enjoyed a great vogue in the 1960s, it was originally scathingly reviewed and went out of print in 1948 after selling a mere 1,025 copies. *Time* magazine called it "the most distinguished failure of the season."

Rallying from critical buffets during his Bleecker Street tenancy, Agee created the screenplay for *The African Queen* and worked as a movie critic for both *Time* and *The Nation.* He had to move from this walk-up apartment after he suffered a heart attack.

Nearby, the quintessential Village corner of Bleecker and MacDougal is a good spot for a breakfast break.

TAKE A BREAK
Café Figaro (✆ **212/677-1100**) at 184–186 Bleecker St. is an old beat-generation haunt. In 1969, Village residents were disheartened to see the Figaro close and in its place arise an uninspired and sterile Blimpie's. In 1976, the present owner completely restored Figaro to its earlier appearance, replastering its walls once again with shellacked copies of the French newspaper *Le Figaro.* Stop in for pastries and coffee or an omelet and absorb the atmosphere, or sit at a sidewalk table to watch the Village parade by.

On the opposite corner is:

5 189 Bleecker St.

For several decades, beginning in the late 1920s, the San Remo (today Carpo's Cafe), an Italian restaurant at the corner of Bleecker and MacDougal Streets, was a writer's hangout frequented by James Baldwin, William Styron, Jack Kerouac, James Agee, Frank O'Hara, Gregory Corso, Dylan Thomas, William Burroughs, and Allen Ginsberg. John Clellon Holmes wrote about the San Remo in his 1952 novel, *Go,* one of the first published works of the beat generation.

Take a right and head north on MacDougal Street to the:

6 Minetta Tavern

Located at 113 MacDougal St. at Minetta Lane (✆ **212/475-3850**), the Minetta Tavern was a speakeasy called the Black Rabbit during Prohibition. The most unlikely event to take place here in those wild days was the founding of De Witt Wallace's very unbohemian *Reader's Digest* on the premises in 1923; the magazine was published in the basement in its early days. Since

1937, the Minetta has been a simpatico Italian restaurant and meeting place for writers and other creative folk, including Ezra Pound, e.e. cummings, Louis Bromfield, and Ernest Hemingway.

The Minetta still evokes the old Village. Walls are covered with photographs of famous patrons and caricatures (about 20 of which artist Franz Kline scrawled in exchange for drinks and food), and the rustic pine-paneled back room is adorned with murals of local landmarks. Stop in for a drink or a meal. The Minetta is open daily from noon to midnight and serves traditional Italian fare.

A little farther up and across the street stands an 1852 house fronted by twin entrances and a wisteria-covered portico, at:

7 130–132 MacDougal St.

This house belonged to Louisa May Alcott's uncle, and after the Civil War, Alcott lived and worked here. Historians believe it was here that she penned her best-known work, the autobiographical children's classic *Little Women* (Jo, Amy, Meg, and Beth were based on Alcott and her sisters Abbie, Anna, and Lizzie, respectively). Alcott grew up in Concord, Massachusetts, the daughter of transcendentalist Amos Bronson Alcott. Emerson was a close family friend, and Thoreau taught the young Louisa botany. During the Civil War, Alcott briefly served as a Union hospital nurse in Washington, D.C., until a case of typhoid fever nearly killed her. Alcott later published a book of letters documenting that time under the title *Hospital Sketches.* Mercury poisoning from the medication she was given left her in fragile health the rest of her life.

Across the street, at 133 MacDougal St., is:

8 The Provincetown Playhouse

The playhouse at 133 MacDougal St. (✆ **212/477-5048**) was first established in 1915 on a wharf in Provincetown, Massachusetts. Founders George Cram "Jig" Cook and his wife Susan Glaspell began by producing their own plays. One day, however, an intense 27-year-old named Eugene O'Neill arrived in Provincetown with a trunk full of plays, a few of which he brought for Cook and Glaspell to read. They immediately recognized his genius and were inspired to create a theater dedicated to experimental drama. It moved to this converted stable, where O'Neill managed it through 1927. Many of O'Neill's early plays premiered here: *Bound East for Cardiff, The Hairy Ape, The Long Voyage Home, The Emperor Jones,* and *All God's Chillun's Got Wings.*

Other seminal figures in the theater's early days were Max Eastman, Djuna Barnes, Edna Ferber, and John Reed. Edna St. Vincent Millay, whose unlikely life plan was to support herself as a poet by earning her living as an actress, snagged both the lead in Fred Dell's *An Angel Intrudes* and Dell himself (their love affair inspired her poems "Weeds" and "Journal"). Katharine Cornell, Tallulah Bankhead, Bette Davis (who made her stage debut here), and Eva Le Gallienne also appeared on the Provincetown stage in its early years. The theater was a great success, and O'Neill's plays went on to Broadway. But instead of basking in their popularity, Cook and Glaspell disbanded the company and moved on to Greece, convinced that acceptance by the establishment signaled their failure as revolutionary artists. Though the Provincetown Players gave their last performance on December 14, 1929, this theater, fully restored in 1997, now presents plays by and for young people, as well as community playhouse–produced O'Neill works.

Next door is:

9 137 MacDougal St.

Jack London, Upton Sinclair, Vachel Lindsay, Louis Untermeyer, Max

Eastman, Theodore Dreiser, Lincoln Steffens, and Sinclair Lewis hashed over life theories at the Liberal Club, "A Meeting Place for Those Interested in New Ideas," founded in 1913 on the second floor of the house that once stood here. Margaret Sanger lectured the club on birth control, an on-premises organization called Heterodoxy worked to promote feminist causes, and cubist art was displayed on the walls.

Downstairs were Polly's Restaurant (run by Polly Holladay and Hippolyte Havel) and the radical Washington Square Book Shop, from which Liberal Club members more often borrowed than bought. Holladay, a staunch anarchist, refused to join even the Liberal Club, which, however bohemian, was still an "organization." The apoplectic Havel, who was on the editorial board of *The Masses* (see stop 37), once shouted out at a meeting where fellow members were debating which literary contributions to accept: "Bourgeois pigs! Voting! Voting on poetry! Poetry is something from the soul! You can't vote on poetry!" When Floyd Dell pointed out to Havel that he had once made editorial selections for the radical magazine *Mother Earth,* Havel shot back, "Yes, but we didn't abide by the results!" Hugo Kalmar, a character in O'Neill's *The Iceman Cometh,* is purportedly based on Havel. In a previous incarnation, this building was the home of Nathaniel Currier (of Currier and Ives).

Turn left onto West 4th Street and continue to the corner of:

⑩ Sixth Avenue and West 4th Street

Eugene O'Neill, a heavy drinker, nightly frequented a bar called the Golden Swan (more familiarly known as the "Hell Hole" or "Bucket of Blood") where the small park now stands and later used it as a setting for his play *The Iceman Cometh,* a play that was 12 years in the writing. The bar was patronized by prostitutes, gangsters, longshoremen, anarchists, and politicians, as well as artists and writers. Eccentric owner Tom Wallace, on whom O'Neill modeled saloon proprietor Harry Hope, kept a pig in the basement and seldom ventured off the premises.

Cross Sixth Avenue, angle up the continuation of West 4th Street, and make your first left onto Cornelia Street looking for:

⑪ 33 Cornelia St.

Throughout the 1940s, film critic/poet/novelist/screenwriter James Agee lived on Bleecker Street and worked in a studio at this address. Here he completed final revisions on *Let Us Now Praise Famous Men,* which portrayed the bleak lives of Alabama sharecroppers.

Next door, at 31 Cornelia St., once stood the **Caffè Cino,** which opened in 1958 and served cappuccino in shaving mugs. In the early 1960s, owner Joe Cino encouraged aspiring playwrights, such as Lanford Wilson, Sam Shepard, and John Guare, to stage readings and performances in his cramped storefront space. Experimentation in this tiny cafe gave birth to New York's off-Broadway theater. Plagued by money troubles, Cino committed suicide in 1967; Caffè Cino closed a year later.

Continue down Cornelia Street to Bleecker Street and turn right. Cross Seventh Avenue and angle back to your left into Commerce Street. Near the corner stands:

⑫ 11 Commerce St.

Washington Irving wrote "The Legend of Sleepy Hollow" while living in this quaint three-story brick building. Born into a prosperous New York family, he penned biographies of naval heroes as an officer in the War of 1812. In 1819, under the name Geoffrey Crayon, he wrote *The Sketch Book,* which contained the stories "The Legend of Sleepy Hollow,"

"Westminster Abbey," and "Rip Van Winkle." Irving was one of the elite New Yorkers who served on the planning commission for Central Park and was ambassador to Spain from 1842 to 1846. He coined the phrase "the almighty dollar" and once observed that "A tart temper never mellows with age, and a sharp tongue is the only tool that grows keener with constant use."

Continue walking west on Commerce and turn left at Bedford Street to find:

⓭ 75½ Bedford St.

The narrowest house in the Village (a mere 9½ ft. across), this unlikely three-story brick residence was built on the site of a former carriage alley in 1873. Pretty, redheaded, feminist poet Edna St. Vincent Millay, who arrived in the Village fresh from Vassar, lived here from 1923 (the year she won a Pulitzer Prize for her poetry) to 1925.

Other famous occupants of the narrow house have included a young Cary Grant and John Barrymore.

Return to Commerce Street and turn left, where you'll find:

⓮ The Cherry Lane Theatre

Nestled in a bend at 38 Commerce St., the Cherry Lane Theatre was founded in 1924 by Edna St. Vincent Millay. Famed scenic designer Cleon Throckmorton transformed the Revolutionary-era building (originally a farm silo, later a brewery and a box factory) into a playhouse that presented works by Edward Albee, Samuel Beckett (*Waiting for Godot* and *Endgame* premiered here), Eugene Ionesco, Jean Genet, and Harold Pinter. In 1951, Judith Malina and Julian Beck founded the ultra-experimental Living Theatre on its premises. Before rising to megafame, Barbra Streisand worked as a Cherry Lane usher.

Nearby, in Commerce Street's bend, is **no. 48,** a Greek Revival house fronted by a bona-fide working gas lamp and built in 1844 for malicious merchant maven A.T. Stewart.

Continue around Commerce Street's bend to Barrow Street, where you turn right, and then turn left back onto Bedford Street. A few doors up on the right is:

⓯ Chumley's

Chumley's (86 Bedford St.; ✆ **212/675-4449**) opened in 1926 in a former blacksmith's shop. During Prohibition, it was a speakeasy with a casino upstairs. Its convoluted entranceway with four steps up and four down (designed to slow police raiders), the lack of a sign outside, and a back door that opens on an alleyway are remnants of that era.

Original owner Lee Chumley was a radical labor sympathizer who held secret meetings of the IWW (Industrial Workers of the World) on the premises. Chumley's has long been a writer's bar. Its walls are lined with book jackets of works by famous patrons who, over the years, have included Edna St. Vincent Millay (she once lived upstairs), John Steinbeck, Eugene O' Neill, e.e. cummings, Edna Ferber, John Dos Passos, F. Scott Fitzgerald, Theodore Dreiser, William Faulkner, Gregory Corso, Norman Mailer, William Carlos Williams, Allen Ginsberg, Lionel Trilling, Harvey Fierstein, Calvin Trillin, and numerous others. Even the elusive J.D. Salinger hoisted a few at the bar here, and Simone de Beauvoir came by when she was in town.

With its working fireplaces (converted blacksmith forges), wood-plank flooring, amber lighting, and old, carved-up oak tables, Chumley's lacks nothing in the way of mellowed atmosphere. Think about returning for drinks or dinner. A blackboard menu features fresh pasta and grilled fish. Open nightly from 5pm to an arbitrary closing time, Chumley's also offers brunch on weeknds.

Continue up Bedford to Grove Street, named in the 19th century for its many gardens and groves, and make a right to:

16 17 Grove St.

Parts of this picturesque wood-frame house date to the early 1800s. A friend of James Baldwin's lived here in the 1960s, and Baldwin frequently stayed at the house. Baldwin, whose fiery writings coincided with the inception of the civil rights movement, once said, "The most dangerous creation of any society is that man who has nothing to lose."

Further along this street is:

17 45 Grove St.

Originally a freestanding two-story building, this was, in the 19th century, one of the Village's most elegant mansions, surrounded by verdant lawns with greenhouses and stables. Built in 1830, it was refurbished with Italianate influences in 1870. In the movie *Reds,* which is based on the life of John Reed, 45 Grove was portrayed (inaccurately) as Eugene O'Neill's house.

Ohio-born poet Hart Crane rented a second-floor room at 45 Grove St. in 1923 and began writing his poetic portrait of America, *The Bridge* (Hart depicted the Brooklyn Bridge as a symbol of America's westward expansion). During his childhood, Crane was constantly traveling with his mother, which kept him from finishing school; nonetheless, he was a voracious reader and brilliantly self-educated. By the time he was 17, his poetry had been published in prestigious New York magazines.

In later years, frustrated by frequent rejection from magazines and other exigencies of his craft, Crane would occasionally toss his typewriter out the window. Often moody and despondent, he was chronically in debt, plagued by guilt over homosexual encounters on the nearby docks, and given to almost nightly alcoholic binges; fellow Villager e.e. cummings once found him passed out on a sidewalk, bundled him into a taxi, and had him driven home. In 1932, returning by ship from Mexico (where, on a Guggenheim fellowship, he had been attempting to write an epic poem about Montezuma), Crane made sexual advances to a crew member, was badly beaten up, and jumped into the waters to his death at the age of 33.

Continue up the street to:

18 59 Grove St.

English-born American revolutionary/political theorist/writer Thomas Paine died here in 1809. Paine came to America (with the help of Benjamin Franklin) in 1774, and in 1776 he produced his famous pamphlet, *The Crisis,* which begins with the words: "These are the times that try men's souls." After fighting in the American Revolution, he returned to England to advocate the overthrow of the British monarchy. Indicted for treason, he escaped to Paris and became a French citizen; while imprisoned there during the Terror, he wrote *The Age of Reason.* He returned to the United States in 1802, where he was vilified for his atheism. Benjamin Franklin once said to Paine, "Where liberty is, there is my country." To which Paine replied: "Where liberty is not, there is mine."

The downstairs space has always been a restaurant, which today is called **Marie's Crisis Cafe** (**© 212/243-9323**). Though the building Paine lived in burned down, some of the interior brickwork is original. Of note is a WPA-era mural behind the bar depicting the French and American Revolutions. Up a flight of stairs is another mural (a wood-relief carving) called *La Convention,* depicting Robespierre, Danton, and Thomas Paine. In the 1920s, you might have spotted anyone from Eugene O'Neill to Edward VIII of England here.

At Seventh Avenue, cross to the opposite side of the wide intersection, walk around to the left of the little park, and head half a block up Christopher Street, the hub of New York's gay community, to no. 53:

⑲ The Stonewall

The current bar in this spot shares a name with its more famous predecessor, the Stonewall Inn. This bar was the scene of the Stonewall riots of June 1969, when gay customers decided to resist the police during a routine raid. The event launched the lesbian and gay rights movement and is commemorated throughout the country every year with gay pride parades.

Continue up the block to:

⑳ The Corner of Waverly Place and Christopher Street

The wedge-shaped Georgian Northern Dispensary building dates from 1831. Edgar Allan Poe was treated for a head cold here in 1836, the year he came to New York with his 13-year-old bride for whom he would later compose the pain-filled requiems "Ulalume" and "Annabel Lee":

I was a child and she was a child,
In this kingdom by the sea;
But we loved with a love that was
more than love—
I and my Annabel Lee.

Keep walking up Christopher Street to take a right onto:

㉑ Gay Street

Famous residents of this tiny street (originally a stable alley) have included New York Mayor Jimmy Walker, who owned the 18th-century town house at no. 12. More recently, Frank Paris, creator of Howdy Doody, lived here.

In the 1920s, Ruth McKenney lived in the basement of no. 14 with her sister Eileen, who later married Nathanael West. It was the setting for McKenney's zany *My Sister Eileen* stories, which were first published in the *New Yorker* and then collected into a book. They were then turned into a popular stage comedy that ran on Broadway from 1940 to 1942, followed by a Broadway musical version called *Wonderful Town* and two movie versions.

During Prohibition, the street held several speakeasies.

At the end of the short street, take a left onto Waverly Place and look for:

㉒ 139 Waverly Place

Edna St. Vincent Millay lived here with her sister, Norma, in 1918. Radical playwright Floyd Dell, her lover, who found the apartment for her, commented: "She lived in that gay poverty which is traditional of the Village, and one may find vivid reminiscences of that life in her poetry."

Cross Sixth Avenue to check out:

㉓ 116 Waverly Place

Dating from 1891, the building has hosted William Cullen Bryant, Horace Greeley, Margaret Fuller, poet Fitz-Greene Halleck, and Herman Melville. Here Poe read his latest poem, "The Raven," to assembled literati. Waverly Place, by the way, was named in 1833 for Sir Walter Scott's novel, *Waverley.*

Return to Sixth Avenue and turn left (south) down it. Take another left onto Washington Place to:

㉔ 82 Washington Place

This was the residence from 1908 to 1912 of Willa Cather, whose books celebrated pioneer life and the beauty of her native Nebraska landscape. Cather came to New York in 1906 at the age of 31 to work at the prestigious *McClure's* magazine and rose to managing editor before resigning to write full time. As her career advanced, and she found herself besieged with requests for lectures and interviews, Cather became almost reclusive and fiercely protective of her privacy.

Bandleader John Philip Sousa owned the beautiful 1839 building next door (**no. 80**).

Washington Place ends at:

㉕ Washington Square Park

Once a swamp frequented largely by duck hunters, this is the hub of the Village. Minetta Brook meandered through it. In the 18th and early 19th centuries, it was a potter's field (more than 10,000 people are buried under the park) and an execution site (one of the makeshift gallows survives—a towering English elm in the northwest corner of the park). The park was dedicated in 1826, and elegant residential dwellings, some of which have survived NYU's cannibalization of the neighborhood, went up around the square. At this time, it was the citadel of stifling patrician gentility so evocatively depicted in the novels of Edith Wharton. She defined Washington Square society as "a little set with its private catch-words, observances, and amusements" indifferent to "anything outside its charmed circle."

The white marble Memorial Arch (1892) at the Fifth Avenue entrance, which replaced a wooden arch erected in 1889 to commemorate the centenary of Washington's inauguration, was designed by Stanford White. One night in 1917, a group of Liberal Club pranksters climbed the Washington Square Arch, fired cap guns, and proclaimed the "independent republic of Greenwich Village," a utopia dedicated to "socialism, sex, poetry, conversation, dawn-greeting, anything—so long as it is taboo in the Middle West." Today, Washington Square Park would probably surpass any of this group's most cherished anarchist fantasies.

Along the square's north edge stand many of the surviving old homes, including, just west of Fifth Avenue:

㉖ 19 Washington Square North (Waverly Place)

Henry James's grandmother, Elizabeth Walsh, lived at this now-defunct address. (The no. 19 that exists today is a different house, the numbering system having changed since James's day.) Young Henry spent much time at her house, which was the inspiration for his novel *Washington Square.*

Further east is:

㉗ 7 Washington Square North

Edith Wharton, age 20, and her mother lived here in 1882. A wealthy aristocrat, born Edith Jones, Wharton maintained a close friendship with Henry James and, like him, left New York's stultifying upper-class social scene for Europe (Paris) in 1910, where she wrote the Pulitzer Prize–winning *The Age of Innocence.* Both she and James were immensely popular in Europe and were deluged with invitations (James once admitted to accepting 107 dinner invitations in a single year). Wharton wrote almost a book a year her entire adult life, while also finding time to feed French and Belgian refugees during World War I and take charge of 600 Belgian orphans.

Nearby is:

㉘ 3 Washington Square North (today the NYU School of Social Work)

Critic Edmund Wilson, managing editor of the *New Republic,* lived here from 1921 to 1923. Another resident, John Dos Passos, a fiery 1920s radical, wrote *Manhattan Transfer* here.

Make a left at University Place and another immediate left into:

㉙ Washington Mews

This picturesque 19th-century cobblestone street, lined with vine-covered, two-story buildings (converted stables and carriage houses constructed to serve posh Washington Sq. town houses), has had several famous residents, among them John Dos Passos, artist Edward Hopper (no. 14A), and Sherwood Anderson (no. 54). The latter building dates from 1834.

Double back to University Place and turn left to head north to the southeast corner of 9th Street, where stands the first of two possible places to:

TAKE A BREAK
The **Knickerbocker Bar and Grill** (southeast corner of 9th St. and University Place; ✆ **212/228-8490**) is a comfortable wood-paneled restaurant and jazz club that attracts an interesting clientele, including writers (Jack Newfield, E.L. Doctorow, Erica Jong, Sidney Zion, Christopher Cerf) and actors (Richard Gere, F. Murray Abraham, Susan Sarandon, Tim Robbins). Harry Connick Jr. got his start playing piano here and Charles Lindbergh signed the contract for his transatlantic flight at the bar. The restaurant offers an eclectic menu.

For superior light fare (pastries, croissants, sandwiches), head two blocks up to a branch of **Dean and Deluca,** 75 University Place, at 11th Street (✆ **212/869-6890**). to 11pm, and Sunday 9am to 8pm.

This address is also a stop on the tour. When Thomas Wolfe graduated from Harvard in 1923, he came to New York to teach at NYU and lived at the Hotel Albert (depicted as the Hotel Leopold in his novel *Of Time and the River*) at this address. Today the Albert Apartments occupy the site.

From University Place, turn left onto 11th Street.

30 25 East 11th St.

The unhappy and sexually confused poet Hart Crane (whom you met at stop 17) lived here for a short time.

31 21 East 11th St.

Crane's neighbor was Mary Cadwaller Jones, who was married to Edith Wharton's brother. Her home was the setting of literary salons; Henry Adams, Theodore Roosevelt, Augustus Saint-Gaudens, and John Singer Sargent often came to lunch, and Henry James was a houseguest when he visited America from Europe.

Continue to Fifth Avenue, cross it, and turn right. On your right is the:

32 Salmagundi Club

This club, located at 47 Fifth Ave., began as an artist's club in 1871 and was originally located at 596 Broadway. The name comes from the *Salmagundi* papers, in which Washington Irving mocked his fellow New Yorkers and first used the term *Gotham* to describe the city. *Salmagundi,* which means "a stew of many ingredients," was thought an appropriate term to describe the club's diverse membership of painters, sculptors, writers, and musicians. The club moved to this mid-19th-century brownstone mansion in 1917. Theodore Dreiser lived at the Salmagundi in 1897, when it was located across the street where the First Presbyterian Church stands today, and probably wrote *Sister Carrie* there, a work based on the experiences of his own sister, Emma.

Cross 12th Street. At the northwest corner is the:

33 Forbes Magazine Building

Located at 60–62 Fifth Ave., the Forbes Magazine Building houses a museum (✆ **212/206-5548**) featuring exhibits from the varied collections of the late Malcolm Forbes, who was famous as a financier, magazine magnate, frequent Liz Taylor escort, and father of one-time presidential hopeful Steve Forbes. On display are hundreds of model ships; legions formed from a collection of more than 100,000 military miniatures; thousands of signed letters, papers, and other paraphernalia from almost every American president; a remarkable even dozen of Fabergé eggs and other objets d'art fashioned for the czars; the evolution of the game Monopoly (natch); and changing exhibits and art shows. Admission is free. The galleries are open Tuesday to Saturday 10am to 4pm.

Make a left on 12th Street and you'll see:

34 New School for Social Research

The New School (66 West 12th St.) was founded in 1919 as a forum for professors too liberal-minded for Columbia University's then stiflingly traditional attitude. In the 1930s, it became a "University in Exile" for intelligentsia fleeing Nazi Germany. Many great writers have taught or lectured in its classrooms over the decades: William Styron, Joseph Heller, Edward Albee, W.H. Auden, Robert Frost, Nadine Gordimer, Max Lerner, Maya Angelou, Joyce Carol Oates, Arthur Miller, I.B. Singer, Susan Sontag, and numerous others.

Turn right up Sixth Avenue and left onto 13th Street to:

35 138 West 13th St.

Max Eastman and other radicals urged revolution in the pages of the *Liberator,* headquartered in this lovely building on a pleasant tree-lined street. The magazine published works by John Reed, Edna St. Vincent Millay, Ernest Hemingway, Elinor Wylie, e.e. cummings (who later became very right-wing and a passionate supporter of Senator Joseph McCarthy's Communist witch hunts), John Dos Passos, and William Carlos Williams. The *Liberator,* established in 1919, succeeded *The Masses,* an earlier Eastman publication (see stop 37).

Further west along the block is:

36 152 West 13th St.

Offices of the *Dial,* a major avant-garde literary magazine of the 1920s, occupied this beautiful Greek Revival brick town house. The magazine dated from 1840 in Cambridge, Massachusetts, where transcendentalists Margaret Fuller and Ralph Waldo Emerson were its seminal editors. In the '20s, its aim was to offer "the best of European and American art, experimental and conventional." Contributors included Marianne Moore, Hart Crane, Conrad Aiken, Ezra Pound, Theodore Dreiser, T.S. Eliot, and artist Marc Chagall.

Continue west on 13th Street, and make a left on Seventh Avenue, a right on 12th Street, and then another right for some afternoon tea at:

TAKE A BREAK
Tea and Sympathy (✆ 212/807-8329), at 108 Greenwich Ave., is straight out of the English countryside, a charming hole-in-the-wall crammed with just a few tables. The wonderful $14 full afternoon tea includes a tiered serving tray stuffed full of finger sandwiches, cakes, biscuits, scones, jam, and clotted cream, plus, of course, a pot of tea (go for the Typhoo). Cheaper, bona fide British dishes include shepherd's pie and bangers and mash. Open daily from 11:30am to 10:30pm.

From Tea and Sympathy, turn left to walk back down Greenwich Avenue to the corner of 12th Street.

37 91 Greenwich Ave.

At the beginning of the 20th century, Max Eastman was editor of a radical left-wing literary magazine called *The Masses.* The magazine at this address published, among others, John Reed, Carl Sandburg, Sherwood Anderson, Upton Sinclair, Edgar Lee Masters, e.e. cummings, and Louis Untermeyer. John Sloan, Stuart Davis, Picasso, and George Bellows provided art for its pages, which a newspaper columnist dismissed thusly:

They draw nude women for The Masses,
Thick, fat, ungainly lasses—
How does that help the working classes?

The Masses was suppressed by the Justice Department in 1918 because of its opposition to World War I and

Reed, Eastman, political cartoonist Art Young, and writer/literary critic Floyd Dell were put on trial under the Espionage Act and charged with conspiracy to obstruct recruiting and prevent enlistment. Pacifist Edna St. Vincent Millay read poems to the accused to help pass the time while juries were out. The trials all ended in hung juries.

Continue another block down Greenwich Avenue; turn right on Bank Street and look for:

38 1 Bank St.

In 1913, shortly after the publication of *O Pioneers!,* Willa Cather, age 40, moved to a seven-room, second-floor apartment in a large brick house here. She lived with her companion Edith Lewis and wrote *My Antonia* (the third of a trilogy about immigrants in the United States), *Death Comes to the Archbishop,* and several other novels.

When she became successful, Cather rented the apartment above hers and kept it empty to ensure perfect quiet. Her Friday afternoon at-homes here were frequented by D.H. Lawrence, among others. Unlike many Village writers of her day, Cather eschewed the radical scene and took little interest in politics.

From Bank Street, take a left onto Waverly Place, cross 11th Street to take another left on Perry Street, and make a final right back onto Greenwich Avenue to:

39 45 Greenwich Ave.

In 1947, William Styron came to New York from North Carolina to work as a junior editor at McGraw-Hill. He moved here in 1951 after a stint in the marines and the success of his first novel, *Lie Down in Darkness.* Styron originally showed manuscript pages from that novel, begun at age 23, to Hiram Haydn, a Bobbs-Merrill editor whose writing class he was taking at the New School. Haydn told Styron he was too advanced for the class and took an option on the novel.

Continue down Greenwich Avenue to West 10th Street and detour right to:

40 139 West 10th St.

Today an Italian restaurant, this was the site, for decades, of a popular Village bar called the Ninth Circle. But it was in 1954 at a former bar at this location that playwright Edward Albee saw graffiti on a mirror reading, "Who's afraid of Virginia Woolf?" and, years later, appropriated it. He recalled the incident in a *Paris Review* interview: "When I started to write the play, it cropped up in my mind again. And, of course, 'Who's afraid of Virginia Woolf' means . . . who's afraid of living life without false illusions."

Double back up West 10th Street, cross Greenwich Avenue, and walk a block where you will see the gated entry to:

41 Patchin Place

The gate closing off Patchin Place is never locked; feel free to pass through it. This tranquil, tree-shaded cul-de-sac has sheltered many illustrious residents. From 1923 to 1962, e.e. cummings lived at no. 4, where visitors included T.S. Eliot, Ezra Pound, and Dylan Thomas. The highly acclaimed but little-known Djuna Barnes (literary critics have compared her to James Joyce) lived in a tiny one-room apartment at no. 5. Reclusive and eccentric, she almost never left the premises for 40 years, prompting cummings to occasionally shout from his window, "Are you still alive, Djuna?"

Louise Bryant and John Reed maintained a residence at Patchin Place for several years until Reed's death in 1920. During this time, he wrote his eyewitness account of the Russian Revolution, *Ten Days That Shook the World.* To avoid interruptions from callers at Patchin Place, Reed rented a room atop a restaurant at 147 West 4th Street to do his writing. Theodore Dreiser and John Masefield were also Patchin Place residents, the former in 1895 when he was still an unknown journalist.

Turn left out of Patchin Place to cross Sixth Avenue. Continue down West 10th Street, but look to your right as you cross Sixth Avenue to see the:

42 Jefferson Market Library (425 Sixth Ave.)

This library was a former produce market. The turreted, red brick-and-granite, Victorian-Gothic castle was built as a courthouse in 1877 and named for Thomas Jefferson. Topped by a lofty clock/bell tower (originally intended as a fire lookout), with tracery and stained-glass windows, gables, and steeply sloping roofs, the building was inspired by a Bavarian castle. In the 1880s, architects voted it one of the 10 most beautiful buildings in America.

Head east down 10th Street to:

43 50 West 10th St.

After his great success with *Who's Afraid of Virginia Woolf?,* Edward Albee bought this late 19th-century converted carriage house in the early 1960s. It's a gem of a building, with highly polished wooden carriage doors. Albee wrote *Tiny Alice* and *A Delicate Balance* here, the latter being a Pulitzer Prize winner. In 1994, he won a second Pulitzer Prize for *Three Tall Women.*

Now look for:

44 37 West 10th St.

Sinclair Lewis, already a famous writer by the mid-1920s, lived in this early 19th-century house with his wife, journalist Dorothy Thompson, from 1928 to 1929. Lewis fell in love with the recently divorced Thompson at first sight in 1927 and immediately proposed to her. Once, when asked to speak at a dinner party, he stood up and said, "Dorothy, will you marry me?" and resumed his seat. Lewis later followed her to Russia and all over Europe until she accepted his proposal. Unfortunately, the marriage didn't last.

Your final stop is:

45 14 West 10th St.

When Mark Twain came to New York at the turn of the century (at the age of 65), he lived in this gorgeous 1855 mansion. An extremely successful writer (Twain's first book was a travel book, *The Innocents Abroad*), he entertained lavishly. Born Samuel Langhorne Clemens, Twain was once a riverboat captain, and he took his pseudonym from the sing-song calls of the sounding men stationed at the prows of Mississippi paddle boats ("mark twain" meant the waters were a safe 2 fathoms deep). Twain was famous for his witticisms, including a quip on the art of quipping: "How lucky Adam was. He knew when he said a good thing, nobody had said it before."

WALKING TOUR 2 MIDTOWN: THE CONCRETE JUNGLE

Start:	**Grand Central Terminal.**
Subway:	**Take the 4, 5, 6, 7, or the shuttle to 42nd Street/Grand Central.**
Finish:	**The Plaza Hotel.**
Time:	**Approximately 4 hours, not counting time for browsing in shops and galleries.**
Best Time:	**Weekdays, when Midtown is bustling but the attractions aren't as packed as they tend to be on weekends.**
Worst Time:	**Rush hour (weekdays 8:30–9:30am and 4:30–6pm).**

If there's one area that defines New York in the popular imagination, it's Midtown. Concentrated here are the dozens of the towering skyscrapers that are so closely identified with the city and its skyline. Lining Fifth Avenue and 57th Street are blue-chip art galleries, high-toned boutiques, chic department stores, and, increasingly, theme restaurants such as the Hard Rock Cafe that make New York the consumer capital of the world. Midtown is Manhattan at its most glamorous.

From the subway platform, follow the Metro North signs to the main concourse of:

❶ Grand Central Terminal

Commodore Vanderbilt himself named the station "Grand Central" in the 1860s, despite the fact that it was then out in the boondocks. The present terminal was built in 1913. This engineering tour de force combines subways, surface streets, pedestrian malls, underground shopping concourses, and 48 pairs of railroad tracks into one smoothly functioning organism.

Masterfully restored in 1997, the main concourse is breathtaking. It's one of America's most impressive interior spaces, with gleaming marble floors, sweeping staircases, and an aqua vaulted ceiling soaring 125 feet (37m) high. Twenty-five hundred pinpricks of electronic stars litter this "sky" with a view of a Mediterranean winter sky's constellations.

TAKE A BREAK

Grand Central has numerous spots where you can pick up some provisions to fortify yourself for the tour, including **Zaro's Bread Basket, Two Boots Pizzeria,** and a branch of Brooklyn-favorite **Junior's** (try their legendary cheesecake).

For something more substantial, head downstairs to the **Oyster Bar,** where decent seafood is served in a first-rate setting of wide-vaulted ceilings Monday through Friday from 11:30am to 9:30pm.

If you'd like to dine under the stars of Grand Central's celestial ceiling, hit **Métrazur,** perched on a balcony above the rush of the terminal, with an incredible view of the ceiling. Lunch is served 11:30am to 3:00pm, Monday through Friday, and snacks are served every day from 3 to 10pm. The New American menu features such specials as salmon sautéed with grain mustard and served with a frissée salad.

Leave the main concourse via the 42nd Street exit and turn right. Walk west for 2 blocks and then make a left onto Fifth Avenue, where you'll find the:

❷ New York Public Library

The library (✆ **212/930-0830;** www.nypl.org) sits in splendor, resembling a Greek temple with rows of Corinthian columns. Completed in 1911, this beaux arts palace, one of the greatest research libraries in the world, cost $10 million to construct, and President Taft himself attended the dedication ceremony. Everything inside was designed as a unit, from the marble walls to the chairs, stepladders, and wastebaskets.

Climb up the broad stone steps guarded by twin stone lions, named Patience and Fortitude by mayor Fiorello LaGuardia in the 1930s for the qualities he proclaimed New Yorkers would need to survive the Depression. Cafes on either side of the grounds, past fountains marked by classical statuary, offer umbrella tables and food during warm weather. (Bryant Park out back is also littered with cast-iron tables, and it hosts a summer open-air film festival.)

The interior of the library contains manuscripts, maps, journals, prints, and more than 38 million volumes occupying 80 miles (129km) of bookshelves. You can sign up for tours (offered Mon–Sat at 11am and 2pm) at the information desk just inside the lobby. The library is open Monday and Thursday through Saturday 10am to 6pm; Tuesday and Wednesday 11am to 7:30pm.

Turn left out of the library to head uptown on the west side of Fifth Avenue. Look up and to your right as you cross 42nd Street

to get a wonderful perspective view down the block to the:

❸ Chrysler Building

At 1,046 feet (314m), you'll see this Art Deco masterpiece, which reigned briefly in 1930 as the tallest building in the world until the Empire State Building came along. The stainless steel spire with its hubcap ribs and thrusting gargoyles creates one of the most beautiful and distinctive features of the Manhattan skyline.

Continue north on Fifth Avenue for two blocks to 44th Street, where you'll turn left. On the north side of 44th Street, at no. 27, is the Harvard Club, designed by McKim, Mead, and White in 1894 in an architectural style that mimicked Harvard's (at the time). The "Veritas" coat of arms tops the building. A few doors down at no. 37 is the Yacht Club, with a fanciful and flowing concrete facade of captain's cabin windows.

Continue along 44th Street. Near Sixth Avenue stands one of New York's most famous literary landmarks:

❹ The Algonquin Hotel

Baltimorian H. L. Mencken began staying at the Algonquin on his frequent business trips to New York after he became the editor of *Smart Set* in 1914. Under Mencken's stewardship, the magazine published the early works of Eugene O'Neill, James Joyce, and F. Scott Fitzgerald.

As *Smart Set* faded from influence in the 1920s, *Vanity Fair* began to take its place, counting Edna St. Vincent Millay, Elinor Wylie, and Theodore Dreiser among its contributors. In its offices at 19 West 44th St., Dorothy Parker, Robert Benchley, and Robert Sherwood served on the editorial staff. They began hanging out in the Algonquin, and soon their gatherings grew into the famous "Round Table," which also included Alexander Woollcott (drama critic for the *New York Times*), George S. Kaufman, Franklin Adams (columnist for the *New York World*), and Edna Ferber.

The group became famous for its witty, acerbic commentary on theater, literature, and the social scene.

One of the regulars, Harold Ross, took it into his head to start a magazine that would incorporate the group's sophisticated, satirical outlook and rounded up investors to begin publication of the *New Yorker,* with offices set up nearby at 25 West 45th St. The first few issues were extremely uneven, but within a couple of years E.B. White and James Thurber had been added to the staff and were reshaping the magazine into one of the most prestigious publications in the country.

Even after the Round Table stopped gathering at the hotel, the Algonquin continued to count famous writers among its guests, including Gertude Stein and her companion Alice B. Toklas, F. Scott Fitzgerald, and William Faulkner, who wrote the acceptance speech for his 1949 Nobel Prize on Algonquin stationery.

To soak up this hotel's genteel ambience, consider having lunch or weekend brunch in the Rose Room. Or ensconce yourself with a cocktail in a comfortable sofa or armchair of the lobby lounge, where *New Yorker* writers frequently conduct interviews.

Across the street from the Algonquin, but light-years away in design, is the **Royalton Hotel.** Poke your head inside and take a look; the whimsically futuristic Jetsons-style decor, created by Philippe Starck, has to be seen to be believed.

Cross Sixth Avenue (also known as Avenue of the Americas) and turn left. Before the corner of 43rd Street is the midtown branch of the:

❺ International Center of Photography

The ICP (✆ **212/857-0000;** www.icp.org) was massively renovated and expanded in 2000. The center presents around 30 photography shows annually. Celebrating various trends,

Midtown: The Concrete Jungle

artists, and themes, these photo shows are some of the best in the city. See p. 262 for more details, including hours and admission fees.

Double back north along Sixth Avenue to 47th Street, where you'll take a right. This block, between Fifth and Sixth avenues, is the Diamond District, where millions of dollars' worth of gems are traded every day. The business hustle on this block makes an unlikely setting for another literary sight, the:

6 Gotham Book Mart

The store (✆ **212/719-4448**), located on the north side at no. 41, may have moved down the block before you read this; call to check. Originally founded in 1920 on West 45th Street, the store moved here in 1923. H. L. Mencken and his friend Theodore Dreiser once stopped in and, delighted to find some of their own works in stock, began to scribble dedications on many of the books, including the Bible, which they signed "With the compliments of the authors."

The store sells new and used books and has hosted countless book publication parties, and the list of writers toasted here has included Dylan Thomas, W. H. Auden, Joyce Carol Oates, and Tennessee Williams. Today, you might find Arthur Miller and John Updike, who drop in frequently. In 1947, the store became headquarters of the James Joyce Society, whose first membership was purchased by T. S. Eliot.

Owner Frances Steloff (who died in 1989 at the age of 101) was known for lending a hand to perennially cash-strapped artists such as Henry Miller and John Dos Passos (Martha Graham once borrowed $1,000 to stage her first dance performance). This tradition grew into the Writers' Emergency Fund, which still offers loans to struggling scribes.

Turn left up Fifth Avenue to 49th Street. On the right side of the avenue stands one of New York's most famous department stores, Saks Fifth Avenue. Immediately opposite Saks, head west into the promenade of:

7 Rockefeller Center

Enter one of the most handsome urban complexes in New York. It encompasses 24 acres and 19 skyscrapers, extending from 47th to 52nd streets between Fifth and Sixth avenues. People scoffed at John D. Rockefeller in 1929 when he unveiled plans to build this "city within a city," because it was so far removed from what was then the commercial heart of New York. But Rockefeller proved all the critics wrong. His complex remade the map, drawing business uptown and setting the standard for future civic projects by incorporating public art and open spaces.

Stroll west through the **Channel Gardens** to Rockefeller Center's famous **skating rink.** In the summer, this area becomes an outdoor cafe; in cooler months, it's packed with skaters gliding along the ice to music and the twinkle of tiny lights in the trees. Each holiday season, a giant Christmas tree stands here, towering over the promenade. Paul Manship's massive ***Prometheus*** lounges above the skating rink, beneath a quote from Aeschylus. Upscale shops surround the plaza.

Take a look inside the lobby of **30 Rockefeller Plaza,** once the RCA Building and now renamed the GE Building. Above the black marble floors and walls are monumental sepia-toned murals by José Maria Sert. This Art Deco building was featured in the movie *Quiz Show.*

Just to the left of 30 Rockefeller Plaza, head west (right) on 49th Street to Sixth Avenue. You'll pass the wraparound corner windows with a digital news feed where early risers peer through the glass and wave in the hopes of becoming part of the backdrop during filming of **NBC's *Today* show** just inside.

When you reach Sixth Avenue, turn right and head uptown. A building boom in the 1960s and 1970s transformed this area into a canyon of 50-story glass skyscrapers. Although the buildings aren't of great note individually, together they form an urban environment of considerable grandeur.

On the right side of Sixth Avenue, north of 50th Street, stands the first rock center building to open, in 1932:

8 Radio City Music Hall

This wonderful concert hall has been restored to its original Art Deco elegance. Its original owner, Samuel "Roxy" Rothafel of Roxy Theater fame, ran it as a vaudeville house, but the enterprise was a flop, and Rothafel, in poor health, sold out to the Rockefellers. Eventually, it became basically a glorified movie theater with Rockettes, but economic considerations and a 1979 overhaul returned it to live show business. Today, following an extensive 1999 restoration and "pristinization," performances run the gamut from B.B. King to Blues Clues Live!, to the annual Christmas Spectacular starring Radio City's own Rockettes. Pricey hour-long guided tours take place every half-hour daily from 10am (11am Sun) to 5pm. Call ✆ **212/247-4777** for information; buy tickets in the gift shop to the left of the entrance.

Continue up Sixth Avenue and take a right on:

9 West 52nd Street

This block was designated "Swing Street" because it holds a special place in jazz history. It was lined with a number of illicit speakeasies during Prohibition, and after its repeal, many of the establishments became jazz clubs, nurturing such great talents as Billie Holliday, Fats Waller, Dizzy Gillespie, Charlie Parker, and Sarah Vaughan.

The **21 Club,** at 21 West 52nd St. (✆ **212/582-7200**), is still a popular restaurant and one of the few establishments to survive from this era. Operating as a speakeasy during Prohibition, it relied on several clever devices to guard against police raids, including a trap door on the bar that sent everyone's cocktails tumbling into the sewer when a button was pressed. Today, it serves excellent food in a tavern atmosphere—if you can get a reservation in the popular dining room. The club is closed weekends in summer and Sunday year-round.

Continue down 52nd Street. Near the end of the block, take a left through the modern passageway/lobby, numbered **666 Fifth Avenue,** through to 53rd Street. Under here, you'll pass by an undulating stainless steel wall waterfall designed by Isamu Noguchi. When you pop out onto 53rd Street, you'll turn right to continue the tour. However, museum shop aficionados can hang a left and jog half a block down to the **Museum of Modern Art's (MoMA) bookshop** and the design store across the street.

Turning right onto 53rd Street, cross Fifth Avenue and walk two-thirds of 53rd's next block to the second pocket-sized, granite-and-waterfall park, where sits a brief, graffiti-covered stretch of the:

10 Berlin Wall

Return to Fifth Avenue and take a left to cruise past glitzy outposts of high fashion, including Ferragamo, Cartier, and Versace. Between 51st and 50th streets rises the unmistakable neo-Gothic bulk of:

11 St. Patrick's Cathedral

This is the seat of the Archdiocese of New York and the largest Catholic cathedral in America. Designed by James Renwick in 1858 and modeled after Cologne's cathedral, this magnificent structure has twin spires rising 330 feet (99m) above street level. Construction took 21 years. Zelda and F. Scott Fitzgerald were married here in 1920. Masses are held daily.

Across the street as you exit, in front of 630 Fifth Ave., crouches Lee Lawrie's 1937 ***Atlas,*** one of New York's most famous statues, in 15 feet (4.5m) of bronze.

Walk along the north (left) side of the church on 51st Street. Cross Madison Avenue and take a right down it, admiring the Gothic-style tracery on the backside of St. Paddy's across the street. On your left, the block is filled with the brownstone-gone-amok mass of the:

⑫ New York Palace Hotel

The hotel is also known as the Villard Houses after the Bavarian immigrant Henry Villard, who published the *New York Evening Post* and founded the Northern Pacific Railroad. He commissioned the unified buildings from McKim, Mead, and White in 1881. Today it's home to one of New York's most oft-reinvented and posh restaurants, **Le Cirque 2000** (✆ **212/303-7788;** www.lecirque.com); and the **Urban Center** (✆ **212/935-3592**), whose bookshop is a treasure trove of tomes on architecture; and, through the central doors in the hotel itself, a compact architectural fantasyland of gilt, marble, sweeping staircases, crystal chandeliers, and opulent meeting rooms.

Take a left onto 50th Street and walk toward Park Avenue. As you look right down Park Avenue, you'll see the **Helmsley Building,** a lovely structure that sits astride the avenue, crowned with an elaborate cupola. The building is overshadowed by the **Met Life building,** one of New York's greatest architectural travesties.

Across Park Avenue, between 50th and 49th streets, stands one of the most famous hotels in the world:

⑬ The Waldorf=Astoria

For over a century, the Waldorf has been synonymous with wealth and luxury, though this location only dates back to the early 20th century. In 1897, in the midst of a devastating economic depression, society matron Mrs. Bradley Martin decided to hold a costume ball at the Waldorf (in the original building on Fifth Ave.) for 1,200 guests, who were to attend dressed in the style of the court of Versailles. When details of the preparations, rumored to top a quarter of a million dollars, hit the papers, outrage ran high. A huge squad of police officers, personally supervised by police commissioner Teddy Roosevelt (whose wife was inside enjoying the festivities), had to be positioned around the hotel to prevent the great unwashed from venting their resentment.

Cole Porter and his wife lived for many years in one of the permanent apartments in the Waldorf Towers; one of the hotel's dining spots, Peacock Alley, still boasts his piano. Other famous residents have included General Douglas MacArthur, Herbert Hoover, Henry and Clare Booth Luce, and the Duke and Duchess of Windsor. Gangster Lucky Luciano also lived here under an alias until he was forced to leave the Waldorf for less luxurious digs in the state penitentiary.

Between 50th and 51st streets on Park Avenue lies **St. Bartholomew's** (✆ **212/378-0200;** www.stbarts.org), a domed Episcopal church from 1918, which was begun in Romanesque style and switched to Byzantine halfway through construction. The church sports a three-arched main portal by Stanford White that came from the original St. Bart's once located down the street.

TAKE A BREAK

St. Bart's may be the only church in New York with its own terrace cafe, **Café St. Bart's** (no phone, though serious advance planners can book on-line at www.opentable.com). Under large umbrellas, with the Byzantine building shading you, you can dine al fresco on scrumptious fare, like the blue-crab burrito with chili oil, or the St. Bart's Classic—tomato-basil soup and a grilled farmhouse cheese sandwich. Main dishes run from $10 to $14. In summer, the terrace presents live music; in winter, the cafe moves indoors into an uninspired back room of the church's complex. Open for lunch year-round, dinner in summer only.

Walk around the left side of St. Bart's down 51st Street to Lexington Avenue and turn left up the east side of it. The **subway grating** on this block is perhaps the most famous in the world, ever since 1955 when one of its gusts of hot air sent the skirt of **Marilyn Monroe's dress** billowing right into pin-up legend in *The Seven Year Itch.*

Continue north up Lexington to 53rd Street, where the corner office building (no. 599 Lexington) features Frank Stella's *Salto nel Mio Sacco,* a colorful 1985 work, in the lobby. Across 53rd Street from this building is the austere, glass-and-buffed-aluminum pinnacle of Citicorp Center. This pillar of international finance incorporates, at the corner of 54th Street, the modern and angular:

⑭ St. Peter's Lutheran Church

This singularly hip house of worship was built in 1977. Adorned with sculpture by Louise Nevelson (check out the Erol Baeker Chapel of the Good Shepard), St. Peter's is famous for its Sunday evening Jazz Vespers, where many of the greatest names in jazz have performed. Besides the permanent Nevelson sculptures and a Pomodoro *Cross* out front, St. Peter's also regularly displays works by contemporary artists.

Just north of St. Peter's, at 55th Street and across Lexington, is the:

⑮ Central Synagogue

This is one of New York's finest examples of Moorish Revival–style architecture. The oldest synagogue in continuous use in the city, it was dedicated in 1870. It was recently renovated after a fire in 1998, and the results are breathtaking, reflecting the synagogues original design, and adding new ornamental towers and crenellation on the outside, and over 5,000 vividly colored wall stencils inside. Tours are available at 12:45pm on Wednesday.

The longtime home to many of the city's top art galleries and upscale boutiques, 57th Street recently has been filling with theme restaurants and overblown chain retail stores. From Park Avenue, turn left along 57th Street, and you'll come to the beautiful black-and-white:

⑯ Fuller Building

This Art Deco beauty is located at the northeast corner of Madison Avenue and 57th Street. Look at the bronze doors, the marble fixtures, and mosaic floors and plan to spend some time browsing in the many art galleries housed here. Though a changeover from old guard galleries has occurred in recent years, the remaining galleries usually have one or two interesting shows each year.

Across 57th Street at no. 32 is:

⑰ PaceWildenstein Gallery

PaceWildenstein (✆ **212/421-3292**) is a major art gallery with specialty dealers spread out on several floors. The main gallery is devoted to 20th-century painting, drawing, and sculpture. It shows blue-chip artists such as Chuck Close, Jim Dine, Jean Dubuffet, and Pablo Picasso. On the 10th floor are **Pace Primitive Art** and **Pace Master Prints and Drawings.** On the ninth floor is **Pace/MacGill** (20th-century photography) and on the third floor is **Pace Prints,** which carries contemporary prints by many of the same artists who show in the main gallery.

Continue along 57th Street to Fifth Avenue. On your left stretches the bejeweled:

⑱ Tiffany & Co.,

Here it is, with its windows full of amazing gems. (*Note:* Contrary to popular belief, it's not a good place to try and rustle up some breakfast, even if you are Audrey Hepburn.)

Cross Fifth Avenue and continue along West 57th Street. Halfway down the next block on your left at no. 40 (an office atrium entrance hallway down the right side of the passage) is the:

⑲ Marlborough Gallery

Located on the second floor at no. 40 (✆ **212/541-4900;** www.marlborough gallery.com), this is one of the most reputable galleries in the world. Big stars here include the late Francis Bacon (Britain's de Kooning), Fernando Botero, Red Grooms, Richard Estes, Alex Katz, Antonio Lopez Garcia, and Larry Rivers.

Across the street, on the seventh floor of no. 41, is:

20 George Adams

This fine gallery (✆ **212/644-5665**) has been here for 30 years and features ceramicist Robert Arneson and other Bay Area artists, realists Jack Beal and Alfred Leslie, the colorfully eccentric paintings of Peter Saul, and Latin American painters such as Jose Bedia and Arnaldo Roche Rabell.

Return to Fifth Avenue, cross it again, and turn left (uptown) onto it, passing some of the city's most glamorous shops. On the east (right) side of the street, on the fourth floor of no. 745, you'll find:

21 Mary Boone Gallery

This is a world-class gallery (✆ **212/752-2929**) of contemporary art by Richard Artschwager, Ross Bleckner, and Eric Fischl, among others. Also in this building is the McKee Gallery, which shows Philip Guston, a major abstract expressionist, as well as Jake Berthot, David Humphrey, Martin Puryear, and Jeanne Silverthrone.

Continue up Fifth Avenue. Just north of 58th Street is the toy store of every child's dreams:

22 F.A.O. Schwarz

You may remember Tom Hanks's famous dance interpretation of "Heart and Soul," performed here on a giant piano keyboard in the movie *Big*. The store is a wonderland of toys, with a menagerie of stuffed animals; fantastic, mobile Lego creations; squadrons of Barbie dolls; a candy shop; and command centers of video games where anybody can play.

Across from F.A.O. Schwarz stands the landmark:

23 Plaza Hotel

Back then, suites rented for $25 a night. Zelda Fitzgerald turned heads here by making a splash (literally) in the fountain in front of the hotel. The Fitzgeralds stayed here in September 1922 while looking for a home, and F. Scott used the Plaza as the backdrop for a crucial scene in his masterpiece, *The Great Gatsby.* Another famous guest, Frank Lloyd Wright, stayed in a suite overlooking the park while he designed the Guggenheim Museum. Young visitors will be familiar with the Plaza as the heroine's home in the children's classic *Eloise* (you can see her portrait, painted by Eloise illustrator Hilary Knight, across from the Palm Court); movie buffs will recognize it from *Crocodile Dundee, The Cotton Club, North by Northwest, Network, Arthur, Home Alone 2,* and, of course, *Plaza Suite.* Little-known trivia: 1920s Plaza chef Hector Boiardi decided to bottle his Italian pasta-and-sauce dishes for the masses; on the labels he phoneticized his name to Boy-ar-dee.

WINDING DOWN

The **Palm Court in the Plaza** is a great place to relax over tea and cakes after your tour.

For an afternoon cocktail, there's no better place to stop than the bar where the Bloody Mary was invented: the **King Cole Bar in the St. Regis Hotel,** 2 East 55th St. at Fifth Avenue (✆ **212/753-4500**), adorned with a wonderful mural of the merry old monarch himself. An elegant afternoon tea is served in the **Astor Court,** a plush venue with a vaulted ceiling, trompe l'oeil cloud murals, and 22-karat gold leaf on the delicate stuccowork.

The hotel itself is a landmark, built in 1904 by John Jacob Astor and housing some of the most expensive rooms in the city. Ernest Hemingway, Alfred Hitchcock, and Salvador Dalí all stayed at the St. Regis, and John Lennon and Yoko Ono occupied suites here in the early 1970s.

WALKING TOUR 3 THE UPPER EAST SIDE

Start:	**The southeast corner of Central Park, at 59th Street and Fifth Avenue.**
Subway:	**Take the N or R to Fifth Avenue.**
Finish:	**91st Street and Fifth Avenue.**
Time:	**Approximately 3 hours.**
Best Time:	**Weekday afternoons, when museums and restaurants are open but not as crowded as on Saturdays.**
Worst Time:	**Sundays, when most stores and galleries are closed and the streets seem deserted.**

Over a century ago, society watchers predicted that the wealthy and fashionable would settle permanently on the avenues bordering Central Park. Time has proven them right. Fifth Avenue north of Grand Army Plaza, which lies at the southeast corner of the park, is officially called Museum Mile. But the magnificent private mansions built here in the first few decades of this century by some of America's wealthiest industrial tycoons also earned it the title of Millionaires' Row. Judging from old photos, it was something to behold.

Today, patrician mansions still stand along the avenue, though others have ceded their coveted real estate to large apartment houses. But the age of imperial living isn't over by any means. Some of the buildings on Fifth Avenue (as well as on Park Ave. and elsewhere on the East Side) contain apartments every bit as palatial and sumptuous as the vanished mansions. Even New Yorkers are surprised to hear of apartments with 20, 30, or even 40 rooms, but they do exist in this neighborhood.

Start your tour where Fifth Avenue and 59th Street meet at:

1 Grand Army Plaza

The plaza is adorned with a brilliant gold statue of William Tecumseh Sherman, the ruthless but effective Civil War general who devastated the Southern countryside and brought the civilian population to its knees with the Union army's scorched-earth March to the Sea. Created by Augustus Saint-Gaudens, it's a classical equestrian statue of the crusty general with a female Winged Victory striding along in front of the horse.

Now stroll up Fifth Avenue, staying on the park side of the street for the best view of the buildings as you pass. In good weather, bookstalls from The Strand line the sidewalk, full of used volumes at a fraction of the cover price. On the east (right) side of Fifth Avenue, at 61st Street, is:

2 The Pierre

This has been one of Manhattan's priciest and most exclusive hotels since its opening in 1930. In 1932, mystery writer Dashiell Hammett stayed here while working on *The Thin Man,* though, unfortunately, he couldn't pay the bill that he had run up during his stay. He allegedly donned a disguise to sneak out without settling his tab.

At the southeast corner of 62nd Street stands the third home of the:

3 Knickerbocker Club

This club looks a lot like the big private houses that once characterized the avenue. The Georgian brick Knickerbocker, completed in 1915, was the work of a firm called Delano and Aldrich, a favorite of high society in the early 20th century. It retains a very pedigreed image. Ernest Hemingway, looking for peace and quiet, rented an apartment here in 1959 and stayed for about a year.

The next block up is 63rd Street. On the east corner you'll see:

4 820 Fifth Ave.

This is one of the earliest apartment houses built hereabouts and still one of the best. Built in 1916, it has only one apartment on each floor, with five fireplaces and seven bathrooms in each one.

Continue northward on Fifth Avenue to 64th Street. Walk just inside Central Park for a look at:

5 The Arsenal

Built in 1848 when this neighborhood was distant and deserted, the Arsenal now houses zoo administration offices. The structure was once a bunkhouse and weapons depot for Civil War troops (notice the railing made of rifles). The Central Park Zoo is right behind the building.

Head back onto Fifth Avenue. Opposite the park at the southeast corner of 64th Street (**828 Fifth Ave.**) is the former mansion of coal magnate Edward Berwind. This residence dates from 1896 and has been preserved as cooperative apartments.

Head east (away from the park) on 64th Street toward Madison Avenue. This particularly handsome East Side block is lined with architectural extravaganzas. Note in particular:

6 3 E. 64th St.

This opulent beaux arts mansion was built in 1903 for the daughter of Mrs. William B. Astor. The house was designed by Warren and Wetmore, the firm responsible for Grand Central Terminal, and it now houses the Consulate General of India. Also worthy of admiration on this block are nos. 16, 19 (now home to a Wildenstein Gallery open Mon–Fri 10am–5pm), and 20.

At Madison Avenue, turn left and saunter two blocks north to 66th Street. Note the rather fantastic apartment house built in 1900 on the **northeast corner of 66th and Madison,** and then turn left (west) off Madison onto 66th Street, heading back toward Fifth Avenue.

Among the many notable houses on this block is the magnificent French Renaissance–style house at **5 E. 66th St.,** with its heavy wooden doors and elegant stonework detail. Built in 1900, it's now home to the Lotos Club, which is dedicated to literature and the fine arts.

Next door, at 3 E. 66th St., is the:

7 Home of President Ulysses S. Grant

Grant lived from 1881 to 1885. Forced to declare bankruptcy after a disastrous presidency that was marred by scandal, the former Civil War hero retired here to spend his last years penning his memoirs. Though he was battling cancer, Grant managed to hang on just long enough to complete the autobiography, which won favorable literary reviews and earned his family half a million dollars.

Now double back to Madison Avenue, turn left, and continue north for two more blocks, stopping to browse in any of the boutiques that catch your eye. There's Nicole Miller; La Perla for lovely lingerie; Emanuel Ungaro; Godiva, where you can treat yourself to some coffee and a decadent truffle; and Berk for cashmere. At 68th Street, turn right (east) toward Park Avenue. One of the best houses on this block is:

8 58 E. 68th St.

Located on the southwest corner of the intersection with Park Avenue, this house was built in 1919 for Harold J. Pratt, son of Rockefeller partner Charles Pratt.

Walk to the north side of 68th Street to:

9 680 Park Ave.

This neo-Federal town house was built from 1909 to 1911 for banker Percy Rivington Pyne and designed by McKim, Mead, and White. Its style and architecture were copied all along this Park Avenue block. When, from 1948 to 1963, it housed the Soviet Mission to the United Nations, Premier Nikita Khrushchev waved to curious crowds from the balcony during his famous shoe-banging visit to the U.N.

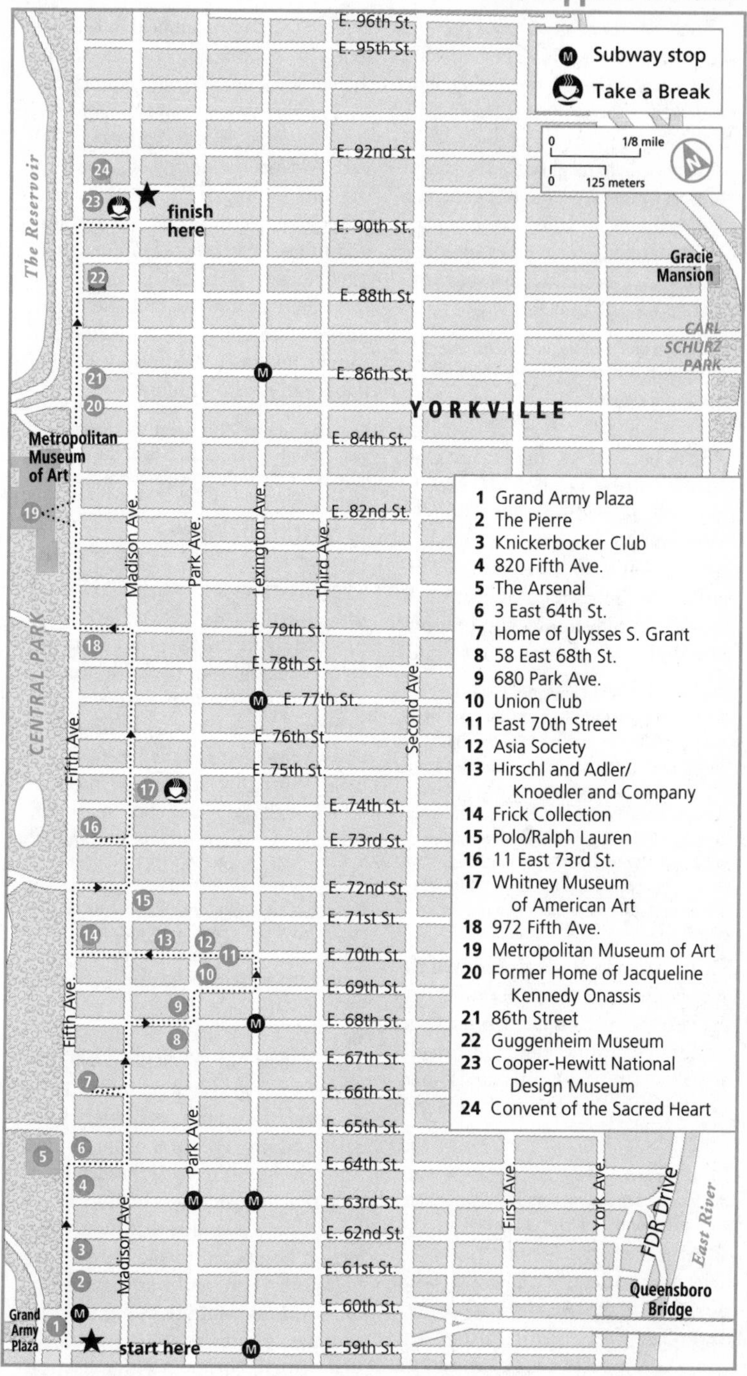
Subway stop
Take a Break
0 1/8 mile
0 125 meters
The Reservoir
CENTRAL PARK
Metropolitan Museum of Art
Grand Army Plaza
finish here
start here
YORKVILLE
Gracie Mansion
CARL SCHURZ PARK
Queensboro Bridge
East River
FDR Drive
Fifth Ave.
Madison Ave.
Park Ave.
Lexington Ave.
Third Ave.
Second Ave.
First Ave.
York Ave.
E. 96th St.
E. 95th St.
E. 92nd St.
E. 90th St.
E. 88th St.
E. 86th St.
E. 84th St.
E. 82nd St.
E. 79th St.
E. 78th St.
E. 77th St.
E. 76th St.
E. 75th St.
E. 74th St.
E. 73rd St.
E. 72nd St.
E. 71st St.
E. 70th St.
E. 69th St.
E. 68th St.
E. 67th St.
E. 66th St.
E. 65th St.
E. 64th St.
E. 63rd St.
E. 62nd St.
E. 61st St.
E. 60th St.
E. 59th St.
1 Grand Army Plaza
2 The Pierre
3 Knickerbocker Club
4 820 Fifth Ave.
5 The Arsenal
6 3 East 64th St.
7 Home of Ulysses S. Grant
8 58 East 68th St.
9 680 Park Ave.
10 Union Club
11 East 70th Street
12 Asia Society
13 Hirschl and Adler/ Knoedler and Company
14 Frick Collection
15 Polo/Ralph Lauren
16 11 East 73rd St.
17 Whitney Museum of American Art
18 972 Fifth Ave.
19 Metropolitan Museum of Art
20 Former Home of Jacqueline Kennedy Onassis
21 86th Street
22 Guggenheim Museum
23 Cooper-Hewitt National Design Museum
24 Convent of the Sacred Heart

The Marquesa de Cuevas bought 680 Park Ave. in 1965, staving off a slated demolition by presenting it to the Americas Society, devoted to educating U.S. citizens about their Western Hemisphere neighbors. The society sponsors public art exhibitions and cultural programs on Latin American and Canadian affairs. The other buildings on this block house the Spanish Institute and the Italian Institute.

Head north on Park Avenue to 69th Street. On the northeast corner stands the:

⑩ Union Club

The Union Club was designed in 1932 to house New York's oldest club. On the other side of 69th Street is Hunter College. Turn right onto 69th Street and continue east toward Lexington Avenue, noting en route 117 E. 69th St., a prototypical, not-so-small, private East Side house with beautiful stained-glass panels around the door.

When you arrive at Lexington Avenue, detour right a few steps to a still-operating branch of Shakespeare and Co. (no. 939), Manhattan's famously literary bookseller whose West Side main branch was put out of business in 1996 when Barnes and Noble strategically built two megastores within walking distance. Double back up Lexington 1½ blocks uptown to 70th Street. Turn left and head back toward Park Avenue along:

⑪ E. 70th Street

This street presents a succession of elegant houses, each more beautiful than the next. Some consider this the finest street in New York. Note in particular no. 125, a post–World War II mansion built for Paul Mellon in a French provincial style.

When you arrive at the Park Avenue end of the block, note the modern building on the northeast corner, which houses the:

⑫ Asia Society

The Asia Society (✆ **212/288-6400** or 212/517-ASIA; www.asiasociety.org) offers workshops, lectures, films, and performances on Asian culture. Major art exhibitions, both ancient and contemporary, are held in the galleries. For more on the museum, including hours and admission fees, see p. 257.

Cross Park Avenue and note 720 Park Ave. on the northwest corner of the intersection. This building is a prime example of the sort of swanky, enormous apartment building that lured former mansion dwellers away from their private houses. The upper stories of buildings like no. 720 often contain apartments with three or four floors and dozens of rooms.

Continue on East 70th Street, crossing Madison, toward Fifth Avenue. Two of the Upper East Side's premier art galleries are along 70th Street.

⑬ Hirschl and Adler

Located at no. 21 (✆ **212/535-8810;** www.hirschlandadler.com), Hirschl and Adler shows quality works of American and European art in many media ranging from the 18th century to current day masterpieces.

Next door, at no. 19, is **Knoedler and Company** (✆ **212/794-0550**), a major gallery for established American artists such as Helen Frankenthaler, Adolph Gottlieb, Nancy Graves, Frank Stella, and John Walker.

Nearing Fifth Avenue, you'll pass a lovely courtyard and lily pond, surrounded by stately black iron gates, before reaching the entrance to my favorite New York museum, the:

⑭ Frick Collection

This collection (✆ **212/288-0700;** www.frick.org) is housed in the 1914 mansion of steel magnate Henry Clay Frick and very evocative of the Gilded Age. The beautiful classic garden overlooking 70th Street was built in 1977. Frick always intended that his art collection be opened to the public after his death. The works are arrayed in rooms, many with Frick's original furnishings, centered around a small, plant-filled atrium with classical styling, a vaulted skylight, and a softly splashing fountain. If you have time for only one museum on this tour, the modestly sized but rich Frick Collection may be your best choice. For more on the collection, including hours and admission fees, see p. 261.

Turn right at the corner of Fifth Avenue, passing a beautiful colonnade on the side of the Frick building. Continue two blocks north, and turn right onto 72nd Street, heading toward Madison Avenue. On your left, at no. 9, is the Lycée Français (a French primary and secondary school), housed in an elaborate 1894 building of the late French Renaissance style. At the southeast corner of 72nd Street and Madison is:

15 Polo/Ralph Lauren

This showcase store, housed in a renovated mansion that dates from 1895, looks for all the world like an English country mansion inside, complete with working fireplaces, Persian rugs, antiques, and a grand baronial staircase. Closed Sunday.

Take Madison Avenue up a block to 73rd Street, passing The Sharper Image (no. 900), the catalog store for the gadget-hound in all of us, and Yumi Katsura (no. 907), a boutique showcasing exquisite wedding gowns for the well-to-do bride. Detour to your left on 73rd Street to see:

16 11 E. 73rd St.

This particularly sumptuous house was built in 1903 by McKim, Mead, and White for Joseph Pulitzer, the Hungarian-born publisher of a once-famous but long-vanished newspaper called the *New York World.* Pulitzer rarely lived in this house because of his extreme sensitivity to sound. At one time, it contained a special soundproof room (mounted on ball bearings to prevent vibrations, no less). When he died in 1911, Pulitzer bequeathed $2 million to the Columbia Graduate School of Journalism, whose trustees bestow the Pulitzer Prizes, annual awards for outstanding achievement in journalism, literature, drama, and musical composition.

Retrace your steps back to Madison Avenue and turn left. At the southeast corner of 75th and Madison you'll see the:

17 Whitney Museum of American Art

Housed in a 1966 architectural masterpiece by Marcel Breuer, the Whitney (✆ **212/570-3676;** www.whitney.org) contains an impressive collection of 20th-century American art, with paintings that reflect trends from naturalism to pop art and abstract expressionism. Roy Lichtenstein, Georgia O'Keeffe, Edward Hopper, and Jasper Johns are just a few of the artists represented here. Hours are Tuesday, Wednesday, Thursday, For more information, including hours and admission fees, see p. 274.

TAKE A BREAK
In the museum's basement, **Sarabeth's at the Whitney** (✆ **212/570-3670**) is much more than your average museum cafeteria—and more expensive, with main lunch dishes starting at $13.70 and brunches starting at $6.75—but it's delicious! See the listing for Sarabeth's Kitchen, in chapter 7, for more details.

Leave the museum and continue uptown on Madison Avenue. At 76th Street, you'll pass one of New York's grand old hotels, **the Carlyle,** which has counted two presidents (Harry Truman and John F. Kennedy) among its famous guests. The west side of Madison Avenue from 76th to 77th streets is lined with a procession of intriguing contemporary art galleries, including the **Gagosian Gallery** in the penthouse of no. 980 (20th-century artists, including Frank Stella, Richard Serra, Andy Warhol, Mark di Suervo, Chris Burden, and Walter de Maria) and **David Findlay** at no. 984 (19th- and 20th-century American and European art). On the way to 79th Street, you'll also run into the French gourmet store **Fauchon** (no. 1000) which boasts a stand-up coffee bar and a menagerie of pastries (all pastry ingredients are French-imported, down to the water).

Turn left when you reach 79th Street and return to Fifth Avenue. The impressive row of buildings includes everything from French château-style structures to neo-Georgian town houses. When you reach the corner of Fifth Avenue, turn left for a look at:

18 972 Fifth Ave.

Located between 78th and 79th streets, this building now serves as the French Embassy's Cultural Services Office, but it was built in 1906 as a wedding present for Payne Whitney by his doting (and childless) rich uncle, Oliver Payne, a Civil War officer and one of the benefactors who helped to found Cornell's Medical College. This McKim, Mead, and White opus cost $1 million and was the talk of the town in its day. Step inside for a glance at its neoclassical rotunda. The broken statue on the central pedestal is a replica of one that caused quite a stir in 1995 when a passing art historian pegged it as a long-lost work by Renaissance master Michelangelo. For years having served as a fountain spout, the suddenly famous Cupid (or, depending on who you ask, perhaps a young Apollo or a young archer) sculpture was spirited away until the controversy over its attribution is resolved. Some claim it was by Michelangelo's teacher Bertoldo; others claim that it's a 19th-century fake.

Next door, on **the corner of 78th Street,** is the classic French-style mansion of tobacco millionaire James B. Duke (as in Duke University). His daughter Doris occupied the house intermittently until 1957, when she donated it to New York University. NYU now operates it as a fine arts institute.

Now turn around and walk north on Fifth Avenue. On your left at 82nd Street is the grand entrance to the:

19 Metropolitan Museum of Art

The Met (© **212/535-7710;** www.metmuseum.org) is one of the world's greatest cultural institutions. The block of 82nd Street that faces the museum's mammoth staircase almost acts as a sort of formal court. The museum's collection is enormous—the largest in the Western Hemisphere—and includes an Egyptian wing that boasts tens of thousands of objects. Its Temple of Dendur, circa 15 B.C. from Lower Nubia, was shipped piece by piece to the Met and painstakingly reconstructed. It would take a lifetime to see all of the Met's treasures, so it might be best to save it for another day and merely admire the exterior for now.

For more information, including hours and admission fees, see p. 247.

Continue uptown past 85th Street. The building at 1040 Fifth Avenue was for many years the:

20 Home of Jacqueline Kennedy Onassis

After her first husband's assassination, she moved here so that Caroline could attend school at nearby Sacred Heart. The former first lady adored New York and was often spotted strolling nearby in her beloved Central Park. After her death from cancer in 1994, hundreds of mourners gathered outside this building, many leaving flowers on the sidewalk in her memory.

Continue uptown to:

21 86th Street

The brick and limestone mansion on the southeast corner of Fifth Avenue and 86th Street was built in 1914 for William Star Miller, but was more famously the home of Grace Vanderbilt, once known as the Queen of America's High Society. Grace Graham Wilson was the daughter of a southern Civil War profiteer who moved north and carefully stitched his family into New York High Society. Grace was first engaged to the Vanderbilt's eldest son, William Henry II, but he died in 1892. Then she was betrothed to Cecil Baring—until Baring Bank crashed in 1893 and she broke it off. It's no wonder, then, that the Vanderbilts sniffed a gold digger in the socialite, and when their now-eldest son and heir-apparent Cornelius III became engaged to her as well, they promptly refused their permission. In fact, some historians attribute Cornelius II's disabling 1896 stroke to the result of an argument with his son over the impending marriage. When the younger Cornelius still would not relent, his father disinherited him as primary heir. Cornelius III's brothers were more forgiving, however, and redistributed the inheritance more equally than the will called for after their father's death.

The intelligent Cornelius III went on to grow his wealth through his love of science—he was a consulting engineer on New York's first subway system—and Grace became the primary New York hostess for almost every visiting monarch and merchant-prince. They moved into a mansion at 640 Fifth Avenue, built in the 1880s by Cornelius III's grandfather William Henry I, which was located down on 51st Street and was the first of a concentration of family houses that at the turn of the 20th century caused Fifth Avenue to be called "Vanderbilt Alley." Despite losing over $8 million in the Great Crash of 1929, the Vanderbilts foolishly maintained their lavish lifestyle throughout the Depression. By the end of the 1930s they were, for Vanderbilts, nearly broke (by which I mean they only had $4 million to spare). They had also become pretty much isolated down around 51st Street, surrounded by ghosts of the Vanderbilt past, lots of noisy traffic, and the new office buildings that had replaced many of the other Millionaire's Row mansions done in by the Depression. Grace and her husband ended up having to sell the 640 Fifth Avenue house, and Cornelius III died in 1942. Grace retreated to this 86th Street address in 1944, but the exile appears, at least from the look of this house, to have been comfortable.

Two blocks further up Fifth Avenue is the unmistakable:

㉒ Guggenheim Museum

(✆ **212/423-3500;** www.guggenheim.org), between 88th and 89th streets, whose building piques just as much interest as the collection of 19th- and 20th-century masterpieces it houses. Designed by Frank Lloyd Wright in 1959, it set off a storm of architectural controversy when it was built. Nowadays, New Yorkers have grown to think of the building as a treasured landmark. The structure has a unique spiral shape; visitors generally take an elevator to the top floor, and then walk down the ramp, viewing the works of art hung along the curved walls that include many special exhibitions along with works by Brancusi, Alexander Calder, Marc Chagall, Kadinsky, Paul Klee, Joan Miró, Mondrian, Picasso, and van Gogh.

For more information, including hours and admission fees, see p. 250.

Uptown from the Guggenheim, between 90th and 91st streets, is another major sight, the:

㉓ Cooper-Hewitt National Design Museum

Under the auspices of the Smithsonian Institution, the Cooper-Hewitt (✆ **212/849-8400;** www.si.edu/ndm) is housed in the former Andrew Carnegie mansion. Built in 1901, this Georgianesque palace originally shared the neighborhood with squatters' shanties and roaming pigs. By the time the squatters were gone and the streets were built up with fine houses, Carnegie was dead. His widow lived in the house until 1949. See p. 259 for more details, including exhibitions, hours, and admission fees.

Across 91st Street from the main entrance to the Cooper-Hewitt is the:

㉔ Convent of the Sacred Heart Girls' School

The convent occupies what was once the largest private house ever built in Manhattan. Financier Otto Kahn bought the property from Andrew Carnegie in 1913, and construction of his mansion, which was modeled on the papal chancellery in Rome, was completed in 1918. Other houses on this 91st Street block, notably nos. 7 and 9, are almost as grand.

Take 91st Street east to Madison Avenue and turn right (downtown) if you'd like to end the tour with a pick-me-up.

WINDING DOWN
At the southwest corner of Madison Avenue and 91st Street is **Jackson Hole** (**✆ 212/427-2820**). Many New Yorkers argue that Jackson Hole flips the best burgers in the city, and you certainly get a lot for your money (burgers start at $4.60). In addition to huge, juicy burgers, Jackson Hole offers omelettes, sandwiches, salads, and great desserts.

10

Shopping

At first glance, the size and breadth of the city's shopping scene seems more overwhelming than anything else. The range of possibilities could test the limits of the most die-hard shopaholic. Even as more and more big chains lay down roots in the city, the world's most unique crop of specialty shops continues to thrive right alongside them. From dinosaur fossils to duck eggs, platform shoes to Chanel suits, love potions to love seats—you'll find a world's worth of merchandise in the Big Apple.

1 The Top Shopping Streets & Neighborhoods

Here's a rundown of New York's most interesting shopping areas, with some highlights of each to give you a feel for the neighborhood. If location is not given here, refer to the store's expanded listing under the appropriate category in "Shopping A to Z," later in this chapter.

DOWNTOWN

LOWER MANHATTAN & THE FINANCIAL DISTRICT

The Financial District's shopping scene was devastated by the demise of the World Trade Center, whose underground shopping mall had evolved into the city's best by 2001. Now **South Street Seaport** (✆ **212/732-7678;** subway: 2, 3, 4, 5 to Fulton St.) carries the neighborhood's torch. Familiar names like Abercrombie & Fitch, Bath & Body Works, Brookstone, and the Sunglass Hut line Fulton Street, the Seaport's main cobbled drag, and fill the levels at Pier 17, a waterfront barge-turned-shopping mall. There's nothing here you can't get anywhere else in Manhattan; come for the historic ambience, the wonderful harbor views, and to spend a few dollars in Lower Manhattan, which needs all the support it can get. For a complete store list, visit **www.southstreetseaport.com.**

Lower Manhattan continues to shine in the discount department. New Yorkers were thrilled in spring 2002 when the king of discount department stores, **Century 21,** reopened its doors against all odds. (The store is across the street from the World Trade Center site.) Electronics mega-mart **J&R** is still going strong, now occupying a full city block with great prices on everything from cameras and computers to CDs and software.

CHINATOWN

Don't expect to find the purchase of a lifetime on Chinatown's streets, but there's some quality browsing to be had. The fish markets along Canal, Mott, Mulberry, and Elizabeth streets are fun for their bustle and exotica. Dispersed among them (especially along **Canal St.**), you'll find a mind-boggling collection of knock-off sunglasses and watches, cheap backpacks, discount leather goods, and exotic souvenirs. It's a fun daytime browse, but don't expect quality—and be sure to bargain before you buy. (Also, skip the bootleg CDs, video, and software—these are stolen goods, and you *will* be disappointed with the product.) **Mott Street,**

Tips **Sales Tax**

New York City sales tax is 8.25%, but it is not added to clothing and footwear items under $110. If you're visiting from out of state, consider having your purchases shipped directly home to avoid paying sales tax.

between Pell Street and Chatham Square, boasts the most interesting of Chinatown's off-Canal shopping, with an antiques shop or two dispersed among the tiny storefronts selling blue-and-white Chinese dinnerware. The definite highlight is the two-stop **Pearl River** Chinese emporium (see "Gifts" in "Shopping A to Z," later in this chapter).

THE LOWER EAST SIDE

The bargains aren't quite what they used to be in the **Historic Orchard Street Shopping District**—which basically runs from Houston to Canal along Allen, Orchard, and Ludlow streets, spreading outward along both sides of Delancey Street—but prices on leather bags, shoes, luggage, and fabrics on the bolt are still quite good. Be aware, though, that the hard sell on Orchard Street can be pretty hard to take. Still, the district is a nice place to discover a part of New York that's disappearing. Come during the week, since most stores are Jewish-owned and, therefore, close Friday afternoon and all day Saturday. Sunday tends to be a madhouse.

The artists and other trendsetters who have been turning this neighborhood into a bastion of hip have also added a cutting edge to its shopping scene in recent years, too. You'll find a growing—and increasingly upscale—crop of alterna-shops south of Houston and north of Grand Street, between Allen and Clinton streets to the east and west, specializing in up-to-the-minute fashions and edgy club clothes for cutting-edge 20-somethings, plus funky retro furnishings, Japanese toys, and other offbeat items. Before you browse, stop into the **Lower East Side Visitor Center,** 261 Broome St., between Orchard and Allen streets (✆ **888/825-8374** or 212/226-9010; subway: F to Delancey St.), for a shopping guide that includes vendors both old-world and new. Or you can preview the list online at **www.lowereastsideny.com**.

SOHO

People love to complain about superfashionable SoHo—it's become too trendy, too tony, too Mall of America. True, **J. Crew** is only one of many big names that have supplanted the artists and galleries that used to inhabit its historic cast-iron buildings. But SoHo is still one of the best shopping 'hoods in the city—and few are more fun to browse. It's the epicenter of cutting-edge fashion and still boasts plenty of unique boutiques. The streets are chock-full of tempting stores, so just come and browse.

SoHo's prime shopping grid is from Broadway east to Sullivan Street, and from Houston down to Broome, although Grand Street, 1 block south of Broome, has been sprouting shops of late. **Broadway** is the most commercial strip, with such recognizable names as **Pottery Barn** and **A/X Armani Exchange.** But the real tone of the neighborhood is set by the big names in avant-garde fashion (see "Clothing" in "Shopping A to Z," later in this chapter). Fabulous accessories shops—like the **Hat Shop,** 120 Thompson St., between Prince and Spring (✆ **212/219-1445**), a full-service milliner for women that also features plenty of off-the-rack toppers, and shoe stores galore—plus high-end home design and housewares boutiques add to the appeal.

NOLITA

Just a few years ago, **Elizabeth Street** was a nondescript adjunct to Little Italy and the no-man's-land east of SoHo. Today it's one of the hottest shopping strips in town, the star of the neighborhood known as Nolita. Elizabeth and neighboring Mott and Mulberry streets are dotted with an increasing number of shops between Houston and Spring streets, with a few pushing 1 more block south to Kenmare. It's an easy walk from the Broadway/Lafayette stop on the F, V line to the neighborhood, since it starts just east of Lafayette Street; you can also take the 6 to Spring Street, or the N, R to Prince Street and walk east from there.

This may be a burgeoning neighborhood, but don't expect cheap—Nolita is clearly the stepchild of SoHo. Its boutiques are largely the province of sophisticated shopkeepers specializing in high-quality fashion-forward products and design. **Mott Street** is an accessories bonanza, with eye-popping **Jamin Puech** for handbags, **Push** and others for gorgeous offbeat jewelry designs, and **Sigerson Morrison** for shoes. The boutique density is most intense on Elizabeth, where offerings range from whimsical milliner **Kelly Christy** at no. 235 (**© 212/965-0686**) to **Area . . . id,** no. 262 (**© 212/219-9903**), for sleek vintage Danish everything. You'll find more standouts in the listings in "Shopping A to Z," later in this chapter, but just cruising the blocks will do the trick.

THE EAST VILLAGE

The East Village personifies bohemian hip. **Kmart,** 770 Broadway (**© 212/673-1540**), between 8th and 9th streets, is so out of place that it's marvelous camp: Japanese kids stare and marvel at gargantuan boxes of laundry detergent as if they were Warhol designed, while multipierced and mohawked locals navigate the name-brand maze alongside stroller-pushing housewives. The easiest subway access is the 6 train to Astor Place, which lets you right out at Kmart and **Astor Wines & Spirits;** from here, it's just a couple blocks east to the prime hunting grounds.

East 9th Street between Second Avenue and Avenue A has become one of my favorite shopping strips in the entire city. Lined with an increasingly smart

---

Tips **Additional Sources for Serious Shoppers**

If you're looking for specific items, check the shopping listings at **www.newyork.citysearch.com**, **www.timeoutny.com**, and **www.nymetro.com** before you leave home.

For an online guide to sample sales designer bargains, you can't do better than the free registration site **www.nysale.com**, which will let you in on unadvertised sales taking place throughout the city.

Hard information about current sales, new shops, sample and close-out sales, and special art, craft, and antiques shows is best found in the "Check Out" section of ***Time Out New York*** or the "Sales & Bargains," "Best Bets," and "Smart City" sections of ***New York*** magazine. *New York* also runs daily updates of these features at **www.nymetro.com**, and *Time Out* usually publishes a twice-yearly shopping guide that's usually available on newsstands for about 6 bucks.

---

collection of boutiques, it proves that the East Village isn't just for kids anymore. Up-and-coming designers, including **Jill Anderson** and **Selia Yang,** sell excellent-quality and affordably priced original fashions for women along here. It's also an excellent strip for stylish gifts and little luxuries. The surrounding blocks aren't quite as mature yet, but are on their way.

If it's strange, illegal, or funky, it's probably available on **St. Marks Place,** which takes over for 8th Street, running east from Third Avenue to Avenue A. This skanky strip is a permanent street market, with countless T-shirt and boho jewelry stands. The height of the action is between Second and Third avenues, which is prime hunting grounds for used-record collectors (see "Music," in "Shopping A to Z," later in this chapter).

LAFAYETTE STREET FROM SOHO TO NOHO

Lafayette Street has a retail character all its own, distinct from the rest of SoHo. It has grown into a full-fledged Antiques Row, especially strong in mid-century furniture. Prices are high, but so is quality. The stretch to stroll is between 8th Street to the north and Spring Street to the south. Either take the 6 train to Astor Place and work your way south; get off at Spring Street and walk north; or take the F or V to Broadway-Lafayette and get dropped off in the heart of the action. Highlights include **Guéridon,** at no. 359, between Bleecker and Bond streets (✆ **212/677-7740;** www.gueridon.com), for sophisticated 20th-century European pieces, mainly French, plus some original designs in the same vein; and **City Barn Antiques,** at Lafayette and Prince streets (✆ **212/941-5757;** www.citybarnantiques.com), probably the nation's premier dealer in impeccably restored Heywood Wakefield furnishings. There's much more—furniture hunters and design lovers will be enthralled for hours. Most dealers are well versed in shipping worldwide.

Dispersed among the furniture and design stores are a number of cutting-edge clothiers, such as **Bond 07,** just off Lafayette at 7 Bond St. (✆ **212/677-8487**), featuring artfully displayed collections of classic vintage fashions and accessories.

GREENWICH VILLAGE

The West Village is great for browsing and gift shopping. Specialty book- and record stores, antiques and craft shops, and gourmet food markets dominate. The Village isn't much of a destination for fashion hunters, with the exception of NYU territory—8th Street between Broadway and Sixth Avenue for trendy footwear and affordable fashions, and Broadway from 8th Street south to Houston, anchored by **Urban Outfitters** at 628 Broadway, between Bleecker and Houston Street (✆ **212/475-0009;** www.urbanoutfitters.com) and dotted with skate and sneaker shops. Clothes hounds looking for volume shopping are better off elsewhere.

The prime drag for strolling is bustling **Bleecker Street,** where you'll find lots of "discount" leather shops and record stores interspersed with a good number of interesting and artsy boutiques. Narrow **Christopher Street** is another fun strip, because it's loaded with genuine Village character. Those who really love to browse should also wander **west of Seventh Avenue** and along **Hudson Street,** where charming shops like **House of Cards and Curiosities,** 23 Eighth Ave., between Jane and 12th streets (✆ **212/675-6178**), the Village's own funky take on an old-fashioned nickel-and-dime, are tucked among the brownstones.

MIDTOWN

THE FLATIRON DISTRICT & UNION SQUARE

When 23rd Street was the epitome of New York uptown fashion more than 100 years ago, the major department stores stretched along **Sixth Avenue** for about a mile (1.5km) from 14th Street up. These elegant stores stood in huge cast-iron buildings that were long ago abandoned and left to rust. In the last few years, however, the area has grown into the city's discount shopping center, with superstores and off-pricers filling up the renovated spaces: **Filene's Basement, TJ Maxx,** and **Bed Bath & Beyond** are all at 620 Sixth Ave., while **Old Navy** is next door, and **Barnes & Noble** is just a couple of blocks away at Sixth Avenue near 22nd Street.

On Broadway, just a few blocks north of Union Square is **ABC Carpet & Home,** a magnet for aspiring Martha Stewarts. If it's actually a rug you're looking for, a whole slew of imported carpet dealers line Broadway from ABC north to about 25th Street.

Upscale retailers who have rediscovered the architectural majesty of **lower Fifth Avenue** include **Banana Republic, Victoria's Secret,** and **Kenneth Cole.** You won't find much that's new along here, but it's a pleasing stretch nonetheless.

HERALD SQUARE & THE GARMENT DISTRICT

Herald Square—where 34th Street, Sixth Avenue, and Broadway converge—is dominated by **Macy's,** the self-proclaimed world's biggest department store, and other famous-name shopping like **Old Navy** across from Macy's on 34th Street. At Sixth Avenue and 33rd Street is the **Manhattan Mall** (© **212/465-0500;** www.manhattanmallny.com), home to mall standards like Foot Locker, LensCrafters, and Radio Shack.

A long block over on Seventh Avenue, not much goes on in the grimy, heavily industrial Garment District. This is, however, where you'll find that quintessential New York experience, the **sample sale** (the box titled "Additional Sources for Serious Shoppers" on p. 345 will tell you how to find out about upcoming sample sales).

TIMES SQUARE & THE THEATER DISTRICT

This neighborhood has become increasingly family oriented, hence, Richard Branson's rollicking **Virgin Megastore;** the fabulous new **Toys"R"Us** flagship on Broadway and 44th Street, which even has its own full-scale Ferris wheel; and the mammoth **E-Walk** retail and entertainment complex on 42nd Street between Seventh and Eighth avenues, overflowing with mall-familiar shops like the **Museum Company.**

West 47th Street between Fifth and Sixth avenues is the city's famous **Diamond District;** see "Jewelry & Accessories" in "Shopping A to Z," later in this chapter.

You'll also notice a wealth of **electronics stores** throughout the neighborhood, many suspiciously trumpeting GOING OUT OF BUSINESS sales. These guys have been going out of business since the Stone Age. That's the bait and switch; pretty soon you've spent too much money for not enough stereo. If you want to check out what they have to offer, go in knowing the going price on that PDA or digital camera you're interested in. You can make a good deal if you know exactly what the market is, but these guys will be happy to suck you dry given half a chance.

Tips Open Hours

Open hours can vary significantly from store to store—even different branches of the Gap can keep different schedules depending on location and management. As a rule of thumb, stores open at 10 or 11am on Monday through Saturday, and 7pm is the most common closing hour (although sometimes it's 6pm). Both opening and closing hours tend to get later as you move downtown; stores in the East Village often don't open until 1 or 2pm, and they stay open until 8pm or later.

All of the big department stores are open 7 days a week. However, unlike department stores in suburban malls, most of these stores don't keep a regular 10am to 9pm schedule. The department stores, and shops along major strips like Fifth Avenue, usually stay open later 1 night a week (often Thurs), although not all shops may comply. Sunday hours are usually noon to 5 or 6pm. Most shops are open 7 days a week, but smaller boutiques may close 1 day a week; in addition, some neighborhoods virtually shut down on a particular day—namely the Lower East Side on Saturday, the East Village on Monday, and most of the Financial District for the weekend. But at holiday time, anything goes: Macy's often stays open until midnight for the last couple of weeks before Christmas!

Your best bet is to **call ahead** if your heart's set on visiting a particular store.

FIFTH AVENUE & 57TH STREET

The heart of Manhattan retail is the corner of Fifth Avenue and 57th Street. Time was, only the very rich could shop these sacred crossroads. Such is not the case anymore, now that **Tiffany & Co.,** which has long reigned supreme here, sits a stone's throw from **Niketown** and the **NBA Store.** In addition, a good number of mainstream retailers, like **Banana Republic,** have flagships along Fifth, further democratizing the avenue. Still, you will find a number of big-name, big-ticket designers radiating from the crossroads, including **Versace, Chanel, Dior,** and **Cartier.** You'll also find big-name jewelers along here, as well as chi-chi department stores like **Bergdorf Goodman, Henri Bendel,** and **Saks Fifth Avenue,** all of which help the avenue maintain its classy cachet.

UPTOWN

MADISON AVENUE

Madison Avenue from 57th to 79th streets has usurped Fifth Avenue as *the* tony shopping street in the city. In fact, in 1998, it vaulted ahead of Hong Kong's Causeway Bay to become the most expensive retail real estate in the world. Bring lots of plastic. This ultradeluxe strip is home to the most luxurious designer boutiques in the world—particularly in the high 60s—with **Barneys New York** as the anchor. For a sampling of local designers, see "Clothing" in "Shopping A to Z," later in this chapter.

For those of us without unlimited budgets, the good news is that stores like **Crate & Barrel** and the fabulous **Ann Taylor** flagship make the untouchable Madison Avenue seem approachable and affordable.

Upper Madison, from about 72nd to 86th streets, has become the domain of cozy-chic home stores for the uptown Martha Stewart set, such as **A La Maison,** no. 1078, between 81st and 82nd (✆ **212/396-1020**), for sophisticated country French imports.

THE UPPER WEST SIDE

The Upper West Side's best shopping street is **Columbus Avenue.** Small shops catering to the neighborhood's white-collar mix of young hipsters and families line both sides of the pleasant avenue from 66th Street (where you'll find an excellent branch of **Barnes & Noble**) to about 86th Street. Highlights include **Robert Marc Opticians** and **Maxilla & Mandible** for museum-quality natural science–based gifts (see "Museum Stores," in "Shopping A to Z," later in this chapter), but you won't lack for good browsing along here.

Boutiques also dot Amsterdam Avenue, but main-drag **Broadway** is most notable for its terrific gourmet edibles at **Zabar's** and **Fairway** (2127 Broadway, at 74th St.; ✆ **212/595-1888**) markets, both legends in their own right (see "Edibles," in "Shopping A to Z," later in this chapter).

2 The Big Department Stores

ABC Carpet & Home This two-building emporium is legendary, and it deserves to be: It's the ultimate home fashions and furnishings department store. On the west side of the street is the stunning 10-floor home emporium. Shopping ABC has often been compared to taking a fantasy tour of your ancestor's attic: The goods run the gamut from Moroccan mosaic-tile end tables to hand-painted Tuscan pottery to Tiffany-style lamps to distressed bed frames made up with Frette linens to much, much more, all carefully chosen and exquisitely displayed. There's a whole floor of on-the-bolt upholstery fabrics to die for. Prices aren't bad comparatively speaking, but these are high-end goods. The Parlor floor boasts an eclectic collection of beautiful gift items and housewares, and some of the smaller items are quite affordable. Occasional sales yield substantial discounts. Adjacent is Belgian import Le Pain Quotidien, serving wonderful lunch fare and elegant desserts (see chapter 7). Across the street is the multifloor carpet store, which boasts a stunning collection of area rugs. 881 & 888 Broadway (at 19th St.). ✆ **212/473-3000.** www.abccarpet.com. Subway: L, N, R, 4, 5, 6 to 14th St./Union Sq.

Barneys New York After financial woes that forced the closure of the original Chelsea store a few years back, New York's self-made temple of chic is back on top. The Madison Avenue store exudes impeccable high style—and a frostiness that I can't seem to overcome, but designer-fashion fans probably won't mind. While the store focuses on hot-off-the-runway women's wear, its menswear runs the gamut from classic to cutting edge. The fragrance department works hard to offer offbeat and unusual scents as well as the classics. Chelsea Passage is one of the world's best gift and tabletop departments. Bring your platinum card, because nothing comes cheap here.

Downtown, **Barneys Co-Op** has blossomed into a real fashion hotspot with its own strong identity, sisterly but separate from the chic Barneys New York Madison Avenue headquarters. At Barneys Co-Op, edgier, artsier, more downtown-casual fashions for men and women—from such vanguard designer names as Daryl K., Comme des Garçons, Herve Chapelier, and Urchin—set the tone. Prices are more reasonable than at the uptown flagship, but you should still be prepared to pay designer prices. 660 Madison Ave. (at 61st St.). ✆ **212/826-8900.** www.barneys.com. Subway: N, R to Fifth Ave. Barneys Co-op at 236 W. 18th St. (btwn Seventh and Eighth aves.); ✆ 212/593-7800. Subway: 1, 9 to 18th St.

Bergdorf Goodman Bergdorf's is a museum of haute couture. The store is beautifully designed on an intimate scale, and many claim that it lacks the nouveau riche feel of Bendel's, but its formality and quiet just make me feel uncomfortable (or maybe it's just that I can't afford anything here?). The customer base is primarily composed of ladies who lunch and businesswomen with gobs of money but little time for nonsense. Still, there's an unparalleled gift and tabletop floor, worth a browse alone; finely tuned designer salons representing both couture powerhouses and downtown darlings; and unparalleled designer handbag and bridal collections. The ladies' shoe department is tops for one-stop designer shopping in the $300-a-pair range, with styles ranging from uptown sleek to funky chic. Just across the street is **Bergdorf Goodman Man,** a palace of fine men's fashion. 754 Fifth Ave. (at 57th St.). © **212/753-7300.** Subway: E, F to Fifth Ave.

Bloomingdale's This is my second-favorite of New York's big department stores (after Saks Fifth Avenue), and my favorite for actual buying. It's more accessible than Barneys or Bergdorf's and more affordable than Saks, but it still has the New York pizzazz that Macy's and Lord & Taylor now largely lack. Taking up the space of a city block, Bloomie's has just about anything you could want, from clothing (both designer and everyday basics) and fragrances to housewares and furniture. It pays to make a reconnaissance trip to get the overview, then move in for the kill. The main entrance is on Third Avenue, but pop up to street level from the 59th Street station and you'll be right at the Lexington Avenue entrance. *Note:* At press time, rumor had it that a second, smaller SoHo branch is in the works, supplanting the Canal Jean Co. at 504 Broadway. 1000 Third Ave. (Lexington Ave. at 59th St.). © **212/705-2000.** www.bloomingdales.com. Subway: 4, 5, 6 to 59th St.

Century 21 *Value* Despite severe damage resulting from its location just across the street from the World Trade Center site, Century 21 pulled off the Herculean feat of reopening its doors on March 1, 2002. The legendary designer discount store is back, and it's better than ever.

Prices on designer goods are 40 to 70% off what you would pay at a department store or designer boutique. Don't think that $250 Armani blazer is a bargain? Look again at the tag—the retail price on it is upward of $800. This is the place to find those $5 Liz Claiborne tees, $20 Todd Oldham pants, or the $50 Bally loafers you've been dreaming of—not to mention underwear, hosiery, and ties so cheap that they're almost free. Kids' clothes, linens, and housewares are also part of the extensive stock. The price you used to pay to get these amazing deals was wrestling with the aggressive, ever-present throngs, but it's hard to say what the ambience will be now. Still, sticking with the traditional wisdom can't hurt: Avoid the weekday lunch hour and Saturdays, if you can help it. 22 Cortlandt St. (btwn Broadway and Church St.). © **212/227-9092.** www.c21stores.com. Subway: 1, 2, 3, 4, 5, M to Fulton St.; A, C to Broadway/Nassau St.; E to Chambers St.

Henri Bendel *Finds* This gorgeous Fifth Avenue store is a lot of fun to browse. It feels like you're shopping in the town house of a confident, monied old lady who doesn't think twice about throwing on a little something by Anna Sui and an outrageously wide-brimmed hat to go out shopping for the day—and she's got the panache to pull it off. It's a superstylish, high-ticket collection for ladies with a flair for the funky and frilly—but the sales are good, and there's always some one-of-a-kind accessories that make affordable souvenirs (and earn you one of the black-and-white striped shopping bags, the best in town). The interior is divine, so take a break from perusing the racks to look around every once in a while. The only downside is that there's no shoe department. The pretty tearoom looks out on Fifth Avenue through Lalique windows. 712 Fifth Ave. (btwn 55th and 56th sts.). ✆ **212/247-1100.** Subway: N, R to Fifth Ave.

Lord & Taylor Okay, so maybe Lord & Taylor isn't the first place you'd go for a vinyl miniskirt. But I like Lord & Taylor's understated, elegant mien. It now operates under the May Company banner but maintains its own sensibility. Long known as an excellent source for women's dresses and coats, L&T stocks all the major labels for men and women, with a special emphasis on American designers. Their house-brand clothes (khakis, blazers, turtlenecks, and summer sportswear) are well made and a great bargain. Sales, especially around holidays, can be stellar. The store is big enough to have a good selection (especially for petites), but doesn't overwhelm—I wish the lighting were better, though, but it's a minor complaint. The Christmas window displays are an annual delight. 424 Fifth Ave. (at 39th St.). ✆ **212/391-3344.** www.lordandtaylor.com. Subway: F, V to 42nd St.

Macy's *Overrated* A four-story sign on the side of the building trumpets, MACY'S, THE WORLD'S LARGEST STORE—a hard fact to dispute, since the 10-story behemoth covers an entire city block, even dwarfing Bloomie's on the other side of town. Macy's is a hard place to shop: The size is unmanageable, the service is dreadful, and the incessant din from the crowds on the ground floor alone will kick your migraine into action. But they do sell *everything.* Massive renovation over the past few years has redesigned many departments into more manageable "ministores"—there's a Metropolitan Museum Gift Shop, a Swatch boutique, and cafes and makeup counters on several floors—but the store's one-of-a-kind flair that I remember so well from my childhood is just a memory now. Still, sales run constantly, holiday or no (1-day sales are popular on Wed and Sat), so bargains are guaranteed. And because so many feel adrift in this retail sea, the store provides personal guides/shoppers at absolutely no charge. My advice: Get the floor plan, and consult it often to avoid wandering off into the sportswear netherworld. At Christmastime, come as late as you can manage (the store is usually open until midnight in the final shopping days). At Herald Square, W. 34th St. and Broadway. ✆ **212/695-4400.** www.macys.com. Subway: B, D, F, N, Q, R, 1, 2, 3, 9 to 34th St.

Saks Fifth Avenue There are branches of Saks all over the country now, but this is it: Saks *Fifth Avenue.* No other store better typifies the Big Apple these days than this legendary flagship store, which is well worth your time—and the smaller-than-most size makes it quite manageable. There's something for everyone here. Saks carries a wide range of clothing; departments err on the pricey designer side (stay out of the lingerie department if you're looking for affordable basics) but run the gamut to affordable house-brand basics. The men's department is the finest in the city. The cosmetics and fragrance departments on the main floor are justifiably noteworthy—they carry many hard-to-find and brand-new brands, including Laura Mercier, the Big Apple's own Kiehl's, and more—as are the extensive fine and costume jewelry counters. And the location, right across from Rockefeller Center, makes it a convenient stop for those on the sightseeing circuit. Don't miss the holiday windows, which are often the city's best. 611 Fifth Ave. (btwn 49th and 50th sts.). ✆ **212/753-4000.** www.saksfifthavenue.com. Subway: B, D, F, Q to 47th–50th sts./Rockefeller Center; E, F to Fifth Ave.

Takashimaya *Finds* This petite branch of Japan's most famous department store chain outpost exudes an appealingly austere, Japanese-tinged French country charm. Come to see some of the city's most beautiful displays of tableware and boudoir fashions. Paris's most famous florist, Christian Tortu, has a main-floor boutique that's a work of art in its own right. The cosmetics department on the top floor is a must for fans of high-end designer brands looking for something special. The serenely elegant Tea Box specializes in delicate bento lunches and beautiful sweets. Aesthetes shouldn't miss this place; it's a wonderful spot for delicate, elegant gifts. 693 Fifth Ave. (btwn 54th and 55th sts.). ✆ **212/350-0100**. Subway: E, F to Fifth Ave.

3 Shopping A to Z

ANTIQUES & COLLECTIBLES

Antiques hounds will dazzle at the bounty that New York has to offer, from Louis XIV settees to vintage DeFranco Family lunchboxes. Be prepared, however—you will pay top dollar for everything.

Traditionalists will love the blocks off **Broadway near 10th and 11th Streets,** where the bounty includes Kentshire Galleries (see below); and **East 59th, 60th, and 61st streets** around Second Avenue, not far from the Manhattan Art & Antiques Center (see below), where about two dozen high-end dealers line the street and spill over onto surrounding blocks. Fans of mid-century furniture and Americana with a twist should browse **Lafayette Street** in SoHo/NoHo. Just about any dealer you visit will have the current issue of the free *Greyrock Antiques Guide* and/or *Antiques New York,* which will lead you to specialty dealers around the city.

Most call it the 26th Street flea market; the famous **Annex Antiques Fair and Flea Market** (✆ **212/243-5343;** www.annexantiques.citysearch.com) is an outdoor emporium of nostalgia, filling a few parking lots along Sixth Avenue between 24th and 27th streets on weekends year-round. The assemblage is hit or miss—some days you'll find treasures galore, and others it seems like there's nothing but junk. A few quality vendors are almost always on hand, though, making it well worth the $1 admission fee. The truly dedicated arrive at 6:30am, but the browsing is still plenty good as late as 4pm. Sunday is always best, since there's double the booty on hand. The website will also link you to other flea markets around the city.

Also check out "Jewelry & Accessories," below, if that's what you're in the market for.

Alphaville This gallery specializes in 1940s, '50s, and '60s toys and movie posters, all in mint condition and beautifully displayed. Space toys are an emphasis. Well worth a look for nostalgic baby boomers, even if you have no intention of buying. 226 W. Houston St. (btwn Sixth Ave. and Varick St.). ✆ **212/675-6850**. www.alphaville.com. Subway: 1, 9 to Houston St.

Chelsea Antiques Building Right around the corner from New York's best flea market (see Annex Antiques Fair and Flea Market, above), this 12-floor building houses more than 100 dealers and is open daily. The permanent stalls run the gamut from 18th-century antiques to rare books to early 20th-century radios, jewelry, and toys. Prices are so good that it's known as a dealer's source, and shoppers are the type who love to prowl, touch everything, and sniff out a bargain. 110 W. 25th St. (btwn Sixth and Seventh aves.). ✆ **212/929-0909**. Subway: F to 23rd St.

Chisolm Gallery Here's the city's best source for collectible-quality vintage travel and advertising posters. Every piece in the collection, which spans the last

100 years, is well chosen and beautifully restored; expect lots of French adverts in the mix. With top quality comes steep prices, so expect to dig deep if you fall in love with a piece. 55 W. 17th St. (just east of Sixth Ave.), 6th floor. ✆ **212/243-8834.** www.vintagepostersnyc.com. Subway: F to 14th St.

The End of History *Finds* This marvelous West Village shop specializes in Murano, Blenko, Holmegaard, and other European glass, with a strong emphasis on the '60s. The constantly changing collection features lots of dazzling shapes and colors, all fetchingly displayed on select pieces of for-sale furnishings, which often have a Scandinavian or mod flair. Everything is so creatively put together that you'll have a blast browsing even if these collectibles aren't your thing. 548½ Hudson St. (btwn Perry and Charles sts.). ✆ **212/647-7598.** Subway: 1, 9 to Christopher St.

Form & Function Co-owned by Fred Schneider of the B-52s, this gallery specializes in lesser-known designers and design trends from 1945 to 1975—a boon to those of us who have seen enough Heywood-Wakefield to last a lifetime. This is a serious gallery, not a mid-century kitsch-fest, so come for the high quality of the home designs. Vintage electronics are featured, too. 95 Vandam St. (1 block north of Spring St., btwn Hudson and Greenwich sts.). ✆ **212/414-1800.** Subway: 1, 9 to Houston St.

J. Fields Studio & Gallery Right next door to Chisolm (see above), this terrific gallery is the place for vintage and contemporary film posters, both foreign and domestic. A limited supply of music posters is on hand, too (including a good selection of psychedelic "Bill Graham Presents" posters from the '60s). J. Fields is considered the best vintage-poster restorer in the city, so quality is first-rate. Prices are high, but with vintage lobby cards starting at $15, even those with small budgets can own a piece of movie history. 55 W. 17th St. (just east of Sixth Ave.), 6th floor. ✆ **212/989-4520.** www.avidcollectorposters.com. Subway: F to 14th St.

Kentshire Galleries Still going strong after a half-century, this large and lovely gallery is the city's prime stop for 18th- and 19th-century English antiques, ranging from jewelry and tabletop items to formal furnishings. Furniture is displayed in richly appointed rooms that make for great browsing. 37 E. 12th St. (btwn University Place and Broadway). ✆ **212/673-6644.** www.kentshire.com. Subway: N, R, L, 4, 5, 6 to 14th St./Union Sq.

La Belle Epoque This shop specializes in original Art Deco and Art Nouveau posters—mostly European advertisements—from the 1890s through the 1950s, as well as conservation framing. If you're a buff with a limited budget, smaller framed pieces in the $100 to $200 range mean that you can buy rather than just browse. 280 Columbus Ave. (at 73rd St.). ✆ **212/362-1770.** www.la-belle-epoque.com. Subway: B, C to 72nd St.

Lost City Arts Lost City features vintage modern furnishings and a quirky selection of accessories (station signs, 3-D photos, and the like), plus their own new midcentury-inspired furniture and accessories, including one inspired by the otherwise forbiddingly expensive custom designs of Machine Age genius Warren MacArthur. A real treat. 18 Cooper Sq. (Fourth Ave. at 5th St.). ✆ **212/375-0500.** www.lostcityarts.com. Subway: N, R to 8th St.

Manhattan Art & Antiques Center This tranquil three-floor emporium of fine antiques boasts more than 100 stalls representing just about every genre of collecting on the map, from perfume bottles and porcelain to Flemish tapestries and Chinese jade to arms and armor. 1050 Second Ave. (btwn 55th and 56th sts.). ✆ **212/355-4400.** www.the-maac.com. Subway: N, R to Lexington Ave.

Going . . . Going . . . Sold!

Auctions specialize in anything collectible, from animation cels to fine wines to Chinese ceramics to Academy Awards fashions. The two major auction houses are **Christie's,** at 20 Rockefeller Plaza, 49th Street between Fifth and Sixth avenues (✆ **212/636-2000;** www.christies.com), and 219 E. 67th St., between Second and Third avenues (✆ **212/606-0400**); and **Sotheby's,** 1334 York Ave., at 72nd Street (✆ **212/606-7000;** www.sothebys.com). Every now and then a celebrity estate goes up for auction (like Jackie O's and the duke and duchess of Windsor's so famously did). No matter what the auction, viewings are free and open to the public; full calendars are available online. If you plan to participate, be sure to review the catalog for price estimates beforehand and attend the sale preview for an advance look at the merchandise.

New York has other auction houses that are less well known (and less fraught with controversy) that you might want to consider, including **Guernsey's,** 108½ East 73rd St., between Park and Lexington aves. (✆ **212/794-2280;** www.guernseys.com), which focuses on modern collections and memorabilia (they auctioned off Jerry Garcia's guitars in spring 2002); and **Tepper Galleries,** 110 East 25th St., between Park and Lexington aves. (✆ **212/677-5300;** www.teppergalleries.com), the city's oldest privately owned auction house, specializing in fine and decorative arts shows and estate sales.

Mood Indigo This dandy of a shop is the city's top dealer in glassware, dishware, and kitchen accessories from the 1930s through the 1950s. The charming shopkeepers also specialize in bakelite jewelry and 1939 World's Fair memorabilia and boast a whopping collection of '50s novelty salt-and-pepper shakers. Everything is pristine, so expect to pay accordingly. 181 Prince St. (btwn Sullivan and Thompson sts.). ✆ **212/254-1176.** Subway: C, E to Spring St.; N, R to Prince St.

Newel Art Galleries This wonderful gallery houses six floors of the best furniture from ages past—be it a throne that would make King Arthur proud or an Art Deco vanity that Carole Lombard might've loved. Browsing hardly gets better. 425 E. 53rd St. (btwn First Ave. and Sutton Place). ✆ **212/758-1970.** www.newel.com. Subway: 6 to 51st St.

ART

See the box titled "Art for Art's Sake: The Gallery Scene," on p. 268.

BEAUTY

C.O. Bigelow Who'd think that a 162-year-old apothecary would carry the city's most eclectic, enjoyable, and international collection of healthy skin and personal care products? The goodies run the gamut from the complete line of oh-so-hip Neals Yard Remedies and Dr. Harris shave creams, both London imports, to French Elgydium toothbrushes and Irish Euthymol toothpaste in bracing cinnamon flavor. Domestic treats include Philip B's botanical hair care products and Bigelow's own line of essential oils. 414 6th Ave. (btwn 8th and 9th sts.). ✆ **212/533-2700.** www.bigelowchemists.com. Subway: A, C, E, F, V to W. 4th St.

Floris London Fragrance lovers shouldn't miss this gorgeous new-world outpost of the marvelous British fragrance house (in business since 1730). Princess

Di was a big fan, and who could blame her? These scents epitomize English botanical splendor and elegance. Floris sells scented candles and home fragrances, too, and expanded their fragrance line in 2000. 703 Madison Ave. (btwn 62nd and 63rd sts.). ✆ **800/5-FLORIS** or 212/935-9100. www.florislondon.com. Subway: N, R to Fifth Ave.; B, Q to Lexington Ave.

Jo Malone *Finds* Any regular *Oprah* watcher is well aware of how much the daytime diva adores London parfumier Jo Malone's light and refreshing floral and fruit scents, as well as her delightfully ungimmicky skin-care line. Ms. Malone opened her first stateside boutique in March 2001, and Big Apple women are rejoicing. On the way to becoming collectors' items, the lovely black-and-white packaging is worth a purchase alone. Don't miss the divine Grapefruit cologne (really). If you can't make it here, Jo Malone also has counters at Saks Fifth Avenue and Bergdorf Goodman. In the Flatiron Building, 949 Broadway (btwn 22nd and 23rd sts). ✆ **212/673-2220.** www.jomalone.com. Subway: N, R to 23rd St.

Kiehl's Kiehl's is more than a store: It's a virtual cult. Models, stockbrokers, foreign visitors, and just about everyone else stops by this always-packed old-time apothecary for its simply packaged, wonderfully formulated products for women and men. Lip Balm no. 1 is the perfect antidote for the biting winds of city or slope. Kiehl's now has a counter at Saks, too (evidence of how they've really moved up in the world), but stop into the original if you can. 109 Third Ave. (btwn 13th and 14th sts.). ✆ **212/677-3171.** Subway: L, N, R, 4, 5, 6 to 14th St./Union Sq.

Sephora The Rock Center branch of the French beauty superstore is a dazzling three-floor bonanza of beauty. You'll find everything you could want here, from scents to nail color to skin cleansers to bath salts to makeup brushes to hair accessories—you get the picture—in a phenomenal number of lines that run the gamut from upscale spa lines Babor, Philip Thomas Roth, and Murad to funky names like Philosophy, Urban Decay, and Hard Candy. An incredible store, with an encyclopedic staff and testers galore. At Rockefeller Center, 636 Fifth Ave. (at 51st St.). ✆ **212/245-1633.** www.sephora.com. Subway: E, F to 51st St. Also at: 1500 Broadway, btwn 43rd and 44th sts. (✆ 212/944-6789; subway: N, R, S, 1, 2, 3, 7, 9 to 42nd St/Times Sq.); 130 W. 34th St., btwn Broadway and Seventh Ave. (✆ 212/629-9315; subway: B, D, F, Q to 34th St./Herald Sq.); 119 Fifth Ave., at 17th St. (✆ 212/674-3570; subway: N, R to 23rd St.); 555 Broadway, btwn Prince and Spring sts. (✆ 212/625-1309; subway: N, R to Prince St.); 1129 Third Ave., at 67th St. (✆ 212/452-3336; subway: 6 to 68th St.); and 2103 Broadway, btwn 73rd and 74th sts. (✆ 212/362-1500; subway: 1, 2, 3, 9 to 72nd St.

BOOKS

THE BIG CHAINS

Barnes & Noble B&N dominates the urban landscape with more locations than any other chain. The Union Square location is my favorite: The selection is huge and well organized, the store is comfortable and never feels overcrowded, and you're welcome to browse—or nab a comfy chair and read—for as long as you like. There's a cafe, of course, and an extensive magazine stand. Many locations host an active calendar of readings and author appearances, often starring such luminaries as Martin Amis and Elmore Leonard. On Union Square, 33 E. 17th St. ✆ **212/253-0810.** www.bn.com. Subway: L, N, R, 4, 5, 6 to 14th St./Union Sq. Also at: 1972 Broadway, at 66th St. (✆ 212/595-6859; subway: 1, 9 to 66th St.); 4 Astor Place, btwn Broadway and Lafayette St. (✆ 212/420-1322; subway: 6 to Astor Place); 675 Sixth Ave., near 22nd St. (✆ 212/727-1227; subway: F to 23rd St.); 160 E. 54th St., at Third Ave. (✆ 212/750-8033; subway: 6 to 51st St.); 600 Fifth Ave., at 48th St. (✆ 212/765-0590; subway: E, F to Fifth Ave.);

Citicorp Center, 160 E. 54th St., btwn Lexington and Third aves. (© 212/750-8033; subway: 6 to 51st St.); 2289 Broadway, at 82nd St. (© 212/362-8835; subway: 1, 9 to 79th St.); 105 Fifth Ave., at 18th St. (© 212/807-0099; subway: F to 14th St.); and 240 E. 86th St., btwn Second and Third aves. (© 212/794-1962; subway: 4, 5, 6 to 86th St.).

Borders The selection of both books and music at Borders is extensive, service is great, and the stores host a wealth of in-store events, including appearances from best-selling authors to musicians like Lou Reed to ethereal pup Mr. Winkle. 461 Park Ave. (at 57th St.). © **212/980-6785.** www.bordersstores.com. Subway: 4, 5, 6 to 59th St. Also at 550 Second Ave., at 32nd St. (© 212/685-3938; subway: 6 to 33rd St.).

SPECIALTY BOOKSTORES

Archivia New, imported, and rare books on architecture, the decorative arts, gardening, and interior design. A book- and design-lover's dream. 1063 Madison Ave. (btwn 80th and 81st sts.), 2nd floor. © **212/439-9194.** www.archivia.com. Subway: 6 to 77th St.

Argosy Books Antiquarian-book hounds should check out this stately 75-year-old store, with high ceilings, packed shelves, a quietly intellectual air, and an outstanding collection of rarities, including 18th- and 19th-century prints, maps, and autographs. 116 E. 59th St. (btwn Park and Lexington aves.). © **212/753-4455.** www.argosybooks.com. Subway: 4, 5, 6 to 59th St.

Bauman Rare Books Dealing strictly in highly prized volumes in topics ranging from philosophy and science to children's classics, Bauman's is one of the foremost resources for serious collectors willing to spend big money for pristine first editions, ranging from Milton's *Paradise Lost* (1669) to Harper Lee's *To Kill a Mockingbird* (1960) signed by the author. 535 Madison Ave. (btwn 54th and 55th sts.). © **800/99-BAUMAN** or 212/751-0011. www.baumanrarebooks.com. Subway: 6 to 51st St. Smaller location at the Waldorf=Astoria Hotel, 301 Park Ave., btwn 49th and 50th sts. (© 212/759-8300; subway: 6 to 51st St.).

Books of Wonder *Kids* You don't have to be a kid to fall in love with this charming bookstore, which served as the model for Meg Ryan's shop in *You've Got Mail.* (Meg even worked here for a spell to train for the role.) Kids will love BOW's story readings; call or check the website for the latest schedule. 16 W. 18th St. (btwn Fifth and Sixth aves.). © **212/989-3270.** www.booksofwonder.com. Subway: L, N, R, 4, 5, 6 to 14th St./Union Sq.

Complete Traveller Whether your destination is Texas or Tibet, you'll find what you need in this, possibly the world's best, travel bookstore. There are maps and travel accessories as well, plus a rare collection of antiquarian travel books whose facts may be outdated but whose writers' perceptions continue to shine. The staff is attentive. 199 Madison Ave. (at 35th St.). © **212/685-9007.** Subway: 6 to 33rd St.

Forbidden Planet Here's the city's largest collection of sci-fi, comics, and graphic-illustration books. The proudly geeky staff really knows what's what. Great sci-fi-themed toys, too. 840 Broadway (at 13th St.). © **212/473-1576.** www.forbiddenplanetnyc.com. Subway: L, N, R, 4, 5, 6 to 14th St./Union Sq.

Gotham Book Mart Paris may have had its Sylvia Beach, but New York was lucky enough to have Frances Steloff. She opened Gotham Book Mart in 1920, and quickly became a defender of the First Amendment rights of authors. She championed such once-banned works as Henry Miller's *Tropic of Cancer,* and numbered among her admirers Ezra Pound, Saul Bellow, and Jackie Kennedy

Onassis. Frances has since passed on, but her aura lives. As always, the emphasis is on poetry, literature, and the arts. This is New York's undisputed literary landmark; look for the sign that says WISE MEN FISH HERE. *Note:* The store is scheduled to move sometime in the near future, but the location and date were unknown at press time; call before you go. 41 W. 47th St. (btwn Fifth and Sixth aves.). ✆ **212/719-4448.** Subway: B, D, F, V to 47th–50th sts./Rockefeller Center.

Hagstrom Map & Travel Center This bookstore sells travel guides and an incredible selection of cartography to meet just about any map need, including some of the best Big Apple maps available. 57 W. 43rd St. (btwn Fifth and Sixth aves.). ✆ **212/398-1222.** Subway: B, D, F, V to 42nd St. Also at 125 Maiden Lane, at Water St. (✆ 212/785-5343; subway: A, C, 2, 3, 4, 5 to Fulton St.).

Housing Works Used Books Cafe *Finds* Here's a way to do something good for yourself and others at the same time: Buy your reading material at this spacious yet quietly cozy used bookshop, sporting 45,000 books and records to browse. It's part of Housing Works, a not-for-profit organization that provides housing, services, and advocacy for homeless people living with HIV and AIDS. The collection is terrific and well organized, with lots of well-priced paperbacks, hardbacks, advance copies, and coffee-table books. There's a comfortable cafe in back that serves coffee and tea as well as freshly prepared sandwiches, sweets, and other light bites, plus beer and wine. The bookstore often hosts readings by well-known writers as well as occasional music performances on Wednesday and Thursday evenings; call or check the website for the current calendar. 126 Crosby St. (south of Houston St.). ✆ **212/334-3324.** www.housingworksubc.com. Subway: F, V to Broadway/Lafayette St.; 6 to Spring St.

Kitchen Arts & Letters Foodies, take note: Here's the ultimate cook's and food-lover's bookstore. You'll be wowed by the depth of the selection, which includes rare, out-of-print, and foreign-language titles focusing on food and wine. The staff will conduct free searches for hard-to-find titles. The shop is an overstuffed jumble, but if this is your bag, you'll be browsing for hours. 1435 Lexington Ave. (btwn 93rd and 94th sts.). ✆ **212/876-5550.** www.kitchenartsandletters.com. Subway: 6 to 96th St.

Madison Avenue Bookshop With the sad demise of Coliseum Books, this lovely shop is now my favorite general-interest bookstore if I want knowledgeable staff to point me to a great read. Author signings are a regular part of the calendar. 883 Madison Ave. (btwn 69th and 70th sts.). ✆ **212/535-6130.** www.madisonavenuebookshop.com. Subway: 6 to 68th St.

Murder Ink Murder, she wrote, he wrote, they wrote—this specialty bookstore claims to be the world's oldest mystery bookstore. They purport to sell every mystery in print, and also have a huge selection of out-of-print paperbacks, hard-to-find imports, and signed first editions. 2486 Broadway (btwn 92nd and 93rd sts.). ✆ **800/488-8123** or 212/362-8905. www.murderink.com. Subway: 1, 9 to 96th St.

Oscar Wilde Bookshop The world's oldest gay and lesbian bookstore is still going strong. The nice staff makes browsing in this landmark a pleasure. 15 Christopher St. (btwn Sixth and Seventh aves.) ✆ **212/255-8097.** www.oscarwildebooks.com. Subway: 1, 9 to Christopher St.

Partners & Crime This West Village shop is as much fun as a good thriller. The new and used collections include signed first editions. Readings and book signings by well-known scribes are a regular event, and live actors perform a

1940s mystery radio show, complete with organist and sound effects, on the first Saturday of the month at 6 and 8pm ($5). 44 Greenwich Ave. (at Charles St.). ✆ **212/243-0440.** www.crimepays.com. Subway: A, B, C, D, E, F, Q to W. 4th (use 8th St. exit).

Rand McNally Travel Store Sheet maps, globes, city maps, international maps, laminated maps—so many maps that you might never get lost again. Offers wide range of travel guides, atlases, and such travelers' aids as voltage converters and inflatable pillows, too. www.randmcnally.com. 150 E. 52nd St. (btwn Lexington and Third aves.). ✆ **212/758-7488.** Subway: E, F to Lexington Ave.; 6 to 51st St. Also at 555 Seventh Ave., btwn 39th and 40th sts. (✆ 212/944-4477; subway: 1, 2, 3, 7, 9, N, R, S to 42nd St./Times Sq.).

Rizzoli This clubby Italian bookstore is the classiest—and most relaxing—spot in town to browse for visual art and design books, plus quality fiction, gourmet cookbooks, and other upscale reading. There's a decent selection of foreign-language, music, and dance titles as well. 31 W. 57th St. (btwn Fifth and Sixth aves.). ✆ **212/759-2424.** Subway: N, R to Fifth Ave.

St. Mark's Bookshop Established in 1977, this left-of-center East Village bookshop is a great place to browse. You'll find lots of terrific alternative and small-press fiction and poetry, plus cultural criticism, Eastern philosophy, and mainstream literature with an edge. You'll also find art, photography, and design books as well as an alternative 'zine rack. Lots of spoken-word CDs and cassettes, too. 31 Third Ave. (at 9th St.). ✆ **212/260-7853.** www.stmarksbookshop.com. Subway: 6 to Astor Place.

The Scholastic Store *Kids* This mammoth store is located at the ground level of the headquarters for children's book publisher Scholastic (which also introduced a boy named Harry Potter to America). The 6,200-foot (1,860m) retail space is a veritable interactive playground for kids. Books, toys, and software products feature Scholastic's top-selling brands, from Clifford the Big Red Dog to Captain Underpants. Needless to say, Hogwarts is well represented. A full slate of in-store events, from author signings to craft workshops, also keeps kids busy; check the website or call for the current schedule. 557 Broadway (btwn Prince and Spring sts.). ✆ **212/343-6166.** www.scholastic.com/sohostore. Subway: N, R to Prince St.

Shakespeare & Co. This boutiquelike bookstore stocks the latest bestsellers, and has a generally well-rounded inventory. The displays are quite enticing if you're looking for something new to read. 716 Broadway (at Washington Place). ✆ **212/529-1330.** www.shakeandco.com. Subway: N, R to 8th St. Also at: 939 Lexington Ave., at 69th St. (✆ 212/570-0201; subway: 6 to 68th St.); 135 E. 23rd St., at Lexington Ave. (✆ 212/505-2021; subway: 6 to 23rd St.); and 1 Whitehall St., at Broadway, next to U.S. Customs House, 1 block from Staten Island Ferry (✆ 212/742-7025; subway: 4, 5 to Bowling Green; N, R to Whitehall St.).

The Strand *Value* Something of a New York legend, The Strand is worth a visit for its staggering "eight miles of books" as well as its extensive inventory of review copies and bargain titles at up to 85% off list price. It's unquestionably the city's best book deal—there's almost nothing marked at list price—and the selection is phenomenal in all categories (there's even a rare book department on the third floor). Still, you'll work for it: The narrow aisles mean you're always getting bumped; the books are only roughly alphabetized; and there's no air-conditioning in summer. Nevertheless, it's a used-book-lover's paradise. Note that the Lower Manhattan location is significantly smaller. 828 Broadway (at 12th St.). ✆ **212/473-1452.** www.strandbooks.com. Subway: L, N, R, 4, 5, 6 to 14th St./Union Sq. Strand Annex at 95 Fulton St., btwn William and Gold sts. (✆ 212/732-6070; subway: 4, 5, 6 to Fulton St.).

Traveler's Choice This small and friendly travel bookstore can meet all of your travel guide needs, from Antarctica to Zimbabwe. 2 Wooster St. (between Grand and Canal sts.). ✆ **212/941-1535**. Subway: A, C, E to Canal St.

Urban Center Books Housed in an architectural landmark, McKim, Mead & White's 1882 Villard Houses, the Municipal Art Society's bookstore boasts a terrific selection of new books on architecture, urban planning, and landscape design. In the Villard Houses, 457 Madison Ave. (at 51st St.). ✆ **800/352-1880** or 212/935-3592. www.urbancenterbooks.com. Subway: 6 to 51st St.

CLOTHING

RETAIL FASHIONS

The Top Designers

The legendary locale for the classic designer names has always been Fifth Avenue and 57th Street. There's been some exodus to Madison Avenue (see below), but the opening of the **Gianni Versace** shop at 647 Fifth Ave., between 51st and 52nd streets (✆ **212/317-0224;** www.versace.com), just before the designer's death has heralded a new era of respect for the avenue. Other deluxe designer tenants from Italy's haute couture world are **Prada** (see "For Men & Women," below); **Salvatore Ferragamo,** no. 661, between 52nd and 53rd streets (✆ **212/759-3822;** www.ferragamo.com); and knit queen **Laura Biagiotti** at 4 W. 57th, just off Fifth Avenue (✆ **212/399-2533**). Tom Ford's stellar **Gucci** is at Fifth Avenue and 54th Street (✆ **212/826-2600;** www.gucci.com), while classic **Chanel** is at 15 E. 57th St., between Fifth and Madison avenues (✆ **212/355-5050**), with the freshly hip tartans of **Burberry** just down the block at 10 W. 57th St. (✆ **212/371-5010;** www.burberry.com). *Note:* Burberry is scheduled to move into its new flagship store just down the block on 57th in fall 2002.

The Upper East Side's Madison Avenue is the heartland of haute couture these days. The biggest names in clean-lined modern design line up along the platinum-coated boulevard; between 59th and 80th streets, you'll find **Calvin Klein, Giorgio Armani, Valentino, Bottega Veneta, Dolce & Gabanna, Emmanuel Ungaro, Givenchy, Hermès, Issey Miyake, Krizia, Max Mara, Prada** (see below), **Polo/Ralph Lauren** (see below), **Versace** (see above), and many more; the density is greatest in the high 60s.

Established avant-garde designers hang out in SoHo. Highlights include **Anna Sui,** 113 Greene St., just south of Prince Street (✆ **212/941-8406;** www.annasui.com), who specializes in slinky fashions with a glam edge; she also has a terrific new beauty line now. **Marc Jacobs,** 163 Mercer St., between Houston and Prince (✆ **212/343-1490;** www.marcjacobs.com), excels at modern takes on classic cuts. Trend-busting designs are the specialty of legendary Brit **Vivienne Westwood,** 71 Greene St., between Spring and Broome (✆ **212/334-5200**). Girlish designs are the specialty of **Cynthia Rowley,** 108 Wooster St., between Prince and Spring (✆ **212/334-1144**), while **Vivienne Tam,** 99 Greene St., between Prince and Spring (✆ **212/966-2398**), specializes in pretty and playful Asian motifs. SoHo has become so designer hot that plenty of established names have moved in as well, including **Louis Vuitton,** 116 Greene St., between Prince and Spring (✆ **212/274-9090;** www.vuitton.com); always-avant **Helmut Lang,** 80 Greene St., near Spring Street (✆ **212/925-7214**); **Burberry,** 131 Spring St., between Greene and Wooster streets (✆ **212/925-9300;** www.burberry.com), and, in the same block, **Chanel,** 139 Spring St. (✆ **212/334-0055**).

Talented up-and-comers have set up shop on and around **Bond Street** in NoHo; on **Elizabeth, Mott,** and **Mulberry streets** in Nolita; along **East 9th Street** in the East Village (see "For Men & Women," below); and on the **Lower East Side,** in the blocks south of Houston Street.

Fashion Flagships

Some New York flagship stores of the major brands are an experience you won't catch in your nearest mall. These stores are display cases for the complete line of fashions, so you'll often find much more to choose from than in your at-home branch. You'll find other locations throughout the city, but these are meant to be the biggest and best: Check out the gorgeous **Ann Taylor** at 645 Madison Ave., at 60th Street (✆ **212/832-2010;** www.anntaylor.com); the **Banana Republic** flagship at Rockefeller Center, 626 Fifth Ave., at 50th Street (✆ **212/974-2350;** www.bananarepublic.com); **Eddie Bauer,** 1960 Broadway, at 67th Street (✆ **212/877-7629;** www.eddiebauer.com), which also carries the AKA Eddie Bauer line and the sports and mountaineering line; **Liz Claiborne,** 650 Fifth Ave., at 52nd Street (✆ **212/956-6505;** www.lizclaiborne.com), which carries all of Liz's lines; and **DKNY,** 655 Madison Ave., at 60th Street (✆ **212/223-DKNY;** www.dkny.com). **J. Crew** has a big bi-level SoHo store at 100 Prince St., between Mercer and Greene streets (✆ **212/966-2739;** www.jcrew.com), as well as a large store on Rockefeller Plaza at 50th Street (✆ **212/765-4227**). **Old Navy** has a huge flagship featuring its affordable basics and signature sense of humor at 610 Sixth Ave., at 18th Street (✆ **212/645-0663;** www.oldnavy.com).

For Men & Women

Brooks Brothers The perfect definition of all that is preppy lies behind this clubby storefront. The label is synonymous with quality, quiet taste, and classic tailoring. The cut of the man's suit is a tad boxy, making it great for the full American body. 346 Madison Ave. (at 44th St.). ✆ **212/682-8800.** www.brooksbrothers.com. Subway: S, 4, 5, 6, 7 to 42nd St./Grand Central. Also at 666 Fifth Ave., btwn 52nd and 53rd sts. (✆ 212/261-9440; subway: 6 to 51st St.).

H&M *Value* The Swedish superdiscounter Hennes & Mauritz took New York by storm in early 2000 with its high-style fashions at budget-minded prices. The colorful, loud, bustling stores are mammoth, but the departments are better organized than those at most full-retail department stores. The men's and women's clothing is ultrachic, and the prices are low, low, low. A real fave with teens, in particular. The main Herald Square store carries all lines, including babies, children's, and maternity wear. 1328 Broadway (at 34th St.). ✆ **212/564-9922.** www.hm.com. Subway: B, D, F, N, R, V, W to 34th St./Herald Sq. Also at 640 Fifth Ave., at 51st St. (✆ 212/489-0390; subway: E, F to Fifth Ave.). Smaller location at 558 Broadway, btwn Prince and Spring sts. (✆ 212/343-8313; subway: N, R to Prince St.).

Jeffrey New York At the end of a deserted street in the still-industrial Meat-Packing District is this oasis of cutting-edge haute couture. Jeffrey New York caters to the Barneys crowd, but this outpost of the famed Atlanta megaboutique is much more accessible and user-friendly. Great accessories and shoes galore. The collection is mostly geared to women, but there's a notable men's department, too, and a deejay to keep tag-alongs entertained. A worthy schlep for style hounds. 449 W. 14th St. (near Tenth Ave.). ✆ **212/206-1272.** Subway: A, C, E, L to 14th St.

Kenneth Cole This two-story Rock Center flagship carries Kenneth Cole's complete lines of stylish clothing and footwear, including his affordable Reaction line. An ideal blend of clean-lined comfort and casual glamour for both men and women. The leather jackets are particularly divine; good accessories, too. Check out the new **Reaction** boutique for a full selection of Cole's midprice line. *Note:* Some secondary locations focus on shoes and leather goods, and carry only limited clothing selections. 610 Fifth Ave. (at 48th St.). ✆ **212-373-5800.** www.kennethcole.com. Also at: 95 Fifth Ave., at 17th St. (✆ 212/675-2550; subway: N, R to 23rd St.); 353 Columbus Ave., near 77th St. (✆ 212/873-2061; subway: B, C to 81st St./Museum of Natural History); 597 Broadway, just south of Houston St. (✆ 212/965-0283; subway: F, V to Broadway-Lafayette St.; N, R to Prince St.); 95 Fifth Ave., at 17th St. (✆ 212/675-2550; subway: 4, 5, 6, N, R, Q, W, L to 14th St./Union Sq.); and Street level at Grand Central Terminal, 107 E. 42nd St. (✆ 212/949-8079; subway: 4, 5, 6, 7, S to 42nd St./Grand Central). **Reaction** boutique at 130 E.57th St., at Lexington Ave. (✆ **212/688-1670;** subway: 4, 5, 6 to 59th St.).

Nicole Fahri *Finds* This cool-chic British import specializes in the same kind of simple, clean-lined casual urban wear as Banana Republic, but it's for those who can afford better. Expect great cuts, neutral colors, and natural fabrics. There's a stylish home store and Modern British cuisine at Nicole's, a terrific *New York Times* two-star winner. 10 E. 60th St. (just east of Fifth Ave.). ✆ **212/223-8811** (✆ 212/223-2288 for reservations at Nicole's). Subway: N, R to Fifth Ave.

Patricia Field The wildest club kids and trendiest trendsetters know Patricia Field as *the* place to shop. Pat Field has been the leading doyenne of cutting-edge chic and downtown cool for more than 2 decades now, and she still reigns—just in case you're not sure, she's the clothing designer for *Sex in the City.* Her shop sports the city's grooviest, most outrageous men's and women's club wear (including no shortage of fetish wear). The wild makeup counter will appear tame once you see the outlandish dos in the wacky wig and hair salon. There's nothing understated about this place—it's a hoot to browse. Carrie Bradshaw's horseshoe necklaces are available here by special order, I'm told. Field's **Hotel Venus** store is more upscale, but no less funky. 10 E. 8th St. (btwn Fifth Ave. and University Place). ✆ **212/254-1699.** www.patriciafield.com. Subway: 6 to Astor Place. **Hotel Venus** at 382 W. Broadway, btwn Spring and Broome sts. (✆ 212/966-4066; subway: C, E to Spring St.).

Paul Stuart Paul Stuart is a touch more hip and a touch more expensive than Brooks Brothers. Stuart is the classic New York haberdasher—gorgeous fabrics, impeccable tailoring, high price tags on everything from suits to weekend wear; there's women's wear, too, but I find Paul Stuart to be all about men. This is a way-of-life store for those who subscribe. Madison Ave. at 45th St. ✆ **212/682-0320.** www.paulstuart.com. Subway: 4, 5, 6, 7, S to 42nd St./Grand Central.

Polo/Ralph Lauren Among all the high-ticket designers whose shops line Madison Avenue, Ralph Lauren deserves special mention for the stunning beauty of his flagship store, housed in a landmark Rhinelander mansion. One of New York's first important freestanding American designer shops, it has continued to wear as well as the classics Ralph churns out. Housewares and infants' clothing as well as women's and men's clothes are for sale. The active wear and sporty country looks are at Polo Sport. 867 & 888 Madison Ave. (at 72nd St.). ✆ **212/606-2100** or 212/434-8000. www.ralphlauren.com. Subway: 6 to 68th St. **Polo Sport** at 379 Broadway, btwn Spring and Broome sts. (✆ 212/625-1660; subway: C, E to Spring St.).

Prada No designer label is more body-conscious, cachet-laden, and downright chic than this sleek Italian line, which reaches beyond clothing to embrace shoes, accessories, and the hippest handbags on the globe (yes, still). SoHo's **Prada Sport** and **Miu Miu** is the destination for under-30 fashionistas with platinum cards. 724 Fifth Ave. (btwn 56th and 57th sts.). ✆ **212/664-0010.** www.prada.com. Subway: N, R to 5th Ave. Also at 841 Madison Ave., at 70th St. (✆ 212/327-4200; subway: 6 to 68th St.). **Prada Sport** at 116 Wooster St., btwn Prince and Spring sts. (✆ 212/925-2221; subway: C, E to Spring St.). **Miu Miu** at 100 Prince St., btwn Mercer and Greene sts. (✆ **212/334-5156;** www.miumiu.com; subway: C, E to Spring St.).

Seize sur Vingt *Finds* This smart Nolita shop custom-tailors Egyptian cotton shirts in bright colors and bold patterns for men and women—perfect for adding a bit of individual flair to your corporate threads. They've also reinvented the bespoke suit in clean, slim, contemporary lines. 243 Elizabeth St. (btwn Houston and Prince sts.). ✆ **866/343-0476** or 212/343-0476. www.16sur20.com. Subway: F, V to Broadway/ Lafayette St; 6 to Spring St.

Shanghai Tang *Finds* This Hong Kong clothier boasts one of the loveliest, wittiest stores on Madison Avenue. The designs are irreverent takes on Chinese classics—Mandarin-collared jackets, ankle-length cheongsams—done in shimmering silks, lustrous velvets, and rich jacquards, and a vibrant palette that runs the gamut from the hot pink to electric blue (plus black, for those of us who prefer to tone down rather than up). The line includes styles for men, women, and children, plus divine home accessories in equally eye-catching colors. 714 Madison Ave. (btwn 63rd and 64th sts.). ✆ **212/888-0111.** www.shanghaitang.com. Subway: N, R to Fifth Ave.; 4, 5, 6 to 59th St.

Thomas Pink One of London's most revered shirtmakers has set up camp on a prime Madison Avenue corner. This shop specializes in beautifully made presized cotton shirts for men and women, crafted from the finest quality twofold pure cotton poplin. While the name Thomas Pink bespeaks tradition to anyone who knows fine shirt making, don't expect stuffy: The tailors work in a broad and lively palette, in both classic and modern styles. The huge selection of men's ties is equally eye-catching, with some of the richest jewel tones I've seen. 520 Madison Ave. (at 53rd St.). ✆ **212/838-1928.** www.thomaspink.co.uk. Subway: E, F to Fifth Ave.; 6 to 51st St. Also at 1155 Sixth Ave., at 50th St. (✆ 212/840-9663; subway: B, D, F, V to 47th–50th sts./Rockefeller Center).

Tristan & America *Value* This Canadian retailer sells affordable, nicely tailored clothing in muted palettes to men and women who love Banana Republic's clothes, but need a break from the high prices there. Look for great men's sweaters, affordable women's suits, and nicely cut trousers and A-line skirts. Excellent sales. 1230 Sixth Ave. (at 49th St.). ✆ **212/246-2354.** www.tristan-america.com. Subway: B, D, F, V to 47th–50th sts./Rockefeller Center.

X-Large Your trend-obsessed teen (or the trend-obsessed teen in you) will love you for taking him to this prime pit stop (co-owned by Beastie Boy Mike D) for upscale skate, street, hip-hop wear. 267 Lafayette St. (btwn Prince and Spring sts.). ✆ **212/334-4480.** www.xlarge.com. Subway: 6 to Spring St.

Just Women

Anthropologie Funky, slightly exotic, and affordable wearables and accessories mix with fun gifts, furniture, and home decorating items. Geared to funky-chic postcollegiate young women who've outgrown Urban Outfitters. 375 W. Broadway (btwn Spring and Broome sts.). ✆ **212/343-7070.** www.anthropologie.com. Subway: C, E to Spring St. Also at 85 Fifth Ave., at 15th St. (✆ 212/627-5885; subway: L, N, R, 4, 5, 6 to Union Sq.).

DVF—The Shop The doyenne of '70s chic, Diane vonFurstenberg, is fashion-forward once again. You need the bod to wear Ms. vonFurstenberg's sheer, clingy, body-conscious styles—but if you've got it, there's no better way to flaunt it. Don't be surprised if you run into such style hounds as Paris and Nicky Hilton browsing the racks at this mod Meat-Packing District boutique. 385 West 12th St. (at Washington St.). ✆ **646/486-4800.** www.dvf.com. Subway; A, C, E, L to 14th St.

Eileen Fisher Making their way around the nation in her own shops and through outlets like Saks and the Garnet Hill catalog, Eileen Fisher's separates are a dream come true for stylish women looking for easy-to-wear classic pieces that transcend the latest fads. She designs fluid clothes in a pleasing neutral palette and uses natural fibers that don't sacrifice comfort for chic. The A-line styles look a bit droopy on shorter women, but otherwise suit all figure types well; petites and plus sizes are carried as well. The superior quality, fabrics, and style make these clothes worth every penny. This beautifully austere SoHo location is Fisher's prime showcase. The semiannual consolidation sales, in March and August, are a bargain hunter's delight. Note that only the SoHo flagship sells the complete line, including both the petite and woman's collections. The closet-size East 9th Street location basically functions as an outlet store, with lots of sale merchandise and seconds on hand. 395 W. Broadway (btwn Spring and Broome sts.). ✆ **212/431-4567.** www.eileenfisher.com. Subway: C, E to Spring St. Also at: 166 Fifth Ave., near 21st and 22nd sts. (✆ 212/924-4777; subway: N, R to 23rd St.); 521 Madison Ave., at 53rd St. (✆ 212/759-9888; subway: 6 to 51st St.); 341 Columbus Ave., near 77th St. (✆ 212/362-3000; subway: B, C to 81st St.); 1039 Madison Ave., btwn 79th and 80th sts. (✆ 212/879-7799; subway: 6 to 77th St.); and 314 E. 9th St., btwn First and Second aves. (✆ 212/529-5715; subway: 6 to Astor Place).

Harriet Love Harriet's clothes are for women who prefer flowing lines and comfy fabrics over the slinky couture duds that threaten to overrun SoHo's boutiques. They're stylish without being trendy; you'll be able to wear them well after the season ends. Expect beautiful sweaters and accessories galore from an eclectic mix of American and European designers. Angelica Huston's a fan—I've spotted her browsing and buying here. 126 Prince St. (btwn Greene and Wooster sts.). ✆ **212/966-2280.** Subway: N, R to Prince St.

Intermix The place to dress and accessorize like your favorite *Sex and the City* gals, at not-too-expensive prices. The Flatiron location is the original, and remains the best. 125 Fifth Ave. (btwn 19th and 20th sts.). ✆ **212/533-9720.** Subway: N, R to 23rd St. Also at 210 Columbus Ave., btwn 69th and 70th sts. ✆ 212/769 9116; subway: B, C to 72nd St.

Jill Anderson *Finds* Finally, a New York designer who designs affordable clothes for real women to wear for real life—not just for 22-year-old size-2s to match with a pair of Pradas and wear out club-hopping. This narrow, peaceful shop and studio is lined on both sides with Jill's simple, clean-lined designs, which drape beautifully and accentuate a woman's form without clinging. They're wearable for all ages and many figure types. (Her small sizes are small enough to fit petites, and her larges generally fit a full-figured size 14.) Her clothes are feminine without being frilly, retro-reminiscent but completely modern, understated, and utterly stylish. 331 E. 9th St. (btwn First and Second aves.). ✆ **212/253-1747.** www.jillanderson.com. Subway: 6 to Astor Place.

Lucy Barnes *Finds* This joyous fashion designer and her light-filled boutique played a major role in drawing fashionistas to the Meat-Packing District; in spring 2002, she relocated to a larger space to accommodate her growing line. The Edinburgh native uses vintage fabrics, buttons, beads, and embroideries in up-to-date shapes that are playful, pretty, and wear well from day to evening. 117 Perry St. (btwn Greenwich and Hudson sts.). ✆ **212/647-0149.** Subway: A, C, E, L to 14th St.

Marianne Novobatzky *Finds* Marianne Novobatzky crafts couture and ready-to-wear evening wear in simple, sexy, clean-lined sheath styles using satins and other seductive fabrics in jewel tones and other gorgeous solid colors. Some beautifully classic businesswear is on hand, too. Brides can be custom-fit by the designer herself for a stunning sheath dress. 65 Mercer St. (just north of Broome St.). ✆ **212/431-4120.** Subway: J, M, N, R, Q, W to Canal St.

Meg If Audrey Hepburn were alive today, this is probably where she'd shop. Meghan Kinney specializes in gorgeous, figure-flattering separates with elegantly straight lines in fabrics that stretch and cling just a bit, but not too much. 312 E. 9th St. (btwn First and Second aves.). ✆ **212/260-6329.** Subway: 6 to Astor Place.

Nicolina This charming and sophisticated shop is a Theater District anomaly. Come for fashionable basics in high-quality natural materials: wide-legged linen pants, flowing A-line and princess-cut dresses in silk and cotton, and sweaters from labels like Beyond Threads and Sarah Arizona in fine wools, cotton, and silk. Great accessories, too. 247 W. 46th St. (btwn Broadway and Eighth Ave.). ✆ **212/302-NICO.** Subway: N, R, S, 1, 2, 3, 9 to 42nd St./Times Sq.

Selia Yang *Finds* This divinely inspired young designer fashions stunning cocktail and evening dresses out of the simple sheath. Her looks are a little younger, a littler softer, a little more flowing and bare-shouldered than Marianne Novobatzky's (above). Her beaded dresses, in particular, are showstoppers, as are her gorgeous bridal gowns. 328 E. 9th St. (btwn First and Second aves.). ✆ **212/254-9073.** www.seliayang.com. Subway: 6 to Astor Place.

Vera Wang The petite powerhouse is still the hottest name in bridal fashions. Vera clothes scads of top stars (particularly petite ones with great figures) on their big day or for the Oscars in her simple, elegant designs. Vera's studio is open by appointment only, so brides-to-be looking for the best should call ahead. There's also a Vera Wang salon on the third floor at Bergdorf's (p. 350). Ask about the annual warehouse sale, usually in September. 991 Madison Ave. (at 77th St.). ✆ **212/628-3400.** www.verawang.com. Subway: 6 to 77th St. Bridesmaids' store at 980 Madison Ave., btwn 76th and 77th sts., 3rd Floor (✆ 212/628-9898; subway: 6 to 77th St.).

Just Men

Frank Stella This refined shop sells casually elegant clothes for the well-dressed 21st-century man, including clean-lined blazers, quality knits, and beautifully cut trousers. 440 Columbus Ave. (at 81st St.). ✆ **212/877-5566.** Subway: B, C to 81st St. Also at 921 Seventh Ave., at 58th St. (✆ 212/957-1600; subway: A, B, C, D, 1, 9 to 59th St./ Columbus Circle).

Paul Smith This temple of new English fashion is a can't miss. When it comes to menswear that's at once fashion forward and undisputedly classic, Paul Smith wins the prize, with jackets, suits, pants, shoes, sportswear, and accessories that are superpricey but worth every cent. 108 Fifth Ave. (at 16th St.). ✆ **212/627-9770.** www.paulsmith.co.uk. Subway: F to 14th St.

Saint Laurie Merchant Tailors *Finds* Family-owned since 1913, this custom tailor offers a huge selection of fabrics, from Scottish worsted wools to Italian silks, and offers you a selection of styles to choose from. The custom job is about $1,000 for a suit (less when sales are going), substantially less for a blazer. 350 Park Ave. (between 51st and 52nd sts.). ✆ **212/317-8700.** www.saintlaurie.com. Subway: 6 to 51st St.

Just Kids

If you need the basics, you'll find branches of **Gap Kids** and **Baby Gap** all over town—it's harder to avoid one than to find one. The department stores are also great sources, of course.

Bu & the Duck *Finds* This divine shop sells its own unique vintage-inspired clothing and shoes that your kids can really wear. Delightful sock puppets and other vintage-inspired toys are also in the mix. 106 Franklin St. (btwn Church St. and W. Broadway). ✆ **212/431-9226.** www.buandtheduck.com. Subway: 1, 9 to Franklin St.

Greenstones et Cie Cute, funky, upscale sportswear from such European lines as Kenzo, Miniman, Clayeux, and Petit Boy. Many of the clothes are one-of-a-kind or handcrafted items, so expect to pay accordingly. 442 Columbus Ave. (btwn 81st and 82nd sts.). ✆ **212/580-4322.** Subway: 1, 9 to 79th St. Also at 1184 Madison Ave., btwn 86th and 87th sts. (✆ 212/427-1665; subway: 4, 5, 6 to 86th St.).

rockstarbaby Here's the place to clad your kid in the coolest glad rags around. This brand-new line of newborn and infant clothing is a collaboration between rocker Tico Torres (Bon Jovi) and designer Cinzia Spinetti. Despite the pedigree and attitude (how 'bout a bib that says BORN TO ROCK for your favorite newborn?), these are gorgeous, practical, and moderately priced wearables. 298 Elizabeth St. (just north of Houston St.). ✆ **212/226-2771.** www.rockstarbaby.com. Subway: 6 to Bleecker St.

Shoofly Top-quality clothing, footwear, and accessories for kids from newborns through teens. You'll find lots of distinctive stuff here, including imported lines. The shoe selection, in particular, is terrific, and not too pricey. The downtown store also sells toys and infant gifts. 465 Amsterdam Ave. (at 82nd St.). ✆ **212/580-4390.** www.shooflynyc.com. Subway: 1, 9 to 79th St. Also at 42 Hudson St., btwn Duane and Thomas sts. (✆ 212/406-3270; subway: 1, 2, 3, 9 to Chambers St.).

Wicker Garden Charlotte turned to this dreamy store to create the perfect *Sex in the City* baby shower for Miranda, so look no further for the city's most stylish imported baby wear and gear. Prices are commensurate with the Upper East Side location and high Victorian-inspired style. 1318–1327 Madison Ave. (btwn 93rd and 94th sts.) ✆ **212/410-7001.** www.wickergarden.com. Subway: 6 to 96th St.

Vintage & Consignment Clothing

Allan & Suzi *Finds* Make it past the freaky windows and inside you'll find one of the best consignment shops in the city. Allan and Suzi have specialized in gently worn 20th-century designer wear for well over a decade now, and their selection is marvelous. Their extensive vintage and contemporary couture collection—which ranges from conservative Chanel to over-the-top Halston, Mackie, and Versace—is so well priced that it's well within reach of the average shopper looking for something extraglamorous to wear. 416 Amsterdam Ave. (at 80th St.). ✆ **212/724-7445.** Subway: 1, 9 to 79th St.

Michael's *Value* This consignment boutique boasts top-drawer designer wear for women—including such names as Chanel, YSL, Prada, Gucci, Richard Tyler, and Escada—at a fraction of the original cost. The bridal salon is an unbeatable find for engaged gals looking for a top-quality dress at an off-the-rack price. 1041 Madison Ave. (btwn 79th and 80th sts.), 2nd floor. ✆ **212/737-7273.** www.michaelsconsignment.com. Subway: 6 to 77th St.

New & Almost New *Finds* This gorgeous closet brims with well-chosen contemporary and retro designer wear, all in like-new condition and at great prices. 65 Mercer St. (just north of Broome St.). ✆ **212/226-6677.** Subway: J, M, N, R, Q, W to Canal St.

Screaming Mimi's *Value* Think you hate vintage shopping? Think again: Screaming Mimi's is as neat and well organized as any high-priced boutique—yet prices are surprisingly reasonable, especially given the pricey vintage shops that have popped up around the city in recent years. The vintage housewares department is a wonderful cornucopia of kitsch, and includes a selection of New York memorabilia; prices start under $10. 382 Lafayette St. (btwn E. 4th and Great Jones sts.). ✆ **212/677-6464.** Subway: 6 to Astor Place.

EDIBLES

Chelsea Market Located in an old Nabisco factory, this big, dazzling food mall is the city's largest. Come for both raw and ready-to-eat foods, including divinely inspired baked goods and cappuccino from **Amy's Bread;** yummy soups from **Hale and Hearty;** Manhattan's best brownie at **Fat Witch Bakery;** and much more, including the wonderful **Chelsea Wine Vault** (p. 381). **Chelsea Market Baskets** is a great place to pick up gifts for home. 75 Ninth Ave. (btwn 15th and 16th sts.). ✆ **212/243-5678.** www.chelseamarket.com. Subway: A, C, E, L to 14th St.

Dean & Deluca This bright, clean-lined store is the best of New York's gourmet supermarkets. The quality is superb across the board: In addition to the excellent butcher, fish, cheese, and dessert counters (check out the stunning cakes and the great character cookies) and beautiful fruits and veggies, you'll find a dried fruit and nut bar, a huge coffee bean selection, a gorgeous cut-flower selection, lots of imported waters and beers in the refrigerator case, and a limited but quality selection of kitchenware in back. A small cafe up front makes a great stop for a cappuccino break from SoHo shopping. 560 Broadway (at Prince St.). ✆ **212/431-1691.** www.dean-deluca.com. Subway: N, R to Prince St.

Grand Central Market Gloriously restored Grand Central Terminal now has its own smallish but terrific gourmet food hall at street level, easily accessible from 42nd Street, with such pleasing vendors as **Adriana's Caravan** for exotic spices; **Ninth Avenue Cheese** for a gourmet selection; **Corrado Bread & Pastry** carrying loaves and pastries from Bouley Bakery; and much more. A delight to browse! If you want wine to go with your bounty, don't miss Grande Harvest (p. 381). 42nd St. at Park Ave. www.grandcentralterminal.com. Subway: S, 4, 5, 6, 7 to 42nd St./Grand Central.

Zabar's More than any other of New York's gourmet food stores, Zabar's is an institution. This giant deli sells prepared foods, packaged goods from around the world, coffee beans, excellent fresh breads, and much more (no fresh veggies, though). This is the place for lox, and the rice pudding is the best I've ever tasted. You'll also find an excellent—and well-priced—collection of housewares and restaurant-quality cookware on the second floor. Prepare yourself for serious crowds. The attached cafe serves terrific sandwiches and takeout—ideal for a Central Park picnic. 2245 Broadway (at 80th St.). ✆ **212/787-2000.** Subway: 1, 9 to 79th St.

BAGELS

No one should visit New York without tasting a real New York bagel. H&H, below, is my (and most New Yorkers') favorite, but for excellent bagels and sit-down service, head to **Ess-A-Bagel** (p. 216) instead.

H&H Bagel The king of New York bagel makers. Stop in at this bare-bones shop for a piping-hot bagel, so good it needs no accompaniment. Cream cheese, lox, and the like are sold in refrigerator cases for take-home use. All locations are open around the clock, so come by for a bagel fix anytime (although I'm told that the Second Ave. branch is run independently, and is not quite as good). If you crave more H&H when you get home, call ✆ **800/NY-BAGEL** or visit their website to order; they ship almost anywhere. 2239 Broadway (at 80th St.). ✆ **212/595-8003.** www.hhbagels.com. Subway: 1, 9 to 79th St. Also at 639 W. 46th St., at Twelfth Ave., across from the Intrepid (✆ 212/595-8000; subway: A, C, E to 42nd St.). Also at 1551 Second Ave., btwn 80th and 81st sts. (✆ 212/734-7441; subway: 6 to 77th St.).

SWEETS

Fauchon This Parisian chocolatier operates a large, elegant boutique featuring an ultra-charming tea salon (at the larger Park Ave. location only), and sparkling glass cases display a gorgeous array of chocolates and sweet treats flown in daily; the candied fruits are among the most gorgeous foods I've ever seen. Afternoon tea is served daily from noon to 6pm (to 5pm on Sun); you can choose between a two-course tea ($30) or a lovely array of salads, quiches, and so forth. Beautifully packaged candies, biscuits, preserves, and the like make elegant and pretty take-home treats. 442 Park Ave. (at 56th St.). ✆ **212/308-5919.** www.fauchon.com. Subway: 4, 5, 6 to 59th St. Also at 1000 Madison Ave., at 77th St. (✆ 212/570-2211; subway: 6 to 77th St.).

Li-Lac Chocolates Li-Lac is one of the few chocolatiers anywhere still making sweets by hand. In business in the same location since 1923, this supremely charming West Village shop whips up its chocolate and maple-walnut fudge fresh every day, and it's a fudge-lover's dream come true. They also make pralines, caramels, and other hand-dipped chocolates, including specialty sweets for the holidays (hollow bunnies and chocolate eggs for Easter, chocolate Santas for Christmas, and so on). 120 Christopher St. (btwn Bleecker and Hudson sts.). ✆ **800/624-4784** or 212/242-7374. Subway: 1, 9 to Christopher St. Also at Grand Central Market, Grand Central Terminal (✆ 212/370-4866; subway: 4, 5, 6, 7 to 42nd St./Grand Central).

Minamoto Kitchoan Wagashi *Finds* In this genuine Japanese confectionery (*wagashi* means "confectionery" in Japanese), the sweets are so beautifully displayed and wrapped, and the glass cases so highly polished, that it feels almost like Tiffany's. Try anything with sweet red bean—you won't be sorry. For less adventuresome palates, the green tea cake is also divine. 608 Fifth Ave. (at 49th St.). ✆ **212/489-3747.** www.kitchoan.com. Subway: B, D, F, Q to 47th–50th sts./Rockefeller Center.

Teuscher Chocolates of Switzerland At $50 a pound, you'd think they were selling gold bouillon. Teuscher makes mints, pralines, and wondrous marzipan, but it's the truffles that folks write home about. Splurge on one or two justifiably famous champagne truffles, and you'll weep with joy. At the Channel Gardens in Rockefeller Center, 620 Fifth Ave. (btwn 49th and 50th sts.). ✆ **800/554-0924** or 212/246-4416. www.teuscherchocolate.com. Subway: B, D, F, Q to 47th–50th sts./Rockefeller Center. Also at 25 E. 61st St., east of Madison Ave. (✆ 212/751-8482; subway: 4, 5, 6, to 59th St.).

ELECTRONICS

J&R Music & Computer World This block-long Financial District emporium is the city's top discount computer, electronics, small appliance, and office equipment retailer. The sales staff is knowledgeable but can get pushy if you don't buy at once or know exactly what you want. Don't succumb—take your time and find exactly what you need. Or better yet, peruse the store's copious catalog or extensive website, both of which make advance research, mail order, and comparison shopping easy. Park Row (at Ann St., opposite City Hall Park). ✆ **800/221-8180** or 212/238-9100. www.jandr.com. Subway: 2, 3 to Park Place; 4, 5, 6 to Brooklyn Bridge/City Hall.

Sony Style Don't expect bargains, but electronics buffs will enjoy perusing the full line of Sony products. On street level is the gadget store, full of small electronics from Sony PlayStations to bookshelf stereo systems. Downstairs, the "Home Entertainment Lounge" is a stylish setting for the complete line of audio components and home-entertainment systems. 550 Madison Ave. (btwn 55th and 56th sts.). ✆ **212/833-8000.** www.sonystyle.com. Subway: E, F to Fifth Ave.

EYEWEAR

Robert Marc Opticians The city overflows with designer eyewear shops, but this is the best. The gorgeous lines, including Robert Marc's own, particularly excel at updates on classic styles, including retro-cool wires and streamlined horn-rims in gorgeous colors. 575 Madison Ave. (btwn 56th and 57th sts.). ✆ **212/319-2000.** www.robertmarc.com. Subway: 4, 5, 6, to 59th St. Also at: 190 Columbus Ave., btwn 68th and 69th sts. (✆ 212/799-4600; subway: 1, 9 to 66th St.); 400 Madison Ave., btwn 47th and 48th sts. (✆ 212/319-2900; subway: 6 to 51st St.); 782 Madison Ave., btwn 66th and 67th sts. (✆ 212/737-6000; subway: 6 to 68th St.); 1046 Madison Ave., btwn 79th and 80th sts. (✆ 212/988-9600; subway: 6 to 77th St.); and 1300 Madison Ave., btwn 92nd and 93rd sts. (✆ 212/722-1600; subway: 6 to 96th St.).

GIFTS

If you're looking for a special gift for a creative spirit, check out the shops that line **East 9th Street** in the East Village; the side streets of **SoHo,** where a good number of unusual boutiques still survive; **Nolita;** and Greenwich Village, especially in the wonderful cadre of one-of-a-kind shops in the **West Village.** See "The Top Shopping Streets & Neighborhoods," earlier in this chapter.

For first-rate Fifth Avenue gifts, don't forget **Tiffany & Co.,** whose upper level boasts wonderful small gifts, all crafted in signature Tiffany silver or crystal and wrapped in the unmistakable blue box (see "Jewelry & Accessories," below).

For additional suggestions, see "Antiques & Collectibles," earlier in this chapter, and "Home Design & Housewares," below.

auto. If a Lucite tic-tac-toe set sounds like a good idea to you, don't miss this witty Meat-Packing District boutique. The mod and minimalist home accessories and gift items—mostly original designs by Brooklyn-based artists—are both well conceived and good-humored. 805 Washington St. (btwn Gansevoort and Horatio sts.). ✆ **212/229-2292.** www.thisisauto.com. Subway: A, C, E, L to 14th St.

Extraordinary* *Finds* This warm, friendly gallery-cum-gift shop is well worth going out of your way to discover. Owner J. R. Sanders, an interior designer who has created lauded exhibits at many city museums, has directed his copious talents to assembling a gorgeous and beautifully displayed collection of gifts from around the world. Lacquered crackle-egg shell trays from Vietnam, carved mango bowls from the Philippines, clever rosewood serving utensils camouflaged as tree branches from Africa, creative cheese servers and wine goblets by American glassblowers, and much, much more—all eye candy for those who thrive on whimsy and good design. Best of all, prices are shockingly reasonable—you'd pay twice as much at any other gallery or boutique—and late hours (usually daily to 10:30pm) make it easy to visit before or after dinner at Guastavino's (see chapter 7). Truly extraordinary! 251 E. 57th St. (just west of Second Ave.). ✆ **212/223-9151.** Subway: 4, 5, 6 to 59th St.

Jack Spade Looking for a gift for the man who has everything? Then head to Jack Spade, which specializes in vintage and new "guy toys." The inventory changes constantly, but expect goodies along the lines of vintage phonog and microscopes, old maps and globes, cool desk accessories, and the like. Th new shop was launched by the husband of Kate Spade (she of chic handbags and paper goods fame), so you can expect a smart, upmarket collection. 56 Greene St. (btwn Spring and Broome sts.). ✆ **212/625-1820.** Subway: C, E to Spring St.; N, R to Prince St.; C, E to Spring St.

Pearl River *Value* This three-floor Chinese mall overflows with affordable Asian exotica, from paper lanterns to Chinese snack foods to Mandarin-collared silk pajamas to mah-jongg sets to Hong Kong action videos. This fascinating place can keep you occupied for hours. *Note:* Look for the main store to move one block north on Broadway, on the west side of the street, by the time you arrive; you won't be able to miss it. 277 Canal St. (at Broadway). ✆ **212/431-4770.** www.pearlriver.com. Subway: N, R to Canal St. Also at 200 Grand St., btwn Mott and Mulberry sts. (✆ 212/966-1010; subway: B, D, Q to Grand St.).

Steuben This is the flagship store for America's premier manufacturer of fine glass and crystal, said to be the world's purest. The store is gorgeous, and the pieces—which run the gamut from fruit bowls to elaborate sculptures—are spectacularly crafted and refract light beautifully. Prices start around $200 for a "hand cooler" (a small collectible, often animal-shaped, that fits in your palm) and run into the five figures. The Corning Gallery, on the lower level, hosts rotating art exhibits. 667 Madison Ave. (at 61st St). ✆ **212752-1441.** www.steuben.com. Subway: N, R to Fifth Ave.

HANDBAGS & LEATHER GOODS

Jamin Puech *Finds* This narrow shop carries exceptionally beautiful handbags, from pressed leather baguettes to silk-screened carryalls, all original and handmade in France by a supremely talented husband-and-wife team. Expensive, but worth it if you're looking for a one-of-a-kind tote. 252 Mott St. (btwn Houston and Prince sts.). ✆ **212/334-9730.** Subway: B, D, F, Q to Broadway/Lafayette St.; 6 to Spring St.

Jutta Neumann *Finds* If you stop into this workmanlike shop, you're likely to find the artist herself behind the counter, cutting and stitching her geometric, bold-hued leather goods—bags, wallets, boots, and more. Her mules and strappy sandals made a big splash in summer 2001. 158 Allen St. (btwn Stanton and Rivington sts.). ✆ **212/982-7048.** www.juttaneumann-newyork.com. Subway: F to Delancey/Essex sts.

kate spade Kate Spade revolutionized the high-end handbag market with her practical yet chic rectangular handbags, which have seemingly taken over the planet. They come in a wide range of fabrics and sizes, from pretty seersuckers to groovy prints to fashionable flannel to basic black, plus a wide range of solids. The daintier evening line is charming, particularly the grosgrain silks. The line has expanded to include chic baby bags, luggage, sexy shoes, and comfy pajamas. You can also find the signature bags at Saks, Barneys, Bergdorf Goodman, and Bloomingdale's. 454 Broome St. (at Mercer St.). ✆ **212/274-1991.** www.katespade.com. Subway: N, R to Prince St. **kate spade travel** at 59 Thompson St., btwn Spring and Broome sts. (✆ 212/965-8654; subway: C, E to Spring St.).

Manhattan Portage Ltd. Store Come here for the hippest nylon and canvas carryalls in town. True to its name, Manhattan Portage manufactures all its bags right in the city, and they're made from hard-wearing materials that can stand up to an urban lifestyle. Popular styles include all-purpose messenger bags, deejay bags, and backpacks (in both standard and nouveau one-shoulder styles) from iridescent yellow to camouflage. Manhattan Portage rough other outlets, but you'll find the most complete selec- St. (btwn First and Second aves.). ✆ **212/995-5490.** www.manhattan ay: 6 to Astor Place.

For the sexiest top-quality luggage around, don't miss this . The colors—deep red, cobalt blue, tweed, black—are gorgeous, as contrast stitching, the shapes are practical, and the styles are both eye-catching yet classic. (Think Coach, but without the in-every-mall ubiquitousness.) Sure, it's expensive, but it lasts a lifetime. 445 Park Ave. (at 56th St.). ✆ **212/750-9797.** www.tanthony.com. Subway: 4, 5, 6 to 59th St.

Village Tannery *Finds* The cream of the Greenwich Village leather crop, with gorgeous and well-priced handbags, backpacks, wallets, and organizers. 173 Bleecker St. (btwn Macdougal and Sullivan sts.). ✆ **212/673-5444.** Subway: 1, 9 to Houston St. Also at 742 Broadway, btwn Astor Place and Waverly St. (✆ 212/979-0013; subway: 6 to Astor Place).

HOME DESIGN & HOUSEWARES

Attention, Oriental rug and kilim fans: Dealers line **Broadway** around the queen of home furnishings department stores, **ABC Carpet & Home** (see "The Big Department Stores," earlier in this chapter). The second floor of **Zabar's** (see "Edibles," above) is another excellent source for high-end kitchenware.

The Apartment *Finds* This clever shop has caused a SoHo sensation with its mod home designs and just-like-home setup (if you lived in a million-dollar downtown loft, of course). You can browse in and buy from every room, including kitchen and bath. A can't-miss for avowed modernists. 101 Crosby St. (btwn Prince and Spring sts.) ✆ **212/219-3661.** www.theapt.com. Subway: 6 to Spring St.

Broadway Panhandler If you're looking for restaurant-quality cookware and kitchen tools, you've found your place. The best combination of selection, prices, and service in town. Don't just take it from me—*New York* magazine gave Broadway Panhandler the "Best Pots and Pans" nod in 2000. 477 Broome St. (btwn Greene and Wooster sts.) ✆ **212/966-3434.** Subway: C, E to Spring St.

Fishs Eddy *Value* What a great idea—selling remainders of kitschy, custom-designed china left over from yesteryear. Ever wanted a dish that *really* says "Blue Plate Special"? Or how about a coffee mug with the terse logo "Cup o' Joe to Go"? The store is Browse Heaven, and prices on its American industrial china are low enough. The store's own designs are equally wonderful, especially its New York skyline line. Other items for sale include basic vintage and retro-inspired flatware, heavy crockery bowls, and classic restaurant-supply glassware that can be hard to find in regular stores, like soda-fountain and pint glasses. 889 Broadway (at 19th St.). ✆ **212/420-9020.** www.fishseddy.com. Subway: L, N, R, 4, 5, 6 to 14th St./Union Sq. Also at 2176 Broadway, at 77th St. (✆ 212/873-8819; subway: 1, 9 to 79th St.).

Frette This Italian linen maker has taken the hotel world by storm with its silky cotton sheets and ultraplush terry towels and robes. If you've slept on some and now you want your own, head to this dedicated boutique or ABC Carpet & Home (earlier in this chapter) for the best selections. Also at Saks, Bloomingdale's, and Bergdorf's. 799 Madison Ave. (btwn 67th and 68th sts.). ✆ **212/988-5221.** www.frette.com. Subway: 6 to 68th St.

Galileo *Finds* An excellent mix of contemporary wares and 20th-century vintage pieces. The selection of fine-quality linens and kitchen towels is small but smart. There are usually a few pieces of furniture scattered about, often blond-wood postwar pieces from the likes of Heywood-Wakefield or Paul McCobb. Gorgeous accessories galore, including a pristine selection of vintage glassware—tumblers, highballs, cocktails, and more—and one-of-a-kind jewelry pieces. Registry is available. 37 Seventh Ave. (at 13th St.). ✆ **212/243-1629.** Subway: 1, 2, 3, 9 to 14th St.

Global Table The place to shop for some of the most beautiful tableware imports, especially if you like Asian ware: bamboo bowls from Vietnam, ceramic tea sets from China, silver mint julep cups from India, lacquered chopsticks from Japan, and much more. 107–109 Sullivan St. (btwn Prince and Spring sts.). ✆ **212/431-5839.** www.globaltable.com. Subway: C, E to Spring St.

Jonathan Adler Anybody who has been reading shelter magazines over the last couple of years will recognize this hot potter's bold vases and lamps instantly. His style merges organic shapes, geometric patterns, natural hues, and mod ideas into a one-of-a-kind style that works in almost any decor—really. Good throw pillows, too. 465 Broome St. (btwn Greene and Mercer sts.). ✆ **212/941-8950.** www.jonathanadler.com. Subway: N, R to Canal St.

kar'ikter *Finds* New York's biggest collection of sleek and playful Alessi housewares from Italy (including Michael Graves's iconic teakettle with bird whistle), as well as European animation cells and toys starring Tintin, Babar, and Asterix. 19 Prince St. (btwn Elizabeth and Mott sts.). ✆ **212/274-1966.** www.karikter.com. Subway: 6 to Spring St.

Leader Restaurant Equipment & Supplies *Value* The Bowery is the place to find restaurant-supply-quality kitchenware, and Leader is the best dealer on the block. This big, bustling, friendly shop is a particularly good source for Chinese and Japanese wares—chopsticks, rice and noodle bowls, sushi plates, sake cups, and the like. You'll see a lot of the same styles you'd find at the high-end home stores in SoHo or the Village but at a fraction of the prices (this is where they buy, too). 191 Bowery (btwn Spring and Delancey sts.). ✆ **800/666-6888** or 212/677-1982. Subway: 6 to Spring St.

Moss *Finds* If you have any interest in modern industrial design, don't miss this sleek, brightly lit store. All kinds of everyday objects are reinvented by cutting-edge European designers, from staplers to flatware to shelving units. The products were designed with 21st-century homes in mind, so they're surprisingly utilitarian and space-efficient. 146 & 150 Greene St. (btwn Houston and Prince sts.). ✆ **212/226-2190.** www.mossonline.com. Subway: N, R to Prince St.

Oriental Lamp Shade Co. The place to dress your favorite fixtures. The range of shades is immense; if you don't see a style or size you like, they'll custom craft one for you. They also carry a wonderful selection of antique and new table and floor lamps as well as ceiling fixtures. 223 W. 79th St. (just east of Broadway). ✆ **212/873-0812.** www.orientallampshade.com. Subway: 1, 9 to 79th St. Also at 816 Lexington Ave., btwn 62nd and 63rd sts. (✆ 212/832-8190; subway: N, R to Lexington Ave.).

Royal Hut After traveling the globe with her husband, Island Records founder Chris Blackwell, Mary Vinson merged her design degree and her world-travel experience to create her own line of cross-cultural home furnishings. Her own gorgeous line of textiles has been handcrafted by weavers and dyers in Europe, Africa, and Asia. Also expect a stunning collection of dishware, glassware, vessels, and accessories in a riot of Asian- and African-inspired color and texture—ideal for the global home. 328 E. 59th St. (btwn First and Second aves.). ✆ **212/207-3027.** www.royalhut.com. Subway: 4, 5, 6, to 59th St.

Terence Conran Shop Sir Terence Conran rules the London design and restaurant world, and now he's looking to make inroads in America with the bold new Bridgemarket complex, housing the stunning Guastavino's restaurant (see chapter 7) and this sleek home shop. It's like an upscale—and, frankly, overpriced—version of IKEA, with lots of sleek contemporary lines, lightweight materials (chrome, blond woods, colorful plastic), and fun twists on standard household goods. Still, he set the tone for affordable contemporary design, and that alone makes this bright, browseable multilevel shop well worth a look. 407 E. 59th St. (at First Ave.). ✆ **212/755-9079.** www.conran.com. Subway: 4, 5, 6 to 59th St.

Totem Design *Finds* Totem is dedicated to manufacturing and distributing new furniture and objects by talented young domestic and international designers. Designs range from minimalist to whimsical to superswanky, but the threefold theme of form, function, and affordability is common throughout. 71 Franklin St. (btwn Church St. and Broadway). ✆ **212/925-5506.** www.totemdesign.com. Subway: 1, 9 to Franklin St. The Totem Gallery is at 83 Grand St. (btwn Greene and Wooster sts.). Subway: N, R to Canal St.

Waterworks The place to give that most sacred of rooms, the bath, a whole new, luxurious look. Half the store displays top-quality, hard-to-find designer hardware and fixtures, while the other half is dedicated to thick Egyptian terry towels, robes, and bathmats, plus stylish accessories for easy reinvention. 469 Broome St. (at Greene St.). ✆ **212/966-0605.** www.waterworks.com. Subway: 6 to Canal St.; N, R to Prince St. Also at 225 E. 57th St., btwn Second and Third aves. (✆ 212/371-9266; subway: 4, 5, 6 to 59th St.).

JEWELRY & ACCESSORIES

Every big-name international jewelry merchant has a shop on Fifth Avenue in the 50s: glam Italian jeweler **Bulgari,** 730 Fifth Ave., at 57th Street (✆ **212/315-9000;** www.bulgari.com); royal jeweler **Asprey & Garrard,** no. 725, at 56th Street (✆ **212/688-1811**); ultraglamorous **Harry Winston,** no. 718, also at 56th Street (✆ **212/245-2000;** www.harrywinston.com); **Cartier,** housed in a stunningly restored mansion at 653 Fifth Avenue, at 52nd Street (✆ **212/753-0111;** www.cartier.com), as well as 828 Madison Ave., at 69th Street (✆ **212/472-6400**); and, best of all, **Van Cleef & Arpels,** 744 Fifth Ave., at 57th Street (✆ **212/644-9500**), which also has a boutique at Bergdorf's.

Some of the smaller boutique names are on Madison Avenue in the '60s; **Fred Leighton,** 773 Madison Ave., at 66th Street (✆ **212/288-1872**), specializes in magnificent estate jewelry.

Boucher *Finds* This jewel box of a store sparkles on a gentrifying corner of the still-industrial Meatpacking District. Designer Laura Mady and her staff meticulously handcraft feminine, nature-inspired necklaces, earrings, and other jewelry using unusual gemstones in organic shapes and freshwater pearls in soft ice-cream hues. Affordable, and ideal for dressing up or everyday wear. 9 Ninth Ave. (near Little W. 12th St., next to Pastis). ✆ **212/206-3775.** www.badcow.com. Subway: A, C, E, L to 14th St.

Doyle & Doyle *Finds* Elizabeth Doyle's lovely antiques boutique offers further evidence of the transformation of the Lower East Side from old-world cheap to exceptionally chic. Doyle & Doyle specializes in fine antique and estate jewelry, from the Georgian period to the 1950s, plus finely crafted vintage costume jewelry. Pieces are all carefully chosen and beautifully displayed. 189 Orchard St.

Value The Diamond District

West 47th Street between Fifth and Sixth avenues is the city's famous Diamond District. Apparently more than 90% of the diamonds sold in the United States come through this neighborhood first, so there are some great deals to be had if you're in the market for a nice rock or another piece of fine jewelry. The street is lined shoulder-to-shoulder with showrooms; be ready to wheel and deal with the largely Hasidic dealers, who offer quite a juxtaposition to the crowds. For a complete introduction to the district, including smart buying tips, point your Web browser to **www.47th-street.com**. If you're in the market for wedding rings, there's only one place to go: Herman Rotenberg's **1,873 Unusual Wedding Rings,** 4 W. 47th St., booth 86 (✆ **800/877-3874** or 212/944-1713; www.unusualweddingrings.com). For semiprecious stones, head a block over to the **New York Jewelry Mart,** 26 W. 46th St. (✆ **212/575-9701**). Virtually all of these dealers are open Monday through Friday only.

(between Houston and Stanton sts.). ✆ **212/677-9991.** www.doyledoyle.com. Subway: F to Second Ave. (exit at the front of the train and walk one block east).

Fortunoff *Value* Despite the high-ticket facade, Fortunoff is a good resource for Swatch watches and a nice place to start pricing classic pieces: gold earrings, necklaces, bracelets, and the like. The styles aren't innovative, but the store tries to keep up an image as a discounter, and prices are low. Great for silver and wedding gifts, too. 681 Fifth Ave. (btwn 53rd and 54th sts.). ✆ **800/FORTUNOFF** or 212/758-6660. www.fortunoff.com. Subway: E, F to Fifth Ave.

Jill Platner *Finds* I adore Platner's aborigine- and nature-inspired silver pieces, which are bold enough to look great on both men and women. Many are strung on brightly colored tenara (a Gortex-like thread) for a prehistoric-meets-21st-century feel. Prices are quite reasonable; it's easy to find a cool pair of earrings or a groovy ring for a just little more than $100. 113 Crosby St. (btwn Houston and Prince sts.). ✆ **212/324-1298.** www.jillplatner.com. Subway: N, R to Prince St.

Push Often featuring rough-hewn finishes and asymmetrical gems and stones, Karen Karch's eye-catching jewelry has attracted an A-list clientele to her atmospheric Nolita shop. Six degrees of separation moment: If you buy one of her pieces, you'll take home a work of art from the designer who worked with Ethan Hawke to design Uma Thurman's wedding ring. 240 Mulberry St. (btwn Prince and Spring sts.). ✆ **212/965-9699.** Subway: 6 to Spring St.

Robert Lee Morris Sculptural silver jewelry is this renowned designer's thing, but he's always got something new and original in his SoHo store. His new Candy Couture collection features divinely simple glass-beaded pieces in electrifying colors; his work with pastel-hued South Sea pearls and delicate water stones is also worth checking out. 400 W. Broadway (btwn Spring and Broome sts.). ✆ **212/431-9405.** www.robertleemorris.com. Subway: C, E to Spring St.

Stuart Moore Those interested in sleek, minimal, angular modern design should head for this sizable store, which showcases the works of Stuart Moore and other supremely talented contemporary designers. Ultramodern, elegant, and simply terrific—I could browse here for hours. 128 Prince St. (at Wooster St.). ✆ **212/941-1023.** www.stuartmoore.com. Subway: N, R to Prince St.

Tiffany & Co. The most famous jewelry store in New York—and maybe the world—deserves all the kudos. This wonderful multilevel store offers a breathtaking selection of jewelry, signature watches, table and stemware, and a handful of surprisingly affordable gift items. I particularly like the whimsical designs, like butterfly brooches and other playful shapes. The store is so full of tourists that it's easy to browse without having any intention of buying. Believe it or not, it's not hard to find a lovely wearable piece in silver (Tiffany's best color, in my opinion) for around $200. If you do indulge, anything you buy—even a $50 silver bookmark or key chain—comes wrapped in that unmistakable blue box with a classic white ribbon tied just so. 727 Fifth Ave. (at 57th St.). ✆ **212/755-8000.** www.tiffany.com. Subway: N, R to Fifth Ave.

Tourneau Time Machine The snazzy three-floor emporium on East 57th Street is the world's largest watch store, carrying more than 90 brands and 8,000 different styles. The mind-boggling selection runs the gamut from Swatch to Rolex; Swiss Army knives, too. 12 E. 57th St. (btwn Fifth and Madison aves.). ✆ **212/758-7300.** www.tourneau.com. Subway: N, R to Fifth Ave. Also at: 500 Madison Ave., at 52nd St. (✆ 212/758-6098; subway: 6 to 51st St.); and 635 Madison Ave., at 59th St. (✆ 212/758-6688; subway: 4, 5, 6 to 59th St.).

LOGO STORES

Mets Clubhouse Shop Stop in for goods galore—baseball caps, T-shirts, posters, Piazza jerseys, '69 Miracle Mets memorabilia, and much more amazin' merchandise. You can buy regular season game tix here, too. 143 E. 54th St. (btwn Lexington and Third aves.). ✆ **212/888-7508.** www.mets.com. Subway: E, F to Lexington Ave.

The MTV Store This petite boutique sits street side, just below the MTV studio. There's not much here—but your kids will surely find something they want anyway, whether it's a Celebrity Deathmatch T-shirt or one of any number of TRL souvenirs. Flyers are sometimes on hand at the register, advertising for audience members for MTV shows—yet another reason for your teen to drag you in. 1515 Broadway (at 44th St.). **212/258-8000.** Subway: 1, 2, 3, 7, 9, N, R, S to 42nd St./Times Sq.

NBA Store For all things NBA and WNBA, head to this three-level megastore, a multimedia celebration of pro hoops, complete with a bleacher-seated arena for player appearances and signings. 666 Fifth Ave. (at 52nd St.). ✆ **212/515-NBA1.** www.nbastore.com. Subway: B, D, F, V to 47th–50th sts./Rockefeller Center

NBC Experience This mammoth, neon-lit store sits directly across from the *Today* show studio and sells all manner of NBC-themed merchandise, from Matt and Katie's favorite mugs to *ER* scrubs to *Frasier* umbrellas to *West Wing* T-shirts to . . . you get the picture. Your kids will enjoy the silly interactive features, like the virtual-reality "Conan O'Brien's Wild Desk Ride," as well as the second-level candy shop. NBC Studio Tours also leave from here; call for details. 30 Rockefeller Plaza (at 49th St.). ✆ **212/664-3700.** www.nbcsuperstore.com. Subway: B, D, F, V to 47th–50th sts./Rockefeller Center.

New York Firefighter's Friend *Finds* What better way to spend your souvenir budget than by saluting New York's bravest? Here's the place to purchase FDNY logo wear, including T-shirts, sweatshirts, hats, and more. The goods are all top-quality, and a portion of profits go in support of the widows and children of the 343 firefighter victims lost in the World Trade Center terrorist attacks. 263 Lafayette St. (btwn Prince and Spring sts.). ✆ **212/226-3142.** www.nyfirestore.com. Subway: 6 to Spring St.

New York 911 *Finds* Adjacent to Firefighter's Friend (above) is the place to shop for not only NYPD logo wear, but also EMT, FBI, and NYC coroner gear. The bounty includes shirts, caps, badge pins, patches, logo toys, and much more. (Not all of the products are licensed by the city, however; I suggest trying to stick with those that are.) The store is well stocked and fun to browse, making it a great place to buy souvenirs and gifts for the folks back home. A portion of proceeds go to NYPD-related charities. 263 Lafayette St. (btwn Prince and Spring sts.). ✆ **888/723-3907** or 212/219-3907. www.ny911.com. Subway: 6 to Spring St.

Niketown More multimedia advertorial than sportswear store, Niketown is surprisingly low key and attractive, with five floors of shoes and athletic wear displayed in stark Lucite and polished metal surroundings. "Museum" cases display Sneakers of the Rich and Famous, and everywhere you're assailed by images of celebrity pitchmen and women. No sales or bargains here—plan on paying top dollar for the high-style athletic wear. Somebody's gotta pay for this place! 6 E. 57th St. (btwn Fifth and Madison aves.). ✆ **212/891-6453.** www.nike.com/niketown_offline. Subway: N, R to Fifth Ave.

The Pop Shop *Finds* For affordable and wearable art that makes supercool souvenirs, come to the Pop Shop. This groovy store is chock-full of items based on designs by artist Keith Haring, who died in 1990. T-shirts, posters, calendars, stationery, toys, notebooks, neat transparent backpacks all sport the vivid primary colors and loopy stick-figure drawings that Haring made famous. Best of all, the Pop Shop is a nonprofit organization, offering continued support to the AIDS-related and children's charities that the young artist championed in life. 292 Lafayette St. (btwn Houston and Prince sts.). ✆ **212/219-2784.** www.haring.com. Subway: F, V to Broadway/Lafayette St.

WWE New York The place to pick up all the World Wrestling Entertainment logo gear you can afford, from Ts to mugs and much more. 1501 Broadway (at 43rd St.). ✆ **212/398-2563.** http://newyork.wwe.com. Subway: 1, 2, 3, 7, 9, N, R, S to 42nd St./Times Sq.

Yankees Clubhouse Shop For all your Bronx Bombers needs—hats, jerseys, jackets, and so on. Tickets for regular-season home games are also for sale, and there's a limited selection of other New York team jerseys. 245 W. 42nd St. (btwn Seventh and Eighth aves.). ✆ **212/768-9555.** www.yankees.com. Subway: A, C, E to 42nd St./Port Authority. Also at 393 Fifth Ave., btwn 36th and 37th sts. (✆ 212/685-4693; subway: 6 to 33rd St.). Also at: 110 E. 59th St., btwn Park and Lexington aves. (✆ 212/758-7844; subway: 4, 5, 6 to 59th St.); and 8 Fulton St., in the South Street Seaport (✆ 212/514-7182; subway: 2, 3, 4, 5 to Fulton St.).

MUSEUM STORES

In addition to these standouts, other noteworthy museum shops worth seeking out include the **New York Public Library,** the **Museum for African Art,** the **Jewish Museum,** and the **American Folk Art Museum** (see chapter 8).

American Craft Museum The nation's top showcase for contemporary crafts boasts an impressive collection of crafts in its museum store, too. Come for exquisite handblown glassware, one-of-a-kind jewelry, original pottery, and other artistic treasures, all beautifully displayed. 40 W. 53rd St. (btwn Fifth and Sixth aves.). ✆ **212/956-3535.** www.americancraftmuseum.org. Subway: E, F to Fifth Ave.

Maxilla & Mandible *Finds* This shop is not affiliated with the American Museum of Natural History, but a visit here makes a good adjunct to your trip to the museum (which is right around the corner). It may look like a freak shop at first glance, but it's really a fascinating natural history emporium. Inside you'll find unusual rocks and shells from around the world, luminescent butterflies in display boxes, even surprisingly affordable real fossils containing prehistoric fish and insects that come with details on their history and where they were excavated. There's also a good variety of natural history–themed toys for the kids. 451 Columbus Ave. (btwn 81st and 82nd sts.). ✆ **212/724-6173.** www.maxillaandmandible.com. Subway: B, C to 81st St.

Metropolitan Museum of Art Store Given the scope of the museum itself, it's no wonder that the gift shop is outstanding. Many treasures from the museum's collection have been reproduced as jewelry, china, and other objets d'art. The range of art books is dizzying, and upstairs is an equally comprehensive selection of posters and inventive children's toys. 1000 Fifth Ave. (at 82nd St.). ✆ **212/570-3894.** www.metmuseum.org/store. Subway: 4, 5, 6 to 86th St. Also at: Rockefeller Center, 15 W. 49th St. (✆ 212/332-1360; subway: B, D, F, V to 47th–50th sts./Rockefeller Center); 113 Prince St., at Greene St. (✆ 212/614-3000; subway: N, R to Prince St.); and on mezzanine level at Macy's, 34th St. and Sixth Ave. (✆ 212/268-7266; subway: B, D, F, Q, N, R to 34th St./Herald Sq.).

MoMA Design Store Across the street from the Museum of Modern Art is this terrific shop, whose stock ranges from museum posters and clever toys for kids to fully licensed reproductions of many of the classics of modern design, including free-form Alvar Aalto vases, Frank Lloyd Wright chairs, and Eames recliners. If these high-design items are out of your reach, choose from plenty of more affordable outré home accessories. The new SoHo store is equally fabulous. *Note:* The museum store will remain open while the museum is closed for renovation. 44 W. 53rd St. (btwn Fifth and Sixth aves.). ✆ **212/767-1050.** www.moma.org. Subway: E, F to Fifth Ave.; B, D, F, Q to 47th–50th sts./Rockefeller Center. Also at 81 Spring St., at Crosby St. (✆ 646/613-1367; subway: 6 to Spring St.).

New York Transit Museum Store Lots of nifty transportation-themed gifts—the cufflinks made out of vintage subway tokens are just great. Grand Central Terminal (on the main level, in the shuttle passage next to the Station Masters' office), 42nd Street and Lexington Ave. ✆ **212/878-0106.** Subway: 4, 5, 6, 7, S to 42nd St./Grand Central.

MUSIC

AUDIO & VIDEO

Music buffs will find a wealth of new-and-used shops lining Bleecker and Carmine streets in the West Village. Standouts include **Rockit Scientist,** just off Bleecker at 43 Carmine St. (✆ **212/242-0066**), a tiny place with a huge folk and psych collection. Unfortunately, **Bleecker Bob's Golden Oldies,** 118 W. 3rd St. (✆ **212/475-9677**), has outlived its legend; it's now a dirty little hole-in-the-wall with lots of worn, badly organized vinyl.

Grungy **St. Marks Place** between Third and Second avenues in the East Village is another great bet. **Mondo Kim's** (✆ **212/598-9985;** www.kimsvideo.com) is a standout for indie music, video, and 'zines.

Academy Records & CDs This Flatiron District shop has a cool intellectual air that's more reminiscent of a good used-book store than your average used-record store. Academy is always filled with classical, opera, and jazz junkies perusing the extensive and well-priced collection of used CDs and vinyl. In addition to the extensive classical and jazz collection is a variety of other audiophile favorites, from rare '60s pop songsters to spoken word. 12 W. 18th St. (btwn Fifth and Sixth aves.). ✆ **212/242-3000.** www.academy-records.com. Subway: L, N, R, 4, 5, 6 to 14th St./Union Sq.

Bleecker St. Records This sizable, well-lit space is great for one-stop shopping. The clean, well-organized CD and LP collections run the gamut from rock, oldies, jazz, folk, and blues to Oi! punk. You'll find lots of imports, collectible, and out-of-print records (including singles), a terrific collection of used CDs, and a mix of casual listeners and serious collectors cruising the bins. 239 Bleecker St. (near Carmine St., just west of Sixth Ave.). ✆ **212/255-7899.** Subway: A, C, E, F, V to W. 4th St.

Colony Music Center This long-lived Theater District shop ("since 1948") is housed in the legendary Brill Building, the Tin Pan Alley of '50s and '60s pop, where legendary songwriters like Goffin and King and producers like Don Kirschner and Phil Spector crafted the soundtrack for a generation. It's the perfect home for Colony, a nostalgia emporium filled with a pricey but excellent collection of vintage vinyl and new CDs. You'll find a great collection of Broadway scores and cast recordings; decades worth of recordings by pop song stylists both legendary and obscure; the city's best collection of sheet music (including some hard-to-find international stuff); and a great selection of original theater and movie posters. You can stock up your in-home karaoke machine here, too. 1619 Broadway (at 49th St.). ✆ **212/265-2050.** www.colonymusic.com. Subway: N, R to 49th St.; 1, 9 to 50th St.

Footlight *Finds* If you like Colony (see above), also check out this dreamy collection of vintage vinyl, strong in jazz and pop vocalists, soundtracks, and show tunes. 113 E. 12th St. (btwn Third and Fourth aves.). ✆ **212/533-1572.** www.footlight.com. Subway: L, N, R, 4, 5, 6 to 14th St./Union Sq.

Generation Records *Value* This tidy little store sells mostly CDs and is an excellent source for "import" live recordings. Originally specializing in hardcore, punk, and heavy metal, the new collection upstairs still has a heavy edge but has since diversified appreciably. Downstairs is a well-organized and well-priced used CD selection that's not as picked over as most and runs the genre gamut; there's also a good selection of used LPs. Despite the help's tough look, they're actually quite friendly and helpful. 210 Thompson St. (btwn Bleecker and 3rd sts.). ✆ **212/254-1100.** Subway: A, C, E, F, V to W. 4th St.

Jazz Record Center *The* place to find rare and out-of-print jazz records. In addition to the extensive selection of CDs and vinyl (including 78s), videos, books, posters, magazines, photos, and other memorabilia are available. Prices start at $5 for vinyl, $10 for CDs, and soar from there, befitting the rarity of the stock. Owner Frederick Cohen is extremely knowledgeable, so come here if you're trying to track down something obscure (Cohen does mail-order business as well). 236 W. 26th St. (btwn Seventh and Eighth aves.), 8th floor. ✆ **212/675-4480.** www.jazzrecordcenter.com. Subway: 1, 9 to 28th St.

NYCD *Value* This neat, narrow little store is home to one of the city's best collections of used rock CDs thanks to its off-the-beaten-track Upper West Side location. Downtown trollers simply don't make it this far uptown to prune the selection, so it's easy to find lots of top titles among the pickings. 426 Amsterdam Ave. (btwn 80th and 81st sts.). ✆ **212/724-4466.** Subway: 1, 9 to 79th St.

Other Music *Finds* Head to Other Music for the wildest sounds in town. You won't find a major label here (that's what Tower, across the street, is for). This shop focuses exclusively on small international labels, especially those on the cutting edge. The bizarro runs the gamut from underground Japanese spin doctors to obscure Irish folk; needless to say, the world music selection is terrific—fascinating and bound to be filled with music you've never heard of. The sales staff really knows their stuff, so ask away. 15 E. 4th St. (btwn Broadway and Lafayette St.). ✆ **212/477-8150.** www.othermusic.com. Subway: F, V to Broadway/Lafayette St.; 6 to Astor Place.

Throb A popular stop for dance-club deejays, this CD/vinyl shop specializes in electronic genres: house, ambient, jungle, drum-and-bass, lounge-core, trance, trip hop. Imports are big business here. You'll also find record bags and T-shirts. 211 E. 14th (btwn Second and Third aves.). ✆ **212/533-2328.** www.throb.com. Subway: L to Third Ave.

Tower Records A mighty chain it may be, but it's hard to complain about Tower. Both main locations are huge multimedia superstores brimming with an encyclopedic collection of music—classical, jazz, rock, world, you name it. The Village location also stocks a very good selection of indie and alternative labels. Just behind it at West 4th and Lafayette is **Tower Books and Video** (✆ **212/228-5100**), where you'll find videos, books, and magazines (although the video selection isn't as good as you might expect). Look for in-stores by big names in music, usually advertised in the *Time Out New York* and *Village Voice.* 692 Broadway (at W. 4th St.). ✆ **212/505-1500.** www.towerrecords.com. Subway: N, R to 8th St.; 6 to Astor Place. Also at 1961 Broadway, at 66th St. (✆ 212/799-2500; subway: 1, 9 to 66th St.).

Virgin Megastore Right in the heart of Times Square, this superstore bustles day and night. For the size of it, the selection isn't as wide as you'd think; still, you're likely to find what you're looking for among the two levels of domestic and imported CDs and cassettes. Other plusses are an extensive singles department, a phenomenal number of listening posts, plus a huge video department. There's also a bookstore, a cafe, and a multiplex movie theater, and you can even arrange airfare on Virgin Atlantic with the on-site travel agent. As at Tower, look for a busy schedule of in-store appearances at both locations. 1540 Broadway (at 45th St.). ✆ **212/921-1020.** www.virginmega.com. Subway: N, R, 1, 2, 3, 7, 9 to Times Sq./42nd St. Also at 52 E. 14th St., at Broadway (✆ 212/598-4666; subway: 4, 5, 6, N, R, L to 14th St./Union Sq.).

INSTRUMENTS

Dan's Chelsea Guitars Although small (and more than a tad dusty), this eclectic shop has a good selection of both new and vintage guitars and amps. It's a good place to browse, as the friendly guys behind the counter aren't going to pressure you. If you're buying, there seems to be some negotiation room. Even if you just stroll by, don't miss the "rare birds" in the front window. 220 W. 23rd St. (btwn Seventh and Eighth aves.). ✆ **212/675-4993.** Subway: 1, 9 to 23rd St.

Sam Ash In business since 1924, mammoth Sam Ash is the place to shop for Marshall stacks, Flying Vs, Yamaha drum kits, digital keyboards, MIDI systems, turntables, pro deejay equipment, and much, much more—including a complete selection of orchestral instruments. Sam's is sort of like the Barnes & Noble of guitar shops—a great place to just pick an ax off the wall and play. You'll even find soundproofed acoustic guitar rooms if you don't want the Metallica fans to ruin your unplugged sound. 160 W. 48th St. (btwn Sixth and Seventh aves.). ✆ **212/719-2299.** www.samashmusic.com. Subway: N, R to 49th St.

PAPER & STATIONERY

Kate's Paperie Three cheers to Kate's for keeping the art of letter writing alive in our computer age. I could browse for hours among this delightful shop's handmade stationery and wrap, innovative invitations and thank-yous, imported notebooks, writing tools, and other creative paper products, including cool paper lampshades. Lovely art cards, too—perfect for writing the folks back home—a joy! The SoHo location is best. 561 Broadway (btwn Prince and Spring sts.). ✆ **212/941-9816.** www.katespaperie.com. Subway: N, R to Prince St. Also at 8 W. 13th St., btwn Fifth and Sixth aves. (✆ 212/633-0570; subway: F to 14th St.); and 1282 Third Ave., btwn 73rd and 74th sts. (✆ 212/396-3670; subway: 6 to 77th St.).

SHOES

Designer shoe shops start on **East 57th Street** and amble up **Madison Avenue,** becoming pricier as you move uptown. **SoHo** is an excellent place to search for the latest styles; the streets are overrun with terrific shoe stores. Cheaper copies of the trendiest styles are sold along **8th Street** between Broadway and Sixth Avenue in the Village, which some people call Shoe Row.

Most department stores have two sizable shoe departments—one for designer stuff and one for daily wearables. See "The Top Shopping Streets & Neighborhoods" and "The Big Department Stores," earlier in this chapter. For **Prada** and **Kenneth Cole,** see "Clothing," and for **Niketown,** see "Logo Stores," both earlier in this section.

In addition to the choices below, you might also consider **Jutta Neumann** and **kate spade,** both listed under "Handbags & Leather Goods," earlier in this chapter.

Arche This French comfort-shoe designer makes some of the best walking shoes on the planet for women. The selection reaches beyond the standard black and brown to embrace a sherbet rainbow of rich Nubuck suedes and buttery leathers. 128 W. 57th St. (btwn Sixth and Seventh aves.). ✆ **212/262-5488.** www.archeshoes.com. Subway: B, Q, W or N, R to 57th St. Also at: 995 Madison Ave., at 77th St. (✆ 212/439-0700; subway: 6 to 77th St.); 1035 Third Ave., at 62nd St. (✆ 212/838-1933; subway: 4, 5, 6 to 59th St.); and 10 Astor Place, btwn Broadway and Lafayette St. (✆ 212/529-4808; subway: 6 to Astor Place).

Camper This Big Apple outpost features the full line of made-in-Spain Camper footwear for men and women. These are the hippest walking shoes and boots on the planet, hands down—ideal for those with an eye for style and a craving for comfort. 125 Prince St. (at Wooster St.). ✆ **212/358-1842.** www.camper.com. Subway: N, R to Prince St.; C, E to Spring St.

Giraudon New York This French designer makes fashionable, well-made street shoes for hip men and women who want something clean lined and stylish but not too chunky or trendy. Not cheap, but not overpriced—these shoes last forever. Prices run $115 to $200, and sales are excellent. 152 Eighth Ave. (btwn 17th and 18th sts.). ✆ **212/633-0999.** www.giraudonnewyork.com. Subway: A, C, E, L to 14th St.

Jimmy Choo Here it is: *the* boutique for *Sex in the City* stilettos. I've hardly seen shoes displayed more beautifully than at this sophisticated three-floor emporium. 645 Fifth Ave. (at 51st St.). ✆ **212/593-0800.** www.jimmychoo.com. Subway: E, F to Fifth Ave.

Manolo Blahnik These wildly sexy women's shoes are notorious for their cut and sway, and the way they shape the leg. Most famous are the catch-me-if-you-can high heels, but there are plenty of flats and low heels, too. Custom shoes in your own fabric are also a possibility. 31 W. 54th St. (btwn Fifth and Sixth aves.). ✆ **212/582-3007.** Subway: E, F to Fifth Ave.

Sacco Mostly Italian-made women's shoes that cross style with supreme comfort. I especially love the fall and winter boots, which are comfortable enough to carry me around the city on even the most arduous of research days. Good prices and sales, too. 94 Seventh Ave. (btwn 15th and 16th sts.). ✆ **212/675-5180.** www.saccoshoes.com. Subway: 1, 9 to 18th St. Also at: 14 E. 17th St., btwn Fifth Ave. and Broadway (243-2070; subway: N, R, L, S, 4, 5, 6 to 14th St./Union Sq.); 111 Thompson St., btwn Prince and Spring sts. (✆ 212/925-8010; subway: C, E to Spring St.); 324 Columbus Ave., btwn 75th and 76th sts. (✆ 212/799-5229; subway: B, C to 81st St.); and 2355 Broadway, at 86th St. (✆ 212/874-8362; subway: 1, 9 to 86th St.).

Sigerson Morrison *Finds* Women who love shoes and are willing to pay in the neighborhood of $200 to $300 for something really special should make a beeline for this Nolita shop. These fashion-forward originals wow with their immaculate details, bright color palette, and sexy, strappy retro appeal—worth every penny. You'll also find some of their styles at Bergdorf Goodman and Saks if you don't want to go downtown. Attention, bargain-hunters: Check out the January winter and August summer sales; prices drop to less than half of retail as the sales wind down. 28 Prince St. (btwn Mott and Elizabeth sts.). ✆ **212/219-3893.** www.sigersonmorrison.com. Subway: B, D, F, Q to Broadway/Lafayette St.; N, R to Prince St.; 6 to Spring St.

Stapleton Shoe Company *Value* If Imelda Marcos had been a man, her first stop would have been this shoe store, right next to the American Stock Exchange. Stapleton sells men's brands like Bally and Johnston & Murphy, all at discounts so deep it'll feel like insider trading. 68 Trinity Place (at Rector St., 3 blocks south of the World Trade Center). ✆ **212/964-6329.** Subway: N, R to Rector St.

Tip Top Shoes If you find yourself discovering that the shoes you thought were so comfortable just aren't cutting it in the Big Apple—trust me, it happens a lot—head over to Tip Top, New York's premier walking-shoe shop (since 1940). You'll find all of the top brands here for men and women, including Rockport, Mephisto, Clark's, and hip Campers, plus tennies from New Balance and Puma. 155 W. 72nd St. (btwn Broadway and Columbus Ave.). ✆ **800/WALKING** or 212/787-4960. www.tiptopshoes.com. Subway: 1, 2, 3, 9 to 72nd St.

SPORTING GOODS

Paragon Sporting Goods The emphasis at this excellent all-purpose sporting goods store—New York's best—is on equipment and athletic wear for virtually every sport, from tennis to biking to mountain climbing. End-of-the-season sales, especially on sneakers and outdoor clothing, bring serious discounts. 867 Broadway (at 18th St.). ✆ **800/961-3030** or 212/255-8036. www.paragonsports.com. Subway: L, N, R, 4, 5, 6 to 14th St./Union Sq.

Patagonia Expensive though it may be, Patagonia deserves kudos for its commitment to producing efficient and ecofriendly sports and adventure wear—fleece pullovers made from recycled plastic soda bottles, shell jackets in ultralight weatherproof materials, and organic cotton T-shirts. 101 Wooster St. (btwn Prince and Spring sts.). ✆ **212/343-1776.** www.patagonia.com. Subway: N, R to Prince St.; C, E to Spring St. Also at 426 Columbus Ave., btwn 80th and 81st sts. (✆ 917/441-0011; subway: B, C to 81st St.).

TOYS

If your kids love to read, don't miss **Books of Wonder** (p. 356). For vintage toys, check out **Alphaville** (p. 352).

Enchanted Forest *Finds* Here's a shop for kids and grown-ups alike. This joyful shop overflows with stuffed animals and puppets, plus the kinds of simple but absorbing games that parents remember well from the days before Sony PlayStation, like PickUp Sticks and Chinese Checkers. There's also a terrific book nook specializing in reissued classics like *The Phantom Toll Booth* and small-print children's and adult gift books—truly a special place. 85 Mercer St. (btwn Spring and Broome sts.). ✆ **212/925-6677.** www.sohotoys.com. Subway: N, R to Prince St.

FAO Schwarz The best-loved toy store in America was designed with an eye for fun: The elevator is shaped like a huge toy soldier, and there are plenty of hands-on displays to keep the little ones occupied for hours. (Although the new Toys"R"Us, below, gives FAO a real run for its money.) Entire areas are devoted to specific toy makers (Lego, Fisher Price, *Star Wars* action figures, Barbie). You and the kids will find plenty of affordable little gifts to take home as souvenirs (the front-left corner specializes in pre-wrapped gifts for moms and dads on business trips). 767 Fifth Ave. (at 58th St.). ✆ **212/644-9400.** www.fao.com. Subway: N, R to Fifth Ave.

Kidding Around This boutique stocks pricey high-quality toys, many imported from Europe. The emphasis is on the old-fashioned—low-tech goodies like puzzles, rocking horses, and tops. One wall is devoted exclusively to tub toys, windups, and other stocking stuffers. 60 W. 15th St. (btwn Fifth and Sixth aves.). ✆ **212/645-6337.** Subway: F to 14th St. Also at 68 Bleecker St., btwn Broadway and Lafayette St. (✆ 212/598-0228; subway: 6 to Bleecker St.).

Toys"R"Us Geoffrey the Giraffe must be mighty pleased with this new multilevel, high-tech home. It occupies almost an entire city block in the heart of Times Square, and even boasts its own full-scale Ferris wheel kids can ride for free. The huge collection is very well organized, and the store's "ambassadors" are abundant and very helpful; they'll even point you to restaurants and kid-friendly attractions in the neighborhood. Don't miss it if you're traveling with kids. 1514 Broadway (at 44th St.). ✆ **800/869-7787.** Subway: 1, 2, 3, 7, 9 to 42nd St. Also at 24–30 Union Square (✆ 212/674-8697; subway: 4, 5, 6, N, R, L, S to 14th St./Union Sq.).

WINE & SPIRITS

Acker Merrall & Condit Co. In business since 1820—which makes Acker America's oldest wine shop—this attractive little store is the Upper West Side's best wine source. There are no bad bottles here. The careful selection is well displayed, with opinionated cards attached to each bin to help you choose. A supremely knowledgeable staff is on hand for additional assistance. 160 W. 72nd St. (btwn Broadway and Columbus aves.). ✆ **212/787-1700.** www.ackerwines.com. Subway: 1, 2, 3, 9 to 72nd St.

Astor Wines & Spirits *Value* This large store is the source for excellent values on liquor and wine; their stock is deep and diverse. The staff is always willing to recommend a vintage. Astor hosts excellent wine tastings two to three afternoons a week, often paired with edibles from local restaurants and gourmet shops; call or check the website for the schedule. 12 Astor Place (at Lafayette St.). ✆ **212/674-7500.** www.astoruncorked.com. Subway: 6 to Astor Place.

Chelsea Wine Vault *Finds* This extra-large shop in the historic Chelsea Market is like the best kind of bookstore: friendly, well stocked, well organized, and staffed strictly with wine gurus who will never steer you wrong. Tastings are a regular event. 75 Ninth Ave. (at 15th St.). ✆ **212/462-4244.** www.chelseawinevault.com. Subway: A, C, E, L to 14th St.

Grande Harvest Wines There isn't a dud to be found in this stylish shop just off Grand Central's main concourse. You'll pay a little more than elsewhere, but it's well worth it for the convenience, great service, and guarantee of a good bottle. In Grand Central Terminal, main concourse, opposite track 17. ✆ **212/682-5855.** Subway: 4, 5, 6, 7, S to 42nd St./Grand Central.

Morrell & Company One of the leading retailers in America boasts a friendly, helpful staff, and has a Fine Wine Division that hosts high-profile auctions. Adjacent is the **Morrell Wine Bar & Cafe** (✆ **212/262-7700;** www.morrellwinebar.com), an ideal place to sample the goods in comfort. 1 Rockefeller Plaza (at 49th St.). ✆ **212/688-9370.** www.morrellwine.com. Subway: B, D, F, V to 47th–50th sts./Rockefeller Center.

Sherry-Lehmann Zagat's has called Sherry-Lehmann "the Rolls-Royce" of wine shops, and the readers of *Decanter* magazine just named it best wine merchant in the United States. Their vast inventory is mind-boggling and includes ritzy gift baskets that make luxurious gifts. Service is excellent and free wine tastings are often on hand. Although expensive, this is the place to come if you're looking for a special bottle. 679 Madison Ave. (btwn 61st and 62nd sts.). ✆ **212/838-7500.** www.sherry-lehmann.com. Subway: N, R to Lexington Ave.; 4, 5, 6 to 59th St.

11

New York City After Dark

New York's nightlife scene is an embarrassment of riches. There's so much to see and do in this city after the sun goes down that your biggest problem is probably going to be choosing among the many temptations.

There's no way that I can tell you in these pages what's going to be on the calendar while you're in town. For the latest, most comprehensive nightlife listings, from theater and performing arts to live rock, jazz, and dance club coverage, ***Time Out New York*** (www.timeoutny.com) is my favorite weekly source; a new issue hits newsstands every Thursday. The free weekly ***Village Voice*** (www.villagevoice.com), the city's legendary alterna-paper, is available late Tuesday downtown and early Wednesday in the rest of the city. The arts and entertainment coverage couldn't be more extensive, and just about every live music venue advertises its shows here. The ***New York Times*** (www.nytoday.com) features terrific entertainment coverage, particularly in the two-part Friday "Weekend" section. The cabaret, classical music, and theater guides are particularly useful. Other great weekly sources are the ***New Yorker*** (www.newyorker.com), in its "Goings on About Town" section; and ***New York*** magazine (www.nymetro.com), whose back "Cue" features the latest happenings. *New York*'s **www.nymetro.com** site is an excellent Web source.

Barhoppers shouldn't pass up the comprehensive paperpack ***Shecky's New York Bar, Club & Lounge Guide,*** printed annually. The website (**newyork.sheckys.com**) is even more current, as is **Shecky's Bar Phone** at **© 212/777-BARS,** which offers up-to-the minute nightlife news for the cost of a phone call.

NYC/Onstage (**© 212/768-1818;** www.tdf.org) is a recorded service providing complete schedules, descriptions, and other details on theater and the performing arts. The bias is toward plays, but NYC/Onstage is a good source for chamber and orchestral music (including all Lincoln Center events), dance, opera, cabaret, and family entertainment, too.

In addition to the wealth of choices below, you might want to consider one of the **sunset** or **dinner cruises** that circle Manhattan, taking in the twinkling lights of the skyline from all sides. See "Harbor Cruises" under "Organized Sightseeing Tours," in chapter 8.

1 All the City's a Stage: The Theater Scene

Nobody does theater better than New York. No other city—not even London—has a theater scene with so much breadth and depth, with so many wide-open alternatives. Broadway, of course, gets the most ink and the most airplay, and deservedly so: Broadway is where you'll find the big stage productions, from crowd-pleasing warhorses like *The Lion King* to phenomenal newer successes like *The Producers.* But today's scene is thriving beyond the bounds of just

Worth Seeking Out

Legendary among Off-Broadway theaters is the **Public Theater,** 425 Lafayette St. (✆ **212/260-2400,** or TeleCharge at 212/239-6200; www.publictheater.org or www.telecharge.com), the legacy of the late visionary theater producer Joseph Papp. Now under the direction of George C. Wolfe, the Public always draws top talent to the stage with its groundbreaking stagings of Shakespeare's plays—past schedules have featured F. Murray Abraham as Lear and Liev Schreiber as Hamlet—as well as new plays, classical dramas, and solo performances. The Public also produces Broadway shows rather regularly, such as *Bring in 'Da Noise, Bring in 'Da Funk* and 2002's *Elaine Stritch at Liberty,* and hosts New York's best annual alfresco event, Shakespeare in the Park, each summer (see the "Park It! Shakespeare, Music & Other Free Fun" box on p. 398). If that's not enough, it's also home to Joe's Pub (p. 408). Definitely worth seeking out!

Broadway—smaller, "alternative" theater has taken hold of the popular imagination, too. With bankable stars on stage, crowds lining up for hot tickets, and hits popular enough to generate major-label cast albums, Off Broadway isn't just for culture vultures anymore.

I can't tell you precisely what will be on while you're in town, so check the publications listed at the start of this chapter or the websites listed in "Online Sources for Theatergoers & Performing Arts Fans," below, to get an idea of what you might like to see. Another useful source is the **Broadway Line** (✆ **888/BROADWAY** or 212/302-4111; www.broadway.org), where you can obtain details and descriptions on current Broadway shows, hear about special offers and discounts, and choose to be transferred to TeleCharge or Ticketmaster to buy tickets. There's also **NYC/Onstage** (✆ **212/768-1818;** www.tdf.org), providing the same kind of service for both Broadway and Off-Broadway productions.

Helping to assure the recent success of the New York theater scene has been the presence of Hollywood stars like Kevin Spacey, Glenn Close, Patrick Stewart, Molly Ringwald, Brooke Shields, Kevin Bacon, Liam Neeson, and Dame Judi Densch. But keep in mind that stars' runs are often very short, and tickets tend to sell out fast. If you hear that there's a celeb you'd like to see coming to the New York stage, don't put off your travel and ticket-buying plans. (The box office can tell you how long a star is contracted for a role.)

THE BASICS

The terms **Broadway, Off-Broadway,** and **Off-Off-Broadway** refer to theater size, pay scales, and other arcane details, not location—or, these days, even star wattage. Most of the Broadway theaters are in Times Square, huddled around the thoroughfare the scene is named for, but not directly on it: Instead, you'll find them dotting the side streets that intersect Broadway, mostly in the mid-40s between Sixth and Eighth avenues (44th and 45th sts. in particular) but running north as far as 53rd Street. There's even a Broadway theater outside Times Square: the Vivian Beaumont in Lincoln Center, on the Upper West Side at Broadway and 65th Street.

Off-Broadway, on the other hand, is not that exacting an expression. With the increasing popularization of off-the-beaten-track productions, the distinction

Broadway Theaters

Ambassador **11**	Gershwin **7**	Palace **32**
American Airlines **45**	Helen Hayes **40**	Playwright's Horizons **48**
American Place **34**	Imperial **18**	Plymouth **29**
Barrymore **26**	John Golden **20**	Richard Rogers **17**
Belasco **36**	Longacre **15**	Royale **24**
Booth **30**	Lunt-Fontanne **28**	Samuel Beckett **47**
Broadhurst **23**	Lyceum **35**	St. James **22**
Broadway **4**	Majestic **21**	Shubert **39**
Brooks Atkinson **16**	Marquis **31**	Stardust **8**
Circle in the Square **10**	Martin Beck **19**	Studio 54 **3**
City Center Stage **2**	Minskoff **38**	Town Hall **37**
Cort **33**	Mitzi E. Newhouse **1**	Virginia **5**
Douglas Fairbanks **49**	Music Box **25**	Vivian Beaumont **1**
Duffy **27**	Nederlander **43**	Walter Kerr **13**
Ethel Barrymore **14**	Neil Simon **6**	WestSide **46**
Eugene O'Neill **12**	New Amsterdam **42**	Winter Garden **9**
Ford Center for the Performing Arts **44**	New Victory **41**	

between Off- and Off-Off-Broadway productions has become fuzzier. Off-Off-Broadway shows tend to be more avant-garde, experimental, and/or nomadic. Off- and Off-Off-Broadway productions tend to be based downtown, but pockets show up in Midtown and on the Upper West Side. Broadway shows tend to keep pretty regular **schedules.** There are usually eight performances a week: evening shows Tuesday through Saturday, plus matinees on Wednesday, Saturday, and Sunday. Evening shows are usually at 8pm, while matinees are usually at 2pm on Wednesday and Saturday, and 3pm on Sunday, but schedules can vary, especially Off-Broadway. Shows usually start on the dot, or within a few minutes of starting time; if you arrive late, you may have to wait until after the first act to take your seat, which can really be a drag.

Ticket prices for Broadway shows vary dramatically. Expect to pay for good seats; the high end for any given show is likely to be between $60 and $100. The cheapest end of the price range can be as low as $20 or as high as $50, depending on the theater configuration. If you're buying tickets at the very low end of a wide available range, be aware that you may be buying obstructed-view seats. If all tickets are the same price or the range is small, you can pretty much count on all of the seats being pretty good. Otherwise, price is your barometer. Note that legroom can be tight in these old theaters, and you'll usually get more in the orchestra seats.

Off-Broadway and Off-Off-Broadway shows tend to be cheaper, with tickets often as low as $10 or $15. However, seats for the most established shows and those with star power can command prices as high as $50.

Don't let price be a deterrent to enjoying the theater. There are ways to pay less if you're willing to make the effort and be flexible, with a few choices at hand as to what you'd like to see. Read on.

TOP TICKET-BUYING TIPS

BEFORE YOU LEAVE HOME

Phone ahead or go online for tickets to the most successful or popular shows as far in advance as you can—in the case of shows like *The Lion King,* it's never too early.

Buying tickets can be simple, if the show you want to see isn't sold out. You need only call such general numbers as **TeleCharge** (✆ **212/239-6200;** www.telecharge.com), which handles most Broadway and Off-Broadway shows and some concerts; or **Ticketmaster** (✆ **212/307-4100;** www.ticketmaster.com), which also handles Broadway and Off-Broadway shows and most concerts. If you're an American Express gold or platinum cardholder, check to see if tickets are being sold through **American Express Gold Card Events** (✆ **800/448-TIKS;** www.americanexpress.com/gce). You'll pay full price just as you would through TeleCharge or Ticketmaster, but Amex has access to blocks of preferred seating specifically set aside for gold cardholders, so you may be able to get tickets to a show that's otherwise sold out, or better seats than you would otherwise be able to buy.

Theatre Direct International (TDI) is a ticket broker that sells tickets to select Broadway and Off-Broadway shows—including some of the most popular crowd-pleasers, like *Oklahoma!* and *Cabaret*—direct to individuals and travel agents. Check to see if they have seats to the shows you're interested in by calling ✆ **800/BROADWAY** or 212/541-8457; you can also order tickets through TDI via their commercial website, **www.broadway.com**. (Disregard the discounted prices, unless you're buying for a group of 20 or more.) Because there's

Good Tickets for a Good Deed

One option for finding hard-to-get tickets is more expensive than most, but good for your self-esteem. **Broadway Cares/Equity Fights AIDS CareTix** program gets producers, theater owners, celebrities, and other Broadway types to donate their coveted house seats to Broadway and Off-Broadway shows. They sell these tickets for double the face value ($130 for a $65 ticket, for example), with the proceeds donated to people living with the disease. Not only do you get what are probably the best seats in the house but also 50% of your purchase is tax deductible. Call ✆ **212/840-0770,** ext. 229 or 230, for ticket choices, which are limited in number. Ticket requests are taken the month prior to the dates you're interested in on the first day of the month (starting Mar 1 if you're interested in seeing a show in Apr, for instance); mark your calendar if you're trying to snag coveted tix like *The Lion King.* For other shows, call at least 48 hours in advance. Hot concert tickets are often available, too. For more on Broadway Cares/Equity Fights AIDS, as well as an online store where you support the cause by buying all manner of Broadway show-themed merchandise, visit **www.broadwaycares.org**.

a minimum service charge of $15 per ticket, you'll definitely do better by trying Ticketmaster or TeleCharge first; but because they act as a consolidator, TDI may have tickets left for a specific show even if the major outlets don't.

Other reputable ticket brokers include **Keith Prowse & Co.** (✆ **800/669-8687** or 212/398-4175; www.keithprowse.com) and **Global Tickets Edwards & Edwards** (✆ **800/223-6108;** www.globaltickets.com). For a list of other licensed ticket brokers recommended by the New York Convention & Visitors Bureau, get a copy of the Official NYC Visitor Kit (see "Visitor Information," in chapter 3, for details). All kinds of ticket brokers list ads in the Sunday *New York Times* and other publications, but don't take the risk. Stick with a licensed broker recommended by the NYCVB.

You may have heard about a new development on the Broadway ticket scene: **Broadway Inner Circle** (✆ **212/563-2929**), the ticket agency that, in a supposed effort to circumvent scalpers, has arranged with select in-demand shows—at this writing, *The Producers* and the revival of Arthur Miller's *The Crucible*—to sell select premium seats for prices close to $500 a ticket. Whether this will outlast *Producers* mania now that original stars Matthew Broderick and Nathan Lane have left the cast is anybody's guess.

If you don't want to pay even a service charge, try calling the **box office** directly. Broadway theaters don't sell tickets over the telephone—the one major exception, the **Roundabout Theatre Company** (✆ **212/719-1300;** www.roundabouttheatre.org), charges a $5-per-ticket "convenience" fee—but a good number of Off-Broadway theaters do.

Also, before you resort to calling broker after broker to snag tickets to a hot show, consider calling the **concierge** at the hotel where you'll be staying. If you've chosen a hotel with a well-connected concierge, he or she may be able to have tickets waiting for you when you check in—for a premium, of course. For more on this, see "When You Arrive," below.

For details on how to obtain advance-purchase theater tickets at a discount, see "Reduced-Price Ticket Deals," below.

Kids Take the Stage: Family-Friendly Theater

The family-friendly theater scene is flourishing these days. There's so much going on that it's best to check *New York* magazine, *Time Out New York,* or the Friday *New York Times* for current listings. Besides larger-than-life general audience Broadway shows, the following offer some dependable kid-targeted entertainment options.

The stunningly renovated **New Victory Theater,** 209 W. 42nd St., between Seventh and Eighth avenues (✆ **646/223-3020;** www.newvictory.org), reopened in 1995 as the city's first full-time family oriented performing arts center and has hosted companies ranging from the Trinity Irish Dance Company to the astounding Flaming Idiots, who juggle everything from fire and swords to bean-bag chairs.

The **Paper Bag Players** (✆ **212/362-0431;** www.paperbagplayers.org), called "the best children's theater in the country" by *Newsweek,* perform funny tales for children 4 to 9 in a set made from bags and boxes, in winter only, at Hunter College's Sylvia and Danny Kaye Playhouse, 68th Street between Park and Lexington avenues (✆ **212/772-4448**). If you can't make it to the Kaye, call the players to inquire whether they'll be staging other performances about town.

TADA! Youth Theater, 120 W. 28th St., between Sixth and Seventh avenues (✆ **212/627-1732;** www.tadatheater.com), is a terrific youth ensemble that performs musicals and plays with a multiethnic perspective for kids, teens, and their families.

The **Swedish Cottage Marionette Theatre** (✆ **212/988-9093;** www.centralpark.org) puts on marionette shows for kids at its 19th-century Central Park theater throughout the year. Reservations are a must.

The "World Voices Club" of the **New Perspectives Theatre,** 750 Eighth Ave., between 46th and 47th streets (✆ **212/730-2030;** www.newperspectivestheatre.org), has a different puppet show based on

ONLINE SOURCES FOR THEATERGOERS & PERFORMING ARTS FANS Some of your best, most comprehensive and up-to-date information sources for what's going on about town are in cyberspace.

CultureFinder (**www.culturefinder.com**) is an excellent site for all arts and entertainment events in New York City, with an emphasis on museum shows, theater, and classical music. You'll find direct links to ticket sellers, plus exclusive discount ticket offers.

Three competing commercial sites—**Broadway.com** (**www.broadway.com**), **Playbill Online** (**www.playbill.com** or www.playbillclub.com), and **TheaterMania** (**www.theatermania.com**)—offer complete information on Broadway and Off-Broadway shows, with links to the ticket-buying agencies once you've selected your show. Each offers an **online theater club** that's free to join and can yield substantial savings—as much as 50%—on advance-purchase theater tickets for select Broadway and Off-Broadway shows. All you have to do is register, and you'll have access to discounts that can range from a few dollars to as much as 50% off regular ticket prices. You can sign up to be notified by e-mail as offers change. By far, I like the *Playbill Club* best; it was the first of the bunch, and its fables from different world cultures each month.

While David Mamet hardly seems like a playwright for the kiddies, the "Atlantic for Kids" series is making a go of it at the **Atlantic Theater Company,** 453 16th St., between Ninth and Tenth avenues (✆ **212/691-5919;** www.atlantictheater.org), which Mamet cofounded with Academy Award–nominated actor William H. Macy. Two of their hilariously offbeat productions made *Time Out New York*'s Best of 2000 list, and Mamet's own version of *The Frog Prince* entertained crowds in winter 2002, so it's worth seeing what's on while you're in town.

Another excellent troupe that excels at children's theater is the **Vital Theatre Company,** 432 W. 42nd St., between Ninth and Tenth avenues (✆ **212/592-4508;** www.vitaltheatre.org); it's well worth seeing what's on.

If you want to introduce your kids to the magic of live opera, check out the "Opera in Brief" program, which runs most Saturdays at 11:30am, at **Amato Opera** (p. 391). For kid-friendly classical music, see what's on at **Bargemusic** (p. 392), which presents chamber-music concerts for kids throughout their regular season. Look for Young People's Concerts and Kidzone Live!, in which kids get to interact with orchestra members prior to curtaintime, at the **New York Philharmonic** (p. 393). Also check to see what's on for the entire family at **Carnegie Hall** (p. 395), which offers family concerts for a bargain-basement ticket price of just $5, plus the CarnegieKids program, which introduces kids ages 3 to 6 to basic musical concepts through a 45-minute music and storytelling performance. Finally, don't forget "Jazz for Young People," Wynton Marsalis's stellar family concert series at **Jazz at Lincoln Center** (p. 396).

discounts offers tend to be the most wide ranging, often including the best Broadway and Off-Broadway shows, while TheaterMania's **TM Insider** is the runner-up; the Broadway.com site wants a bit too much personal information for my taste. Nothing prevents you from signing up with all of them and taking advantage of the best deals.

As an information source, you can't beat **LiveBroadway.com** (**www.livebroadway.com**), the official website of Broadway, sponsored by the League. Theater buffs will also enjoy perusing the **Internet Broadway Database** (**www.ibdb.com**), the official archival database for Broadway theater information, past and present.

WHEN YOU ARRIVE

Once you arrive in the city, getting your hands on tickets can take some street smarts—and failing those, cold hard cash. Even if it seems unlikely that seats are available, always **call the box office** before attempting any other route. Single seats are often easiest to obtain, so people willing to sit apart may find themselves in luck.

You should also try the **Broadway Ticket Center,** run by the League of American Theatres and Producers (the same people behind the Broadway Line, above) at the Times Square Visitors Center, 1560 Broadway, between 46th and 47th streets (open Mon–Sat 9am–7pm, Sun 10am–6pm). They often have tickets available for otherwise sold-out shows, both for advance and same-day purchase, and only charge about $5 extra per ticket.

Even if saving money isn't an issue for you, check the boards at the **TKTS Booth** in Times Square; more on that under "Reduced-Price Ticket Deals," below.

In addition, your **hotel concierge** may be able to arrange tickets for you. These are usually purchased through a broker and a premium will be attached, but they're usually good seats and you can count on them being legitimate. (A $20 tip to the concierge for this service is reasonable—perhaps even more if the tickets are for an extremely hot show, like *The Producers.* By the time you've paid this tip, you might come out better by contacting a broker or ticket agency yourself.) If you want to deal with a licensed broker direct, **Keith Prowse & Co.** has a local office that accommodates drop-ins at 234 W. 44th St., between Seventh and Eighth avenues, Suite 1000 (© **800/223-6108;** open Mon–Sat 9am–6pm).

If you buy from one of the **scalpers** selling tickets in front of the theater doors, you're taking a risk. They may be perfectly legitimate—a couple from the 'burbs whose companions couldn't make it for the evening, say—but they could be swindlers passing off fakes for big money. It's a risk that's not worth taking.

One preferred **insiders' trick** is to make the rounds of Broadway theaters at about 6pm, when unclaimed house seats are made available to the public. These tickets—reserved for VIPs, friends of the cast, the press, or other hangers-on—offer great locations and are sold at face value.

Also, note that **Monday** is often a good day to cop big-name show tickets. Though most theaters are dark on that day, some of the most sought-after choices aren't. Locals are at home on the first night of the workweek, so all the odds are in your favor. Your chances will always be better on weeknights, or for Wednesday matinees, rather than weekends.

REDUCED-PRICE TICKET DEALS

Your best bet is to try before you go. You may be able to purchase **reduced-price theater tickets** in advance over the phone (or in person at the box office) by joining one or more of the online theater clubs. Membership is free and can garner you discounts of up to 50% on select Broadway and Off-Broadway shows. For further details, see "Online Sources for Theatergoers & Performing Arts Fans," above.

Broadway shows—even blockbusters—sometimes have a limited number of cheaper tickets set aside for students and seniors, and they may even be available at the last minute; call the box office direct to inquire. *Rent* has offered all kinds of bargains to keep younger theatergoers coming.

The best deal in town on same-day tickets for both Broadway and Off-Broadway shows is at the **Times Square Theatre Centre,** better known as the **TKTS** booth run by the nonprofit Theatre Development Fund in the heart of the Theater District at Duffy Square, 47th Street and Broadway (open 3–8pm for evening performances, 10am–2pm for Wed and Sat matinees, from 11am on Sun for all performances). Tickets for that day's performances are usually offered at half price, with a few reduced only 25%, plus a $2.50 per ticket service charge. Boards outside the ticket windows list available shows; you're unlikely to find certain perennial or outsize smashes, but most other shows turn up. Only cash and traveler's checks are accepted (no credit cards). There's often a huge line, so show up early for the best availability and be prepared to wait—but frankly, the crowd is all part of the fun. If you don't care much what you see and you'd just like to go to a show, you can walk right up to the window later in the day and something's always available.

Run by the same group and offering the same discounts is the **TKTS DowntownTheatre Centre,** on the plaza in the Financial District's Bowling Green Park (open Mon–Friday 11am–5:30pm, Sat 11am–3:30pm; subway: 4, 5 to Bowling Green). All the same policies apply. The advantages to coming down here are that the lines are generally shorter, and matinee tickets are available the day before, so you can plan ahead.

Visit **www.tdf.org** or call **NYC/Onstage** at ✆ **212/768-1818** and press "8" for the latest TKTS information.

2 Opera, Classical Music & Dance

While Broadway is the Big Apple's greatest hit, many other performing arts also flourish in this culturally rich and entertainment-hungry town.

In addition to the listings below, see what's happening at **Carnegie Hall** and the **Brooklyn Academy of Music,** two of the most respected—and enjoyable—multifunctional performing arts venues in the city. The marvelous **92nd Street Y** also regularly hosts events that are worth considering. I've listed the operatic and symphonic companies housed at **Lincoln Center** below; also check the center's full calendar for all offerings. See "Major Concert Halls & Landmark Venues," below.

OPERA

New York has grown into one of the world's major opera centers. The season generally runs September through May, but there's usually something going on at any time of year.

Amato Opera Theatre *Finds* This cozy, off-the-beaten-track venue functions as a showcase for talented young American singers. The intimate 100-plus-seat house celebrated its 50th season last year amid a rising reputation and increasing ticket sales. The staple is full productions of Italian classics—Verdi's *La Traviata,* Puccini's *Madame Butterfly,* Bizet's *Carmen,* with an occasional Mozart tossed in—at great prices for regular performances ($28, $23 for seniors and kids). Performances, usually held on Saturday and Sunday, now regularly sell out, so it's a good idea to reserve 3 weeks in advance.

Note for parents: On one Saturday a month, "Opera in Brief" offers fully costumed, kid-length versions of the classics interwoven with narration so Mom and Dad have a palatable forum in which to introduce the little ones to opera. At $15 or so per ticket, these matinee performances are wallet-friendly, too. 319 Bowery (at 2nd St.). ✆ **212/228-8200.** www.amato.org. Subway: F to Second Ave.; 6 to Bleecker St.

Metropolitan Opera Tickets can cost a small fortune—anywhere from $25 to $275 (individual ticket prices were not yet set for 2002–03 at press time). But for its full productions of the classic repertory and schedule packed with world-class grand sopranos and tenors, the Metropolitan Opera ranks first in the world. Millions are spent on fabulous stagings, and the venue itself is a wonder of acoustics. The 2002–03 season sees two notable premieres for the company (Vincenzo Bellini's *Il Pirata* and William Bolcom's *A View from the Bridge,* based on the Arthur Miller Play), plus Plácido Domingo as Louis Ipanov in Giordano's *Fedora* and repertory favorites *Faust, Carmen, Die Fledermaus,* and *Don Giovanni.*

To guarantee that its audience understands the words, the Met has outfitted the back of each row of seats with screens for subtitles—translation help for those who want it, minimum intrusion for those who don't. James Levine continues his role as the brilliant and popular conductor of the orchestra. At the Metropolitan Opera House, Lincoln Center, Broadway and 64th St. ✆ **212/362-6000.** www.metopera.org. Subway: 1, 9 to 66th St.

New York City Opera The New York City Opera is a superb company, with a delightful duality to its approach: It not only attempts to reach a wider audience than the Met with its more "human" scale and significantly lower prices ($25–$98) but it's also committed to adventurous premieres, newly composed operas, the occasional avant-garde work, American musicals presented as fresh, innovated operettas (Stephen Sondheim's *Sweeney Todd, Porgy and Bess*), and even obscure works by mainstream or lesser-known composers. Its mix stretches from the "easy" works of Puccini and Verdi and Gilbert and Sullivan to the more challenging oeuvres of the likes of Arnold Schönberg and Philip Glass. For the 2002–03 season, look for the groundbreaking debut of *Dead Man Walking,* based on Sister Helen Prejean's book (and the film of the same name); a new production of *Little Women;* and a double whammy from Puccini: *Madame Butterfly* and *La Bohème.* At the New York State Theater, Lincoln Center, Broadway and 64th St. ✆ **212/870-5570** (information or box office), or 212/307-4100 for Ticketmaster. www.nycopera.com or www.ticketmaster.com. Subway: 1, 9 to 66th St.

New York Gilbert and Sullivan Players If you're in the mood for lighthearted operetta, try this lively company, which specializes in Gilbert and Sullivan's 19th-century English comic works. Tickets are affordable, usually in the $30 to $50 range (exact prices for 2002–03 season were not yet determined at press time). The annual calendar generally runs from October through April and includes four shows a year, with some performances held at City Center (p. 394). At Symphony Space, Broadway and 95th St. ✆ **212/864-5400** or 212/769-1000. www.nygasp.org. Subway: 1, 2, 3, 9 to 96th St.

CLASSICAL MUSIC

Bargemusic *Finds* Many thought Olga Bloom peculiar, if not deranged, when she transformed a 40-year-old barge into a chamber music concert hall. More than 20 years later, Bargemusic is an internationally renowned recital room boasting more than 100 first-rate chamber music performances a year. Visiting musicians love the chance to play in such an intimate setting, so the roster regularly includes highly respected international musicians as well as local stars like violinist Cynthia Phelps.

There are three shows per week, on Thursday and Friday evenings at 7:30pm and Sunday afternoon at 4pm. The musicians perform on a small stage in a cherry-paneled, fireplace-lit room accommodating 130. The barge may creak a bit and an occasional boat may speed by, but the music rivals what you'll find in almost any other New York concert hall—and the panoramic view through the glass wall behind the stage can't be beat. Neither can the price: Tickets are just $35 ($20 students), or $40 for performances by larger ensembles. Reserve well in advance. At Fulton Ferry Landing (just south of the Brooklyn Bridge), Brooklyn. ✆ **718/624-2083** or 718/624-4061. www.bargemusic.org. Subway: 2, 3 to Clark St.; A, C to High St.

The Juilliard School *Value* During its school year, the nation's premier music education institution sponsors about 550 performances of the highest quality—

at the lowest prices. With most concerts free and $20 as a maximum ticket price, Juilliard is one of New York's greatest cultural bargains. Though most would assume that the school presents only classical music concerts, Juilliard also offers other music as well as drama, dance, opera, and interdisciplinary works. The best way to find out about the wide array of productions is to call, visit the school's website (click on "Calendar of Events"), or consult the bulletin board in the building's lobby. Note that tickets are sometimes required even for free performances. Watch for master classes and discussions open to the public featuring celebrity guest teachers. 60 Lincoln Center Plaza (Broadway at 65th St.). ✆ **212/769-7406**, or 212/721-6500 for charge tickets. www.juilliard.edu. Subway: 1, 9 to 66th St.

New York Philharmonic Symphony-wise, you'd be hard-pressed to do better than the New York Philharmonic. Now that legendary music director Kurt Masur has retired, the country's oldest orchestra is now under the guidance of distinguished conductor Lorin Maazel, formerly of the Bavarian Radio Symphony Orchestra. Don't expect quality to falter one bit. Highlights of the 2002–03 season include a New Year's Eve Gershwin gala, a wealth of crowd pleasers from Beethoven's Ninth to Yo Yo Ma, and a season finale of Mahler's *Resurrection* symphony. There's a summer season in July, when themed classics brighten the hall, as well as summer concerts in Central Park that are worth checking into.

Tickets range from $36 to $68; opt for a rush-hour concert or a matinee for the lowest across-the-board prices. If you can afford it—and if the tickets are available—it's well worth it to pay for prime seats. The acoustics of the hall are

---

Tips Last-Minute Ticket-Buying Tips

Most seats at New York Philharmonic performances are sold to subscribers, with just a few left for the rest of us. But there are still ways to get tickets. Periodically, a number of same-day orchestra tickets are made available at the philharmonic, and sold first thing in the morning for $25 a pop (maximum 2). They usually go on sale at 10am weekdays, 1pm Saturday (noon if there's a matinee). And when subscribers can't attend, they may turn their tickets back to the theaters, which then resell them at the last moment. These can be in the most coveted rows of the orchestra. Ticket holders can donate unwanted tickets until curtain time, so tickets that are not available first thing in the morning may become available later in the day. The hopeful form "cancellation lines" 2 hours or more before curtain time for a crack at returned tickets on a first-come, first-served basis. Senior/student/disabled rush tickets may be available for $10 (maximum two) on concert day, but never at Friday matinees or Saturday evening performances. To check availability for any of these programs at all performances, call Audience Services at ✆ **212/875-5656** before you head to the box office.

Note that Lincoln Center's **Alice Tully Hall** (where the Chamber Music Society performs and other concerts are held), the **Metropolitan Opera,** the **New York City Opera,** and **Carnegie Hall** offer similar last-minute and discount programs (the **New York City Ballet** offers Student Rush tickets only). It makes sense to call the box office first to check on same-day availability before heading to the theater—or, if you're willing to risk coming away empty-handed, be there at opening time for first crack.

---

such that, at the midrange price points, I prefer the second tier (especially the boxes) over the more expensive rear orchestra seats. Go cheap if you have to; you're sure to enjoy the program from any vantage. At Avery Fisher Hall, Lincoln Center, Broadway at 65th St. © **212/875-5656** for audience services, 212/875-5030 for box office information or Center Charge at 212/721-6500 for tickets. www.newyorkphilharmonic.org. Subway: 1, 9 to 66th St.

DANCE

In general, dance seasons run September through February and then March through June, but there's almost always something going on. In addition to the major troupes below, some other names to keep in mind are the **Brooklyn Academy of Music,** the **92nd Street Y, Radio City Music Hall,** and **Town Hall** (see "Major Concert Halls & Landmark Venues," below). For particularly innovative works, see what's on at the **Dance Theater Workshop,** in the Bessie Schönberg Theater, 219 W. 19th St., between Seventh and Eighth avenues (© **212/691-6500** or 212/924-0077; www.dtw.org), a first-rate launching pad for nearly a quarter-century.

In addition to regular appearances at City Center (below), the **American Ballet Theatre** (www.abt.org) takes up residence at Lincoln Center's Metropolitan Opera House (© **212/362-6000**) for 8 weeks each spring; their recent reinterpretation of *Swan Lake* caused quite a stir. The same venue also hosts such visiting companies as the Kirov, Royal, and Paris Opéra ballets.

The weekly ***Time Out New York,*** available on newsstands around town, maintains a section dedicated to dance events around town that's an invaluable resource to fans.

City Center Modern dance usually takes center stage in this Moorish dome-topped performing arts palace. The companies of Merce Cunningham, Martha Graham, Paul Taylor, Alvin Ailey, Twyla Tharp, the Dance Theatre of Harlem (celebrating its 30th year this season), and the American Ballet Theatre are often on the calendar. Don't expect cutting edge—but do expect excellence. Sight lines are terrific from all corners, and a new acoustical shell means the sound is pitch-perfect. 131 W. 55th St. (btwn Sixth and Seventh aves.). © **877/581-1212** or 212/581-1212. www.citycenter.org. Subway: F, N, Q, R, W to 57th St.; B, D, E to Seventh Ave.

Joyce Theater Housed in an old Art Deco movie house, the Joyce has grown into one of the world's greatest modern dance institutions. You can see everything from Native American ceremonial dance to Maria Benites Teatro Flamenco to the innovative works of Pilobolus to the Martha Graham Dance Company. In residence annually is Eliot Feld's ballet company, Ballet Tech, which WQXR radio's Francis Mason called "better than a whole month of namby-pamby classical ballets." The Joyce has a second space, **Joyce SoHo,** where you can see rising young dancers and experimental works in the intimacy of a 70-seat performance space. 175 Eighth Ave. (at 19th St.). © **212/242-0800.** www.joyce.org. Subway: C, E to 23rd St.; 1, 9 to 18th St. Joyce SoHo at 155 Mercer St. (btwn Houston and Prince sts.). © **212/431-9233.** Subway: N, R to Prince St.

New York City Ballet Highly regarded for its unsurpassed technique, the New York City Ballet is the world's best. The company renders with happy regularity the works of two of America's most important choreographers: George Balanchine, its founder, and Jerome Robbins. Under the direction of Ballet Master in Chief Peter Martins, the troupe continues to expand its repertoire and performs to a wide variety of classical and modern music. The cornerstone of the annual season is the Christmastime production of *The Nutcracker,* for which tickets usually become available in early October. Ticket prices for most events run $28 to $66. At the New York State Theater at Lincoln Center, Broadway and 64th St. ✆ **212/870-5570.** www.nycballet.com. Subway: 1, 9 to 66th St.

3 Major Concert Halls & Landmark Venues

Apollo Theatre Built in 1914, this legendary Harlem theater launched or abetted the careers of countless musical icons—including Bessie Smith, Billie Holiday, Dinah Washington, Duke Ellington, Ella Fitzgerald, Sarah Vaughan, Count Basie, Aretha Franklin, and the Jackson Five—and is in large part responsible for the development and worldwide popularization of black music in America. By the 1970s, it had fallen on hard times, but a 1986 restoration breathed new life into the landmark. Today the Apollo is internationally renowned for its African-American acts of all musical genres, from hip-hop acts to Wynton Marsalis's "Jazz for Young People" events. Wednesday's "Amateur Night at the Apollo" is a loud, fun-filled night that draws in young talents from all over the country with high hopes of making it big (a very young Lauryn Hill started out here—and didn't win!). 253 W. 125th St. (btwn Adam Clayton Powell and Frederick Douglass blvds.). ✆ **212/749-5838,** or 212/889-3532 for information on attending a "Showtime at the Apollo" taping. Subway: 1, 9 to 125th St.

Brooklyn Academy of Music *Finds* BAM is the city's most renowned contemporary arts institution, presenting cutting-edge theater, opera, dance, and music. Offerings have included historically informed presentations of baroque opera by William Christie and Les Arts Florissants; pop opera from Lou Reed; Marianne Faithfull singing the music of Kurt Weill; dance by Mark Morris and Mikhail Baryshnikov; the Philip Glass ensemble accompanying screenings of *Koyannisqatsi* and Lugosi's original *Dracula;* the Royal Dramatic Theater of Sweden directed by Ingmar Bergman; and many more experimental works by both renowned and lesser-known international artists as well as visiting companies from all over the world.

Of particular note is the **Next Wave Festival,** September through December, this country's foremost showcase for new experimental works (see the "New York City Calendar of Events" in chapter 3). The **BAM Rose Cinemas** show first-run independent films, and there's free live music every Thursday, Friday, and Saturday night at **BAMcafé,** which can range from atmospheric electronica from cornetist Graham Haynes to radical jazz from the Harold Rubin Trio to the tango band Tanguardia! ($10 food minimum). Inquire about the gospel brunch on select Sundays from 2 to 4pm. 30 Lafayette Ave. (off Flatbush Ave.), Brooklyn. ✆ **718/636-4100.** www.bam.org. Subway: 2, 3, 4, 5, M, N, Q, R, W to Pacific St./Atlantic Ave.

Carnegie Hall Perhaps the world's most famous performance space, Carnegie Hall offers everything from grand classics to the music of Ravi Shankar. The **Issac Stern Auditorium,** the 2,804-seat main hall, welcomes visiting orchestras from across the country and the world. Many of the world's premier soloists and ensembles give recitals. The legendary hall is both visually and acoustically brilliant; don't miss an opportunity to experience it if there's something on that interests you.

There's also the intimate 268-seat **Weill Recital Hall,** usually used to showcase chamber music and vocal and instrumental recitals. Carnegie Hall has also reclaimed the ornate underground Zankel Concert Hall, occupied by a movie theater for 38 years; it should reopen as a 650-seat third stage in 2003. For last-minute ticket-buying tips, see the box on p. 393. 881 Seventh Ave. (at 57th St.). ✆ **212/247-7800.** www.carnegiehall.org. Subway: B, N, Q, R to 57th St.

Lincoln Center for the Performing Arts New York is the world's premier performing arts city, and Lincoln Center is its premier institution. Whenever you're planning an evening's entertainment, check the offerings here—which can include opera, dance, symphonies, jazz, theater, film, and more, from the classics to the contemporary. Lincoln Center's many buildings serve as permanent homes to their own companies as well as major stops for world-class performance troupes from around the globe.

Resident companies include the following: The **Chamber Music Society of Lincoln Center** (✆ **212/875-5788;** www.chambermusicsociety.org), performs at Alice Tully Hall or the Daniel and Joanna S. Rose Rehearsal Studio, often in the company of such high-caliber guests as Anne Sofie Von Otter and Midori. The **Film Society of Lincoln Center** (✆ **212/875-5600;** www.filmlinc.com) screens a daily schedule of movies at the Walter Reade Theater, and hosts a number of important annual film and video festivals as well as the Reel to Real program for kids, pairing silent screen classics with live performance. **Jazz at Lincoln Center** (✆ **212/258-9800;** www.jazzatlincolncenter.org) is led by the incomparable Wynton Marsalis, with the orchestra usually performing at Alice Tully Hall; the "Jazz at the Penthouse" program, where great jazz pianists like Ellis Marsalis and Tommy Flanagan play in a spectacular candlelit setting overlooking the Hudson River, is the hottest ticket in town. **Lincoln Center Theater** (✆ **212/362-7600;** www.lct.org) consists of the Vivian Beaumont Theater, a modern and comfortable venue with great sight lines that has been home to much good Broadway drama (at press time, the Tony award–winning *Contact*), and the Mitzi E. Newhouse Theater, a well-respected Off-Broadway house that has also boasted numerous theatrical triumphs. Past seasons have included excellent productions of Tom Stoppard's *Arcadia, Carousel* in revival, and David Hare's one-man show, *Via Dolorosa.*

For details on the **Metropolitan Opera,** the **New York City Opera,** the **New York City Ballet,** the **Juilliard School,** the phenomenal **New York Philharmonic,** and the **American Ballet Theatre,** which takes up residence here every spring, see "Opera, Classical Music & Dance," earlier in this chapter.

Most of the companies' **major seasons** run from about September or October to April, May, or June. **Special series** like Great Performers and the new American Songbook, showcasing classic American show tunes, help round out the calendar. Indoor and outdoor events are held in warmer months: Summer kicks off with the **JVC Jazz Festival** in June; July sees **Midsummer Night's Swing** with partner dancing, lessons, and music on the plaza; August's **Mostly Mozart** attracts talents like Alicia de Larrocha and André Watts; the 3-year-old **Lincoln Center Festival** celebrates the best of the performing arts; **Lincoln Center Out-of-Doors** is a series of free alfresco music and dance performances also in August; there's also the **New York Film Festival,** and more. Check the "Calendar of Events," in chapter 3, or Lincoln Center's website to see what special events will be on while you're in town.

Tickets for all performances at Avery Fisher and Alice Tully halls can be purchased through **CenterCharge** (✆ **212/721-6500**) or online at www.lincolncenter.org (click on "Box Office & Schedule" in the upper-right corner). Tickets for all Lincoln Center Theater performances can be purchased thorough **TeleCharge** (✆ **212/239-6200;** www.telecharge.com). Tickets for New York

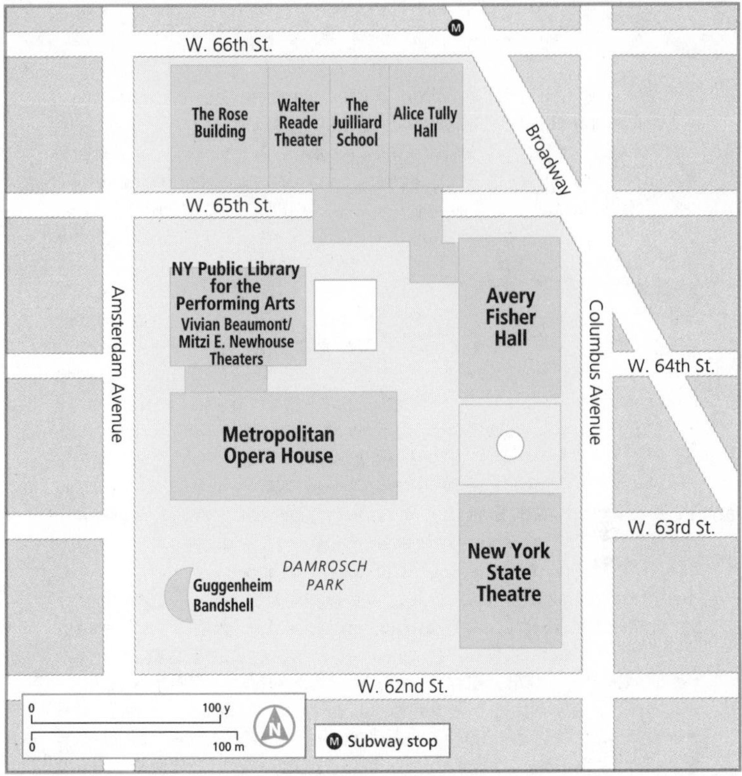

State Theater productions (New York City Opera and Ballet companies) are available through **Ticketmaster** (© **212/307-4100;** www.ticketmaster.com), while tickets for films showing at the Walter Reade Theater can be bought up to 7 days in advance by calling © **212/496-3809.** For last-minute ticket-buying tips, see the box on p. 393.

Lincoln Center is also home to the **New York Public Library for the Performing Arts** (© **212/870-1630;** www.nypl.org), which is now reopened after a major renovation.

Offered daily, 1-hour **guided tours** of Lincoln Center tell the story of the great performing arts complex, and even offer glimpses of rehearsals; call © **212/875-5350.** 70 Lincoln Center Plaza (at Broadway and 64th St.). © **212/546-2656** or 212/875-5456 www.lincolncenter.org. Subway: 1, 9 to 66th St.

Madison Square Garden U2, Springsteen, Tina Turner, Lauryn Hill, and other monsters of rock and pop regularly fill this 20,000-seat arena, which is also home to the Knicks, the Rangers, and the WNBA's Liberty. A cavernous concrete hulk, it's better suited to sports than to concerts, or in-the-round events such as the Ice Capades, Ringling Bros. Barnum & Bailey Circus, or the International Cat Show. End up in the back for The Who, and you'd better bring binoculars.

You'll find far better sight lines at the **Theater at Madison Square Garden,** an amphitheater-style auditorium with 5,600 seats that has also played host to

Park It! Shakespeare, Music & Other Free Fun

As the weather warms, New York culture comes outdoors to play.

Shakespeare in the Park, held at Central Park's Delacorte Theater, is by far the city's most famous alfresco arts event. Organized by the late Joseph Papp's Public Theater, the schedule consists of two summertime productions, usually two of the Bard's plays. Productions often feature big names and range from traditional interpretations (Andre Braugher as an armor-clad *Henry V*) to avant-garde presentations (Morgan Freeman, Tracey Ullman, and David Alan Grier in *Taming of the Shrew* as a Wild West showdown). Patrick Stewart's role as Prospero in *The Tempest* a few years back was so popular that the show was propelled onto Broadway for an award-winning run. The theater itself, next to Belvedere Castle near 79th Street and West Drive, is a dream—on a beautiful starry night, there's no better stage in town. Tickets are given out free on a first-come, first-served basis (two per person), at 1pm on the day of the performance at the theater. The Delacorte might have 1,881 seats, but each is a hot commodity, so people generally line up on the baseball field next to the theater about 2 to 3 hours in advance (even earlier if a big box-office name is involved). You can also pick up same-day tickets between 1 and 3pm at the Public Theater, at 425 Lafayette St., where the Shakespeare Festival continues throughout the year. For more information, call the Public Theater at ✆ **212/539-8750** or the Delacorte at ✆ **212/861-7277,** or go online at **www.publictheater.org.**

With summer also comes the sound of music to Central Park, where the **New York Philharmonic** and the **Metropolitan Opera** regularly entertain beneath the stars; for the current schedule, call ✆ **212/360-3444,** 212/875-5709, or 212/362-6000, or visit **www.lincolncenter.org.**

some major pop stars, from Barbra Streisand to Roxy Music. Watch for annual stagings of *The Wizard of Oz; A Christmas Carol;* and family shows such as *Sesame Street Live.* Newest at MSG is the **Comedy Garden** (www.comedygarden.com), the Garden's own comedy club at the Theater, where talent runs the gamut from well-known local comics to Robin Williams and Joan Rivers.

The box office is located at Seventh Avenue and 32nd Street. Or you can purchase tickets through **Ticketmaster** (✆ **212/307-7171;** www.ticketmaster.com). On Seventh Ave. from 31st to 33rd sts. ✆ **212/465-MSG1.** www.thegarden.com. Subway: A, C, E, 1, 2, 3, 9 to 34th St.

92nd Street Y Tisch Center for the Arts *Value* This generously endowed community center offers a phenomenal slate of top-rated cultural happenings, from classical to folk to jazz to world music to cabaret to lyric theater and literary readings. Just because it's the "Y," don't think this place is small potatoes: Great classical performers—Isaac Stern, Janos Starker, Nadja Salerno-Sonnenberg—give recitals here. In addition, the full concert calendar often includes luminaries such as Max Roach, John Williams, and Judy Collins; Jazz at the Y from Dick Hyman and guests; the long-standing Chamber Music at the Y series; the classical Music from the Jewish Spirit series; and regular cabaret programs. The lectures and literary readings calendar is unparalleled, with featured speakers ranging from Lorne

The most active music stage in the park is **SummerStage,** at Rumsey Playfield, midpark around 72nd Street, which has featured everyone from the Godfather of Soul, James Brown, to the angel poet of punk, Patti Smith. Recent offerings have included concerts by Hugh Masekela, Sugarhill Gang, the Jon Spencer Blues Explosion, and Marianne Faithfull; and "Viva, Verdi!" festival performances by the New York Grand Opera; cabaret nights; and more. The season usually lasts from mid-June to early August. While some big-name shows charge admission, tickets aren't usually required; donations are warmly accepted, however. For the latest performance info, call the SummerStage hot line at ✆ **212/360-2777** or visit **www.summerstage.org**.

Central Park may be the most happening park in town, but the calendar of free events heats up throughout the city's parks in summertime. You can find out what's happening by calling the **Parks and Recreation Special Events Hot Line** at ✆ **888/NY-PARKS** or 212/360-3456, or pointing your Web browser to **nycparks.completeinet.net**.

Additionally, most of the city's top museums offer free music and other programs after regular hours on select nights. The **Metropolitan Museum of Art** has an extensive slate of offerings each week, including live classical music and cocktails on Friday and Saturday evenings. There's lots of fun to be had at others as well, including the **Guggenheim,** whose weekend Worldbeat Jazz series is a big hit; the **American Museum of Natural History,** which features live jazz in the Hall of the Universe in the new Rose Center for Earth and Space; and the **Brooklyn Museum of Art,** which hosts the remarkably eclectic **First Saturday** program monthly. For details, see the museum listings in chapter 8.

Michaels to David Halberstam to Ralph Nader to Katie Couric to Erica Jong to Ken Burns to Elie Wiesel to Alan Dershowitz to A. S. Byatt to . . . the list goes on and on. There's a regular schedule of modern dance, too, through the Harkness Dance Project. Best of all, readings and lectures are usually priced between $20 and $30 for nonmembers, dance is usually $20, and concert tickets generally go for $15 to $50—half or a third of what you'd pay at comparable venues. Additionally, a full calendar of entertainment targeted to the culturally aware in their 20s and 30s—from poetry readings to film screenings to live music from talent as wide ranging as Middle Eastern instrumentalist Omar Faruk Tekbilek and folk troubadour John Wesley Harding—is offered at the Upper West Side community center **Makor,** 35 W. 67th St. (✆ **212/601-1000;** www.makor.org; subway: 1, 9 to 66th St.). 1395 Lexington Ave. (at 92nd St.). ✆ **212/996-1100,** or 212/415-5500 for tickets. www.92ndsty.org. Subway: 4, 5, 6 to 86th St.; 6 to 96th St.

Radio City Music Hall This stunning 6,200-seat Art Deco theater, with interior design by Donald Deskey, opened in 1932. After an extensive renovation in 1999, legendary Radio City continues to be a choice venue, where the theater alone adds a dash of panache to any performance. Star of the Christmas season is the **Radio City Music Hall Christmas Spectacular,** starring the legendary Rockettes. Visiting pop chart-toppers, from Patti LaBelle to Radiohead, also perform here. Thanks to perfect acoustics and uninterrupted sight lines, there's hardly a bad seat in the house. The theater also hosts dance performances, family entertainment, and a number of annual awards shows—such as the Essence Awards, the GQ Man of the Year Awards, and anything MTV is holding in town—so this is a good place to celeb-spot on show nights. 1260 Sixth Ave. (at 50th St.). ✆ **212/247-4777,** or 212/307-7171 for Ticketmaster. www.radiocity.com or www.ticketmaster.com. Subway: B, D, F, V to 49th–50th sts./Rockefeller Center.

Town Hall This intimate landmark theater—a National Historic Site designed by McKim, Mead & White—is blessed with outstanding acoustics, making it an ideal place to enjoy many kinds of performances, including theater, dance, lectures, drama, comedy, film, and pop and world music. The calendar regularly includes such offerings as American tap and Brazilian tango exhibitions; Native American music and global rhythms; comedy from the *Kids in the Hall* Reunion Tour or Eddie Izzard; live tapings of "A Prairie Home Companion" with Garrison Keillor or spoken word from Henry Rollins; lectures by luminaries such as Marianne Williamson and Frank Gehry; concerts by the likes of David Sandborn or the reunited Blondie; symphony, opera, and ballet companies from around the world; and much more. The grade is extremely steep, so unless Lurch sits in front of you, fellow audience members shouldn't block your view. 123 W. 43rd St. (btwn Sixth and Seventh aves.). ✆ **212/840-2824,** or 212/307-4100 for Ticketmaster. www.the-townhall-nyc.org or www.ticketmaster.com. Subway: N, Q, R, S, W, 1, 2, 3, 7, 9 to 42nd St./Times Sq.; B, D, F, V to 42nd St.

4 Live Rock, Jazz, Blues & More

I discuss the top venues, both large and small, below. But there are far more than these, and new ones are popping up all the time. For the latest, be sure to check the publications discussed in the introduction to this chapter as well as the online sources outlined in "Online Sources for Live Music Fans," below.

LARGER VENUES

For coverage of **Madison Square Garden,** the **Theater at MSG,** and **Town Hall,** see "Major Concert Halls & Landmark Venues," earlier in this chapter.

Beacon Theatre This pleasing midsize Upper West Side venue—a 1928 Art Deco movie palace with an impressive lobby, stairway, and auditorium seating about 2,700—hosts mainly pop music performances, usually for the over-30 crowd. Featured acts have ranged from street-smart pop diva Sheryl Crow to handsome-as-ever Bryan Ferry to befuddled Beach Boy Brian Wilson to Grateful Dead heirs apparent Phish to not-yet-deads the Allman Brothers. You'll also find such special events as the bodybuilding "Night of Champions" on the mix-and-match calendar. 2124 Broadway (at 74th St.). ✆ **212/496-7070.** www.livetonight.com. Subway: 1, 2, 3, 9 to 72nd St.

Hammerstein Ballroom In the past couple of years, this midsize venue has become one of the city's most popular rock stages, hosting such acts as Everything But the Girl, Moby, Bush, Belle & Sebastian, the Cranberries, Youssou N'Dour, prefab boy band O-Town, and Fatboy Slim (who hosted a fabulous deejay party). The sound system is very good, and the stage is mounted high enough that sight lines are decent even from the main floor. The side balconies are always reserved for VIPs, but the main balcony level, graded for good views and boasting comfortable theater-style seating, is usually open to regular Joes and Janes like us. However, you have to have a mezzanine-level ticket to gain

Tips Ticket-Buying Tips

Tickets for events at all larger theaters as well as at Hammerstein Ballroom, Roseland, Irving Plaza, B.B. King's, and S.O.B.'s can be purchased through **Ticketmaster** (**© 212/307-7171;** www.ticketmaster.com).

Advance tickets for an increasing number of shows at smaller venues—including CBGB's, Bowery Ballroom, Mercury Lounge, Village Underground, and Fez Under Time Cafe—can be purchased through **Ticketweb** (**© 212/269-4TIX;** www.ticketweb.com). Do note, however, that Ticketweb can sell out in advance of actual ticket availability. Just because Ticketweb doesn't have tickets left for an event doesn't mean it's completely sold out, so be sure and check with the venue directly.

Even if a show is sold out doesn't mean you're out of luck. There's usually a number of people hanging around at show time trying to get rid of extra tickets for friends who didn't show, and they're usually happy to pass them off for face value. You'll also see professional scalpers, who often peddle forgeries and are best avoided—it doesn't take a rocket scientist to tell the difference. Be aware, of course, that all forms of resale are illegal.

access, so request one when you're buying if you want one (there's usually no cost difference). Otherwise, you'll end up on the general-admission, standing-room-only floor, which some (not me!) prefer. At the Manhattan Center, 311 W. 34th St. (btwn Eighth and Ninth aves.). **© 212/485-1534.** www.concerthotline.com. Subway: A, C, E to 34th St./Penn Station.

Roseland This old warhorse of a venue, a 1919 ballroom gone to seed, has been under threat of the wrecking ball for years now. Everybody has played at this too-huge-for-its-own-good 2,500-capacity general-admission hall, from Marc Anthony to Fiona Apple to Busta Rhymes to Smashmouth to Rage Against the Machine to Jeff Beck. Bands who tend to inspire mosh pits like to book here (think Nine Inch Nails, The Offspring) because there's plenty of space for slamming and surfing at the front of the stage. Thankfully, there's also lots of room to steer clear and still enjoy the show. Advance tickets can be purchased at the Irving Plaza box office (p. 402) without the service fee that Ticketmaster charges. Take a moment on your way through the lobby to check out the cases memorializing Roseland's postwar heydays as the city's premier dance hall. Ballroom dancing still takes place Sunday from 2:30 to 10pm; admission is $10. 239 W. 52nd St. (btwn Broadway and Eighth Ave.). **© 212/777-6800,** 212/247-0200, or 212/307-7171 for Ticketmaster. www.roselandballroom.com or www.livetonight.com. Subway: C, E, 1, 9 to 50th St.

MIDSIZE & MULTIGENRE VENUES

Also see what's on at the stellar **Joe's Pub** (p. 408), a top-flight cabaret that hosts intimate shows by pop acts.

B.B. King Blues Club & Grill This snazzy 550-seat venue is one of the prime anchors of Times Square's "new" 42nd Street. Despite its name, B.B. King's seldom sticks to the blues; instead, what you're likely to find is a bill full of familiar pop, funk, and rock names, mainly from the past. The big-ticket talent runs the gamut from the Four Tops, Rick James, and Nile Rodgers and Chic (cool!)

Online Sources for Live Music Fans

These websites are your top online sources for live music schedules:

- **Local Music:** www.localmusic2.com
- **Live Tonight:** www.livetonight.com
- **Metropolitan Concert Hot Line:** www.concerthotline.com
- **Clear Channel Entertainment:** www.cc.com
- **Ticketmaster:** www.ticketmaster.com

Additionally, Web source **Citysearch (www.citysearch.com),** ***Time Out New York*** **(www.timeoutny.com),** and all of the hard-copy resources (and their corresponding websites) listed at the start of this chapter offer a wealth of live-music listings.

to Tower of Power to Dream Theater and Blue Oyster Cult. A few more (relatively) esoteric acts take the stage on occasion, such as Luther "Guitar Junior" Johnson and Shemikia Copeland. Tourist-targeted pricing place makes for a very expensive night on the town, word is that the food isn't as good as it was in the beginning, and seating policies can be terribly convoluted, but there's no arguing with the quality of the talent. The Sunday gospel lunch is a genuine slice of joy. 42nd St. btwn Seventh and Eighth aves. ✆ **212/997-4144,** or 212/307-7171 for tickets. www.bbkingblues.com. Subway: A, C, E, Q, W, 1, 2, 3, 7, 9 to 42nd St.

The Bottom Line The Bottom Line built its reputation by serving as a showcase for the likes of Bruce Springsteen and the Ramones, and it remains one of the city's most well-respected venues. With table seating, wait service, decent burgers and fries, and a no-smoking policy, it's one of the city's most comfortable, too. The Bottom Line is renowned for its excellent sound and bookings of the best rock and folk singer/songwriters in the business. Shawn Colvin, Marshall Crenshaw, Robyn Hitchcock, Lucinda Williams, Steve Forbert, Emmylou Harris, Tower of Power, and David Johansen (and alter-ego Buster Poindexter, natch) are among the many artists who make this their favored venue for area appearances. There are usually two shows nightly. 15 W. 4th St. (at Mercer St.). ✆ **212/502-3471** or 212/228-6300. www.bottomlinecabaret.com. Subway: N, R to Astor Place; A, C, E, F, V to W. 4th St.

Bowery Ballroom This marvelous space is run by the same people behind the pleasing Mercury Lounge (see below). The Bowery space is bigger, accommodating a crowd of 500 or so, and even better. The stage is big and raised to allow good sight lines from every corner. The sound couldn't be better, and Art Deco details give the place a sophistication that doesn't come easy to general-admission halls. My favorite spot is on the balcony, which has its own bar and seating alcoves. This place is a favorite with alt-rockers like Vic Chesnutt, Travis, Cracker, Rinocerose, Shudder to Think, and the marvelous Toshi Reagon, as well as more established acts (Warren Zevon, Neil Finn, Patti Smith), who thrive in an intimate setting. Save on the service charge by buying advance tickets at Mercury's box office. 6 Delancey St. (at Bowery). ✆ **212/533-2111.** www.boweryballroom.com. Subway: F, J, M, Z to Delancey St.

Irving Plaza This high-profile midsize music hall is the prime stop for national-name rock bands that aren't quite big enough yet (or anymore) to sell out Hammerstein, Roseland, or the Beacon. Think Five for Fighting, the Eels, Jars of Clay, Badly Drawn Boy, the Reverend Horton Heat, the resurrected

Television, Kenny Wayne Shepherd, Cowboy Junkies, and Cheap Trick. From time to time, big-name artists also perform—Bob Dylan, Trent Reznor, and AJ McLean of the Backstreet Boys have all played "secret" shows here. All in all, a very nice place to see a show, with a well-elevated stage and lots of open space even on sold-out nights. There's an upstairs balcony that offers unparalleled views, but come early for a spot. 17 Irving Place (1 block west of Third Ave. at 15th St.). ✆ **212/777-1224** or 212/777-6800. www.irvingplaza.com. Subway: L, N, R, 4, 5, 6 to 14th St./ Union Sq.

The Knitting Factory New York's premier avant-garde music venue has four separate spaces, each showcasing performances ranging from experimental jazz and acoustic folk to spoken-word and poetry readings to out-there multimedia works. Regulars who use the Knitting Factory as their lab of choice include former Lounge Lizard John Lurie; around-the-bend experimentalist John Zorn; guitar gods Vernon Reid, Eliot Sharp, and David Torn; innovative sideman (to Tom Waits and Elvis Costello, among others) Marc Ribot; and Television's Richard Lloyd. (If these names mean nothing to you, chances are good that the Knitting Factory is not for you.) The schedule is peppered with edgy star turns from the likes of Yoko Ono, Taj Mahal, Faith No More's Mike Patton, and Lou Reed. There are often two show times a night in the remarkably pleasing main performance space, so it's easy to work a show around other activities. The Old Office Lounge offers an extensive list of microbrews and free live entertainment. 74 Leonard St. (btwn Broadway and Church St.). ✆ **212/219-3006.** www.knittingfactory.com. Subway: 1, 9 to Franklin St.

(MOSTLY) ROCK CLUBS

In addition to the choices below, rock fans on the hunt for diamonds in the rough might also want to see what's on at folk rock's legendary **Bitter End,** 147 Bleecker St., between Thompson and LaGuardia streets in the heart of the Village (✆ **212/673-7030;** www.bitterend.com).

Arlene Grocery This casual Lower East Side club boasts a friendly bar and a good sound system; unfortunately, music isn't always free anymore, but the quality of the artists is usually pretty high, and the cover usually tops out at $5. Arlene Grocery primarily serves as a showcase for hot bands looking for a deal or promoting their self-pressed record. The crowd is an easygoing mix of club-hoppers, rock fans looking for a new fix, and industry scouts looking for new blood. 95 Stanton St. (btwn Ludlow and Orchard sts.). ✆ **212/358-1633.** www.arlene-grocery.com. Subway: F to Second Ave.

Brownie's This bare-bones East Village showcase gets points for quantity with its great sound system, easygoing vibe, and nightly jam-packed lineup, which on occasion features such alterna-stars as J. Mascis (Dinosaur Jr.) and Craig Wedren (Shudder to Think). 169 Ave. A (btwn 10th and 11th sts.). ✆ **212/420-8392.** www.browniesnyc.com. Subway: L to First Ave.

CBGB The original downtown rock club has seen better days, but no other spot is so rich with rock-and-roll history. This was the launching pad for New York punk and New Wave: the Ramones, Blondie, the Talking Heads, the Cramps, Patti Smith, Stiv Bators and the Dead Boys—everybody got started here. These days, you've probably never heard of most acts performing here. Never mind—CB's still rocks. Expect loud and cynical, and you're unlikely to come away disappointed. Come early if you have hopes of actually seeing the stage.

More today than yesterday is **CB's 313 Gallery,** a welcome spin-off that showcases alternative art on the walls and mostly acoustic singer/songwriters on stage. Same goes for CB's **lounge,** which has a more cerebral alt edge to its sounds, plus regular poetry slams. Within striking distance of the history, but more pleasant all the way around. 315 Bowery (at Bleecker St.). ✆ **212/982-4052,** or 212/677-0455 for CB's 313 Gallery. www.cbgb.com. Subway: F to Second Ave.; 6 to Bleecker St.

Fez Under Time Cafe You have to reserve a seat a few days ahead for the wildly popular Thursday night Mingus Big Band, when the low-ceilinged basement performance space is filled with the cool sounds of jazz. The rest of the week brings an eclectic live music-and-performance art mix, which can range from Patti Rothberg to drag grande dame Hedda Lettuce to fun lounge-lizardy tributes to acts like Queen and ABBA from Loser's Lounge. You never know who's gonna pop up; Joan Rivers even did a few shows here in mid-2002. The stage is fronted by tightly packed picnic-style tables and a few coveted booths. Time Cafe's pleasing, well-priced menu is served during performances (see chapter 7). I would love this sophisticated space if it were just better ventilated; if you need to escape the rampant cigarette smoke, head upstairs to the relaxing lounge and bar with an *Arabian Nights* ambience. 380 Lafayette St. (at Great Jones St.). ✆ **212/533-2680.** www.feznyc.com. Subway: 6 to Bleecker St.

Mercury Lounge The Merc is everything a top-notch live music venue should be: unpretentious, extremely civilized, and outfitted with a killer sound system. The rooms themselves are nothing special: a front bar and an intimate back-room performance space with a low stage and a few tables along the wall. The calendar is filled with a mix of accomplished local rockers and national acts like Frank Black, the Mekons, and Spacehog. The crowd is grown-up and easygoing. The only downside is that it's consistently packed thanks to the high quality of the entertainment and all-around pleasing nature of the experience. 217 E. Houston St. (at Essex St./Ave. A). ✆ **212/260-4700.** www.mercuryloungenyc.com. Subway: F to Second Ave.

Rodeo Bar *Value* Here's New York's oldest—and finest—honky-tonk. Hike up your Wranglers and head those Fryes inside, where you'll find longhorns on the walls, peanut shells underfoot, first-class margaritas at the bar, and Tex-Mex on the menu. But this place is really about the music: urban-tinged country, foot-stompin' bluegrass, swinging rockabilly, Southern-flavored rock. Bigger names like Brian Setzer and up-and-comers on the tour circuit like Hank Williams III occasionally grace the stage, but regular acts like Dixieland swingers the Flying Neutrinos, cowpunk goddess Rosie Flores, and the good-time BBQ Bob and the Spareribs usually supply free music, keeping the urban cowboys plenty happy. A 10-gallon hat full o' fun. It's Happy Hour until 7pm; the music starts around 9:30pm nightly, and goes till at least 3am. 375 Third Ave. (at 27th St.). ✆ **212/683-6500.** www.rodeobar.com. Subway: 6 to 28th St.

Village Underground *Finds* The folks behind dearly departed Tramps have opened this intimate, comfortable, and even somewhat romantic subterranean venue. Some surprisingly big-name talent has been in the house of late, including Lisa Loeb, the Calling, Phantom Planet, Buckwheat Zydeco, Evan Dando, bluesman Otis Rush, and R&B legend Solomon Burke (on the heels of his 2001 Rock and Roll Hall of Fame induction). But even if you don't recognize the names, you can count on a night of quality music. Advance tickets can be purchased online at **www.tickeweb.com** or by calling ✆ **866/468-7619.** 130 W. 3rd St. (btwn Sixth Ave. and MacDougal St.). ✆ **212/777-7745.** www.thevillageunderground.com. Subway: A, C, E, F, V to W. 4th (use W. 3rd St. exit).

JAZZ, BLUES, LATIN & WORLD MUSIC

Be aware that a night at a top-flight jazz club can be expensive. Cover charges can vary dramatically—from as little as $10 to as high as $65, depending on who's taking the stage—and there's likely to be an additional two-drink minimum (or a dinner requirement, if you choose an early show). Call ahead so you know what you're getting into; reservations are also an excellent idea at top spots.

For those of you who like your jazz with an edge, see what's on at the **Knitting Factory** (p. 403). Trad fans should also consider the Thursday Mingus Big Band Workshop at **Fez Under Time Cafe** (p. 404), while swingsters should consider **Swing 46** (p. 425). Weekends at **Carnegie Club** (p. 418) are ideal for Sinatra fans looking to relive the moment.

Despite its name, **B.B. King Blues Club & Grill** extends well beyond the blues genre to embrace over-the-hill acts of just about any ilk, from Morris Day and the Time to Blue Oyster Cult. Still, venerable bluesman does take the stage from time to time, so you might want to see what's on; turn to p. 401.

You might also consider **The Kitchen,** 512 W. 19th St., between Tenth and Eleventh avenues (✆ **212/255-5793;** www.thekitchen.org), for a full slate of live music and performance art. In association with the 92nd Street Y, **Makor** (p. 399) offers a similarly eclectic mix, as does **Joe's Pub** (p. 408), which adds a cabaret spin.

There's also world-beat jazz every Friday and Saturday from 5 to 8pm in the rotunda at the **Guggenheim Museum;** see chapter 8. And don't forget **Jazz at Lincoln Center,** the nation's premier forum for the traditional and developing jazz canon; see p. 396.

Birdland This legendary club abandoned its distant uptown roost in 1996 for a more convenient Midtown nest, where it has established itself once again as one of the city's premier jazz spots. While the legend of Parker, Monk, Gillespie, and other bebop pioneers still holds sway, this isn't a crowded, smoky joint of yesteryear. The big room is spacious, comfy, and classy, with an excellent sound system and top-notch talent roster any night of the week. Expect lots of accomplished big bands and jazz trios, plus occasional appearances by stars like Pat Metheny and Dave Brubeck. You can't go wrong with the regular Sunday night show, starring Chico O'Farrell's smokin' Afro-Cuban Jazz Big Band. At press time, Tuesday was the domain of the Duke Ellington Orchestra, lead by Duke's 20-year-old grandson Paul Ellington every other week. The southern-style food is even pretty good. 315 W. 44th St. (btwn Eighth and Ninth aves.). ✆ **212/581-3080.** www.birdlandjazz.com. Subway: A, C, E to 42nd St.

Blue Note The Blue Note attracts the biggest names in jazz to its intimate setting. Those who've played here include just about everyone of note: Lionel Hampton, Dave Brubeck, Ray Charles, B.B. King, Manhattan Transfer, Dr. John, George Duke, Chick Corea, David Sanborn, Arturo Sandoval, Gato Barbieri, and the superb Oscar Peterson. The sound system is excellent, and every seat in the house has a sight line to the stage. A night here can get expensive, but how often do you get to enjoy jazz of this caliber? There are two shows per night, and dinner is served. 131 W. 3rd St. (at Sixth Ave.). ✆ **212/475-8592.** www.bluenote.net. Subway: A, C, E, F, V to W. 4th St.

Iridium This well-respected and snazzily designed jazz club has relocated from its longtime perch across from Lincoln Center to an even better heart-of-the-Theater District location. Everything else remains the same, including the accomplished talent and big-name acts that always take the stage. Like the

Energizer bunny, Les Paul keeps on going, still playing every Monday night. Other top-notch performers who often appear include Nicholas Payton, Mose Allison, McCoy Tyner and Bobby Hutcherson, and the excellent Jazz Messengers. A full, rather sophisticated dinner menu is served. 1650 Broadway (at 51st St.). © **212/582-2121.** www.iridiumjazzclub.com. Subway: 1, 9 to 50th St.

Jazz at the Cajun *Finds* This cozy, rather casual New Orleans–themed supper club is the best venue in town for genuine prewar big-band and Dixieland jazz—think Jelly Roll Morton, Scott Joplin, early Duke. The fanatical crowd comes from all walks of life, united in their love of the old school. Cajun is home base for Vince Giordano's Nighthawks, who are pure masters of yesteryear—a real joy to watch!—but the place jumps no matter what top-notch crew takes the stage. The food is affordable and just fine; be sure to reserve in advance. 129 Eighth Ave. (btwn 16th and 17th sts.). © **212/691-6174.** www.jazzatthecajun.com. Subway: A, C, E, L to 14th St.

Jazz Standard *Finds* Kudos to the newly renovated Jazz Standard, where both the food and music meet all expectations. Boasting a sophisticated retro-speakeasy vibe, the Jazz Standard is one of the city's largest jazz clubs, with well-spaced tables seating 150 and a reasonable $15 cover. The rule is straightforward, mainstream jazz by new and established musicians, including such stars as Branford Marsalis. Now that the restaurant is **Blue Smoke** from Danny Meyer (Union Square Cafe, Gramercy Tavern), serving gourmet Southern barbecue, you really can't go wrong here. This joint makes for one fantastic night on the town. 116 E. 27th St. (btwn Park Ave. S. and Lexington Ave.). © **212/576-2232.** www.jazzstandard.net. Subway: 6 to 28th St.

Lenox Lounge Harlem's best jazz club is this beautifully renovated classic. Said to be a favorite of Billie Holliday's, the intimate, Art Deco-cool back room—complete with zebra stripes on the walls built-in banquettes—hosts top-flight live jazz vocalists, trios, and quartets for a crowd that comes to listen and be wowed. Blues and R&B are the province of Thursday. The cover never goes higher than $15, which makes Lenox Lounge a good value to boot. There's a warm, cozy, and immensely popular bar up front. Good soul food is served—or, better yet, pair your visit with dinner at nouveau Creole Bayou or soul-food landmark Sylvia's (see chapter 7). Well worth the trip uptown for those who want a genuine Harlem jazz experience. 288 Malcolm X Blvd. (Lenox Ave.; btwn 124th and 125th sts.). © **212/427-0253.** Subway: 2, 3 to 125th St.

Small's *Finds* Here's a great destination for committed jazzophiles: If you just don't want to stop grooving after the other clubs close, head to this cozy basement hideaway, which stays open all night. Scheduled performers, which often

Take the A Train

Harlem's jazz scene has taken on new energy in recent years. In addition to **Lenox Lounge** (see below), serious jazz fans might also want to consider **Showmans Cafe,** 375 W. 125th St., between St. Nicholas and Morningside avenues (© **212/864-8941;** subway: A, B, C, D to 125th St.), which hosts nightly (except Sun) music ranging from soulful jazz to funky bebop. The music attracts music lovers and players from all walks of life, and the service is just as friendly whether you come from the neighborhood, downtown, or out of town.

include cutting-edge unsigned acts or overlooked talents, play from around 10pm to 2am, followed by a nightly jam session until dawn (and often beyond). No alcohol is served, but that doesn't keep the crowds away—they're happy to come just for the music. Drinks are free with the $10 cover (you're also welcome to BYO), and all ages are welcome. 183 W. 10th St. (just off Seventh Ave.). ✆ **212/929-7565.** www.smallsjazz.com. Subway: 1, 9 to Christopher St.

S.O.B.'s If you like your music hot, hot, hot, S.O.B.'s is the place for you. This is the city's top world-music venue, specializing in Brazilian, Caribbean, and Latin sounds. The packed house dances and sings along nightly to calypso, samba, mambo, African drums, reggae, or other global grooves, united in the high-energy, feel-good vibe. Bookings include top-flight performers from around the globe; Astrud Gilberto, Ruben Blades, King Sunny Ade, Eddie Palmieri, Buckwheat Zydeco, Beausoleil, and the unsurpassed Celia Cruz are only a few of the names who have graced this lively stage. The room's Tropicana Club style has island pizzazz that carries through to the Caribbean-influenced cooking and extensive tropical drinks menu. This place is so popular that it's an excellent idea to book in advance, especially if you'd like table seating. Monday is dedicated to Latin sounds, Tuesday to reggae; Friday features a late-night French Caribbean dance party, while Saturday is reserved for samba. 204 Varick St. (at Houston St.). ✆ **212/243-4940.** www.sobs.com. Subway: 1, 9 to Houston St.

The Village Vanguard What CBGB's is to rock, the Village Vanguard is to jazz. One look at the photos on the walls will show you who's been through since 1935, from Coltrane, Miles, and Monk to recent appearances by Wynton Marsalis and Joshua Redman. Expect a mix of established names and high-quality local talent, including the Vanguard's own jazz orchestra on Monday nights. The sound is great, but sight lines are terrible, so come early for a front table. The crowd can seem either overly serious or overly touristy, but don't let that stop you—you'll always find great music. 178 Seventh Ave. South (just below 11th St.). ✆ **212/255-4037.** www.villagevanguard.net. Subway: 1, 2, 3, 9 to 14th St.

5 Cabaret

An evening spent at a sophisticated cabaret just might be the quintessential New York night on the town. It isn't cheap: Covers can range from $10 to $60, depending on the showroom and the act, and also require two-drink or dinner-check minimums. Always reserve ahead, and get the complete lowdown when you do.

Cafe Carlyle Cabaret doesn't get any better than this. First of all, this is where you'll find Bobby Short—and that's all those who know cabaret need to know. Nothing evokes the essence of Manhattan more than an evening with this quintessential interpreter of Porter and the Gershwins. When he's not in residence, you'll find such rarefied talents as Eartha Kitt and Betty Buckley. The room is intimate and as swanky as they come. Expect a high tab—admission is $60 with $30 per-person minimum; dinner and two people could easily spend $300—but if you're looking for the best of the best, look no further. Value-minded cabaret fans can save by reserving standing room (which usually results in a spot at the bar) for just $35. On most Mondays, Woody Allen joins the Eddy Davis New Orleans Jazz Band on clarinet to swing Dixie style ($75 cover). At the Carlyle hotel, 781 Madison Ave. (at 76th St.). ✆ **212/570-7189.** Closed July–Aug. Subway: 6 to 77th St.

Feinstein's at the Regency *Finds* This intimate and elegant cabaret-style nightclub is the first from Grammy-winning song impresario Michael Feinstein. Cover charges can soar, but you can count on a memorable night of first-quality dining and song, and no other cabaret merges old-school cool and hipster appeal so well. Recent high-wattage talent has included Rosemary Clooney, Keely Smith, Jimmy Webb, the Smothers Brothers, and the man himself. Call ahead to reserve; you can also purchase tickets through Ticketmaster. At the Regency Hotel, 540 Park Ave. (at 61st St.). ✆ **212/339-4095,** or 212/307-4100 for Ticketmaster. www.feinsteinsattheregency.com or www.ticketmaster.com. Subway: 4, 5, 6 to 59th St.

Joe's Pub Joe's Pub isn't exactly your daddy's cabaret. Still, this beautiful—and hugely popular—cabaret and supper club, eloquently named for the legendary Joseph Papp, is everything a New York cabaret should be. Done in an elegant retro-style, the multilevel space serves up an American menu and top-notch entertainment from a more eclectic mix of talent than you'll find on any other cabaret calendar. The sophisticated crowd comes for music and spoken word that ranges from operatic diva Diamanda Galas to solo shows from Broadway stars like Daphne Rubin-Vega (*Rent*) and Tom Wopat (*Annie Get Your Gun*) to first-class pop from husband-and-wife singer/songwriters Michael Penn and Aimee Mann to modern rumba masters Los Munequitos de Matanzas. There's always jazz on the calendar, and don't be surprised if Broadway actors show up on off-nights to exercise their substantial chops. Deejays take over during the late-night hours. At the Joseph Papp Public Theater, 425 Lafayette St. (btwn Astor Place and 4th St.). ✆ **212/539-8777,** or TeleCharge at 212/239-6200 (for advance tickets). www.joespub.com. Subway: 6 to Astor Place.

The Oak Room Recently refurbished to recall its glory days, the Oak Room is one of the city's most intimate, elegant, and sophisticated spots for cabaret. Headliners include such first-rate talents as Andrea Marcovicci, Steve Ross, Dave Frishberg, the marvelous Julie Wilson, and cool-cat jazz guitarist John Pizzarelli, plus occasional lesser names that are destined for greatness. At the Algonquin hotel, 59 W. 44th St. (btwn Fifth and Sixth aves.). ✆ **212/840-6800.** Closed July–Aug. Subway: B, D, F, V to 42nd St.

6 Stand-Up Comedy

Cover charges are generally in the $8 to $20 range, with all-star Carolines going as high as $30 on occasion. Many clubs also have a two-drink minimum. Be sure to ask about the night's cover when you make reservations, which are strongly recommended, *especially* on weekends.

You might also see who's taking the stage at Madison Square Garden's new laugh-a-minute offshoot, **Comedy Garden** (p. 398), where even Robin Williams books in to hone his stand-up chops every once in awhile.

Carolines on Broadway Caroline Hirsch presents today's hottest headliners in her upscale Theater District showroom, which doesn't have a bad seat in the house. You're bound to recognize at least one or two of the established names and hot up-and-comers on the bill in any given week, like Dave Chapelle, Janeane Garofalo, Colin Quinn, Lewis Black, Kathy Griffin, Robert Wuhl, Jimmie Walker ("Dyn-o-mite!"), Pauly Shore, or Jay Mohr. Monday is usually New Talent Night, while HOT97 radio hosts up-and-coming black comedians on select Tuesdays. 1626 Broadway (btwn 49th and 50th sts.). ✆ **212/757-4100.** www.carolines.com. Subway: N, R to 49th St.; 1, 9 to 50th St.

Comedy Cellar *Finds* This intimate subterranean club is the club of choice for stand-up fans in the know, thanks to the best, most consistently impressive lineups in the business. I'll always love the Comedy Cellar for introducing an uproariously funny unknown comic named Ray Romano to me a few years back. 117 MacDougal St. (btwn Bleecker and W. 3rd sts.). ✆ **212/254-3480.** www.comedycellar.com. Subway: A, C, E, F, V, S to W. 4th St. (use 3rd St. exit).

Dangerfield's Dangerfield's is the nightclub version of the comedy club, with a mature crowd and a straight-outta-Vegas atmosphere. The comedians are all veterans of the comedy-club and late-night talk-show circuit. 1118 First Ave. (btwn 61st and 62nd sts.). ✆ **212/593-1650.** www.dangerfieldscomedyclub.com. Subway: N, R to Lexington Ave.; 4, 5, 6, to 59th St.

Gotham Comedy Club *Finds* Here's the city's trendiest, most comfortable, and most sophisticated comedy club. The young talent—Tom Rhodes, Sue Costello, Mitch Fatel, Lewis Black of the *Daily Show*—is red hot. Robert Klein was a regular Wednesday fixture at this writing. Jerry Seinfeld has also been exercising his chops here of late. Look for theme nights like "Comedy Salsa" and "A Very Jewish Christmas." Tuesday is set aside for new talent. 34 W. 22nd St. (btwn Fifth and Sixth aves.). ✆ **212/367-9000.** www.gothamcomedyclub.com. Subway: F, N, R to 23rd St.

Stand-Up New York The Upper West Side's premier stand-up comedy club hosts some of the brightest young comics in the business, plus frequent drop-ins like Dennis Leary, Caroline Rhea, Robin Williams, and Mr. Upper West Side himself, Jerry Seinfeld. 236 W. 78th St. (at Broadway). ✆ **212/595-0850.** www.standupny.com. Subway: 1, 9 to 79th St.

7 Bars & Cocktail Lounges

Rise Bar Rise Bar is doing a lovely job of filling the fancy-cocktails-with-a-side-of-spectacular views bill now that the World Trade Center's glorious Greatest Bar on Earth is gone. Situated on the 14th floor of Ritz-Carlton's brand-new Battery Park hotel (p. 110), this sleek and lovely bar boasts fantastic harbor views starring Lady Liberty, plus a massive waterfront terrace for enjoying warm-weather libations. The bar also benefits from Ritz-Carlton's first-class food service, here featuring sushi and innovative finger foods beautifully presented on tiered serving plates. Reservations are accepted, if you want to guarantee yourself a prime seat. In the Ritz-Carlton New York, Battery Park, 2 West St. (at the end of West St., just north of Battery Place). ✆ **917/790-2525.** Subway: 4, 5 to Bowling Green.

Wall St. Kitchen & Bar Want to rub elbows with some genuine bulls and bears after a hard day of downtown sightseeing? Head to this surprisingly appealing and affordable bar, housed in a spectacular former bank, which specializes in on-tap beers (around 50 are on offer at any given time) and "flight" menus of wines and microbrews for tasting. The familiar bar food is well prepared and reasonably priced. Come on a weekday to enjoy the crowd. Like the true Financial District institution it is, Wall St. Kitchen is open Monday through Friday only. 70 Broad St. (btwn Beaver and S. William sts., about 1½ blocks south of New York Stock Exchange). ✆ **212/797-7070.** Subway: J, M, Z to Broad St.; 4, 5 to Bowling Green.

TRIBECA

Anotherroom This candlelit, comfortably chic wine and beer lounge is the ideal spot for visitors who want a grown-up scene, but one more relaxed, and not quite, well, so *expensive* as that found at the Bubble Lounge (below). Expect a choice selection of brews and wines by the glass, plus friendly service and an atmosphere conducive to conversation. 249 W. Broadway (between N. Moore and Beach sts.). ✆ **212/226-1418.** Subway: A, C, E, 1, 9 to Canal St.

Bubble Lounge From the first cork that popped, this wine bar dedicated to the bubbly was an effervescent hit. More than 300 champagnes and sparkling wines are served in this glamorous living-room setting, more than 30 of them by the glass, to pair with caviar, foie gras, cheese, and elegant sweets. No jeans, sneakers, or baseball caps. There' s live bluesy jazz on Monday and Tuesday. 228 W. Broadway (btwn Franklin and White sts.). ✆ **212/431-3443.** www.bubblelounge.com. Subway: 1, 9 to Franklin St.

Church Lounge The big, superstylish Larry Bogdanow–designed atrium lobby bar and restaurant at the Tribeca Grand Hotel (p. 112) is not quite as trendsetting as it was a year ago, but it's still makes a great place to enjoy a top-flight cocktail and rub elbows with the neighborhood's chic locals (which include just about anybody who has business with Miramax). Dress well, call ahead if you want to experience the height of the action—around 11pm—or if you want a table in the nonsmoking area. 2 Sixth Ave. (at White and Church sts.). ✆ **212/519-6600.** Subway: 1, 9 to Franklin St.; A, C, E to Canal St.

Grace *Finds* This spacious and surprisingly unpretentious lounge has made itself right at home with a sophisticated yet down-to-earth vibe; a good selection of classic cocktails, single-malt scotches, and on-tap beers from the sweeping, welcoming mahogany bar; and an affordable menu of elegant yet unpretentious Pan-Asian–influenced New American dishes. There's an airy dining room in back, too, if you'd like to reserve a nook for yourself. 114 Franklin St. (btwn W. Broadway and Church St.). ✆ **212/343-4200.** www.gracebarandrestaurant.com. Subway: 1, 9 to Franklin St.

The Sporting Club The city's best sports bar is a guy's joint if there ever were one. The space is as big as a linebacker, with giant TV screens at every turn tuned to just about every game on the planet. (Wall Streeters bring their international cohorts here to catch everything from English football to Japanese sumo.) The menu is what you'd expect: wings, burgers, club sandwiches, and *lots* of beer. Reservations accepted (a good idea when a big game's on). When the games are over, this turns into a surprisingly popular singles place. 99 Hudson St. (btwn Franklin and Leonard sts.). ✆ **212/219-0900.** www.thesportingclub.net. Subway: 1, 9 to Franklin St.

Walker's *Finds* Walker's is an old holdout from prefabulous TriBeCa. It's got some charm, with a tin ceiling, a long wooden bar, oldies on the sound system, and cozy tables where you can dine on good, affordable meat-and-potatoes fare. Don't get fancy with your drink orders; stick with Guinness or one of the other drafts. 16 N. Moore St. (at Varick St.). ✆ **212/941-0142.** Subway: 1, 9 to Franklin St.

CHINATOWN

Double Happiness *Finds* The only indicator to the subterranean entrance is a vertical WATCH YOUR STEP sign. Once through the door, you'll find a beautifully designed speakeasy-ish lounge with artistic nods to the neighborhood throughout, plus a wonderfully low-key vibe. The space is large, but a low ceiling and intimate nooks add a hint of romance. The fabulous food is from the upstairs restaurant, Wyanoka, so this is a great place to satisfy the munchies, too. Don't miss the green tea martini, an inspired house creation. 173 Mott St. (btwn Grand and Broome sts.). ✆ **212/941-1282.** Subway: 6 to Spring St.

THE LOWER EAST SIDE

Also consider **Le Pere Pinard,** 175 Ludlow St., south of Houston (✆ **212/777-4917**), a terrific—and *très français*—wine bar; see p. 173.

Abaya *Finds* A flight of cool new hangouts continues to energize the bar scene, and the best of the bunch is Abaya. The *Clockwork Orange*–inspired '70s-chic club offers both style and substance: The design is futuristic but comfortable, the Mediterranean finger-foods menu is *Zagat*-worthy, the deejay talent spinning eclectic house music is first-rate, and the one-of-a-kind cocktails include the tasty Tang martini. 244 E. Houston St. (btwn aves. A and B). ✆ **212/777-7467.** Subway: F to Second Ave.

Barramundi *Finds* This nice little lounge is most notable for its fairy-tale outdoor garden, extremely friendly staff, and settled-in feel in a neighborhood overrun by hipster copycats in recent years. Come on a weeknight to snare a table in the little corner of heaven out back. A crackling fireplace makes Barramundi almost as appealing on cool nights, too. 147 Ludlow St. (btwn Stanton and Rivington sts.). ✆ **212/569-6900.** Subway: F to Second Ave.

Idlewild *Value* It may look unapproachable from the street, with nothing but an unmarked stainless-steel facade, but inside you'll find a fun, easygoing bar that's perfect for lovers of retro-kitsch. The interior is a larger-scale repro of a jet airplane, complete with reclining seats, tray tables, and too-small bathrooms that will transport you back to your favorite midair moments. The crowd is a cool mix of downtown locals and hip tourists, and the deejay spins a listener-friendly mix of light techno, groovy disco in the funkadelic vein, and '80s tunes. Drinks are downright affordable. 145 E. Houston St. (btwn First and Second aves. on the south side of Houston). ✆ **212/477-5005.** Subway: F to Second Ave.

Lansky Lounge & Grill This faux speakeasy is a wonderful throwback to the retro-cool '30s. Lansky Lounge is one of the Lower East Side's classiest scenes, with a cool-as-a-cucumber zoot-suit vibe that has outlived New York's flirtation with neoswing. The special martinis and infused vodkas are terrific, and the 10-ounce Cosmos are some of the best in town. Come on a weeknight, when the crowd is more local than bridge-and-tunnel. They've now taken over the adjoining Ratner's dining room and transformed it into a stylish chophouse, in case you want to eat, too. Look for the neon-red "L." 104 Norfolk St. (btwn Rivington and Delancey sts.). ✆ **212/677-9489.** www.lanskylounge.com. Subway: F to Delancey St.

Whiskey Ward *Finds* Here's the second-best bar in town for serious whiskey fans (only behind the East Village's dba): First-class single malts and bourbons to choose from, and absolutely no pretensions. Nice on-tap and bottled beer selection, too. 121 Essex St. (btwn Rivington and Delancey sts.). ✆ **212/477-2998.** Subway: F to Delancey St.

SOHO

You might also consider the easygoing Down Under bar **24/8 Lounge,** located below Aussie restaurant **Eight Mile Creek** (p. 176), 240 Mulberry St., between Prince and Spring streets (✆ **212/431-4635;** www.eightmilecreek.com). Thursday is deejay night, while Sunday is set aside for groovy live music.

Fanelli's Cafe *Value* Deep in the heart of trendy SoHo, this place is classic New York pub: The long bar is propped up by regulars, and the corner door and pressed-tin ceiling have locked in the 1847 atmosphere (this is the second-oldest continuously operating establishment in the city), the goliath burgers are great, and the on-tap beer is parceled out in pint glasses. Beware: The noise level really starts to escalate around 7pm. 94 Prince St. (at Mercer St.). ✆ **212/226-9412.** Subway: N, R to Prince St.

Merc Bar Notable for its long tenure in the fickle world of beautiful-people bars, upscale Merc Bar has mellowed nicely. The decor bespeaks civilized rusticity with warm woods, a canoe over the bar, copper-top tables, and butter-leather banquettes—think SoHo goes to Yosemite. A great place to nestle into a comfortable couch with your honey and enjoy the scene. The European martini (Stoli raspberry and Chambord) is divine. Look carefully, because there's no sign. 151 Mercer St. (btwn Prince and Houston sts.). ✆ **212/966-2727.** www.mercbar.com. Subway: N, R to Prince St.

Ñ On a charming cobbled street that somehow escaped gentrification, Ñ (pronounced like the Spanish letter, *eh*-nyeh) is long, narrow, candlelit, and hip. Despite its cool, the staff is warm, and the extensive, award-winning sherry list is excellent. There's also a nice, fruity sangria, plus a full bar for non-Spanish tastes. You can order some of the city's best tapas, which come out of a very tiny kitchen in back. 33 Crosby St. (btwn Grand and Broome sts.). ✆ **212/219-8856.** Subway: N, R to Prince St.; 6 to Spring St.

Pravda This Bolshevik-chic lounge (which careful watchers might recognize from *Sex and the City*) makes pricey but perfect martinis for a classy crowd drawn in by the romantic pre-Gorbachev revolutionary vibe. More than 70 vodkas are on hand from 18 countries. There's plenty of Russian caviar on hand to wash down with those pricey cocktails, plus a full humidor for the cigar-bar crowd. There's no sign, so look for the light that says "281" on the east side of the street and walk down the stairwell. 281 Lafayette St. (btwn Houston and Prince sts.). ✆ **212/226-4944** or 212/334-5015. Subway: N to Prince St.

Puck Fair *Finds* This gleaming pub looks as if it could have been lifted wholesale out of an equally stylish corner of London and plunked down on this side of the pond. It's genuine through and through, but a young crowd and a hip soundtrack make it feel fresh rather than old man-neighborhoody (like Fanelli's). Twenty beers are on tap (including Guinness, of course). If you can snare a table, the petite mezzanine makes a great spot to sit down and dig into the surprisingly good pub grub. 298 Lafayette St. (just south of Houston St.). ✆ **212/431-1200.** www.puckfair.citysearch.com. Subway: F to Broadway/Lafayette St.

THE EAST VILLAGE & NOHO

In addition to the choices below, also consider the magical **Fez,** 380 Lafayette St., at Great Jones St. (✆ **212/533-2680;** www.feznyc.com), a dimly lit Moroccan-themed bar and lounge that I much prefer to the downstairs performance space.

B Bar & Grill Originally a Gulf gas station, this cavernous bar/dining room is '60s modern and attractive, with high ceilings, comfy booths, retro-style mood lighting, a large central bar, and the latest alterna-hits on the sound system. But the 6,500-square-foot tree-filled courtyard—alfresco space that's otherwise unheard of in this city—is the biggest draw. The bar offers a regular selection of signature drinks, including a Ketel One martini that even Bond could love. The reasonably priced food is better than you'd expect. Come early for quiet, later for a pretentious party guarded by a velvet rope and peopled by a cliquish crowd. 40 E. 4th St. (at Bowery). ✆ **212/475-2220.** www.bbarandgrill.com. Subway: 6 to Bleecker St.

Burp Castle *Finds* This oddball theme bar is a must for serious beer lovers. It's styled as a "Temple of Beer Worship," complete with medieval-inspired decor, choral music on the sound system, and soft-spoken waiters in monkish garb. Before you have time to let the weirdness of it all sink in, you'll be distracted by the incomparable beer list. There are more than 500 bottled and on-tap beers to choose from—including a phenomenal collection of Trappist ales, of course. 41 E. 7th St. (btwn Second and Third aves.). ✆ **212/982-4576.** Subway: 6 to Astor Place.

dba *Finds* One of my New York favorites, dba has completely bucked the loungey trend that has taken over the city, instead remaining firmly and resolutely an unpretentious neighborhood bar. dba is a beer- and scotch-lover's paradise, with a massive drink menu on giant chalkboards. Owner Ray Deter specializes in British-style cask-conditioned ales (the kind that you pump by hand) and stocks a phenomenal collection of single-malt scotches. Ray has enclosed the back garden, transforming it into a cozy East Village beer garden. Excellent jukebox, too. 41 First Ave. (btwn 2nd and 3rd sts.). ✆ **212/475-5097.** www.drinkgoodstuff.com. Subway: F to Second Ave.

Temple Bar *Finds* One of the first comers to New York's lounge scene, Temple Bar is still a gorgeous deco hangout, with a long L-shaped bar leading to a lovely seating area with velvet drapes, romantic backlighting, and Sinatra crooning in the background. Cocktails simply don't get any better than the classic martini (with just a kiss of vermouth) or the smooth-as-penoir silk Manhattan (Johnnie Walker Black, sweet vermouth, bitters). Elegant finger foods provide a reason to never leave. Bring a date—and feel free to invite me along anytime. Look for the petroglyph-like lizards on the otherwise-unmarked facade. 332 Lafayette St. (just north of Houston St., on the west side of the street). ✆ **212/925-4242.** Subway: 6 to Bleecker St.

Tom & Jerry's (288 Bar) *Finds* Here's an extremely pleasing neighborhood bar minus the grunge factor that usually plagues such joints. The place has an authentic local vibe, and the youngish, artsy crowd is unpretentious and chatty. The beer selection is very good and the mixed drinks are better than average. Flea-market hounds will enjoy the vintage collection of "Tom & Jerry" punch-bowl sets behind the bar, and creative types will enjoy the rotating collection of works from local artists, which changes monthly. There's no sign, but you'll spy the action through the plate-glass window on the east side of Elizabeth Street just north of Houston. 288 Elizabeth St. ✆ **212/260-5045.** Subway: 6 to Bleecker St.

GREENWICH VILLAGE & THE MEAT-PACKING DISTRICT

Bowlmor/Pressure *Finds* Super-cool Bowlmor isn't your daddy's bowling alley: deejays spin, martinis flow, candy-colored balls knock down day-glo pins, and strikes and spares are automatically tallied into the wee hours. Frankly, Bowlmor is a blast. Once you're finished with your 10-pin—or while you're waiting for your lane—head upstairs to the palatial rooftop lounge Pressure, housed in a 16,000-square-foot inflated bubble and boasting designer-mod furnishings, a sexy cocktail menu that includes a luscious chocolate martini (infused with Godiva chocolate liquer), a fleet of pool tables, and always-on movie screens adding an arty-party flair. 110 University Pl. (btwn 12th and 13th sts.). ✆ **212/255-8188** (Bowlmor) or 212/352-1161 (Pressure). www.bowlmor.com or www.pressurenyc.com. Subway: 4, 5, 6, L, N, R to 14th St./Union Sq.

Chumley's A classic. Many bars in New York date their beginnings to Prohibition, but Chumley's still has the vibe. The crowd doesn't date back nearly as far,

Late-Night Bites

All this barhopping and clubbing really works up an appetite. Where to eat?

Open until 4am nightly, **Blue Ribbon,** 97 Sullivan St., between Prince and Spring streets in SoHo (© **212/274-0404**), is where the city's top chefs come to unwind after they close their own kitchens for the night. Thanks to a top-drawer oyster bar and excellent comfort food, this cozy bistro is always packed, so expect a wait.

Other great choices for after-hours eats include the funky Francophile diner **Florent** (p. 187), and authentic bistro **Pastis** (p. 186), both in the red-hot Meat-Packing District. TriBeCa has the **Odeon** (p. 169), an attractive and affordable Art Deco bistro that's one of the top after-hours eateries in town, but I prefer **Le Zinc** (p. 169), a warm and welcoming bistro from the folks behind chic Chanterelle. A quintessential late-night choice in far west Chelsea is the **Empire Diner** (p. 189), a throwback shrine to the slicked-up all-American diner where the after-hours crowd may be the best people-watching in town. In SoHo, consider sexy siren **Balthazar** (p. 174), the Claudette Colbert of bistros, which serves until 1:30am weeknights, 2:30am weekends.

In the East Village, head to **Veselka** (p. 182), a comfortable and appealing diner offering authentic Eastern European fare at rock-bottom prices; **Katz's Delicatessen** (p. 173) for first-class Jewish deli eats Friday and Saturday until 2:30am; or **First** (p. 178) for splashier late-night fare courtesy of chef Sam DeMarco. Everybody's favorite Chinatown restaurant, **New York Noodletown** (p. 172), is open until 3:30am nightly, while nearby **Umberto's Clam House** (p. 171), serves up authentic Little Italy eats and ambience until 4am.

In the Theater District, French brasserie **Pigalle** (p. 204) has seriously stylized the 24-hour dining scene, while **Won Jo** (p. 209) offers Midtowners Korean barbecue as a round-the-clock option. Theatergoers can also feast on first-class pastrami and cheesecake until 3:45am at **Carnegie Deli** (p. 210), until 2am at the **Stage Deli** (p. 210).

Also, remember that many of the bars and cocktail lounges listed in this chapter—like Bongo, Grace, Justin's, Lansky Lounge, Lot 61, Merchant's, Old Town, Puck Fair, Spread, Kanvas, Double Happiness, Flute, the Russian Vodka Room, and Heartland Brewery—serve food, from full meals to munchies, into the wee hours.

however. Come to warm yourself by the fire and indulge in a once-forbidden pleasure: beer. There's actually a good selection of on-taps and microbrews. The door is unmarked, with a metal grille on the small window; another entrance is at 58 Barrow St., which takes you in through a back courtyard. 86 Bedford St. (at Barrow St.). © **212/675-4449.** Subway: 1, 9 to Christopher St.

Hogs & Heifers This roadhouse-style bar is it: the *Coyote Ugly* bar, complete with "bra tree," bar-top hip shaking, and free-flowing shots. It's pretty much devoid of its original rough-and-tumble local appeal, but still offers a good bit of fun for those who don't mind the tourist trappings. The bridge-and-tunnel, frat-boyish crowd gets pretty wild as the night wears on, especially on weekends. 859 Washington St. (at 13th St.). ✆ **212/929-0655.** Subway: A, C, E, L to 14th St. Also at 1843 First Ave., btwn 95th and 96th sts. (✆ **212/722-8635;** subway: 6 to 96th St.).

Hudson Bar & Books This former exclusive gentleman's club maintains a similar appeal as an elegant bar. Among the draws are cool jazz, a magnificent copper-topped marble bar, good lighting, comfortable seating, and an extensive—and expensive—champagne, cocktails, cognacs, and malts menu. Pleasantly, the crowd is comprised more of at-home locals than preening tourists. A great date place. 636 Hudson St. (btwn Horatio and Jane sts.). ✆ **212/229-2642.** Subway: A, C, E, L to 14th St.

White Horse Tavern Poets and literary buffs pop into this 1880 pub to pay their respects to Dylan Thomas, who tipped his last jar here before shuffling off this mortal coil. Best enjoyed in the warm weather when there's outdoor drinking, or at happy hour for the cheap drafts that draw in a big frat-boy and post-frat yuppie crowd. 567 Hudson St. (at 11th St.). ✆ **212/243-9260.** Subway: 1, 9 to Christopher St.

CHELSEA

Bongo *Value* This casual, comfortable mid-century-modern lounge is the place to come for cocktails that are well made and a great value considering their bathtub size. Don't miss the French martini, made with Vox vodka and Lillet—yum! Even better: Bongo boasts a full raw-bar menu—a half dozen varieties of oysters, cherrystones and littlenecks, even lobster and caviar—and an excellent lobster roll. The crowd is hip, but, happily, not too trendy. Come early if you want to have space to sit and eat. 299 Tenth Ave. (btwn 27th and 28th sts.). ✆ **212/947-3654.** Subway: C, E to 23rd St.

Chelsea Brewing Company Decent American pub grub, good house-label brews, and great Hudson River views from a terrific waterfront terrace make this an excellent choice for a few beers and some easygoing socializing. Even if it's too cold (or crowded) for alfresco enjoyment, you'll find an attractive, high-ceilinged wood-and-brass brewpub inside—nothing unique, but comfortable and view-endowed. At Pier 59, Chelsea Piers, Eleventh Ave. and 18th St. ✆ **212/336-6440.** www.chelseabrewingco.com. Subway: C, E to 23rd St.

Justin's Surprise, surprise—Sean "P. Diddy" Combs's tony soul fooder is the hangout of choice for hip-hop stars and music industry execs. You can dine here on upscale Caribbean soul food (reservations suggested), but come instead for the late-night scene in the sophisticated bar if you're up for some top-notch people-watching. Be prepared for the velvet rope on busy nights (Tuesday is particularly rife with industry folks). 31 W. 21st St. (btwn Fifth and Sixth aves.). ✆ **212/352-0599.** Subway: F, N, R to 23rd St.

Kanvas Apropos to its location, just a stone's throw from west Chelsea's clutch of cutting-edge art gallery, this sleek Chelsea lounge doubles as art gallery itself, so it makes a great place to commune with an artsy crowd. It's a plush designer space, with a classic long-wood bar up front, cozy banquettes in back, and artwork that rotates monthly. The martini menu boasts 2 dozen varieties, including a mint chocolate chip version; the Brazilian *caipirinhas* are also notable, and the finger foods are better than at most similar spots. While the mood is usually relaxed, art-opening nights can be unpleasantly hectic. 219 Ninth Ave. (btwn 23rd and 24th sts.). ✆ **212/727-2616.** www.kanvasnyc.com. Subway: C, E to 23rd St.

Lot 61 This cavernous hot spot in far west Chelsea has always been my favorite of the shallow fashionista hangouts, and it's as hot as ever. The warehouse-meets-*Wallpaper* design is so humorously high style that you just gotta love it—where else are you going to recline on rubber sofas rescued from mental hospitals, surrounded by oversize art from contemporary bad boys like Damien Hirst? Even the martini menu is a hoot, boasting 61 versions of the classic cocktail (this must be a record). So as not to find yourself cramped into the front bar, make a reservation in the lounge, where you can sip Cosmos and graze from a surprisingly terrific menu of finger foods and other light dishes. Earlier is better; let the Giselle Bündchens in training fill up the room around you. Dress well, take a taxi, look carefully for the door (the logo is faint), and brush off the withering looks from the help. It's easy to catch a cab on the way out, as there's a garage on the same block. 550 W. 21st St. (near 11th Ave.). ✆ **212/243-6555.** www.lot61.com. Subway: C, E to 23rd St.

Merchant's New York New York's young working crowd just loves this place. For good reason: It's attractive, comfortable, and mixes a great straight-ahead cocktail. On the ground floor is a stylish living room–like bar, with a mezzanine for dinner. In the downstairs lounge a fireplace roars, usually year-round; there's also streetside seating in warm weather. The food is good, too. 112 Seventh Ave. So. (btwn 16th and 17th sts.). ✆ **212/366-7267.** Subway: 1, 9 to 18th St.

Serena *Finds* Unwilling to await the first signs of flagging, this plush and popular basement boîte has managed to stay fresh by reinventing itself in 2002. Done in deep, sexy reds, Serena is again as hip as can be—I've even spotted mixmaster Moby here. It's relatively unpretentious considering its hot-spot status; still, dress the part if you want to make it past the doorman, especially on weekends. The crowd is young and pretty, and the schizophrenic music mix is a blast—think Fatboy Slim meets ABBA meets Foghat, and you'll get the picture. In the basement level of the Hotel Chelsea, 222 W. 23rd St. (btwn Seventh and Eighth aves.). ✆ **212/255-4646.** Subway: C, E, 1, 9 to 23rd St.

THE FLATIRON DISTRICT, UNION SQUARE & GRAMERCY PARK

Also consider the **Old Town Bar & Restaurant** (p. 194), 45 E. 18th St., between Broadway and Park Avenue South (✆ **212/529-6732**), a genuine tin-ceiling 19th-century bar that makes a terrific place to soak up some old New York atmosphere.

Eugene *Finds* This sumptuous Art-Deco supper club was born out of the 1930s golden-age-of-nightclubs tradition, but it's thoroughly modern in style and attitude. It's the party venue of choice among celebs, and for good reason: Eugene always hosts a party that's both sophisticated and kick-up-your-heels fun. Come in early to sink into a sumptuous club chair and toss back a couple of perfectly mixed cocktails, or make dinner reservations in top toque Sam DeMarco's sleek New American dining room. Come 10pm, put on your dancing shoes, because the dance floor is spacious and the deejay spins fun, listener-friendly dance tracks. A real find! Be sure to dress well. 27 W. 24th St. (btwn Fifth and Sixth aves.). ✆ **212/462-0999.** www.eugene.nyc.com. Subway: N, R to 23rd St.

Flute *Finds* This ultra-romantic bubbly bar is a Flatiron District favorite among a chic crowd drawn by the luxe setting and the city's best fleet of champagnes in the cooler. I like it better than TriBeCa's Bubble Lounge (p. 410) thanks to the gorgeous bi-level design, the terrific French-Vietnamese finger food, and the sophisticated but not snooty ambience. Probably the best date place in town. Reservations never hurt, especially if you're a small party. 40 E. 20th St. (btwn Broadway and Park Ave. South). ✆ **212/529-7870.** Subway: 6 to 23rd St. Also at 205 W. 54th St., (btwn Seventh Ave. and Broadway). ✆ **212/265-5169;** subway: B, D, E to Seventh Ave.; 1, 9 to 50th St.

Heartland Brewery The food leaves a bit to be desired, but the house-brewed beers are first-rate. Great American Beer Festival three-time award-winner Farmer Jon's Oatmeal Stout is always on hand, as are three or four hand-crafted ales and a lager or two. A good selection of single malts and tequilas, too. The wood-paneled two-level bar is big and appealing, but expect a loud, boisterous after-work crowd, plus a good number of Germans and Brits (testament to the quality of the brew). 35 Union Sq. West (at 16th St.). ✆ **212/645-3400.** www.heartlandbrewery.com. Subway: L, N, R, 4, 5, 6 to 14th St./Union Sq. Also at 1285 Sixth Ave. (at 51st St., across from Radio City Music Hall). ✆ **212/582-8244.** Subway: B, D, F, V to 47th–50th sts./Rockefeller Center.

Park Avenue Country Club This place bills itself as a "sports cafe," and it is indeed more polished than your average beer-and-pretzels sports bar. That said, it's a very comfortable place to hunker down over a club sandwich and a beer to watch the game. There are TVs at every turn (including ten giant screens), with satellite dishes pulling in practically every game happening on the globe. 381 Park Ave. So. (at 27th St.). ✆ **212/685-3636.** www.parkavenuecountryclub.com. Subway: 6 to 28th St.

Pete's Tavern The oldest continually operating establishment in the city, Pete's opened while Lincoln was still president. It reeks of genuine history—and, more importantly, there's Guinness on tap, a terrific happy hour, and a St. Patrick's Day party that makes the neighbors crazy. The crowd is a mix of locals from ritzy Gramercy Park and more down-to-earth types. 129 E. 18th St. (at Irving Place). ✆ **212/473-7676.** Subway: L, N, R, 4, 5, 6 to 14th St./Union Sq.

Slate The former Chelsea Billiards has been upscaled into Slate, the sleekest, chicest pool hall in town; in fact, *Sex and the City* has even filmed here. The room is dressed in fiery reds and cool greys with sexy fiber optics playing light tricks at the bar; a deejay spins hip-hop, top 40, and easy techno tunes as you rack 'em up. Still, don't be fooled: This is a serious billiard palace, with 34 top-flight Steel and Brunswick tables. Excellent selection of international beers as well as cocktail-esque libations. 54 W. 21st St. (btwn Fifth and Sixth aves.). ✆ **212/989-0096.** www.chelseabilliard.citysearch.com. Subway: N, R to 23rd St.

Spread/Coal *Finds* This sexy lounge/restaurant hybrid is the best of a popular new breed thanks to low-slung designer interiors, inspired cocktails, chef Michael Navarro's innovative small-plates menu and terrific sushi bar, and an ambience long on comfort and short on attitude. Seating is in living room–style nooks; a savvy deejay adds to the lounge-style allure. You can enjoy just cocktails, a light appetizer spread, a full meal, or just dessert: The coconut sushi—rice soaked in coconut milk, topped with slices of pineapple and kiwi, chocolate sauce instead of soy, candied ginger, and shaved chocolate chopsticks—is one of the best sweet finishes in town. Or head downstairs to subterranean lounge Coal, which offers all comers a VIP vibe in an almost futuristic setting; a cozy spot next to the fireplace will definitely impress your date. At the Marcel hotel, 323 Third Ave. (at 24th St.). ✆ **212/683-8880.** www.spreadnyc.com. Subway: 6 to 23rd St.

TIMES SQUARE & MIDTOWN WEST

Joe Allen (p. 203), the legendary Broadway pub on Restaurant Row, 326 W. 46th St., between Eighth and Ninth avenues (✆ **212/581-6464**), is an excellent choice for an after-theater beer or cocktail even if you don't dine here. For a top-flight microbrew, visit the second branch of **Heartland Brewery** (p. 417) across from Radio City at 1285 Sixth Ave., at 51st Street (© **212/582-8244**). Additionally, the original location of **Flute** (p. 416) is a swanky subterranean champagne lounge that makes an ideal place for couples to canoodle over glasses of bubbly and elegant light bites.

Algonquin Bar The splendid oak-paneled lobby of this venerable literati-favored Arts-and-Crafts hotel is the comfiest and most welcoming in the city, made to linger over pre- or post-theater cocktails. You'll feel the spirit of Dorothy Parker and the legendary Algonquin Round Table that pervades the room. Try the Matilda, a light, refreshing blend of orange juice, Absolut Mandarin, triple sec, and champagne, named after the Algonquin's legendary feline in residence. Adjacent is the pubby, clubby **Blue Bar,** home to a rotating collection of Hirschfeld drawings that's well worth checking out. 59 W. 44th St. (btwn Fifth and Sixth aves.). © **212/840-6800.** Subway: B, D, F, V to 42nd St.

Carnegie Club *Finds* Like sister lounge Campbell Apartment (p. 420), this swellegant lounge is another architecturally magnificent space with soaring ceilings and an intimate mezzanine, plus a grand stone fireplace—a Gothic mood warmed up with plush, contemporary furnishings and a romantic vibe. "Weekends with Sinatra" stars Cary Hoffman and the Stan Rubin Orchestra in a wonderfully evocative—and surprisingly exact—cabaret show featuring the music of Frank Sinatra (two shows nightly on Sat; cover $30, plus $15 minimum). There's also live swing on Friday. Reservations are recommended on live music nights. 156 W. 56th St. (btwn Sixth and Seventh aves.). © **212/957-9676.** Subway: B, Q to 57th St.

Hudson Bar The Hudson, the newest hotel from enfant terrible duo Ian Schrager and Philippe Starck, also boasts one of the best and hottest new bars on the scene. Outfitted like a futuristic canteen, Hudson Bar glows from below with an underlit floor, while the low ceiling wears a Crayola-like fresco by Francesco Clemente. In between you'll find a tony, older-than-you'd-expect crowd. The one-of-a-kind cocktail menu is terrific, too. Enter at street level, on the Ninth Avenue side of the hotel's main entrance; dress well to avoid attitude. 356 W. 58th St. (btwn Eighth and Ninth aves.), New York, NY 10019. © **212/554-6000.** Subway: A, B, C, D, 1, 9 to 59th St./Columbus Circle.

M Bar *Finds* This library-style lounge transcends its hotel-bar status with a lovely circular bar, a first-rate cocktail menu, comfortable seating, a dark and romantic Art Deco mood, and a warmth that will make pretension-phobes feel right at home. Prices are reasonable too, especially considering the neighborhood. The weekly Wednesday jazz night has turned into a big hit with locals—so much so that the calendar has expanded to include cabaret nights and wine tastings. A real gem! Adjacent to the Mansfield hotel, 12 W. 44th St. (btwn Fifth and Sixth aves.). © **212/944-6050.** Subway: B, D, F, V to 42nd St.

Mickey Mantle's Of course, it's terribly sad that the Mick, who gave his life to the bottle, should have his name on a bar. But if you're a fan, it's definitely worth a visit to his classic mahogany-and-brass sports bar and restaurant, which chronicles his life and career in photos. The crowd is a laid-back mix of white-collar after-workers and interested tourists. Classic moderately priced burger fare is available, plus the requisite souvenirs. A great place to watch the game. 42 Central Park South (btwn Fifth and Sixth aves.). © **212/688-7777.** www.mickeymantles.com. Subway: F to 57th St.

Morrell Wine Bar & Cafe One of the leading wine stockists in America (p. 382) has created the ideal place to sample the first-rate collection of vintages in comfort. Situated at the heart of Rockefeller Center, just across the alley from the plaza, the bi-level space is contemporary and comfortable and attended by an extremely knowledgeable wait staff. In addition to the extensive bar and lounge space, a nice New American menu is also served; make reservations for dinner. 1 Rockefeller Plaza (at 49th St.). ✆ **212/262-7700.** www.morrellwinebar.com. Subway: B, D, F, V to 47th–50th sts./Rockefeller Center.

Rainbow Room Closed to the public a few years back, the legendary Rainbow Room is now back in the mix. The Grill Room is open daily for lunch and dinner, serving overpriced a la carte Continental fare plus a mammoth Sunday all-you-can-eat brunch, but don't bother. Instead, head up to the bar in the Grill Room, where you can sit for the price of a too-expensive cocktail, soaking in the ambience, views, and live piano music. No jeans or sneakers, please. 30 Rockefeller Plaza (entrance on 49th St. between Fifth and Sixth aves.), 64th floor. ✆ **212/632-5000.** www.cipriani.com/rainbowroom.html. Subway: B, D, F, V to 47th–50th sts./Rockefeller Center.

Russian Vodka Room *Finds* This terrific old-school lounge is a real Theater District find. It's not going to win any style awards, but it's extremely comfortable and knows what's what when it comes to vodkas. There are more than 50 on hand, plus the RVR's own miraculous infusions; you can order an iced rack of six if you can't decide between such yummy flavors as cranberry, apple cinnamon, ginger, horseradish, and more (the raspberry makes a perfect Cosmo). The 30-something-and-up crowd is peopled with post-Soviet imports as well as New Yorkers in the know about this best-kept secret. The Russian nibbles are top flight, too, and you can reserve a table for full dinner in the back dining room. Come early if you want to snag a bar table. 265 W. 52nd St. (btwn Broadway and Eighth Ave.). ✆ **212/307-5835.** Subway: C, E, 1, 9 to 50th St.

Tír Na Nóg This festive place is a standout among the Irish pubs that line Eighth Avenue in the shadow of Penn Station. The handsome decor lends the place a genuine Celtic vibe, as does the Murphy's on tap and the lilt of the friendly bartender. The bar has quickly established itself among both locals and bridge-and-tunnel types for its unpretentious, lively air. There's good upscale pub grub, a small dance floor, and live foot-stompin' Irish music Friday and Saturday nights. The ideal place to celebrate St. Patrick's Day. 5 Penn Plaza (Eighth Ave. between 33rd and 34th sts.). ✆ **212/630-0249.** www.tirnanognyc.com. Subway: A, C, E to 34th St./Penn Station.

MIDTOWN EAST & MURRAY HILL

Cozying up to the long bar at **Guastavino's** (p. 212), 409 E. 59th St., between First and York avenues (✆ **212/980-2455**), makes a great way to admire this under-the-59th Street–bridge restaurant's soaring architecture for the mere price of a drink.

Beekman Bar & Books Located just off tony Beekman Place, this genteel library-inspired lounge boasts cherry bookcases lined with leather-bound volumes, cozy seating alcoves, and a roaring fireplace. A jazz trio plays on Friday and Saturday. Behind Bar & Books is the renowned **Cigar Bar,** an exquisite space reminiscent of an old-world gentleman's club, and regarded as the first dedicated cigar lounge in the country. 889 First Ave. (at 50th St.). ✆ **212/980-9314.** Subway: 6 to 51st St.

Bull & Bear The Bull & Bear is like a gentlemen's pub, with brass-studded red leather chairs, a waistcoated staff, and a grand troika-shaped mahogany bar

Tips Additional Sources for Bar- & Club-Hoppers

If you want even more bars and clubs to choose from, pick up the pocket-size ***Shecky's Bar, Club & Lounge Guide*** or the annual ***Time Out New York Eating & Drinking*** guide, both produced annually and available in most city bookstores. A copy of glossy weekly city guide ***Time Out New York*** will also do the trick, especially if you're looking for the latest dance parties or other scheduled events, from comedy to cabaret.

You'll find a wealth of current bar and club listings—far more than we have room to include in these pages—at **Shecky's online** ★ **(newyork.sheckys.com)**; Shelly's also maintains a hot line for up-to-the-minute nightlife news at ✆ **212/777-BARS.**

Other useful online sources include **www.nymetro.com, www.newyork.citysearch.com,** and **www.digitalcity.com/newyork.**

polished to a high sheen at the center of the room. Still, it's plenty comfy for casual drinkers. Ask Oscar, who's been here for more than 30 years, or one of the other accomplished bartenders to blend you a classic cocktail. Or just order a beer—either way, you'll be right at home here. An ideal place to kick back after a hard day of sightseeing. At the Waldorf=Astoria. 301 Park Ave. (btwn 49th and 50th sts.). ✆ **212/872-4900.** Subway: 6 to 51st St.

Cellar Bar Midtown's latest attention-grabbing boîte is a sumptuous, barrel-vaulted lounge attracting a well-heeled cocktail crowd with pricey but perfect cocktails and international deejay talent, including Parisian turntable superstar Stéphane Pompougnac, who spins monthly. Ideal for a romantic tête-a-tête on quieter nights. In the Bryant Park Hotel, 40 W. 40th St. (btwn Fifth and Sixth aves.). ✆ **212/642-2260.** Subway: B, D, F, V to 42nd St.

The Campbell Apartment This swank lounge on the mezzanine level at Grand Central Terminal has been created out of the former business office of prewar businessman John W. Campbell, who transformed the space into a pre-Renaissance palace worthy of a Medici. The high-ceilinged room has been restored to its full Florentine glory, and serves wines and champagnes by the glass, single-malt scotches, fine stogies, and haute noshies to a well-heeled commuting crowd. Try to snag a seat in the little-used upstairs room if you want some quiet. Call ahead before heading over, as the space tends to be closed for private parties on a rather frequent basis. No sneakers, baseball caps, athletic wear, or ripped jeans. In Grand Central Terminal, 15 Vanderbilt Ave. ✆ **212/953-0409.** Subway: S, 4, 5, 6, 7 to 42nd St./Grand Central.

The Ginger Man The big bait at this appealing upscale beer bar is the 66 gleaming tap handles lining the wood-and-brass bar, dispensing everything from Sierra Nevada and Hoegaarden to cask-conditioned ales. The cavernous space has a clubby feel. Cohiba-toking Wall Streeters (and the young men and women they flirt with) lounge on sofas and chairs, while non-smokers have a comfortable room all to themselves. The limited menu is well prepared, and prices are better than you'd expect from an upmarket place like this. 11 E. 36th St. (btwn Fifth and Madison aves.). ✆ **212/532-3740.** Subway: 6 to 33rd St.

King Cole Room The birthplace of the Bloody Mary, this theatrical spot may just be New York's best classic hotel bar. The Maxfield Parrish mural alone is worth the price of a classic cocktail (ask the bartender to tell you about the "hidden" meaning of the painting). The sophisticated setting demands proper attire, so dress for the occasion. Avoid the after-work hours at holiday time, when the oppressive crowd can ruin the mood. An elegant bar-food menu is available. At the St. Regis hotel, 2 E. 55th St. (at Fifth Ave.). © **212/339-6721.** Subway: E, F to 53rd St.

Monkey Bar This legendary bar and restaurant has experienced quite a resurgence since—you guessed it—Carrie and Mr. Big hooked up here on *Sex and the City*. It definitely deserved the attention: The swanky space is dolled up like a Hollywood supper club circa the 1930s, the drinks are faultless, and the legendary monkey murals are worth a look alone. Skip the dining room and head directly to the piano bar for the ultimate Monkey Bar experience. At the Hotel Elysee, 60 E. 54th St. (btwn Madison and Park aves.). © **212/838-2600.** Subway: 6 to 51st St.

Oak Bar And they do mean oak! The rich wood sets an elegant tone throughout this clubby, almost medieval beer hall. Sumptuous, high-backed red chairs and old-time waiters set the right mood for the after-work power crowd. The bar gets very crowded after 5pm, but the atmosphere always remains sophisticated and old world. For something a bit more casual, try the hotel's **Oyster Bar,** a wonderfully authentic British Isles pub, instead. At the Plaza hotel, 768 Fifth Ave. (at 59th St.). © **212/759-3000.** Subway: N, R to 60th St.

Pen-Top Bar & Terrace *Moments* This petite penthouse bar offers some of Midtown's most dramatic views, straight down fabulous Fifth Avenue in both directions. Best of all is the huge rooftop patio, Midtown's best open-air spot on warm evenings; it's much bigger than the bar itself. Expect an extremely well-heeled crowd that doesn't mind the big tab that follows cocktails here. The Pen-Top is extremely popular, so don't be surprised if you can't get in, especially on nights when the weather isn't accommodating to alfresco revelers. On the 23rd floor of the Peninsula hotel, 700 Fifth Ave. (at 55th St.). © **212/956-2888.** Subway: E, F to Fifth Ave.

Villard Bar & Lounge This decadent two-floor lounge is a divine place to celebrate over a cocktail and enjoy the opulent McKim, Mead & White architecture of the Villard Houses if you can't—or don't want to—pay for dinner at adjoining Le Cirque. Word is the sage and pineapple martini is a real treat. Be sure to dress well to fit in with the Prada-suited, Manolo-heeled crowd. In the New York Palace hotel, 24 E. 51st St. (at Madison Ave.). © **212/303-7757.** Subway: E, F to Fifth Ave.; 6 to 51st St.

THE UPPER WEST SIDE

All State Cafe *Finds* This subterranean pub is one of Manhattan's undiscovered treasures—the quintessential neighborhood "snugger." It's easy to miss from the street, and the regulars like it that way. The All State attracts a grown-up neighborhood crowd drawn in by the casual ambience, the great burgers, and an outstanding jukebox. 250 W. 72nd St. (btwn Broadway and West End Ave.). © **212/874-1883.** Subway: 1, 2, 3, 9 to 72nd St.

Amsterdam Billiard Club A straight-ahead, top-flight billiard bar with a completely unpretentious ambience, good beers on tap, and a lively local crowd make this one of the best pool bars in NYC. 344 Amsterdam Ave. (btwn 76th and 77th sts.). © **212/496-8180.** Subway: 1, 9 to 79th St. 210 E. 86th St. (btwn Second and Third aves.). © 212/570-4545; subway: 6 to 86th St.

Evelyn Lounge This subterranean bar is one of the more chic spots on the Upper West Side. Expect an attractive Victorian-modern space outfitted with velveteen sofas and a stylishly dressed yuppie crowd on the make. There's the requisite cigar room, plus live music a few nights a week. Prices are reasonable. Expect quiet mid-week, chino-wearing crowds on weekends. 380 Columbus Ave. (at 78th St.). ✆ **212/724-2363.** Subway: B, C to 81st St./Museum of Natural History.

Hi-Life Bar & Grill Here's a page out of the days when men wore grey flannel suits and everybody had a doozy of a before-dinner cocktail. This casual bar and restaurant is a longtime neighborhood favorite. The bar prides itself on its excellent classic cocktails, particularly its martinis, and they are terrific. But if you just want to pony up to the bar in your sweats and order a Bud, come on in—the Hi-Life is that kind of joint. The food is decent, too, and there's a nice alfresco patio. 477 Amsterdam Ave. (at 83rd St.). ✆ **212/787-7199.** Subway: 1, 9 to 79th St. Also at 1340 First Ave. (at 72nd St.). ✆ **212/249-3600.** Subway: 6 to 68th St.

Shark Bar This perennially popular and always-classy spot is well known for its good soul food and even better singles' scene. It's also a favorite hangout for sports celebs, so don't be surprised if you spot a New York Knick or two—in fact, be surprised if you don't. 307 Amsterdam Ave. (btwn 74th and 75th sts.). ✆ **212/874-8500.** Subway: 1, 2, 3, 9 to 72nd St.

THE UPPER EAST SIDE

There's also an outpost of the Meat-Packing District *Coyote Ugly* roadhouse **Hogs & Heifers** (p. 414) at 1843 First Ave., between 95th and 96th streets (✆ **212/722-8635;** subway: 6 to 96th St.). Despite its offshoot status, this one's slightly more laidback and boasts more genuine saloon style than the original. If you have a laidback game of pool in mind, head to the east side branch of the **Amsterdam Billiard Club** (p. 421), 210 E. 86th St., between Second and Third avenues (✆ **212/570-4545;** subway: 6 to 86th St.). Also look for another retro-cool and neighborhood branch of the **Hi-Life** (p. 422), at 1340 First Ave., at 72nd Street (✆ **212/249-3600;** subway: 6 to 68th St.).

Bemelmans Bar Named after children's book illustrator Ludwig Bemelmans, who created the Madeline books after he painted the whimsical mural here, this is a supremely luxurious spot for cocktails. Tuck into a dark, romantic corner and nurse a classic martini or the sublime Millionaire's Margarita. Jazz vocalist Barbara Carroll has been singing here for 15 years; expect to find her or other relaxing live entertainment Monday through Saturday from 9:30am to 1am ($15 cover). At the Carlyle hotel, 35 E. 76th St. (at Madison Ave.). ✆ **212/744-1600.** Subway: 6 to 77th St.

Brandy's Piano Bar A mixed crowd—Upper East Side locals, waiters off work, gays, straights, all ages—comes to this intimate, old-school piano bar for the friendly atmosphere and nightly entertainment. The talented wait staff does most of the singing while waiting for their big break, but enthusiastic patrons regularly join in. 235 E. 84th St. (btwn Second and Third aves.). ✆ **212/650-1944.** Subway: 4, 5, 6 to 86th St.

Elaine's *The Big Chill* claimed that Elaine's was over and done with way back when. They were dreaming. Glittering literati still come here for dinner and book parties. Look for regulars like Woody Allen and other A-list types. If you can't get a table, you can always scan the room from the upfront bar. 1703 Second Ave. (btwn 88th and 89th sts.). ✆ **212/534-8103.** Subway: 4, 5, 6 to 86th St.

Great Hall Balcony Bar *Moments* One of Manhattan's best cocktail bars is only open on Friday and Saturday—and only from 4 to 8:30pm, to boot. The

Metropolitan Museum of Art transforms the lobby's mezzanine level into a cocktail-and-classical music lounge twice weekly, offering a marvelous only-in-New York experience. The music is usually provided by a grand piano and string quartet. You'll have to pay the $10 admission, but the galleries are open until 9pm. At the Metropolitan Museum of Art, Fifth Ave. at 82nd St. ✆ **212/535-7710.** www.metmuseum.org. Subway: 4, 5, 6 to 86th St.

Mark's Bar If the more high-profile luxe hotel bars like Bemelmans or the King Cole are just too full, head to this lesser-known but equally appealing compatriot. The space is outfitted like an elegant living room with a romantic flair. The crowd tends to be older and quite used to sipping expensive cocktails. Sophisticated nibbles are also served. In the Mark hotel, 25 E. 77th St. (at Madison Ave.). ✆ **212/744-4300.** Subway: 6 to 77th St.

8 Dance Clubs & Party Scenes

Nothing in New York nightlife is as mutable as the club scene. In this world, hot spots don't even get 15 minutes of fame—their time in the limelight is usually more like a commercial break.

First things first: Finding and going to the latest hot spot is not worth agonizing over. Clubbers spend their lives obsessing over the scene. My rule of thumb is that if I know about a place, it must not be hip anymore. Even if I could tell you where the hippest club kids hang out today, they'll have moved on by the time you arrive in town.

"Clubs" as actual, physical spaces don't mean much anymore. The hungry-for-nightlife crowd now follows events of certain party "producers" who switch venues and times each week. A number of bars and lounges listed in the previous section host "club" scenes on various nights of the week.

The tracking game is best left to the perennial party crowd who know the rest of the crowd as well as the guy at the door (who lets them in for free) and someone at the bar (who comps them drinks). You're not likely to get that well connected in your week of vacation. Just find someplace that amuses you, and enjoy the crowd that enjoys it with you.

I've concentrated on a wide variety of club scenes below, from performance artsy to perennially popular discos, most of which are generally easy to make your way into. You can find listings for the most current hot spots and movable parties in the **publications and online sources** listed in at the start of this chapter and in the note called "Additional Sources for Bar- & Club-Hoppers" on p. 420. Additional online sources that might score you discount admissions to select clubs include **www.promony.com**. You can also check **newyork.sheckys.com** for VIP guest list access.

No matter what, **always call ahead,** because schedules change constantly and can do so at the last minute. Even better: You also may be able to put your name on a guest list that will save you a few bucks at the door.

New York nightlife starts late. With the exception of places that have scheduled performances, clubs stay almost empty until about 11pm. Don't depend on plastic—bring cash, and plan on dropping a wad at most places. Cover charges run anywhere from $7 to $30, and often get more expensive as the night wears on.

Baktun This club has been hot, hot, hot since the word go. Sleek Baktun was conceived in 2000 as a multimedia lounge, and as such incorporates avant-garde video projections (shown on a clever double-sided video screen) into its raging

Getting Beyond the Velvet Rope

If your heart's set on getting into an exclusive club or lounge, here are a few pointers that may help to tip the scale in your favor:

- **Dress well and fashionably.** Like it or not, the doorman is sizing you up to decide if you're hip enough to make the scene. If you want to get in, you have to play along.
- **Arrive early.** Frankly, the bouncers are just not as vigilant at 9pm, when the place is half empty, as they are at 11pm—and once you're inside, you're in for the night. Weeknights are also a better bet. Clubbers may tell you that eager beavers are disdained for arriving too early, but I find earlier to almost always be more successful than later.
- **Be polite.** No matter how obnoxious the doorman may be, giving attitude back won't help. And who knows? You might just charm him with your winning personality.
- **Don't try to talk your way in.** Don't drop names or make up some story to get in the door. These guys have heard it all. If you're not wanted, why bother? Take your business to a friendlier establishment, where you'll be happier in the long run.

dance parties as well as live cybercasts. The music tends toward electronica, with some live acts in the mix. At press time, Saturday's Direct Drive was the key drum 'n' bass party in town. 418 W. 14th St. (btwn Ninth Ave. and Washington St.). © **212/206-1590.** www.baktun.com. Subway: A, C, E, L to 14th St.

Cafe Wha? You'll find a carefree crowd dancing in the aisles of this casual basement club just about any night of the week. From Wednesday through Sunday, the stage features the house's own Wha Band, which does an excellent job of cranking out crowd-pleasing covers of familiar rock-and-roll hits from the '70s, '80s, and '90s. Monday night is the hugely popular Brazilian Dance Party, while Tuesday night is Classic Funk Night. Expect to be surrounded by lots of Jersey kids and out-of-towners on the weekends, but so what? Reservations are a good idea. The cover runs from free to $10. 115 MacDougal St. (btwn Bleecker and W. 3rd sts.). © **212/254-3706.** www.cafewha.com. Subway: A, B, C, E, FV to W. 4th St.

Centro-Fly Anyone who remembers the old rock-and-roll joint Tramps won't believe the swank Op Art club that fills the space now. It's so fab, in fact, that Mary J. Blige used it as a video set. The sunken bar must be the coolest in town. Despite the fabulousness of the place, Centro-Fly is quite welcoming. The places lures top-notch deejay talent ranging from Junior Sanchez to Dimitri from Paris to Grandmaster Flash. Depending on the night, look for deep house, hip-hop, or another edgy music mix. The Friday-night funky-soulful British house party GBH (www.gbh.tv), New York's longest-running house party, may be the best reason to come. 45 W. 21st St. (btwn Fifth and Sixth aves.). © **212/627-7770,** or 212/539-3916 for GBH info/guest lists www.centrofly.com. Subway: F to 23rd St.; N, R to 23rd St.

Culture Club This silly, '80s-themed club dance club attracts a big bridge-and-tunnel and tourist crowd looking for some good, clean fun. It's decidedly unhip and very accessible, offering lots of retro enjoyment for those with a touch of nostalgia for Duran Duran, Pac Man, and Boy Toy–era Madonna. If the 70's are more your thing, head instead to sister club **Polly Esther's,** 186 W. 4th St., between Sixth and Seventh avenues (© **212/924-5707**), where BeeGees-era disco is still the sound of choice on Friday and Saturday nights. 179 Varick St. (btwn King and Charlton sts.) ✆ **212/243-1999.** Subway: 1, 9 to Houston St.

Decade *Finds* Finally—somewhere to dance until nearly dawn for the baby boomers. This upscale hybrid supper/dance club attracts a well-dressed, well-heeled crowd who lounge in the cigar and champagne bars in between dancing to a fun mix of tunes from the '70s, '80s, and '90s. The food is quite tasty and the service is top-notch, too. Nights can sell out, so it pays to reserve ahead. 1117 First Ave. (at 61st St.). ✆ **212/835-5979.** www.decadeny.com. Subway: N, R to Lexington Ave.; 4, 5, 6 to 59th St.

Exit *Time Out* calls Exit the "supermall of nightclubs," and for good reason—because it covers 45,000 square feet and is able to accommodate more than 5,000 partyers, any velvet rope scene is pure posturing. The main floor is a mammoth atrium with a deejay booth—usually housing the top talent of the moment spinning tunes—suspended above. The space was made for crazy carnival acts like Antigravity, a bizarre club-land take on the Flying Wallendas. Upstairs is a warren of ultraplush VIP rooms, each with its own deejay. With capacity this big, expect club-goers of all stripes to show up on any given night. 610 W. 56th St. (btwn Eleventh and Twelfth aves.). ✆ **212/582-8282.** www.exitnyc.com. Subway: A, B, C, D, 1, 9 to 59th St./Columbus Circle.

Fun Despite its less-than-appealing location, this eye-popping club underneath the Brooklyn Bridge is a blast on any night, thanks to a wild assault from giant multimedia projection screens that pushes Fun over the experimental edge into colorful, high-tech haywire. The result is entertaining and upbeat, in an anything-goes kind of way. The crowd is young, hip, outgoing, and—for once—not uniformed in basic black. The program changes depending on the night, but expect an eclectic mix of soul, funk, hip-hop, techno, R&B, break beats, and the like. 130 Madison St. (btwn Pike and Market sts.). ✆ **212/964-0303.** www.fun.citysearch.com. Subway: F to East Broadway.

Nell's If you're going to spend one night out on the town, here's the place to do it. Nell's calls itself "The Classic New York Nightclub," and it has well earned the moniker. Nell's was the first to establish a loungelike atmosphere years ago and it has been endlessly copied by restaurateurs and nightclub owners. Nell's attracts a grown-up crowd that ranges from homeboys to Wall Streeters. Although the entertainment can run the gamut from comedy and spoken word to Cuban sounds, most of the parties have a soulful edge. Dress nicely—Nell's deserves respect. 246 W. 14th St. (btwn Seventh and Eighth aves.). ✆ **212/675-1567.** www.nells.com. Subway: A, C, E, 1, 2, 3, 9 to 14th St.

Shine Shine draws a well-dressed crowd to TriBeCa with a loungey vibe and a few well-placed 21st-century twists—most notably, great cocktails, terrific deejay talent from around the globe, and a blessedly attitude-free door policy, especially for a dance scene this cool. The cavernous, high-ceilinged space and elevated center stage allows for all manner of cabaret and performance art, which can run the gamut from classic to kooky and can include risqué circus acts, burlesque, or live reggae bands. 285 W. Broadway (just south of Canal St.). ✆ **212/941-0900.** www.shinelive.com. Subway: A, C, E, 1, 9 to Canal St.

Swing 46 *Finds* Swing is a nightly affair at this Theater District jazz and supper club (supper not required). Music is live nightly except Monday, when a deejay takes over, and runs the gamut from big band to boogie-woogie to jump blues. Do not miss Vince Giordano and His Nighthawks if they're on the bill, especially if sharp-dressed Casey McGill is singing and strumming his ukulele too. The Harlem Renaissance Orchestra is another great choice. Even first-timers can join in the fun, as free swing lessons are offered Wednesday through Saturday at 9:15pm. No jeans or sneakers. 349 W. 46th St. (btwn Eighth and Ninth aves.). ✆ **212/262-9554.** www.swing46.com. Subway: C, E to 50th St.

Vinyl *Finds* No alcohol is served at Vinyl—but that doesn't keep the rapturous masses at bay, which just goes to show how terrific this dance club really is. This commodious TriBeCa club welcomes a big, mixed black/white, gay/straight crowd to the best roster of weekly parties on the planet—mainly hip-hop- and house-flavored party nights ruled by a first-rate crop of deejays. The now-legendary Body and Soul (www.bodyandsoul-nyc.com) is a Sunday afternoon party extraordinaire. Even better is Friday's Be Yourself, superstar deejay Danny Tenaglia's weekly rave, which doesn't relent until the Saturday-morning cartoon hours. 6 Hubert St. (btwn Hudson and Greenwich sts.). ✆ **212/343-1379.** Subway: A, C, E to Canal St.; 1, 9 to Franklin St.

The World With more than 4,000 square feet of dance floors, mind-blowing sound and video systems, and top-flight international deejay talent, WWE New York transforms into Times Square's hottest dance party every Saturday night. The place loses all traces of its Wrestlemania identity for the night. Big-name artists perform on select weeknights. At WWE New York, 1501 Broadway (at 43rd St.). ✆ **212/398-2563** or 212/398-3439. http://newyork.wwe.com or http://clubworldnyc.com. Subway: 1, 2, 3, 7, 9, N, Q, R, S, W to 42nd St./Times Sq.

9 The Gay & Lesbian Scene

To get a thorough, up-to-date take on what's happening in gay and lesbian nightlife, pick up copies of ***HX*** (www.hx.com), ***New York Blade*** (www.nyblade.com), ***Next*** (www.nextnyc.com), or ***LGNY*** (www.lgny.com). They're available for free in bars and clubs all around town or at the **Lesbian and Gay Community Center,** at 208 W. 13th St., between Seventh and Eighth avenues (✆ **212/620-7310;** www.gaycenter.org). The interdisciplinary weekly ***Time Out New York*** boasts a terrific gay and lesbian section that some consider to be the city's best source; another great source is the legendary free weekly ***Village Voice.*** Always remember that asking people in one bar can lead you to discover another that fits your tastes.

These days, many bars, clubs, cabarets, and cocktail lounges are neither gay nor straight but a bit of both, either catering to a mixed crowd or to varying orientations on different nights of the week. In addition to the choices below, most of the clubs listed in "Dance Clubs & Party Scenes," above, cater to a gay crowd, some predominantly so. Be sure to see what's happening at such clubs as **Exit** and **Vinyl,** which regularly cater to gay and/or gay/straight mixed crowds.

Barracuda Chelsea is central to gay life—and gay bars. This trendy, loungey place is a continuing favorite, regularly voted "Best Bar" by *HX* and *New York Press* magazines, while *Paper* singles out the hunky bartenders. There's a sexy bar for cruising out front and a comfy lounge in back. Look for the regular drag shows. 275 W. 22nd St. (btwn Seventh and Eighth aves.). ✆ **212/645-8613.** Subway: C, E, 1, 9 to 23rd St.

Big Cup Big Cup isn't a bar but a coffeehouse—a really great one. Still, you'd be hard-pressed to find a cooler, comfier pickup joint, or a more preening crowd. This is where all the Chelsea boys hang. 228 Eighth Ave. (btwn 21st and 22nd sts.). ✆ **212/206-0059.** Subway: C, E to 23rd St.

Boiler Room This down-to-earth East Village bar is everybody's favorite gay dive. Despite the mixed guy-girl crowd, it's a serious cruising scene for well-sculpted beautiful boys and a perfectly fine hangout for those who'd rather play pool. 86 E. 4th St. (btwn First and Second aves.). ✆ **212/254-7536.** Subway: F to Second Ave.

Chase *Finds* This serene and stylish multiroom lounge on the northern fringe of Hell's Kitchen is symbolic of how far this trash-to-treasure neighborhood has come over the last half dozen years. The pretty-boy staff is welcoming to locals and visitors alike. 255 W. 55th St. (btwn Broadway and Eighth Ave.). ✆ **212/333-3400.** Subway: A, B, C, D, 1, 9 to 59th St./Columbus Circle.

The Cock *Finds* This gleefully seedy East Village joint is the most envelope-pushing gay club in town. A self-proclaimed "rock and sleaze fag bar" is dedicated to good-natured depravity. Head elsewhere if you're the retiring type. 188 Ave. A (at 12th St.). ✆ **212/777-6254.** Subway: L to First Ave.

Crazy Nanny's This long-standing lesbian bar is huge, friendly, wildly popular, and perpetually trendy. There's two floors, two bars, a groovy jukebox, dancing, a pool table, video games, and a variety of theme nights, including Dance Party on Thursday, and Karaoke on Sunday and Wednesday. Out-of-towners are welcome. 21 Seventh Ave. South (at Leroy St.). ✆ **212/366-6312.** www.crazynannys.com. Subway: 1, 9 to Houston St.

Duplex Cabaret The heart of the gay cabaret and piano-bar scene. Expect a high camp factor and lots of good-natured fun that runs the gamut from mini-musicals to drag revues to stand-up comedy. 61 Christopher St. (at Seventh Ave.). ✆ **212/255-5438.** Subway: 1, 9 to Christopher St.

g Big crowds of muscular, designer-dressed men have made this lovely, relaxed lounge a popular style scene for meeting dream dates. Deejays spin suave sounds nightly. There's a nonalcoholic juice bar, too, and magazines that invite early hours lounging. 225 W. 19th St. (btwn Seventh and Eighth aves.). ✆ **212/929-1085.** www.glounge.com. Subway: 1, 9 to 18th St.

Hell This glamorous lounge is a sexy haven for a predominantly gay weekend crowd in the hipper-than-hell Meat-Packing District. The cocktails are well mixed, and plenty of comfy sofas are on hand for getting cozy. 59 Gansevoort St. (btwn Washington and Greenwich sts.). ✆ **212/727-1666.** Subway: A, C, E to 14th St.

Henrietta Hudson *Finds* This friendly and extremely popular women's bar/lounge is known for drawing in an attractive, upmarket lipstick lesbian crowd that comes for the great jukebox and videos as well as the pleasingly low-key atmosphere. There's a $5 to $7 cover on weekends, when deejays spin tunes (Fri and Sat) and live bands are in the house (Sun). 438–444 Hudson St. (at Morton St.). ✆ **212/924-3347.** www.henriettahudsons.com. Subway: 1, 9 to Houston St.

Meow Mix This funky, divey East Villager is a great lesbian hangout. It draws in a young, attractive, artsy riot grrrl crowd with nightly diversions like groovy deejays and live bands. 269 E. Houston St. (at Suffolk St.) ✆ **212/254-0689.** www.meowmixchix.com. Subway: F to Second Ave.

Splash/SBNY After ten years, this campy and fun gay dance club still manages to be one of the hottest scenes on the men's circuit. In fact, an end-of-2001 rebirth has breathed new life into the scene; *New York* magazine even chose it best gay dance club for 2002. Beautiful bartenders, video screens playing campy scenes, New York's best drag queens—Splash has it all. Theme nights are a big deal. Best of the bunch is Musical Mondays, dedicated to Broadway video clips and music. Musical Mondays' now-famous singalongs are such a blast that it regularly draws a crossover gay/straight mixed crowd as well as celebs like Nathan Lane and the cast of Abba musical *Mamma Mia!* 50 W. 17th St. (btwn Fifth and Sixth aves.). ✆ **212/691-0073.** www.splashbar.com. Subway: F, V to 14th St.; 4, 5, 6, N, R, L, Q, W to 14th St./Union Sq.

Stonewall Bar The spot where it all started. A mixed gay and lesbian crowd—old and young, beautiful and great personalities—makes this an easy place to begin. At least pop in to relive a defining moment in queer history. 53 Christopher St. (east of Seventh Ave.). ✆ **212/463-0950.** Subway: 1, 9 to Christopher St.

Townhouse Bar Here's a first-class watering hole for men who want to relax rather than cruise. Friendly and open to all. 236 E. 58th St. (btwn Second and Third aves.). ✆ **212/754-4649.** Subway: 4, 5, 6 to 59th St.

Ty's Bar This very friendly, unassuming gay bar has been a part of the Village men's cruise scene for about a million years. 114 Christopher St. (btwn Bleecker and Bedford sts.). ✆ **212/741-9641.** www.tys.citysearch.com. Subway: 1, 9 to Christopher St.

View Bar *Finds* Up front is a very attractive and comfortable lounge, in back is a pool room with the name-worthy view; throughout you'll find friendly bartenders, affordable drinks, and Kenneth Cole–dressed boys who could pass on either side of bi. A welcome addition to the scene. 232 Eighth Ave. (btwn 21st and 22nd sts.). ✆ **212/929-2243.** Subway: C, E to 23rd St.

Index

See also Restaurant index, below.

GENERAL INDEX

Restaurants

FROMMER'S® COMPLETE TRAVEL GUIDES

Alaska
Alaska Cruises & Ports of Call
Amsterdam
Argentina & Chile
Arizona
Atlanta
Australia
Austria
Bahamas
Barcelona, Madrid & Seville
Beijing
Belgium, Holland & Luxembourg
Bermuda
Boston
Brazil
British Columbia & the Canadian Rockies
Budapest & the Best of Hungary
California
Canada
Cancún, Cozumel & the Yucatán
Cape Cod, Nantucket & Martha's Vineyard
Caribbean
Caribbean Cruises & Ports of Call
Caribbean Ports of Call
Carolinas & Georgia
Chicago
China
Colorado
Costa Rica
Denmark
Denver, Boulder & Colorado Springs
England
Europe
European Cruises & Ports of Call
Florida
France
Germany
Great Britain
Greece
Greek Islands
Hawaii
Hong Kong
Honolulu, Waikiki & Oahu
Ireland
Israel
Italy
Jamaica
Japan
Las Vegas
London
Los Angeles
Maryland & Delaware
Maui
Mexico
Montana & Wyoming
Montréal & Québec City
Munich & the Bavarian Alps
Nashville & Memphis
Nepal
New England
New Mexico
New Orleans
New York City
New Zealand
Northern Italy
Nova Scotia, New Brunswick & Prince Edward Island
Oregon
Paris
Philadelphia & the Amish Country
Portugal
Prague & the Best of the Czech Republic
Provence & the Riviera
Puerto Rico
Rome
San Antonio & Austin
San Diego
San Francisco
Santa Fe, Taos & Albuquerque
Scandinavia
Scotland
Seattle & Portland
Shanghai
Singapore & Malaysia
South Africa
South America
South Florida
South Pacific
Southeast Asia
Spain
Sweden
Switzerland
Texas
Thailand
Tokyo
Toronto
Tuscany & Umbria
USA
Utah
Vancouver & Victoria
Vermont, New Hampshire & Maine
Vienna & the Danube Valley
Virgin Islands
Virginia
Walt Disney World® & Orlando
Washington, D.C.
Washington State

FROMMER'S® DOLLAR-A-DAY GUIDES

Australia from $50 a Day
California from $70 a Day
Caribbean from $70 a Day
England from $75 a Day
Europe from $70 a Day
Florida from $70 a Day
Hawaii from $80 a Day
Ireland from $60 a Day
Italy from $70 a Day
London from $85 a Day
New York from $90 a Day
Paris from $80 a Day
San Francisco from $70 a Day
Washington, D.C. from $80 a Day

FROMMER'S® PORTABLE GUIDES

Acapulco, Ixtapa & Zihuatanejo
Amsterdam
Aruba
Australia's Great Barrier Reef
Bahamas
Berlin
Big Island of Hawaii
Boston
California Wine Country
Cancún
Charleston & Savannah
Chicago
Disneyland®
Dublin
Florence
Frankfurt
Hong Kong
Houston
Las Vegas
London
Los Angeles
Los Cabos & Baja
Maine Coast
Maui
Miami
New Orleans
New York City
Paris
Phoenix & Scottsdale
Portland
Puerto Rico
Puerto Vallarta, Manzanillo & Guadalajara
Rio de Janeiro
San Diego
San Francisco
Seattle
Sydney
Tampa & St. Petersburg
Vancouver
Venice
Virgin Islands
Washington, D.C.

FROMMER'S® NATIONAL PARK GUIDES

Banff & Jasper
Family Vacations in the National Parks
Grand Canyon
National Parks of the American West
Rocky Mountain
Yellowstone & Grand Teton
Yosemite & Sequoia/ Kings Canyon
Zion & Bryce Canyon

Frommer's® Memorable Walks

Chicago
London
New York
Paris
San Francisco
Washington, D.C.

Frommer's® Great Outdoor Guides

Arizona & New Mexico
New England
Northern California
Southern New England
Vermont & New Hampshire

Suzy Gershman's Born to Shop Guides

Born to Shop: France
Born to Shop: Hong Kong, Shanghai & Beijing
Born to Shop: Italy
Born to Shop: London
Born to Shop: New York
Born to Shop: Paris

Frommer's® Irreverent Guides

Amsterdam
Boston
Chicago
Las Vegas
London
Los Angeles
Manhattan
New Orleans
Paris
Rome
San Francisco
Seattle & Portland
Vancouver
Walt Disney World
Washington, D.C.

Frommer's® Best-Loved Driving Tours

Britain
California
Florida
France
Germany
Ireland
Italy
New England
Northern Italy
Scotland
Spain
Tuscany & Umbria

Hanging Out™ Guides

Hanging Out in England
Hanging Out in Europe
Hanging Out in France
Hanging Out in Ireland
Hanging Out in Italy
Hanging Out in Spain

The Unofficial Guides®

Bed & Breakfasts and Country Inns in:
California
Great Lakes States
Mid-Atlantic
New England
Northwest
Rockies
Southeast
Southwest
Best RV & Tent Campgrounds in:
California & the West
Florida & the Southeast
Great Lakes States
Mid-Atlantic
Northeast
Northwest & Central Plains
Southwest & South Central Plains
U.S.A.
Beyond Disney
Branson, Missouri
California with Kids
Chicago
Cruises
Disneyland®
Florida with Kids
Golf Vacations in the Eastern U.S.
Great Smoky & Blue Ridge Region
Inside Disney
Hawaii
Las Vegas
London
Mid-Atlantic with Kids
Mini Las Vegas
Mini-Mickey
New England and New York with Kids
New Orleans
New York City
Paris
San Francisco
Skiing in the West
Southeast with Kids
Walt Disney World®
Walt Disney World® for Grown-ups
Walt Disney World® with Kids
Washington, D.C.
World's Best Diving Vacations

Special-Interest Titles

Frommer's Adventure Guide to Australia & New Zealand
Frommer's Adventure Guide to Central America
Frommer's Adventure Guide to India & Pakistan
Frommer's Adventure Guide to South America
Frommer's Adventure Guide to Southeast Asia
Frommer's Adventure Guide to Southern Africa
Frommer's Britain's Best Bed & Breakfasts and Country Inns
Frommer's Caribbean Hideaways
Frommer's Exploring America by RV
Frommer's Fly Safe, Fly Smart
Frommer's France's Best Bed & Breakfasts and Country Inns
Frommer's Gay & Lesbian Europe
Frommer's Italy's Best Bed & Breakfasts and Country Inns
Frommer's New York City with Kids
Frommer's Ottawa with Kids
Frommer's Road Atlas Britain
Frommer's Road Atlas Europe
Frommer's Road Atlas France
Frommer's Toronto with Kids
Frommer's Vancouver with Kids
Frommer's Washington, D.C., with Kids
Israel Past & Present
The New York Times' Guide to Unforgettable Weekends
Places Rated Almanac
Retirement Places Rated